DRAMA
OF THE
ENGLISH
RENAISSANCE

MODERN LIBRARY COLLEGE EDITIONS

DRAMA
OF THE
English
Renaissance

EDITED BY

M. L. WINE

NEW YORK

MODERN LIBRARY

DISTRIBUTED BY McGRAW-HILL, INC.

Library of Congress Catalog
Card Number: 68–20031
17 18 19 BAH BAH 9 9

The Modern Library
is published by
Random House, Inc.

Manufactured in the United States of America

ISBN: 0–07–553569–6

Preface

The modernized texts of English Renaissance plays, exclusive of Shakespeare, in this volume are based on the first or very early editions as noted in the introductory material to each play. Square brackets indicate editorial alterations or emendations of the copy texts that have been introduced on the authority of other early editions or of modern scholarship. Misplaced stage directions have been silently transposed, verse relineated wherever necessary, abbreviations expanded, proper names regularized, older forms of words silently modernized (as *burden* from *burthen*, *lose* from *loose*, *show* from *shew*, etc.), and for the sake of clarity a small number of imperative stage directions inserted. To preserve the sense of the fluid and unrestricted staging before 1642, the modern practice of localizing scenes has not been followed; instead, scenic divisions are indicated marginally in brackets, where they do not obtrude upon the text. Footnotes explain, for the most part, words whose meanings are obsolete or where modern usage does not accurately convey the nuances of the original. The bibliographies list authors or editors cited specifically in the introductions and works of general and specific scholarship or criticism that influenced the writing of them. E. K. Chambers' *The Elizabethan Stage* and G. E. Bentley's *The Jacobean and Caroline Stage* were especially useful.

I wish to acknowledge the generosity of the libraries or institutions (cited in the introductions) granting permission to use their original editions as copy texts for the present collection; the many courtesies, in particular, of the staff of the Henry E. Huntington Library of San Marino, California; my indebtedness to previous editors of the plays; the helpful suggestions of Ann Englander and Charles Holmes; the valiant labors of my manuscript editors, Anne Olin and Carol Green; and an incalculable debt to Allan Casson for his untiring assistance.

Contents

Introduction

Drama is the characteristic mode of expression of the English Renaissance during its two greatest periods, the Elizabethan and the Jacobean. Yet, were it not for the brainstorm (and shrewd business sense) of a noted actor, James Burbage, the Golden Age of English drama—unbelievable as it may seem to us today—might not have come to pass. In 1576, to counter the hostility of the city fathers of London against the small itinerant troupes of actors that tried to eke out a livelihood by performing in the courtyards of inns, Burbage, with financial assistance from his grocer brother-in-law, John Brayne, leased land in the Shoreditch "fields" just north of the city and outside its jurisdiction, and built the first permanent theater in England. Modeled after the open bear-baiting rings and the semicircular inn courtyards with their several galleries, and named with manifesto-like simplicity the Theater, its construction assured the continuance and development of the much-harassed acting profession, which had been seeking recognition and status since about the middle of the fifteenth century. The rising tide of Reformation sentiment had militated strongly against a repertoire that had largely grown out of the medieval Catholic church; and the mode of the strolling players' existence subjected them to antivagrancy laws that made them liable to arrest and even imprisonment. Only the sponsorship of a nobleman or other person of rank, whose livery they wore as "servants," enabled them to ply their craft more freely.

Despite official hostility, sufficient evidence exists that the populace at large, accustomed for several centuries to visits from these companies, responded warmly to them. The numerous progeny of the Theater during the decades immediately following bears witness to the soundness of Burbage's instincts: the nearby Curtain within the next year (1577), a theater at Newington Butts shortly thereafter, the Rose (1587), the Swan (1595), the Fortune (1600), the Red Bull (around 1605), and the Hope (1613). Most of these were on the Bankside, a district south of the Thames and also outside the city's jurisdiction. In 1599, following a legal entanglement with the landlord leasing the land on which the commercially prosperous Theater was standing, James Burbage's sons, Cuthbert and Richard, and five other shareholders in the company, Shakespeare among them, demolished the building and, with a genuine sense of poetic justice, erected on the Bankside, phoenix-like from its timbers, the most famous of all theaters in English theatrical history—the Globe, home of England's greatest company (the Lord Chamberlain's men), one of its greatest actors (Richard Burbage), and its greatest playwright.

The prestige for which the acting profession had so long struggled came rapidly within these years. One of James I's first acts, upon ascending the throne in 1603, was to confer the badge of his livery upon the Lord Chamberlain's men, known thereafter as the Servants of His Majesty; but the gesture in a sense only symbolized the eminence that this company, and the profession in general, already had achieved in the public estimation. With the stability of permanent homes and large, regular audiences comprised of all the strata of the population of England's chief metropolis, the companies expanded into guilds of sorts—with as many as ten actors, apprentices, and hired hands. But, more important for posterity, the burgeoning profession attracted, in the place of the anonymous or near-anonymous writers of earlier years, many writers who were destined to become the glory of English letters—men who might otherwise never have written for the theater at all. As it happens, their drama derives its lifeblood from a vital association with an active and prosperous theatrical environment and not from the closet or academy. To a dying repertoire they brought enrichment in form and ideas and transformed the jangling rhymes of medieval drama to the supplest blank verse and to the most versatile prose. In a little more than a decade after the building of the Theater, any young man with a literary talent and ambitions for name and fortune—whether a glover's son from Stratford-on-Avon or a Cambridge scholarship student from Canterbury—might have been found writing for one of the London companies.

The Tragicall History
of the Life and Death
of *Doctor Faustus.*

Written by *Ch. Marklin.*

LONDON,
Printed for *John Wright,* and are to be sold at his shop
without Newgate, at the ſ. . . . . . . he

Introduction

English drama is religious in origin, stemming from the great
cosmic drama that is Christianity: the rebellion of Lucifer
against God, the creation of the world and of man, the fall of
man and his redemption by the birth, crucifixion, and resur-
rection of Christ. Beginning with little playlets introduced
by anonymous priests near the end of the tenth century into
the Easter, and later into the Christmas, services, the whole
Bible story came to be dramatized for a largely unlettered
populace. In the following centuries great cycles of these
"miracle plays" came into being. By the fourteenth century,
although still under the ægis of the church, production
passed into the hands of the craft guilds, each play in the
cycle often ingeniously assigned—as the Noah play to the
water drawers, the crucifixion to the pinmakers and painters.
Christ is, of course, the protagonist of each cycle; but man
is actually at the center: Christ is the ideal human whose
example all men must endeavor to imitate. Not surprisingly
then, in the fourteenth century, side by side with the miracle
plays, the morality play that explicitly allegorized the
moral implicit in the miracle plays developed: Everyman,
beset on all sides by the distracting temptations of the world,
is now the protagonist in a divine comedy that guides him
to a lasting judgment of salvation.

From the beginning of the sixteenth century until the
building of the Theater in 1576, drama in England went
through a transitional period. The growing Protestantism of
the Reformation caused the Catholic-inspired miracle plays,
except for isolated performances, to decline in popularity;

and the guilds, for economic reasons, lost interest in sponsoring them. Strolling bands of players, most of them originally members of guilds (James Burbage himself was, like Shakespeare's Snug, a joiner), continued to keep alive the dramatic tradition and to seek desperately for new material. As even the morality tradition was threatened with extinction, a new, and more secularized, form developed—the so-called "hybrid morality," in which historical or pseudo-historical figures, a King John or a Cambises, replaced the generalized Everyman in basically the same kind of plot. In the meantime, with the advent of humanism, an amateur dramatic tradition was springing up in schools and universities and in the homes of wealthy patrons, where the plays of Terence and Plautus and Seneca and the Italian comedians of the Renaissance were being either translated or refurbished by schoolmasters or gentlemen playwrights. The establishment of permanent theaters and permanent repertory companies at a professional level brought about a cross-fertilization of academic and "popular," or professional, drama, and the great age of Elizabethan drama ushered in complete secularization and widespread experimentation. Polonius' list is not an exaggeration: "tragedy, comedy, history, pastoral, pastoral-comical, historical-pastoral, tragical-historical, tragical-comical-historical-pastoral; scene individable, or poem unlimited."

But however it may seem to differ from the religious drama of an earlier age, Elizabethan drama drew its greatest vitality from its original source by renewing the form of Everyman's conflict of conscience in subtler, contemporary, and highly individualistic terms. In an age distinguished by the discovery of rich and brave new worlds and by greater social mobility not permitted under a feudalistic system, the choice of the later Everyman was no longer an easy one to make—even with Knowledge at his side. Finding his loyalties strongly divided between rival claims of the world and of the spirit, he might create—as for a while he seemed to—a delicate harmony between them when total acceptance or rejection of either was not quite possible; more likely he was to find them irreconcilable.

More hauntingly than any other play of its time, Marlowe's *The Tragical History of the Life and Death of Doctor Faustus* dramatizes this tragic pull between world and spirit. Alone among the earlier playwrights, Marlowe is the first to raise the question that later writers were to ask with greater frequency and urgency as Elizabethan optimism surrendered to Jacobean pessimism: "For what is a man profited, if he shall gain the whole world, and lose his own soul?" And the difficulty of answering, in contrast to the assured ease with which an earlier age could answer, makes the dramatic mode inevitable. Now generally dated about 1592, *Doctor Faustus* at first seems like an anomaly at this late date with its obvious trappings of the medieval morality play: the Good and Bad Angels, Lucifer and his cohorts, the vision of hell, and the parade of the Seven Deadly Sins. Even the Chorus that acts as Prologue and Epilogue functions in part like the "moral doctor" who steps forth at the end of the older plays to pointedly drive home the inescapable moral:

> Cut is the branch that might have grown full straight,
> And burnèd is Apollo's laurel bough
> That sometime grew within this learned man.
> Faustus is gone: regard his hellish fall,
> Whose fiendful fortune may exhort the wise
> Only to wonder at unlawful things,
> Whose deepness doth entice such forward wits
> To practice more than heavenly power permits.

The play holds up a mirror for the spectator's edification: the penalties for losing sight of the end for which man was created are clearly visible. Dissatisfied with the limitations of "mere man, Faustus sells his soul to the devil to become a god; but, like Icarus flying too close to the sun, he burns his wings and falls.

Orthodox as its theme is, *Doctor Faustus* could not have been written earlier, and not merely because a particularized Faustus, tragically damning himself, replaces a generalized Everyman, who has been saved in the eternal scheme of things. What is new is the way Marlowe manipulates a dramatic form that by the nature of its didactic commitment directs the spectator to look down judgingly upon the protagonist while at the same time urging from him an irrationally sympathetic response. From a rational point of view, Faustus is an absurd figure who, knowing that the heavens call him to repentance, nevertheless separates himself from God. From an irrational view, Faustus embraces his tragedy by striving for a fate absolving him from human limitations.

Explicitly, an audience can never doubt that Faustus deserves his condemnation, that his crime—his willful separation from God, from ultimate meaning—is in fact his punishment: despair. Not only does the Chorus make distant the main action by framing it, and thereby making it seem like a play within a play, but the Prologue, in its appeal to "patient judgments," also removes suspense that might detract from judging: "His waxen wings did mount above his reach,/ And melting, heavens conspired his overthrow." The ambivalent shifting of the sequence of tenses in the Prologue indicates, in a sense, that the action is over even before it begins, but the moral of Faustus' "fortunes" is applicable in the present lives of all men.

The Faustus who sits in his study as the play opens and surveys all the known fields of knowledge is, in fact, a "fond [i.e., foolish] worldling" who confounds wisdom with knowledge. With all his learning, Faustus has rejected "learning's golden gifts," which should teach him to value the moral paternity of his soul instead of denying it. Having lost the good of his intellect, he is so benighted with "aspiring pride and insolence" that, even with the extreme example of Mephostophilis as a walking hell on earth, he rejects the knowledge before him, as well as the promptings of his conscience in the form of the Good Angel, to satisfy himself that "hell is a fable." Refusing to face the ugliness of hell, of a life cut off from the source of meaning, he loses also the vision of the beauty that is heaven and like a schoolboy gloats over the silly parade of the Seven Deadly Sins that Lucifer conjures up for him. The farcical episodes that follow the signing of the pact with the devil, whether written by Marlowe or by his conjectured collaborators, reveal the true nature of his achievement: like the clowns of the subplot, Faustus leads a life that is a hollow farce—"sleeping, eating, walking, and disputing." Even as he evokes, in the most famous passage in all of Marlowe, the sight of Helen of Troy to "glut the longing of my heart's desire," the presence of the Old Man, "whose faith is great," functions as a distancing Chorus to show that Faustus is making love to a destructive shadow, not the genuine substance of faith. With nothing more substantial Faustus' longings can only disintegrate into despair. By having let "sin by custom grow . . . into nature," he suffers the ultimate punishment of being unable to weep tears of repentance although earlier God had congealed his blood to stop him from signing the foolish pact. Truly damned, Faustus yearns even for what he fears.

Strangely and ironically, as medieval as the form of the play appears to be, Marlowe has managed to impose upon it a unity that evokes the foreboding aura of classical Greek tragedy. Uninterrupted by act or scene changes, the action of the play is resolutely single, arising entirely from Faustus' initial decision to defy God. And the effect of that action's working itself out on the bare Elizabethan stage is to concentrate the locale almost entirely in the mind of Faustus; even the clowning scenes have relevance only in context of his decision. Furthermore, the play's extreme dramatic compression of time, morally exemplifying the meaninglessness of worldly time under the aspect of eternity, dramatically reveals Faustus as the fated or tragic victim of time. The action supposedly covers twenty-four years, but the play gives us to understand that these are no more than a single day, twenty-four hours, in the life of a man. At the end of the first scene, Faustus says, "This night I'll conjure though I die therefore"; after the signing of the pact, Lucifer tells Faustus that "at midnight I will send for thee"; and in the final scene, twenty-four years later at midnight, Lucifer indeed sends for Faustus, who dies "therefore." Even an hour is no more than a few minutes; Faustus' eleventh-hour soliloquy is a masterpiece of dramatic compression. All his attempts to stop time are irrational—from denying the knowledge of his senses to glutting them; but it is in his unreason that the deeper power of the play lies.

Faustus thus is both a moral exemplum, in the medieval sense, of a man who absurdly throws his life away and at the same time a kind of classical tragic hero—misguided though that heroism may be—who stands at the center of an action that he has willed in defiance of a life filled with ambiguity and in which the unceasing process of time inexorably mocks man's efforts to "resolve [him] of all ambiguities." Without a comparable vision from heaven to balance Lucifer's, Faustus, unable to make a leap to greater faith, conjures against time a world of imaginative beauty. His failure to square with reality, and his final realization of that failure, is tragic.

The Playwright

CHRISTOPHER MARLOWE (1564–1593) was born in Canterbury, the son of a well-to-do shoemaker, who also served as a parish clerk. A scholarship student at the King's School in Canterbury and also later at Corpus Christi College, Cambridge, Marlowe received his B.A. in 1584 and his M.A. in 1587. Before leaving the university, he seems to have served the Privy Council on a secret political mission. As an Archbishop Parker scholarship student at Cambridge, he was expected to be a candidate for holy orders; but in 1587 he went to London and began his playwrighting career with the immensely successful first part of *Tamburlaine*. On May 12, 1593, the playwright Thomas Kyd (author of *The Spanish Tragedy*) was arrested on a libel charge; among his papers were certain heretical documents that he claimed belonged to Marlowe, with whom he once had shared a room. The Privy Council issued a warrant for Marlowe's arrest in Kent on May 18, and on May 20 ordered him to remain in daily attendance. But ten days later, before the Council could take up the charges, Marlowe was fatally stabbed in a quarrel at Eleanor Bull's tavern in Deptford. The circumstances surrounding his death are still somewhat obscure despite outstanding research. What is certain is that the career of the most promising dramatist of the age, save Shakespeare, came to an untimely end.

The Play

The present text of *The Tragical History of the Life and Death of Doctor Faustus* is based on the 1616 "enlarged" quarto of the play in the British Museum, collated with the 1604 quarto in the Bodleian Library of Oxford University and Sir Walter Greg's brilliant conjectural reconstruction. The editions of Boas, Jump, and Ribner have also been consulted. Greg argues that the 1604 edition represents a reconstruction from memory of the original acting version but shortened and adapted for a touring company in the provinces, whereas the later quarto is based on the author's drafts and on the earlier edition where the drafts proved illegible. Boas argues for Samuel Rowley's collaboration, particularly in the comic scenes. In the following text, readings from the 1604 quarto are enclosed within double brackets [[   ]]. The play is now generally dated 1592. The Admiral's Company, with Edward Alleyn in the title role, performed the play twenty-four times from October 1594 to October 1597.

SELECTED BIBLIOGRAPHY

The Complete Plays of Christopher Marlowe, ed. I. Ribner. New York: Odyssey Press, 1963.

Marlowe's "Doctor Faustus" 1604–1616: Parallel Texts, ed. W. W. Greg. Oxford: The Clarendon Press, 1950.

The Tragical History of Doctor Faustus, 2nd ed., ed. F. S. Boas. London: Methuen, 1949.

Doctor Faustus, ed. R. Gill. New York: Hill and Wang, 1966. (The New Mermaids.)

The Tragical History of the Life and Death of Doctor Faustus, ed. J. D. Jump. London: Methuen; Cambridge, Mass.: Harvard University Press, 1962. (The Revels Plays.)

The Tragical History of the Life and Death of Doctor Faustus by Christopher Marlowe: A Conjectural Reconstruction, ed. W. W. Greg. Oxford: The Clarendon Press, 1950.

Bakeless, J. *The Tragicall History of Christopher Marlowe.* 2 vols. Cambridge, Mass.: Harvard University Press, 1942.

Bevington, D. M. *From "Mankind" to Marlowe: Growth of Structure in the Popular Drama of Tudor England.* Cambridge, Mass.: Harvard University Press, 1962.

Boas, F. S. *Christopher Marlowe: A Biographical and Critical Study,* rev. ed. Oxford: The Clarendon Press, 1953.

Brockbank, J. P. *Marlowe: "Doctor Faustus."* Studies in English Literature 6. London: Edward Arnold, 1962.

Cole, D. W. *Suffering and Evil in the Plays of Marlowe.* Princeton, N.J.: Princeton University Press, 1962.

Davidson, C. "Doctor Faustus of Wittenberg," *Studies in Philology,* LIX (1962), 514–523.

Gardner, H. "Milton's 'Satan' and the Theme of Damnation in

Elizabethan Tragedy," *English Studies*, new series I (1948), 48–53.

Greg, W. W. "The Damnation of Faustus," *Modern Language Review*, XLI (1946), 97–107.

Hawkins, S. "The Education of Faustus," *Studies in English Literature*, VI (1966), 193–209.

Hotson, J. L. *The Death of Christopher Marlowe*. London: Nonesuch; Cambridge, Mass.: Harvard University Press, 1925.

Kaula, D. "Time and the Timeless in *Everyman* and *Doctor Faustus*," *College English*, XXII (1960), 9–14.

Kirschbaum, L. "Marlowe's *Faustus*: A Reconsideration," *Review of English Studies*, XIX (1943), 225–241.

Kocher, P. H. *Christopher Marlowe: A Study of His Thought, Learning, and Character*. Chapel Hill: University of North Carolina Press, 1946.

Leech, C., ed. *Marlowe: A Collection of Critical Essays*. Englewood Cliffs, N.J.: Prentice-Hall, 1964.

Levin, H. *The Overreacher: A Study of Christopher Marlowe*. Cambridge, Mass.: Harvard University Press, 1952.

Mahood, M. M. "Marlowe's Heroes," in *Poetry and Humanism*. London: Cape, 1950. Pp. 54–86.

Maxwell, J. C. "The Plays of Christopher Marlowe," in *The Age of Shakespeare*, rev. ed., ed. B. Ford. Baltimore, Md.: Penguin Books, 1964. Pp. 162–178.

Ornstein, R. "The Comic Synthesis in *Doctor Faustus*," *Journal of English Literary History*, XXII (1955), 165–172.

Palmer, D. J. "Magic and Poetry in *Doctor Faustus*," *The Critical Quarterly*, VI (1964), 56–67.

Poirier, M. *Christopher Marlowe*. London: Chatto and Windus, 1951.

Sachs, A. "The Religious Despair of Doctor Faustus," *Journal of English and Germanic Philology*, LXIII (1964), 625–647.

Sewall, R. B. "Doctor Faustus," in *The Vision of Tragedy*. New Haven, Conn.: Yale University Press, 1959. Pp. 57–67, 159–160.

Smith, J. "Marlowe's *Doctor Faustus*," *Scrutiny*, VIII (1930), 36–55.

Smith, W. D. "The Nature of Evil in *Doctor Faustus*," *Modern Language Review*, LX (1965), 171–175.

Snyder, S. "Marlowe's *Doctor Faustus* as an Inverted Saint's Life," *Studies in Philology*, LXIII (1966), 565–577.

Steane, J. B. *Marlowe: A Critical Study*. Cambridge: Cambridge University Press, 1964.

Tulane Drama Review, VIII, no. 4 (1964): "Marlowe Issue."

Westlund, J. "The Orthodox Christian Framework of Marlowe's *Faustus*," *Studies in English Literature*, III (1963), 191–205.

Wilson, F. P. *Marlowe and the Early Shakespeare*. Oxford: The Clarendon Press, 1954.

[DRAMATIS PERSONAE

*

CHORUS.
DOCTOR JOHN FAUSTUS *of Wittenberg.*
WAGNER, *a student, Faustus' servant.*
VALDES } *his friends; magicians.*
CORNELIUS }
THREE SCHOLARS, *students under Faustus.*
An OLD MAN.

POPE ADRIAN.
RAYMOND, *King of Hungary.*
BRUNO, *rival Pope appointed by Emperor Charles V.*
CARDINALS OF FRANCE *and* PADUA.
ARCHBISHOP OF RHEIMS.

CHARLES V, *Emperor of Germany.*
MARTINO } *gentlemen at his*
FREDERICK } *court.*
BENVOLIO }
The DUKE OF SAXONY.

The DUKE OF VANHOLT.
The DUCHESS OF VANHOLT.

ROBIN *or* CLOWN.
DICK.
A VINTNER.
A HORSE-COURSER.
A CARTER.
A HOSTESS.
GOOD ANGEL.
BAD ANGEL *or* SPIRIT.
MEPHOSTOPHILIS.
LUCIFER.
BEËLZEBUB.
PRIDE
COVETOUSNESS
ENVY
WRATH } *the Seven Deadly Sins.*
GLUTTONY
SLOTH
LECHERY
A PIPER
ALEXANDER THE GREAT
His PARAMOUR
DARIUS, *King of Persia* } *spirits*
HELEN OF TROY
Two CUPIDS

Devils, Bishops, Monks, Friars, Soldiers, and Attendants.]

The Tragical History of the Life and Death of Doctor Faustus

[Prologue]

Enter CHORUS.

CHORUS. Not marching in the fields of Trasimene*
    Where Mars did mate* the warlike Carthagens,
    Nor sporting in the dalliance of love
    In courts of kings where state* is overturned,
    Nor in the pomp of proud audacious deeds
    Intends our muse to vaunt his heavenly verse.
    Only this, gentles: we must now perform
    The form of Faustus' fortunes, good or bad;
    And so to patient judgments we appeal
    And speak for Faustus in his infancy.   10
    Now is he born, of parents base of stock,
    In Germany, within a town called Rhode;
    At riper years to Wittenberg he went,
    Whereas* his kinsmen chiefly brought him up.
    So much he profits in divinity,

Trasimene: Lake Trasimene in Italy where, in 217 B.C., the
Carthaginian general, Hannibal, led his army to victory.
mate: join with, ally himself with.
state: government.
whereas: where.

[[The fruitful plot of scholarism graced,]]
That shortly he was graced with doctor's name,
Excelling all, and sweetly can dispute
In th'heavenly matters of theology;
Till, swoll'n with cunning* of a self-conceit,   20
His waxen wings did mount above his reach,
And melting,* heavens conspired his overthrow;
For, falling to a devilish exercise,
And glutted now with learning's golden gifts,
He surfeits upon cursèd necromancy;
Nothing so sweet as magic is to him,
Which he prefers before his chiefest bliss.
And this the man that in his study sits.

                                              [[*Exit.*]]

[i]

                    FAUSTUS *in his study.*
FAUSTUS. Settle thy studies, Faustus, and begin
To sound the depth of that thou wilt profess;
Having commenced,* be a divine in show,
Yet level * at the end of every art
And live and die in Aristotle's works.
Sweet Analytics, 'tis thou hast ravished me!
[*He reads.*]
Bene disserere est finis logices:
Is to dispute well logic's chiefest end?
Affords this art no greater miracle?
Then read no more; thou hast attained that end.   10
A greater subject fitteth Faustus' wit.
Bid *on kai me on** farewell, Galen* come,
[*He reads.*]
[[Seeing *ubi desinit philosophus, ibi incipit medicus*]].*
Be a physician, Faustus; heap up gold

cunning: knowledge.
his waxen wings . . . melting: as befell Icarus.
commenced: graduated (with a degree).
level: aim.
on kai me on: being and not being (transliterated from the Greek).
Galen: noted medieval physician.
ubi . . . medicus: where the philosopher stops, there the physician begins.

And be eternized for some wondrous cure.
[*He reads.*]
Summum bonum medicinæ sanitas:
The end of physic is our body's health.
Why, Faustus, hast thou not attained that end?
[[Is not thy common talk sound aphorisms?]]
Are not thy bills° hung up as monuments,   20
Whereby whole cities have escaped the plague
And thousand desperate maladies been cured?
Yet art thou still but Faustus and a man.
Couldst thou make men to live eternally
Or, being dead, raise them to life again,
Then this profession were to be esteemed.
Physic, farewell! Where is Justinian?
[*He reads.*]
Si una eademque res legatu[r] duobus,
Alter rem, alter valorem rei, etc.°
A petty case of paltry legacies!   30
[*He reads.*]
Exhereditar[e] filium non potest pater nisi—°
Such is the subject of the Institute
And universal body of the law.
This study fits a mercenary drudge
Who aims at nothing but external trash,
Too servile and illiberal for me.
When all is done, divinity is best.
Jerome's Bible,° Faustus, view it well:
[*He reads.*]
Stipendium peccati mors est. Ha! *Stipendium, etc.*
The reward of sin is death? That's hard.   40
[*He reads.*]
Si peccasse negamus, fallimur,

---

bills: medicinal prescriptions.

si . . . etc.: if one and the same thing is willed to two persons,
let one of them have the thing, the other the value of the thing,
etc. (Derived from the *Institute* of Justinian, the 6th-century
Roman emperor of Constantinople who was responsible for the
codification of Roman law.)

exhereditar[e] . . . nisi: a father cannot disinherit his son except—

Jerome's Bible: the Vulgate. Faustus quotes (and translates)
from Romans, vi:23, and I John, i:8.

Et nulla est in nobis veritas:
If we say that we have no sin,
We deceive ourselves, and there is no truth in us.
Why, then, belike we must sin
And so consequently die.
Ay, we must die an everlasting death.
What doctrine call you this? *Che sarà, sarà:*
What will be, shall be! Divinity, adieu!　　　　　④　　50
These metaphysics of magicians
And necromantic books are heavenly.
Lines, circles, [signs,] letters [[and]] characters!
Ay, these are those that Faustus most desires.
O, what a world of profit and delight,
Of power, of honor, [[of]] omnipotence
Is promised to the studious artisan!
All things that move between the quiet poles
Shall be at my command. Emperors and kings
Are but obeyed in their several provinces,
[[Nor can they raise the wind or rend the clouds]];　　60
But his dominion that exceeds in this
Stretcheth as far as doth the mind of man.
A sound magician is a demi-god;
Here tire,° my brains, to get° a deity!　Lucifer's sin (original sin)

Enter WAGNER.

Wagner, commend me to my dearest friends,
The German Valdes and Cornelius;
Request them earnestly to visit me.
WAGNER. I will, sir.

　　　　　　　　　　　　　　　　　　　　　Exit.

FAUSTUS. Their conference will be a greater help to me
Than all my labors, plod I ne'er so fast.　　70
Enter the ANGEL *and* SPIRIT.°
GOOD ANGEL. O, Faustus, lay that damnèd book aside
And gaze not on it lest it tempt thy soul
And heap God's heavy wrath upon thy head.
Read, read the Scriptures. *That* is blasphemy.
BAD ANGEL. Go forward, Faustus, in that famous art
Wherein all nature's treasury is contained.

---

tire: i.e., tire yourselves out.
get: beget.
spirit: i.e., evil spirit.

Be thou on earth as Jove is in the sky,
Lord and commander of these elements.

                                        Exeunt Angels.

FAUSTUS. How am I glutted with conceit* of this!
Shall I make spirits fetch me what I please,   80
Resolve me of* all ambiguities,
Perform what desperate enterprise I will?
I'll have them fly to India for gold,
Ransack the ocean for orient pearl,
And search all corners of the new-found world
For pleasant fruits and princely delicates.
I'll have them read me strange philosophy
And tell the secrets of all foreign kings;
I'll have them wall all Germany with brass
And make swift Rhine circle fair Wittenberg.   90
I'll have them fill the public schools with [silk]
Wherewith the students shall be bravely* clad.
I'll levy soldiers with the coin they bring
And chase the Prince of Parma from our land
And reign sole king of all our provinces.*
Yea, stranger engines for the brunt of war
Than was the fiery keel at Antwerp's bridge*
I'll make my servile spirits to invent.

                    Enter VALDES *and* CORNELIUS.

Come, German Valdes and Cornelius,
And make me blessed with your sage conference.   100
Valdes, sweet Valdes, and Cornelius,
Know that your words have won me at the last
To practice magic and concealèd arts;
[[Yet not your words only but mine own fantasy
That will receive no object, for my head
But ruminates on necromantic skill]].
Philosophy is odious and obscure;
Both law and physic are for petty wits;

_____

conceit: notion (of attaining).
resolve me of: resolve for me.
bravely: finely, splendidly.
provinces: the Netherlands, where the Prince of Parma was the
Spanish governor-general.
fiery . . . bridge: the fire-ship that the Dutch employed to
destroy the bridge that Parma had constructed across the Scheldt
river to blockade Antwerp.

[Faustus does none of these things w/ Mephistopheles]

[[Divinity is basest of the three,
Unpleasant, harsh, contemptible, and vile]].   110
'Tis magic, magic, that hath ravished me.
Then, gentle friends, aid me in this attempt,
And I, that have with subtle syllogisms
Gravelled° the pastors of the German church
And made the flow'ring pride of Wittenberg
[[Swarm]] to my problems° as the infernal spirits
On sweet Musæus when he came to hell,
Will be as cunning as Agrippa° was,
Whose shadow[[s]] made all Europe honor him.
VALDES. Faustus, these books, thy wit, and our experi-
      ence   120
Shall make all nations to canonize us.
As Indian Moors° obey their Spanish lords,
So shall the spirits of every element
Be always serviceable to us three:
Like lions shall they guard us when we please,
Like Almain rutters° with their horsemen's staves
Or Lapland giants trotting by our sides,
Sometimes like women or unwedded maids,
Shadowing more beauty in their airy brows
Than has the white breasts of the queen of love.   130
From Venice shall they drag huge argosies,
And from America the golden fleece
That yearly stuffed old Philip's treasury,
If learned Faustus will be resolute.
FAUSTUS. Valdes, as resolute am I in this
As thou to live; therefore, object it not.
CORNELIUS. The miracles that magic will perform
Will make thee vow to study nothing else.
He that is grounded in astrology,
Enriched with tongues, well seen in minerals,   140
Hath all the principles magic doth require.
Then doubt not, Faustus, but to be renowned

---

gravelled: perplexed, amazed.
problems: lectures; public debates.
Agrippa: the German physician, Henry Cornelius Agrippa
(1486–1535), accredited with the power to raise "shadows" from
the dead.
Indian Moors: American Indians.
Almain rutters: German cavalrymen (with "staves" or lances).

And more frequented for this mystery
Than heretofore the Delphian oracle.
The spirits tell me they can dry the sea
And fetch the treasure of all foreign wrecks,
Yea, all the wealth that our forefathers hid
Within the massy entrails of the earth.
Then tell me, Faustus, what shall we three want?

FAUSTUS. Nothing, Cornelius. O, this cheers my soul!   150
Come, show me some demonstrations magical,
That I may conjure in some [[lusty]]* grove
And have these joys in full possession.

VALDES. Then haste thee to some solitary grove
And bear wise Bacon's and Abanus'* works,
The Hebrew Psalter, and New Testament;
And whatsoever else is requisite
We will inform thee ere our conference cease.

CORNELIUS. Valdes, first let him know the words of art,
And then, all other ceremonies learned,   160
Faustus may try his cunning by himself.

VALDES. First, I'll instruct thee in the rudiments,
And then wilt thou be perfecter than I.

FAUSTUS. Then come and dine with me, and after meat
We'll canvas every quiddity* thereof;
For ere I sleep I'll try what I can do:
This night I'll conjure though I die therefore.

*Exeunt omnes.**

[ii]

Enter two SCHOLARS.

1 SCHOLAR. I wonder what's become of Faustus, that
was wont to make our schools ring with *sic probo.**

2 SCHOLAR. That shall we presently* know; here comes
his boy.

---

lusty: pleasant.
Bacon's and Abanus': Roger Bacon (1214?–1294) and Pietro
d'Abano (1250?–1316?)—both considered as magicians in the medieval period.
quiddity: essence of a thing (scholastic).
omnes: all.
sic probo: thus I prove (scholastic).
presently: at once, immediately.

Enter WAGNER.

1 SCHOLAR. How now, sirrah, where's thy master?

WAGNER. God in heaven knows.

2 SCHOLAR. Why, dost not thou know then?

WAGNER. Yes, I know; but that follows not.

1 SCHOLAR. Go to, sirrah, leave your jesting and tell us
where he is.   10

WAGNER. That follows not by force of argument, which
you, being licentiates,* should stand upon; therefore,
acknowledge your error and be attentive.

2 SCHOLAR. Then you will not tell us?

WAGNER. You are deceived, for I will tell you. Yet, if
you were not dunces, you would never ask me such
a question. For is he not *corpus naturale?** and is not
that *mobile?* Then wherefore should you ask me such
a question? But that I am by nature phlegmatic, slow
to wrath, and prone to lechery (to love, I would say),   20
it were not for you to come within forty foot of the
place of execution although I do not doubt but to see
you both hanged the next sessions. Thus having triumphed over you, I will set my countenance like a
precisian* and begin to speak thus:

Truly, my dear brethren, my master is within at dinner with Valdes and Cornelius as this wine, if it could
speak, would inform your worships. And so, the Lord
bless you, preserve you, and keep you, my dear brethren.   30

Exit.

1 SCHOLAR. O Faustus, then I fear that which I have
long suspected:

That thou art fall'n into that damnèd art

For which they two are infamous through the world.

2 SCHOLAR. Were he a stranger, not allied to me,

The danger of his soul would make me mourn.

But come, let us go and inform the rector;

It may be his grave counsel may reclaim him.

---

licentiates: graduates.

corpus naturale: a natural body (*corpus naturale seu mobile:*
scholastic terminology for the subject matter of physics).

precisian: puritan.

1 SCHOLAR. I fear me nothing will reclaim him now.
2 SCHOLAR. Yet let us see what we can do.

Exeunt.

[iii]
     Thunder. Enter LUCIFER *and four Devils [above].*
       [[Enter FAUSTUS *to conjure.]]*
FAUSTUS. Now that the gloomy shadow of the night,
   Longing to view Orion's drizzling look,
   Leaps from th'antarctic world unto the sky
   And dims the welkin° with her pitchy breath,
   Faustus, begin thine incantations
   And try if devils will obey thy hest,
   Seeing thou hast prayed and sacrificed to them.
   Within this circle is Jehovah's name,
   Forward and backward anagrammatized,
   Th'abbreviated names of holy saints,   °
   Figures of every adjunct to the heavens,
   And characters of signs and [[erring]] stars,°
   By which the spirits are enforced to rise.
   Then fear not, Faustus, to be resolute
   And try the utmost magic can perform.
   (*Thunder.*)
   Sint mihi dei Acherontis propitii! Valeat numen triplex
   Jehovæ! Ignei, ærii, aquatani spiritus, salvete! Orientis
   princeps, Beëlzebub, inferni ardentis monarcha, et
   Demogorgon, propitiamus vos ut appareat et surgat
   Mephostophilis.   20
   (*Dragon [above].*)
   [Quid tu moraris?] Per Jehovam, Gehennam, et conse-
   cratam aquam quam nunc spargo, signumque crucis
   quod nunc facio, et per vota nostra, ipse nunc surgat
   nobis dicat[u]s Mephostophilis.°

---

welkin: sky; world.
signs . . . stars: the Zodiac and the Planets.
sint mihi . . . Mephostophilis: may the gods of Acheron be favorably inclined toward me! Away with the triple name of Jehovah!
Hail, spirits of fire, air, [and] water. Prince of the East, Beëlzebub,
monarch of burning hell, and Demogorgon, we pray to you that
Mephostophilis may appear and rise. . . . Why do you delay? By
Jehovah, Gehenna, and the holy water which I now sprinkle, and
by the sign of the cross which I now make, and by our prayers, let
Mephostophilis himself, evoked by us, now rise!

Enter a Devil.

I charge thee to return and change thy shape;
Thou art too ugly to attend on me.
Go, and return an old Franciscan friar;
That holy shape becomes a devil best.

Exit Devil.

I see there's virtue in my <u>heavenly</u> words.
Who would not be proficient in this art?   30
How pliant is this Mephostophilis,
Full of <u>obedience and humility!</u>
Such is the force of magic and my spells.
[[Now, Faustus, thou art conjuror laureate,
That canst command great Mephostophilis.
Quin re[d]is, Mephostophilis, fratris imagine!]]*

Enter MEPHOSTOPHILIS.

MEPHOSTOPHILIS. Now, Faustus, what wouldst thou have me do?

FAUSTUS. I charge thee wait upon me whilst I live,
To do whatever Faustus shall command,
Be it to make the moon drop from her sphere   40
Or the ocean to overwhelm the world.

MEPHOSTOPHILIS. I am a servant to great Lucifer
And may not follow thee without his leave;
No more than he commands must we perform.

FAUSTUS. Did not he charge thee to appear to me?

MEPHOSTOPHILIS. No, I came now hither of mine own accord.

FAUSTUS. Did not my conjuring [[speeches]] raise thee? Speak!

MEPHOSTOPHILIS. That was the cause, but yet *per acciden[s]:*
For when we hear one rack the name of God,
Abjure the Scriptures and his Savior Christ,   50
We fly in hope to get his glorious soul;
Nor will we come unless he use such means
Whereby he is in danger to be damned.
Therefore, the shortest cut for conjuring
Is stoutly to abjure [[the Trinity]]
And pray devoutly to the prince of hell.

---

quin . . . imagine: Why not return, Mephostophilis, in the disguise of a friar!

FAUSTUS. So Faustus hath already done and holds this
    principle:
There is no chief but only Beëlzebub,
To whom Faustus doth dedicate himself.
This word "damnation" terrifies not me,   60
For I confound hell in Elysium.
My ghost be with the old philosophers!
But, leaving these vain trifles of men's souls,
Tell me, what is that Lucifer thy lord?

MEPHOSTOPHILIS. Arch-regent and commander of all
    spirits.

FAUSTUS. Was not that Lucifer an angel once?

MEPHOSTOPHILIS. Yes, Faustus, and most dearly loved
    of God.

FAUSTUS. How comes it then that he is prince of devils?

MEPHOSTOPHILIS. O, by aspiring pride and insolence,
For which God threw him down from the face of
    heaven.   70

FAUSTUS. And what are you that live with Lucifer?

MEPHOSTOPHILIS. Unhappy spirits that live with Lucifer,
Conspired against our God with Lucifer,
And are forever damned with Lucifer.

FAUSTUS. Where are you damned?

MEPHOSTOPHILIS.   In hell.

FAUSTUS. How comes it then that thou art out of hell?

MEPHOSTOPHILIS. Why, this is hell, nor am I out of it.
Think'st thou that I [[who]] saw the face of God
And tasted the eternal joys of heaven
Am not tormented with ten thousand hells   80
In being deprived of everlasting bliss?
O Faustus, leave these frivolous demands,
Which strike a terror to my fainting soul.

FAUSTUS. What, is great Mephostophilis so passionate
For being deprived of the joys of heaven?
Learn thou of Faustus manly fortitude
And scorn those joys thou never shalt possess.
Go bear these tidings to great Lucifer:
Seeing Faustus hath incurred eternal death
By desperate thoughts against Jove's deity,   90
Say he surrenders up to him his soul
So he will spare him four and twenty years,
Letting him live in all voluptuousness,
Having thee ever to attend on me,

    To give me whatsoever I shall ask,
    To tell me whatsoever I demand,
    To slay mine enemies [[and aid]] my friends,
    And always be obedient to my will.
    Go, and return to mighty Lucifer,
    And meet me in my study at <u>midnight</u>,   100
    And then resolve me of thy master's mind.
MEPHOSTOPHILIS. I will, Faustus.

Q: as the break between night and day

Exit.

FAUSTUS. Had I as many souls as there be stars,
    I'd give them all for Mephostophilis.
    By him I'll be great emperor of the world
    And make a bridge th[o]rough the moving air
    To pass the ocean with a band of men.
    I'll join the hills that bind the Afric shore
    And make that country continent to Spain
    And both contributory to my crown.   110
    The Emperor shall not live but by my leave,
    Nor any potentate of Germany.
    Now that I have obtained what I desire,
    I'll live in speculation of this art
    Till Mephostophilis return again.

                                                        Exit.
                            [*Exeunt* LUCIFER *and four Devils.*]

[iv]
                Enter WAGNER *and* [ROBIN,] *the* CLOWN.

WAGNER. Come hither, sirrah boy.
ROBIN. Boy! O, disgrace to my person! Zounds, boy in
    your face! You have seen many boys with [[such
    pickedevants°]], I am sure.
WAGNER. Sirrah, hast thou no comings in?°
ROBIN. Yes, and goings out too, you may see, sir.
WAGNER. Alas, poor slave! See how poverty jests in his
    nakedness. I know the villain's out of service, and so
    hungry that I know he would give his soul to the
    devil for a shoulder of mutton though it were blood-   10
    raw.

    ———

    pickedevants: pointed beards.
    comings in: earnings.

ROBIN. Not so neither! I had need to have it well roasted,
and good sauce to it, if I pay so dear, I can tell you.

WAGNER. Sirrah, wilt thou be my man and wait on me,
and I will make thee go like *Qui mihi discipulus?**

ROBIN. What, in verse?

WAGNER. No,.slave, in beaten* silk and stavesacre.

ROBIN. Stavesacre! That's good to kill vermin; then, belike, if I serve you, I shall be lousy.

WAGNER. Why, so thou shalt be whether thou dost it or   20
no; for, sirrah, if thou dost not presently bind thyself
to me for seven years, I'll turn all the lice about thee
into familiars* and make them tear thee in pieces.

ROBIN. Nay, sir, you may save yourself a labor, for they
are as familiar with me as if they paid for their meat
and drink, I can tell you.

WAGNER. Well, sirrah, leave your jesting and take these
guilders.

ROBIN. Yes, marry, sir, and I thank you too.

WAGNER. So, now thou art to be at an hour's warning,   30
whensoever and wheresoever the devil shall fetch thee.

ROBIN. Here, take your guilders [[again]]; I'll none of
'em.

WAGNER. Not I. Thou art pressed;* prepare thyself, for
I will presently raise up two devils to carry thee away.
—Banio! Belcher!

ROBIN. Belcher! And Belcher come here, I'll belch him.
I am not afraid of a devil.

Enter two Devils [[and the CLOWN [ROBIN] *runs up and
down crying]].*

WAGNER. How now, sir, will you serve me now?

ROBIN. Ay, good Wagner; take away the devil then.   40

WAGNER. Spirits, away! [*Exeunt Devils.*] Now, sirrah,
follow me.

ROBIN. I will, sir. But hark you, master, will you teach
me this conjuring occupation?

WAGNER. Ay, sirrah, I'll teach thee to turn thyself to a
dog, or a cat, or a mouse, or a rat, or anything.

---

qui mihi discipulus: you who are my pupil (beginning of a
didactic poem by the Elizabethan schoolmaster William Lily).
beaten: embroidered.
familiars: attendant spirits or demons.
pressed: impressed (as impressment of troops); hired.

ROBIN. A dog, or a cat, or a mouse, or a rat! O brave
    Wagner!
WAGNER. Villain, call me Master Wagner, and see that
    you walk attentively, and let your right eye be always   50
    diametrally fixed upon my <u>left heel</u>, that thou mayst
    *quasi vestigiis nostras insistere.**
ROBIN. Well, sir, I warrant you.

                                          Exeunt.

[v]
               Enter FAUSTUS *in his study.*
FAUSTUS. Now, Faustus, must thou needs be damned,
    [[And]] canst thou not be saved?
    What boots it then to think on God or heaven?
    Away with such vain fancies and despair;
    Despair in God, and trust in Beëlzebub.
    Now go not backward. Faustus, be resolute!
    Why waver'st thou? O, something soundeth in mine
        ear:
    "Abjure this magic; turn to God again!"
    [[Ay, and Faustus will turn to God again.
    To God?]] He loves thee not.   10
    The god thou serv'st is <u>thine own appetite</u>,
    Wherein is fixed the love of Beëlzebub:
    To him I'll build an altar and a church
    And offer <u>lukewarm</u> blood of new-born babes.
                 Enter the two Angels.
BAD ANGEL. Go forward, Faustus, in that famous art.
GOOD ANGEL. Sweet Faustus, leave that execrable art.
FAUSTUS. <u>Contrition, prayer, repentance</u>—what of these?
GOOD ANGEL. O, they are means to bring thee unto heaven.
BAD ANGEL. Rather illusions, fruits of lunacy,
    That make [[men]] foolish that do use them most.   20
GOOD ANGEL. Sweet Faustus, think of heaven and heav-
    enly things.
BAD ANGEL. No, Faustus, think of <u>honor</u> and of <u>wealth</u>.
                           Exeunt Angels.
FAUSTUS. Wealth! Why, the signory of Emden* shall be
    mine.

---

    quasi . . . insistere: as if to follow hard on my footsteps.
    Emden: German port with which England carried on heavy
trading.

When Mephostophilis shall stand by me,
What power can hurt me? Faustus, thou art safe.
Cast no more doubts! Mephostophilis, come
And bring glad tidings from great Lucifer.
Is't not midnight? Come, Mephostophilis.
Veni,° *veni, Mephostophile!*

> *Enter* MEPHOSTOPHILIS.

Now tell me what saith Lucifer thy lord?   30
[[MEPHOSTOPHILIS.]] That I shall wait on Faustus whilst
  he lives,
So he will buy my service with his soul.
FAUSTUS. Already Faustus hath hazarded that for thee.
MEPHOSTOPHILIS. But now thou must bequeath it sol-
  emnly
And write a deed of gift with thine own blood,
For that security craves Lucifer.
If thou deny it, I must back to hell.
FAUSTUS. Stay, Mephostophilis, and tell me
What good will my soul do thy lord?
MEPHOSTOPHILIS.   Enlarge his kingdom.
FAUSTUS. Is that the reason why he tempts us thus?   40
MEPHOSTOPHILIS. *Solamen miseris socios habuisse do-*
  loris.°
FAUSTUS. Why, have you any pain that torture [[others]]?
MEPHOSTOPHILIS. As great as have the human souls of
  men.
But tell me, Faustus, shall I have thy soul?
And I will be thy slave and wait on thee
And give thee more than thou hast wit to ask.
FAUSTUS. Ay, Mephostophilis, I'll give it him.
MEPHOSTOPHILIS. Then, Faustus, stab thy arm coura-
  geously,
And bind thy soul that at some certain day
Great Lucifer may claim it as his own;   50
And then be thou as great as Lucifer.
FAUSTUS. Lo, Mephostophilis, for love of thee
  [*He stabs his arm.*]
Faustus hath cut his arm, and with his proper° blood

---

veni: come.

solamen . . . doloris: a consolation to the unfortunate is to have
had partners in suffering.   *proper:* own.

Assures his soul to be great Lucifer's,
Chief lord and regent of perpetual night.
View here this blood that trickles from mine arm,
And let it be propitious for my wish.
MEPHOSTOPHILIS. But, Faustus,
Write it in manner of a deed of gift.
FAUSTUS. Ay, so I do. But, Mephostophilis,   60
My blood congeals, and I can write no more.
MEPHOSTOPHILIS. I'll fetch thee <u>fire</u> to dissolve it straight.

> *Exit.*

FAUSTUS. What might the staying of my blood portend?
Is it unwilling I should write this bill?
Why streams it not that I may write afresh?
"Faustus gives to thee his soul." O, there it stayed.
Why shouldst thou not? Is not thy soul thine own?
Then write again: "Faustus gives to thee his soul."
> *Enter* MEPHOSTOPHILIS *with the chafer of fire.*
MEPHOSTOPHILIS. See, Faustus, here is fire; set it on.
FAUSTUS. So, now the blood begins to clear again.   70
Now will I make an end immediately.
[*He writes.*]
MEPHOSTOPHILIS [*aside*]. What will not I do to obtain
his soul!
FAUSTUS. <u>*Consummatum est:*</u>* this bill is ended,
And Faustus hath bequeathed his soul to Lucifer.
But what is this inscription on mine arm?
Homo fuge! * Whither should I fly?
If unto [[God]], he'll throw me down to hell.
My senses are deceived; here's nothing writ.
O yes, I see it plain. Even here is writ
Homo fuge! Yet shall not Faustus fly.   80
MEPHOSTOPHILIS [*aside*]. I'll fetch him somewhat to de-
light his mind.

> *Exit.*

> *Enter Devils, giving crowns and rich apparel*
> *to* FAUSTUS. *They dance and then depart.*
> *Enter* MEPHOSTOPHILIS.
FAUSTUS. What means this show? Speak, Mephostophilis.

---

consummatum est: it is finished (the last words of Christ on the
cross, John, xix, 30).
homo fuge: fly, man!

MEPHOSTOPHILIS. Nothing, Faustus, but to delight thy
    mind
And let thee see what magic can perform.
FAUSTUS. But may I raise such spirits when I please?
MEPHOSTOPHILIS. Ay, Faustus, and do greater things
    than these. _allusion_
FAUSTUS. Then, Mephostophilis, receive this scroll,
    A deed of gift of body and of soul:
    But yet conditionally that thou perform
    All covenants and articles between us both.   90
MEPHOSTOPHILIS. Faustus, I swear by hell and Lucifer
    To effect all promises between us [made].
FAUSTUS. Then hear me read it, Mephostophilis.
    On these conditions following:
       First, that Faustus may be a spirit in form and sub-
    stance;
       Secondly, that Mephostophilis shall be his servant
    and [[at his command]];
       Thirdly, that Mephostophilis shall do for him and
    bring him whatsoever;   100
       Fourthly, that he shall be in his chamber or house
    invisible;
       Lastly, that he shall appear to the said John Faustus
    at all times in what [[form or shape]] soever he please;
       I, John Faustus of Wittenberg, doctor, by these
    presents do give both body and soul to Lucifer, Prince
    of the East, and his minister, Mephostophilis, and fur-
    thermore grant unto them that, four and twenty years
    being expired, [[the]] articles above written inviolate,
    full power to fetch or carry the said John Faustus,   110
    body and soul, flesh, blood, [[or goods]], into their
    habitation wheresoever.

                     By me, John Faustus.
MEPHOSTOPHILIS. Speak, Faustus. Do you deliver this
    as your deed?
FAUSTUS. Ay, take it, and the devil give thee good of it!
MEPHOSTOPHILIS. So now, Faustus, ask me what thou
    wilt.
FAUSTUS. First [[will I question with]] thee about hell.
    Tell me, where is the place that men call hell?
MEPHOSTOPHILIS. Under the heavens.
FAUSTUS. Ay, so are all things else; but whereabouts?   120
MEPHOSTOPHILIS. Within the bowels of these elements,

Where we are tortured and remain for ever.
Hell hath no limits, nor is circumscribed
In one self place, but where we are is hell,
And where hell is there must we ever be.
And, to be short, when all the world dissolves
And every creature shall be purified,
All places shall be hell that is not heaven.

FAUSTUS. I think hell's a fable.

MEPHOSTOPHILIS. Ay, think so still till experience change
   thy mind.   130

FAUSTUS. Why, dost thou think that Faustus shall be
   damned?

MEPHOSTOPHILIS. Ay, of necessity, for here's the scroll
In which thou hast given thy soul to Lucifer.

FAUSTUS. Ay, and body too; but what of that?
Think'st thou that Faustus is so fond* to imagine
That after this life there is any pain?
No, these are trifles and mere old wives' tales.

MEPHOSTOPHILIS. But I am an instance to prove the contrary,
For I tell thee I am damned and now in hell.

FAUSTUS. Nay, and this be hell, I'll willingly be damned.   140
What! Sleeping, eating, walking, and disputing! But,
leaving this, let me have a wife, the fairest maid in
Germany; for I am wanton and lascivious and cannot
live without a wife.

MEPHOSTOPHILIS. [[How, a wife! I prithee, Faustus, talk
not of a wife.

FAUSTUS. Nay, sweet Mephostophilis, fetch me one, for
I will have one.

MEPHOSTOPHILIS. Well, thou wilt have one. Sit there till   150
I come; I'll fetch thee a wife in the devil's name.

                                      [Exit.]

   [Re-]enter [MEPHOSTOPHILIS] *with a Devil dressed
     like a woman, with fireworks.*]]

FAUSTUS. What sight is this?

MEPHOSTOPHILIS. [[Tell [me], Faustus, how dost thou
like thy wife?

FAUSTUS. A plague on her for a hot whore!]] No, I'll no
wife.

MEPHOSTOPHILIS. Marriage is but a ceremonial toy;

---

fond: foolish.

And, if thou lovest me, think no more of it.
I'll cull thee out the fairest courtesans
And bring them every morning to thy bed:
She whom thine eye shall like, thy heart shall have,
Were she as chaste as was Penelope,*
As wise as Saba,* or as beautiful   160
As was bright Lucifer before his fall.
[[Hold; take this book; peruse it thoroughly.]]
The iterating of these lines brings gold;
The framing of this circle on the ground
Brings thunder, whirlwinds, storm, and lightning.
Pronounce this thrice devoutly to thyself
And men in harness* shall appear to thee,
Ready to execute what thou command'st.
FAUSTUS. Thanks, Mephostophilis, for this sweet book.
This will I keep as chary as my life.   170

                                              Exeunt.

[vi]
        Enter FAUSTUS *in his study and* MEPHOSTOPHILIS.
FAUSTUS. When I behold the heavens, then I repent
    And curse thee, wicked Mephostophilis,
    Because thou hast deprived me of those joys.
MEPHOSTOPHILIS. 'Twas thine own seeking, Faustus;
    thank thyself.
    But think'st thou heaven is such a glorious thing?
    I tell thee, Faustus, it is not half so fair
    As thou or any man that breathes on earth.
FAUSTUS. How prov'st thou that?
MEPHOSTOPHILIS. 'Twas made for man; then he's more
    excellent.
FAUSTUS. If heaven was made for man, 'twas made for
    me: 10
    I will renounce this magic and repent.
                Enter the two Angels.
GOOD ANGEL. Faustus, repent; yet God will pity thee.
BAD ANGEL. Thou art a spirit;* God cannot pity thee.

Penelope: Ulysses' faithful wife.
Saba: Sheba.
harness: armor.
exeunt: editors conjecture a missing scene at this point.
spirit: i.e., evil spirit.

FAUSTUS. Who buzzeth in mine ears I am a spirit?
  Be I a devil, yet God may pity me;
  Yea, God will pity me if I repent.
BAD ANGEL. Ay, but Faustus never shall repent.
                                    [[*Exeunt*]] *Angels.*
FAUSTUS. My heart is hardened; I cannot repent.
  Scarce can I name salvation, faith, or heaven,
  [[But fearful echoes thunders in mine ears,   20
  "Faustus, thou art damned!" Then swords and knives,
  Poison, guns, halters, and envenomed steel]]
  Are laid before me to dispatch myself.
  And long ere this I should have done the deed
  Had not sweet pleasure conquered deep despair.
  Have not I made blind Homer sing to me
  Of Alexander's* love and Oenon's death?
  And hath not he,* that built the walls of Thebes
  With ravishing sound of his melodious harp,
  Made music with my Mephostophilis?
  Why should I die, then, or basely despair?
  I am resolved Faustus shall not repent.—
  Come, Mephostophilis, let us dispute again   30
  And reason of divine astrology.
  Speak; are there many spheres above the moon?
  Are all celestial bodies but one globe
  As is the substance of this centric earth?
MEPHOSTOPHILIS. As are the elements, such are the heav-
    ens,
  Even from the moon unto the empyreal orb,
  Mutually folded in each other's spheres,   40
  And jointly move upon one axle-tree,
  Whose terminè is termed the world's wide pole;
  Nor are the names of Saturn, Mars, or Jupiter
  Feigned, but are erring stars.
FAUSTUS.   But have they all
  One motion, both *situ et tempore?**
MEPHOSTOPHILIS. All move from east to west in four and
  twenty hours upon the poles of the world but differ in
  their motions upon the poles of the zodiac.

  Alexander: or Paris, whose desertion of the nymph Oenone
caused her death.
  he: Amphion, son of Zeus and Antiope.
  situ et tempore: in place and time.

FAUSTUS. These slender questions Wagner can decide.
Hath Mephostophilis no greater skill?   50
Who knows not the double motion of the planets?
That the first is finished in a natural day?
The second thus: Saturn in thirty years;
Jupiter in twelve; Mars in four; the sun, Venus, and
Mercury in a year; the moon in twenty-eight days?
These are freshmen's [[suppositions]]. But tell me,
hath every sphere a dominion or *intelligentia?*

MEPHOSTOPHILIS. Ay.

FAUSTUS. How many heavens or spheres are there?

MEPHOSTOPHILIS. Nine: the seven planets, the firma-   60
ment, and the empyreal heaven.

FAUSTUS. But is there not *cœlum igneum? et crystallinum?**

MEPHOSTOPHILIS. No, Faustus, they be but fables.

FAUSTUS. Resolve me then in this one question: Why are
not conjuctions, oppositions, aspects, eclipses all at one
time, but in some years we have more, in some less?

MEPHOSTOPHILIS. *Per inæqualem motum respectu totius.**

FAUSTUS. Well, I am answered. Now tell me who made   70
the world?

MEPHOSTOPHILIS. I will not.

FAUSTUS. Sweet Mephostophilis, tell me.

MEPHOSTOPHILIS. Move me not, Faustus.

FAUSTUS. Villain, have not I bound thee to tell me any
thing?

MEPHOSTOPHILIS. Ay, that is not against our kingdom.
This is. Thou art damned; think thou of hell.

FAUSTUS. Think, Faustus, upon <u>God</u> that made the
world.

MEPHOSTOPHILIS. Remember this!   80

                                                                Exit.

FAUSTUS. Ay, go accursèd spirit, to thy ugly hell!
'Tis thou hast damned distressèd Faustus' soul.
Is't not too late?

                    Enter the two Angels.

------

cœlum . . . *crystallinum:* fiery and crystaline spheres.
per . . . *totius:* because of their unequal motion regarding the
whole.

BAD ANGEL. Too late.

GOOD ANGEL. Never too late if Faustus will repent.

BAD ANGEL. If thou repent, devils will tear thee in pieces.

GOOD ANGEL. Repent, and they shall never raze thy skin.

Exeunt Angels.

FAUSTUS. O Christ, my Savior, my Savior,
Help to save distressèd Faustus' soul.

Enter LUCIFER, BEËLZEBUB, *and* MEPHOSTOPHILIS.

LUCIFER. Christ cannot save thy soul, for he is just.   90
There's none but I have interest in the same.

FAUSTUS. O, what art thou that look'st so terribly?

LUCIFER. I am Lucifer,
And this is my companion prince in hell.

FAUSTUS. O Faustus, they are come to fetch thy soul.

BEËLZEBUB. We are come to tell thee thou dost injure us.

LUCIFER. Thou call'st on Christ contrary to thy promise.

BEËLZEBUB. Thou shouldst not think on God.

LUCIFER. Think on the devil.

BEËLZEBUB. And his dam, too.   100

FAUSTUS. Nor will Faustus henceforth. Pardon [[me in]]
this,
And Faustus vows never to look to heaven,
[[Never to name God or to pray to him,
To burn his Scriptures, slay his ministers,
And make my spirits pull his churches down]].

LUCIFER. So shalt thou show thyself an obedient servant,
And we will highly gratify thee for it.

BEËLZEBUB. Faustus, we are come from hell in person
to show thee some pastime. Sit down, and thou shalt
behold the Seven Deadly Sins appear to thee in their   110
own proper shapes and likeness.

FAUSTUS. That sight will be as pleasant to me as Paradise
was to Adam the first day of his creation.

LUCIFER. Talk not of Paradise or creation, but mark the
show.——Go, Mephostophilis, fetch them in.

[Exit MEPHOSTOPHILIS.*]*

Enter the Seven Deadly Sins [led in by MEPHOSTOPHILIS
and a Piper].

BEËLZEBUB. Now, Faustus, question them of their names
and dispositions.

FAUSTUS. That shall I soon.——What art thou, the first?

PRIDE. I am Pride. I disdain to have any parents. I am

like to Ovid's flea; I can creep into every corner of a   120
wench. Sometimes, like a periwig, I sit upon her brow;
next, like a necklace, I hang about her neck; then, like
a fan of feathers, I kiss her [[lips]]; and, then, turning
myself to a wrought° smock, do what I list. But fie,
what a smell is here! I'll not speak [[another word]]
unless the ground be perfumed and covered with cloth
of arras.

FAUSTUS. Thou art a proud knave indeed.—What art
thou, the second?

COVETOUSNESS. I am Covetousness, begotten of an old   130
churl in a leather bag; and, might I now obtain my
wish, this house, you and all, should turn to gold, that
I might lock you safe into my chest. O my sweet gold!

FAUSTUS. And what art thou, the third?

ENVY. I am Envy, begotten of a chimney-sweeper and an
oyster-wife. I cannot read and therefore wish all books
burned. I am lean with seeing others eat. O, that there
would come a famine over all the world, that all might
die, and I live alone! Then thou shouldst see how fat
I'd be. But must thou sit and I stand? Come down,   140
with a vengeance!

FAUSTUS. Out, envious wretch!—But what art thou, the
fourth?

WRATH. I am Wrath. I had neither father nor mother; I
leaped out of a lion's mouth when I was scarce an hour
old, and ever since have run up and down the world
with [[this]] case of rapiers, wounding myself when I
could get none to fight withal. I was born in hell—and
look to it, for some of you shall be my father.

FAUSTUS. And what art thou, the fifth?   150

GLUTTONY. I am Gluttony. My parents are all dead, and
the devil a penny they have left me but a small pension, and that buys me thirty meals a day and ten
bevers°—a small trifle to suffice nature. I come of a
royal pedigree: my father was a gammon of bacon,
and my mother was a hogshead of claret wine. My
godfathers were these: Peter Pickled-herring and Martin Martlemas-beef. But my godmother, O, she was [[a
jolly gentlewoman, and well beloved in every good

---

wrought: embroidered.
bevers: light snacks.

town and city; her name was Mistress Margery March-   160
beer]]. Now, Faustus, thou hast heard all my progeny;° wilt thou bid me to supper?

FAUSTUS. [[No, I'll see thee hanged! Thou wilt eat up all
my victuals.]]

GLUTTONY. Then the devil choke thee!

FAUSTUS. Choke thyself, glutton!—What art thou, the
sixth?

SLOTH. Heigh-ho! I am Sloth. I was begotten on a sunny
bank, [[where I have lain ever since; and you have
done me great injury to bring me from thence. Let me   170
be carried thither again by Gluttony and Lechery]].
Heigh-ho! I'll not speak a word more for a king's ransom.

FAUSTUS. And what are you, Mistress Minx, the seventh
and last?

LECHERY. Who? [[I, sir?]] I am one that loves an inch
of raw mutton° better than an ell of fried stockfish,
and the first letter of my name begins with Lechery.

LUCIFER. Away, to hell, away! On, piper!

                Exeunt the Seven Sins [and the Piper].

FAUSTUS. O, how this sight doth delight my soul!   180

LUCIFER. But, Faustus, in hell is all manner of delight.

FAUSTUS. O, might I see hell and return again safe, how
happy were I then!

LUCIFER. Faustus, thou shalt; at midnight I will send
for thee. Meanwhile, peruse this book and view it
thoroughly, and thou shalt turn thyself into what shape
thou wilt.

FAUSTUS. Thanks, mighty Lucifer. This will I keep as
chary as my life.

LUCIFER. Now, Faustus, farewell.   190

FAUSTUS. Farewell, great Lucifer.—Come, Mephostophilis.

                Exeunt omnes, several ways.

[vii]

            Enter the CLOWN [ROBIN].

ROBIN. What, Dick, look to the horses there till I come
again. I have gotten one of Doctor Faustus' conjuring
books, and now we'll have such knavery as't passes.

_____

progeny: lineage.   raw mutton: prostitute.

Enter DICK.

DICK. What, Robin, you must come away and walk the horses.

ROBIN. I walk the horses! I scorn't, 'faith; I have other matters in hand. Let the horses walk themselves and they will. [*He reads.*] "A *per se,** a; t, h, e, the; o *per se,* o; *deny orgon, gorgon.*"* Keep further from me, O thou illiterate and unlearned hostler.   10

DICK. 'Snails,* what has thou got there, a book? Why, thou canst not tell ne'er a word on't.

ROBIN. That thou shalt see presently. Keep out of the circle, I say, lest I send you into the hostry* with a vengeance.

DICK. That's like, 'faith! You had best leave your foolery; for, an my master come, he'll conjure you, 'faith.

ROBIN. My master conjure me! I'll tell thee what: an my master come here, I'll clap as fair a pair of horns* on's head as e'er thou sawest in thy life.   20

DICK. Thou needst not do that, for my mistress hath done it.

ROBIN. Ay, there be of us here that have waded as deep into matters as other men if they were disposed to talk.

DICK. A plague take you! I thought you did not sneak up and down after her for nothing. But I prithee tell me in good sadness,* Robin, is that a conjuring book?

ROBIN. Do but speak what thou't have me to do, and I'll do't. If thou't dance naked, put off thy clothes, and I'll conjure thee about presently. Or, if thou't go   30 but to the tavern with me, I'll give thee white wine, red wine, claret wine, sack, muscadine, malmsey, and whippincrust.* Hold, belly, hold, and we'll not pay one penny for it.

---

per se: by itself (a *per se,* a: "a" by itself spells "a").

deny orgon, gorgon: Robin is trying to make out the word *Demogorgon* (see iii. 19).

'snails: contraction of "by God's nails!"

hostry: inn.

horns: traditional sign of a cuckold.

in good sadness: in earnest.

whippincrust: hippocras (?).

DICK. O brave! Prithee let's to it presently, for I am as
   dry as a dog.
ROBIN. Come, then, let's away.

Exeunt.

[Chorus I]
                    Enter the CHORUS.
CHORUS. Learned Faustus,
   To find the secrets of astronomy,
   Graven in the book of Jove's high firmament,
   Did mount him up to scale Olympus' top,
   Where, sitting in a chariot burning bright
   Drawn by the strength of yokèd dragons' necks,
   He views the clouds, the planets, and the stars,
   The tropic[s], zones, and quarters of the sky,
   From the bright circle of the hornèd moon
   Even to the height of *Primum Mobile;** 10
   And, whirling round with this circumference
   Within the concave compass of the pole,
   From east to west his dragons swiftly glide
   And in eight days did bring him home again.
   Not long he stayed within his quiet house
   To rest his bones after his weary toil,
   But new exploits do hale him out again;
   And, mounted then upon a dragon's back,
   That with his wings did part the subtle air,
   He now is gone to prove* cosmography, 20
   That measures coasts and kingdoms of the earth,
   And, as I guess, will first arrive at Rome
   To see the Pope and manner of his court
   And take some part of holy Peter's feast,
   The which this day is highly solemnized.

Exit.

[viii]
                    Enter FAUSTUS *and* MEPHOSTOPHILIS.
FAUSTUS. Having now, my good Mephostophilis,
   Passed with delight the stately town of Trier,

Primum Mobile: First Mover; outermost sphere of creation (in
Ptolemaic astronomy).
   prove: test, explore.

Environed round with airy mountain tops,
With walls of flint and deep-entrenchèd lakes,*
Not to be won by any conquering prince;
From Paris next, coasting the realm of France,
We saw the river Main fall into Rhine,
Whose banks are set with groves of fruitful vines;
Then up to Naples, rich Campania,
[With] buildings fair and gorgeous to the eye,   10
[Whose] streets straight forth, and paved with finest
    brick,
[[Quarters the town in four [equivalents]]].
There saw we learned Maro's* golden tomb,
The way he cut an English mile in length
[[Thorough]] a rock of stone in one night's space.
From thence to Venice, Padua, and the [[rest,
In midst]] of which a sumptuous temple stands,
That threats the stars with her aspiring top,
Whose frame is paved with sundry colored stones
And roofed aloft with curious * work in gold.   20
Thus hitherto hath Faustus spent his time.
But tell me now, what resting place is this?
Hast thou, as erst I did command,
Conducted me within the walls of Rome?

MEPHOSTOPHILIS. I have, my Faustus, and for proof
    thereof
This is the goodly palace of the Pope;
And, 'cause we are no common guests,
I choose his privy chamber for our use.

FAUSTUS. I hope his holiness will bid us welcome.

MEPHOSTOPHILIS. All's one, for we'll be bold with his
    ven[i]son.   30
But now, my Faustus, that thou mayst perceive
What Rome contains for to delight thine eyes,
Know that this city stands upon seven hills
That underprop the groundwork of the same.
Just through the midst runs flowing Tiber's stream,
With winding banks that cut it in two parts,
Over the which [[four]] stately bridges lean,

---

lakes: moats.
Maro: Virgil, famous as a magician in the middle ages.
curious: expert; intricate.

That make safe passage to each part of Rome.
Upon the bridge called Pont[e] Angelo
Erected is a castle passing strong,   40
Where thou shalt see such store of ordinance
As that the double cannons forged of brass
Do [[match]] the number of the days contained
Within the compass of one complete year;
Beside the gates and high pyramides*
That Julius Cæsar brought from Africa.

FAUSTUS. Now, by the kingdoms of infernal rule,
Of Styx, of Acheron, and the fiery lake
Of ever-burning Phlegeton, I swear
That I do long to see the monuments   50
And situation of bright-splendent Rome.
Come, therefore, let's away.

MEPHOSTOPHILIS. Nay, stay, my Faustus. I know you'd
    see the Pope
And take some part of holy Peter's feast,
The which [[in state and]] high solemnity
This day is held through Rome and Italy
In honor of the Pope's triumphant victory.

FAUSTUS. Sweet Mephostophilis, thou pleasest me. → PLEASURE
Whilst I am here on earth, let me be cloyed
With all things that delight the heart of man.   60
My four and twenty years of liberty ? → pseudo-liberty
I'll spend in pleasure and in dalliance,
That Faustus' name, whilst this bright frame doth
    stand,
May be admirèd through the furthest land. ★ FAME (q

MEPHOSTOPHILIS. 'Tis well said, Faustus; come, then,
    stand by me
And thou shalt see them come immediately.

FAUSTUS. Nay, stay, my gentle Mephostophilis,
And grant me my request, and then I go.
Thou know'st within the compass of eight days
We viewed the face of heaven, of earth, and hell.   70
So high our dragons soared into the air
That looking down the earth appeared to me
No bigger than my hand in quantity.
There did we view the kingdoms of the world,

---

pyramides: obelisk before the gates of Saint Peter's in Rome.

And what might please mine eye I there beheld.
Then in this show let me an actor be,
That this proud Pope may Faustus' [cunning] see.
MEPHOSTOPHILIS. Let it be so, my Faustus, but first stay
And view their triumphs* as they pass this way!
And then devise what best contents thy mind   80
By [cunning] in thine art to cross the Pope
Or dash the pride of this solemnity,
To make his monks and abbots stand like apes
And point like antics* at his triple crown,
To beat the beads about the friars' pates
Or clap huge horns upon the cardinals' heads,
Or any villainy thou canst devise,
And I'll perform it, Faustus. Hark, they come!
This day shall make thee be admired in Rome.
> *Enter the Cardinals and Bishops, some bearing*
> *crosiers, some the pillars; Monks and Friars*
> *singing their procession. Then the* POPE
> *and* RAYMOND, *King of Hungary, with*
> BRUNO, *led in chains.*

POPE. Cast down our footstool.
RAYMOND.   Saxon Bruno, stoop,   90
Whilst on thy back his holiness ascends
Saint Peter's chair and state pontifical.
BRUNO. Proud Lucifer, that state belongs to me;
But thus I fall to Peter, not to thee.
POPE. To me and Peter shalt thou groveling lie
And crouch before the papal dignity.—
Sound trumpets, then, for thus Saint Peter's heir
From Bruno's back ascends Saint Peter's chair.
(*A flourish while he ascends.*)
Thus, as the gods creep on with feet of wool
Long ere with iron hands they punish men,   100
So shall our sleeping vengeance now arise
And smite with death thy hated enterprise.
Lord Cardinals of France and Padua,
Go forthwith to our holy consistory
And read amongst the statutes decretal
What, by the holy council held at Trent,

---

triumphs: processions; spectacular displays.
antics: clowns, fools.

    The sacred synod hath decreed for him
    That doth assume the papal government
    Without election and a true consent.
    Away, and bring us word with speed.   110
1 CARDINAL. We go, my lord.

                            Exeunt Cardinals.

POPE. Lord Raymond!
    [*The* POPE *and* RAYMOND *talk apart.*]
FAUSTUS. Go, haste thee, gentle Mephostophilis,
    Follow the cardinals to the consistory
    And, as they turn their superstitious books,
    Strike them with sloth and drowsy idleness;
    And make them sleep so sound that in their shapes
    Thyself and I may parley with this Pope,
    This proud confronter of the Emperor,
    And in despite of all his holiness   120
    Restore this Bruno to his liberty
    And bear him to the states of Germany.
MEPHOSTOPHILIS. Faustus, I go.
FAUSTUS.   Dispatch it soon;
    The Pope shall curse that Faustus came to Rome.
             [*Exeunt*] FAUSTUS *and* MEPHOSTOPHILIS.
BRUNO. Pope Adrian, let me have some right of law;
    I was elected by the Emperor.
POPE. We will depose the Emperor for that deed
    And curse the people that submit to him;
    Both he and thou shalt stand excommunicate
    And interdict from church's privilege   130
    And all society of holy men.
    He grows too proud in his authority,
    Lifting his lofty head above the clouds,
    And like a steeple overpeers the church.
    But we'll pull down his haughty insolence;
    And, as Pope Alexander, our progenitor,
    Trod on the neck of German Frederick,°
    Adding this golden sentence to our praise,
    "That Peter's heirs should tread on emperors
    And walk upon the dreadful adder's back,   140

    German Frederick: Frederick Barbarossa, who at Canossa acknowledged the papal supremacy of Pope Alexander III (1159–1181).

Treading the lion and the dragon down,
And fearless spurn the killing basilisk," *
So will we quell that haughty schismatic
And by authority apostolical
Depose him from his regal government.

BRUNO. Pope Julius swore to princely Sigismund,
For him and the succeeding popes of Rome,
To hold the emperors their lawful lords.

POPE. Pope Julius did abuse the church's [rights],
And therefore none of his decrees can stand.   150
Is not all power on earth bestowed on us?
And therefore, though we would, we cannot err.
Behold this silver belt, whereto is fixed
Seven golden [keys] fast sealed with seven seals
In token of our sevenfold power from heaven,
To bind or loose, lock fast, condemn, or judge,
Resign or seal, or whatso pleaseth us.
Then he and thou and all the world shall stoop
Or be assurèd of our dreadful curse
To light as heavy as the pains of hell.   160
    Enter FAUSTUS *and* MEPHOSTOPHILIS *like the Cardinals.*

MEPHOSTOPHILIS. Now tell me, Faustus, are we not fitted
    well?

FAUSTUS. Yes, Mephostophilis, and two such cardinals
Ne'er served a holy pope as we shall do.
But whilst they sleep within the consistory
Let us salute his reverend fatherhood.

RAYMOND. Behold, my lord, the cardinals are returned.

POPE. Welcome, grave fathers. Answer presently,
What have our holy council there decreed
Concerning Bruno and the Emperor,
In quittance of their late conspiracy   170
Against our state and papal dignity?

FAUSTUS. Most sacred patron of the church of Rome,
By full consent of all the synod
Of priests and prelates, it is thus decreed:
That Bruno and the German Emperor
Be held as Lollards* and bold schismatics

---

basilisk: a fabled serpent whose glance was fatal.
Lollards: followers of the reformer John Wyclif (1320?–1384);
more generally, as here, heretics.

And proud disturbers of the church's peace.
And if that Bruno by his own assent,
Without enforcement of the German peers,
Did seek to wear the triple diadem   180
And by your death to climb Saint Peter's chair,
The statutes decretal have thus decreed:
He shall be straight condemned of heresy
And on a pile of faggots burned to death.
POPE. It is enough. Here, take him to your charge
And bear him straight to Pont[e] Angelo,
And in the strongest tower enclose him fast.
Tomorrow, sitting in our consistory
With all our college of grave cardinals,
We will determine of his life or death.   190
Here, take his triple crown along with you
And leave it in the church's treasury.
Make haste again, my good lord cardinals,
And take our blessing apostolical.
MEPHOSTOPHILIS. So, so! Was never devil thus blessed
    before.
FAUSTUS. Away, sweet Mephostophilis, be gone!
The cardinals will be plagued for this anon.
        Exeunt FAUSTUS *and* MEPHOSTOPHILIS [*with* BRUNO].
POPE. Go presently and bring a banquet forth,
That we may solemnize Saint Peter's feast
And with Lord Raymond, King of Hungary,   200
Drink to our late and happy victory.

                                                Exeunt.

[ix]
        *A sennet while the banquet is brought in; and then
    enter* FAUSTUS *and* MEPHOSTOPHILIS *in their own shapes.*
MEPHOSTOPHILIS. Now, Faustus, come, prepare thyself
    for mirth.
The sleepy cardinals are hard at hand
To censure Bruno, that is posted hence
And on a proud-paced steed as swift as thought
Flies o'er the Alps to fruitful Germany,
There to salute the woeful Emperor.
FAUSTUS. The Pope will curse them for their sloth today,
That slept both Bruno and his crown away.

But now, that Faustus may delight his mind
And by their folly make some merriment,   10
Sweet Mephostophilis, so charm me here
That I may walk invisible to all
And do whate'er I please, unseen of any.
MEPHOSTOPHILIS. Faustus, thou shalt; then kneel down
      presently:
            Whilst on thy head I lay my hand
            And charm thee with this magic wand.
            First wear this girdle, then appear
            Invisible to all are here:
            The planets seven, the gloomy air,
            Hell, and the Furies' forkèd hair,   20
            Pluto's blue fire, and Hecate's tree
            With magic spells so compass thee
            That no eye may thy body see.
So, Faustus, now for all their holiness,
Do what thou wilt, thou shalt not be discerned.
FAUSTUS. Thanks, Mephostophilis. Now, friars, take
      heed
Lest Faustus make your shaven crowns to bleed.
MEPHOSTOPHILIS. Faustus, no more; see where the
      cardinals come.
            [*Sound a sennet.*] *Enter* POPE *and all the Lords.*
            Enter the Cardinals with a book.
POPE. Welcome, lord cardinals. Come, sit down.
Lord Raymond, take your seat. Friars, attend,   30
And see that all things be in readiness,
As best beseems this solemn festival.
1 CARDINAL. First, may it please your sacred holiness
To view the sentence of the reverend synod
Concerning Bruno and the Emperor.
POPE. What needs this question? Did I not tell you
Tomorrow we would sit i' th' consistory
And there determine of his punishment?
You brought us word even now; it was decreed
That Bruno and the cursèd Emperor   40
Were by the holy council both condemned
For loathèd lollards and base schismatics.
Then wherefore would you have me view that book?
1 CARDINAL. Your grace mistakes; you gave us no such
      charge.

RAYMOND. Deny it not; we all are witnesses
　　That Bruno here was late delivered you,
　　With his rich triple crown to be reserved
　　And put into the church's treasury.
AMBO° CARDINALS. By holy Paul, we saw them not.
POPE. By Peter, you shall die　　　　　　　　　　　50
　　Unless you bring them forth immediately.
　　Hale them to prison; lade their limbs with gyves!
　　False prelates, for this hateful treachery
　　Cursed be your souls to hellish misery.
　　　　　　　　　[Exeunt Cardinals with Attendants.]
FAUSTUS. So, they are safe. Now, Faustus, to the feast;
　　The Pope had never such a frolic guest.
POPE. Lord Archbishop of Rheims, sit down with us.
ARCHBISHOP. I thank your holiness.
FAUSTUS. Fall to! The devil choke you an you spare!
POPE. Who's that spoke? Friars, look about.　　　　60
[[FRIAR. Here's nobody, if it like your holiness.]]
POPE. Lord Raymond, pray fall to. I am beholding
　　To the Bishop of Milan for this so rare a present.
FAUSTUS. I thank you, sir.
　　[[*Snatch it.*]]
POPE. How now! Who snatched the meat from me?
　　Villains, why speak you not?—
　　My good Lord Archbishop, here's a most dainty dish
　　Was sent me from a cardinal in France.
FAUSTUS. I'll have that too.
　　[*He snatches it.*]
POPE. What Lollards do attend our holiness　　　　70
　　That we receive such great indignity?
　　Fetch me some wine.
FAUSTUS. Ay, pray do, for Faustus is a-dry.
POPE. Lord [R]aymond, I drink unto your grace.
FAUSTUS. I pledge your grace.
　　[*He snatches the cup.*]
POPE. My wine gone too? Ye lubbers, look about
　　And find the man that doth this villainy,
　　Or by our sanctitude you all shall die.—
　　I pray, my lords, have patience at this
　　Troublesome banquet.　　　　　　　　　　　　80

---

ambo: both.

ARCHBISHOP. Please it your holiness, I think it be some
  ghost crept out of purgatory and now is come unto
  your holiness for his pardon.
POPE. It may be so:
  Go, then, command our priests to sing a dirge
  To lay the fury of this same troublesome ghost.—
                                        [*Exit Attendant.*]

  [[Once again, my lord, fall to.
  (*The Pope crosseth himself.*)]]
FAUSTUS. How now?
  Must every bit be spicèd with a cross?
  Nay, then, take that!   90
  [FAUSTUS *hits him a box of the ear.*]
POPE. O, I am slain! Help me, my lords!
  O, come and help to bear my body hence.
  Damned be this soul for ever for this deed.
                          Exeunt the POPE *and his Train.*
MEPHOSTOPHILIS. Now, Faustus, what will you do now?
  For I can tell you you'll be cursed with bell, book, and
  candle.*
FAUSTUS. Bell, book, and candle; candle, book, and
    bell—
  Forward and backward, to curse Faustus to hell!
  Enter the Friars with bell, book, and candle for the dirge.
1 FRIAR. Come, brethren, let's about our business with
  good devotion.   100
  [[Sing *this.*]]
    *Cursed be he that stole his holiness' meat from the
      table.*
        *Maledicat Dominus!**
    *Cursed be he that struck his holiness a blow [[on]]
      the face.*
        Maledicat Dominus!
    *Cursed be he that struck Friar Sandelo a blow on
      the pate.*
        Maledicat Dominus!
    Cursed be he that disturbeth our holy dirge.
        Maledicat Dominus!

---

cursed . . . candle: as in the rite of excommunication.
maledicat Dominus: may the Lord curse him!

> *Cursed be he that took away his holiness' wine.*
> *Maledicat Dominus!* 110
> [[*Et omnes sancti!** Amen.*]]
>
> > [FAUSTUS *and* MEPHOS-
> > TOPHILIS] *beat the Fri-*
> > *ars, fling firework*[[*s*]]
> > *among them, and* [[*so*]]
> > *exeunt.*

[x]
> *Enter* CLOWN [ROBIN] *and* DICK, *with a cup.*

DICK. Sirrah Robin, we were best look that your devil can answer the stealing of this same cup, for the vintner's boy follows us at the hard heels.

ROBIN. 'Tis no matter; let him come. An he follow us, I'll so conjure him as he was never conjured in his life, I warrant him. Let me see the cup.

> *Enter* VINTNER.

DICK. Here 'tis. Yonder he comes. Now, Robin, now or never show thy cunning.

VINTNER. O, are you here? I am glad I have found you. You are a couple of fine companions! Pray, where's the 10 cup you stole from the tavern?

ROBIN. How, how? We steal a cup? Take heed what you say; we look not like cup-stealers, I can tell you.

VINTNER. Never deny't, for I know you have it, and I'll search you.

ROBIN. Search me? Ay, and spare not. [*Aside to* DICK.] Hold the cup, Dick.—Come, come, search me, search me.

[*The* VINTNER *searches* ROBIN.]

VINTNER. Come on, sirrah, let me search you now.

DICK. Ay, ay, do, do. [*Aside to* ROBIN.] Hold the cup, 20 Robin.—I fear not your searching; we scorn to steal your cups, I can tell you.

VINTNER. Never outface me for the matter, for sure the cup is between you two.

ROBIN. Nay, there you lie; 'tis beyond us both.

---

et omnes sancti: and all the saints.

VINTNER. A plague take you! I thought 'twas your knavery to take it away. Come, give it me again.

ROBIN. Ay, much! When? Can you tell?—Dick, make
me a circle, and stand close at my back, and stir not
for thy life.—Vintner, you shall have your cup anon.   30
—Say nothing, Dick.—*O per se, o; Demogorgon,
Belcher, and Mephostophilis!*

Enter MEPHOSTOPHILIS.

MEPHOSTOPHILIS. You princely legions of infernal rule,
How am I vexèd by these villains' charms!
From Constantinople have they brought me now
Only for pleasure of these damnèd slaves.

[*Exit* VINTNER, *running.*]

ROBIN. By Lady, sir, you have had a shrewd° journey
of it. Will it please you to take a shoulder of mutton
to supper and a tester° in your purse, and go back
again.   40

DICK. Ay, I pray you heartily, sir; for we called you but
in jest, I promise you.

MEPHOSTOPHILIS. To purge the rashness of this cursèd
deed,
First be thou turnèd to this ugly shape,
For apish deeds transformèd to an ape.

ROBIN. O brave, an ape! I pray, sir, let me have the
carrying of him about to show some tricks.

MEPHOSTOPHILIS. And so thou shalt. Be thou transformed to a dog, and carry him upon thy back. Away,
be gone!   50

ROBIN. A dog! That's excellent. Let the maids look well
to their porridge pots, for I'll into the kitchen presently. Come, Dick, come.

Exeunt the two Clowns.

MEPHOSTOPHILIS. Now with the flames of ever-burning
fire
I'll wing myself and forthwith fly amain
Unto my Faustus, to the Great Turks' court.

Exit.

---

shrewd: tiresome; poor.
tester: sixpence (slang).

[Chorus 2]°
[[*Enter* CHORUS.

CHORUS. When Faustus had with pleasure ta'en the view
      Of rarest things and royal courts of kings,
      He stayed his course and so returnèd home,
      Where such as bare his absence but with grief—
      I mean his friends and nearest companions—
      Did gratulate his safety with kind words;
      And in their conference of what befell
      Touching his journey through the world and air
      They put forth questions of astrology,
      Which Faustus answered with such learned skill   10
      As they admired and wondered at his wit.
      Now is his fame spread forth in every land.
      Amongst the rest the Emperor is one,
      Carolus the Fifth,° at whose palace now
      Faustus is feasted 'mongst his noblemen.
      What there he did in trial of his art
      I leave untold, your eyes shall see performed.

                                                    Exit.]]

[xi]
      Enter MARTINO *and* FREDERICK, *at several doors.*
MARTINO. What ho, officers, gentlemen,
      Hie to the presence° to attend the Emperor!
      Good Frederick, see the rooms be voided straight;
      His majesty is coming to the hall.
      Go back, and see the state° in readiness.
FREDERICK. But where is Bruno, our elected Pope,
      That on a fury's back came post from Rome?
      Will not his grace consort the Emperor?
MARTINO. O yes, and with him comes the German con-
            juror,
      The learned Faustus, fame of Wittenberg,   10
      The wonder of the world for magic art;

      Chorus 2: follows scene ix in 1604 quarto; placed here by Boas.
      Carolus the Fifth: Charles V, Emperor of the Holy Roman Em-
pire (1519–1556).
      presence: presence-chamber.
      state: throne; canopied chair of state.

And he intends to show great Carolus
The race of all his stout progenitors,
And bring in presence of his majesty
The royal shapes and warlike semblances
Of Alexander and his beauteous paramour.

FREDERICK. Where is Benvolio?

MARTINO. Fast asleep, I warrant you.
He took his rouse with stoups* of Rhenish wine
So kindly yesternight to Bruno's health   20
That all this day the sluggard keeps his bed.

FREDERICK. See, see, his window's ope; we'll call to him.

MARTINO. What ho, Benvolio!

> *Enter* BENVOLIO *above at a window, in his*
> *nightcap, buttoning.*

BENVOLIO. What a devil ail you two?

MARTINO. Speak softly, sir, lest the devil hear you;
For Faustus at the court is late arrived,
And at his heels a thousand furies wait
To accomplish whatsoever the doctor please.

BENVOLIO. What of this?

MARTINO. Come, leave thy chamber first, and thou shalt
see   30
This conjuror perform such rare exploits
Before the Pope and royal Emperor
As never yet was seen in Germany.

BENVOLIO. Has not the Pope enough of conjuring yet?
He was upon the devil's back late enough;
And, if he be so far in love with him,
I would he would post with him to Rome again.

FREDERICK. Speak; wilt thou come and see this sport?

BENVOLIO.   Not I.

MARTINO. Wilt thou stand in thy window and see it
then?

BENVOLIO. Ay, and I fall not asleep i' th' meantime.   40

MARTINO. The Emperor is at hand, who comes to see
What wonders by black spells may compassed be.

BENVOLIO. Well, go you attend the Emperor. I am content for this once to thrust my head out at a window,
for they say if a man be drunk overnight the devil
cannot hurt him in the morning. If that be true, I have

---

took . . . stoups: went on a binge.

a charm in my head shall control him as well as the
conjuror, I warrant you.

> [*Exeunt* FREDERICK *and* MARTINO,
> BENVOLIO *remaining at window
> throughout next scene.*]

[xii]

> *A sennet.* CHARLES, *the German Emperor,* BRUNO,
> [DUKE OF] SAXONY, FAUSTUS, MEPHOSTOPHILIS,
> FREDERICK, MARTINO, *and Attendants.*

EMPEROR. Wonder of men, renowned magician,
Thrice-learned Faustus, welcome to our court.
This deed of thine, in setting Bruno free
From his and our professèd enemy,
Shall add more excellence unto thine art
Than if by powerful necromantic spells
Thou couldst command the world's obedience.
Forever be beloved of Carolus;
And, if this Bruno thou hast late redeemed*
In peace possess the triple diadem   10
And sit in Peter's chair despite of chance,
Thou shalt be famous through all Italy
And honored of the German Emperor.
FAUSTUS. These gracious words, most royal Carolus,
Shall make poor Faustus to his utmost power
Both love and serve the German Emperor
And lay his life at holy Bruno's feet.
For proof whereof, if so your grace be pleased,
The doctor stands prepared by power of art
To cast his magic charms that shall pierce through   20
The ebon gates of ever-burning hell
And hale the stubborn furies from their caves
To compass whatsoe'er your grace commands.
BENVOLIO. Blood! He speaks terribly. But, for all that,
I do not greatly believe him; he looks as like [a] con-
juror as the Pope to a costermonger.
EMPEROR. Then, Faustus, as thou late didst promise us,
We would behold that famous conqueror,
Great Alexander, and his paramour
In their true shapes and state majestical,   30

---

redeemed: rescued.

That we may wonder at their excellence.

FAUSTUS. Your majesty shall see them presently.—
Mephostophilis, away,
And with a solemn noise of trumpets' sound
Present before this royal Emperor
Great Alexander and his beauteous paramour.

MEPHOSTOPHILIS. Faustus, I will.

[*Exit.*]

BENVOLIO. Well, master doctor, an° your devils come
not away quickly, you shall have me asleep presently.
Zounds, I could eat myself for anger to think I have   40
been such an ass all this while to stand gaping after
the devil's governor° and can see nothing.

FAUSTUS. I'll make you feel something anon if my art
fail me not.—
My lord, I must forewarn your majesty
That when my spirits present the royal shapes
Of Alexander and his paramour
Your grace demand no questions of the king,
But in dumb silence let them come and go.

EMPEROR. Be it as Faustus please; we are content.

BENVOLIO. Ay, ay, and I am content too. And thou bring   50
Alexander and his paramour before the Emperor, I'll
be Actæon° and turn myself to a stag.

FAUSTUS. And I'll play Diana and send you the horns
presently.

*Sennet. Enter at one [door] the Emperor ALEXANDER,
at the other DARIUS. They meet; DARIUS is thrown
down; ALEXANDER kills him, takes off his crown, and,
offering to go, his PARAMOUR meets him. He
embraceth her and sets DARIUS' crown upon her
head; and, coming back, both salute the
EMPEROR, who, leaving his state, offers
to embrace them, which FAUSTUS seeing
suddenly stays him. Then trumpets cease,
and music sounds.*

---

an: if.
governor: tutor.
Actæon: turned into a stag by Diana, whom he came upon
bathing with her nymphs.

My gracious lord, you do forget yourself;
These are but shadows, not substantial.

EMPEROR. O, pardon me; my thoughts are so ravishèd
With sight of this renownèd Emperor
That in mine arms I would have compassed him.
But, Faustus, since I may not speak to them
To satisfy my longing thoughts at full,   60
Let me this tell thee: I have heard it said
That this fair lady, whilst she lived on earth,
Had on her neck a little wart or mole;
How may I prove that saying to be true?

FAUSTUS. Your majesty may boldly go and see.

EMPEROR. Faustus, I see it plain,
And in this sight thou better pleasest me
Than if I gained another monarchy.

FAUSTUS. Away! Be gone!

Exit Show.

See, see, my gracious lord, what strange beast is yon,   70
that thrusts his head out at [the] window.

EMPEROR. O, wondrous sight! See, Duke of Saxony,
Two spreading horns most strangely fastenèd
Upon the head of young Benvolio.

SAXONY. What? Is he asleep or dead?

FAUSTUS. He sleeps, my lord, but dreams not of his
horns.

EMPEROR. This sport is excellent. We'll call and wake
him.—What ho, Benvolio!

BENVOLIO. A plague upon you! Let me sleep awhile.   80

EMPEROR. I blame thee not to sleep much, having such
a head of thine own.

SAXONY. Look up, Benvolio; 'tis the Emperor calls.

BENVOLIO. The Emperor! Where? O, zounds, my head!

EMPEROR. Nay, and thy horns hold, 'tis no matter for
thy head, for that's armed sufficiently.

FAUSTUS. Why, how now, sir knight? What, hanged by
the horns? This [is] most horrible. Fie, fie, pull in your
head for shame; let not all the world wonder at you.

BENVOLIO. Zounds, doctor, is this your villainy?   90

FAUSTUS. O, say not so, sir; the doctor has no skill,
No art, no cunning to present these lords
Or bring before this royal Emperor

The mighty monarch, warlike Alexander.
If Faustus do it, you are straight resolved
In bold Actæon's shape to turn a stag.
And therefore, my lord, so please your majesty,
I'll raise a kennel of hounds shall hunt him so
As all his footmanship shall scarce prevail
To keep his carcass from their bloody fangs.—   100
Ho, Belimote, Argiron, Asterote!

BENVOLIO. Hold, hold! Zounds, he'll raise up a kennel of
devils, I think, anon. Good my lord, entreat for me.
'Sblood, I am never able to endure these torments.

EMPEROR. Then, good master doctor,
Let me entreat you to remove his horns;
He has done penance now sufficiently.

FAUSTUS. My gracious lord, not so much for injury done
to me as to delight your majesty with some mirth hath
Faustus justly requited this injurious° knight; which   110
being all I desire, I am content to remove his horns.—
Mephostophilis, transform him.—And hereafter, sir,
look you speak well of scholars.

BENVOLIO [aside]. Speak well of ye! 'Sblood, and scholars be such cuckold-makers to clap horns of honest
men's heads o'this order, I'll ne'er trust smooth faces
and small ruffs° more. But, an I be not revenged for
this, would I might be turned to a gaping oyster and
drink nothing but salt water.

EMPEROR. Come, Faustus, while the Emperor lives,   120
In recompense of this thy high desert,
Thou shalt command the state of Germany
And live beloved of mighty Carolus.

                                            Exeunt omnes.

[xiii]
      Enter BENVOLIO, MARTINO, FREDERICK, *and Soldiers.*

MARTINO. Nay, sweet Benvolio, let us sway thy thoughts
From this attempt against the conjuror.

BENVOLIO. Away! You love me not to urge me thus.
Shall I let slip so great an injury

---

injurious: insulting.
smooth . . . ruffs: "beardless scholars in academic garb"
(Boas).

When every servile groom jests at my wrongs
And in their rustic gambols proudly say,
"Benvolio's head was graced with horns today"?
O, may these eyelids never close again
Till with my sword I have that conjuror slain.
If you will aid me in this enterprise,   10
Then draw your weapons and be resolute;
If not, depart. Here will Benvolio die
But* Faustus' death shall quit* my infamy.
FREDERICK. Nay, we will stay with thee, betide what
    may,
And kill that doctor if he come this way.
BENVOLIO. Then, gentle Frederick, hie thee to the grove
And place our servants and our followers
Close in an ambush there behind the trees.
By this, I know, the conjuror is near:
I saw him kneel and kiss the Emperor's hand   20
And take his leave laden with rich rewards.
Then, soldiers, boldly fight; if Faustus die,
Take you the wealth; leave us the victory.
FREDERICK. Come, soldiers, follow me unto the grove.
Who kills him shall have gold and endless love.
                    Exit FREDERICK *with the Soldiers.*
BENVOLIO. My head is lighter than it was by th' horns,
But yet my heart['s] more ponderous than my head
And pants until I see that conjuror dead.
MARTINO. Where shall we place ourselves, Benvolio?
BENVOLIO. Here will we stay to bide the first assault.   30
O, were that damnèd hell-hound but in place,
Thou soon shouldst see me quit my foul disgrace.
                    Enter FREDERICK.
FREDERICK. Close, close! The conjuror is at hand
And all alone comes walking in his gown.
Be ready then and strike the peasant down.
BENVOLIO. Mine be that honor, then. Now, sword, strike
    home.
For horns he gave, I'll have his head anon.
                    Enter FAUSTUS *with the false head.*
MARTINO. See, see, he comes.

---

but: unless.
quit: requite, pay for.

BENVOLIO.   No words! This blow
    ends all.
    Hell take his soul; his body thus must fall.
    [*He strikes* FAUSTUS.]
FAUSTUS. O!   40
FREDERICK. Groan you, master doctor?
BENVOLIO. Break may his heart with groans! Dear Fred-
    erick, see,
    Thus will I end his griefs immediately.
MARTINO. Strike with a willing hand. His head is off.
    [BENVOLIO *cuts off* FAUSTUS' *false head.*]
BENVOLIO. The devil's dead; the furies now may laugh.
FREDERICK. Was this that stern aspect, that awful frown,
    Made the grim monarch of infernal spirits
    Tremble and quake at his commanding charms?
MARTINO. Was this that damnèd head whose heart con-
    spired
    Benvolio's shame before the Emperor?   50
BENVOLIO. Ay, that's the head; and here the body lies,
    Justly rewarded for his villainies.
FREDERICK. Come, let's devise how we may add more
    shame
    To the black scandal of his hated name.
BENVOLIO. First, on his head, in quittance of my wrongs,
    I'll nail huge forkèd horns and let them hang
    Within the window where he yoked me first,
    That all the world may see my just revenge.
MARTINO. What use shall we put his beard to?
BENVOLIO. We'll sell it to a chimney-sweeper: it will   60
    wear out ten birchen brooms, I warrant you.
FREDERICK. What shall [his] eyes do?
BENVOLIO. We'll put out his eyes, and they shall serve
    for buttons to his lips to keep his tongue from catch-
    ing cold.
MARTINO. An excellent policy! And now, sirs, having
    divided him, what shall the body do?
    [FAUSTUS *stands up.*]
BENVOLIO. Zounds,* the devil's alive again!
FREDERICK. Give him his head, for God's sake!

---

zounds: contraction of "by God's wounds!"

FAUSTUS. Nay, keep it. Faustus will have heads and
    hands,   70
  [Ay, all] your hearts to recompense this deed.
  Knew you not, traitors, I was limited
  For four-and-twenty years to breathe on earth?
  And had you cut my body with your swords,
  Or hewed this flesh and bones as small as sand,
  Yet in a minute had my spirit returned
  And I had breathed a man made free from harm.
  But wherefore do I dally my revenge?—
  Asteroth, Belimoth, Mephostophilis!
      Enter MEPHOSTOPHILIS *and other Devils.*
  Go, horse these traitors on your fiery backs   80
  And mount aloft with them as high as heaven;
  Thence pitch them headlong to the lowest hell.
  Yet stay; the world shall see their misery,
  And hell shall after plague their treachery.
  Go, Belimoth, and take this caitiff hence,
  And hurl him in some lake of mud and dirt;
  Take thou this other; drag him through the woods
  Amongst the pricking thorns and sharpest briers
  Whilst with my gentle Mephostophilis
  This traitor flies unto some steepy rock   90
  That, rolling down, may break the villain's bones
  As he intended to dismember me.
  Fly hence; dispatch my charge immediately!
FREDERICK. Pity us, gentle Faustus. Save our lives!
FAUSTUS. Away!
FREDERICK.   He must needs go that the devil
  drives.
              Exeunt Spirits with the Knights.
          Enter the ambushed Soldiers.
1 SOLDIER. Come, sirs, prepare yourselves in readiness.
  Make haste to help these noble gentlemen;
  I heard them parley with the conjuror.
2 SOLDIER. See where he comes. Dispatch, and kill the
  slave.
FAUSTUS. What's here? An ambush to betray my life?   100
  Then, Faustus, try thy skill.—Base peasants, stand!
  For lo, these trees remove* at my command

---

remove: change positions.

And stand as bulwarks 'twixt yourselves and me
To shield me from your hated treachery.
Yet to encounter this your weak attempt,
Behold an army comes incontinent.°

> (FAUSTUS *strikes the
> door, and enter a Devil
> playing on a drum,
> after him another bear-
> ing an ensign, and div-
> ers with weapons,* ME-
> PHOSTOPHILIS *with fire-
> works; they set upon
> the Soldiers and drive
> them out.* [*Exit* FAUS-
> TUS.])

[xiv]

Enter at several doors BENVOLIO, FREDERICK, *and*
MARTINO, *their heads and faces bloody and besmeared
with mud and dirt, all having horns on their heads.*

MARTINO. What ho, Benvolio!

BENVOLIO.   Here! What, Frederick,
  ho!

FREDERICK. O help me, gentle friend. Where is Martino?

MARTINO. Dear Frederick, here,
  Half smothered in a lake of mud and dirt,
  Through which the furies dragged me by the heels.

FREDERICK. Martino, see! Benvolio's horns again!

MARTINO. O misery! How now, Benvolio?

BENVOLIO. Defend me, heaven! Shall I be haunted°
  still?

MARTINO. Nay, fear not, man; we have no power to kill.

BENVOLIO. My friends transformèd thus! O hellish spite,   10
  Your heads are all set with horns!

FREDERICK.   You hit it right.
  It is your own you mean; feel on your head.

BENVOLIO. Zounds, horns again!

---

incontinent: immediately.
haunted: "(1) bewitched (2) hunted, pursued (since he is a
stag)" (Ribner).

MARTINO.   Nay, chafe not, man;
    we all are sped.*
BENVOLIO. What devil attends this damned magician,
    That, spite of spite, our wrongs are doublèd?
FREDERICK. What may we do that we may hide our
    shames?
BENVOLIO. If we should follow him to work revenge,
    He'd join long asses' ears to these huge horns
    And make us laughing-stocks to all the world.
MARTINO. What shall we then do, dear Benvolio?   20
BENVOLIO. I have a castle joining near these woods,
    And thither we'll repair and live obscure
    Till time shall alter [these] our brutish shapes.
    Sith* black disgrace hath thus eclipsed our fame,
    We'll rather die with grief than live with shame.

                         Exeunt omnes.

[xv]

        [[*Enter* FAUSTUS *and* MEPHOSTOPHILIS.]

FAUSTUS. Now, Mephostophilis, the restless course
    That time doth run with calm and silent foot,
    Short'ning my days and thread of vital life,
    Calls for the payment of my latest years;
    Therefore, sweet Mephostophilis, let us
    Make haste to Wi[t]tenberg.
MEPHOSTOPHILIS. What, will you go on horseback or on
    foot?
FAUSTUS. Nay, till I am past this fair and pleasant green,
    I'll walk on foot.

                   [*Exit* MEPHOSTOPHILIS.]
        Enter a HORSE-COURSER.

HORSE-COURSER. I have been all this day seeking one   10
    Master Fustian. Mass, see where he is. God save you,
    master doctor!
FAUSTUS. What, horse-courser! You are well met.]]
HORSE-COURSER. I beseech your worship, accept of these
    forty dollars.
FAUSTUS. Friend, thou canst not buy so good a horse for
    so small a price. I have no great need to sell him; but,

---

    sped: done for, done in.
    sith: since, seeing that.

if thou likest him for ten dollars more, take him because I see thou hast a good mind to him.

HORSE-COURSER. I beseech you, sir, accept of this. I am   20
a very poor man and have lost very much of late by
horse-flesh, and this bargain will set me up again.

FAUSTUS. Well, I will not stand° with thee. Give me the
money. Now, sirrah, I must tell you that you may ride
him o'er hedge and ditch and spare him not. But—do
you hear?—in any case ride him not into the water.

HORSE-COURSER. How, sir? Not into the water? Why,
will he not drink of all waters?

FAUSTUS. Yes, he will drink of all waters, but ride him
not into the water; o'er hedge and ditch, or where   30
thou wilt, but not into the water. Go, bid the hostler
deliver him unto you, and remember what I say.

HORSE-COURSER. I warrant you, sir. O, joyful day! Now
am I a made man forever.

Exit.

FAUSTUS. What art thou, Faustus, but a man condemned
to die?
Thy fatal time draws to a final end;
Despair doth drive distrust into my thoughts.
Confound these passions with a quiet sleep.
Tush, Christ did call the thief upon the cross;
Then rest thee, Faustus, quiet in conceit.°   40
(*He sits to sleep.*)
Enter the HORSE-COURSER *wet.*

HORSE-COURSER. O, what a cozening doctor was this! I,
riding my horse into the water, thinking some hidden
mystery° had been in the horse, I had nothing under
me but a little straw and had much ado to escape
drowning. Well, I'll go rouse him and make him give
me my forty dollars again.—Ho, sirrah doctor, you
cozening scab!° Master doctor, awake and rise, and
give me my money again; for your horse is turned to
a bottle° of hay. Master doctor!
(*He pulls off his leg.*)

---

stand: bargain.
conceit: thought, mind.
mystery: quality.
scab: scoundrel.
bottle: bundle.

Alas, I am undone! What shall I do? I have pulled off 50
his leg.

FAUSTUS. O, help, help! The villain hath murdered me.

HORSE-COURSER. Murder or not murder, now he has but
one leg I'll outrun him and cast this leg into some
ditch or other.

[*Exit.*]

FAUSTUS. Stop him, stop him, stop him!—Ha, ha, ha!
Faustus hath his leg again, and the horse-courser a
bundle of hay for his forty dollars.

Enter WAGNER.

How now, Wagner, what news with thee?

WAGNER. If it please you, the Duke of Vanholt doth 60
earnestly entreat your company and hath sent some
of his men to attend you with provision fit for your
journey.

FAUSTUS. The Duke of Vanholt's an honorable gentleman, and one to whom I must be no niggard of my
cunning. Come away!

Exeunt.

[xvi]

Enter CLOWN [ROBIN], DICK, HORSE-COURSER,
and a CARTER.

CARTER. Come, my masters, I'll bring you to the best
beer in Europe.—What ho, hostess! Where be these
whores?

Enter HOSTESS.

HOSTESS. How now, what lack you? What, my old
gues[t]s, welcome!

ROBIN. Sirrah, Dick, dost thou know why I stand so
mute?

DICK. No, Robin; why is't?

ROBIN. I am eighteen pence on the score. But say nothing; see if she have forgotten me. 10

HOSTESS. Who's this that stands so solemnly by himself?
What, my old guest!

ROBIN. O, hostess, how do you? I hope my score stands
still.

HOSTESS. Ay, there's no doubt of that, for methinks you
make no haste to wipe it out.

DICK. Why, hostess, I say, fetch us some beer.

HOSTESS. You shall presently. Look up into th'hall there, ho!

Exit.

DICK. Come, sirs, what shall we do now till mine hostess   20
comes?

CARTER. Marry, sir, I'll tell you the bravest tale how a conjuror served me. You know Doctor Fauster?

HORSE-COURSER. Ay, a plague take him! Here's some on's have cause to know him. Did he conjure thee, too?

CARTER. I'll tell you how he served me. As I was going to Wittenberg t'other day with a load of hay, he met me and asked me what he should give me for as much hay as he could eat. Now, sir, I, thinking that a little   30
would serve his turn, bade him take as much as he would for three farthings. So he presently gave me my money and fell to eating; and, as I am a cursen* man, he never left eating till he had eat up all my load of hay.

ALL. O monstrous! Eat a whole load of hay!

ROBIN. Yes, yes, that may be; for I have heard of one that has eat a load of logs.

HORSE-COURSER. Now, sirs, you shall hear how villain-ously he served me. I went to him yesterday to buy   40
a horse of him, and he would by no means sell him under forty dollars. So, sir, because I knew him to be such a horse as would run over hedge and ditch and never tire, I gave him his money. So, when I had my horse, Doctor Fauster bade me ride him night and day and spare him no time. "But," quoth he, "in any case ride him not into the water." Now, sir, I, think-ing the horse had some quality that he would not have me know of, what did I but rid him into a great river? And, when I came just in the midst, my horse   50
vanished away, and I sat straddling upon a bottle of hay.

ALL. O brave doctor!

HORSE-COURSER. But you shall hear how bravely I served him for it. I went me home to his house, and there I found him asleep. I kept a hallooing and whooping

---

cursen: christened (hence, a Christian).

in his ears, but all could not wake him. I, seeing that, took him by the leg and never rested pulling till I had pulled me his leg quite off; and now 'tis at home in mine hostry.   60

ROBIN. And has the doctor but one leg then? That's excellent, for one of his devils turned me into the likeness of an ape's face.

CARTER. Some more drink, hostess!

ROBIN. Hark you, we'll go into another room and drink awhile, and then we'll go seek out the doctor.

Exeunt omnes.

[xvii]

Enter the DUKE OF VANHOLT, *his* DUCHESS, FAUSTUS, *and* MEPHOSTOPHILIS.

DUKE. Thanks, master doctor, for these pleasant sights. Nor know I how sufficiently to recompense your great deserts in erecting that enchanted castle in the air, the sight whereof so delighted me as nothing in the world could please me more.

FAUSTUS. I do think myself, my good lord, highly recompensed in that it pleaseth your grace to think but well of that which Faustus hath performed. But, gracious lady, it may be that you have taken no pleasure in those sights; therefore, I pray you, tell me what is the   10 thing you most desire to have: be it in the world, it shall be yours. I have heard that great-bellied women do long for things are rare and dainty.

DUCHESS. True, master doctor; and, since I find you so kind, I will make known unto you what my heart desires to have. And, were it now summer, as it is January, a dead time of the winter, I would request no better meat than a dish of ripe grapes.

FAUSTUS. This is but a small matter.—Go, Mephostophilis, away!   20

Exit MEPHOSTOPHILIS.

Madam, I will do more than this for your content.

Enter MEPHOSTOPHILIS *again with the grapes.*

Here, now taste ye these; they should be good, for they come from a far country, I can tell you.

DUKE. This makes me wonder more than all the rest, that at this time of the year, when every tree is barren of his fruit, from whence you had these ripe grapes.

FAUSTUS. Please it your grace, the year is divided into
two circles over the whole world, so that, when it is
winter with us, in the contrary circle it is likewise
summer with them, as in India, Saba, and such coun-   30
tries that lie far east, where they have fruit twice a
year. From whence, by means of a swift spirit that I
have, I had these grapes brought as you see.

DUCHESS. And, trust me, they are the sweetest grapes
that e'er I tasted.

(*The Clowns bounce* at the gate, within.*)

DUKE. What rude disturbers have we at the gate?
Go, pacify their fury, set it ope,
And then demand of them what they would have.

(*They knock again and call out to talk with* FAUSTUS.)

A SERVANT. Why, how now, masters, what a coil * is
there!
What is the reason you disturb the duke?   40

DICK. We have no reason for it; therefore a fig for him!

SERVANT. Why, saucy varlets, dare you be so bold?

HORSE-COURSER. I hope, sir, we have wit enough to be
more bold than welcome.

SERVANT. It appears so. Pray be bold elsewhere,
And trouble not the duke.

DUKE.   What would they have?

SERVANT. They all cry out to speak with Doctor Faustus.

CARTER. Ay, and we will speak with him.

DUKE. Will you, sir? Commit the rascals!

DICK. Commit * with us! He were as good commit with   50
his father as commit with us.

FAUSTUS. I do beseech your grace, let them come in;
They are good subject for a merriment.

DUKE. Do as thou wilt, Faustus; I give thee leave.

FAUSTUS. I thank your grace.

> *Enter the* CLOWN [ROBIN], DICK, CARTER,
> *and* HORSE-COURSER.

                              Why, how now, my good
friends?

---

bounce: bang, knock
coil: disturbance.
commit: fornicate.

'Faith, you are too outrageous,* but come near;
I have procured your pardons. Welcome all!

ROBIN. Nay, sir, we will be welcome for our money, and
we will pay for what we take.—What ho! Give's half
a dozen of beer here, and be hanged. 60

FAUSTUS. Nay, hark you, can you tell me where you are?

CARTER. Ay, marry, can I; we are under heaven.

SERVANT. Ay, but, sir sauce-box, know you in what
place?

HORSE-COURSER. Ay, ay, the house is good enough to
drink in. Zouns, fill us some beer, or we'll break all
the barrels in the house and dash out all your brains
with your bottles.

FAUSTUS. Be not so furious; come, you shall have beer.
My lord, beseech you give me leave awhile; 70
I'll gage my credit 'twill content your grace.

DUKE. With all my heart, kind doctor, please thyself;
Our servants and our court's at thy command.

FAUSTUS. I humbly thank your grace.—Then fetch some
beer.

HORSE-COURSER. Ay, marry, there spake a doctor indeed;
and, 'faith, I'll drink a health to thy wooden leg for
that word.

FAUSTUS. My wooden leg? What dost thou mean by that?

CARTER. Ha, ha, ha! Dost hear him, Dick? He has forgot 80
his leg.

HORSE-COURSER. Ay, ay, he does not stand much upon
that.

FAUSTUS. No, 'faith, not much upon a wooden leg.

CARTER. Good Lord, that flesh and blood should be so
frail with your worship! Do not you remember a horse-
courser you sold a horse to?

FAUSTUS. Yes, I remember I sold one a horse.

CARTER. And do you remember you bid he should not
ride [him] into the water? 90

FAUSTUS. Yes, I do very well remember that.

CARTER. And do you remember nothing of your leg?

FAUSTUS. No, in good sooth.

CARTER. Then I pray remember your curtsy.

FAUSTUS. I thank you, sir.

---

outrageous: violent.

CARTER. 'Tis not so much worth. I pray you, tell me one
    thing.

FAUSTUS. What's that?

CARTER. Be both your legs bedfellows every night to-
    gether?   100

FAUSTUS. Wouldst thou make a Colossus* of me, that
    thou shouldst askest me such questions?

CARTER. No, truly, sir; I would make nothing of you,
    but I would fain know that.

                     Enter HOSTESS *with drink.*

FAUSTUS. Then I assure thee certainly they are.

CARTER. I thank you; I am fully satisfied.

FAUSTUS. But wherefore dost thou ask?

CARTER. For nothing, sir; but methinks you should have
    a wooden bedfellow of one of 'em.

HORSE-COURSER. Why, do you hear, sir; did not I pull   110
    off one of your legs when you were asleep?

FAUSTUS. But I have it again now I am awake. Look you
    here, sir.

ALL. O horrible! Had the doctor three legs?

CARTER. Do you remember, sir, how you cozened me
    and eat up my load of—

    (FAUSTUS *charms him dumb.*)

DICK. Do you remember how you made me wear an
    ape's—

    [FAUSTUS *charms him dumb.*]

HORSE-COURSER. You whoreson conjuring scab, do you
    remember how you cozened me with a ho—   120
    [FAUSTUS *charms him dumb.*]

ROBIN. Ha' you forgotten me? You think to carry it away
    with your "hey-pass" and "re-pass." Do you remember
    the dog's fa—

    [FAUSTUS *charms him dumb.*]

                          Exeunt Clowns.

HOSTESS. Who pays for the ale? Hear you, master doctor,
    now you have sent away my gues[t]s, I pray who shall
    pay me for my a—

    [FAUSTUS *charms her dumb.*]

                            Exit HOSTESS.

    Colossus: referring to the Colossus of Rhodes, a giant statue that
supposedly straddled the entrance to the harbor of that city.

DUCHESS. My lord,
  We are much beholding to this learned man.
DUKE. So are we, madam, which we will recompense
  With all the love and kindness that we may. 130
  His artful sport drives all sad thoughts away.

                Exeunt.

[xviii]
   *Thunder and lightning. Enter Devils with covered
     dishes.* MEPHOSTOPHILIS *leads them into*
     FAUSTUS' *study. Then enter* WAGNER.
WAGNER. I think my master means to die shortly.
  He has made his will and given me his wealth,
  His house, his goods, and store of golden plate,
  Besides two thousand ducats ready coined.
  I wonder what he means. If death were nigh,
  He would not frolic thus. He's now at supper
  With the scholars, where there's such belly-cheer
  As Wagner in his life ne'er saw the like.
  And see where they come; belike the feast is done.

                Exit.

  Enter FAUSTUS, MEPHOSTOPHILIS, *and two or three*
            SCHOLARS.
1 SCHOLAR. Master Doctor Faustus, since our conference 10
  about fair ladies, which was the beautifulest in all the
  world, we have determined with ourselves that Helen
  of Greece was the admirablest lady that ever lived.
  Therefore, master doctor, if you will do us so much
  favor as to let us see that peerless dame of Greece,
  whom all the world admires for majesty, we should
  think ourselves much beholding unto you.
FAUSTUS. Gentlemen,
  For that I know your friendship is unfeigned,
  [[And Faustus' custom is not to deny]] 20
  The just request[[s]] of those that wish him well,
  You shall behold that peerless dame of Greece,
  No otherwise for pomp [[and]] majesty
  Than when Sir Paris crossed the seas with her
  And brought the spoils to rich Dardania.°
  Be silent, then, for danger is in words.

Dardania: Troy.

Music sound[[s]]. MEPHOSTOPHILIS *brings in* HELEN;
she passeth over the stage.

[[2 SCHOLAR. Too simple is my wit to tell her praise
Whom all the world admires for majesty.

3 SCHOLAR. No marvel though the angry Greeks pursued
With ten years' war the rape of such a queen,   30
Whose heavenly beauty passeth all compare.

1 SCHOLAR. Since we have seen the pride of nature's
works
And only paragon of excellence,
Let us depart; and for this glorious deed
Happy and blessed be Faustus evermore.

FAUSTUS. Gentlemen, farewell; the same I wish to you.
Exeunt Scholars.]]

Enter an OLD MAN.

OLD MAN. O gentle Faustus, leave this damnèd art,
This magic, that will charm thy soul to hell   *fallen nature*
And quite bereave thee of salvation.
Though thou hast now offended like a man,   *initial sin*   40
Do not persevere in it like a devil. *choice to sin*
Yet, yet, thou hast an amiable° soul
If sin by custom grow not into nature:
Then, Faustus, will repentance come too late;
Then thou art banished from the sight of heaven;
No mortal can express the pains of hell.
It may be this my exhortation
Seems harsh and all unpleasant; let it not,
For, gentle son, I speak it not in wrath
Or envy° of thee, but in tender love   50
And pity of thy future misery.
And so have hope that this my kind rebuke,
Checking thy body, may amend thy soul.

FAUSTUS. Where art thou, Faustus? Wretch, what hast
thou done?
[[Damned art thou, Faustus, damned; despair and
die!]]
Hell claims his right and with a roaring voice
Says, "Faustus, come; thine hour is almost come";
And Faustus now will come to do thee right.

---

amiable: capable of receiving (divine) love.
envy: ill-will.

(MEPHOSTOPHILIS *gives him a dagger.*)

OLD MAN. O, stay, good Faustus, stay thy desperate
     steps!
   I see an angel hover o'er thy head   60
   And with a vial full of precious grace
   Offers to pour the same into thy soul;
   Then call for mercy, and avoid despair.

FAUSTUS. [[Ah, my sweet]] friend, I feel thy words
   To comfort my distressèd soul.
   Leave me awhile to ponder on my sins.

OLD MAN. Faustus, I leave thee, but with grief of heart,
   Fearing the enemy of thy hapless soul.

                                                            Exit.

FAUSTUS. Accursèd Faustus, [[where is mercy now?]]
   I do repent, and yet I do despair;   70
   Hell strives with grace for conquest in my breast.
   What shall I do to shun the snares of death?

MEPHOSTOPHILIS. Thou traitor, Faustus, I arrest thy soul
   For disobedience to my sovereign lord.
   Revolt,° or I'll in piecemeal tear thy flesh.

FAUSTUS. I do repent I e'er offended him.
   Sweet Mephostophilis, entreat thy lord
   To pardon my unjust presumption,
   And with my blood again I will confirm
   The former vow I made to Lucifer.   80

[[MEPHOSTOPHILIS.]] Do it, then, Faustus, with un-
     feignèd heart,
   Lest greater dangers do attend thy drift.°
   [FAUSTUS *stabs his arm and again signs the contract
   in blood.*]

[[FAUSTUS.]] Torment, sweet friend, that base and aged
     man
   That durst dissuade me from thy Lucifer
   With greatest torment that our hell affords.

MEPHOSTOPHILIS. His faith is great; I cannot touch his
     soul,
   But what I may afflict his body with
   I will attempt, which is but little worth.

FAUSTUS. One thing, good servant, let me crave of thee

---

   revolt: return to your contract with Lucifer
   drift: drifting.

To glut the longing of my heart's desire: 90
That I may have unto my paramour
That heavenly Helen which I saw of late,
Whose sweet embraces may extinguish clear
Those thoughts that do dissuade me from my vow
And keep [[mine oath]] I made to Lucifer.

MEPHOSTOPHILIS. This or what else my Faustus shall
    desire
Shall be performed in twinkling of an eye.
        Enter HELEN *again, passing over between two*
                        Cupids.

FAUSTUS. Was this the face that launched a thousand
    ships
And burnt the topless towers of Ilium?
Sweet Helen, make me immortal with a kiss.   100
[*She kisses him.*]
Her lips suck forth my soul—see where it flies!
Come, Helen, come, give me my soul again.
Here will I dwell, for heaven is in these lips,
And all is dross that is not Helena.
                [[*Enter* OLD MAN.]]
I will be Paris, and for love of thee
Instead of Troy shall Wittenberg be sacked;
And I will combat with weak Menelaus°
And wear thy colors on my plumèd crest;
Yea, I will wound Achilles in the heel
And then return to Helen for a kiss.   110
O, thou art fairer than the evening's air
Clad in the beauty of a thousand stars;
Brighter art thou than flaming Jupiter
When he appeared to hapless Semele;°
More lovely than the monarch of the sky
In wanton Arethusa's° azure[[d]] arms;
And none but thou shalt be my paramour.
                        Exeunt [*all but* OLD MAN].
[[OLD MAN. Accursèd Faustus, miserable man,
    That from thy soul exclud'st the grace of heaven

Menelaus: husband of Helen of Troy.
Semele: who was consumed by Zeus' lightning.
Arethusa: a nymph who gave her name to a spring.

And fliest the throne of his tribunal seat!   120
                    Enter the Devils.
Satan begins to sift me with his pride.
As in this furnace God shall try my faith,
My faith, vile hell, shall triumph over thee!
Ambitious fiends, see how the heavens smiles
At your repulse and laughs your state to scorn!
Hence, hell, for hence I fly unto my God.

                                    Exeunt.]]

[xix]
              Thunder. Enter LUCIFER, BEËLZEBUB, *and*
                    MEPHOSTOPHILIS [*above*].
LUCIFER. Thus from infernal Dis° do we ascend
    To view the subjects of our monarchy,
    Those souls which sin seals the black sons of hell,
    'Mong which as chief, Faustus, we come to thee,
    Bringing with us lasting damnation
    To wait upon thy soul. The time is come
    Which makes it forfeit.
MEPHOSTOPHILIS.   And this gloomy night
    Here in this room will wretched Faustus be.
BEËLZEBUB. And here we'll stay
    To mark him how he doth demean himself.   10
MEPHOSTOPHILIS. How should he but in desperate lu-
        nacy?
    Fond worldling, now his heart-blood dries with grief,
    His conscience kills it, and his laboring brain
    Begets a world of idle fantasies
    To overreach the devil—but all in vain:
    His store of pleasures must be sauced with pain.
    He and his servant Wagner are at hand,
    Both come from drawing Faustus' latest will.
    See where they come.
                  Enter FAUSTUS *and* WAGNER.
FAUSTUS. Say, Wagner, thou hast perused my will;   20
    How dost thou like it?
WAGNER.   Sir, so wondrous well
    As in all humble duty I do yield

Dis: Hades.

My life and lasting service for your love.
Enter the Scholars.

FAUSTUS. Gramercies,° Wagner. Welcome, gentlemen.

[*Exit* WAGNER.]

1 SCHOLAR. Now, worthy Faustus, methinks your looks
are changed.

FAUSTUS. [[Ah,]] gentlemen!

2 SCHOLAR. What ails Faustus?

FAUSTUS. Ah, my sweet chamber-fellow, had I lived with   30
thee, then had I lived still, but now must die eternally.
Look, sirs, comes he not? Comes he not?

1 SCHOLAR. O my dear Faustus, what imports this fear?

2 SCHOLAR. Is all our pleasure turned to melancholy?

3 SCHOLAR. He is not well with being over-solitary.

2 SCHOLAR. If it be so, we'll have physicians, and
Faustus shall be cured.

3 SCHOLAR. 'Tis but a surfeit, sir; fear nothing.

FAUSTUS. A surfeit of deadly sin that hath damned both
body and soul.   40

2 SCHOLAR. Yet, Faustus, look up to heaven and remember [[God's]] mercy is infinite.

FAUSTUS. But Faustus' offence can ne'er be pardoned.
The serpent that tempted Eve may be saved, but not
Faustus. [[Ah,]] gentlemen, hear [[me]] with patience
and tremble not at my speeches. Though my heart
pant[[s]] and quiver[[s]] to remember that I have
been a student here these thirty years, O, would I had
never seen Wittenberg, never read book! And what
wonders I have done all Germany can witness, yea,   50
all the world, for which Faustus hath lost both Germany and the world, yea, heaven itself—heaven, the
seat of God, the throne of the blessed, the kingdom
of joy—and must remain in hell for ever. Hell, [[ah,]]
hell, for ever! Sweet friends, what shall become of
Faustus, being in hell for ever?

[[3 SCHOLAR.]] Yet, Faustus, call on God.

FAUSTUS. On God, whom Faustus hath abjured? On God,
whom Faustus hath blasphemed? [[Ah,]] my God, I
would weep, but the devil draws in my tears. Gush   60

---

gramercies: thanks.

forth blood instead of tears, yea, life and soul! O, he
stays my tongue! I would lift up my hands, but see,
they hold 'em, they hold 'em.

ALL. Who, Faustus?

FAUSTUS. Why, Lucifer and Mephostophilis. [[Ah,]]
gentlemen, I gave them my soul for my cunning.

ALL. O, God forbid!

FAUSTUS. God forbade it, indeed; but Faustus hath done
it. For the vain pleasure of four and twenty years hath
Faustus lost eternal joy and felicity. I writ them a bill   70
with mine own blood. The date is expired; this is the
time, and he will fetch me.

1 SCHOLAR. Why did not Faustus tell us of this before,
that divines might have prayed for thee?

FAUSTUS. Oft have I thought to have done so; but the
devil threatened to tear me in pieces if I named God,
to fetch me body and soul if I once gave ear to divinity; and now 'tis too late. Gentlemen, away, lest you
perish with me!

2 SCHOLAR. O, what may we do to save Faustus?   80

FAUSTUS. Talk not of me, but save yourselves and depart.

3 SCHOLAR. God will strengthen me; I will stay with
Faustus.

1 SCHOLAR. Tempt not God, sweet friend; but let us into
the next room and [[there]] pray for him.

FAUSTUS. Ay, pray for me, pray for me; and, what noise
soever you hear, come not unto me, for nothing can
rescue me.

2 SCHOLAR. Pray thou, and we will pray that God may
have mercy upon thee.   90

FAUSTUS. Gentlemen, farewell. If I live till morning, I'll
visit you; if not, Faustus is gone to hell.

ALL. Faustus, farewell.

Exeunt Scholars.

MEPHOSTOPHILIS. Ay, Faustus, now thou hast no hope
of heaven;
Therefore despair. Think only upon hell,
For that must be thy mansion, there to dwell.

FAUSTUS. O thou bewitching fiend, 'twas thy temptation
Hath robbed me of eternal happiness.

MEPHOSTOPHILIS. I do confess it, Faustus, and rejoice.

'Twas I that, when thou wert i'the way to heaven,   100
Dammed up thy passage; when thou took'st the book
To view the Scriptures, then I turned the leaves
And led thine eye.
What, weep'st thou? 'Tis too late. Despair! Farewell!
Fools that will laugh on earth must weep in hell.

Exit.

Enter the GOOD ANGEL *and the* BAD ANGEL
at several doors.

GOOD ANGEL. O Faustus, if thou hadst given ear to me,
Innumerable joys had followed thee;
But thou didst love the world.
BAD ANGEL.   Gave ear to me,
And now must taste hell's pains perpetually.
GOOD ANGEL. O, what will all thy riches, pleasures,
   pomps   110
Avail thee now?
BAD ANGEL.   Nothing but vex thee more,
To want in hell, that had on earth such store.
   (*Music while the throne descends.*)
GOOD ANGEL. O, thou hast lost celestial happiness,
Pleasures unspeakable, bliss without end.
Hadst thou affected sweet divinity,
Hell or the devil had had no power on thee.
Hadst thou kept on that way, Faustus, behold
In what resplendent glory thou hadst s[a]t
In yonder throne, like those bright shining saints,
And triumphed over hell; that hast thou lost.   120
And now, poor soul, must thy good angel leave thee;
The jaws of hell are open to receive thee.

Exit.

(*Hell is discovered.*)
BAD ANGEL. Now, Faustus, let thine eyes with horror
   stare
Into that vast perpetual torture-house.
There are the furies tossing damnèd souls
On burning forks; their bodies [boil] in lead.
There are live quarters broiling on the coals,
That ne'er can die. This ever-burning chair
Is for o'er-tortured souls to rest them in.
These that are fed with sops of flaming fire   130

Were gluttons and loved only delicates
And laughed to see the poor starve at their gates.
But yet all these are nothing; thou shalt see
Ten thousand tortures that more horrid be.

FAUSTUS. O, I have seen enough to torture me.

BAD ANGEL. Nay, thou must feel them, taste the smart
of all.
He that loves pleasure must for pleasure fall.
And so I leave thee, Faustus, till anon;
Then wilt thou tumble in confusion.

Exit.

(The clock strikes eleven.)

FAUSTUS. [[Ah,]] Faustus,   140
Now hast thou but one bare hour to live,
And then thou must be damned perpetually.
Stand still, you ever-moving spheres of heaven,
That time may cease and midnight never come.
Fair nature's eye, rise, rise again, and make
Perpetual day; or let this hour be but
A year, a month, a week, a natural day,
That Faustus may repent and save his soul.
O lente, lente currite noctis equi! *
The stars move still, time runs, the clock will strike,   150
The devil will come, and Faustus must be damned.
O, I'll leap up to [[my God!]] Who pulls me down?
[[See, see where Christ's blood streams in the firma-
ment!
One drop would save my soul, half a drop. Ah,]] my
Christ!—
Rend not my heart for naming of my Christ;
Yet will I call on him. O, spare me, Lucifer!—
Where is it now? 'Tis gone; and see [[where God
Stretcheth out his arm and bends his ireful brows]].
Mountains and hills, come, come, and fall on me,
And hide me from the heavy wrath of [[God!   160
No, no!]]
Then will I headlong run into the earth.
[[Earth, gape!]] O, no, it will not harbor me.

---

o . . . equi: o slowly, slowly, run, horses of the night! (adapted
from Ovid's *Amores,* I. xiii. 40).

You stars that reigned at my nativity,
Whose influence hath allotted death and hell,
Now draw up Faustus like a foggy mist
Into the entrails on yon laboring cloud,
That, when you vomit forth into the air,
My limbs may issue from your smoky mouths,
[[So that my soul may but]] ascend to heaven.   170
(*The watch strikes.*)
[[Ah,]] half the hour is passed; 'twill all be passed
    anon!
O [[God,
If thou wilt not have mercy on my soul,
Yet for Christ's sake, whose blood hath ransomed
    me,]]
Impose some end to my incessant pain.
Let Faustus live in hell a thousand years,
A hundred thousand, and at last be saved.
[[O,]] no end is limited to damnèd souls.
Why wert thou not a creature wanting soul?
Or why is this immortal that thou hast?   180
[[Ah,]] Pythagoras' *metempsychosis,*° were that true,
This soul should fly from me and I be changed
Into some brutish beast.
All beasts are happy, for when they die
Their souls are soon dissolved in elements;
But mine must live still to be plagued in hell.
Cursed be the parents that engendered me!
No, Faustus, curse thyself, curse Lucifer
That hath deprived thee of the joys of heaven.
(*The clock strikes twelve.*)
[[O,]] it strikes, it strikes! Now, body, turn to air,   190
Or Lucifer will bear thee quick° to hell!
O soul, be changed into [[little]] water drops,
And fall into the ocean, ne'er be found.
            Thunder, and enter the Devils.
[[My God, my God!]] Look not so fierce on me!

Pythagoras' *metempsychosis:* Pythagoras of Samos (6th century
B.C.), who was credited with the doctrine of the transmigration
of souls.
quick: living, alive.

Adders and serpents, let me breathe awhile!
Ugly hell, gape not! Come not, Lucifer!
I'll burn my books!—[[Ah,]] Mephostophilis!

Exeunt with him.

[xx]

Enter the Scholars.

1 SCHOLAR. Come, gentlemen, let us go visit Faustus,
For such a dreadful night was never seen
Since first the world's creation did begin;
Such fearful shrieks and cries were never heard.
Pray heaven the doctor have escaped the danger.

2 SCHOLAR. O, help us, heaven! See, here are Faustus'
limbs,
All torn asunder by the hand of death.

3 SCHOLAR. The devils whom Faustus served have torn
him thus:
For, 'twixt the hours of twelve and one, methought
I heard him shriek and call aloud for help,   10
At which self time the house seemed all on fire
With dreadful horror of these damnèd fiends.

2 SCHOLAR. Well, gentlemen, though Faustus' end be
such
As every Christian heart laments to think on,
Yet for he was a scholar, once admired
For wondrous knowledge in our German schools,
We'll give his mangled limbs due burial;
And all the students, clothed in mourning black,
Shall wait upon his heavy° funeral.

Exeunt.

[Epilogue]

Enter CHORUS.

[CHORUS]. Cut is the branch that might have grown full
straight,
And burnèd is Apollo's laurel bough
That sometime grew within this learned man.
Faustus is gone: regard his hellish fall,
Whose fiendful fortune may exhort the wise

---

heavy: sorrowful.

Only to wonder at unlawful things,
Whose deepness doth entice such forward wits
To practice more than heavenly power permits.   [*Exit.*]

*Terminat hora diem; terminat Author opus.**

FINIS.

---

terminat . . . *opus:* the hour ends the day; the author ends his work.

THE
SHOMAKERS
Holiday.
OR
The Gentle Craft.

With the humorous life of Simon
Eyre, ſhoomaker, and Lord Maior
of London.

As it was acted before the Queenes moſt excellent Ma-
ieſtie on New-yeares day at night laſt, by the right
honourable the Earle of Notingham, Lord high Ad-
mirall of England, his ſeruants.

Printed by Valentine Sims dwelling at the foote of Adling
hill, neere Bainards Caſtle, at the ſigne of the White
Swanne, and are there to be ſold.
1 6 0 0.

Introduction

> FAUSTUS. *Where are you damned?*
> MEPHOSTOPHILIS. *In hell.*
> FAUSTUS. *How comes it then that thou art out of hell?*
> MEPHOSTOPHILIS. *Why, this is hell, nor am I out of it.*
> (Doctor Faustus, *scene iii*)

The bare Elizabethan stage, open to the sky and projecting into a large audience comprising every class of English society, is itself a little world that metaphorically suggests the larger world: "All the world's a stage,/ And all the men and women merely players"; and on the stage of the world men make their own heaven or hell. In *Doctor Faustus* that world is hell on earth, a place that entices man but ultimately makes a mockery of his endeavors to master it. Faustus' failure to make a brazen world golden looks ahead, however, to the next decade; the drama of the 1590s mainly celebrates a harmonious world and social order symbolized in "fair Eliza," God's vicar in this His earthly city. Shakespeare's history plays, all written in these years as a tribute to the Tudor ideal of government, reveal how delicate is the balance that maintains this order. The destructive forces that man's devastating drive for earthly power unleashes are contained only with difficulty by a sustaining vision of "this earth of majesty."

Dekker's *The Shoemakers' Holiday: A Pleasant Comedy of the Gentle Craft*, a play of 1599 and performed before Her

Majesty on the first night of the New Year of 1600, might be considered, for all its frankly uninhibited celebration of life, the swan song of the Elizabethan drama of enchantment. On the same scenery-less stage where Faustus experienced hell, Dekker created a semblance of heaven on earth. In Wittenberg Faustus learned his "devilish exercise"; but there Dekker's noble Lacy learns the shoemaker's trade and thus, by proving that he is no "silken" courtier, becomes worthy of marrying a lord mayor's daughter. The juxtaposition of comic and serious scenes in *Doctor Faustus* serves to deny meaning to Faustus' existence; in *The Shoemakers' Holiday* it tends to affirm and to glorify a divinely ordered society, reflected especially in the opening scene, where all classes of the realm come together, as they did in the Elizabethan theater, and in the final scene, where the king himself breaks bread with his loyal and loving subjects. Dekker's king is no mere *deus ex machina* brought in to resolve the plot to a happy ending; he, like the "bright mirror of true chastity" before whom the servants of the lord high admiral performed the play, is God's anointed deputy who walks freely in the demi-paradise that is his realm. He forgives "vile treason," and his compassionate tolerance preserves the social fabric. In a reign of love, discord ultimately has no place. On the domestic level the "madcap" Simon Eyre imitates his beloved monarch with the same results.

Dekker shares with Shakespeare a sense of life's sweetness and meaningful purpose, which, for all Faustus' attractions to the world, Marlowe so rigorously excludes from his work. Yet Dekker is never sentimental; like Shakespeare also, he is aware of life's harsh realities. The play opens with conscription for war (the threat of a new Armada from Spain was serious in the summer of 1599); in the middle Rafe returns lame and cannot find his wife; and the couplet that concludes the play has the king remind players and audience alike:

When all our sports and banquetings are done,
Wars must right wrongs which Frenchmen have begun.
Every day is not playing holiday, as Jane so poignantly reminds us: "I cannot live by keeping holiday." "It is," as Eyre says, "a hard world"; but holidays are necessary to remind men, by refreshing their tired spirits, that life is a gift and a blessing that continues to revitalize itself. When "cold's the wind and wet's the rain," the only remedy is to

"troll the bowl," to down it merrily even while singing a dirge. "Pull up a good heart," Hodge advises Rafe; and Eyre dares urge the king himself to "let care vanish!" In fact, "Avaunt, avoid, Mephostophilus!" might be considered Eyre's lusty and infectious rebuke to Faustus.

The Playwright

THOMAS DEKKER (c. 1572–c. 1632), a Londoner by birth, is mentioned in Henslowe's diary as a playwright for the Admiral's men in 1598; but little is known definitely about his personal life or career. Although he wrote plays sporadically throughout his life, his main dramatic output, mostly in collaboration, falls between 1598 and 1602. In the early seventeenth century he turned to pamphleteering, and in a chapter of *The Gull's Hornbook* (1609) he left an engaging record of the contemporary theatrical scene. An active career as a writer did not keep him from want, and from 1613 to 1619 he served in King's Bench for debt. Only a few of the over forty plays in which he had a hand have survived.

The Play

The present text of *The Shoemakers' Holiday* is based on copies of the first quarto of 1600 in the Henry E. Huntington and the Folger Shakespeare libraries that have been collated with the old-spelling edition of Fredson Bowers. The original quarto has no act or scene divisions. Dekker wrote the play in 1599, and the Admiral's men performed it at court on the night of January 1, 1600.

SELECTED BIBLIOGRAPHY

The Dramatic Works of Thomas Dekker, ed. F. Bowers. 4 vols.
Cambridge: Cambridge University Press, 1953–1961.
The Non-dramatic Works of Thomas Dekker, ed. A. B. Grosart. 5
vols. London: Huth Library, 1884–1886.
The Shoemakers' Holiday, ed. P. C. Davies. Edinburgh: Oliver
and Boyd, 1968.
The Shoemaker's Holiday, ed. J. B. Steane. Cambridge: Cambridge
University Press, 1965.

Jones-Davies, M. T. *Un peintre de la vie londonienne: Thomas
Dekker.* Paris: Didier [1958].
Knights, L. C. *Drama and Society in the Age of Jonson.* London:
Chatto and Windus, 1937.
Novarr, D. "Dekker's Gentle Craft and the Lord Mayor of Lon-
don," *Modern Philology,* LVII (1960), 233–239.
Toliver, H. E. *"The Shoemaker's Holiday:* Theme and Image,"
Boston University Studies in English, V (1961), 208–218.

[DRAMATIS PERSONAE

*

The KING OF ENGLAND.
The EARL OF CORNWALL.
SIR HUGH LACY, *Earl of Lincoln.*
ROWLAND LACY, *mainly in disguise as* HANS MEULTER } *his nephews.*
ASKEW
SIR ROGER OATLEY, *Lord Mayor of London.*
MASTER HAMMON }
MASTER WARNER } *citizens of London.*
MASTER SCOTT }
SIMON EYRE, *a shoemaker, afterwards Lord Mayor.*
ROGER, *commonly called* HODGE, *foreman to Eyre.*
FIRKE }
RAFE DAMPORT } *journeymen to Eyre.*
LOVELL, *a courtier.*
DODGER, *parasite to the Earl of Lincoln.*
A DUTCH SKIPPER.
BOY, *apprentice to Eyre.*
BOY, *servant to Oatley.*

ROSE, *daughter to Oatley.*
MARGERY, *wife to Eyre.*
JANE, *wife to Rafe Damport.*
SYBIL, *maid to Rose.*

Courtiers, Officers, Soldiers, Huntsmen, Shoemakers, Apprentices,
Servants, and Attendants.
Time: Middle of the Fifteenth Century.]

To All Good Fellows, Professors° of the
Gentle Craft, of What Degree Soever.

Kind gentlemen and honest boon companions, I present you here with a merry conceited° comedy called *The Shoemakers' Holiday*, acted by my Lord Admiral's Players this present Christmas before the Queen's most excellent Majesty, for the mirth and pleasant matter by Her Highness graciously accepted, being indeed no way offensive. The argument of the play I will set down in this epistle: Sir Hugh Lacy, Earl of Lincoln, had a young gentleman of his own name, his near kinsman, that loved the lord mayor's daughter of London; to prevent and cross which love, the Earl caused his kinsman to be sent coronel° of a company into France: who resigned his place to another gentleman, his friend, and came disguised like a Dutch shoemaker to the house of Simon Eyre in Tower Street, who served the mayor and his household with shoes; the merriments that passed in Eyre's house, his coming to be mayor of London, Lacy's getting his love, and other accidents,° with two merry three-men's songs. Take all in good worth that is well intended, for nothing is purposed but mirth; mirth length'neth long life, which, with all other blessings, I heartily wish you.

Farewell!

The First Three-man's Song.

O, the month of May, the merry month of May,
So frolic, so gay, and so green, so green, so green!
O, and then did I unto my true love say,
"Sweet Peg, thou shalt be my summer's queen!

"Now the nightingale, the pretty nightingale,
The sweetest singer in all the forest's choir,

---

professors . . . craft: shoemakers; so called by Hugh, their patron saint.
conceited: imaginatively constructed.
coronel: colonel.
accidents: events, occurrences.

Entreats thee, sweet Peggy, to hear thy true love's tale:
Lo, yonder she sitteth, her breast against a brier.

"But, O, I spy the cuckoo, the cuckoo, the cuckoo;
See where she sitteth—come away, my joy;   10
Come away, I prithee. I do not like the cuckoo
Should sing where my Peggy and I kiss and toy."

  O, the month of May, the merry month of May,
  So frolic, so gay, and so green, so green, so green!
  And then did I unto my true love say,
  "Sweet Peg, thou shalt be my summer's queen!"

The Second Three-man's Song.
(*This is to be sung at the latter end.*)

      Cold's the wind, and wet's the rain—
        Saint Hugh be our good speed.
      Ill is the weather that bringeth no gain,
        Nor helps good hearts in need.

      Troll the bowl, the jolly nut-brown bowl,
        And here, kind mate, to thee!
      Let's sing a dirge for Saint Hugh's soul,
        And down it merrily.

      Down a-down, hey down a-down,
        Hey derry derry down a-down,   10
      (Close with the tenor boy.)
      Ho, well done; to me let come!
        Ring compass, *gentle joy.*

      Troll the bowl, the nut-brown bowl,
        And here, kind, &c.
      (As often as there be men to drink.)

      (At last, when all have drunk, this verse:)

      Cold's the wind, and wet's the rain—
        Saint Hugh be our good speed.

---

ring compass: sound the full range of one's voice.

Ill is the weather that bringeth no gain,
Nor helps good hearts in need.

The Prologue,
as it was pronounced before the Queen's Majesty

As wretches in a storm, expecting day,
With trembling hands and eyes cast up to heaven,
Make prayers the anchor of their conquered hopes,
So we, dear goddess, wonder of all eyes,
Your meanest vassals, through mistrust and fear
To sink into the bottom of disgrace
By our imperfit pastimes, prostrate thus
On bended knees, our sails of hope do strike,
Dreading the bitter storms of your dislike.
Since then, unhappy men, our hap is such   10
That to ourselves ourselves no help can bring
But needs must perish if your saintlike ears,
Locking the temple where all mercy sits,
Refuse the tribute of our begging tongues,
O, grant, bright mirror of true chastity,
From those life-breathing stars, your sunlike eyes,
One gracious smile: for your celestial breath
Must send us life or sentence us to death.

The Shoemakers' Holiday

A Pleasant Comedy of the Gentle Craft

[i]

Enter LORD MAYOR, LINCOLN.

LINCOLN. My lord mayor, you have sundry times
  Feasted myself and many courtiers more;
  Seldom or never can we be so kind
  To make requital of your courtesy.
  But, leaving this, I hear my cousin° Lacy
  Is much affected° to your daughter Rose.

LORD MAYOR. True, my good lord, and she loves him so well
  That I mislike her boldness in the chase.

LINCOLN. Why, my lord mayor, think you it then a shame
  To join a Lacy with an Oatley's name?   10

LORD MAYOR. Too mean is my poor girl for his high birth;
  Poor citizens must not with courtiers wed,
  Who will in silks and gay apparel spend
  More in one year than I am worth by far.
  Therefore your honor need not doubt° my girl.

LINCOLN. Take heed, my lord; advise you what you do!
  A verier unthrift lives not in the world
  Than is my cousin, for I'll tell you what:

---

cousin: denoting close relationship.
affected: in love with.
doubt: fear.

'Tis now almost a year since he requested
To travel countries for experience;   20
I furnished him with coin, bills of exchange,
Letters of credit, men to wait on him,
Solicited my friends in Italy
Well to respect him. But, to see the end:
Scant had he journeyed through half Germany
But all his coin was spent, his men cast off,
His bills embezzled;° and my jolly coz,
Ashamed to show his bankrupt presence here,
Became a shoemaker in Wittenberg—
A goodly science for a gentleman   30
Of such descent! Now judge the rest by this:
Suppose your daughter have a thousand pound,
He did consume me more in one half year;
And, make him heir to all the wealth you have,
One twelvemonth's rioting will waste it all.
Then seek, my lord, some honest citizen
To wed your daughter to.
LORD MAYOR.   I thank your lordship.
    [*Aside.*] Well, fox, I understand your subtlety.—
As for your nephew, let your lordship's eye
But watch his actions; and you need not fear,   40
For I have [sent] my daughter far enough.
And yet your cousin Rowland might do well
Now he hath learned an occupation.
    [*Aside.*] And yet I scorn to call him son-in-law.
LINCOLN. Ay, but I have a better trade for him.
I thank his grace he hath appointed him
Chief colonel of all those companies
Mustered in London and the shires about
To serve his highness in those wars of France.
See where he comes!—
              Enter LOVELL, LACY, *and* ASKEW.
                       Lovell, what news with you?   50
LOVELL. My Lord of Lincoln, 'tis his highness' will
That presently° your cousin ship for France
With all his powers; he would not for a million
But they should land at Dieppe within four days.

------

embezzled: wasted.
presently: at once, immediately.

LINCOLN. Go certify his grace it shall be done.—

Exit LOVELL.

Now, cousin Lacy, in what forwardness
Are all your companies?
LACY.   All well prepared.
The men of Hertfordshire lie at Mile End;
Suffolk and Essex train in Tothill Fields;
The Londoners and those of Middlesex,   60
All gallantly prepared in Finsbury,
With frolic spirits long for the parting hour.
LORD MAYOR. They have their imprest,° coats, and fur-
    niture;°
And, if it please your cousin Lacy come
To the Guildhall, he shall receive his pay;
And twenty pounds besides my brethren
Will freely give him, to approve° our loves
We bear unto my lord your uncle here.
LACY. I thank your honor.
LINCOLN.   Thanks, my good lord
    mayor.
LORD MAYOR. At the Guildhall we will expect° your
    coming.   70

Exit.

LINCOLN. To approve your loves to me? No! Subtlety!—
Nephew, that twenty pound he doth bestow
For joy to rid you from his daughter Rose.
But, cousins both, now here are none but friends,
I would not have you cast an amorous eye
Upon so mean a project as the love
Of a gay, wanton, painted citizen.
I know this churl even in the height of scorn
Doth hate the mixture of his blood with thine.
I pray thee, do thou so! Remember, coz,   80
What honorable fortunes wait on thee.
Increase the king's love, which so brightly shines
And gilds thy hopes. I have no heir but thee:
And yet not thee if, with a wayward spirit,

---

imprest: advance pay.
furniture: equipment.
approve: demonstrate.
expect: await.

Thou start° from the true bias of my love.
LACY. My lord, I will—for honor, not desire
  Of land or livings, or to be your heir—
  So guide my actions in pursuit of France
  As shall add glory to the Lacys' name.
LINCOLN. Coz, for those words here's thirty Portuguese.°   90
  And, nephew Askew, there's a few for you.
  Fair Honor in her loftiest eminence
  Stays in France for you till you fetch her thence.
  Then, nephews, clap swift wings on your designs.
  Begone, begone! Make haste to the Guildhall;
  There presently I'll meet you. Do not stay:
  Where Honor [beckons], Shame attends delay.

                                                                    Exit.

ASKEW. How gladly would your uncle have you gone!
LACY. True, coz, but I'll o'erreach his policies.
  I have some serious business for three days,   100
  Which nothing but my presence can dispatch.
  You, therefore, cousin, with the companies
  Shall haste to Dover; there I'll meet with you
  Or, if I stay past my prefixèd time,
  Away for France: we'll meet in Normandy.
  The twenty pounds my lord mayor gives to me
  You shall receive, and these ten Portuguese,
  Part of mine uncle's thirty. Gentle coz,
  Have care to our great charge; I know your wisdom
  Hath tried itself in higher consequence.   110
ASKEW. Coz, all myself am yours; yet have this care,
  To lodge in London with all secrecy.
  Our uncle Lincoln hath (besides his own)
  Many a jealous eye, that in your face
  Stares only to watch means for your disgrace.
LACY. Stay, cousin! Who be these?
          Enter SIMON EYRE, *his* WIFE, HODGE, FIRKE,
          JANE, *and* RAFE *with a piece* [*of leather*].
EYRE. Leave whining, leave whining! Away with this
  whimp'ring, this puling, these blubb'ring tears, and
  these wet eyes! I'll get thy husband discharged, I war-
  rant thee, sweet Jane; go to!   120
HODGE. Master, here be the captains.

---

start: turn away from.
Portuguese: gold coins.

EYRE. Peace, Hodge; hushed, ye knave, hushed!

FIRKE. Here be the cavaliers and the coronels, master.

EYRE. Peace, Firke; peace, my fine Firke! Stand by with
your pishery-pashery. Away! I am a man of the best
presence; I'll speak to them and° they were popes.—
[*To* IACY *and* ASKEW.] Gentlemen, captains, colonels,
commanders! Brave men, brave leaders, may it please
you to give me an audience. I am Simon Eyre, the
mad shoemaker of Tower Street. This wench with the   130
mealy mouth that will never tire is my wife, I can tell
you. Here's Hodge, my man and my foreman. Here's
Firke, my fine firking° journeyman. And this is blub-
bered Jane. All we come to be suitors for this honest
Rafe. Keep him at home and, as I am a true shoemaker and a gentleman of the Gentle Craft, buy spurs
yourself and I'll find° ye boots these seven years.

WIFE. Seven years, husband?

EYRE. Peace, midriff, peace! I know what I do. Peace!

FIRKE. Truly, master cormorant,° you shall do God good   140
service to let Rafe and his wife stay together. She's
a young new-married woman. If you take her husband
away from her a-night, you undo her. She may beg in
the daytime, for he's as good a workman at a prick
and an awl as any is in our trade.

JANE. O, let him stay; else I shall be undone!

FIRKE. Ay, truly, she shall be laid at one side like a pair
of old shoes else and be occupied for no use.

LACY. Truly, my friends, it lies not in my power.
The Londoners are pressed,° paid, and set forth   150
By the lord mayor; I cannot change a man.

HODGE. Why, then you were as good be a corporal as a
colonel if you cannot discharge one good fellow. And,
I'll tell you true, I think you do more than you can
answer, to press a man within a year and a day of his
marriage.

EYRE. Well said, melancholy Hodge. Gramercy, my fine
foreman.

---

and: if.

firking: prankish.

find: provide.

cormorant: a colonel or, like the bird of prey, a greedy officer
forcing a soldier from his home.

pressed: impressed (as troops).

WIFE. Truly, gentleman, it were ill done for such as you
to stand so stiffly against a poor young wife, consider-   160
ing her case; she is new-married—but let that pass.
I pray, deal not roughly with her; her husband is a
young man and but newly entered—but let that pass.

EYRE. Away with your pishery-pashery, your pols and
your edipols!° Peace, mid[riff]! Silence, Cicely Bum-
trinket! Let your head speak!

FIRKE. Yea, and the horns too, master.

EYRE. Too soon, my fine Firke, too soon! Peace, scoundrels! See you this man? Captains, you will not release
him? Well, let him go. He's a proper shot; let him   170
vanish! Peace, Jane, dry up thy tears; they'll make his
powder dankish. Take him, brave men! Hector of
Troy was an hackney to him; Hercules and Terma-
gant scoundrels; Prince Arthur's Round Table—by
the Lord of Ludgate—ne'er fed such a tall,° such a
dapper swordsman. By the life of Pharaoh, a brave,
resolute swordsman! Peace, Jane! I say no more, mad
knaves.

FIRKE. See, see, Hodge, how my master raves in commendation of Rafe!   180

HODGE. Rafe, th'art a gull,° by this hand, and thou
goest [not].

ASKEW. I am glad, good Master Eyre, it is my hap
To meet so resolute a soldier.
Trust me, for your report and love to him,
A common slight regard shall not respect him.

LACY. Is thy name Rafe?

RAFE.   Yes, sir.

LACY.   Give me thy hand.
Thou shalt not want, as I am a gentleman.—
Woman, be patient. God, no doubt, will send
Thy husband safe again; but he must go—   190
His country's quarrel says it shall be so.

HODGE. Th'art a gull, by my stirrup, if thou dost not go.
I will not have thee strike thy gimlet into these weak
vessels; prick thine enemies, Rafe.

---

pols and edipols: by Pollux!
tall: brave.
gull: fool, dupe.

Enter DODGER.

DODGER. My lord, your uncle on the Tower Hill
　　Stays with the lord mayor and the aldermen,
　　And doth request you will all speed you may
　　To hasten thither.

ASKEW. 　　　　　　　Cousin, [let us] go.

LACY. Dodger, run you before; tell them we come.—

Exit DODGER.

　　This Dodger is mine uncle's parasite,　　　　　　　　　200
　　The arrant'st varlet that e'er breathed on earth.
　　He sets more discord in a noble house
　　By one day's broaching of his pickthank* tales
　　Than can be salved again in twenty years.
　　And he, I fear, shall go with us to France
　　To pry into our actions.

ASKEW. 　　　　　　Therefore, coz,
　　It shall behoove you to be circumspect.

LACY. Fear not, good cousin.—Rafe, hie to your colors.

[*Exeunt* LACY *and* ASKEW.]

RAFE. I must because [there is] no remedy.
　　But, gentle master and my loving dame,　　　　　　　　210
　　As you have always been a friend to me,
　　So in mine absence think upon my wife.

JANE. Alas, my Rafe!

WIFE. 　　　　　　　She cannot speak for weeping.

EYRE. Peace, you cracked groats, you mustard tokens!*
　　Disquiet not the brave soldier.—Go thy ways, Rafe!

JANE. Ay, ay, you bid him go. What shall I do when he
　　is gone?

FIRKE. Why, be doing with me or my fellow Hodge; be
　　not idle.

EYRE. Let me see thy hand, Jane. This fine hand, this　220
　　white hand, these pretty fingers must spin, must card,
　　must work. Work, you bombast* cotton-candle*
　　quean;* work for your living, with a pox to you!—Hold
　　thee, Rafe; here's five sixpences for thee. Fight for the

---

pickthank: flattering.
tokens: yellow plague spots.
bombast: cotton-wool.
cotton-candle: cotton-wick candle (hence, cheap).
quean: harlot, prostitute.

honor of the Gentle Craft, for the gentlemen shoemakers, the courageous cordwainers, the flower of
Saint Martin's, the mad knaves of Bedlam, Fleet
Street, Tower Street, and Whitechapel. Crack me the
crowns of the French knaves, a pox on them! Crack
them! Fight, by the Lord of Ludgate! Fight, my fine   230
boy!

FIRKE. Here, Rafe, here's three twopences. Two carry
into France; the third shall wash our souls at parting
(for sorrow is dry). For my sake, firk the *Basa mon
cues.**

HODGE. Rafe, I am heavy at parting; but here's a shilling
for thee. God send thee to cram thy slops* with
French crowns and thy enemies' bellies with bullets.

RAFE. I thank you, master, and I thank you all.
Now, gentle wife, my loving, lovely Jane,   240
Rich men at parting give their wives rich gifts,
Jewels and rings to grace their lily hands.
Thou know'st our trade makes rings for women's
    heels.
Here, take this pair of shoes cut out by Hodge,
Stitched by my fellow Firke, seamed by myself,
Made up and pinked* with letters for thy name.
Wear them, my dear Jane, for thy husband's sake;
And, every morning when thou pull'st them on,
Remember me and pray for my return.
Make much of them, for I have made them so   250
That I can know them from a thousand mo.*

>   *Sound drum. Enter* LORD MAYOR, LINCOLN, LACY,
>   ASKEW, DODGER, *and Soldiers. They pass over
>   the stage.* RAFE *falls in amongst them;* FIRKE
>   *and the rest cry "Farewell," etc., and so exeunt.*

[ii]
>   *Enter* ROSE, *alone, making a garland.*

ROSE. Here sit thou down upon this flow'ry bank
And make a garland for thy Lacy's head.

---

firk . . . cues: trounce the kiss-my-tails (cf. French slang *Baisez
mon queue*).
slops: wide, baggy breeches.
pinked: perforated.
mo: more.

These pinks, these roses, and these violets,
These blushing gillyflowers, these marigolds,
The fair embro[i]dery of his coronet,
Carry not half such beauty in their cheeks
As the sweet count'nance of my Lacy doth.
O my most unkind father! O my stars,
Why lowered you so at my nativity
To make me love, yet live robbed of my love?   10
Here as a thief am I imprisonèd
For my dear Lacy's sake within those walls
Which by my father's cost were builded up
For better purposes. Here must I languish
For him that doth as much lament, I know,
Mine absence as for him I pine in woe.

Enter SYBIL.

SYBIL. Good morrow, young mistress. I am sure you
make that garland for me, against* I shall be Lady of
the Harvest.

ROSE. Sybil, what news at London?   20

SYBIL. None but good. My lord mayor, your father, and
Master Philpot, your uncle, and Master Scott, your
cousin, and Mistress Frigbottom by Doctors' Commons do all, by my troth, send you most hearty commendations.

ROSE. Did Lacy send kind greetings to his love?

SYBIL. O, yes, out of cry.* By my troth, I scant knew
him. Here 'a* wore [a] scarf, and here a scarf; here
a bunch of feathers, and here precious stones and jewels and a pair of garters—O, monstrous!—like one of   30
our yellow silk curtains at home here in Old Ford
House, here in Master Bellymount's chamber. I stood
at our door in Cornhill, looked at him, he at me indeed, spake to him, but he not to me, not a word.
"Marry, g'up," thought I, "with a wanion!"* He
passed by me as proud—"Marry, foh! Are you grown
humorous?"* thought I, and so shut the door, and in
I came.

---

against: for the time when.
out of cry: beyond description.
'a: he.
wanion: bad luck or a vengeance (variant of *waniand*).
humorous: capricious, moody; ill-humored.

ROSE. O Sybil, how dost thou my Lacy wrong!
   My Rowland is as gentle as a lamb;   40
   No dove was ever half so mild as he.
SYBIL. Mild? Yea, as a bushel of stamped crabs.° He
   looked upon me as sour as verjuice. "Go thy ways!"
   thought I; "thou mayst be much in my gaskins,° but
   nothing in my netherstocks."° This is your fault, mistress, to love him that loves you not. He thinks scorn
   to do as he's done to; but, if I were as you, I'd cry,
   "Go by, Jeronimo, go by!"°
     I'd set mine old debts against my new driblets,
     And the hare's foot against the goose giblets;   50
     For, if ever I sigh when sleep I should take,
     Pray God I may lose my maidenhead when I wake.
ROSE. Will my love leave me, then, and go to France?
SYBIL. I know not that, but I am sure I see him stalk
   before the soldiers. By my troth, he is a proper man;
   but he is proper that proper doth. Let him go snick-
   up,° young mistress.
ROSE. Get thee to London, and learn perfectly
   Whether my Lacy go to France or no.
   Do this, and I will give thee for thy pains   60
   My cambric apron and my Romish gloves,
   My purple stockings and a stomacher
   Say, wilt thou do this, Sybil, for my sake?
SYBIL. Will I, quoth 'a? At whose suit? By my troth, yes,
   I'll go. A cambric apron, gloves, a pair of purple
   stockings, and a stomacher! I'll sweat in purple, mis-
   tress, for you; I'll take anything that comes o' God's
   name! O, rich! A cambric apron! Faith, then have at
   up tails all.° I'll go jiggy-joggy to London and be
   here in a trice, young mistress.   70
                                                  Exit.

---

   stamped crabs: crushed crab apples.
   gaskins: wide trousers.
   netherstocks: stockings ("we may know each other, but we're
not intimate").
   go by . . . by: a popular catch phrase, inaccurately cited by
Sybil, from Kyd's revenge play *The Spanish Tragedy* (c. 1589).
   snick-up: hang.
   have . . . all: hasten and be off.

ROSE. Do so, good Sybil.—Meantime, wretched I
  Will sit and sigh for his lost company.

Exit.

[iii]
    Enter ROWLAND LACY, *like a Dutch shoemaker.*
LACY. How many shapes have gods and kings devised
  Thereby to compass their desired loves!
  It is no shame for Rowland Lacy, then,
  To clothe his cunning with the Gentle Craft,
  That, thus disguised, I may unknown possess
  The only happy presence of my Rose.
  For her have I forsook my charge in France,
  Incurred the king's displeasure, and stirred up
  Rough hatred in mine uncle Lincoln's breast.
  O love, how powerful art thou, that canst change   10
  High birth to bareness, and a noble mind
  To the mean semblance of a shoemaker!
  But thus it must be: for her cruel father,
  Hating the single union of our souls,
  Hath secretly conveyed my Rose from London
  To bar me of her presence; but I trust
  Fortune and this disguise will further me
  Once more to view her beauty, gain her sight.
  Here in Tower Street, with Eyre the shoemaker,
  Mean I a while to work. I know the trade;   20
  I learnt it when I was in Wittenberg.
  Then cheer thy hoping sprites, be not dismayed;
  Thou canst not want. Do Fortune what she can,
  The Gentle Craft is living for a man.

Exit.

[iv]
    Enter EYRE, *making himself ready.*
EYRE. Where be these boys, these girls, these drabs,
  these scoundrels? They wallow in the fat brewis* of
  my bounty and lick up the crumbs of my table, yet
  will not rise to see my walks cleansed. Come out, you
  powder-beef* queans! What, Nan! What, Madge Mum-

---

brewis: meat broth.
powder-beef: salted beef.

blecrust! Come out, you fat midriff swagbelly whores, and sweep me these kennels* that the noisome stench offend not the nose of my neighbors. What, Firke, I say! What, Hodge! Open my shop windows! What, Firke, I say! 10

Enter FIRKE.

FIRKE. O Master, is't you that speak bandog and bed-lam* this morning? I was in a dream and mused what madman was got into the street so early. Have you drunk this morning that your throat is so clear?

EYRE. Ah, well said, Firke; well said, Firke! To work, my fine knave, to work! Wash thy face, and thou't be more blessed.

FIRKE. Let them wash my face that will eat it. Good master, send for a souse-wife* if you'll have my face cleaner. 20

Enter HODGE.

EYRE. Away, sloven! Avaunt, scoundrel!—Good morrow, Hodge; good morrow, my fine foreman.

HODGE. O master, good morrow; y'are an early stirrer. Here's a fair morning.—Good morrow, Firke. I could have slept this hour. Here's a brave day towards!

EYRE. O, haste to work, my fine foreman, haste to work.

FIRKE. Master, I am as dry as dust to hear my fellow Roger talk of fair weather. Let us pray for good leather, and let clowns and plowboys and those that work in the fields pray for brave days. We work in 30 a dry shop; what care I if it rain?

Enter Eyre's WIFE.

EYRE. How now, Dame Margery, can you see to rise? Trip and go; call up the drabs, your maids.

WIFE. See to rise? I hope 'tis time enough; 'tis early enough for any woman to be seen abroad. I marvel how many wives in Tower Street are up so soon. God's me, 'tis not noon! Here's a yawling!

EYRE. Peace, Margery, peace! Where's Cicely Bumtrin ket, your maid? She has a privy fault—she farts in her sleep. Call the quean up. If my men want shoe- 40 thread, I'll swinge her in a stirrup.

---

kennels: gutters.
bandog and bedlam: like a chained bloodhound and madman.
souse-wife: pig-pickler.

FIRKE. Yet that's but a dry beating; here's still a sign of drought.

> Enter LACY singing [, *disguised as* HANS, *a Dutch shoemaker*].

LACY.   *Der was een bore van Galderland,*
>   *Frolick si byen!*
>   *He was als dronck he could nyet stand,*
>   *Upsolce se byen!*
>   *Tap eens de canneken;*
>   *Drincke, scho[n]e mannekin.**

FIRKE. Master, for my life, yonder's a brother of the   50
Gentle Craft. If he bear not Saint Hugh's bones,* I'll
forfeit my bones. He's some uplandish° workman.
Hire him, good master, that I may learn some gibble-
gabble. 'Twill make us work the faster.

EYRE. Peace, Firke! A hard world! Let him pass, let him
vanish. We have journeymen enow. Peace, my fine
Firke!

WIFE. Nay, nay, y'are best to follow your man's counsel;
you shall see what will come on't. We have not men
enow but we must entertain every butterbox°—but   60
let that pass.

HODGE. Dame, 'fore God, if my master follow your counsel, he'll consume little beef. He shall be glad of men
and he can catch them.

FIRKE. Ay, that he shall.

HODGE. 'Fore God, a proper man and, I warrant, a fine
workman. Master, farewell. Dame, adieu. If such a
man as he cannot find work, Hodge is not for you.
(*Offer[s] to go.*)

EYRE. Stay, my fine Hodge.

FIRKE. Faith, and your foreman go, dame, you must   70

Lacy's song: There was a boor from Gelderland,
>   Jolly they be!
>   He was so drunk he could not stand,
>   Drunken they be!
>   Tap once the cannikin;
>   Drink, pretty mannikin.

Saint Hugh's bones: the bones of Saint Hugh, the patron saint of the Gentle Craft, were believed to have been turned into shoe-makers' tools.

uplandish: foreign.

butterbox: Dutchman.

take a journey to seek a new journeyman. If Roger
remove, Firke follows. If Saint Hugh's bones shall
not be set a-work, I may prick mine awl in the walls
and go play. Fare ye well, master. Goodbye, dame.

EYRE. Tarry, my fine Hodge, my brisk foreman! Stay,
Firke! Peace, pudding-broth! By the Lord of Ludgate,
I love my men as my life. Peace, you gallimaufry!*
Hodge, if he want work, I'll hire him. One of you, to
him—Stay, he comes to us.

LACY. *Goeden dach, meester, ende u, vro, oak.*   80

FIRKE. Nails!* If I should speak after him without drinking, I should choke. —And you, friend Oak, are you
of the Gentle Craft?

LACY. *Yaw, yaw; ik bin den skomawker.*

FIRKE. "Den skomaker," quoth 'a! And hark you, *skomaker*, have you all your tools? A good rubbing pin,
a good stopper, a good dresser, your four sorts of
awls, and your two balls of wax, your paring knife,
your hand-and-thumb-leathers, and good Saint Hugh's
bones to smooth up your work?   90

LACY. *Yaw, yaw; be niet vorveard. Ik hab all de dingen
voour mack skoes groot and cleane.*

FIRKE. Ha, ha! Good master, hire him; he'll make me
laugh so that I shall work more in mirth than I can
in earnest.

EYRE. Hear ye, friend, have ye any skill in the mystery*
of cordwainers?

LACY. *Ik weet neit wat yow seg; ich verstaw you niet.*

FIRKE. Why, thus, man [*imitating a shoemaker at work*]:
"Ich verste u niet," quoth 'a.   100

LACY. *Yaw, yaw, yaw; ick can dat wel doen.*

FIRKE. "Yaw, yaw!" He speaks yawing like a jackdaw
that gapes to be fed with cheese curds. O, he'll give
a villainous pull at a can of double beer; but Hodge

---

gallimaufry: hotch potch.
goeden . . . oak: good day, master, and you, wife, too.
nails: contraction of "by God's nails!"
yaw, . . . skomawker: yes, yes; I am the shoemaker.
yaw, . . . cleane: yes, yes; be not afraid. I have all the things
to make shoes big and little.
mystery: profession.
ik . . . neit: I know not what you say; I understand you not.

and I have the vantage—we must drink first because
we are the eldest journeymen.

EYRE. What is thy name?

LACY. Hans—Hans Meulter.

EYRE. Give me thy hand; th'art welcome.—Hodge, entertain him. Firke, bid him welcome. Come, Hans.   110
Run, wife; bid your maids, your trullibubs,° make
ready my fine men's breakfasts. To him, Hodge!

HODGE. Hans, th'art welcome. Use thyself friendly, for
we are good fellows; if not, thou shalt be fought with,
wert thou bigger than a giant.

FIRKE. Yea, and drunk with, wert thou Gargantua. My
master keeps no cowards, I tell thee.—Ho, boy! Bring
him an heel-block; here's a new journeyman.

Enter BOY.

LACY. *O, ich wersto you; ich moet een halve dossen cans
betaelen.*—*Here, boy, nempt dis skilling; tap eens free-*   120
licke.°

Exit BOY.

EYRE. Quick, snipper-snapper, away! Firke, scour thy
throat; thou shalt wash it with Castilian liquor.

Enter BOY.

Come, my last of the fives,° give me a can. Have to
thee, Hans! Here, Hodge! Here, Firke! Drink, you
mad Greeks, and work like true Trojans, and pray for
Simon Eyre, the shoemaker.—Here, Hans, and th'art
welcome.

FIRKE. Lo, dame, you would have lost a good fellow
that will teach us to laugh. This beer came hopping in   130
well.

WIFE. Simon, it is almost seven.

EYRE. Is't so, Dame Clapperdudgeon?° Is't seven o'
clock, and my men's breakfast not ready? Trip and
go, you soused conger, away! Come, you mad Hyper-
boreans. Follow me, Hodge. Follow me, Hans. Come
after, my fine Firke. To work, to work awhile, and
then to breakfast!

Exit.

---

trullibubs: sluts.

o . . . freelicke: o, I understand you; I must pay for a half-
dozen cans.—Here, boy, take this shilling; tap once freely.

last of the fives: smallest one.

clapperdudgeon: beggar; making noise like a beggar's dish.

FIRKE. Soft! *Yaw, yaw,* good Hans. Though my master
  have no more wit but to call you afore me, I am not   140
  so foolish to go behind you, I being the elder journeyman.

Exeunt.

[v]

Hallooing within. Enter WARNER *and* HAMMON, *like hunters.*

HAMMON. Cousin, beat every brake; the game's not far.
  This way with wingèd feet he fled from death
  Whilst the pursuing hounds, scenting his steps,
  Find out his high way to destruction.
  Besides, the miller's boy told me even now
  He saw him take soil,° and he hallooed him,
  Affirming him so embossed,°
  That long he could not hold.

WARNER.   If it be so,
  'Tis best we trace these meadows by Old Ford.

    A noise of Hunters within. Enter a BOY.

HAMMON. How now, boy? Where's the deer? Speak!   10
  Saw'st thou him?

BOY. O, yea; I saw him leap through a hedge and then
  over a ditch; then, at my lord mayor's pale, over he
  skipped me and in he went me, and "Holla" the hunters cried and "There, boy; there, boy!" But there he
  is, o' mine honesty.

HAMMON. Boy, God amercy! Cousin, let's away;
  I hope we shall find better sport today.

Exeunt.

    Hunting within. Enter ROSE *and* SYBIL.

ROSE. Why, Sybil, wilt thou prove a forester?

SYBIL. Upon some, no! Forester? Go by! No, faith, mis-   20
  tress, the deer came running into the barn through the
  orchard and over the pale. I wot° well I looked as
  pale as a new cheese to see him. But "Whip!" says
  Goodman Pinclose, up with his flail, and our Nick
  with a prong, and down he fell, and they upon him,
  and I upon them. By my troth, we had such sport,

---

  take soil: take to water (for refuge).
  embossed: exhausted; foaming at the mouth.
  wot: know.

and in the end we ended him: His throat we cut,
flayed him, unhorned him, and my lord mayor shall
eat of him anon when he comes.

(*Horns sound within.*)

ROSE. Hark, hark, the hunters come! Y'are best take
    heed;   30
They'll have a saying to you for this deed.

    Enter HAMMON, WARNER, *Huntsmen, and* BOY.

HAMMON. God save you, fair ladies.

SYBIL.   Ladies! O, gross!

WARNER. Came not a buck this way?

ROSE.   No, but two does.

HAMMON. And which way went they? Faith, we'll hunt
    at those.

SYBIL. At those? Upon some, no! When, can you tell?

WARNER. Upon some, ay!

SYBIL.   Good Lord!

WARNER.   Wounds!°
    Then farewell.

HAMMON. Boy, which way went he?

BOY.   This way, sir, he
    ran.

HAMMON. This way he ran indeed. Fair mistress Rose,
    Our game was lately in your orchard seen.

WARNER. Can you advise which way he took his flight?   40

SYBIL. Follow your nose; his horns will guide you right.

WARNER. Th'art a mad wench.

SYBIL.   O, rich!

ROSE.   Trust me,
    not I.
  It is not like the wild forest deer
  Would come so near to places of resort.
  You are deceived; he fled some other way.

WARNER. Which way, my sugar candy, can you show?

SYBIL. Come up, good honeysops; upon some, no!

ROSE. Why do you stay and not pursue your game?

SYBIL. I'll hold° my life their hunting nags be lame.

HAMMON. A deer more dear is found within this place.   50

ROSE. But not the deer, sir, which you had in chase.

---

wounds: contraction of "by God's wounds!"
hold: wager, bet.

HAMMON. I chased the deer, but this dear chaseth me.

ROSE. The strangest hunting that ever I see.

But where's your park?

(*She offers to go away.*)

HAMMON.   'Tis here—O, stay!

ROSE. Impale me, and then I will not stray.

WARNER [*to* SYBIL]. They wrangle, wench; we are more
    kind than they.

SYBIL. What kind of hart is that dear heart you seek?

WARNER. A hart, dear heart!

SYBIL.   Who ever saw the like?

ROSE. To lose your heart, is't possible you can?

HAMMON. My heart is lost.

ROSE.   Alack, good gentleman!   60

HAMMON. This poor lost heart would I wish you might
    find.

ROSE. You, by such luck, might prove your hart a hind.

HAMMON. Why, Luck had horns, so have I heard some
    say.

ROSE. Now, God, and't be His will, send Luck into your
    way.

            Enter LORD MAYOR *and Servants.*

LORD MAYOR. What, Master Hammon! Welcome to Old
    Ford!

SYBIL [*to* WARNER]. God's pitikins, hands off, sir! Here's
    my lord.

LORD MAYOR. I hear you had ill luck and lost your game.

HAMMON. 'Tis true, my lord.

LORD MAYOR.   I am sorry for the same.

What gentleman is this?

HAMMON.   My brother-in-law.

LORD MAYOR. Y'are welcome both. Sith° Fortune offers
    you   70

Into my hands, you shall not part from hence

Until you have refreshed your wearied limbs.—

Go, Sybil, cover the board.—You shall be guest

To no good cheer but even a hunter's feast.

HAMMON. I thank your lordship.—[*Aside to* WARNER.]
    Cousin, on my life,

For our lost venison I shall find a wife.

                          Exeunt [*all but the* LORD MAYOR].

---

sith: since.

LORD MAYOR. In, gentlemen; I'll not be absent long.—
This Hammon is a proper gentleman,
A citizen by birth, fairly allied.
How fit an husband were he for my girl!   80
Well, I will in and do the best I can
To match my daughter to this gentleman.

Exit.

[vi]

    Enter LACY [*as* HANS], SKIPPER, HODGE, *and* FIRKE.

SKIPPER. *Ick sal yow wat seggen, Hans: dis skip dat
comen from Candy is al vol, by Got's sacrament, van
sugar, civet, almonds, cambrick, end alle dingen—
towsand, towsand ding. Nempt it, Hans, nempt it
vor u meester. Daer be de bils van laden. Your
meester, Simon Eyre, sal hae good copen.** Wat seggen you, Hans?*

FIRKE. *Wat seggen de reggen de copen, slopen*—Laugh,
Hodge, laugh!

LACY. *Mine liever broder Firke, bringt Meester Eyre* [*t*]*ot*   10
*den signe un Swannekin; daer sal you finde dis skipper
end me. Wat seggen you, broder Firke? Doot it,
Hodge.** Come, skipper.

Exeunt [LACY *and* SKIPPER].

FIRKE. "Bring him," quoth you? Here's no knavery, to
bring my master to buy a ship worth the lading of two
or three hundred thousand pounds! Alas, that's nothing! A trifle, a bable,* Hodge.

HODGE. The truth is, Firke, that the merchant owner of
the ship dares not show his head; and therefore this
skipper that deals for him, for the love he bears to   20
Hans, offers my master Eyre a bargain in the commodities. He shall have a reasonable day of payment;

---

ick . . . copen: I'll tell you what, Hans: this ship that is come
from Candia is all full, by God's sacrament, of sugar, civet, almonds, cambric, and all things—a thousand thousand things. Take
it, Hans, take it for your master. There are the bills of lading. Your
master, Simon Eyre, shall have a good bargain.
mine . . . Hodge: my dear brother Firke, bring Master Eyre to
the sign of the Swan; there shall you find this skipper and me.
What say you, brother Firke? Do it, Hodge.
bable: bauble, trifle.

he may sell the wares by that time and be an huge
gainer himself.

FIRKE. Yea, but can my fellow Hans lend my master
twenty porpentines as an earnest penny?

HODGE. Portuguese, thou wouldst say. Here they be,
Firke. Hark, they jingle in my pocket like Saint
Mary [O]very's bells.

Enter EYRE *and his* WIFE [*and a Boy*].

FIRKE. Mum! Here comes my dame and my master.   30
She'll scold, on my life, for loitering this Monday; but
all's one—let them all say what they can, Monday's
our holiday.

WIFE. You sing, Sir Sauce, but I beshrew* your heart.
I fear for this your singing we shall smart.

FIRKE. Smart for me, dame? Why, dame, why?

HODGE. Master, I hope you'll not suffer my dame to take
down your journeymen.

FIRKE. If she take me down, I'll take her up—yea, and
take her down too, a button-hole lower.   40

EYRE. Peace, Firke! Not I, Hodge, by the life of Pharaoh, by the Lord of Ludgate, by this beard, every
hair whereof I value at a king's ransom, she shall not
meddle with you.—Peace, you bombast cotton-candle
quean! Away, Queen of Clubs! Quarrel not with me
and my men, with me and my fine Firke. I'll firk you
if you do!

WIFE. Yea, yea, man; you may use me as you please.
But let that pass.

EYRE. Let it pass, let it vanish away! Peace! Am I not   50
Simon Eyre? Are not these my brave men? Brave
shoemakers, all gentlemen of the Gentle Craft? Prince
am I none, yet am I nobly born, as being the sole son
of a shoemaker. Away, rubbish! Vanish! Melt like
kitchen stuff.

WIFE. Yea, yea, 'tis well; I must be called rubbish,
kitchen stuff, for a sort* of knaves.

FIRKE. Nay, dame, you shall not weep and wail in woe
for me. Master, I'll stay no longer. Here's a venentory
of my shop tools. Adieu, master. Hodge, farewell.   60

---

beshrew: curse.
sort: crowd, group, pack.

HODGE. Nay, stay, Firke. Thou shalt not go alone.

WIFE. I pray let them go. There be mo maids than Mawkin, more men than Hodge, and more fools than Firke.

FIRKE. Fools? Nails! If I tarry now, I would my guts might be turned to shoe-thread!

HODGE. And, if I stay, I pray God I may be turned to a Turk and set in Finsbury for boys to shoot at.—Come, Firke.

EYRE. Stay, my fine knaves, you arms of my trade, you pillars of my profession! What, shall a tittle-tattle's 70
words make you forsake Simon Eyre?—Avaunt, kitchen stuff! Rip, you brown-bread Tannikin,° out of my sight! Move me not! Have not I ta'en you from selling tripes in Eastcheap, and set you in my shop, and made you hail-fellow with Simon Eyre the shoemaker? And now do you deal thus with my journeymen? Look, you powder-beef quean, on the face of Hodge; here's a face for a lord.

FIRKE. And here's a face for any lady in Christendom.

EYRE. Rip, you chitterling! Avaunt, boy! Bid the tapster 80
of the Bore's Head fill me a dozen cans of beer for my journeymen.

FIRKE. A dozen cans? O, brave! Hodge, now I'll stay.

EYRE [*aside to Boy*]. And the knave fills any more than two, he pays for them.—[*Exit Boy.—Aloud.*] A dozen cans of beer for my journeymen!

> [*Enter Boy with two cans, and exit.*]

Here, you mad Mesopotamians. Wash your livers with this liquor. Where be the odd ten?—[*Aside.*] No more, Madge, no more.—Well said. Drink and to work!—What work dost thou, Hodge? What work? 90

HODGE. I am a-making a pair of shoes for my lord mayor's daughter, Mistress Rose.

FIRKE. And I a pair of shoes for Sybil, my lord's maid. I deal with her.

EYRE. Sybil? Fie, defile not thy fine workmanly fingers with the feet of kitchen stuff and basting ladles! Ladies of the court, fine ladies, my lads, commit their feet to our appareling. Put gross work to Hans. Yark° and seam, yark and seam!

Tannikin: Anna (Dutch diminutive).
yark: draw stitches tight in shoemaking.

FIRKE. For yarking and seaming let me alone, and I   100
come to't.

HODGE. Well, master, all this is from the bias. Do you
remember the ship my fellow Hans told you of? The
skipper and he are both drinking at the Swan. Here
be the Portuguese to give earnest. If you go through
with it, you cannot choose but be a lord at least.

FIRKE. Nay, dame, if my master prove not a lord and
you a lady, hang me.

WIFE. Yea, like enough, if you may loiter and tipple
thus.   110

FIRKE. Tipple, dame? No, we have been bargaining with
Skellum Skanderbag Can-You-Dutch-Spreaken for a
ship of silk cyprus,° laden with sugar candy.

EYRE. Peace, Firke! Silence, Tittle-tattle! Hodge, I'll go
through with it. Here's a seal ring, and I have sent for
a guarded° gown and a damask cassock.

Enter the Boy with a velvet coat and an Alderman's
gown.

See where it comes. Look here, Maggy. (EYRE *puts*
it on.) Help me, Firke. Apparel me, Hodge. Silk and
satin, you mad Philistines, silk and satin!

FIRKE. Ha, ha! My master will be as proud as a dog in   120
a doublet, all in beaten° damask and velvet.

EYRE. Softly, Firke, for rearing of the nap and wearing
threadbare my garments. How dost thou like me,
Firke? How do I look, my fine Hodge?

HODGE. Why, now you look like yourself, master. I warrant you, there's few in the City but will give you the
wall and come upon you with the "Right Worshipful."

FIRKE. Nails! My master looks like a threadbare cloak
new turned and dressed. Lord, Lord, to see what good
raiment doth! Dame, dame, are you not enamored?   130

EYRE. How sayst thou, Maggy? Am I not brisk? Am I not
fine?

WIFE. Fine? By my troth, sweetheart, very fine! By my
troth, I never liked thee so well in my life, sweetheart.
But let that pass. I warrant there be many women in

Cyprus: black lawn; cypress.
guarded: decorated, ornamented.
beaten: embroidered.

the City have not such handsome husbands but only
for their apparel. But let that pass too.

Enter [LACY *as*] HANS *and* SKIPPER.

LACY. *Godden day, mester. Dis be de skipper dat heb
de skip van marchandice. De commodity ben good;
nempt it, master, nempt it.*°   140

EYRE. God-a-mercy, Hans. Welcome, skipper. Where lies
this ship of merchandise?

SKIPPER. *De skip ben in r[e]vere. Dor be van sugar,
civet, almonds, cambrick, and a towsand towsand
tings. Gotz sacrament, nempt it, mester! Yo sall heb
good copen.*°

FIRKE. To him, master! O sweet master! O sweet wares!
Prunes, almonds, sugar candy, carrot roots, turnips! O
brave, fatting meat! Let not a man buy a nutmeg but
yourself.   150

EYRE. Peace, Firke! Come, skipper, I'll go ab[oar]d with
you.—Hans, have you made him drink?

SKIPPER. *Yaw, yaw, ic heb veale gedrunck.*°

EYRE. Come, Hans, follow me. Skipper, thou shalt have
my countenance in the City.

Exeunt [EYRE, SKIPPER, *and* LACY].

FIRKE. "Yaw, heb veale gedrunck," quoth 'a. They may
well be called butterboxes when they drink fat veal
and thick beer too. But come, dame, I hope you'll
chide us no more.

WIFE. No, faith, Firke. No, perdy,° Hodge. I do feel   160
honor creep upon me and, which is more, a certain
rising in my flesh—but let that pass.

FIRKE. Rising in your flesh do you feel, say you? Ay, you
may be with child. But why should not my master feel
a rising in his flesh, having a gown and a gold ring
on? But you are such a shrew, you'll soon pull him
down.

---

godden . . . it: good day, master. This is the skipper that has
the ship of merchandise. The commodity is good; take it, master,
take it.

de . . . copen: the ship is in the river. There are sugar, civit,
almonds, cambric, and a thousand thousand things. God's sacrament, take it, master! You shall have a good bargain.

yaw, . . . gedrunck: yes, yes. I have drunk much.

perdy: truly (French *par Dieu*).

WIFE. Ha, ha! Prithee, peace! Thou mak'st my worship
   laugh, but let that pass. Come, I'll go in. Hodge,
   prithee go before me. Firke, follow me.   170
FIRKE. Firke doth follow.—Hodge, pass out in state.

                                        Exeunt.

[vii]
Enter LINCOLN *and* DODGER.

LINCOLN. How now, good Dodger, what's the news in
   France?
DODGER. My lord, upon the eighteen day of May
   The French and English were prepared to fight;
   Each side with eager fury gave the sign
   Of a most hot encounter. Five long hours
   Both armies fought together. At the length,
   The lot of victory fell on our sides.
   Twelve thousand of the Frenchmen that day died,
   Four thousand English, and no man of name
   But Captain Hyam and young Ardington,   0
   Two gallant gentlemen—I knew them well.
LINCOLN. But, Dodger, prithee tell me, in this fight
   How did my cousin Lacy bear himself?
DODGER. My lord, your cousin Lacy was not there.
LINCOLN. Not there?
DODGER.   No, my good lord.
LINCOLN.   Sure, thou
   mistakest.
   I saw him shipped, and a thousand eyes beside
   Were witnesses of the farewells which he gave
   When I, with weeping eyes, bid him adieu.
   Dodger, take heed.
DODGER.   My lord, I am advised   20
   That what I spake is true. To prove it so,
   His cousin Askew, that supplied his place,
   Sent me for him from France, that secretly
   He might convey himself hither.
LINCOLN.   Is't even so?
   Dares he so carelessly venture his life
   Upon the indignation of a king?
   Hath he despised my love and spurned those favors
   Which I with prodigal hand poured on his head?
   He shall repent his rashness with his soul.

Since of my love he makes no estimate,
I'll make him wish he had not known my hate.   30
Thou hast no other news?
DODGER.   None else, my lord.
LINCOLN. None worse I know thou hast. Procure the
    king
To crown his giddy brows with ample honors!
Send him chief colonel, and all my hope
Thus to be dashed! But 'tis in vain to grieve;
One evil cannot a worse relieve.
Upon my life, I have found out his plot!
That old dog, Love, that fawned upon him so,
Love to that puling girl, his fair-cheeked Rose,
The lord mayor's daughter, hath distracted him;   40
And in the fire of that love's lunacy
Hath he burnt up himself, consumed his credit,
Lost the king's love, yea, and, I fear, his life,
Only to get a wanton to his wife.
Dodger, it is so.
DODGER.   I fear so, my good lord.
LINCOLN. It is so—nay, sure it cannot be!
I am at my wits' end. Dodger—
DODGER.   Yea, my lord.
LINCOLN. Thou art acquainted with my nephew's haunts.
Spend this gold for thy pains; go seek him out.
Watch at my lord mayor's. There if he live,   50
Dodger, thou shalt be sure to meet with him.
Prithee, be diligent.—Lacy, thy name
Lived once in honor, now dead in shame.—
Be circumspect.

                                                    Exit.

DODGER.   I warrant you, my lord.

                                                    Exit.

[viii]
            Enter LORD MAYOR *and* MASTER SCOTT.
LORD MAYOR. Good Master Scott, I have been bold with
    you
To be a witness to a wedding knot
Betwixt young Master Hammon and my daughter.
O, stand aside; see where the lovers come.
            Enter HAMMON *and* ROSE.

ROSE. Can it be possible you love me so?
No, no! Within those eyeballs I espy
Apparent likelihoods of flattery.
Pray now, let go my hand.
HAMMON.   Sweet Mistress Rose,
Misconstrue not my words, nor misconceive
Of my affection, whose devoted soul   10
Swears that I love thee dearer than my heart.
ROSE. As dear as your own heart? I judge it right:
Men love their hearts best when th'are out of sight.
HAMMON. I love you, by this hand!
ROSE.   Yet hands off now!
If flesh be frail, how weak and frail's your vow!
HAMMON. Then by my life I swear.
ROSE.   Then do not brawl;
One quarrel loseth wife and life and all.
Is not your meaning thus?
HAMMON.   In faith, you jest.
ROSE. Love loves to sport; therefore, leave love, y'are
    best.
LORD MAYOR. What? Square* they, Master Scott?
SCOTT.   Sir,
    never doubt,   20
Lovers are quickly in and quickly out.
HAMMON. Sweet Rose, be not so strange in fancying me.
Nay, never turn aside! Shun not my sight.
I am not grown so fond to fond* my love
On any that shall quit* it with disdain.
If you will love me, so; if not, farewell.
LORD MAYOR. Why, how now, lovers, are you both
    agreed?
HAMMON. Yes, faith, my lord.
LORD MAYOR.   'Tis well; give me your
    hand.
Give me yours, daughter.—How now? Both pull back!
What means this, girl?
ROSE.   I mean to live a maid.   30
HAMMON (aside). But not to die one; pause ere that be
    said.

---

square: quarrel.
so fond to fond: so foolish as to bestow.
quit: requite.

LORD MAYOR. Will you still cross me, still be obstinate?

HAMMON. Nay, chide her not, my lord, for doing well;
  If she can live an happy virgin's life,
  'Tis far more blessed than to be a wife.

ROSE. Say, sir, I cannot. I have made a vow:
  Whoever be my husband, 'tis not you.

LORD MAYOR. Your tongue is quick.—But, Master [Hammon], know,
  I bade you welcome to another end.

HAMMON. What, would you have me pule and pine and pray   40
  With "lovely lady," "mistress of my heart,"
  "Pardon your servant," and the rhymer play,
  Railing on Cupid and his tyrant's dart?
  Or shall I undertake some martial spoil,
  Wearing your glove at tourney and at tilt,
  And tell how many gallants I unhorsed?
  Sweet, will this pleasure you?

ROSE.   Yea; when wilt begin?
  What? Love rhymes, man? Fiè on that deadly sin!

LORD MAYOR. If you will have her, I'll make her agree.

HAMMON. Enforcèd love is worse than hate to me.—   50
  [*Aside.*] There is a wench keeps shop in the Old Change;
  To her will I. It is not wealth I seek;
  I have enough and will prefer her love
  Before the world.—My good lord mayor, adieu.
  Old love for me; I have no luck with new.

                                                        Exit.

LORD MAYOR. Now, mammet,* you have well behaved yourself!
  But you shall curse your coyness if I live.—
  Who's within there? See you convey your mistress
  Straight to th' Old Ford. I'll keep you straight enough.
  'Fore God, I would have sworn the puling girl   60
  Would willingly accepted Hammon's love.
  But banish him my thoughts!—Go, minion, in!

                                                Exit ROSE.

  Now, tell me, Master Scott, would you have thought
  That Master Simon Eyre, the shoemaker,
  Had been of wealth to buy such merchandise?

------

mammet: doll, puppet.

SCOTT. 'Twas well, my lord, your honor and myself
　　Grew partners with him, for your bills of lading
　　Show that Eyre's gains in one commodity
　　Rise at the least to full three thousand pound,
　　Besides like gain in other merchandise.   70
LORD MAYOR. Well, he shall spend some of his thousands
　　now,
　　For I have sent for him to the Guildhall.

　　　　　　　　　　　Enter EYRE.

　　See where he comes.—Good morrow, Master Eyre.
EYRE. Poor Simon Eyre, my lord, your shoemaker.
LORD MAYOR. Well, well, it likes° yourself to term you
　　so.

　　　　　　　　　　　Enter DODGER.

　　Now, Master Dodger, what's the news with you?
DODGER. I'd gladly speak in private to your honor.
LORD MAYOR. You shall, you shall.—Master Eyre and
　　Master Scott,
　　I have some business with this gentleman.
　　I pray, let me entreat you to walk before   80
　　To the Guildhall; I'll follow presently.
　　Master Eyre, I hope ere noon to call you sheriff.
EYRE. I would not care, my lord, if you might call me
　　King of Spain.—Come, Master Scott.

　　　　　　　　　　　[*Exeunt* EYRE *and* SCOTT.]

LORD MAYOR. Now, Master Dodger, what's the news
　　you bring?
DODGER. The Earl of Lincoln by me greets your lordship
　　And earnestly requests you, if you can,
　　Inform him where his nephew Lacy keeps.
LORD MAYOR. Is not his nephew Lacy now in France?
DODGER. No, I assure your lordship, but disguised   90
　　Lurks here in London.
LORD MAYOR.　　　　　London? Is't even so?
　　It may be; but, upon my faith and soul,
　　I know not where he lives or whether he lives;
　　So tell my Lord of Lincoln. Lur[k] in London?
　　Well, Master Dodger, you perhaps may start° him;
　　Be but the means to rid him into France,

　　─────────────

　　likes: pleases.
　　start: find.

I'll give you a dozen angels° for your pains.
So much I love his honor, hate his nephew,
And prithee so inform thy lord from me.
DODGER. I take my leave.
LORD MAYOR.   Farewell, good Master
    Dodger.—   100

                                                            Exit DODGER.

Lacy in London? I dare pawn my life
My daughter knows thereof and for that cause
Denied young Master Hammon in his love.
Well, I am glad I sent her to Old Ford.
God's Lord, 'tis late! To Guildhall I must hie;
I know my brethren stay° my company.

                                                                    Exit.

[ix]

    Enter FIRK, *Eyre's* WIFE, [LACY *as*] HANS, *and* ROGER.
WIFE. Thou goest too fast for me, Roger. [O, Firke!]
FIRKE. Ay, forsooth.
WIFE. I pray thee, run (do you hear?), run to Guildhall
    and learn if my husband, Master Eyre, will take that
    worshipful vocation of master sheriff upon him. Hie
    thee, good Firke.
FIRKE. Take it? Well, I go; and he should not take it,
    Firke swears to forswear him. Yes, forsooth, I go to
    Guildhall.
WIFE. Nay, when? Thou art too compendious and te-   10
    dious.
FIRKE. O, rare! Your Excellence is full of eloquence.—
    [*Aside.*] How like a new cartwheel my dame speaks!
    And she looks like an old, musty ale bottle° going to
    scalding.
WIFE. Nay, when? Thou wilt make me melancholy.
FIRKE. God forbid your worship should fall into that
    humor. I run.

                                                                    Exit.

WIFE. Let me see now, Roger and Hans.
HODGE. Ay, forsooth, dame—mistress, I should say, but   20

───────────────

angels: gold coins.
stay: await.
ale bottle: made of leather.

the old term so sticks to the roof of my mouth I can hardly lick it off.

WIFE. Even what thou wilt, good Roger. Dame is a fair name for any honest Christian, but let that pass. How dost thou, Hans?

HANS. *Mee tanck you, vro.*

WIFE. Well, Hans and Roger, you see God hath blessed your master; and, perdy, if ever he comes to be master sheriff of London (as we are all mortal), you shall see I will have some odd thing or other in a corner for   30
you. I will not be your back-friend,* but let that pass. Hans, pray thee tie my shoe.

HANS. *Yaw, ic sal, vro.*

WIFE. Roger, thou know'st the length of my foot; as it is none of the biggest, so, I thank God, it is handsome enough. Prithee, let me have a pair of shoes made— cork, good Roger, wooden heel too.

HODGE. You shall.

WIFE. Art thou acquainted with never a farthingale maker nor a French-hood maker? I must enlarge my   40
bum. Ha, ha! How shall I look in a hood, I wonder? Perdy, oddly, I think.

HODGE [*aside*]. As a cat out of a pillory.—Very well, I warrant you, mistress.

WIFE. Indeed, all flesh is grass. And, Roger, canst thou tell where I may buy a good hair?

HODGE. Yes, forsooth, at the poulterer's in Gracious Street.

WIFE. Thou art an ungracious wag, perdy; I mean a false hair for my periwig.   50

HODGE. Why, mistress, the next time I cut my beard, you shall have the shavings of it; but they are all true hairs.

WIFE. It is very hot. I must get me a fan or else a mask.

HODGE [*aside*]. So you had need, to hide your wicked face.

WIFE. Fie upon it! How costly this world's calling is, perdy! But that it is one of the wonderful works of God, I would not deal with it. Is not Firke come yet? Hans, be not so sad; let it pass and vanish, as my hus-   60
band's worship says.

---

back-friend: a reluctant friend.

HANS. *Ick bin vrolick; lot see yow soo.**
HODGE. Mistress, will you drink* a pipe of tobacco?
WIFE. O, fie upon it, Roger, perdy! These filthy tobacco
  pipes are the most idle, slavering bables that ever I
  felt. Out upon it! God bless us, men look not like men
  that use them.

Enter RAFE, *being lame.*

HODGE. What! Fellow Rafe? Mistress, look here—Jane's
  husband! Why, how now, lame? Hans, make much of
  him; he's a brother of our trade, a good workman, and   70
  a tall soldier.
HANS. *You be welcome, broder.*
WIFE. Perdy, I knew him not. How dost thou, good
  Rafe? I am glad to see thee well.
RAFE. I would God you saw me, dame, as well
  As when I went from London into France.
WIFE. Trust me, I am sorry, Rafe, to see thee impotent.
  Lord, how the wars have made him sunburnt! The
  left leg is not well. 'Twas a fair gift of God the in-
  firmity took not hold a little higher, considering thou   80
  camest from France. But let that pass.
RAFE. I am glad to see you well, and I rejoice
  To hear that God hath blessed my master so
  Since my departure.
WIFE. Yea, truly Rafe, I thank my Maker. But let that
  pass.
HODGE. And, sirrah Rafe, what news, what news in
  France?
RAFE. Tell me, good Roger, first, what news in England?
  How does my Jane? When didst thou see my wife?   90
  Where lives my poor heart? She'll be poor indeed
  Now I want limbs to get whereon to feed.
HODGE. Limbs? Hast thou not hands, man? Thou shalt
  never see a shoemaker want bread though he have but
  three fingers on a hand.
RAFE. Yet all this while I hear not of my Jane.
WIFE. O Rafe, your wife—perdy, we know not what's
  become of her. She was here awhile and, because she
  was married, grew more stately than became her. I
  checked her, and so forth. Away she flung, never re-   100

---

ick . . . soo: I am merry; let's see you so.
drink: smoke.

turned, nor said bye nor bah. And, Rafe, you know "ka me, ka thee." * And so, as I tell ye.—Roger, is not Firke come yet?

HODGE. No, forsooth.

WIFE. And so, indeed, we heard not of her; but I hear she lives in London. But let that pass. If she had wanted, she might have opened her case to me or my husband or to any of my men. I am sure there's not any of them, perdy, but would have done her good to his power.—Hans, look if Firke be come.   110

LACY. *Yaw, i[c] sal, vro.*

                                                    Exit [LACY *as*] HANS.

WIFE. And so, as I said—but, Rafe, why dost thou weep? Thou knowest that naked we came out of our mother's womb and naked we must return; and, therefore, thank God for all things.

HODGE. No, faith, Jane is a stranger here; but, Rafe, pull up a good heart—I know thou hast one. Thy wife, man, is in London. One told me he saw her a while ago very brave and neat. We'll ferret her out and London hold her.   120

WIFE. Alas, poor soul, he's overcome with sorrow. He does but as I do—weep for the loss of any good thing. But, Rafe, get thee in, call for some meat and drink. Thou shalt find me worshipful towards thee.

RAFE. I thank you, dame. Since I want limbs and lands, I'll to God, my good friends, and to these my hands.

                                                                    Exit.

Enter [LACY *as*] HANS, *and* FIRKE *running.*

FIRKE. Run, good Hans! O, Hodge! O, Mistress! Hodge, heave up thine ears. Mistress, smug up* your looks. On with your best apparel! My master is chosen, my master is called, nay, condemned by the cry of the   130 country to be sheriff of the City for this famous year now to come and time now being. A great many men in black gowns were asked for their voices and their hands, and my master had all their fists about his ears presently. And they cried, "Ay, ay, ay, ay"; and so I came away.

---

ka . . . thee: "tit for tat"; "scratch me and I'll scratch you."
smug up: smarten up.

Wherefore, without all other grieve,*
I do salute you, Mistress Shrieve.*

LACY. *Yaw, my mester is de groot man, de shrieve.*

HODGE. Did not I tell you, mistress? Now I may boldly   140
say, "Good morrow to your worship."

WIFE. Good morrow, good Roger. I thank you, my good
people all.—Firke, hold up thy hand; here's a three-
penny piece for thy tidings.

FIRKE. 'Tis but three halfpence, I think. Yes, 'tis threepence; I smell the rose.*

HODGE. But, mistress, by ruled by me, and do not speak
so pulingly.

FIRKE. 'Tis her worship speaks so and not she. No, faith,
mistress, speak me in the old key: "To it, Firke! There,   150
good Firke! Ply your business, Hodge! Hodge, with a
full mouth! I'll fill your bellies with good cheer till
they cry twang."

Enter SIMON EYRE, *wearing a gold chain.*

LACY. *See, myn liever broder, heer compt my meester!* *

WIFE. Welcome home, Master Shrieve! I pray God continue you in health and wealth.

EYRE. See here, my Maggy, a chain, a gold chain for
Simon Eyre! I shall make thee a lady. Here's a French
hood for thee—on with it, on with it! Dress thy brows
with this flap of a shoulder of mutton to make thee   160
look lovely. Where be my fine men? Roger, I'll make
over my shop and tools to thee. Firke, thou shalt be
the foreman. Hans, thou shalt have an hundred for
twenty. Be as mad knaves as your master Sim Eyre
hath been, and you shall live to be sheriffs of London.
—How dost thou like me, Margery? Prince am I none,
yet am I princely born. Firke, Hodge, and Hans!

ALL THREE. Ay, forsooth, what says your worship, [Mas-
ter] Sheriff?

EYRE. Worship and honor, you Babylonian knaves, for   170
the Gentle Craft! But I forg[e]t myself. I am bidden
by my lord mayor to dinner to Old Ford. He's gone

---

grieve: (beyond any other) sheriff.
shrieve: sheriff.
rose: on the coin.
see . . . meester: see, my dear brothers, here comes my master!

before; I must after. Come, Madge, on with your
trinkets. Now, my true Trojans, my fine Firke, my
dapper Hodge, my honest Hans, some device, some
odd crotchets, some morris, or suchlike, for the honor
of the gentle shoemakers. Meet me at the Old Ford.
You know my mind.
Come, Madge, away!
Shut up the shop, knaves, and make holiday!   180

                             Exeunt [EYRE *and* WIFE].

FIRKE. O, rare! O, brave! Come, Hodge. Follow me,
   Hans.
We'll be with them for a morris dance.

                                              Exeunt.

[x]

    Enter LORD MAYOR, EYRE, *his* WIFE [*in a French
       hood*], SYBIL, *and other Servants.*

LORD MAYOR. Trust me, you are as welcome to Old
   Ford
As I myself.
WIFE.   Truly, I thank your lordship.
LORD MAYOR. Would our bad cheer were worth the
   thanks you give.
EYRE. Good cheer, my lord mayor, fine cheer! A fine
   house, fine walls, all fine and neat.
LORD MAYOR. Now, by my troth, I'll tell thee, Master
   Eyre,
It does me good and all my brethren
That such a madcap fellow as thyself
Is entered into our society.
WIFE. Ay, but, my lord, he must learn now to put on
   gravity.   10
EYRE. Peace, Maggy! A fig for gravity! When I go to
   Guildhall in my scarlet gown, I'll look as demurely
   as a saint and speak as gravely as a justice of peace.
   But now I am here at Old Ford, at my good lord
   mayor's house, let it go by! Vanish, Maggy! I'll be
   merry. Away with flip-flap, these fooleries, these
   gulleries! What, honey? Prince am I none, yet am I
   princely born. What says my lord mayor?
LORD MAYOR. Ha, ha, ha! I had rather than a thousand
   pound

I had a heart but half so light as yours. 20

EYRE. Why, what should I do, my lord? A pound o'
care pays not a dram of debt. Hum, let's be merry
whiles we are young; old age, sack, and sugar will
steal upon us ere we be aware.*

LORD MAYOR. It's well done. Mistress Eyre, pray give
good counsel to my daughter.

WIFE. I hope Mistress Rose will have the grace to take
nothing that's bad.

LORD MAYOR. Pray God she do; for, i'faith, Mistress
Eyre,

I would bestow upon that peevish girl 30
A thousand marks more than I mean to give her
Upon condition she'd be ruled by me.
The ape still crosseth me. There came of late
A proper gentleman, of fair revenues,
Whom gladly I would call son-in-law;
But my fine cockney would have none of him.—
You'll prove a coxcomb* for it ere you die:
A courtier, or no man, must please your eye.

EYRE. Be ruled, sweet Rose. Th'art ripe for a man.
Marry not with a boy that has no more hair on his 40
face than thou hast on thy cheeks. A courtier! Wash,
go by! Stand not upon pishery-pashery. Those silken
fellows are but painted images—outsides, outsides,
Rose! Their inner linings are torn. No, my fine mouse,
marry me with a gentleman grocer like my lord mayor,
your father. A grocer is a sweet trade—plums, plums!
Had I a son or daughter should marry out of the
generation and blood of the shoemakers, he should
pack. What! The Gentle Trade is a living for a man
through Europe, through the world. 50

(*A noise within of a tabor and a pipe.*)

LORD MAYOR. What noise is this?

EYRE. O my lord mayor, a crew of good fellows that for
love to your honor are come hither with a morris
dance.—Come in, my Mesopotamians, cheerily!

Eyre's speech: "The First Three-man's Song" is sometimes inserted at this place.
coxcomb: fool.

Enter HODGE, [LACY *as*] HANS, RAFE, FIRKE, *and
other Shoemakers in a morris; after a little dancing,
the* LORD MAYOR *speaks.*

LORD MAYOR. Master Eyre, are all these shoemakers?

EYRE. All cordwainers, my good lord mayor.

ROSE [*aside*]. How like my Lacy looks yond shoemaker!

LACY [*aside*]. O, that I durst but speak unto my love!

LORD MAYOR. Sybil, go fetch some wine to make these
    drink.—
  You are all welcome.   60

ALL. We thank your lordship.

(ROSE *takes a cup of wine and goes to* HANS.)

ROSE. For his sake whose fair shape thou represent'st,
  Good friend, I drink to thee.

LACY. *Ic bedancke, good frister.*°

WIFE. I see, Mistress Rose, you do not want judgment:
  you have drunk to the properest man I keep.

FIRKE. Here be some have done their parts to be as
  proper as he.

LORD MAYOR. Well, urgent business calls me back to
  London.
  Good fellows, first go in and taste our cheer   70
  And, to make merry as you homeward go,
  Spend these two angels in beer at Stratford Bow.

EYRE. To these two, my mad lads, Sim Eyre adds another. Then cheerily, Firke. Tickle it, Hans. And all
  for the honor of shoemakers.

                                    (*All go dancing out.*)

LORD MAYOR. Come, Master Eyre, let's have your company.

            Exeunt [LORD MAYOR, EYRE *and Eyre's* WIFE].

ROSE. Sybil, what shall I do?

SYBIL.   Why, what's the matter?

ROSE. That Hans the shoemaker is my love Lacy,
  Disguised in that attire to find me out.
  How should I find the means to speak with him?   80

SYBIL. What, mistress, never fear. I dare venture my
  maidenhead to nothing—and that's great odds—that
  Hans the Dutchman, when we come to London, shall
  not only see and speak with you, but in spite of all

ic . . . frister: I thank you, good maid.

your father's policies steal you away and marry you.
Will not this please you?

ROSE. Do this, and ever be assured of my love.

SYBIL. Away, then, and follow your father to London,
    lest your absence cause him to suspect something.
    Tomorrow, if my counsel be obeyed,   90
    I'll bind you prentice to the Gentle Trade.

                                      Exeunt.

[xi]

> *Enter* JANE *in a seamster's shop, working;*
> *and* HAMMON, *muffled, at another door.*
> *He stands aloof.*

HAMMON. Yonder's the shop, and there my fair love sits.
    She's fair and lovely, but she is not mine.
    O, would she were! Thrice have I courted her;
    Thrice hath my hand been moistened with her hand
    Whilst my poor famished eyes do feed on that
    Which made them famish. I am infortunate:
    I still love one, yet nobody loves me.
    I muse in other men what women see
    That I so want! Fine Mistress Rose was coy,
    And this too curious! * O, no, she is chaste;   10
    And, for she thinks me wanton, she denies
    To cheer my cold heart with her sunny eyes.
    How prettily she works! O, pretty hand!
    O, happy work! It doth me good to stand
    Unseen to see her. Thus I oft have stood
    In frosty evenings, a light burning by her,
    Enduring biting cold, only to eye her.
    One only look hath seemed as rich to me
    As a king's crown—such is love's lunacy.
    Muffled, I'll pass along, and by that try   20
    Whether she know me.

JANE.   Sir, what is't you buy?
    What is't you lack, sir? Calico? Or lawn?
    Fine cambric shirts or bands? What will you buy?

HAMMON [*aside*]. That which thou wilt not sell. Faith,
    yet I'll try.—
    How do you sell this handkercher?

---

curious: scrupulous, fastidious.

JANE.   Good cheap.

HAMMON. And how these ruffs?

JANE.   Cheap too.

HAMMON.   And how
    this band?

JANE. Cheap too.

HAMMON.   All cheap! How sell you then this
    hand?

JANE. My hands are not to be sold.

HAMMON.   To be given then.
    Nay, faith, I come to buy.

JANE.   But none knows when.

HAMMON. Good sweet, leave work a little while. Let's
    play.   30

JANE. I cannot live by keeping holiday.

HAMMON. I'll pay you for the time which shall be lost.

JANE. With me you shall not be at so much cost.

HAMMON. Look how you wound this cloth; so you wound
    me.

JANE. It may be so.

HAMMON.   'Tis so.

JANE.   What remedy?

HAMMON. Nay, faith, you are too coy.

JANE.   Let go my hand.

HAMMON. I will do any task at your command;
    I would let go this beauty, were I not
    Enjoined to disobey you by a power
    That controls kings. I love you!

JANE.   So, now part.   40

HAMMON. With hands I may, but never with my heart.
    In faith, I love you.

JANE.   I believe you do.

HAMMON. Shall a true love in me breed hate in you?

JANE. I hate you not.

HAMMON.   Then you must love.

JANE.   I do.
    What? Are you better now? I love not you.

HAMMON. All this I hope is but a woman's fray
    That means "Come to me" when she cries, "Away!"
    In earnest, mistress, I do not jest;
    A true chaste love hath entered in my breast.
    I love you dearly as I love my life;   50
    I love you as a husband loves a wife.

That and no other love my love requires.
Thy wealth, I know, is little; my desires
Thirst not for gold. Sweet, beauteous Jane, what's
    mine
Shall (if thou make myself thine) all be thine.
Say, judge, what is thy sentence—life or death?
Mercy or cruelty lies in thy breath.

JANE. Good sir, I do believe you love me well;
  For 'tis a silly conquest, silly pride,
  For one like you (I mean a gentleman)   60
  To boast that by his love tricks he hath brought
  Such and such women to his amorous lure.
  I think you do not so; yet many do
  And make it even a very trade to woo.
  I could be coy, as many women be,
  Feed you with sunshine smiles and wanton looks;
  But I detest witchcraft. Say that I
  Do constantly believe you, constant have—

HAMMON. Why dost thou not believe me?

JANE.   I believe
    you.

  But yet, good sir, because I will not grieve you   70
  With hopes to taste fruit which will never fall,
  In simple truth this is the sum of all:
  My husband lives—at least I hope he lives.
  Pressed was he to these bitter wars in France;
  Bitter they are to me by wanting him.
  I have but one heart, and that heart's his due.
  How can I then bestow the same on you?
  Whilst he lives, his I live, be it ne'er so poor,
  And rather be his wife than a king's whore.

HAMMON. Chaste and dear woman, I will not abuse thee   80
  Although it cost my life if thou refuse me.
  Thy husband, pressed for France, what was his name?

JANE. Rafe Damport.

HAMMON.   Damport? Here's a letter sent
  From France to me from a dear friend of mine,
  A gentleman of place; here he doth write
  Their names that have been slain in every fight.

JANE. I hope death's scroll contains not my love's name.

HAMMON. Cannot you read?

JANE.   I can.

HAMMON.   Peruse the same.

To my remembrance such a name I read
Amongst the rest. See here!

JANE.   Ay me, he's dead!   90
He's dead! If this be true, my dear heart's slain.

HAMMON. Have patience, dear love.

JANE.   Hence, hence!

HAMMON.   Nay, sweet Jane,
Make not poor sorrow proud with these rich tears.
I mourn thy husband's death because thou mourn'st.

JANE. That bill is forged; 'tis signed by forgery.

HAMMON. I'll bring thee letters sent besides to many
Carrying the like report. Jane, 'tis too true.
Come, weep not; mourning, though it rise from love,
Helps not the mournèd, yet hurts them that mourn.

JANE. For God's sake, leave me.

HAMMON.   Whither dost thou   100
turn?
Forget the dead; love them that are alive.
His love is faded; try how mine will thrive.

JANE. 'Tis now no time for me to think on love.

HAMMON. 'Tis now best time for you to think on love
Because your love lives not.

JANE.   Though he be dead,
My love to him shall not be buricd.
For God's sake, leave me to myself alone.

HAMMON. 'Twould kill my soul to leave thee drowned in
moan.
Answer me to my suit, and I am gone;
Say to me yea or no.

JANE.   No.

HAMMON.   Then farewell!—   110
One farewell will not serve—I come again.
Come, dry these wet cheeks. Tell me, faith, sweet
Jane,
Yea or no, once more.

JANE.   Once more I say no.
Once more be gone, I pray, else will I go.

HAMMON. Nay then, I will grow rude. By this white
hand,
Until you change that cold "no," here I'll stand
Till by your hard heart—

JANE.   Nay, for God's love, peace!
My sorrows by your presence more increase.

Not that you thus are present, but all grief
Desires to be alone; therefore in brief   120
Thus much I say, and saying bid adieu:
If ever I wed man, it shall be you.

HAMMON. O blessed voice! Dear Jane, I'll urge no more;
Thy breath hath made me rich.

JANE.   Death makes me
poor.

Exeunt.

[xii]

Enter HODGE *at his shopboard,* RAFE, FIRKE,
[LACY *as*] HANS, *and a Boy at work.*

ALL [*singing*]. *Hey, down a-down, down derry!*

HODGE. Well said, my hearts. Ply your work today; we
loitered yesterday. To it pell-mell that we may live to
be lord mayors or aldermen at least.

FIRKE.   *Hey, down a-down, derry!*

HODGE. Well said, i'faith! How sayst thou, Hans? Doth
not Firke tickle it?

HANS. *Yaw, mester.*

FIRKE. Not so neither; my organ pipe squeaks this morning for want of liquoring.   10
Hey, down a-down, derry!

HANS. *Forwar[e], Firke; tow best un jolly yongster.
Hort I, mester, ic bid yo cut me un pair [vampies]
vor Mester Jeffres' bootes.**

HODGE. Thou shalt, Hans.

FIRKE. Master!

HODGE. How now, boy?

FIRKE. Pray, now you are in the cutting vein, cut me
out a pair of counterfeits, or else my work will not pass
current.   20
Hey, down a-down!

HODGE. Tell me, sirs, are my cousin Mistress Priscilla's
shoes done?

FIRKE. Your cousin? No, master; one of your aunts,*
hang her! Let them alone!

---

forware, . . . bootes: go on, Firke; thou art a jolly youngster.
Hear me, master, I pray you cut me a pair of vamps for Master
Jeffrey's boots.
aunts: prostitutes.

RAFE. I am in hand with them. She gave charge that
none but I should do them for her.

FIRKE. Thou do for her? Then 'twill be a lame doing,
and that she loves not. Rafe, thou mightst have sent
her to me; in faith, I would have yerked and firked   30
your Priscilla.
Hey, down a-down, derry!
This gear° will not hold.

HODGE How sayst thou, Firke? Were we not merry at
Old Ford?

FIRKE. How, merry? Why, our buttocks went jiggy-joggy
like a quagmire. Well, Sir Roger Oatmeal, if I thought
all meal of that nature, I would eat nothing but bag-
puddings.

RAFE. Of all good fortunes my fellow Hans had the best. 40

FIRKE. 'Tis true because Mistress Rose drank to him.

HODGE. Well, well, work apace. They say seven of the
aldermen be dead or very sick.

FIRKE. I care not; I'll be none.

RAFE. No, nor I; but then my Master Eyre will come
quickly to be lord mayor.

Enter Sybil.

FIRKE. Whoop! Yonder comes Sybil.

HODGE. Sybil, welcome, i'faith. And how dost thou, mad
wench?

FIRKE. Syb-whore, welcome to London.   50

SYBIL. Godamercy, sweet Firke. Good Lord, Hodge,
what a delicious shop you have got! You tickle it,
i'faith.

RAFE. Godamercy, Sybil, for our good cheer at Old
Ford.

SYBIL. That you shall have, Rafe.

FIRKE. Nay, by the Mass, we had tickling cheer, Sybil.
And how the plague dost thou and Mistress Rose and
my lord mayor? I put the women in first.

SYBIL. Well, Godamercy. But, God's me, I forget myself! 60
Where's Hans the Fleming?

FIRKE. Hark, butterbox, now you must yelp out some
spreken.

LACY. *Vat begaie [you]? Vat vod [you], frister?°*

___

gear: matter, business.
vat . . . frister: what do you want? What would you, girl?

SYBIL. Marry, you must come to my young mistress, to
  pull on her shoes you made last.
LACY. *Vare ben your e[d]le fro? Vare ben your mistris?* *
SYBIL. Marry, here at our London house in Corn[hill].
FIRKE. Will nobody serve her turn but Hans?
SYBIL. No, sir. Come, Hans, I stand upon needles.   70
HODGE. Why then, Sybil, take heed of pricking.
SYBIL. For that let me alone; I have a trick in my budget.
  —Come, Hans.
LACY. *Yaw, yaw, ic sall meete yo gane.* *
HODGE. Go, Hans, make haste again.

                                    [*Exeunt* LACY] *and* SYBIL.
  —Come, who lacks work?
FIRKE. I, master, for I lack my breakfast. 'Tis munching
  time, and past.
HODGE. Is't so? Why then, leave work, Rafe. To break-
  fast! Boy, look to the tools. Come, Rafe; come, Firke.   80
                                                Exeunt.

[xiii]
                    Enter a SERVING-MAN.

SERVING-MAN. Let me see now, the sign of the Last in
  Tower Street. Mass, yonder's the house.—What, haw!
  Who's within?

                       Enter RAFE.

RAFE. Who calls there? What want you, sir?
SERVING-MAN. Marry, I would have a pair of shoes made
  for a gentlewoman against tomorrow morning. What,
  can you do them?
RAFE. Yes, sir, you shall have them. But what length's
  her foot?
SERVING-MAN. Why, you must make them in all parts   10
  like this shoe; but, at any hand, fail not to do them,
  for the gentlewoman is to be married very early in the
  morning.
RAFE. How? By this shoe must it be made? By this? Are
  you sure, sir, by this?
SERVING-MAN. How, "by this? Am I sure, sir, by this"?
  Art thou in thy wits? I tell thee I must have a pair of

---

  vare . . . mistris: where is your noble lady? Where is your mistress?

  yaw, . . . gane: yes, yes, I shall go with you.

shoes, dost thou mark me? A pair of shoes, two shoes,
made by this very shoe, this same shoe, against tomorrow morning by four o'clock. Dost understand me.   20
Canst thou do't?

RAFE. Yes, sir, yes—I—I—I can do't. By this shoe, you
say? I should know this shoe. Yes, sir, yes, by this shoe.
I can do't. Four o'clock? Well. Whither shall I bring
them?

SERVING-MAN. To the sign of the Golden Ball in Watling
Street. Inquire for one Master Hammon, a gentleman,
my master.

RAFE. Yea, sir. By this shoe, you say?

SERVING-MAN. I say Master Hammon at the Golden Ball.   30
He's the bridegroom, and those shoes are for his bride.

RAFE. They shall be done by this shoe. Well, well, Master
Hammon at the Golden Shoe—I would say the Golden
Ball. Very well, very well. But I pray you, sir, where
must Master Hammon be married?

SERVING-MAN. At Saint Faith's Church under Paul's, but
what's that to thee? Prithee, dispatch those shoes, and
so farewell.

Exit.

RAFE. "By this shoe," said he. How am I amazed
At this strange accident! Upon my life,   40
This was the very shoe I gave my wife
When I was pressed for France—since when, alas,
I never could hear of her. It is the same,
And Hammon's bride no other but my Jane.

Enter FIRKE.

FIRKE. 'Snails,* Rafe! Thou hast lost thy part of three
pots a countryman of mine gave me to breakfast.

RAFE. I care not; I have found a better thing.

FIRKE. A thing? Away! Is it a man's thing or a woman's
thing?

RAFE. Firke, dost thou know this shoe?   50

FIRKE. No, by my troth, neither doth that know me. I
have no acquaintance with it; 'tis a mere stranger to
me.

RAFE. Why, then, I do: this shoe, I durst be sworn,
Once coverèd the instep of my Jane.

'snails: contraction of "By God's nails!"

This is her size, her breadth; thus trod my love;
These true love knots I pricked. I hold my life,
By this old shoe I shall find out my wife.

FIRKE. Ha, ha! Old shoe, that wert new—how a mur-
rain° came this ague fit of foolishness upon thee?   60

RAFE. Thus, Firke: even now here came a serving-man;
By this shoe would he have a new pair made
Against tomorrow morning for his mistress
That's to be married to a gentleman.
And why may not this be my sweet Jane?

FIRKE. And why mayst not thou be my sweet ass? Ha,
ha!

RAFE. Well, laugh and spare not, but the truth is this:
Against tomorrow morning I'll provide
A lusty crew of honest shoemakers
To watch the going of the bride to church.   70
If she prove Jane, I'll take her in despite
From Hammon and the devil, were he by.
If it be not my Jane, what remedy?
Hereof am I sure, I shall live till I die
Although I never with a woman lie.

Exit.

FIRKE. Thou lie with a woman to build nothing but
Cripplegates!° Well, God sends fools fortune, and it
may be he may light upon his matrimony by such a
device—for wedding and hanging goes by destiny.

Exit.

[xiv]

Enter [LACY *as*] HANS *and* ROSE, *arm in arm.*

LACY. How happy am I by embracing thee!
O, I did fear such cross mishaps did reign
That I should never see my Rose again.

ROSE. Sweet Lacy, since fair opportunity
Offers herself to further our escape,
Let not too overfond esteem of me

---

murrain: plague.
Cripplegates: one of the gates of the city of London (pulled
down in 1762); the 16th-century historian Stow claimed that it
derived its name from "cripples begging there."

Hinder that happy hour. Invent the means,
And Rose will follow thee through all the world.

LACY. O, how I surfeit with excess of joy,
Made happy by thy rich perfection!   10
But, since thou pay'st sweet int'rest to my hopes,
Redoubling love on love, let me once more,
Like to a bold-faced debtor, crave of thee
This night to steal abroad and at Eyre's house,
Who now by death of certain aldermen
Is mayor of London, and my master once,
Meet thou thy Lacy, where, in spite of change,
Your father's anger, and mine uncle's hate,
Our happy nuptials will [w]e consummate.

                      Enter SYBIL.

SYBIL. O God, what will you do, mistress? Shift for   20
    yourself—your father is at hand! He's coming, he's
    coming! Master Lacy, hide yourself in my mistress!
    For God's sake, shift for yourselves!

LACY. Your father come! Sweet Rose, what shall I do?
    Where shall I hide me? How shall I escape?

ROSE. A man, and want wit in extremity?
    Come, come, be Hans still; play the shoemaker;
    Pull on my shoe.

                Enter [former] LORD MAYOR.

LACY.   Mass, and that's well remembered.

SYBIL. Here comes your father.

LACY. *Forware, metresse, 'tis un good skow; it sal vel*   30
    *dute, or ye sal neit betallen.**

ROSE. O God, it pincheth me! What will you do?

LACY [*aside to* ROSE]. Your father's presence pincheth,
    not the shoe.

LORD MAYOR. Well done; fit my daughter well, and she
    shall please thee well.

LACY. *Yaw, yaw, ick weit dat well. Forware, 'tis un good*
    *skoo; 'tis gimait van neits leither, se ever, mine here.**

                    Enter a PRENTICE.

LORD MAYOR. I do believe it.—What's the news with
    you?

---

forware, . . . betallen: indeed, mistress, 'tis a good shoe; it shall
fit well, or you shall not pay.

yaw, . . . here: yes, yes, I know that well. Indeed, 'tis a good
shoe; 'tis made of neat's leather, see here, my lord.

PRENTICE. Please you, the Earl of Lincoln at the gate
　Is newly lighted and would speak with you.　　　　　40
LORD MAYOR. The Earl of Lincoln come [to] speak with
　　me?
　Well, well, I know his errand.—Daughter Rose,
　Send hence your shoemaker. Dispatch, have done!—
　Syb, make things handsome.—Sir boy, follow me.
　　　　　　　　　　　　　　Exit [*with* PRENTICE].
LACY. Mine uncle come! O, what may this portend?
　Sweet Rose, this of our love threatens an end.
ROSE. Be not dismayed at this; whate'er befall,
　Rose is thine own. To witness I speak truth,
　Where thou appoints the place, I'll meet with thee.
　I will not fix a day to follow thee　　　　　　　　50
　But presently steal hence—do not reply.
　Love which gave strength to bear my father's hate
　Shall now add wings to further our escape.
　　　　　　　　　　　　　　　　　　Exeunt.
　　Enter [*former*] LORD MAYOR *and* LINCOLN.
LORD MAYOR. Believe me, on my credit, I speak truth;
　Since first your nephew Lacy went to France,
　I have not seen him. It seemed strange to me
　When Dodger told me that he stayed behind,
　Neglecting the high charge the king imposed.
LINCOLN. Trust me, Sir Roger Oatley, I did think
　Your counsel had given head to this attempt,　　　60
　Drawn to it by the love he bears your child.
　Here I did hope to find him in your house,
　But now I see mine error and confess
　My judgment wronged you by conceiving so.
LORD MAYOR. Lodge in my house, say you? Trust me,
　　my lord,
　I love your nephew Lacy too too dearly
　So much to wrong his honor; and he hath done so
　That first gave him advice to stay from France.
　To witness I speak truth, I let you know
　How careful I have been to keep my daughter　　70
　Free from all conference or speech of him.
　Not that I scorn your nephew, but in love
　I bear your honor, lest your noble blood
　Should by my mean worth be dishonorèd.
LINCOLN [*aside*]. How far the churl's tongue wanders
　　from his heart!—

Well, well, Sir Roger Oatley, I believe you,
With more than many thanks for the kind love
So much you seem to bear me. But, my lord,
Let me request your help to seek my nephew,
Whom, if I find, I'll straight embark for France.   80
So shall [your] Rose be free, [my] thoughts at rest,
And much care die which now [l]ies in my breast.

Enter SYBIL.

SYBIL. O Lord! Help, for God's sake! My mistress! O,
   my young mistress!

LORD MAYOR. Where is thy mistress? What's become of
   her?

SYBIL. She's gone! She's fled!

LORD MAYOR. Gone! Whither is she fled?

SYBIL. I know not, forsooth. She's fled out of doors with
   Hans the shoemaker. I saw them scud, scud, scud,
   apace, apace!   90

LORD MAYOR. Which way? What, John! Where be my
   men? Which way?

SYBIL. I know not, and it please your worship.

LORD MAYOR. Fled with a shoemaker! Can this be true?

SYBIL. O Lord, sir, as true as God's in heaven.

LINCOLN [*aside*]. Her love turned shoemaker? I am glad
   of this.

LORD MAYOR. A Fleming butterbox, a shoemaker!
   Will she forget her birth, requite my care
   With such ingratitude? Scorned she young Hammon
   To love a honnikin,° a needy knave?
   Well, let her fly; I'll not fly after her.   100
   Let her starve if she will; she's none of mine.

LINCOLN. Be not so cruel, sir.

Enter FIRKE *with shoes.*

SYBIL [*aside*].   I am glad she's 'scaped.

LORD MAYOR. I'll not account of her as of my child.
   Was there no better object for her eyes
   But a foul drunken lubber, swill-belly,
   A shoemaker? That's brave!

FIRKE. Yea, forsooth, 'tis a very brave shoe, and as fit as
   a pudding.

LORD MAYOR. How now? What knave is this? From
   whence comest thou?

---

honnikin: low-born person.

FIRKE. No knave, sir. I am Firke the shoemaker, lusty 110
Roger's chief lusty journeyman; and I come hither to
take up the pretty leg of sweet Mistress Rose, and
thus hoping your worship is in as good health as I
was at the making hereof, I bid you farewell, Yours,
Firke.

LORD MAYOR. Stay, stay, sir knave!

LINCOLN. Come hither, shoemaker.

FIRKE. 'Tis happy the knave is put before the shoemaker, or else I would not have vouchsafed to come
back to you. I am moved, for I stir. 120

LORD MAYOR. My lord, this villain calls us knaves by
craft.

FIRKE. Then 'tis by the Gentle Craft, and to call one
knave gently is no harm. Sit your worship merry!—
[*Aside to* SYBIL.] Syb, your young mistress—I'll so
bob° the[m], now my master, Master Eyre, is lord
mayor of London.

LORD MAYOR. Tell me, sirrah, whose man are you?

FIRKE. I am glad to see your worship so merry. I have
no maw° to this gear, no stomach as yet to a red petticoat. 130

(*Pointing to* SYBIL.)

LINCOLN. He means not, sir, to woo you to his maid,
But only doth demand whose man you are.

FIRKE. I sing now to the tune of "Rogero." Roger, my
fellow, is now my master.

LINCOLN. Sirrah, know'st thou one Hans, a shoemaker?

FIRKE. Hans, shoemaker? O, yes; stay, yes, I have him!
I tell you what (I speak it in secret), Mistress Rose
and he are by this time—no, not so, but shortly are to
come over one another with "Can you dance the shaking of the sheets?"° It is that Hans.—[*Aside.*] I'll so 140
gull these diggers!

LORD MAYOR. Know'st thou, then, where he is?

FIRKE. Yes, forsooth; yea, marry!

LINCOLN. Canst thou, in sadness°—

FIRKE. No, forsooth; no, marry!

bob: fool.
maw: appetite.
can . . . sheets: a popular dance song.
in sadness: in earnest.

LORD MAYOR. Tell me, good honest fellow, where he is,
And thou shalt see what I'll bestow of thee.

FIRKE. Honest Fellow? No, sir, not so, sir. My profession
is the Gentle Craft. I care not for seeing; I love feeling. Let me feel it here—*aurium tenus*, ten pieces of   150
gold; *genuum tenus*,* ten pieces of silver; and then
Firke is your man in a new pair of stretchers.*

LORD MAYOR. Here is an angel, part of thy reward,
Which I will give thee. Tell me where he is.

FIRKE. No point! Shall I betray my brother? No! Shall I
prove Judas to Hans? No! Shall I cry treason to my
corporation? No! I shall be firked and yerked then.
But give me your angel; your angel shall tell you.

LINCOLN. Do so, good fellow. 'Tis no hurt to thee.

FIRKE. Send simpering Syb away.   160

LORD MAYOR. Huswife, get you in.

Exit SYBIL.

FIRKE. Pitchers have ears, and maids have wide mouths;
but for Hans Prans, upon my word, tomorrow morning he and young Mistress Rose go to this gear. They
shall be married together, by this rush, or else turn
Firke to a firkin of butter to tan leather withal.

LORD MAYOR. But art thou sure of this?

FIRKE. Am I sure that Paul's steeple is a handful higher
than London Stone? Or that the Pissing Conduit leaks
nothing but pure Mother Bunch?* Am I sure I am   170
lusty Firke? God's nails! Do you think I am so base
to gull you?

LINCOLN. Where are they married? Dost thou know the
church?

FIRKE. I never go to church, but I know the name of it.
It is a swearing church. Stay a while! 'Tis—ay, by the
Mass! No, no! 'Tis—ay, by my troth! No, nor that.
'Tis—ay, by my faith, that, that, 'tis—Ay! By my
Faith's Church under Paul's Cross! There they shall
be knit like a pair of stockings in matrimony; there
they'll be incony.*   180

---

aurium tenus, . . . *genuum tenus:* up to the ears, up to the
knees.

stretchers: shoe stretchers (used punningly for "lies").

Mother Bunch: tavern hostess noted for watering her ale.

incony: fine, nice (?).

LINCOLN. Upon my life, my nephew Lacy walks
   In the disguise of this Dutch shoemaker.
FIRKE. Yes, forsooth.
LINCOLN. Doth he not, honest fellow?
FIRKE. No, forsooth; I think Hans is nobody but Hans,
   no spirit.
LORD MAYOR. My mind misgives me now, 'tis so, indeed.
LINCOLN. My cousin speaks the language, knows the
   trade.
LORD MAYOR. Let me request your company, my lord.
   Your honorable presence may, no doubt,   190
   Refrain their headstrong rashness when myself
   Going alone perchance may be o'erborne.
   Shall I request this favor?
LINCOLN.   This, or what else.
FIRKE. Then you must rise betimes, for they mean to
   fall to their "hey-pass and repass," "pindy-pandy,*
   which hand will you have," very early.
LORD MAYOR. My care shall every way equal their haste.
   This night accept your lodging in my house;
   The earlier shall we stir, and at Saint Faith's
   Prevent this giddy, hair-brained nuptial.   200
   This traffic of hot love shall yield cold gains;
   They ban our loves, and we'll forbid their banns.

                                                   [*Exit.*]

LINCOLN. At Saint Faith's Church, thou sayst?
FIRKE. Yes, by my troth.
LINCOLN. Be secret, on thy life.

                                                   [*Exit.*]

FIRKE. Yes, when I kiss your wife! Ha, ha! Here's no
   craft in the Gentle Craft. I came hither of purpose
   with shoes to Sir Roger's worship whilst Rose, his
   daughter, be cony-catched* by Hans. Soft now! These
   two gulls will be at Saint Faith's Church tomorrow   210
   morning to take Master Bridegroom and Mistress
   Bride napping; and they, in the meantime, shall chop
   up the matter at the Savoy. But the best sport is: Sir
   Roger Oatley will find my fellow, lame Rafe's wife
   going to marry a gentleman, and then he'll stop her

---

pindy-pandy: handy-dandy.
cony-catched: hoodwinked, cheated.

instead of his daughter. O, brave! There will be fine
tickling sport. Soft now, what have I to do? O, I
know now. A mess of shoemakers meet at the Wool-
sack in Ivy Lane to cozen my gentleman of lame
Rafe's wife; that's true.   220

> *Alack, alack!*
> *Girls, hold out tack!**
> *For now smocks for this jumbling*
> *Shall go to wrack.*

Exit.

[xv]

Enter EYRE, *his* WIFE, [LACY *as*] HANS, *and* ROSE.

EYRE. This is the morning, then. Stay, my bully, my
honest Hans, is it not?

LACY. This is the morning that must make us two
Happy or miserable; therefore, if you—

EYRE. Away with these if's and and's, Hans, and these
et ceteras! By mine honor, Rowland Lacy, none but
the king shall wrong thee. Come, fear nothing. Am
not I Sim Eyre? Is not Sim Eyre lord mayor of London? Fear nothing, Rose. Let them all say what they
can. "Dainty, come thou to me."*—Laughest thou?   10

WIFE. Good my lord, stand her friend in what thing you
may.

EYRE. Why, my sweet Lady Madgy, think you Simon
Eyre can forget his fine Dutch journeyman? No, vah!
Fie, I scorn it! It shall never be cast in my teeth that
I was unthankful. Lady Madgy, thou hadst never
covered thy Saracen's head with this French flap,
nor loaden thy bum with this farthingale ('tis trash,
trumpery, vanity); Simon Eyre had never walked in
a red petticoat nor worn a chain of gold but for my   20
fine journeyman's Portuguese. And shall I leave him?
No! Prince am I none, yet bear a princely mind.

LACY. My lord, 'tis time for us to part from hence.

EYRE. Lady Madgy, Lady Madgy, take two or three of
my piecrust eaters, my buff-jerkin varlets that do
walk in black gowns at Simon Eyre's heels; take them,

---

hold out tack: be firm.
dainty . . . me: popular song.

good Lady Madgy. Trip and go, my brown Queen of
Periwigs, with my delicate Rose and my jolly Rowland, to the Savoy. See them linked; countenance the
marriage; and, when it is done, cling, cling together,   30
you Hamborough turtledoves. I'll bear you out. Come
to Simon Eyre. Come dwell with us, Hans. Thou shalt
eat minced pies and marchpane.° Rose, away, cricket!
Trip and go, my Lady Madgy, to the Savoy! Hans,
wed and to bed; kiss and away! Go, vanish!

WIFE. Farewell, my lord.

ROSE. Make haste, sweet love.

WIFE. She'd fain the deed were done.

LACY. Come, my sweet Rose; faster than deer we'll run.

                                   (They go out.)

EYRE. Go, vanish, vanish! Avaunt, I say! By the Lord of   40
Ludgate, it's a mad life to be a lord mayor. It's a stirring life, a fine life, a velvet life, a careful life. Well,
Simon Eyre, yet set a good face on it, in the honor of
Saint Hugh. Soft! The king this day comes to dine
with me, to see my new buildings. His majesty is welcome; he shall have good cheer, delicate cheer, princely cheer. This day my fellow prentices of London
come to dine with me too; they shall have fine cheer,
gentlemanlike cheer. I promised the mad Cappado-
cians, when we all served at the Conduit together,   50
that, if ever I came to be mayor of London, I would
feast them all; and I'll do't—I'll do't, by the life of
Pharaoh! By this beard, Sim Eyre will be no flincher!
Besides, I have procured that upon every Shrove
Tuesday, at the sound of the pancake bell, my fine
dapper Assyrian lads shall clap up their shop windows, and away. This is the day, and this day they
shall do't, they shall do't!

    Boys, that day are you free; let masters care,
And prentices shall pray for Simon Eyre.   60

                                        Exit.

[xvi]

    Enter HODGE, FIRKE, RAFE, *and five or six*
    Shoemakers, all with cudgels or such weapons.

---

marchpane: marzipan.

HODGE. Come, Rafe; stand to it, Firke. My masters, as
we are the brave bloods of the shoemakers, heirs apparent to Saint Hugh, and perpetual benefactors to all
good fellows, thou shalt have no wrong. Were Hammon a king of spades, he should not delve in thy
close* without thy sufferance. But tell me, Rafe, art
thou sure 'tis thy wife?

RAFE. Am I sure this is Firke? This morning, when I
stroked on her shoes, I looked upon her, and she upon
me, and sighed, asked me if ever I knew one Rafe.   10
"Yes," said I. "For his sake," said she, tears standing
in her eyes, "and for thou art somewhat like him,
spend this piece of gold." I took it. My lame leg and
my travel beyond sea made me unknown. All is one
for that; I know she's mine.

FIRKE. Did she give thee this gold? O glorious, glittering
gold! She's thine own, 'tis thy wife, and she loves
thee; for I'll stand to't there's no woman will give
gold to any man but she thinks better of him than she
thinks of them she gives silver to. And for Hammon,   20
neither Hammon nor hangman shall wrong thee in
London. Is not our old master Eyre lord mayor?
Speak, my hearts.

ALL. Yes, and Hammon shall know it to his cost.

          Enter HAMMON, *his Man,* JANE, *and Others.*

HODGE. Peace, my bullies; yonder they come.

RAFE. Stand to't, my hearts. Firke, let me speak first.

HODGE. No, Rafe, let me.—Hammon, whither away so
early?

HAMMON. Unmannerly, rude slave, what's that to thee?

FIRKE. To him, sir? Yes, sir, and to me, and others. Good   30
morrow, Jane, how dost thou? Good Lord, how the
world is changed with you! God be thanked!

HAMMON. Villains, hands off! How dare you touch my
love?

ALL. Villains? Down with them! Cry clubs for prentices!

HODGE. Hold, my hearts! Touch her, Hammon? Yea, and
more than that, we'll carry her away with us. My
masters and gentlemen, never draw your bird-spits;
shoemakers are steel to the back, men every inch of
them, all spirit.

---

close: field.

ALL OF HAMMON'S SIDE. Well, and what of all this?   40

HODGE. I'll show you. Jane, dost thou know this man?
'Tis Rafe, I can tell thee. Nay, 'tis he in faith though
he be lamed by the wars. Yet look not strange, but
run to him, fold him about the neck and kiss him.

JANE. Lives then my husband? O God, let me go,
Let me embrace my Rafe.

HAMMON.   What means my Jane?

JANE. Nay, what meant you to tell me he was slain?

HAMMON. Pardon me, dear love, for being misled.—
[*To* RAFE.] 'Twas rumored here in London thou wert
dead.

FIRKE. Thou seest he lives. Lass, go pack home with   50
him. Now, Master Hammon, where's your mistress,
your wife?

SERVANT. 'Swounds,* master, fight for her! Will you
thus lose her?

ALL. Down with that creature! Clubs! Down with him!

HODGE. Hold, hold!

HAMMON. Hold, fool! Sirs, he shall do no wrong.—
Will my Jane leave me thus and break her faith?

FIRKE. Yea, sir! She must, sir! She shall, sir! What then?
Mend it.   60

HODGE. Hark, fellow Rafe, follow my counsel: set the
wench in the midst and let her choose her man and
let her be his woman.

JANE. Whom should I choose? Whom should my
thoughts affect
But him whom heaven hath made to be my love?
Thou art my husband, and these humble weeds
Makes thee more beautiful than all his wealth.
Therefore, I will but put off his attire,
Returning it into the owner's hand,
And after ever be thy constant wife.   70

HODGE. Not a rag, Jane! The law's on our side; he that
sows in another man's ground forfeits his harvest. Get
thee home, Rafe; follow him, Jane. He shall not have
so much as a busk-point* from thee.

FIRKE. Stand to that, Rafe; the appurtenances are thine
own. Hammon, look not at her!

'swounds: contraction of "by God's wounds!"
busk-point: lace of a corset.

SERVANT. O, 'swounds, no!

FIRKE. Blue coat, be quiet. We'll give you a new livery
else; we'll make Shrove Tuesday Saint George's Day
for you.°—Look not, Hammon; leer not! I'll firk you!   80
For thy head now, one glance, one sheep's eye, anything, at her! Touch not a rag, lest I and my brethren
beat you to clouts.

SERVANT. Come, Master Hammon, there's no striving
here.

HAMMON. Good fellows, hear me speak. And, honest
Rafe,
Whom I have injured most by loving Jane,
Mark what I offer thee. Here in fair gold
Is twenty pound; I'll give it for thy Jane.
If this content thee not, thou shalt have more.

HODGE. Sell not thy wife, Rafe. Make her not a whore.   90

HAMMON. Say, wilt thou freely cease thy claim in her,
And let her be my wife?

ALL.   No, do not, Rafe!

RAFE. Sirrah Hammon, Hammon, dost thou think a
shoemaker is so base to be a bawd to his own wife
for commodity? Take thy gold. Choke with it! Were
I not lame, I would make thee eat thy words.

FIRKE. A shoemaker sell his flesh and blood? O indignity!

HODGE. Sirrah, take up your pelf and be packing.

HAMMON. I will not touch one penny; but in lieu   100
Of that great wrong I offerèd thy Jane,
To Jane and thee I give that twenty pound.
Since I have failed of her, during my life
I vow no woman else shall be my wife.
Farewell, good fellows of the Gentle Trade.
Your morning's mirth my mourning day hath made.
                         Exeunt [HAMMON *and Servants*].

FIRKE [*to Servant going out*]. Touch the gold, creature,
if you dare! Y'are best be trudging.—Here, Jane, take
thou it. Now let's home, my hearts.

HODGE. Stay! Who comes here? Jane, on again with thy   110
mask!

we'll make . . . for you: we'll beat you until you are blue like
your livery.

Enter LINCOLN, [*former*] LORD MAYOR, *and Servants.*

LINCOLN. Yonder's the lying varlet mocked us so.

LORD MAYOR. Come hither, sirrah!

FIRKE. I, sir? I am "sirrah"? You mean me, do you not?

LINCOLN. Where is my nephew married?

FIRKE. Is he married? God give him joy, I am glad of it. They have a fair day, and the sign is in a good planet—Mars in Venus.

LORD MAYOR. Villain! Thou told'st me that my daughter Rose

This morning should be married at Saint Faith's.   120

We have watched there these three hours at the least,

Yet see we no such thing.

FIRKE. Truly, I am sorry for't. A bride's a pretty thing.

HODGE. Come to the purpose. Yonder's the bride and bridegroom you look for, I hope. Though you be lords, you are not to bar by your authority men from women, are you?

LORD MAYOR. See, see, my daughter's masked!

LINCOLN.   True, and my nephew,

To hide his guilt, counterfeits him lame.

FIRKE. Yea, truly, God help the poor couple! They are   130
lame and blind.

LORD MAYOR. I'll ease her blindness.

LINCOLN.   I'll his lameness cure.

FIRKE [*aside to the Shoemakers*]. Lie down, sirs, and laugh! My fellow Rafe is taken for Rowland Lacy, and Jane for Mistress Damask Rose. This is all my knavery.

LORD MAYOR. What, have I found you, minion?

LINCOLN.   O, base wretch!

Nay, hide thy face. The horror of thy guilt

Can hardly be washed off. Where are thy powers?

What battles have you made? O, yes, I see   140

Though fought'st with Shame, and Shame hath conquered thee.

This lameness will not serve.

LORD MAYOR.   Unmask yourself.

LINCOLN. Lead home your daughter.

LORD MAYOR.   Take your nephew
    hence.

RAFE. Hence! 'Swounds, what mean you? Are you mad?
    I hope you cannot enforce my wife from me. Where's
    Hammon?

LORD MAYOR. Your wife?

LINCOLN. What Hammon?

RAFE. Yea, my wife; and, therefore, the proudest of you
    that lays hands on her first, I'll lay my crutch across   150
    his pate.

FIRKE. To him, lame Rafe! Here's brave sport!

RAFE. Rose call you her? Why, her name is Jane. Look
    here else; do you know her now?
    [*He unmasks* JANE.]

LINCOLN. Is this your daughter?

LORD MAYOR.   No, nor this your
    nephew.
    My Lord of Lincoln, we are both abused
    By this base, crafty varlet.

FIRKE. Yea, forsooth, no varlet. Forsooth, no base. For-
    sooth, I am but mean;* no crafty neither, but of the
    Gentle Craft.   160

LORD MAYOR. Where is my daughter Rose? Where is
    my child?

LINCOLN. Where is my nephew Lacy marrièd?

FIRKE. Why, here is good laced mutton,* as I promised
    you.

LINCOLN. Villain, I'll have thee punished for this wrong.

FIRKE. Punish the journeyman villain, but not the jour-
    neyman shoemaker.

                        Enter DODGER.

DODGER. My lord, I come to bring unwelcome news:
    Your nephew Lacy and your daughter Rose
    Early this morning wedded at the Savoy,   170
    None being present but the lady mayoress.
    Besides, I learned among the officers
    The lord mayor vows to stand in their defense
    'Gainst any that shall seek to cross the match.

LINCOLN. Dares Eyre the shoemaker uphold the deed?

---

mean: of low birth.
laced mutton: prostitute.

FIRKE. Yes, sir, shoemakers dare stand in a woman's
quarrel, I warrant you, as deep as another, and
deeper too.

DODGER. Besides, his grace today dines with the mayor,
Who on his knees humbly intends to fall   180
And beg a pardon for your nephew's fault.

LINCOLN. But I'll prevent him. Come, Sir Roger Oatley;
The king will do us justice in this cause.
Howe'er their hands have made them man and wife,
I will disjoin the match or lose my life.

Exeunt [LINCOLN, LORD MAYOR, DODGER, *and Servants*].

FIRKE. Adieu, Monsieur Dodger! Farewell, fools! Ha,
ha! O, if they had stayed, I would have so lammed
them with flouts! O, heart! My codpiece point is ready
to fly in pieces every time I think upon Mistress Rose.
But let that pass, as my lady mayoress says.   190

HODGE. This matter is answered. Come, Rafe; home
with thy wife. Come, my fine shoemakers; let's to our
master's, the new lord mayor, and there swagger this
Shrove Tuesday. I'll promise you wine enough, for
Madge keeps the cellar.

ALL. O, rare! Madge is a good wench.

FIRKE. And I'll promise you meat enough, for simp'ring
Susan keeps the larder. I'll lead you to victuals, my
brave soldiers. Follow your captain. O, brave! Hark!
Hark!   200

(Bell rings.)

ALL. The pancake bell rings! The pancake bell! Trilill,
my hearts!

FIRKE. O, brave! O sweet bell! O delicate pancakes!
Open the doors, my hearts, and shut up the windows!
Keep in the house; let out the pancakes! O, rare, my
hearts! Let's march together for the honor of Saint
Hugh to the great new hall in Gracious Street corner,
which our master, the new lord mayor, hath built.

RAFE. O, the crew of good fellows that will dine at my
lord mayor's cost today!   210

HODGE. By the Lord, my lord mayor is a most brave
man. How shall prentices be bound to pray for him
and the honor of the gentlemen shoemakers! Let's
feed and be fat with my lord's bounty.

FIRKE. O musical bell, still! O Hodge! O my brethren!

There's cheer for the heavens. Ven'son pasti[es] walk
up and down piping hot like sergeants; beef and
brewis comes marching in dry fats;* fritters and pancakes comes trolling in in wheelbarrows; hens and
oranges hopping in porters' baskets, collops and eggs   220
in scuttles; and tarts and custards comes quavering in
in malt shovels.

Enter more Prentices.

ALL. Whoop! Look here, look here!

HODGE. How now, mad lads, whither away so fast?

1 PRENTICE. Whither? Why, to the great new hall.
Know you not why? The lord mayor hath bidden all
the prentices in London to breakfast this morning.

ALL. O brave shoemaker! O brave lord of incompre-
hensible good fellowship! Whoo! Hark you! The pancake bell rings.   230

(*Cast up caps.*)

FIRKE. Nay, more, my hearts! Every Shrove Tuesday is
our year of jubilee; and, when the pancake bell rings,
we are as free as my lord mayor. We may shut up our
shops and make holiday. I'll have it called Saint
Hugh's Holiday.

ALL. Agreed, agreed! Saint Hugh's Holiday!

HODGE. And this shall continue forever.

ALL. O, brave! Come, come, my hearts. Away, away!

FIRKE. O, eternal credit to us of the Gentle Craft!
March fair, my hearts! O rare!   240

Exeunt.

[xvii]

Enter KING *and his Train over the stage.*

KING. Is our lord mayor of London such a gallant?

NOBLEMAN. One of the merriest madcaps in your land.
Your grace will think, when you behold the man,
He's rather a wild ruffian than a mayor.
Yet thus much I'll ensure your majesty,
In all his actions that concern his state
He is as serious, provident, and wise,
As full of gravity amongst the grave,
As any mayor hath been these many years.

KING. I am with child till I behold this huff-cap.   10

---

fats: vats.

But all my doubt is, when we come in presence,
His madness will be dashed clean out of countenance.
NOBLEMAN. It may be so, my liege.
KING.   Which to prevent,
Let someone give him notice 'tis our pleasure
That he put on his wonted merriment.
Set forward!
ALL.   On afore!

Exeunt.

[xviii]
> *Enter* EYRE, HODGE, FIRKE, RAFE, *and other*
> *Shoemakers, all with napkins on their shoulders.*

EYRE. Come, my fine Hodge, my jolly gentlemen shoemakers. Soft! Where be these cannibals, these varlets,
my officers? Let them all walk and wait upon my brethren; for my meaning is that none but shoemakers,
none but the livery of my company, shall in their satin
hoods wait upon the trencher of my sovereign.
FIRKE. O my lord, it will be rare!
EYRE. No more, Firke. Come, lively! Let your fellow
prentices want no cheer. Let wine be plentiful as
beer, and beer as water. Hang these penny-pinching   10
fathers that cram wealth in innocent lambskins. Rip,
knaves! Avaunt! Look to my guests.
HODGE. My lord, we are at our wits' end for room. Those
hundred tables will not feast the fourth part of them.
EYRE. Then cover me those hundred tables again, and
again, till all my jolly prentices be feasted. Avoid,
Hodge! Run, Rafe! Frisk about, my nimble Firke!
Carouse me fathom healths to the honor of the shoemakers. Do they drink lively, Hodge? Do they tickle
it, Firke?   20
FIRKE. Tickle it? Some of them have taken their liquor
standing so long that they can stand no longer. But
for meat, they would eat it and they had it.
EYRE. Want they meat? Where's this swag-belly, this
greasy kitchen-stuff cook? Call the varlet to me. Want
meat! Firke, Hodge, lame Rafe, run, my tall men,
beleaguer the shambles,° beggar all Eastcheap, serve
me whole oxen in chargers, and let sheep whine upon

---

beleaguer the shambles: besiege the meat market.

the tables like pigs for want of good fellows to eat
them. Want meat! Vanish, Firke! Avaunt, Hodge!   30
HODGE. Your lordship mistakes my man Firke. He means
their bellies want meat, not the boards, for they have
drunk so much they can eat nothing.*

Enter [LACY *still dressed as*] HANS, ROSE, *and* WIFE.

WIFE. Where is my lord?
EYRE. How now, Lady Madgy?
WIFE. The king's most excellent majesty is new come.
He sends me for thy honor. One of his most worship-
ful peers bade me tell thou must be merry and so
forth. But let that pass.
EYRE. Is my sovereign come? Vanish, my tall shoemak-   40
ers, my nimble brethren! Look to my guests, the pren-
tices—yet stay a little! How now, Hans? How looks
my little Rose?
LACY. Let me request you to remember me.
I know your honor easily may obtain
Free pardon of the king for me and Rose,
And reconcile me to my uncle's grace.
EYRE. Have done, my good Hans, my honest journeyman. Look cheerily! I'll fall upon both my knees till
they be as hard as horn, but I'll get thy pardon.   50
WIFE. Good my lord, have a care what you speak to his
grace.
EYRE. Away, you Islington whitepot!* Hence, you happer*-arse, you barley pudding full of maggots! You
broiled carbonado,* avaunt! Avaunt, avoid, Mephostophilus! Shall Sim Eyre [learn] to speak of you, Lady
Madgy? Vanish, Mother Miniver-cap, vanish! Go, trip
and go! Meddle with your partlets* and your pishery-
pashery, your flues and your whirligigs. Go, rub! Out
of mine alley! Sim Eyre knows how to speak to a pope, 60
to Sultan Soliman, to Tamburlaine and he were here.
And shall I melt, shall I droop before my sovereign?
No, come, my Lady Madgy! Follow me, Hans! About

Hodge's speech: "The Second Three-man's Song" is sometimes
inserted at this place.
Islington whitepot: a custard.
happer: shaped like a hopper or vat for hops.
carbonado: steak; piece of flesh.
partlets: ruffs.

your business, my frolic freebooters! Firke, frisk about
and about and about, for the honor of mad Simon
Eyre, lord mayor of London.

FIRKE. Hey, for the honor of the shoemakers!

Exeunt.

[xix]

A long flourish or two. Enter KING, *Nobles,* EYRE,
his WIFE, LACY [*as himself*], ROSE. LACY *and*
ROSE *kneel.*

KING. Well, Lacy, though the fact was very foul
Of your revolting from our kingly love
And your own duty, yet we pardon you.
Rise both, and Mistress Lacy, thank my lord mayor
For your young bridegroom here.

EYRE. So, my dear liege, Sim Eyre and my brethren, the
gentlemen shoemakers, shall set your sweet majesty's
image cheek by jowl by Saint Hugh for this honor you
have done poor Simon Eyre. I beseech your grace,
pardon my rude behavior; I am a handicraftsman, yet   10
my heart is without craft. I would be sorry at my soul
that my boldness should offend the king.

KING. Nay, I pray thee, good lord mayor, be even as merry
As if thou wert among thy shoemakers.
It does me good to see thee in this humor.

EYRE. Sayst thou me so, my sweet Dioclesian? Then,
hump! Prince am I none, yet am I princely born. By
the Lord of Ludgate, my liege, I'll be as merry as a
pie.*

KING. Tell me, in faith, mad Eyre, how old thou art.   20

EYRE. My liege, a very boy, a stripling, a younker. You
see not a white hair on my head, not a gray in this
beard. Every hair, I assure thy majesty, that sticks in
this beard, Sim Eyre values at the King of Babylon's
ransom. Tama[r] Cham's beard was a rubbing brush
to't. Yet I'll shave it off and stuff tennis balls with it
to please my bully king.

KING. But all this while I do not know your age.

EYRE. My liege, I am six-and-fifty year old, yet I can
cry "hump!" with a sound heart for the honor of Saint   30

---

pie: magpie.

Hugh. Mark this old wench, my king: I danced the
shaking of the sheets with her six-and-thirty years
ago, and yet I hope to get two or three young lord
mayors ere I die. I am lusty still, Sim Eyre still. Care
and cold lodging brings white hairs. My sweet majesty, let care vanish! Cast it upon thy nobles; it will
make thee look always young like Apollo. And cry
"hump!" Prince am I none, yet am I princely born.

KING. Ha, ha! Say, Cornwall, didst thou ever see his like.

NOBLEMAN. Not I, my lord.

        Enter LINCOLN *and* [*former*] LORD MAYOR.

KING.   Lincoln, what news with
    you?   40

LINCOLN. My gracious lord, have care unto yourself,
    For there are traitors here.

ALL.   Traitors? Where? Who?

EYRE. Traitors in my house? God forbid! Where be my
    officers? I'll spend my soul ere my king feel harm.

KING. Where is the traitor, Lincoln?

LINCOLN [*pointing to* LACY].   Here he stands.

KING. Cornwall, lay hold on Lacy!—Lincoln, speak.
    What canst thou lay unto thy nephew's charge?

LINCOLN. This, my dear liege: your grace, to do me
    honor,
    Heaped on the head of this degenerous* boy
    Desertless favors; you made choice of him   50
    To be commander over powers in France.
    But he—

KING.   Good Lincoln, prithee pause awhile.
    Even in thine eyes I read what thou wouldst speak.
    I know how Lacy did neglect our love,
    Ran himself deeply (in the highest degree)
    Into vile treason.

LINCOLN.   Is he not a traitor?

KING. Lincoln, he was; now have we pardoned him.
    'Twas not a base want of true valor's fire
    That held him out of France, but love's desire.

LINCOLN. I will not bear his shame upon my back.   60

KING. Nor shalt thou, Lincoln; I forgive you both.

LINCOLN. Then, good my liege, forbid the boy to wed

_____

    degenerous: ignoble.

One whose mean birth will much disgrace his bed.

KING. Are they not married?

LINCOLN.   No, my liege.

BOTH [ROSE *and* LACY].   We are!

KING. Shall I divorce them then? O, be it far
That any hand on earth should dare untie
The sacred knot knit by God's majesty.
I would not for my crown disjoin their hands
That are conjoined in holy nuptial bands.
How sayst thou, Lacy? Wouldst thou lose thy Rose?   70

LACY. Not for all India[']s wealth, my sovereign.

KING. But Rose, I am sure, her Lacy would forgo.

ROSE. If Rose were asked that question, she'd say no!

KING. You hear them, Lincoln?

LINCOLN.   Yea, my liege, I do.

KING. Yet canst thou find i'th' heart to part these two?
Who seeks, besides you, to divorce these lovers?

LORD MAYOR. I do, my gracious lord; I am her father.

KING. Sir Roger Oatley, our last mayor, I think?

NOBLEMAN. The same, my liege.

KING.   Would you offend
Love's laws?
Well, you shall have your wills. You sue to me   80
To prohibit the match. Soft, let me see—
You both are married, Lacy, art thou not?

LACY. I am, dread sovereign.

KING.   Then, upon thy life,
I charge thee not to call this woman wife.

LORD MAYOR. I thank your grace.

ROSE.   O my most gracious
lord!
(*Kneel[s].*)

KING. Nay, Rose, never woo me. I tell you true,
Although as yet I am a bachelor,
Yet I believe I shall not marry you.

ROSE. Can you divide the body from the soul,
Yet make the body live?

KING.   Yea, so profound?   90
I cannot, Rose, but you I must divide.
Fair maid, this bridegroom cannot be your bride.°—

---

bride: applied to both sexes.

Are you pleased, Lincoln? Oatley, are you pleased?

BOTH. Yes, my lord.

KING.   Then must my heart be eased;
For, credit me, my conscience lives in pain
Till these whom I divorced be joined again.
Lacy, give me thy hand. Rose, lend me thine.
Be what you would be! Kiss now! So, that's fine.
At night, lovers, to bed!—Now let me see
Which of you all mislikes this harmony?   100

LORD MAYOR. Will you then take from me my child
    perforce?

KING. Why, tell me, Oatley, shines not Lacy's name
As bright in the world's eye as the gay beams
Of any citizen?

LINCOLN.   Yea, but, my gracious lord,
I do mislike the match far more than he:
Her blood is too too base for me.

KING.   Lincoln, no more!
Dost thou not know that love respects no blood,
Cares not for difference of birth or state?
The maid is young, well born, fair, virtuous,
A worthy bride for any gentleman.   110
Besides, your nephew for her sake did stoop
To bare necessity and, as I hear,
Forgetting honors and all courtly pleasures,
To gain her love became a shoemaker.
As for the honor which he lost in France,
Thus I redeem it: Lacy, kneel thee down!
Arise, Sir Rowland Lacy! Tell me now,
Tell me in earnest, Oatley, canst thou chide,
Seeing thy Rose a lady and a bride?

LORD MAYOR. I am content with what your grace hath
    done.   120

LINCOLN. And I, my liege, since there's no remedy.

KING. Come on, then, all shake hands. I'll have you
    friends;
Where there is much love, all discord ends.
What says my mad lord mayor to all this love?

EYRE. O my liege, this honor you have done to my fine
    journeyman here, Rowland Lacy, and all these favors
    which you have shown to me this day in my poor

house will make Simon Eyre live longer by one dozen
of warm summers more than he should.

KING. Nay, my mad lord mayor (that shall be thy name),   130
If any grace of mine can length thy life,
One honor more I'll do thee: that new building,
Which at thy cost in Cornhill is erected,
Shall take a name from us; we'll have it called
The Leadenhall because in digging it
You found the lead that covereth the same.

EYRE. I thank your majesty.

WIFE.   God bless your grace!

KING. Lincoln, a word with you!
    Enter HODGE, FIRKE, RAFE, *and more Shoemakers.*

EYRE. How now, my mad knaves? Peace, speak softly!
Yonder is the king.   140

KING. With the old troop which there we keep in pay,
We will incorporate a new supply.
Before one summer more pass o'er my head,
France shall repent England was injurèd.
What are all those?

LACY.   All shoemakers, my liege,
Sometimes my fellows. In their companies
I lived as merry as an emperor.

KING. My mad lord mayor, are all these shoemakers?

EYRE. All shoemakers, my liege; all gentlemen of the
Gentle Craft, true Trojans, courageous cordwainers.   150
They all kneel to the shrine of holy Saint Hugh.

ALL [THE] SHOEMAKERS. God save your majesty!

KING. Mad Simon, would they anything with us?

EYRE. Mum, mad knaves! Not a word! I'll do't, I warrant
you. They are all beggars, my liege, all for themselves. And I for them all on both my knees do entreat
that, for the honor of poor Simon Eyre and the good
of his brethren, these mad knaves, your grace would
vouchsafe some privilege to my new Leadenhall: that
it may be lawful for us to buy and sell leather there   160
two days a week.

KING. Mad Sim, I grant your suit; you shall have patent
To hold two market days in Leadenhall,
Mondays and Fridays—those shall be the times.
Will this content you?

ALL.   Jesus bless your grace!

EYRE. In the name of these my poor brethren shoemakers, I most humbly thank your grace. But, before
I rise, seeing you are in the giving vein and we in the
begging, grant Sim Eyre one boon more.

KING. What is it, my lord mayor?   170

EYRE. Vouchsafe to taste of a poor banquet that stands
sweetly waiting for your sweet presence.

KING. I shall undo thee, Eyre, only with feasts.
Already have I been too troublesome,
Say, have I not?

EYRE. O my dear king, Sim Eyre was taken unawares
upon a day of shroving * which I promised long ago
to the prentices of London. For, and't please your
highness, in time past, I bare the water tankard, and   180
my coat sits not a whit the worse upon my back. And
then, upon a morning, some mad boys (it was a Shrove
Tuesday, even as 'tis now) gave me my breakfast;
and I swore then by the stopple of my tankard, if
ever I came to be lord mayor of London, I would feast
all the prentices. This day, my liege, I did it; and the
slaves had an hundred tables five times covered. They
are gone home and vanished.
        Yet add more honor to the Gentle Trade:
        Taste of Eyre's banquet, Simon's happy made.

KING. Eyre, I will taste of thy banquet and will say   190
I have not met more pleasure on a day.—
Friends of the Gentle Craft, thanks to you all.
Thanks, my kind lady mayoress, for our cheer.—
Come, lords, awhile let's revel it at home!
When all our sports and banquetings are done,
Wars must right wrongs which Frenchmen have begun.

                                                    Exeunt.

                            FINIS.
_____
    shroving: rejoicing, merrymaking.

VOLPONE,

OR

THE FOXE.

A Comœdie.

Acted in the yeere 1605. By
the K. Maiesties
Servants.

The Author B. I.

HORAT.

Simul & iucunda, & idonea dicere vitæ.

———————————————

LONDON,
Printed by VVILLIAM STANSBY.

M. DC. XVI.

Art No. 3 for Volpone

Introduction

> WIFE. . . . *How costly this world's calling is, perdy! But that it is one of the wonderful works of God, I would not deal with it.*
>
> (The Shoemakers' Holiday, *scene ix.*)

Over the twilight hours of his aging monarch's long-lived reign Dekker casts the halo of romance. Like Margery the shoemaker's wife, aware of "how costly this world's calling is," he deals with it for the same reason only. *The Shoemakers' Holiday,* most fittingly "acted before the Queen's most excellent Majesty on New Year's day at night last," closes out the century in an almost nostalgic evocation of a golden age of England in which love maintains order. But the dominant mood that ushers in the new century and, after 1603, the reign of the Stuarts is bitterly satiric or tragic; sometimes it is difficult to distinguish between the two. Disenchantment, in a word, is the keynote to the drama of the entire century; but it is deepest in the first decade when playwrights suddenly became aware that the Elizabethan ceremony of innocence was drowning in the bitter corruptions of Jacobean life. In the years when, as Keynes has pointed out, modern capitalism was born, not all men were sharing the famed prosperity of the times. Prices were rising continually, but wages remained fixed; and in the depressed

economy of the last years of Elizabeth's reign the plight of
those with fixed incomes seemed hopeless while those with
the means of attaining and producing capital—the "new"
men of the rising middle class, the big merchants, investors,
large-scale farmers who benefited from land enclosures—
were having a field day. Moreover, the changing economy
was undermining the old, more feudal and agrarian, way of
life. When money began to talk, traditional values began
to fall silent. The result in drama was that, as the new century dawned, the playwrights—the brief chroniclers of their
time—began to ponder the question that only Marlowe
seriously, and despairingly, had considered earlier: what
profits it a man to gain the world and lose his soul? A world
dominated by the profit motive is, they felt, unnatural; and
play after play of the first decade, the "dark" comedies and
the great tragedies, dramatizes the medieval sin of usury,
the chief manifestation of avarice. In a usorious world, where
gold is unnaturally creative, the truly *natural* relationships
are overturned: child rebels against parent, wife against
husband, subject against ruler, servant against master, friend
against friend. "When degree is shaked," as Shakespeare saw
in *Troilus and Cressida* (late 1601?), will becomes appetite,
and appetite "an universal wolf."

As a portrayal of the unnatural begetting of the unnatural,
Jonson's comedy of early 1606, *Volpone; or, The Fox*, voices
the desperation of a society that is rapidly losing its traditional bearings and has not yet succeeded in redefining itself.
Moreover, in a world thronged with acquisitive parasites,
such as Mosca describes at the beginning of Act III, redefini-
tion seems doomed to failure; for, where riches "mak'st men
do all things," integrity of self becomes meaningless. The
unreality of playacting, symbolized by Volpone's mountebank
masquerade in Act II, characterizes the acquisitive society:
men don disguises and "change shapes" to deceive others
and, in fact, themselves, to be anything other than men
created in God's image. Volpone's offspring are naturally
monstrous. When men have lost the good of the intellect that
enables them to distinguish appearance from reality, the
natural from the unnatural, only the beast survives—as it
does in almost every character, except Celia and Bonario,
in the play. Thus the punishments meted out at the end—a
procedure not conventional in comedy, as Jonson well knew

—are in a Dantesque sense, as with Faustus, the crimes themselves: a totally predatory existence, with appetite incapable of satisfaction, must prove futile.

Whatever laughter this dark comedy evokes is of a savage, uncomfortable sort. Jonson himself thought laughter a corruption of the true office of comedy, which was "to inform men in the best reason of living." The ordinary beast fable, the literary form that the play resembles most in spirit, normally invites us to laugh at animals made to enact human roles; and in reading a fable of this type (or in watching the movie of Orwell's *Animal Farm*) we can accept more easily the moral because of our superior knowledge that we are, after all, not animals. But to watch humans acting out their descriptions as "birds of prey" and other animals— Volpone the fox, Mosca the fly, Voltore the vulture, Corbaccio the raven, Corvino the crow, Sir Pol the parrot—is too frightening for outright laughter. Only in the subplot involving the antics of Sir Pol does Jonson permit a freer laughter, but here the theme is folly rather than vice.

As an imaginative re-creation of a hellish world, *Volpone* forces an audience, by means of its language as well as by its inverted beast fable, to experience the absurdity of the unnatural at the same time that it must judge the unnatural. Judgment assumes awareness of "the best reason of living." In a world of devils Volpone is, indeed, a magnifico and Mosca something of a prince. Theirs are the grand gestures, and the intensity of their drives and their joy in ghoulish sports compel—like Milton's Satan—a certain admiration. But the grandeur of their expression is, like Faustus', hollow; and an audience must judge how Jonson damns them in the superb poetry that he puts into their mouths. Next to the poetry that they utter, the pious exclamations ("O heaven!") of Celia and Bonario, the only genuinely human characters in the play, *seem* melodramatic and ridiculous; but this discrepancy is part of the meaningful ambivalence that characterizes the language. Volpone's opening speech, for instance, his tribute to gold in Christian images associated with the Deity, is obviously blasphemous; but it is not *simply* blasphemous or *simply* characteristic of his inverted scheme of values. Even as it condemns him an audience is put into the uncomfortable position of asking itself how much it acknowledges the validity of what Volpone is saying:

> *Dear saint,*
> *Riches, the dumb god that giv'st all men tongues,*
> *That canst do naught, and yet makst men do all things;*
> *The price of souls! Even hell, with thee to boot,*
> *Is made worth heaven! Thou art virtue, fame,*
> *Honor, and all things else! Who can get thee,*
> *He shall be noble, valiant, honest, wise—*

The Playwright

BEN(JAMIN) JONSON (1572–1637), the leading man of letters in the early seventeenth century, was born probably in Westminster, the posthumous son of a Scottish minister, and was educated in the classics by William Camden at Westminster School. Poverty forced him to follow for a time the trade of his stepfather, a bricklayer; but around 1592 he volunteered as a soldier in the Low Countries, where, he claimed, he killed an enemy in single combat. By 1597 Henslowe was employing him as an actor and playwright for the Admiral's men—an association that ended abruptly when Jonson killed a fellow actor in a duel. Only recitation of the Latin or "neck-verse" saved him from hanging, but he was branded with an "H" (for "Homicide") on his thumb and sent to prison, where he became a Roman Catholic (to which faith he adhered for the next twelve years). He also suffered imprisonment in 1597 for his share in Nashe's now lost satirical play, *Isle of Dogs,* as he was to again in 1605 for his share in the satire of the Scots in *Eastward Hoe!* Although his main association as a playwright was to be with the King's men, he wrote for both public and private theaters after 1598; and with the production of *The Masque of Blackness* in 1605 he began a long association with the court as a writer of masques. In 1613 he was on the Continent as tutor to the son of Sir Walter Raleigh. In 1616 he oversaw the publication in a folio edition of seven of his comedies, two tragedies, masques and entertainments prepared for the king, epigrams, and occasional verse; and in the same year King James, by conferring a lifetime pension upon him, in effect created him Poet Laureate. To lose weight Jonson went on a walking trip to Scotland in 1619 and was entertained by the poet William Drummond of Hawthornden, who recorded for posterity their conversation. In 1628, upon the death of Middleton, he was appointed chronologer of London; and in the same year he suffered a stroke from which he never fully recovered. A quarrel with Inigo Jones, who designed scenes and costumes for his masques, over the superiority of the poet or designer in the creation of masques lost him court patronage in 1631. Although he never went to a university, both Oxford and Cambridge conferred honorary degrees upon him; and after his death friends honored him with a collection of elegies, *Jonsonus Virbius*. He was buried in Westminster Abbey.

The Play

The present text of *Volpone; or, The Fox* is based on the 1616 folio edition (*The Workes of Benjamin Jonson*) in the Henry E. Huntington Library—which, in turn, is based on a carefully corrected copy of the 1607 quarto—and collated with the Herford and Simpson old-spelling edition. The play is divided into acts and scenes, the latter designated in classical manner by the entrance of a new character onto the stage. The present edition omits commendatory verses and does not preserve Jonson's unusual system of accentuation. The King's men first performed the play at the Globe in 1606 and at Oxford and Cambridge in 1606 or 1607.

SELECTED BIBLIOGRAPHY

Volpone; or, The Fox, ed. A. B. Kernan. The Yale Ben Jonson. New Haven, Conn., and London: Yale University Press, 1962.

Volpone; or, The Fox, ed. J. D. Rea. Yale Studies in English 59. New Haven, Conn.: Yale University Press, 1919.

Works, ed. C. H. Herford, P. and E. M. Simpson. 11 vols. Oxford: The Clarendon Press, 1925–1952.

Barish, J. A., ed. *Ben Jonson: A Collection of Critical Essays.* Englewood Cliffs, N. J.: Prentice-Hall, 1963.

———. "The Double Plot in *Volpone,*" *Modern Philology,* LI (1953), 83–92.

Dessen, A. C. "*Volpone* and the Late Morality Tradition," *Modern Language Quarterly,* XXV (1964), 383–399.

Enck, J. J. *Jonson and the Comic Truth.* Madison: University of Wisconsin Press, 1957.

Goldberg, S. L. "Folly into Crime: the Catastrophe of *Volpone,*" *Modern Language Quarterly,* XX (1959), 233–242.

Hawkins, H. "Folly, Incurable Disease, and *Volpone,*" Studies in English Literature, VIII (1968), 335–348.

Jackson, G. B. *Vision and Judgment in Ben Johnson's Drama.* New Haven, Conn.: Yale University Press, 1968.

Knights, L. C. *Drama and Society in the Age of Jonson.* London: Chatto and Windus, 1937.

Knoll, R. E. *Ben Jonson's Plays: An Introduction.* Lincoln: University of Nebraska Press, 1965.

Levin, H. "Jonson's Metempsychosis," *Philological Quarterly,* XXII (1943), 231–239.

Miller, J. "Volpone: A Study of Dramatic Ambiguity," in *Studies in English Language and Literature,* edd. A. Shalvi and A. A. Mendilow. Jerusalem: The Hebrew University, 1966, pp. 35–95.

Musgrove, S. *Shakespeare and Jonson.* Auckland, New Zealand: University College, 1957.

Partridge, E. B. *The Broken Compass: A Study of the Major Comedies of Ben Jonson.* New York: Columbia University Press, 1958.

Sackton, A. H. *Rhetoric as a Dramatic Language in Ben Jonson.* New York: Columbia University Press, 1948.

Thayer, C. G. *Ben Jonson: Studies in the Plays.* Norman: University of Oklahoma Press, 1963.

TO

THE MOST NOBLE AND MOST EQUAL SISTERS,
THE TWO FAMOUS UNIVERSITIES,
FOR THEIR LOVE AND ACCEPTANCE
SHOWN TO HIS POEM IN THE PRESENTATION,
BEN. JONSON,
THE GRATEFUL ACKNOWLEDGER,
DEDICATES BOTH IT AND HIMSELF.
[*There follows an* Epistle, *if
you dare venture on the length.*]*

Never, most equal sisters, had any man a wit* so
presently* excellent as that it could raise itself; but
there must come both matter, occasion, commenders,
and favorers to it. If this be true, and that the fortune
of all writers doth daily prove it, it behooves the careful to provide well toward these accidents and, having
acquired them, to preserve that part of reputation most
tenderly wherein the benefit* of a friend is also de-
fended. Hence is it that I now render myself grateful and am studious to justify the bounty of your act,   10
to which, though your mere authority were satisfying,
yet, it being an age wherein poetry and the professors*
of it hear so ill on all sides, there will a reason be
looked for in the subject. It is certain, nor can it with
any forehead be opposed, that the too much license
of poetasters in this time hath much deformed their
mistress, that, every day, their manifold and manifest
ignorance doth stick unnatural reproaches upon her;
but for their petulancy it were an act of the greatest
injustice either to let the learned suffer or so divine a   20
skill (which indeed should not be attempted with un-
clean hands) to fall under the least contempt. For, if
men will impartially, and not asquint, look toward the
offices and function of a poet, they will easily conclude
to themselves the impossibility of any man's being the
good poet without first being a good man. He that is said

---

there . . . length: from the 1607 Quarto.   wit: intelligence.
presently: at once, immediately.   benefit: kindness.
professors: practitioners.

to be able to inform* young men to all good disciplines,
inflame grown men to all great virtues, keep old men in
their best and supreme state, or, as they decline to childhood, recover them to their first strength; that comes   30
forth the interpreter and arbiter of nature, a teacher of
things divine no less than human, a master of manners,
and can alone (or with a few) effect the business of
mankind: this, I take him, is no subject for pride and
ignorance to exercise their railing rhetoric upon. But it
will here be hastily answered that the writers of these
days are other things; that not only their manners but
their natures are inverted, and nothing remaining with
them of the dignity of poet but the abused name, which
every scribe usurps; that now, especially in dramatic, or,   40
as they term it, stage poetry, nothing but ribaldry, profa-
nation, blasphemy, all license of offense to God and man
is practiced. I dare not deny a great part of this (and am
sorry I dare not) because in some men's abortive features* (and would they had never boasted the light) it
is overtrue; but that all are embarked in this bold adventure for hell is a most uncharitable thought and,
uttered, a more malicious slander. For my particular, I
can (and from a most clear conscience) affirm that I
have ever trembled to think toward the least profane-   50
ness, have loathed the use of such foul and unwashed
bawdry as is now made the food of the scene.* And,
howsoever I cannot escape, from some, the imputation of
sharpness, but that they will say I have taken a pride,
or lust, to be bitter, and not my youngest infant* but
hath come into the world with all his teeth, I would ask
of these supercilious politics,* what nation, society, or
general order, or state I have provoked? what public
person? whether I have not (in all these) preserved their
dignity, as mine own person, safe? My works are read,   60
allowed* (I speak of those that are entirely mine); look
into them. What broad reproofs have I used? Where
have I been particular? where personal? except to a
mimic, cheater, bawd, or buffoon, creatures for their in-

---

inform: mold, form.   abortive features: defective plays.
scene: stage.   youngest infant: *Sejanus*, 1603.
politics: politicians; intriguers.   allowed: licensed.

solencies worthy to be taxed? Yet to which of these so
pointingly as he might not either ingenuously have confessed or wisely dissembled his disease? But it is not
rumor can make men guilty, much less entitle me to
other men's crimes. I know that nothing can be so inno-
cently writ, or carried, but may be made obnoxious to   70
construction; marry, whilst I bear mine innocence about
me, I fear it not. Application° is now grown a trade with
many, and there are that profess to have a key for the
deciphering of everything; but let wise and noble persons
take heed how they be too credulous, or give leave to
these invading interpreters to be overfamiliar with their
fames, who cunningly, and often, utter their own virulent
malice under other men's simplest meanings. As for those
that will (by faults which charity hath raked up or common honesty concealed) make themselves a name with   80
the multitude, or (to draw their rude and beastly claps)
care not whose living faces they entrench with their
petulant styles, may they do it without a rival, for me!
I choose rather to live graved in obscurity than share
with them in so preposterous a fame. Nor can I blame
the wishes of those severe and wiser patriots, who, pro-
viding° the hurts these licentious spirits may do in a
state, desire rather to see fools, and devils, and those
antique° relics of barbarism retrieved, with all other
ridiculous and exploded follies, than behold the wounds   90
of private men, of princes, and nations. For, as Horace
makes Trebatius speak among these,—*Sibi quisque
timet, qua[m]quam est intactus, et odit.*° And men may
justly impute such rages, if continued, to the writer as
his sports. The increase of which lust in liberty, together
with the present trade of the stage, in all their misc'line°
interludes, what learned or liberal soul doth not already
abhor? where nothing but the filth of the time is uttered,
and that with such impropriety of phrase, such plenty
of solecisms, such dearth of sense, so bold prolepses, so   100
racked metaphors, with brothelry able to violate the ear

---

application: identification of hidden allusions in the plays.
providing: foreseeing.   antique: bizarre, grotesque.
sibi . . . odit: everyone fears for himself, although he is injured,
and is angry. *Sermones,* II. i. 23.
misc'line: mixed, miscellaneous.

of a pagan, and blasphemy to turn the blood of a Christian to water. I cannot but be serious in a cause of this nature, wherein my fame and the reputations of divers honest and learned are the question; when a name° so full of authority, antiquity, and all great mark, is (through their insolence) become the lowest scorn of the age, and those men subject to the petulancy of every vernaculous° orator that were wont to be the care of kings and happiest monarchs. This is it that hath not only rapt me to present indignation, but made me studious heretofore and, by all my actions, to stand off from them: which may most appear in this my latest work (which you, most learned arbitresses, have seen, judged, and, to my crown, approved) wherein I have labored, for their instruction and amendment, to reduce° not only the ancient forms but manners of the scene, the easiness, the propriety, the innocence, and, last, the doctrine, which is the principal end of poesie, to inform men in the best reason of living. And though my catastrophe may, in the strict rigor of comic law, meet with censure, as turning back to my promise, I desire the learned and charitable critic to have so much faith in me to think it was done of industry: for with what ease I could have varied it nearer his scale (but that I fear to boast my own faculty) I could here insert. But my special aim being to put the snaffle in their mouths that cry out, "We never punish vice in our interludes," etc., I took the more liberty, though not without some lines of example, drawn even in the ancients themselves, the goings out° of whose comedies are not always joyful, but ofttimes the bawds, the servants, the rivals, yea, and the masters are mulcted, and fitly, it being the office of a comic poet to imitate justice, and instruct to life, as well as purity of language, or stir up gentle affections. To which I shall take the occasion elsewhere to speak. For the present, most reverenced sisters, as I have cared to be thankful for your affections past, and here made the understanding acquainted with some ground of your favors, let me not despair their continuance to the maturing of some worth-

110

120

130

140

---

name: Horace.   vernaculous: scurrilous.   reduce: revive.
goings out: conclusions, denouements.

ier fruits: wherein, if my muses be true to me, I shall raise the despised head of poetry again and, stripping her out of those rotten and base rags wherewith the times have adulterated her form, restore her to her primitive habit, feature, and majesty, and render her worthy to be embraced and kissed of all the great and master-spirits of our world. As for the vile and slothful, who never affected an act worthy of celebration, or are so inward° with their own vicious natures, as they worthily fear her and think it a high point of policy to keep her in contempt with their declamatory and windy invectives, she shall out of just rage incite her servants (who are *genus irritabile*°) to spout ink in their faces that shall eat, farther than their marrow, into their fames; and not Cinnamus the barber,° with his art, shall be able to take out the brands, but they shall live, and be read, till the wretches die, as things worst deserving of themselves in chief and then of all mankind.

[From my house in the Blackfriars, this 11th day of February, 1607.]°

150

160

---

inward: familiar, intimate.

genus irritabile: the excitable tribe (of poets).

barber: also a surgeon. Martial mentions this particular skill of Cinnamus (*Epigrams,* 6, 64, 26).

1607: 1607 Quarto.

THE PERSONS OF THE PLAY

*

VOLPONE, *a Magnifico.**   PEREGRINE, *a Gent[leman]-*
MOSCA, *his Parasite.*   *traveler.*
VOLTORE, *an Advocate.*   BONARIO, *a young Gentleman.*
CORBACCIO, *an old Gentleman.*   FINE MADAME WOULD-BE, *the*
CORVINO, *a Merchant.*   *Knight's wife.*
AVOCATORI, *four Magistrates.*   CELIA, *the Merchant's wife.*
NOTARIO, *the Register.*   COMMENDATORI, *Officers.*
NANO, *a Dwarf.*   MERCATORI, *three Merchants.*
CASTRONE, *an Eunuch.*   ANDROGYNO, *a Hermaphrodite.*
*Grege.**   SERVITORE, *a Servant.*
[SIR] POLITIC WOULD-BE, *a*   WOMEN.
    Knight.

THE SCENE: *Venice.*

[This comedy was first acted in the year 160[6],
By the King's Majesty's Servants.
The principal comedians were

Richard Burbage   John Heminges
Henry Condell   John Lowin
William Sly   Alexander Cooke

With the allowance of the Master of Revels.]

Magnifico: Venetian nobleman.
Grege: the mob.

The Argument

V OLPONE, childless, rich, feigns sick, despairs,
O ffers his state to hopes of several heirs,
L ies languishing; his Parasite receives
P resents of all, assures, deludes, then weaves
O ther cross plots, which ope' themselves, are told.
N ew tricks for safety are sought; they thrive; when, bold,
E ach tempts th'other again, and all are sold.

Prologue

Now, luck yet send us, and a little wit
 Will serve to make our play hit;
According to the palates of the season,
 Here is rhyme, not empty of reason.
This we were bid to credit from our poet,
 Whose true scope, if you would know it,
In all his poems still° hath been this measure:
 To mix profit with your pleasure;
And not as some (whose throats their envy failing)
 Cry hoarsely, "All he writes is railing,"   10
And, when his plays come forth, think they can flout
  them,
 With saying, "He was a year about them."
To these there needs no lie but this his creature,
 Which was, two months since, no feature;
And, though he dares give them five lives to mend it,
 'Tis known, five weeks fully penned it,
From his own hand, without a coadjutor,
 Novice, journeyman, or tutor.
Yet thus much can I give you as a token
 Of his play's worth: no eggs are broken,   20
Nor quaking custards with fierce teeth affrighted,
 Wherewith your rout are so delighted;
Nor hales he in a gull, old ends reciting,
 To stop gaps in his loose writing,
With such a deal of monstrous and forced action,
 As might make Bedlam° a faction;
Nor made he his play for jests stol'n from each table,

---

still: constantly, always.
Bedlam: Bethlehem Hospital, an asylum for the insane.

But makes jests to fit his fable.
And so presents quick* comedy refined,
    As best critics have designed;   30
The laws of time, place, persons he observeth,
    From no needful rule he swerveth.
All gall and copp'ras* from his ink he draineth,
    Only a little salt remaineth,
Wherewith he'll rub your cheeks till, red with laugh-
    ter,
    They shall look fresh a week after.

---

quick: lively.
copp'ras: vitriol.

Volpone; or, The Fox

ACT I

[I. i]

VOLPONE, MOSCA.

[VOLPONE.] Good morning to the day; and, next, my
  gold!
Open the shrine that I may see my saint.
[MOSCA *opens a curtain, revealing great treasure.*]
Hail the world's soul, and mine! More glad than is
The teeming earth to see the longed-for sun
Peep through the horns of the celestial Ram,
Am I, to view thy splendor darkening his,
That, lying here amongst my other hoards,
Show'st like a flame by night, or like the day
Struck out of chaos, when all darkness fled
Unto the center.° O thou son of Sol,°   10
But brighter than thy father, let me kiss,
With adoration, thee and every relic
Of sacred treasure in this blessed room.
Well did wise poets, by thy glorious name,
Title that age which they would have the best,
Thou being the best of things and far transcending
All style of joy in children, parents, friends,
Or any other waking dream on earth.
Thy looks when they to Venus did ascribe,
They should have giv'n her twenty thousand Cupids;   20

---

center: the earth's center.   Sol: the sun.

Such are thy beauties and our loves! Dear saint,
Riches, the dumb god that giv'st all men tongues,
That canst do naught, and yet mak'st men do all
     things;
The price of souls! Even hell, with thee to boot,
Is made worth heaven! Thou art virtue, fame,
Honor, and all things else! Who can get thee,
He shall be noble, valiant, honest, wise—
MOSCA. And what he will, sir. Riches are in fortune
A greater good than wisdom is in nature.
VOLPONE. True, my belovèd Mosca. Yet, I glory   30
More in the cunning purchase of my wealth
Than in the glad possession since I gain
No common way: I use no trade, no venture;
I wound no earth with ploughshares; fat no beasts
To feed the shambles; have no mills for iron,
Oil, corn, or men, to grind 'hem into poulder;*
I blow no subtle glass; expose no ships
To threat'nings of the furrow-facèd sea;
I turn no monies in the public bank,
Nor usure private—
MOSCA.   No, sir, nor devour   40
Soft prodigals. You shall ha' some will swallow
A melting heir as glibly as your Dutch
Will pills of butter, and ne'er purge for't;
Tear forth the fathers of poor families
Out of their beds and coffin them, alive,
In some kind, clasping prison, where their bones
May be forthcoming when the flesh is rotten.
But your sweet nature doth abhor these courses;
You loathe the widow's or the orphan's tears
Should wash your pavements, or their piteous cries   50
Ring in your roofs, and beat the air for vengeance—
VOLPONE. Right, Mosca, I do loathe it.
MOSCA.   And, besides, sir,
You are not like the thresher that doth stand
With a huge flail, watching a heap of corn,
And, hungry, dares not taste the smallest grain
But feeds on mallows and such bitter herbs;
Nor like the merchant, who hath filled his vaults

_____

poulder: powder.

With Romagnìa and rich Candian wines,
Yet drinks the lees of Lombard's vinegar.
You will not lie in straw whilst moths and worms   60
Feed on your sumptuous hangings and soft beds.
You know the use of riches and dare give, now,
From that bright heap, to me, your poor observer,°
Or to your dwarf, or your hermaphrodite,
Your eunuch, or what other household trifle
Your pleasure allows maint'nance—
VOLPONE.   Hold thee, Mosca,
Take of my hand; thou strik'st on truth in all,
And they are envious term thee parasite.
Call forth my dwarf, my eunuch, and my fool,
And let 'hem make me sport.

                                          [*Exit* MOSCA.]
                              What should I do   70
But cocker up° my genius and live free
To all delights my fortune calls me to?
I have no wife, no parent, child, ally
To give my substance to; but whom I make
Must be my heir: and this makes men observe° me.
This draws new clients, daily, to my house,
Women and men of every sex and age,
That bring me presents, send me plate, coin, jewels,
With hope that when I die (which they expect
Each greedy minute) it shall then return   80
Tenfold upon them; whilst some, covetous
Above the rest, seek to engross me, whole,
And counterwork the one unto the other,
Contend in gifts, as they would seem in love:
All which I suffer, playing with their hopes,
And am content to coin 'hem into profit,
And look upon their kindness, and take more,
And look on that; still bearing them in hand,°
Letting the cherry knock against their lips,
And draw it by their mouths, and back again.—   90
How now!

---

observer: obsequious servant.
cocker up: indulge, pamper.
observe: notice, pander to.
bearing them in hand: deceiving them.

[I. ii]

    NANO, ANDROGYNO, CASTRONE, VOLPONE, MOSCA.

[NANO.] Now, room for fresh gamesters, who do will you
    to know
    They do bring you neither play nor university show;
    And therefore do entreat you that whatsoever they
      rehearse
    May not fare a whit the worse for the false pace* of
      the verse.
    If you wonder at this, you will wonder more, ere we
      pass,
    For know, here
    [*He points to* ANDROGYNO.]
                    is enclosed the soul of Pythagoras,
    That juggler divine, as hereafter shall follow;
    Which soul, fast and loose, sir, came first from Apollo,
    And was breathed into Æthalides, Mercurius his son,
    Where it had the gift to remember all that ever was
      done.   10
    From thence it fled forth and made quick transmigra-
      tion
    To goldy-locked Euphorbus, who was killed, in good
      fashion,
    At the siege of old Troy, by the cuckold of Sparta.
    Hermotimus was next (I find it in my charta)
    To whom it did pass, where no sooner it was missing
    But with one Pyrrhus of Delos it learned to go afishing;
    And thence did it enter into the sophist of Greece.
    From Pythagore, she went into a beautiful piece,
    Hight * Aspasia, the meretrix;* and the next toss of her
    Was, again, of a whore she became a philosopher,   20
    Crates the Cynic (as itself doth relate it).
    Since, kings, knights, and beggars, knaves, lords, and
      fools gat it,
    Besides ox and ass, camel, mule, goat, and brock,*
    In all which it hath spoke, as in the cobbler's cock.*

---

    false pace: uneven or doggeral rhythm.   hight: called, named.
    meretrix: whore, harlot.   brock: badger.
    cobbler's cock: Lucian's dialogue *The Cock* is the source of this
passage.

But I come not here to discourse of that matter,
Or his one, two, or three, or his great oath, "By
   quater!" *
His musics, his trigon,* his golden thigh,
Or his telling how elements shift; but I
Would ask, how of late thou hast suffered translation,
And shifted thy coat in these days of reformation? *   30
ANDROGYNO. Like one of the reformèd, a fool, as you can
   see,
Counting all old doctrine heresy.
NANO. But not on thine own forbid meats hast thou ven-
   tured?
ANDROGYNO. On fish, when first a Carthusian I entered.
NANO. Why, then thy dogmatical silence* hath left thee?
ANDROGYNO. Of that an obstreperous lawyer bereft me.
NANO. O wonderful change! When Sir Lawyer forsook
   thee,
For Pythagore's sake, what body then took thee?
ANDROGYNO. A good, dull moil.*
NANO.   And how! By that
   means
Thou wert brought to allow of the eating of beans?   40
ANDROGYNO. Yes.
NANO.   But from the moil into whom didst
   thou pass?
ANDROGYNO. Into a very strange beast, by some writers
   called an ass;
By others, a precise,* pure, illuminate brother,
Of those devour flesh, and sometimes one another,
And will drop you forth a libel or a sanctified lie
Betwixt every spoonful of a Nativity pie.
NANO. Now quit thee, for heaven, of that profane nation,
And gently report thy next transmigration.
ANDROGYNO. To the same that I am.
NANO.   A creature of de-
   light?

by quater: by the tetractys, a geometrical figure representing the
number 10 as the triangle of 4.   trigon: triangular lyre.
   how . . . reformation: what other transmigrations of the soul
have you experienced since the Protestant Reformation?
   silence: referring to Pythagoras' injunction to his followers of a
five year period of silence.   moil: mule.   precise: puritanical.

And, what is more than a fool, an hermaphrodite?   50
Now, pray thee, sweet soul, in all thy variation,
Which body wouldst thou choose to take up thy
    station?

ANDROGYNO. Troth, this I am in, even here would I tarry.

NANO. 'Cause here the delight of each sex thou canst
    vary?

ANDROGYNO. Alas, those pleasures be stale and forsaken;
No, 'tis your fool wherewith I am so taken,
The only one creature that I can call blessèd;
For all other forms I have proved most distressèd.

NANO. Spoke true, as thou wert in Pythagoras still.
This learned opinion we celebrate will,   60
Fellow eunuch, as behooves us, with all our wit and
    art,
To dignify that whereof ourselves are so great and
    special a part.

VOLPONE. Now, very, very pretty!—Mosca, this
Was thy invention?

MOSCA.   If it please my patron,
Not else.

VOLPONE.   It doth, good Mosca.

MOSCA.   Then it was, sir.

Song

Fools, they are the only nation
Worth men's envy or admiration;
Free from care or sorrow-taking,
Selves and others merry making:
All they speak or do is sterling.   70
Your fool, he is your great man's dearling,°
And your ladies' sport and pleasure;
Tongue and bable° *are his treasure.*
E'en his face begetteth laughter,
And he speaks truth free from slaughter;
He's the grace of every feast
And, sometimes, the chiefest guest;
Hath his trencher and his stool,
When wit waits upon the fool.
    O, who would not be   80
    He, he, he?

(*One knocks without.*)

---

dearling: darling.   bable: babble; bauble; the male organ.

VOLPONE. Who's that? Away! Look, Mosca.

MOSCA.   Fool, begone!

     [*Exeunt* NANO, CASTRONE, *and* ANDROGYNO.]

'Tis Signor Voltore, the advocate;
I know him by his knock.

VOLPONE.   Fetch me my gown,
My furs, and night-caps; say my couch is changing,
And let him entertain himself awhile
Without i'th'gallery.

        [*Exit* MOSCA.]

    Now, now, my clients
Begin their visitation! Vulture, kite,
Raven, and gorcrow,° all my birds of prey,
That think me turning carcass, now they come.   90
I am not for 'hem yet.

     [*Enter* MOSCA.]

       How now? the news?

MOSCA. A piece of plate, sir.

VOLPONE.   Of what bigness?

MOSCA.   Huge,
Massy, and antique, with your name inscribed,
And arms engraven.

VOLPONE.   Good! and not a fox
Stretched on the earth, with fine delusive sleights
Mocking a gaping crow? Ha, Mosca?

MOSCA.   Sharp, sir.

VOLPONE. Give me my furs. Why dost thou laugh so,
 man?

MOSCA. I cannot choose, sir, when I apprehend
What thoughts he has, without, now, as he walks:
That this might be the last gift he should give;
That this would fetch you; if you died today,   100
And gave him all, what he should be tomorrow;
What large return would come of all his ventures;
How he should worshipped be and reverenced;
Ride with his furs and foot-cloths; waited on
By herds of fools and clients; have clear way
Made for his moil, as lettered as himself;
Be called the great and learned advocate:
And then concludes, there's naught impossible.

----

gorcrow: carrion crow.

VOLPONE. Yes, to be learned, Mosca.
MOSCA.   O, no: rich   110
   Implies it. Hood an ass with reverend purple,
   So you can hide his two ambitious° ears,
   And he shall pass for a cathedral doctor.°
VOLPONE. My caps, my caps, good Mosca. Fetch him in.
MOSCA. Stay, sir; your ointment for your eyes.
VOLPONE.   That's
      true;
   Dispatch, dispatch! I long to have possession
   Of my new present.
MOSCA.   That, and thousands more,
   I hope to see you lord of.
VOLPONE.   Thanks, kind Mosca.
MOSCA. And that, when I am lost in blended dust,
   And hundred such as I am, in succession—   120
VOLPONE. Nay, that were too much, Mosca.
MOSCA.   You shall
      live
   Still to delude these harpies.
VOLPONE.   Loving Mosca,
   'Tis well! My pillow now, and let him enter.
                                          [*Exit* MOSCA.]
   Now, my feigned cough, my phthisic, and my gout,
   My apoplexy, palsy, and catarrhs,
   Help, with your forcèd functions, this my posture,
   Wherein, this three year, I have milked their hopes.
   He comes, I hear him—uh! uh! uh! uh! O—

[I. iii]
                   MOSCA, VOLTORE, VOLPONE.
[MOSCA.] You still are what you were, sir. Only you,
   Of all the rest, are he commands his love;
   And you do wisely to preserve it thus,
   With early visitation and kind notes
   Of your good meaning to him, which, I know,
   Cannot but come most grateful.—Patron, sir!
   Here's Signor Voltore is come—
VOLPONE.   What say you?

————————
   ambitious: prominent; flapping.
   cathedral doctor: university professor.

MOSCA. Sir, Signor Voltore is come this morning
  To visit you.
VOLPONE.   I thank him.
MOSCA.   And hath brought
  A piece of antique plate, bought of Saint Mark,*   10
  With which he here presents you.
VOLPONE.   He is welcome.
  Pray him to come more often.
MOSCA.   Yes.
VOLPONE.   What says he?
MOSCA. He thanks you and desires you see him often.
VOLPONE. Mosca!
MOSCA.   My patron?
VOLPONE.   Bring him near; where
  is he?
  I long to feel his hand.
MOSCA.   The plate is here, sir.
VOLTORE. How fare you, sir?
VOLPONE.   I thank you, Signor
  Voltore.
  Where is the plate? Mine eyes are bad.
VOLTORE [*putting the plate into his hands*].   I'm sorry
  To see you still thus weak.
MOSCA [*aside*].   That he is not weaker.
VOLPONE. You are too munificent.
VOLTORE.   No, sir; would to
  heaven
  I could as well give health to you as that plate!   20
VOLPONE. You give, sir, what you can. I thank you. Your
  love
  Hath taste in this and shall not be unanswered.
  I pray you see me often.
VOLTORE.   Yes, I shall, sir.
VOLPONE. Be not far from me.
MOSCA [*to* VOLTORE].   Do you observe that,
  sir?
VOLPONE. Harken unto me still; it will concern you.
MOSCA. You are a happy man, sir; know your good.
VOLPONE. I cannot now last long—
MOSCA [*aside to* VOLTORE].   You are his heir, sir.

Saint Mark: at a goldsmith's shop in Saint Mark's Place.

VOLTORE [*aside*]. Am I?

VOLPONE.   I feel me going—uh! uh! uh! uh!
   I am sailing to my port—uh! uh! uh! uh!
   And I am glad I am so near my haven.   30

MOSCA. Alas, kind gentleman; well, we must all go—

VOLTORE. But, Mosca—

MOSCA.   Age will conquer.

VOLTORE.   Pray thee,
     hear me.
   Am I inscribed his heir for certain?

MOSCA.   Are you?
   I do beseech you, sir, you will vouchsafe
   To write me i' your family. All my hopes
   Depend upon your worship. I am lost
   Except the rising sun do shine on me.

VOLTORE. It shall both shine and warm thee, Mosca.

MOSCA.   Sir,
   I am a man that have not done your love
   All the worst offices: Here I wear your keys,   40
   See all your coffers and your caskets locked,
   Keep the poor inventory of your jewels,
   Your plate, and monies; am your steward, sir,
   Husband your goods here.

VOLTORE.   But am I sole heir?

MOSCA. Without a partner, sir, confirmed this morning;
   The wax is warm yet, and the ink scarce dry
   Upon the parchment.

VOLTORE.   Happy, happy me!
   By what good chance, sweet Mosca?

MOSCA.   Your desert, sir;
   I know no second cause.

VOLTORE.   Thy modesty
   Is loath to know it; well, we shall requite it.   50

MOSCA. He ever liked your course, sir; that first took him.
   I oft have heard him say how he admired
   Men of your large profession, that could speak
   To every cause, and things mere contraries,
   Till they were hoarse again, yet all be law;
   That, with most quick agility, could turn,
   And re-turn; make knots, and undo them;
   Give forkèd counsel; take provoking gold
   On either hand, and put it up. These men,
   He knew, would thrive with their humility.   60

And, for his part, he thought he should be blessed
To have his heir of such a suffering spirit,
So wise, so grave, of so perplexed a tongue,
And loud withal, that would not wag, nor scarce
Lie still, without a fee; when every word
Your worship but lets fall is chequin! °
(*Another knocks.*)
Who's that? One knocks. I would not have you seen,
    sir.
And yet—pretend you came and went in haste;
I'll fashion an excuse. And, gentle sir,
When you do come to swim in golden lard,   70
Up to the arms in honey, that your chin
Is borne up stiff with fatness of the flood,
Think on your vassal; but remember me:
I ha' not been your worst of clients.
VOLTORE.   Mosca—
MOSCA. When will you have your inventory brought, sir?
Or see a copy of the will?—Anon!—
I'll bring 'em to you, sir. Away, be gone;
Put business i' your face.

                                      [*Exit* VOLTORE.]
VOLPONE.   Excellent, Mosca!
Come hither, let me kiss thee.
MOSCA.   Keep you still, sir.
Here is Corbaccio.
VOLPONE.   Set the plate away;   80
The vulture's gone, and the old raven's come.

[I.iv]

                    MOSCA, CORBACCIO, VOLPONE.
[MOSCA.] Betake you to your silence and your sleep.—
Stand there, and multiply.
[*He sets the plate among the treasures.*]
                              —Now shall we see
A wretch who is, indeed, more impotent
Than this can feign to be, yet hopes to hop
Over his grave.
                 [*Enter* CORBACCIO.]
                 Signor Corbaccio!
You're very welcome, sir.

---

chequin: Venetian gold coin.

CORBACCIO.   How does your patron?

MOSCA. Troth, as he did, sir; no amends.

CORBACCIO.   What? Mends
he?

MOSCA. No, sir; he is rather worse.

CORBACCIO.   That's well. Where
is he?

MOSCA. Upon his couch, sir, newly fall'n asleep.

CORBACCIO. Does he sleep well?

MOSCA.   No wink, sir, all this
night,   10
Nor yesterday, but slumbers.

CORBACCIO.   Good! He should take
Some counsel of physicians. I have brought him
An opiate here from mine own doctor—

MOSCA. He will not hear of drugs.

CORBACCIO.   Why? I myself
Stood by while't was made; saw all th'ingredients,
And know it cannot but most gently work.
My life for his, 'tis but to make him sleep.

VOLPONE [*aside*]. Ay, his last sleep if he would take it.

MOSCA.   Sir,
He has no faith in physic.*

CORBACCIO.   Say you? Say you?

MOSCA. He has no faith in physic: he does think   20
Most of your doctors are the greater danger,
And worse disease, t'escape. I often have
Heard him protest that your physician
Should never be his heir.

CORBACCIO.   Not I his heir?

MOSCA. Not your physician, sir.

CORBACCIO.   O, no, no, no,
I do not mean it.

MOSCA.   No, sir, nor their fees
He cannot brook; he says they flay a man
Before they kill him.

CORBACCIO.   Right, I do conceive* you.

MOSCA. And then they do it by experiment,
For which the law not only doth absolve 'hem   30
But gives them great reward; and he is loath
To hire his death so.

---

physic: medicine.   conceive: understand.

CORBACCIO.   It is true, they kill
With as much license as a judge.
MOSCA.   Nay, more;
For he but kills, sir, where the law condemns,
And these can kill him too.
CORBACCIO.   Ay, or me,
Or any man. How does his apoplex?
Is that strong on him still?
MOSCA.   Most violent.
His speech is broken, and his eyes are set,
His face drawn longer than't was wont—
CORBACCIO.   How? how?
Stronger that he was wont?
MOSCA.   No, sir; his face   40
Drawn longer than't was wont.
CORBACCIO.   O, good!
MOSCA.   His mouth
Is ever gaping, and his eyelids hang.
CORBACCIO.   Good.
MOSCA. A freezing numbness stiffens all his joints
And makes the color of his flesh like lead.
CORBACCIO.   'Tis good.
MOSCA. His pulse beats slow and dull.
CORBACCIO.   Good symptoms
still.
MOSCA. And from his brain—
CORBACCIO.   Ha! How? Not from his
brain?
MOSCA. Yes, sir; and from his brain—
CORBACCIO.   I conceive you;
good.
MOSCA. Flows a cold sweat, with a continual rheum,
Forth the resolvèd* corners of his eyes.
CORBACCIO. Is't possible? Yet I am better, ha!   50
How does he with the swimming of his head?
MOSCA. O, sir, 'tis past the scotomy;* he now
Hath lost his feeling and hath left to snort;
You can hardly perceive him that he breathes.
CORBACCIO. Excellent, excellent! Sure I shall outlast him!
This makes me young again, a score of years.
MOSCA. I was a-coming for you, sir.

---

resolvèd: dissolved.   scotomy: dizziness.

CORBACCIO.   Has he made his
　will?
What has he given me?
MOSCA.   No, sir.
CORBACCIO.   Nothing? Ha?
MOSCA. He has not made his will, sir.
CORBACCIO.   O, O, O!
What then did Voltore, the lawyer, here?   60
MOSCA. He smelt a carcass, sir, when he but heard
　My master was about his testament;
　As I did urge him to it for your good—
CORBACCIO. He came unto him, did he? I thought so.
MOSCA. Yes, and presented him this piece of plate.
CORBACCIO. To be his heir?
MOSCA.   I do not know, sir.
CORBACCIO.   True,
　I know it too.
MOSCA [aside].   By your own scale, sir.
CORBACCIO.   Well,
　I shall prevent* him yet. See, Mosca, look;
　Here I have brought a bag of bright chequins
　Will quite weigh down his plate.
MOSCA.   Yea, marry, sir!   70
　This is true physic, this your sacred medicine;
　No talk of opiates to this great elixir!
CORBACCIO. 'Tis *aurum palpabile,** if not *potabile.**
MOSCA. It shall be ministered to him in his bowl?
CORBACCIO. Ay, do, do, do.
MOSCA.   Most blessed cordial!
　This will recover him.
CORBACCIO.   Yes, do, do, do.
MOSCA. I think it were not best, sir.
CORBACCIO.   What?
MOSCA.   To recover him.
CORBACCIO. O, no, no, no; by no means!
MOSCA.   Why, sir, this
　Will work some strange effect if he but feel it.

---

　prevent: anticipate; go before.
　aurum palpabile: palpable gold (can be felt).
　potabile: drinkable (also refers to the gold), supposedly an effi-
cacious medicinal remedy; the philosopher's stone.

CORBACCIO. 'Tis true; therefore forbear. I'll take my
venture;   80
   Give me't again.
MOSCA.   At no hand, pardon me;
   You shall not do yourself that wrong, sir. I
   Will so advise you, you shall have it all.
CORBACCIO. How?
MOSCA.   All, sir; 'tis your right, your own; no
man
   Can claim a part: 'tis yours without a rival,
   Decreed by destiny.
CORBACCIO.   How? How, good Mosca?
MOSCA. I'll tell you, sir. This fit he shall recover—
CORBACCIO. I do conceive you.
MOSCA.   And, on first advantage
   Of his gained sense, will I re-importune him
   Unto the making of his testament   90
   And show him this.
   [*He points to* CORBACCIO's *gift*.]
CORBACCIO.   Good, Good.
MOSCA.   'Tis better yet
   If you will hear, sir.
CORBACCIO.   Yes, with all my heart.
MOSCA. Now would I counsel you, make home with
speed;
   There, frame a will whereto you shall inscribe
   My master your sole heir.
CORBACCIO.   And disinherit
   My son?
MOSCA.   O, sir, the better: for that color°
   Shall make it much more taking.
CORBACCIO.   O, but color?
MOSCA. This will, sir, you shall send it unto me.
   Now, when I come to enforce (as I will do)
   Your cares, your watchings, and your many prayers,   100
   Your more than many gifts, your this day's present,
   And, last, produce your will, where, without thought
   Or least regard unto your proper° issue,
   A son so brave and highly meriting,
   The stream of your diverted love hath thrown you

color: pretense, pretext.   proper: own.

Upon my master, and made him your heir:
He cannot be so stupid, or stone dead,
But out of conscience and mere gratitude—
CORBACCIO. He must pronounce me his?
MOSCA.   'Tis true.
CORBACCIO.   This plot
   Did I think on before.
MOSCA.   I do believe it.   110
CORBACCIO. Do you not believe it?
MOSCA.   Yes, sir.
CORBACCIO.   Mine own
      project.
MOSCA. Which, when he hath done, sir—
CORBACCIO.   Published me
      his heir?
MOSCA. And you so certain to survive him—
CORBACCIO.   Ay.
MOSCA. Being so lusty a man—
CORBACCIO.   'Tis true.
MOSCA.   Yes, sir—
CORBACCIO. I thought on that too. See, how he should be
   The very organ to express my thoughts!
MOSCA. You have not only done yourself a good—
CORBACCIO. But multiplied it on my son?
MOSCA.   'Tis right, sir.
CORBACCIO. Still my invention.
MOSCA.   'Las, sir, heaven knows
   It hath been all my study, all my care   120
   (I e'en grow gray withal), how to work things—
CORBACCIO. I do conceive, sweet Mosca.
MOSCA.   You are he
   For whom I labor here.
CORBACCIO.   Ay, do, do, do.
   I'll straight about it.
MOSCA [aside].   Rook go with you,* raven!
CORBACCIO. I know thee honest.
MOSCA [aside].   You do lie, sir.
CORBACCIO.   And—
MOSCA [aside]. Your knowledge is no better than your
      ears, sir.

_____

rook . . . you: may you be rooked or cheated (pun on "rook"
["gull"], "crow").

CORBACCIO. I do not doubt to be a father to thee.
MOSCA [*aside*]. Nor I to gull my brother of his blessing.
CORBACCIO. I may ha' my youth restored to me; why
    not?
MOSCA [*aside*]. Your worship is a precious ass—
CORBACCIO.   What
    sayst thou?   130
MOSCA. I do desire your worship to make haste, sir.
CORBACCIO. 'Tis done, 'tis done; I go.

                                    [*Exit.*]
VOLPONE [*leaping up from his bed*]. O, I shall burst!
    Let out my sides, let out my sides—
MOSCA.   Contain
    Your flux of laughter, sir; you know this hope
    Is such a bait it covers any hook.
VOLPONE. O, but thy working, and thy placing it!
    I cannot hold; good rascal, let me kiss thee.
    I never knew thee in so rare a humor.
MOSCA. Alas, sir, I but do as I am taught;
    Follow your grave instructions; give 'hem words;   140
    Pour oil into their ears, and send them hence.
VOLPONE. 'Tis true, 'tis true. What a rare punishment
    Is avarice to itself!
MOSCA.   Ay, with our help, sir.
VOLPONE. So many cares, so many maladies,
    So many fears attending on old age;
    Yea, death so often called on as no wish
    Can be more frequent with 'hem; their limbs faint,
    Their senses dull, their seeing, hearing, going,°
    All dead before them; yea, their very teeth,
    Their instruments of eating, failing them.   150
    Yet this is reckoned life! Nay, here was one
    Is now gone home, that wishes to live longer!
    Feels not his gout, nor palsy; feigns himself
    Younger by scores of years, flatters his age
    With confident belying it; hopes he may
    With charms, like Aeson,° have his youth restored;
    And with these thoughts so battens as if fate
    Would be as easily cheated on as he,
    And all turns air!

---

going: faculty of walking.
Aeson: rejuvenated by the magic of Medea, his son Jason's wife

(Another knocks.)
                                    Who's that, there, now? A third?
MOSCA. Close to your couch again; I hear his voice.   160
 It is Corvino, our spruce merchant.
VOLPONE [*lying down again*].   Dead!
MOSCA. Another bout,° sir, with your eyes.—Who's
 there?

[I.v]

     MOSCA, CORVINO, VOLPONE.

[MOSCA.] Signor Corvino! Come most wished for! O,
 How happy were you, if you knew it, now!
CORVINO. Why? What? Wherein?
MOSCA.   The tardy hour is
 come, sir.
CORVINO. He is not dead?
MOSCA.   Not dead, sir, but as good;
 He knows no man.
CORVINO.   How shall I do then?
MOSCA.   Why, sir?
CORVINO. I have brought him here a pearl.
MOSCA.   Perhaps
 he has
 So much remembrance left as to know you, sir;
 He still° calls on you; nothing but your name
 Is in his mouth. Is your pearl orient,° sir?
CORVINO. Venice was never owner of the like.   10
VOLPONE. Signor Corvino!
MOSCA.   Hark!
VOLPONE.   Signor Corvino!
MOSCA. He calls you; step and give it him. He's here,
 sir,
 And he has brought you a rich pearl.
CORVINO.   How do you, sir?
 Tell him it doubles the twelfth caract.
MOSCA.   Sir,
 He cannot understand; his hearing's gone,
 And yet it comforts him to see you—
CORVINO.   Say

---

bout: application of eye ointment used as a disguise.
still: continually. orient: lustrous.

I have a diamond for him, too.

MOSCA.   Best show't, sir;
Put it into his hand; 'tis only there
He apprehends—he has his feeling yet.
See how he grasps it!

CORVINO.   'Las, good gentleman.   20
How pitiful the sight is!

MOSCA.   Tut, forget, sir.
The weeping of an heir should still be laughter
Under a visor.

CORVINO.   Why, am I his heir?

MOSCA. Sir, I am sworn, I may not show the will
Till he be dead. But here has been Corbaccio,
Here has been Voltore, here were others too,
I cannot number 'hem, they were so many,
All gaping here for legacies; but I,
Taking the vantage of his naming you
("Signor Corvino, Signor Corvino!"), took   30
Paper, and pen, and ink, and there I asked him
Whom he would have his heir? "Corvino." Who
Should be executor? "Corvino." And
To any question he was silent to,
I still interpreted the nods he made,
Through weakness, for consent; and sent home
     th'others,
Nothing bequeathed them but to cry and curse.

CORVINO. O, my dear Mosca!
     (*They embrace.*)

                              Does he not perceive us?

MOSCA. No more than a blind harper. He knows no man,
No face of friend, nor name of any servant,   40
Who't was that fed him last, or gave him drink;
Not those he hath begotten, or brought up,
Can he remember.

CORVINO.   Has he children?

MOSCA.   Bastards,
Some dozen, or more, that he begot on beggars,
Gypsies, and Jews, and blackmoors when he was
     drunk.
Knew you not that, sir? 'Tis the common fable.
The dwarf, the fool, the eunuch are all his;
He's the true father of his family,

In all save me, but he has given 'hem nothing.

CORVINO. That's well, that's well! Art sure he does not
    hear us?   50

MOSCA. Sure, sir? Why, look you, credit your own sense.
    [*He shouts in* VOLPONE'S *ear.*]
    The pox approach and add to your diseases
    If it would send you hence the sooner, sir;
    For your incontinence, it hath deserved it
    Throughly° and throughly, and the plague to boot!—
    You may come near, sir.—Would you would once close
    Those filthy eyes of yours that flow with slime
    Like two frog-pits, and those same hanging cheeks,
    Covered with hide instead of skin—Nay, help, sir!—
    That look like frozen dish-clouts set on end!   60

CORVINO. Or like an old smoked wall, on which the rain
    Ran down in streaks!

MOSCA.   Excellent, sir, speak out;
    You may be louder yet: a culverin°
    Dischargèd in his ear would hardly bore it.

CORVINO. His nose is like a common sewer, still running.

MOSCA. 'Tis good! And what his mouth?

CORVINO.   A very draught.

MOSCA. O, stop it up—

CORVINO.   By no means.

MOSCA.   Pray you, let
    me.
    Faith, I could stifle him rarely with a pillow,
    As well as any woman that should keep him.

CORVINO. Do as you will, but I'll be gone.

MOSCA.   Be so;   70
    It is your presence makes him last so long.

CORVINO. I pray you, use no violence.

MOSCA.   No, sir? Why?
    Why should you be thus scrupulous, pray you, sir?

CORVINO. Nay, at your discretion.

MOSCA.   Well, good sir, be
    gone.

CORVINO. I will not trouble him now to take my pearl?

MOSCA. Puh! nor your diamond. What a needless care
    Is this afflicts you! Is not all here yours?

---

    throughly: thoroughly.   culverin: small cannon.

Am not I here whom you have made? Your creature?
That owe my being to you?

CORVINO.   Grateful Mosca!
Thou are my friend, my fellow, my companion,   80
My partner, and shalt share in all my fortunes.

MOSCA. Excepting one.

CORVINO.   What's that?

MOSCA.   Your gallant
wife, sir.

                                 [*Exit* CORVINO.]

Now is he gone; we had no other means
To shoot him hence but this.

VOLPONE.   My divine Mosca!
Thou hast today outgone thyself.
(*Another knocks.*)

                         —Who's there?
I will be troubled with no more. Prepare
Me music, dances, banquets, all delights;
The Turk is not more sensual in his pleasures
Than will Volpone.

                                 [*Exit* MOSCA.]

            Let me see—a pearl!
A diamond! plate! chequins! Good morning's purchase.   90
Why, this is better than rob churches, yet,
Or fat, by eating once a month a man.—

                [*Enter* MOSCA.]

Who is't?

MOSCA.   The beauteous Lady Would-be, sir,
Wife to the English knight, Sir Politic Would-be—
This is the style, sir, is directed me—
Hath sent to know how you have slept tonight
And if you would be visited.

VOLPONE.   Not now.
Some three hours hence—

MOSCA.   I told the squire* so much.

VOLPONE. When I am high with mirth and wine, then,
then.

'Fore heaven, I wonder at the desperate valor   100
Of the bold English, that they dare let loose
Their wives to all encounters!

---

squire: messenger.

MOSCA.   Sir, this knight
  Had not his name for nothing: he is politic,
  And knows, howe'er his wife affect strange airs,
  She hath not yet the face to be dishonest.*
  But had she Signor Corvino's wife's face—
VOLPONE. Has she so rare a face?
MOSCA.   O, sir, the wonder,
  The blazing star of Italy, a wench
  O' the first year! A beauty ripe as harvest!
  Whose skin is whiter than a swan, all over!   110
  Than silver, snow, or lilies! A soft lip,
  Would tempt you to eternity of kissing!
  And flesh that melteth in the touch to blood!
  Bright as your gold! And lovely as your gold!
VOLPONE. Why had not I known this before?
MOSCA.   Alas, sir,
  Myself but yesterday discovered it.
VOLPONE. How might I see her?
MOSCA.   O, not possible;
  She's kept as warily as is your gold;
  Never does come abroad, never takes air
  But at a windore.* All her looks are sweet   120
  As the first grapes or cherries and are watched
  As near as they are.
VOLPONE.   I must see her—
MOSCA.   Sir,
  There is a guard, of ten spies thick, upon her;
  All his whole household; each of which is set
  Upon his fellow, and have all their charge,
  When he goes out, when he comes in, examined.
VOLPONE. I will go see her, though but at her windore.
MOSCA. In some disguise then.
VOLPONE.   That is true. I must
  Maintain mine own shape still the same: we'll think.
                                                              [Exeunt.]

---

  dishonest: unchaste.
  windore: window.

ACT II

[II.i]

[SIR] POLITIC WOULD-BE, PEREGRINE.

[SIR POLITIC.] Sir, to a wise man, all the world's his soil.
  It is not Italy, nor France, nor Europe
  That must bound me if my fates call me forth.
  Yet, I protest, it is no salt° desire
  Of seeing countries, shifting a religion,
  Nor any disaffection to the state
  Where I was bred (and unto which I owe
  My dearest plots) hath brought me out; much less
  That idle, antique, stale, gray-headed project
  Of knowing men's minds and manners, with Ulysses,   10
  But a peculiar humor of my wife's,
  Laid for this height° of Venice, to observe,
  To quote,° to learn the language, and so forth.
  I hope you travel, sir, with license?°
PEREGRINE.   Yes.
SIR POLITIC. I dare the safelier converse. How long, sir,
  Since you left England?
PEREGRINE.   Seven weeks.
SIR POLITIC.   So lately!
  You ha' not been with my lord ambassador?
PEREGRINE. Not yet, sir.
SIR POLITIC.   Pray you, what news, sir, vents
  our climate?
  I heard, last night, a most strange thing reported
  By some of my lord's followers, and I long   20
  To hear how 'twill be seconded.
PEREGRINE.   What was't, sir?
SIR POLITIC. Marry, sir, of a raven, that should build
  In a ship royal of the king's.
PEREGRINE [*aside*].   This fellow,
  Does he gull me, trow?° or is gulled?—Your name,
    sir?
SIR POLITIC. My name is Politic Would-be.

---

salt: inordinate.   height: latitude.
quote: note down; observe.   license: passport.
trow: do you suppose?

PEREGRINE [*aside*].   O, that
    speaks him.—
  A knight, sir?
SIR POLITIC.   A poor knight, sir.
PEREGRINE.   Your lady
  Lies here, in Venice, for intelligence
  Of tires° and fashions and behavior
  Among the courtesans? The fine Lady Would-be?
SIR POLITIC. Yes, sir, the spider and the bee ofttimes   30
  Suck from one flower.
PEREGRINE.   Good Sir Politic!
  I cry you mercy; I have heard much of you.
  'Tis true, sir, of your raven.
SIR POLITIC.   On your knowledge?
PEREGRINE. Yes, and your lion's whelping in the Tower.°
SIR POLITIC. Another whelp!
PEREGRINE.   Another, sir.
SIR POLITIC.   Now,
    heaven!
  What prodigies be these? The fires at Berwick!°
  And the new star!° These things concurring, strange!
  And full of omen! Saw you those meteors?
PEREGRINE. I did, sir.
SIR POLITIC.   Fearful! Pray you, sir, confirm
    me,
  Were there three porpoises seen above the bridge,   40
  As they give out?
PEREGRINE.   Six, and a sturgeon, sir.
SIR POLITIC. I am astonished!
PEREGRINE.   Nay, sir, be not so;
  I'll tell you a greater prodigy than these—
SIR POLITIC. What should these things portend?
PEREGRINE.   The
    very day
  (Let me be sure) that I put forth from London,
  There was a whale discovered in the river,
  As high as Woolwich, that had waited there—

---

  tires: attires, dress.   Tower: of London.
  fires at Berwick: town on the Scottish border where ghostly
armies were reported fighting in 1604.
  new star: discovered by Kepler in 1604.

Few know how many months—for the subversion
Of the Stode fleet.
SIR POLITIC.   Is't possible? Believe it,
'Twas either sent from Spain or the Archduke's!   50
Spinola's* whale, upon my life, my credit!
Will they not leave these projects? Worthy sir,
Some other news.
PEREGRINE.   Faith, Stone the fool is dead;
And they do lack a tavern fool extremely.
SIR POLITIC. Is Mas' Stone dead?
PEREGRINE.   He's dead, sir; why,
    I hope
You thought him not immortal?—[*Aside.*] O, this
    knight,
Were he well known, would be a precious thing
To fit our English stage: He that should write
But such a fellow should be thought to feign
Extremely, if not maliciously.—
SIR POLITIC.   Stone dead!   60
PEREGRINE. Dead. Lord, how deeply, sir, you appre-
    hend it!
He was no kinsman to you?
SIR POLITIC.   That I know of.
Well, that same fellow was an unknown fool.
PEREGRINE. And yet you knew him, it seems?
SIR POLITIC.   I did so.
    Sir,
I knew him one of the most dangerous heads
Living within the state, and so I held him.
PEREGRINE. Indeed, sir?
SIR POLITIC.   While he lived, in action.
He has received weekly intelligence,*
Upon my knowledge, out of the Low Countries,
For all parts of the world, in cabbages;   70
And those dispensed, again, t'ambassadors,
In oranges, musk-melons, apricots,
Lemons, pome-citrons, and suchlike; sometimes
In Colchester oysters, and your Selsey cockles.
PEREGRINE. You make me wonder.

Spinola: Spanish general in the Netherlands.
intelligence: information from spies; communication.

SIR POLITIC.   Sir, upon my
    knowledge.
    Nay, I have observed him at your public ordinary°
    Take his advertisement° from a traveler
    (A concealed statesman) in a trencher of meat;
    And, instantly, before the meal was done,
    Convey an answer in a toothpick.
PEREGRINE.   Strange!   80
    How could this be, sir?
SIR POLITIC.   Why, the meat was cut
    So like his character,° and so laid as he
    Must easily read the cipher.
PEREGRINE.   I have heard
    He could not read, sir.
SIR POLITIC.   So 'twas given out,
    In polity, by those that did employ him;
    But he could read and had your languages,
    And, to't, as sound a noddle—
PEREGRINE.   I have heard, sir,
    That your baboons were spies and that they were
    A kind of subtle nation near to China.
SIR POLITIC. Ay, ay, your Mamuluchi.° Faith, they had   90
    Their hand in a French plot, or two; but they
    Were extremely given to women as
    They made discovery of all; yet I
    Had my advices here, on Wednesday last,
    From one of their own coat, they were returned,
    Made their relations° (as the fashion is)
    And now stand fair for fresh employment.
PEREGRINE [aside].   Heart!
    This Sir Pol will be ignorant of nothing.—
    It seems, sir, you know all.
SIR POLITIC.   Not all, sir. But
    I have some general notions; I do love   100
    To note and to observe: though I live out,
    Free from the active torrent, yet I'ld mark

---

    ordinary: tavern, restaurant.   advertisement: information.
    character: handwriting (accent on second syllable).
    Mamuluchi: soldiers recruited from slaves who converted to
Islamism.   relations: reports.

    The currents and the passages of things
    For mine own private use and know the ebbs
    And flows of state.
PEREGRINE.   Believe it, sir, I hold
    Myself in no small tie° unto my fortunes
    For casting me thus luckily upon you,
    Whose knowledge, if your bounty equal it,
    May do me great assistance in instruction
    For my behavior and my bearing, which   110
    Is yet so rude and raw—
SIR POLITIC.   Why? Came you forth
    Empty of rules for travel?
PEREGRINE.   Faith, I had
    Some common ones, from out that vulgar° grammar,
    Which he that cried Italian taught me.
SIR POLITIC. Why, this it is that spoils all our brave
      bloods,
    Trusting our hopeful gentry unto pedants,
    Fellows of outside and mere bark. You seem
    To be a gentleman, of ingenuous° race—
    I not profess it, but my fate hath been
    To be where I have been consulted with,   120
    In this high kind, touching some great men's sons,
    Persons of blood and honor—
PEREGRINE.   Who be these, sir?

[II. ii]
      MOSCA, [SIR] POLITIC, PEREGRINE, NANO, *Grege*.
      [MOSCA *and* NANO *start to erect a platform*.]
[MOSCA.] Under that windore, there't must be. The
    same.
SIR POLITIC. Fellows to mount a bank! Did your instruc-
    tor
    In the dear tongues never discourse to you
    Of the Italian mountebanks?
PEREGRINE.   Yes, sir.
SIR POLITIC.   Why,
    Here shall you see one.

---

    tie: obligation.   vulgar: common.
    ingenuous: ingenious (with pun?).

PEREGRINE.   They are quacksalvers,
   Fellows that live by venting° oils and drugs.
SIR POLITIC. Was that the character he gave you of
   them?
PEREGRINE. As I remember.
SIR POLITIC.   Pity his ignorance.
   They are the only knowing men of Europe!
   Great general scholars, excellent physicians,   10
   Most admired statesmen, professed favorites
   And cabinet counselors to the greatest princes!
   The only languaged men of all the world!
PEREGRINE. And I have heard they are the most lewd°
   impostors,
   Made all of terms and shreds; no less beliers
   Of great men's favors than their own vile med'cines;
   Which they will utter° upon monstrous oaths,
   Selling that drug for twopence, ere they part,
   Which they have valued at twelve crowns before.
SIR POLITIC. Sir, calumnies are answered best with si-
   lence.   20
   Yourself shall judge.—Who is it mounts, my friends?
MOSCA. Scoto of Mantua,° sir.
SIR POLITIC.   Is't he? Nay, then,
   I'll proudly promise, sir, you shall behold
   Another man than has been phant'sied to you.
   I wonder, yet, that he should mount his bank
   Here, in this nook, that has been wont t'appear
   In face of the Piazza!—Here he comes.
   [*Enter* VOLPONE, *disguised as a mountebank doctor.*]
VOLPONE. Mount, zany.°
GREGE. Follow, follow, follow, follow, follow!
SIR POLITIC. See how the people follow him! He's a man   30
   May write ten thousand crowns in bank here. Note,
   [VOLPONE *mounts the platform.*]
   Mark but his gesture. I do use to observe
   The state he keeps in getting up!

---

   venting: vending, dispensing, selling.
   lewd: ignorant.   utter: sell, vend.
   Scoto of Mantua: an Italian juggler actually in England at this
time.
   zany: a secondary or servant clown; a stock character in the
Commedia dell' arte.

PEREGRINE.   'Tis worth it, sir.

VOLPONE. Most noble gentlemen and my worthy patrons!
It may seem strange that I, your Scoto Mantuano, who
was ever wont to fix my bank in face of the public
Piazza, near the shelter of the Portico to the Procura-
tia, should now, after eight months' absence from this
illustrious city of Venice, humbly retire myself into an
obscure nook of the Piazza.   40

SIR POLITIC. Did not I now object the same?

PEREGRINE.   Peace,
    sir.

VOLPONE. Let me tell you: I am not, as your Lombard
proverb saith, cold on my feet or content to part with
my commodities at a cheaper rate than I accustomed:
look not for it. Nor that the calumnious reports of that
impudent detractor, and shame to our profession
(Alessandro Buttone, I mean), who gave out, in public, I was condemned *a sforzato*° to the galleys for
poisoning the Cardinal Bembo's——cook, hath at all
attached,° much less dejected me. No, no, worthy gen-   50
tlemen; to tell you true, I cannot endure to see the rabble of these ground *ciarlitani*° that spread their cloaks
on the pavement as if they meant to do feats of activity, and then come in lamely, with their moldy tales
out of Boccacio, like stale Tabarine, the fabulist: some
of them discoursing their travels, and of their tedious
captivity in the Turks' galleys, when, indeed, were the
truth known, they were the Christians' galleys, where
very temperately they eat bread and drunk water as a
wholesome penance, enjoined them by their confessors,   60
for base pilferies.

SIR POLITIC. Note but his bearing and contempt of
these.

VOLPONE. These   turdy-facy-nasty-paty-lousy-fartical
rogues, with one poor groatsworth of unprepared
antimony, finely wrapt up in several *scartoccios*,° are
able, very well, to kill their twenty a week, and play;
yet these meager, starved spirits, who have half

---

a sforzato: to hard labor.   attached: in a legal suit.
ciarlitani: petty impostors or charlatans.
scartoccios: waste folds of paper.

stopped the organs of their minds with earthy oppilations,° want not their favorers among your shriveled
salad-eating artisans, who are overjoyed that they may   70
have their half-pe'rth° of physic; though it purge
'hem into another world, 't makes no matter.

SIR POLITIC. Excellent! Ha' you heard better language,
sir?

VOLPONE. Well, let 'hem go. And, gentlemen, honorable
gentlemen, know, that for this time, our bank, being
thus removed from the clamors of the *canaglia,*°
shall be the scene of pleasure and delight; for I have
nothing to sell, little or nothing to sell.

SIR POLITIC. I told you, sir, his end.

PEREGRINE.   You did so, sir.

VOLPONE. I protest, I and my six servants are not able to   80
make of this precious liquor so fast as it is fetched
away from my lodging by gentlemen of your city,
strangers of the Terrafirma,° worshipful merchants,
ay, and senators too, who, ever since my arrival, have
detained me to their uses by their splendidous liberali-
ties. And worthily; for what avails your rich man to
have his magazines stuffed with *moscadelli,*° or of the
purest grape, when his physicians prescribe him, on
pain of death, to drink nothing but water cocted°
with aniseeds? O health! health! the blessing of the   90
rich! the riches of the poor! Who can buy thee at too
dear a rate since there is no enjoying this world without thee? Be not then so sparing of your purses, honorable gentlemen, as to abridge the natural course of
life—

PEREGRINE. You see his end.

SIR POLITIC.   Ay, is't not good?

VOLPONE. For, when a humid flux or catarrh, by the
mutability of air, falls from your head into an arm or
shoulder, or any other part, take you a ducat, or your
chequin of gold, and apply to the place affected: see   100
what good effect it can work. No, no, 'tis this blessed
unguento,° this rare extraction, that hath only power

---

oppilations: obstructions.   half-pe'rth: half-pennyworth.
canaglia: rabble, mob.   terrafirma: mainland.
moscadelli: muscatel wines.   cocted: boiled.
unguento: ointment.

to disperse all malignant humors that proceed either of hot, cold, moist, or windy causes—

PEREGRINE. I would he had put in dry too.

SIR POLITIC. Pray you observe.

VOLPONE. To fortify the most indigest and crude stomach, ay, were it of one that, through extreme weakness, vomited blood, applying only a warm napkin to the place, after the unction and fricace;* for the *vertigine** in the head, putting but a drop into your nostrils, likewise behind the ears; a most sovereign and approved remedy: the *mal-caduco,** cramps, convulsions, paralyses, epilepsies, *tremorcordia,** retired nerves, ill vapors of the spleen, stoppings of the liver, the stone, the strangury, *hernia ventosa, iliaca passio;** stops a *dysenteria* immediately; easeth the torsion of the small guts; and cures *melancholia hypocondriaca*, being taken and applied according to my printed receipt. (*Pointing to his bill and his glass.*) For this is the physician, this the medicine; this counsels, this cures; this gives the direction, this works the effect; and, in sum, both together may be termed an abstract of the theoric and practic in the Æsculapian art. 'Twill cost you eight crowns. And, Zan Fritada, pray thee sing a verse, extempore, in honor of it.

SIR POLITIC. How do you like him, sir?

PEREGRINE. Most strangely, I!

SIR POLITIC. Is not his language rare?

PEREGRINE. But alchemy I never heard the like, or Broughton's books.*

[NANO *sings.*]

Song.

Had old Hippocrates or Galen,
That to their books put med'cines all in,
But known this secret, they had never
(Of which they will be guilty ever)

---

fricace: salve that is rubbed on.   vertigine: vertigo, dizziness.
mal-caduco: epilepsy.   tremorcordia: palpitation of the heart.
iliaca passio: colic.
Broughton's books: Old Testament commentaries by the Puritan minister, Hugh Broughton.

> *Been murderers of so much paper,*
> *Or wasted many a hurtless taper:*
> *No Indian drug had e'er been famèd,*
> *Tobacco, sassafras not namèd;*
> *Ne° yet of guacum one small stick, sir,*
> *Nor Raymund Lully's great elixir.*
> *Ne had been known the Danish Gonswart,*
> *Or Paracelsus, with his long sword.°*   140

PEREGRINE. All this, yet, will not do; eight crowns is
     high.
VOLPONE. No more.—Gentlemen, if I had but time to
     discourse to you the miraculous effects of this my oil,
     surnamed *Oglio del Scoto,* with the countless catalogue
     of those I have cured of th'aforesaid and many more
     diseases; the patents and privileges of all the princes
     and commonwealths of Christendom; or but the de-
     positions of those that appeared on my part before
     the signory of the *Sanita°* and most learned College   150
     of Physicians, where I was authorized, upon notice
     taken of the admirable virtues of my medicaments,
     and mine own excellency in matter of rare and un-
     known secrets, not only to disperse them publicly in
     this famous city but in all the territories that happily
     joy under the government of the most pious and mag-
     nificent states of Italy. But may same other gallant
     fellow say, "O, there be divers that make profession
     to have as good and as experimented receipts as
     yours." Indeed, very many have assayed, like apes,   160
     in imitation of that, which is really and essentially in
     me, to make of this oil; bestowed great cost in fur-
     naces, stills, alembics, continual fires, and preparation
     of the ingredients (as indeed there goes to it six
     hundred several simples, besides some quantity of
     human fat, for the conglutination, which we buy of
     the anatomists), but, when these practitioners come to
     the last decoction, blow, blow, puff, puff, and all flies
     in fumo.° Ha, ha, ha! Poor wretches! I rather pity
     their folly and indiscretion than their loss of time and

---

ne: nor.
Paracelsus . . . sword: in the hilt of which this German physi-
cian-alchemist was supposed to have kept his "essences."
Sanita: medical board of Venice.   *in fumo:* in fumes.

money; for those may be recovered by industry, but to   170
be a fool born is a disease incurable. For myself, I
always from my youth have endeavored to get the
rarest secrets, and book them, either in exchange or
for money; I spared nor cost nor labor where anything
was worthy to be learned. And, gentlemen, honorable
gentlemen, I will undertake, by virtue of chemical art,
out of the honorable hat that covers your head, to
extract the four elements; that is to say, the fire, air,
water, and earth, and return you your felt without
burn or stain. For, whilst others have been at the   180
balloo,° I have been at my book, and am now past
the craggy paths of study and come to the flowery
plains of honor and reputation.

SIR POLITIC. I do assure you, sir, that is his aim.

VOLPONE. But to your price—

PEREGRINE.   And that withal, Sir Pol.

VOLPONE. You all know, honorable gentlemen, I never
valued this *ampulla,* or vial, at less than eight crown;
but for this time I am content to be deprived of it for
six: six crowns is the price, and less in courtesy I know
you cannot offer me; take it or leave it, howsoever,   190
both it and I am at your service. I ask you not as the
value of the thing, for then I should demand of you
a thousand crowns; so the Cardinals Montalto, Fernese,
the great Duke of Tuscany, my gossip,* with divers
other princes have given me; but I despise money.
Only to show my affection to you, honorable gentlemen, and your illustrious state here, I have neglected
the messages of these princes, mine own offices,
framed my journey hither, only to present you with
the fruits of my travels.—Tune your voices once more   200
to the touch of your instruments, and give the honorable assembly some delightful recreation.

PEREGRINE. What monstrous and most painful circum-
      stance
Is here, to get some three or four *gazets!* °
Some threepence i'th' whole, for that 'twill come to.

[NANO *sings.*]

---

balloo: Venetian ball game.   gossip: intimate friend.
gazets: Venetian coins of little worth.

Song.

You that would last long, list to my song;
Make no more coil,° but buy of this oil.
Would you be ever fair? and young?
Stout of teeth? and strong of tongue?
Tart of palate? quick of ear?   210
Sharp of sight? of nostril clear?
Moist of hand? and light of foot?
Or, I will come nearer to't,
Would you live free from all diseases?
Do the act your mistress pleases,
Yet fright all achès from your bones?
Here's a med'cine for the nones.°

VOLPONE. Well, I am in a humor, at this time, to make a
present of the small quantity my coffer contains: to
the rich in courtesy, and to the poor for God's sake.   220
Wherefore, now mark: I asked you six crowns; and
six crowns, at other times, you have paid me; you
shall not give me six crowns, nor five, not four, nor
three, nor two, nor one; nor half a ducat; no, nor a
moccenigo.° Sixpence it will cost you, or six hundred
pound—expect no lower price, for, by the banner of
my front, I will not bate a bagatine;° that I will have,
only, a pledge of your loves, to carry something from
amongst you to show I am not contemned by you.
Therefore, now, toss your handkerchiefs cheerfully,   230
cheerfully; and be advertised that the first heroic
spirit that deigns to grace me with a handkerchief,
I will give it a little remembrance of something beside,
shall please it better than if I had presented it with
a double pistolet.°

PEREGRINE. Will you be that heroic spark, Sir Pol?
(CELIA *at a windo[w] throws down her handkerchief.*)
O, see! the windore has prevented ° you.

VOLPONE. Lady, I kiss your bounty; and for this timely
grace you have done your poor Scoto of Mantua, I   240
will return you, over and above my oil, a secret of that
high and inestimable nature shall make you forever
enamored on that minute wherein your eye first de-

---

coil: disturbance.   nones: occasion.   *moccenigo:* small coin.
bagatine: small Italian coin.   pistolet: Spanish gold coin.
prevented: anticipated.

scended on so mean, yet not altogether to be despised,
an object. Here is a poulder* concealed in this paper,
of which, if I should speak to the worth, nine thousand
volumes were but as one page, that page as a line,
that line as a word: so short is this pilgrimage of man
(which some call life) to the expressing of it. Would
I reflect on the price? Why, the whole world is but as
an empire, that empire as a province, that province as   250
a bank, that bank as a private purse to the purchase
of it. I will only tell you: it is the poulder that made
Venus a goddess (given her by Apollo), that kept her
perpetually young, cleared her wrinkles, firmed her
gums, filled her skin, colored her hair; from her derived to Helen, and at the sack of Troy unfortunately
lost; till now, in this our age, it was as happily recovered, by a studious antiquary, out of some ruins of
Asia, who sent a moiety of it to the court of France
(but much sophisticated*) wherewith the ladies there   260
now color their hair. The rest, at this present, remains
with me; extracted to a quintessence, so that, wherever
it but touches, in youth it perpetually preserves, in
age restores the complexion; seats your teeth, did they
dance like virginal jacks, firm as a wall; makes them
white as ivory, that were black as—

[II. iii]

CORVINO, [SIR] POLITIC, PEREGRINE.
[CORVINO *to* CELIA.] Spite o' the devil, and my shame!
—[*to* VOLPONE.] Come down here;
Come down! No house but mine to make your scene?
Signor Flaminio, will you down, sir? Down?
What, is my wife your Franciscina, sir?
No windores on the whole Piazza here
To make your properties but mine? but mine?
(*He beats away the mountebank, etc.*)
Heart! ere tomorrow I shall be new christened
And called the Pantalone di Besogniosi*
About the town.

poulder: powder.   sophisticated: adulterated.
Pantalone di Besogniosi: literally, "fool of beggars"—a stock
character (the old, cuckolded merchant), along with Flaminio
(head of a noted company of actors) and Franciscina (the light-
of-love serving maid), of the *Commedia dell' arte.*

PEREGRINE.   What should this mean, Sir Pol?
SIR POLITIC. Some trick of state, believe it. I will home.   10
PEREGRINE. It may be some design on you.
SIR POLITIC.   I know not.
  I'll stand upon my guard.
PEREGRINE.   It is your best, sir.
SIR POLITIC. This three weeks, all my advices, all my
      letters,
  They have been intercepted.
PEREGRINE.   Indeed, sir?
  Best have a care.
SIR POLITIC.   Nay, so I will.
PEREGRINE [aside].   This knight,
  I may not lose him for my mirth, till night.

                                                [Exeunt.]

[II. iv]

                    VOLPONE, MOSCA.
[VOLPONE.] O, I am wounded!
MOSCA.   Where, sir?
VOLPONE.   Not with-
      out;
  Those blows were nothing: I could bear them ever.
  But angry Cupid, bolting from her eyes,
  Hath shot himself into me like a flame,
  Where, now, he flings about his burning heat,
  As in a furnace an ambitious* fire
  Whose vent is stopped. The fight is all within me.
  I cannot live except thou help me, Mosca.
  My liver* melts; and I, without the hope
  Of some soft air from her refreshing breath,   10
  Am but a heap of cinders.
MOSCA.   'Las, good sir!
  Would you had never seen her!
VOLPONE.   Nay, would thou
  Hadst never told me of her!
MOSCA.   Sir, 'tis true;
  I do confess I was unfortunate,
  And you unhappy; but I'm bound in conscience,
  No less than duty, to effect my best

  ambitious: swelling.   liver: regarded as the seat of love.

To your release of torment, and I will, sir.
VOLPONE. Dear Mosca, shall I hope?
MOSCA.   Sir, more than
    dear,
I will not bid you despair of aught
Within a human compass.
VOLPONE.   O, there spoke   20
My better angel. Mosca, take my keys,
Gold, plate, and jewels—all's at thy devotion;°
Employ them how thou wilt; nay, coin me too,
So thou in this but crown my longings. Mosca?
MOSCA. Use but your patience.
VOLPONE.   So I have.
MOSCA.   I doubt not
To bring success to your desires.
VOLPONE.   Nay, then,
I not repent me of my late disguise.
MOSCA. If you can horn° him, sir, you need not.
VOLPONE.   True;
Besides, I never meant him for my heir.
Is not the color o' my beard and eyebrows   30
To make me known?
MOSCA.   No jot.
VOLPONE.   I did it well.
MOSCA. So well, would I could follow you in mine
With half the happiness; and, yet, I would
Escape your epilogue.°
VOLPONE.   But were they gulled
With a belief that I was Scoto?
MOSCA.   Sir,
Scoto himself could hardly have distinguished!
I have not time to flatter you now; we'll part,
And, as I prosper, so applaud my art.

                                        [*Exeunt.*]

[II. v]

                CORVINO, CELIA, *Servitore* [*later*].
[CORVINO.] Death of mine honor, with the city's fool?
A juggling, tooth-drawing, prating mountebank?

---

devotion: service, disposal.
horn: give (him) the horns of a cuckold.   epilogue: beating.

And at a public windore? where, whilst he,
With his strained action, and his dole of faces,°
To his drug-lecture draws your itching ears,
A crew of old, unmarried, noted lechers
Stood leering up like satyrs: and you smile
Most graciously, and fan your favors forth,
To give your hot spectators satisfaction!
What, was your mountebank their call? Their whistle?   10
Or were y'enamored on his copper rings?
His saffron jewel, with the toad-stone in't?
Or his embroiderèd suit, with the cope-stitch,
Made of a hearse cloth? Or his old tilt-feather?
Or his starched beard? Well, you shall have him, yes.
He shall come home and minister unto you
The fricace for the mother.° Or, let me see,
I think you had rather mount? Would you not mount?
Why, if you'll mount, you may; yes, truly, you may,
And so you may be seen, down to th' foot.   20
Get you a cittern,° Lady Vanity,°
And be a dealer with the virtuous man;
Make one: I'll but protest myself a cuckold,
And save your dowry. I am a Dutchman, I!
For, if you thought me an Italian,
You would be damned ere you did this, you whore!
Thou'ldst tremble to imagine that the murder
Of father, mother, brother, all thy race,
Should follow as the subject of my justice.
CELIA. Good sir, have patience!
CORVINO.   What couldst thou
    propose°   30
Less to thyself than in this heat of wrath,
And stung with my dishonor, I should strike
This steel unto thee, with as many stabs
As thou wert gazed upon with goatish eyes?
CELIA. Alas, sir, be appeased! I could not think
My being at the windore should more now
Move your impatience than at other times.
CORVINO. No? Not to seek and entertain a parley

---

dole of faces: distribution of grimaces.   mother: hysteria.
cittern: guitar-like instrument; zither.
Lady Vanity: character in the morality plays.   propose: expect.

With a known knave? Before a multitude?
You were an actor with your handkerchief,   40
Which he, most sweetly, kissed in the receipt
And might, no doubt, return it with a letter
And point the place where you might meet: your sis-
    ter's,
Your mother's, or your aunt's might serve these ex-
    cuses?
CELIA. Why, dear sir, when do I make these excuses?
Or ever stir abroad but to the church?
And that so seldom—
CORVINO.   Well, it shall be less;
And thy restraint before was liberty
To what I now decree; and, therefore, mark me.
First, I will have this bawdy light dammed up;   50
And, till't be done, some two or three yards off
I'll chalk a line, o'er which, if thou but chance
To set thy desp'rate foot, more hell, more horror,
More wild, remorseless rage shall seize on thee
Than on a conjuror that had heedless left
His circle's safety ere his devil was laid.*
Then, here's a lock which I will hang upon thee;
And, now I think on't, I will keep thee backwards;*
Thy lodging shall be backwards, thy walks backwards,
Thy prospect—all be backwards, and no pleasure   60
That thou shalt know but backwards. Nay, since you
    force
My honest nature, know it is your own
Being too open makes me use you thus.
Since you will not contain your subtle nostrils
In a sweet room, but they must snuff the air
Of rank and sweaty passengers—
(*Knock within.*)
                        One knocks.
Away, and be not seen, pain of thy life;
Not look toward the windore; if thou dost—
Nay, stay, hear this—let me not prosper, whore,
But I will make thee an anatomy,*   70
Dissect thee mine own self, and read a lecture

---

laid: exorcised.   backwards: in the back of the house.
anatomy: skeleton; cadaver.

Upon thee to the city, and in public.
Away!

[*Exit* CELIA.]

[*Enter* SERVITORE.]

Who's there?

SERVITORE.   'Tis Signor Mosca, sir.

[II. vi]

CORVINO, MOSCA.

[CORVINO.] Let him come in; his master's dead: there's
        yet
Some good to help the bad.—My Mosca, welcome!
I guess your news.

MOSCA.   I fear you cannot, sir.

CORVINO. Is't not his death?

MOSCA.   Rather the contrary.

CORVINO. Not his recovery?

MOSCA.   Yes, sir

CORVINO   I am cursed,
I am bewitched; my crosses meet to vex me
How? how? how? how?

MOSCA.   Why, sir, with Scoto's oil!
Corbaccio and Voltore brought of it
Whilst I was busy in an inner room—

CORVINO. Death! That damned mountebank! But for the
        law   10
Now, I could kill the rascal; 't cannot be
His oil should have that virtue. Ha' not I
Known him a common rogue, come fiddling in
To th' *osterìa,** with a tumbling whore,
And, when he has done all his forced tricks, been glad
Of a poor spoonful of dead wine, with flies in't?
It cannot be. All his ingredients
Are a sheep's gall, a roasted bitch's marrow,
Some few sod * earwigs, pounded caterpillars,
A little capon's grease, and fasting spittle—   20
I know 'hem to a dram.

MOSCA.   I know not, sir;
But some on't, there, they poured into his ears,
Some in his nostrils, and recovered him,
Applying but the fricace.

---

osterìa: inn, hostelry.   sod: sodden, boiled.

CORVINO.   Pox o' that fricace!

MOSCA. And since, to seem the more officious
And flatt'ring of his health, there they have had
(At extreme fees) the College of Physicians
Consulting on him how they might restore him;
Where one would have a cataplasm° of spices,
Another a flayed ape clapped to his breast,   30
A third would ha' it a dog, a fourth an oil
With wild cats' skins. At last, they all resolved
That, to preserve him, was no other means
But some young woman must be straight sought out,
Lusty, and full of juice, to sleep by him;
And to this service, most unhappily
And most unwillingly, am I now employed,
Which here I thought to pre-acquaint you with,
For your advice, since it concerns you most,
Because I would not do that thing might cross   40
Your ends, on whom I have my whole dependence,
    sir.
Yet, if I do it not, they may delate°
My slackness to my patron, work me out
Of his opinion; and there all your hopes,
Ventures, or whatsoever, are all frustrate.
I do but tell you, sir. Besides, they are all
Now striving who shall first present him. Therefore,
I could entreat you briefly, conclude somewhat;
Prevent 'hem if you can.

CORVINO.   Death to my hopes!
This is my villainous fortune! Best to hire   50
Some common courtesan?

MOSCA.   Ay, I thought on that, sir.
But they are all so subtle, full of art,
And age again doting and flexible,
So as—I cannot tell—we may perchance
Light on a quean° may cheat us all.

CORVINO.   'Tis true.

MOSCA. No, no: it must be one that has no tricks, sir,
Some simple thing, a creature made unto it;
Some wench you may command. Ha' you no kins-
    woman?

---

cataplasm: poultice.   delate: denounce; accuse, blame.
quean: harlot, prostitute.

God's so—Think, think, think, think, think, think,
   think, sir.
One o' the doctors offered there his daughter.   60
CORVINO. How!
MOSCA.   Yes, Signor Lupo, the physician.
CORVINO. His daughter!
MOSCA.   And a virgin, sir. Why? Alas,
He knows the state of's body, what it is;
That naught can warm his blood, sir, but a fever,
Nor any incantation raise his spirit;
A long forgetfulness hath seized that part.
Besides, sir, who shall know it? Some one or two—
CORVINO. I pray thee give me leave.
   [*He walks aside.*]
                                   If any man
But I had had this luck—The thing in'tself,
I know, is nothing—Wherefore should not I   70
As well command my blood and my affections
As this dull doctor? In the point of honor,
The cases are all one of wife and daughter.
MOSCA [*aside*]. I hear him coming.
CORVINO.   She shall do't: 'tis
   done.
'Slight,* if this doctor, who is not engaged,
Unless't be for his counsel, which is nothing,
Offer his daughter, what should I that am
So deeply in? I will prevent him. Wretch!
Covetous wretch!—Mosca, I have determined.
MOSCA. How, sir?
CORVINO.   We'll make all sure. The party you
   wot* of   80
Shall be mine own wife, Mosca.
MOSCA.   Sir, the thing,
But that I would not seem to counsel you,
I should have motioned * to you at the first;
And, make your count, you have cut all their throats.
Why, 'tis directly taking a possession!
And, in his next fit, we may let him go.
'Tis but to pull the pillow from his head,

'slight: contraction of "by God's light!"   wot: know.
motioned: proposed.

And he is thr[o]ttled; 't had been done before
But for your scrupulous doubts.
CORVINO.   Ay, a plague on't,
My conscience fools my wit! Well, I'll be brief,   90
And so be thou, lest they should be before us.
Go home, prepare him, tell him with what zeal
And willingness I do it; swear it was
On the first hearing (as thou mayst do, truly)
Mine own free motion.
MOSCA.   Sir, I warrant you,
I'll so possess him with it that the rest
Of his starved clients shall be banished all,
And only you received. But come not, sir,
Until I send, for I have something else
To ripen for your good—you must not know't.   100
CORVINO. But do not you forget to send now.
MOSCA.   Fear not.
                                                        [*Exit.*]

[II.vii]

                        CORVINO, CELIA.
[CORVINO.] Where are you, wife? My Celia? Wife?
                [*Enter* CELIA, *weeping.*]
    What, blubbering?
Come, dry those tears. I think thou thought'st me in
    earnest?
Ha? By this light, I talked so but to try thee.
Methinks the lightness of the occasion
Should ha' confirmed thee. Come, I am not jealous.
CELIA. No?
CORVINO.   Faith, I am not, I, nor never was:
It is a poor, unprofitable humor.
Do not I know if women have a will
They'll do 'gainst all the watches o' the world?
And that the fiercest spies are tamed with gold?   10
Tut, I am confident in thee, thou shalt see't;
And see I'll give thee cause, too, to believe it.
Come, kiss me. Go, and make thee ready straight,
In all thy best attire, thy choicest jewels;
Put 'hem all on, and, with 'hem, thy best looks.
We are invited to a solemn feast

At old Volpone's, where it shall appear
How far I am free from jealousy or fear.

[*Exeunt.*]

ACT III

[III.i]

MOSCA.

[MOSCA.] I fear I shall begin to grow in love
With my dear self and my most prosp'rous parts,
They do so spring and burgeon; I can feel
A whimsy i' my blood. I know not how,
Success hath made me wanton. I could skip
Out of my skin now, like a subtle snake,
I am so limber. O! your parasite
Is a most precious thing, dropped from above,
Not bred 'mongst clods and clo[d]polls here on earth.
I muse the mystery° was not made a science,   10
It is so liberally professed! Almost
All the wise world is little else in nature
But parasites or sub-parasites. And yet
I mean not those that have your bare town-art,
To know who's fit to feed 'hem; have no house,
No family, no care, and therefore mold
Tales for men's ears, to bait that sense; or get
Kitchen-invention° and some stale receipts
To please the belly and the groin; nor those,
With their court-dog-tricks, that can fawn and fleer,   20
Make their revènue out of legs and faces,
Echo my lord, and lick away a moth:
But your fine, elegant rascal, that can rise
And stoop, almost together, like an arrow;
Shoot through the air as nimbly as a star;
Turn short as doth a swallow; and be here,
And there, and here, and yonder, all at once;
Present to any humor, all occasion;
And change a visor swifter than a thought!
This is the creature had the art born with him;   30
Toils not to learn it, but doth practice it

---

mystery: profession.
kitchen-invention: elaborate or ingenious recipes (*receipts*).

Out of most excellent nature: and such sparks
Are the true parsites, others but their zanies.

[III.ii]

MOSCA, BONARIO.

[MOSCA (*aside*).] Who's this? Bonario? Old Corbaccio's
    son?
  The person I was bound to seek.—Fair sir,
  You are happ'ly met.
BONARIO.   That cannot be by thee.
MOSCA. Why, sir?
BONARIO.   Nay, pray thee know thy way and
    leave me:
  I would be loath to interchange discourse
  With such a mate° as thou art.
MOSCA.   Courteous sir,
  Scorn not my poverty.
BONARIO.   Not I, by heaven;
  But thou shalt give me leave to hate thy baseness.
MOSCA. Baseness?
BONARIO.   Ay, answer me, is not thy sloth
  Sufficient argument? Thy flattery?   10
  Thy means of feeding?
MOSCA.   Heaven be good to me!
  These imputations are too common, sir,
  And eas'ly stuck on virtue when she's poor.
  You are unequal ° to me, and howe'er
  Your sentence may be righteous, yet you are not,
  That, ere you know me, thus proceed in censure.
  Saint Mark bear witness 'gainst you, 'tis inhuman!
  [*He weeps.*]
BONARIO [*aside*]. What? Does he weep? The sign is soft
    and good.
  I do repent me that I was so harsh.
MOSCA. 'Tis true that, swayed by strong necessity,   20
  I am enforced to eat my careful ° bread
  With too much obsequy; 'tis true, beside,
  That I am fain to spin mine own poor raiment
  Out of my mere observance,° being not born

---

mate: low fellow.   unequal: unjust, unfair.
careful· acquired with care or difficulty.   observance: service.

To a free fortune; but that I have done
Base offices, in rending friends asunder,
Dividing families, betraying counsels,
Whispering false lies, or mining men with praises,
Trained ° their credulity with perjuries,
Corrupted chastity, or am in love   30
With mine own tender ease, but would not rather
Prove the most rugged and laborious course
That might redeem my present estimation,
Let me here perish, in all hope of goodness.
BONARIO [*aside*]. This cannot be a personated passion!—
I was to blame, so to mistake thy nature;
Pray thee forgive me, and speak out thy business.
MOSCA. Sir, it concerns you; and, though I may seem,
At first, to make a main° offense in manners,
And in my gratitude unto my master,   40
Yet, for the pure love which I bear all right,
And hatred of the wrong, I must reveal it.
This very hour your father is in purpose
To disinherit you—
BONARIO.   How!
MOSCA.   And thrust you forth
As a mere° stranger to his blood; 'tis true, sir.
The work in no way engageth me, but as
I claim an interest in the general state
Of goodness and true virtue, which I hear
T'abound in you, and for which mere respect,°
Without a second aim, sir, I have done it.   50
BONARIO. This tale hath lost thee much of the late trust
Thou hadst with me; it is impossible:
I know not how to lend it any thought
My father should be so unnatural.
MOSCA. It is a confidence that well becomes
Your piety;° and formed, no doubt, it is
From your own simple innocence, which makes
Your wrong more monstrous and abhorred. But, sir,
I now will tell you more. This very minute
It is, or will be doing; and, if you   60
Shall be but pleased to go with me, I'll bring you
(I dare not say where you shall see, but) where

---

trained: tricked, lured.   main: great.   mere: complete.
for . . . respect: for this reason only.   piety: filial love.

Your ear shall be a witness of the deed,
Hear yourself written bastard and professed
The common issue of the earth.

BONARIO.   I'm 'mazed!

MOSCA. Sir, if I do it not, draw your just sword
And score your vengeance on my front and face;
Mark me your villain. You have too much wrong,
And I do suffer for you, sir. My heart
Weeps blood in anguish—

BONARIO.   Lead; I follow thee.   70

                               [*Exeunt.*]

[III.iii]

        VOLPONE, NANO, ANDROGYNO, CASTRONE.

[VOLPONE.] Mosca stays long, methinks. Bring forth your
    sports
And help to make the wretched time more sweet.

NANO. Dwarf, fool, and eunuch, well met here we be.
A question it were now, whether° of us three,
Being all the known delicates of a rich man,
In pleasing him, claim the precedency can?

CASTRONE. I claim for myself.

ANDROGYNO.   And so doth the fool.

NANO. 'Tis foolish indeed; let me set you both to school.
First, for your dwarf, he's little and witty,
And everything, as it is little, is pretty;   10
Else, why do men say to a creature of my shape,
So soon as they see him, "It's a pretty little ape"?
And why a pretty ape but for pleasing imitation
Of greater men's action in a ridiculous fashion.
Beside, this feat° body of mine doth not crave
Half the meat, drink, and cloth one of your bulks will
    have.
Admit your fool's face be the mother of laughter,
Yet, for his brain, it must always come after;
And, though that do feed him, it's a pitiful case
His body is beholding to such a bad face.   20
    (*One knocks.*)

VOLPONE. Who's there? My couch! Away! Look, Nano,
    see!

           [*Exeunt* ANDROGYNO *and* CASTRONE.]

---

whether: which.   feat: neatly formed, delicate.

Give me my caps first—go, inquire.

[Exit NANO.]

Now Cupid

Send it be Mosca, and with fair return.

NANO [within]. It is the beauteous Madam—

VOLPONE.   Would-
    be—is it?

NANO. The same.

VOLPONE.   Now, torment on me! Squire her in,
    For she will enter or dwell here forever.
    Nay, quickly, that my fit were past.
    [He lies down on his couch.]

I fear

    A second hell too, that my loathing this
    Will quite expel my appetite to the other.
    Would she were taking, now, her tedious leave.   30
    Lord, how it threats me what I am to suffer!

[III.iv]

    LADY [WOULD-BE], VOLPONE, NANO, Women 2 [later].

[LADY WOULD-BE to NANO.] I thank you, good sir. Pray
    you signify
    Unto your patron I am here.—This band
    Shows not my neck enough.—I trouble you, sir;
    Let me request you bid one of my women
    Come hither to me. In good faith, I am dressed
    Most favorably today! It is no matter;
    'Tis well enough.
            [Enter 1 WAITING-WOMAN.]

Look, see these petulant things!

    How they have done this!

VOLPONE [aside].   I do feel the fever
    Ent'ring in at mine ears. O, for a charm
    To fright it hence!

LADY WOULD-BE.   Come nearer. Is this curl   10
    In his right place? Or this? Why is this higher
    Than all the rest? You ha' not washed your eyes yet?
    Or do they not stand even i' your head?
    Where's your fellow? Call her.

[Exit 1 WOMAN.]

NANO [aside].   Now, Saint Mark
    Deliver us! Anon she'll beat her women

Because her nose is red.

           [Enter 1 and 2 Women.]

LADY WOULD-BE.   I pray you, view

    This tire,° forsooth; are all things apt, or no?

[1] WOMAN. One hair a little, here, sticks out, forsooth.

LADY WOULD-BE. Dost so, forsooth? And where was your

        dear sight

    When it did so, forsooth? What now! Bird-eyed?   20

    And you, too? Pray you both approach and mend it.

    Now, by that light, I muse you're not ashamed!

    I, that have preached these things, so oft, unto you,

    Read you the principles, argued all the grounds,

    Disputed every fitness, every grace,

    Called you to counsel of so frequent dressings—

NANO [*aside*]. More carefully than of your fame or honor.

LADY WOULD-BE. Made you acquainted what an ample

        dowry

    The knowledge of these things would be unto you,

    Able, alone, to get you noble husbands   30

    At your return; and you, thus, to neglect it!

    Besides, you seeing what a curious° nation

    Th'Italians are, what will they say of me?

    "The English lady cannot dress herself."

    Here's a fine imputation to our country!

    Well, go your ways, and stay i' the next room.

    This fucus° was too coarse, too; it's no matter.—

    Good sir, you'll give 'hem entertainment?

           [Exeunt NANO *and Waiting-Women.]*

VOLPONE [*aside*]. The storm comes toward me.

LADY WOULD-BE.   How

    does my Volp?

VOLPONE. Troubled with noise, I cannot sleep; I dreamt   40

    That a strange fury entered now my house,

    And, with the dreadful tempest of her breath,

    Did cleave my roof asunder.

LADY WOULD-BE.   Believe me, and I

    Had the most fearful dream, could I remember't—

VOLPONE [*aside*]. Out on my fate! I ha' giv'n her the

        occasion

------

    tire: headdress.   curious: fastidious.

    fucus: cosmetic; rouge.

How to torment me: she will tell me hers.

LADY WOULD-BE. Methought the golden mediocrity,
    Polite and delicate—

VOLPONE.   O, if you do love me,
    No more; I sweat, and suffer, at the mention
    Of any dream; feel how I tremble yet.   50

LADY WOULD-BE. Alas, good soul! The passion of the
    heart! *
    Seed-pearl were good now, boiled with syrup of ap-
    ples,
    Tincture of gold, and coral, citron-pills,
    Your elecampane root, myrobalanes—

VOLPONE. Ay me, I have ta'en a grasshopper by the
    wing!

LADY WOULD-BE. Burnt silk and amber. You have mus-
    cadel
    Good i' the house—

VOLPONE.   You will not drink and part?

LADY WOULD-BE. No, fear not that. I doubt * we shall
    not get
    Some English saffron (half a dram would serve),
    Your sixteen cloves, a little musk, dried mints,   60
    Burgloss, and barley-meal—

VOLPONE [aside].   She's in again!
    Before I feigned diseases; now I have one.

LADY WOULD-BE. And these applied with a right scarlet
    cloth.

VOLPONE [aside]. Another flood of words! A very torrent!

LADY WOULD-BE. Shall I, sir, make you a poultice?

VOLPONE.   No,
    no, no;
    I'm very well; you need prescribe no more.

LADY WOULD-BE. I have, a little, studied physic; but
    now
    I'm all for music, save i' the forenoons
    An hour or two for painting. I would have
    A lady, indeed, t'have all—letters and arts,   70
    Be able to discourse, to write, to paint,
    But principal, as Plato holds, your music
    (And so does wise Pythagoras, I take it)

---

passion of the heart: heartburn.   doubt: fear.

Is your true rapture when there is concent *
In face, in voice, and clothes, and is, indeed,
Our sex's chiefest ornament.
VOLPONE.   The poet *
As old in time as Plato, and as knowing,
Says that your highest female grace is silence.
LADY WOULD-BE. Which o' your poets? Petrarch? or
    Tasso? or Dante?
    Guarini? Ariosto? Aretine?   80
    Cieco di Hadria? I have read them all.
VOLPONE [*aside*]. Is everything a cause to my destruc-
    tion?
LADY WOULD-BE. I think I ha' two or three of 'hem
    about me.
VOLPONE [*aside*]. The sun, the sea, will sooner both
    stand still
    Than her eternal tongue! Nothing can 'scape it.
LADY WOULD-BE. Here's *Pastor Fido*—
VOLPONE [*aside*].   Profess obsti-
    nate silence;
    That's now my safest.
LADY WOULD-BE.   All our English writers,
    I mean such as are happy in th'Italian,
    Will deign to steal out of this author, mainly,
    Almost as much as from Montagniè: *   90
    He has so modern and facile a vein,
    Fitting the time, and catching the court-ear.
    Your Petrarch is more passionate, yet he,
    In days of sonneting, trusted 'hem with much.
    Dante is hard, and few can understand him.
    But, for a desperate wit, there's Aretine!
    Only his pictures are a little obscene—
    You mark me not?
VOLPONE.   Alas, my mind's perturbed.
LADY WOULD-BE. Why, in such cases, we must cure
    ourselves,
    Make use of our philosophy—

---

concent: harmony.   poet: Sophocles (*Ajax*, 293).
Pastor Fido: Guarini's pastoral play *The Faithful Shepherd.*
Montagniè: the French essayist Montaigne, pronounced as **four**
syllables.

VOLPONE.   O'y me!   100
LADY WOULD-BE. And, as we find our passions do rebel,
    Encounter 'hem with reason or divert 'hem
    By giving scope unto some other humor
    Of lesser danger: as, in politic bodies,
    There's nothing more doth overwhelm the judgment,
    And clouds the understanding, than too much
    Settling and fixing and, as 'twere, subsiding
    Upon one object. For the incorporating
    Of these same outward things into that part
    Which we call mental leaves some certain feces   110
    That stop the organs and, as Plato says,
    Assassinates our knowledge.
VOLPONE [aside].   Now, the spirit
    Of patience help me!
LADY WOULD-BE.   Come, in faith, I must
    Visit you more now adays and make you well;
    Laugh and be lusty.
VOLPONE [aside].   My good angel save me!
LADY WOULD-BE. There was but one sole man in all the
        world
    With whom I e'er could sympathize; and he
    Would lie you* often, three, four hours together
    To hear me speak, and be sometime so rapt
    As he would answer me quite from the purpose,   120
    Like you; and you are like him, just. I'll discourse
    (And't be but only, sir, to bring you asleep)
    How we did spend our time and loves together,
    For some six years.
VOLPONE.   O, O, O, O, O, O!
LADY WOULD-BE. For we were *coætanei,** and brought
        up—
VOLPONE [aside]. Some power, some fate, some fortune
    rescue me!

[III.v]

            MOSCA, LADY [WOULD-BE], VOLPONE.
[MOSCA.] God save you, madam!
LADY WOULD-BE.   Good sir.
VOLPONE.   Mosca?

———————

lie you: lie.   *coætanei:* of the same age.

Welcome!
Welcome to my redemption.
MOSCA.   Why, sir?
VOLPONE [*aside*].   O,
Rid me of this my torture quickly, there,
My madam with the everlasting voice;
The bells in time of pestilence ne'er made
Like noise or were in that perpetual motion!
The cock-pit comes not near it. All my house,
But now, steamed like a bath with her thick breath.
A lawyer could not have been heard; nor scarce
Another woman, such a hail of words   10
She has let fall. For hell's sake, rid her hence.
MOSCA [*aside*]. Has she presented?
VOLPONE [*aside*].   O, I do not care;
I'll take her absence upon any price,
With any loss.
MOSCA.   Madam—
LADY WOULD-BE.   I ha' brought your patron
A toy, a cap here, of mine own work—
MOSCA.   'Tis well.
I had forgot to tell you I saw your knight
Where you'ld little think it—
LADY WOULD-BE.   Where?
MOSCA.   Marry,
Where yet, if you make haste, you may apprehend
him,
Rowing upon the water in a gondole,
With the most cunning courtesan of Venice.   20
LADY WOULD-BE. Is't true?
MOSCA.   Pursue 'hem, and believe
your eyes.
Leave me to make your gift.

                                   [*Exit* LADY WOULD-BE.]
                                   —I knew 'twould take.
For, lightly,° they that use themselves most license
Are still most jealous.
VOLPONE.   Mosca, hearty thanks
For thy quick fiction and delivery of me.
Now to my hopes, what sayst thou?

---

lightly: generally.

[*Re-enter* LADY WOULD-BE.]

LADY WOULD-BE.   But do you hear,
  sir?
VOLPONE [*aside*]. Again! I fear a paroxysm.
LADY WOULD-BE.   Which way
  Rowed they together?
MOSCA.   Toward the Rialto.
LADY WOULD-BE. I pray you lend me your dwarf.
MOSCA.   I
    pray you take him.
                              [*Exit* LADY WOULD-BE.]
    Your hopes, sir, are like happy blossoms, fair,   30
    And promise timely fruit, if you will stay
    But the maturing; keep you at your couch.
    Corbaccio will arrive straight with the will;
    When he is gone, I'll tell you more.
                                          [*Exit.*]

VOLPONE.   My blood,
    My spirits are returned; I am alive;
    And, like your wanton gamester at primero,
    Whose thought had whispered to him, not go less,
    Methinks I lie and draw—for an encounter.
    [*He draws the curtains across the bed.*]

[III.vi]

                    MOSCA, BONARIO.
[MOSCA.] Sir, here concealed you may hear all. But pray
    you
    Have patience, sir.
    (*One knocks.*)
                        The same's your father
    knocks.
    I am compelled to leave you.
BONARIO.   Do so. Yet
    Cannot my thought imagine this a truth.
    [*He hides himself.*]

[III.vii]

          MOSCA, CORVINO, CELIA, BONARIO, VOLPONE.
[MOSCA.] Death on me! You are come too soon; what
    meant you?
    Did not I say I would send?

CORVINO.   Yes, but I feared
  You might forget it, and then they prevent us.
MOSCA. Prevent!—[*Aside.*] Did e'er man haste so for
    his horns?
  A courtier would not ply it so for a place.—
  Well, now there's no helping it, stay here;
  I'll presently* return.

                                                    [*Exit.*]

CORVINO.   Where are you, Celia?
  You know not wherefore I have brought you hither?
CELIA. Not well, except you told me.
CORVINO.   Now I will.
  Hark hither.
  [*They walk apart.*]
                    [*Re-enter* MOSCA.]
MOSCA (*to* BONARIO). Sir, your father hath sent word,   10
  It will be half an hour ere he come;
  And, therefore, if you please to walk the while
  Into that gallery—at the upper end
  There are some books to entertain the time;
  And I'll take care no man shall come unto you, sir.
BONARIO. Yes, I will stay there.—[*Aside.*] I do doubt
    this fellow.

                                                    [*Exit.*]

MOSCA. There, he is far enough; he can hear nothing;
  And, for his father, I can keep him off.
  [*He draws open the curtains of* VOLPONE'S *bed.*]
CORVINO. Nay, now, there is no starting back, and there-
    fore
  Resolve upon it: I have so decreed.   20
  It must be done. Nor would I move't afore,
  Because I would avoid all shifts and tricks
  That might deny me.
CELIA.   Sir, let me beseech you,
  Affect not these strange trials; if you doubt
  My chastity, why, lock me up forever;
  Make me the heir of darkness. Let me live
  Where I may please your fears, if not your trust.
CORVINO. Believe it, I have no such humor, I.
  All that I speak I mean; yet I am not mad:

―――――――――

presently: immediately.

Not horn-mad,* see you? Go to, show yourself   30
   Obedient and a wife.

CELIA.   O heaven!

CORVINO.   I say it,
   Do so.

CELIA.   Was this the train?*

CORVINO.   I've told you reasons:
   What the physicians have set down; how much
   It may concern me; what my engagements are;
   My means, and the necessity of those means
   For my recovery; wherefore, if you be
   Loyal and mine, be won, respect my venture.

CELIA. Before your honor?

CORVINO.   Honor! Tut, a breath;
   There's no such thing in nature; a mere term
   Invented to awe fools. What, is my gold   40
   The worse for touching? Clothes for being looked on?
   Why, this's no more. An old, decrepit wretch,
   That has no sense, no sinew; takes his meat
   With others' fingers; only knows to gape
   When you do scald his gums; a voice, a shadow;
   And what can this man hurt you?

CELIA.   Lord! What spirit
   Is this hath entered him?

CORVINO.   And for your fame,
   That's such a jig;* as if I would go tell it,
   Cry it, on the Piazza! Who shall know it
   But he that cannot speak it, and this fellow,   50
   Whose lips are i' my pocket, save yourself—
   If you'll proclaim't, you may—I know no other
   Should come to know it.

CELIA.   Are heaven and saints then
      nothing?
   Will they be blind or stupid?

CORVINO.   How?

CELIA.   Good sir,
   Be jealous still, emulate them, and think
   What hate they burn with toward every sin.

CORVINO. I grant you: if I thought it were a sin,

---

   horn-mad: raving mad or jealous (pun on cuckoldry).
   train: stratagem, trick, plot.   jig: farce.

I would not urge you. Should I offer this
To some young Frenchman, or hot Tuscan blood
That had read Aretine, conned all his prints,   60
Knew every quirk within lust's labyrinth,
And were professed critic in lechery,
And I would look upon him, and applaud him,
This were a sin; but here, 'tis contrary,
A pious work, mere charity, for physic
And honest polity to assure mine own.
CELIA. O heaven! canst thou suffer such a change?
VOLPONE [*aside*]. Thou art mine honor, Mosca, and my
    pride,
My joy, my tickling, my delight! Go, bring 'hem.
MOSCA. Please you draw near, sir.
CORVINO.   Come on, what—   70
    You will not be rebellious? By that light—
MOSCA. Sir, Signor Corvino, here, is come to see you.
VOLPONE. O!
MOSCA.   And hearing of the consultation had,
    So lately, for your health, is come to offer,
    Or rather, sir, to prostitute—
CORVINO.   Thanks, sweet Mosca.
MOSCA. Freely, unasked, or unentreated—
CORVINO.   Well.
MOSCA. As the true, fervent instance of his love,
    His own most fair and proper wife, the beauty
    Only of price in Venice—
CORVINO.   'Tis well urged.
MOSCA. To be your comfortress, and to preserve you.   80
VOLPONE. Alas, I am past already! Pray you, thank him
    For his good care and promptness; but for that,
    'Tis a vain labor e'en to fight 'gainst heaven,
    Applying fire to a stone—uh, uh, uh, uh!—
    Making a dead leaf grow again. I take
    His wishes gently, though; and you may tell him
    What I have done for him. Marry, my state is hopeless!
    Will him to pray for me, and t'use his fortune
    With reverence when he comes to't.
MOSCA.   Do you hear, sir?
    Go to him with your wife.
CORVINO.   Heart of my father!   90
    Wilt thou persist thus? Come, I pray thee, come.

Thou seest 'tis nothing, Celia. By this hand
I shall grow violent. Come; do't, I say.
CELIA. Sir, kill me rather. I will take down poison,
Eat burning coals, do anything—
CORVINO.   Be damned!
Heart! I will drag thee hence home by the hair;
Cry thee a strumpet through the streets; rip up
Thy mouth unto thine ears; and slit thy nose,
Like a raw rotchet!°—Do not tempt me, come.
Yield, I am loath—Death! I will buy some slave,   100
Whom I will kill, and bind thee to him, alive;
And at my windore hang you forth, devising
Some monstrous crime, which I, in capital letters,
Will eat into thy flesh with *aquafortis*°
And burning cor'sives° on this stubborn breast.
Now, by the blood thou hast incensed, I'll do't!
CELIA. Sir, what you please, you may; I am your martyr,
CORVINO. Be not thus obstinate; I ha' not deserved it.
Think who it is entreats you. Pray thee, sweet;
Good faith, thou shalt have jewels, gowns, attires,   110
What thou wilt, think and ask. Do but go kiss him.
Or touch him but. For my sake. At my suit.
This once. No? Not? I shall remember this.
Will you disgrace me thus? D'you thirst my undoing?
MOSCA. Nay, gentle lady, be advised.
CORVINO.   No, no.
She has watched her time. God's precious, this is
    scurvy;
'Tis very scurvy; and you are—
MOSCA.   Nay, good sir.
CORVINO. An errant locust, by heaven, a locust! Whore,
Crocodile, that hast thy tears prepared,
Expecting how thou'lt bid 'hem flow.
MOSCA.   Nay, pray you,
    sir!   120
She will consider.
CELIA.   Would my life would serve
To satisfy.
CORVINO.   'Sdeath! If she would but speak to him,

---

rotchet: red fish.   *aquafortis:* sulphuric acid.
cor'sives: corrosives.

And save my reputation, 'twere somewhat;
But, spitefully, to effect my utter ruin!
MOSCA. Ay, now you have put your fortune in her hands.
    Why, i' faith, it is her modesty, I must quit* her.
    If you were absent, she would be more coming;
    I know it, and dare undertake for her.
    What woman can before her husband? Pray you,
    Let us depart and leave her here.
CORVINO.   Sweet Celia,   130
    Thou mayst redeem all yet; I'll say no more.
    If not, esteem yourself as lost. Nay, stay there.
                   [*Exeunt* CORVINO *and* MOSCA.]
CELIA. O God and his good angels! Whither, whither
    Is shame fled human breasts? that with such ease
    Men dare put off your honors, and their own?
    Is that, which ever was a cause of life,
    Now placed beneath the basest circumstance,
    And modesty an exile made for money?
VOLPONE (*He leaps off from his couch*). Ay, in Corvino,
    and such earth-fed minds,
    That never tasted the true heaven of love.   140
    Assure thee, Celia, he that would sell thee,
    Only for hope of gain, and that uncertain,
    He would have sold his part of Paradise
    For ready money had he met a cope-man.*
    Why art thou 'mazed to see me thus revived?
    Rather applaud thy beauty's miracle;
    'Tis thy great work that hath, not now alone,
    But sundry times, raised me in several shapes,
    And, but this morning, like a mountebank,
    To see thee at thy windore. Ay, before   150
    I would have left my practice* for thy love,
    In varying figures I would have contended
    With the blue Proteus or the hornèd flood.
    Now art thou welcome.
CELIA.   Sir!
VOLPONE.   Nay, fly me not.
    Nor let thy false imagination
    That I was bed-rid make thee think I am so:

---

quit: acquit, excuse.   cope-man: chapman; merchant.
practice: deceit, craft.

Thou shalt not find it. I am, now, as fresh,
As hot, as high, and in as jovial plight
As when (in that so celebrated scene
At recitation of our comedy,   160
For entertainment of the great Valois)
I acted young Antinous and attracted
The eyes and ears of all the ladies present,
T'admire each graceful gesture, note, and footing.

Song.

> Come, my Celia, let us prove,*
> While we can, the sports of love;
> Time will not be ours forever;
> He, at length, our good will sever;
> Spend not then his gifts in vain.
> Suns that set may rise again;   170
> But, if once we lose this light,
> 'Tis with us perpetual night.
> Why should we defer our joys?
> Fame and rumor are but toys.
> Cannot we delude the eyes
> Of a few poor household spies?
> Or his easier ears beguile,
> Thus removèd by our wile?
> 'Tis no sin love's fruits to steal
> But the sweet thefts to reveal: 180
> To be taken, to be seen,
> These have crimes accounted been.

CELIA. Some serene* blast me, or dire lightning strike
    This my offending face!
VOLPONE.   Why droops my Celia?
Thou hast in place of a base husband found
A worthy lover: use thy fortune well,
With secrecy and pleasure. See, behold,
What thou art queen of; not in expectation,
As I feed others, but possessed and crowned.
See, here, a rope of pearl, and each more orient*   190
Than that the brave Egyptian queen* caroused;
Dissolve and drink 'hem. See, a carbuncle
May put out both the eyes of our Saint Mark;

---

prove: test, try.   serene: harmful damp evening air.
orient: precious; pure.   queen: Cleopatra.

A diamond would have bought Lollia Paulina*
When she came in like star-light, hid with jewels
That were the spoils of provinces; take these,
And wear, and lose 'hem; yet remains an earring
To purchase them again and this whole state.
A gem but worth a private patrimony
Is nothing; we will eat such at a meal.   200
The heads of parrots, tongues of nightingales,
The brains of peacocks and of estriches*
Shall be our food; and, could we get the phoenix,
Though nature lost her kind, she were our dish.

CELIA. Good sir, these things might move a mind affected
With such delights; but I, whose innocence
Is all I can think wealthy, or worth th'enjoying,
And which, once lost, I have naught to lose beyond it,
Cannot be taken with these sensual baits.
If you have conscience—

VOLPONE.   'Tis the beggar's virtue;   210
If thou hast wisdom, hear me, Celia.
Thy baths shall be the juice of July-flowers,*
Spirit of roses, and of violets,
The milk of unicorns, and panthers' breath
Gathered in bags and mixed with Cretan wines.
Our drink shall be preparèd gold and amber,
Which we will take until my roof whirl round
With the vertigo; and my dwarf shall dance,
My eunuch sing, my fool make up the antic.*
Whilst we, in changèd shapes, act Ovid's tales,   220
Thou like Europa now, and I like Jove,
Then I like Mars, and thou like Erycine;*
So of the rest till we have quite run through
And wearied all the fables of the gods.
Then will I have thee in more modern forms,
Attirèd like some sprightly dame of France,
Brave Tuscan lady, or proud Spanish beauty;
Sometimes unto the Persian Sophy's wife,
Or the Grand Signor's* mistress; and, for change,

Lollia Paulina: wife of a Roman provincial governor who adorned
herself with the jewels plundered by her husband.
estriches: ostriches.   July-flowers: gillyflowers.
antic: grotesque performance.   Erycine: Venus.
Grand Signor: Sultan of Turkey.

To one of our most artful courtesans,   230
Or some quick° Negro, or cold Russian;
And I will meet thee in as many shapes:
Where we may so transfuse our wand'ring souls
Out at our lips and score up sums of pleasures,
    That the curious shall not know
        How to tell° them as they flow;
  And the envious, when they find
        What their number is, be pined.°

CELIA. If you have ears that will be pierced, or eyes
That can be opened, a heart may be touched,   240
Or any part that yet sounds man about you;
If you have touch of holy saints, or heaven,
Do me the grace to let me 'scape. If not,
Be bountiful and kill me. You do know
I am a creature hither ill betrayed
By one whose shame I would forget it were.
If you will deign me neither of these graces,
Yet feed your wrath, sir, rather than your lust
(It is a vice comes nearer manliness),
And punish that unhappy crime of nature,   250
Which you miscall my beauty: flay my face,
Or poison it with ointments for seducing
Your blood to this rebellion. Rub these hands
With what may cause an eating leprosy,
E'en to my bones and marrow; anything
That may disfavor me, save in my honor,
And I will kneel to you, pray for you, pay down
A thousand hourly vows, sir, for your health,
Report and think you virtuous—
VOLPONE.   Think me cold,
Frozen, and impotent, and so report me?   260
That I had Nestor's hernia° thou wouldst think.
I do degenerate and abuse my nation
To play with opportunity thus long;
I should have done the act and then have parleyed.
Yield, or I'll force thee.
  [*He seizes her.*]
CELIA.   O! just God!

———————

quick: lively.   tell: count.   be pined: be made to pine away.
  Nestor's hernia: the impotence of an old man like Homer's
Nestor.

VOLPONE.   In vain—
BONARIO (*He leaps out from where* MOSCA *had placed
    him*). Forbear, foul ravisher! Libidinous swine!
Free the forced lady, or thou diest, impostor!
But that I am loath to snatch thy punishment
Out of the hand of justice, thou shouldst yet
Be made the timely sacrifice of vengeance   270
Before this altar and this dross, thy idol.—
Lady, let's quit the place; it is the den
Of villainy. Fear naught; you have a guard:
And he, ere long, shall meet his just reward.
                            [*Exeunt* BONARIO *and* CELIA.]
VOLPONE. Fall on me, roof, and bury me in ruin!
Become my grave, that wert my shelter! O!
I am unmasked, unspirited, undone,
Betrayed to beggary, to infamy—

[III.viii]

                        MOSCA, VOLPONE.
[MOSCA.] Where shall I run, most wretched shame of
    men,
    To beat out my unlucky brains?
VOLPONE.   Here, here.
What! Dost thou bleed?
MOSCA.   O, that his well-driven
    sword
    Had been so courteous to have cleft me down
    Unto the navel, ere I lived to see
    My life, my hopes, my spirits, my patron, all
    Thus desperately engagèd° by my error!
VOLPONE. Woe on thy fortune!
MOSCA.   And my follies, sir.
VOLPONE. Th'hast made me miserable.
MOSCA.   And myself, sir.
    Who would have thought he would have hearkened
    so?   10
VOLPONE. What shall we do?
MOSCA.   I know not; if my heart
    Could expiate the mischance, I'ld pluck it out.
    Will you be pleased to hang me? Or cut my throat?

———

engagèd: trapped.

And I'll requite you, sir. Let's die like Romans
Since we have lived like Grecians.
(*They knock without.*)

VOLPONE.   Hark! Who's
    there?
I hear some footing; officers, the *Saffi*,*
Come to apprehend us! I do feel the brand
Hissing already at my forehead; now,
Mine ears are boring.

MOSCA.   To your couch, sir; you
    Make that place good, however. Guilty men   20
    Suspect what they deserve still.—Signor Corbaccio!

[III.ix.]

          CORBACCIO, MOSCA, VOLTORE, VOLPONE.

[CORBACCIO.] Why, how now, Mosca?

MOSCA.   O, undone,
    amazed, sir.
Your son, I know not by what accident,
Acquainted with your purpose to my patron,
Touching your will, and making him your heir,
Entered our house with violence, his sword drawn,
Sought for you, called you wretch, unnatural,
Vowed he would kill you.

CORBACCIO.   Me?

MOSCA.   Yes, and my patron.

CORBACCIO. This act shall disinherit him indeed;
    Here is the will.

MOSCA.   'Tis well, sir.

CORBACCIO.   Right and well.
    Be you as careful° now for me.

                [*Enter* VOLTORE *behind.*]

MOSCA.   My life, sir,   10
    Is not more tendered;* I am only yours.

CORBACCIO. How does he? Will he die shortly, think'st
    thou?

MOSCA.   I fear
He'll outlast May.

CORBACCIO.   Today?

_____

    saffi: bailiffs; Venetian police.   careful: concerned.
    tendered: watched over, attended to.

MOSCA.   No, last out May, sir.

CORBACCIO. Couldst thou not gi'him a dram?

MOSCA.   O, by no
    means, sir.

CORBACCIO. Nay, I'll not bid you.

VOLTORE [*coming forward*].   This is a knave, I see.

MOSCA [*aside*]. How! Signor Voltore! Did he hear me?

VOLTORE.   Parasite!

MOSCA. Who's that?—O, sir, most timely welcome.

VOLTORE.   Scarce
    To the discovery of your tricks, I fear.
    You are his only? And mine, also, are you not?

MOSCA. Who? I, sir?

VOLTORE.   You, sir. What device is this   20
    About a will?

MOSCA.   A plot for you, sir.

VOLTORE.   Come,
    Put not your foists° upon me; I shall scent 'hem.

MOSCA. Did you not hear it?

VOLTORE.   Yes, I hear Corbaccio
    Hath made your patron, there, his heir.

MOSCA.   'Tis true,
    By my device, drawn to it by my plot,
    With hope—

VOLTORE.   Your patron should reciprocate?
    And you have promised?

MOSCA.   For your good I did, sir.
    Nay, more, I told his son, brought, hid him here,
    Where he might hear his father pass the deed;
    Being persuaded to it by this thought, sir: 30
    That the unnaturalness, first, of the act,
    And then his father's oft disclaiming° in him
    (Which I did mean t'help on) would sure enrage him
    To do some violence upon his parent.
    On which the law should take sufficient hold,
    And you be stated in a double hope.
    Truth be my comfort, and my conscience,
    My only aim was to dig you a fortune
    Out of these two old, rotten sepulchres—

VOLTORE. I cry thee mercy, Mosca.

---

foists: tricks, deceits.   disclaiming: denying (kinship).

MOSCA.   Worth your pa-   40
  tience,
  And your great merit, sir. And see the change!
VOLTORE. Why? What success?
MOSCA.   Most hapless! You must
  help, sir.
  Whilst we expected th'old raven, in comes
  Corvino's wife, sent hither by her husband—
VOLTORE. What, with a present?
MOSCA.   No, sir, on visitation
  (I'll tell you how anon), and, staying long,
  The youth he grows impatient, rushes forth,
  Seizeth the lady, wounds me, makes her swear
  (Or he would murder her, that was his vow)
  T'affirm my patron to have done her rape,   50
  Which how unlike it is, you see! And hence,
  With that pretext, he's gone t'accuse his father,
  Defame my patron, defeat you—
VOLTORE.   Where's her hus-
  band?
  Let him be sent for straight.
MOSCA.   Sir, I'll go fetch him.
VOLTORE. Bring him to the _Scrutineo_.°
MOSCA.   Sir, I will.
VOLTORE. This must be stopped.
MOSCA.   O, you do nobly, sir.
  Alas, 'twas labored all, sir, for your good;
  Nor was there want of counsel in the plot:
  But Fortune can, at any time, o'erthrow
  The projects of a hundred learned clerks,° sir.   60
CORBACCIO [_straining to hear_]. What's that?
VOLTORE.   Will't
  please you, sir, to go along?
                              [_Exit with_ CORBACCIO.]
MOSCA. Patron, go in and pray for our success.
VOLPONE. Need makes devotion: heaven your labor
  bless!

  Scrutineo: Senate house.   clerks: scholars.

ACT IV

[IV.i]

[SIR] POLITIC, PEREGRINE.

[SIR POLITIC.] I told you, sir, it° was a plot: you see
    What observation is! You mentioned me
    For some instructions; I will tell you, sir
    (Since we are met here in this height of Venice),
    Some few particulars I have set down
    Only for this meridian, fit to be known
    Of your crude traveler; and they are these.
    I will not touch, sir, at your phrase or clothes,
    For they are old.
PEREGRINE.   Sir, I have better.
SIR POLITIC.   Pardon;
    I meant as they are themes.
PEREGRINE.   O, sir, proceed;   10
    I'll slander you no more of wit, good sir.
SIR POLITIC. First, for your garb,° it must be grave and
      serious,
    Very reserved and locked; not tell a secret
    On any terms, not to your father; scarce
    A fable but with caution; make sure choice
    Both of your company and discourse; beware
    You never speak a truth—
PEREGRINE.   How!
SIR POLITIC.   Not to strangers,
    For those be they you must converse with most;
    Others I would not know, sir, but at distance,
    So as I still might be a saver in 'hem.   20
    You shall have tricks else passed upon you hourly.
    And then, for your religion, profess none,
    But wonder at the diversity of all;
    And, for your part, protest, were there no other
    But simply the laws o'th'land, you could content you.
    Nick Machiavel and Monsieur Bodin° both
    Were of this mind. Then must you learn the use
    And handling of your silver fork at meals,
    The metal of your glass (these are main matters

---

    it: the mountebank scene above.   garb: demeanor.
    Machiavel . . . Bodin: the famous Florentine and French political writers.

With your Italian), and to know the hour   30
When you must eat your melons and your figs.
PEREGRINE. Is that a point of state too?
SIR POLITIC.   Here it is.
For your Venetian, if he see a man
Preposterous° in the least, he has him straight;
He has, he strips him. I'll acquaint you, sir.
I now have lived here 'tis some fourteen months;
Within the first week of my landing here,
All took me for a citizen of Venice,
I knew the forms so well—
PEREGRINE [aside].   And nothing else.
SIR POLITIC. I had read Contarine°, took me a house,   40
Dealt with my Jews to furnish it with movables—
Well, if I could but find one man, one man
To mine own heart, whom I durst trust, I would—
PEREGRINE. What, what, sir?
SIR POLITIC.   Make him rich, make him
    a fortune:
He should not think again. I would command it.
PEREGRINE. As how?
SIR POLITIC.   With certain projects that I have,
Which I may not discover.
PEREGRINE [aside].   If I had
But one to wager with, I would lay odds now
He tells me instantly.
SIR POLITIC.   One is (and that
I care not greatly who knows) to serve the state   50
Of Venice with red herrings for three years,
And at a certain rate, from Rotterdam,
Where I have correspondence. There's a letter
Sent me from one o'th'States, and to that purpose;
He cannot write his name, but that's his mark.
PEREGRINE. He is a chandler?
SIR POLITIC.   No, a cheesemonger.
There are some other, too, with whom I treat
About the same negotiation;
And I will undertake it: for 'tis thus

preposterous: incorrect according to convention.
Contarine: Cardinal Contarini, famed for a work on Venice that
was translated into English in 1599.

I'll do't with ease; I've cast* it all. Your hoy*   60
Carries but three men in her and a boy,
And she shall make me three returns a year;
So, if there come but one of three, I save;
If two, I can defalk.* But this is now
If my main project fail.
PEREGRINE.   Then you have others?
SIR POLITIC. I should be loath to draw the subtle air
Of such a place without my thousand aims.
I'll not dissemble, sir; where'er I come
I love to be considerative; and, 'tis true,
I have at my free hours thought upon   70
Some certain goods unto the state of Venice,
Which I do call my cautions,* and, sir, which
I mean, in hope of pension, to propound
To the Great Council, then unto the Forty,
So to the Ten. My means are made already—
PEREGRINE. By whom?
SIR POLITIC.   Sir, one that though his place
    b'obscure,
Yet he can sway, and they will hear him. He's
A *commendatore.*
PEREGRINE.   What, a common sergeant?
SIR POLITIC. Sir, such as they are put it in their mouths
What they should say, sometimes, as well as greater.   80
I think I have my notes to show you—
PEREGRINE.   Good sir—
SIR POLITIC. But you shall swear unto me, on your
    gentry,
Not to anticipate—
PEREGRINE.   I, sir?
SIR POLITIC.   Nor reveal
A circumstance—My paper is not with me.
PEREGRINE. O, but you can remember, sir.
SIR POLITIC.   My first is
Concerning tinderboxes. You must know
No family is here without its box.
Now, sir, it being so portable a thing,
Put case that you or I were ill affected

---

cast: calculated, reckoned.   hoy: small vessel.
defalk: make retrenchments.   cautions: precautions.

Unto the state; sir, with it in our pockets,   90
Might not I go into the Arsenal?
Or you? Come out again? And none the wiser?
PEREGRINE. Except yourself, sir.
SIR POLITIC.   Go to, then. I, there-
    fore,
Advertise to the state how fit it were
That none but such as were known patriots,
Sound lovers of their country, should be suffered
T'enjoy them in their houses; and even those
Sealed at some office and at such a bigness
As might not lurk in pockets.
PEREGRINE.   Admirable!
SIR POLITIC. My next is, how t'inquire, and be resolved   100
By present° demonstration, whether a ship
Newly arrivèd from S[y]ria, or from
Any suspected part of all the Levant,
Be guilty of the plague. And where they use
To lie out forty, fifty days sometimes,
About the *Lazaretto*° for their trial,
I'll save that charge and loss unto the merchant
And in an hour clear the doubt.
PEREGRINE.   Indeed, sir?
SIR POLITIC. Or—I will lose my labor.
PEREGRINE.   My faith, that's
    much.
SIR POLITIC. Nay, sir, conceive* me. 'Twill cost me, in
    onions,   110
Some thirty livres°—
PEREGRINE.   Which is one pound sterling.
SIR POLITIC. Beside my waterworks; for this I do, sir:
First, I bring in your ship 'twixt two brick walls
(But those the state shall venture); on the one
I strain me a fair tarpaulin, and in that
I stick my onions, cut in halves; the other
Is full of loopholes, out at which I thrust
The noses of my bellows; and those bellows
I keep, with waterworks, in perpetual motion,
Which is the easi'st matter of a hundred.   120

---

present: immediate.   *Lazaretto:* island used for quarantine.
conceive: understand.   livres: French coins.

Now, sir, your onion, which doth naturally
Attract th'infection, and your bellows blowing
The air upon him, will show instantly
By his changed color if there be contagion,
Or else remain as fair as the first.
Now 'tis known, 'tis nothing.
PEREGRINE.   You are right, sir.
SIR POLITIC. I would I had my note.
PEREGRINE.   Faith, so would I;
But you ha' done well for once, sir.
SIR POLITIC.   Were I false,
Or would be made so, I could show you reasons
How I could sell this state now to the Turk,   130
Spite of their galleys or their—
[*He searches for his notes.*]
PEREGRINE.   Pray you, Sir Pol.
SIR POLITIC. I have 'hem not about me.
PEREGRINE.   That I feared.
They're there, sir?
SIR POLITIC.   No, this is my diary,
Wherein I note my actions of the day.
PEREGRINE. Pray you let's see, sir. What is here?
[*He reads.*]

                                        "*Notandum,*°
A rat had gnawn my spur leathers; notwithstanding,
I put on new and did go forth; but, first,
I threw three beans over the threshold. *Item,*
I went and bought two toothpicks, whereof one
I burst, immediately, in a discourse   140
With a Dutch merchant 'bout *ragion del stato.*°
From him I went and paid a *moccenigo*
For piecing my silk stockings; by the way,
I cheapened° sprats, and at Saint Mark's I urined."—
Faith, these are politic notes!
SIR POLITIC.   Sir, I do slip
No action of my life, thus but I quote it.
PEREGRINE. Believe me, it is wise!
SIR POLITIC.   Nay, sir, read forth.

---

notandum: let it be noted.
ragion del stato: affairs of the state; politics.
cheapened: bargained for.

[IV.ii]
     LADY [WOULD-BE], NANO, *Women,* [SIR] POLITIC,
                  PEREGRINE.

[LADY WOULD-BE.] Where should this loose knight be,
    trow? Sure, he's housed.°
NANO. Why, then he's fast.
LADY WOULD-BE.   Ay, he plays both° with me.
    I pray you stay. This heat will do more harm
    To my complexion than his heart is worth.
    I do not care to hinder, but to take him.
    [*She rubs her cheeks.*]
    How it comes off!
[1] WOMAN.   My master's yonder.
LADY WOULD-BE.   Where?
[2] WOMAN. With a young gentleman.
LADY WOULD-BE.   That's the same
    party!
    In man's apparel! Pray you, sir, jog my knight.
    I will be tender to his reputation,
    However he demerit.°
SIR POLITIC [*seeing his wife*]. My lady!
PEREGRINE.   Where?   10
SIR POLITIC. 'Tis she indeed, sir; you shall know her.
    She is,
    Were she not mine, a lady of that merit
    For fashion and behavior; and for beauty
    I durst compare—
PEREGRINE.   It seems you are not jealous,
    That dare commend her.
SIR POLITIC.   Nay, and for discourse—
PEREGRINE. Being your wife, she cannot miss that.
SIR POLITIC.   Madam,
    Here is a gentleman; pray you, use him fairly;
    He seems a youth, but he is—
LADY WOULD-BE.   None?
SIR POLITIC.   Yes, one
    Has put his face as soon into the world—
LADY WOULD-BE. You mean, as early? But today?

---

    housed: in a house of prostitution.   plays both: fast and loose.
    demerit: is at fault.

SIR POLITIC.   How's
   this?   20
LADY WOULD-BE. Why, in this habit, sir; you apprehend
   me!
   Well, Master Would-be, this doth not become you;
   I had thought the odor, sir, of your good name
   Had been more precious to you, that you would not
   Have done this dire massàcre on your honor.
   One of your gravity and rank besides!
   But knights, I see, care little for the oath
   They make to ladies, chiefly their own ladies.
SIR POLITIC. Now, by my spurs, the symbol of my
   knighthood—
PEREGRINE [*aside*]. Lord, how his brain is humbled for
   an oath!   30
SIR POLITIC. I reach° you not.
LADY WOULD-BE.   Right sir, your polity
   May bear it through thus.—[*To* PEREGRINE.] Sir, a
   word with you.
   I would be loath to contest publicly
   With any gentlewoman, or to seem
   Froward or violent (as *The Courtier*° says);
   It comes too near rusticity in a lady,
   Which I would shun by all means. And, however
   I may deserve from Master Would-be, yet
   T'have one fair gentlewoman thus be made
   Th'unkind instrument to wrong another,   40
   And one she knows not, ay, and to persèver,
   In my poor judgment, is not warranted
   From being a solecism in our sex,
   If not in manners.
PEREGRINE.   How is this!
SIR POLITIC.   Sweet madam,
   Come nearer to your aim.
LADY WOULD-BE.   Marry, and will, sir.
   Since you provoke me with your impudence
   And laughter of your light land-siren here,
   Your Sporus,° your hermaphrodite—

---

reach: understand.
   The Courtier: the Renaissance handbook of conduct by Casti-
glione.   Sporus: Emperor Nero's favorite.

PEREGRINE.   What's here?
  Poetic fury and historic* storms!
SIR POLITIC. The gentleman, believe it, is of worth   50
  And of our nation.
LADY WOULD-BE.   Ay, your Whitefriars* nation!
  Come, I blush for you, Master Would-be, ay;
  And am ashamed you should ha' no more forehead*
  Than thus to be the patron, or Saint George,
  To a lewd harlot, a base fricatrice,*
  A female devil in a male outside.
SIR POLITIC.   Nay,
  And you be such a one, I must bid adieu
  To your delights! The case appears too liquid.*
                                        [*Exit.*]

LADY WOULD-BE. Ay, you may carry't clear with your
    state-face! *
  But for your carnival * concupiscence,   60
  Who here is fled for liberty of conscience,
  From furious persecution of the marshal,
  Her will I disc'ple.*
PEREGRINE.   This is fine, i'faith!
  And do you use this often? Is this part
  Of your wit's exercise, 'gainst* you have occasion?
  Madam—
LADY WOULD-BE. Go to, sir.
PEREGRINE.   Do you hear me, lady?
  Why, if your knight have set you to beg shirts,
  Or to invite me home, you might have done it
  A nearer way by far.
LADY WOULD-BE.   This cannot work you
  Out of my snare.
PEREGRINE.   Why, am I in it, then?   70
  Indeed, your husband told me you were fair,
  And so you are; only your nose inclines
  (That side that's next the sun) to the queen-apple.*

---

historic: histrionic, dramatic.
Whitefriars: notorious part of London where evildoers were
immune from the law and from arrest.   forehead: shame.
fricatrice: prostitute.   liquid: clear.
state-face: public or official manner.
carnival: with pun on carnal.   disc'ple: discipline.
'gainst: when.   queen-apple: particularly red.

LADY WOULD-BE. This cannot be endured by any patience.

[IV.iii]

 MOSCA, LADY [WOULD-BE], PEREGRINE [,NANO, *Women*].

[MOSCA.]. What's the matter, madam?

LADY WOULD-BE.   If the Senate
 Right not my quest in this, I will protest 'hem
 To all the world no aristocracy.

MOSCA. What is the injury, lady?

LADY WOULD-BE.   Why, the callet °
 You told me of, here I have ta'en disguised.

MOSCA. Who? This! What means your ladyship? The creature
 I mentioned to you is apprehended now
 Before the Senate. You shall see her—

LADY WOULD-BE.   Where?

MOSCA. I'll bring you to her. This young gentleman,
 I saw him land this morning at the port.   10

LADY WOULD-BE. Is't possible? How has my judgment wandered!
 Sir, I must, blushing, say to you, I have erred,
 And plead your pardon.

PEREGRINE.   What! more changes yet?

LADY WOULD-BE. I hope yo' ha' not the malice to remember
 A gentlewoman's passion. If you stay
 In Venice here, please you to use me, sir—

MOSCA. Will you go, madam?

LADY WOULD-BE.   Pray you, sir, use me.
 In faith,
 The more you see me, the more I shall conceive
 You have forgot our quarrel.

         [*Exeunt all but* PEREGRINE.]

PEREGRINE.   This is rare!
 Sir Politic Would-be? No, Sir Politic Bawd,   20
 To bring me thus acquainted with his wife!
 Well, wise Sir Pol, since you have practiced thus
 Upon my freshmanship, I'll try your salt-head, °
 What proof it is against a counterplot.

              [*Exit.*]

———

callet: wanton, wench, strumpet.   salt-head: lechery.

[IV.iv]

VOLTORE, CORBACCIO, CORVINO, MOSCA.

[VOLTORE.] Well, now you know the carriage of the
    business,
  Your constancy is all that is required
  Unto the safety of it.

MOSCA.   Is the lie
  Safely conveyed amongst us? Is that sure?
  Knows every man his burden?

CORVINO.   Yes.

MOSCA.   Then shrink
  not.

CORVINO [aside to MOSCA]. But knows the advocate the
  truth?

MOSCA.   O, sir,
  By no means. I devised a formal tale
  That salved your reputation. But be valiant, sir.

CORVINO. I fear no one but him, that this his pleading
  Should make him stand for a co-heir—

MOSCA.   Co-halter!   10
  Hang him! we will but use his tongue, his noise,
  As we do Croaker's here.
  [He points to CORBACCIO.]

CORVINO.   Ay, what shall he do?

MOSCA. When we ha' done, you mean?

CORVINO.   Yes.

MOSCA.   Why,
  we'll think:
  Sell him for mummia,° he's half dust already.—
  (To VOLTORE.) Do not you smile to see this buffalo,°
  How he doth sport it with his head?—[Aside.] I should
  If all were well and past.—(To CORBACCIO.) Sir, only
    you
  Are he that shall enjoy the crop of all,
  And these not know for whom they toil.

CORBACCIO.   Ay, peace.

MOSCA (to CORVINO). But you shall eat it.—[Aside.]
  Much!

---

mummia: medicine supposedly made from mummies.
buffalo: jest referring to Corvino's horns.

(*Then to* VOLTORE *again.*)
　　　　　—Worshipful sir,　　　　　　　　　　20
Mercury sit upon your thund'ring tongue,
Or the French Hercules,° and make your language
As conquering as his club, to beat along,
As with a tempest, flat, our adversaries;
But much more yours, sir.

VOLTORE.　　　　　　　　Here they come; ha' done.

MOSCA. I have another witness, if you need, sir,
　I can produce.

VOLTORE.　　　Who is it?

MOSCA.　　　　　　　　Sir, I have her.

[IV.v]

Avocatori 4, BONARIO, CELIA, VOLTORE,
　　CORBACCIO, CORVINO, MOSCA, NOTARIO,
　　　　Commendatori.

[AVOCATORE 1.] The like of this the Senate never heard
　of.

AVOCATORE 2. 'Twill come most strange to them when
　we report it.

AVOCATORE 4. The gentlewoman has been ever held
　Of unreprovèd name.

AVOCATORE 3.　　　So the young man.

AVOCATORE 4. The more unnatural part, that of his
　father.

AVOCATORE 2. More of the husband.

AVOCATORE 1.　　　　　　　I not know to
　give
His act a name, it is so monstrous! °

AVOCATORE 4. But the impostor, he is a thing created
　T'exceed example!

AVOCATORE [1].　　　And all after times!

AVOCATORE 2. I never heard a true voluptuary　　　10
　Described but him.

AVOCATORE 3.　　　Appear yet those were cited?

NOTARIO. All but the old magnifico, Volpone.

AVOCATORE 1. Why is not he here?

French Hercules: Ognius, symbol, like Mercury, of eloquence.
monstrous: pronounced as "monsterous."

MOSCA.   Please your father-
    hoods,
    Here is his advocate. Himself's so weak,
    So feeble—
AVOCATORE 4. What are you?
BONARIO.   His parasite,
    His knave, his pander! I beseech the court
    He may be forced to come, that your grave eyes
    May bear strong witness of his strange impostures.
VOLTORE. Upon my faith and credit with your virtues,
    He is not able to endure the air.   20
AVOCATORE 2. Bring him, however.
AVOCATORE 3.   We will see him.
AVOCATORE 4.   Fetch him.
VOLTORE. Your fatherhoods' fit pleasures be obeyed,
                            [*Exeunt Commendatori.*]
    But sure the sight will rather move your pities
    Than indignation. May it please the court,
    In the meantime, he may be heard in me:
    I know this place most void of prejudice,
    And therefore crave it, since we have no reason
    To fear our truth should hurt our cause.
AVOCATORE 3.   Speak free.
VOLTORE. Then know, most honored fathers, I must now
    Discover to your strangely abusèd ears   30
    The most prodigious and most frontless° piece
    Of solid impudence and treachery
    That ever vicious nature yet brought forth
    To shame the state of Venice. This lewd woman,
    That wants no artificial looks or tears
    To help the visor she has now put on,
    Hath long been known a close° adulteress
    To that lascivious youth there; not suspected,
    I say, but known, and taken in the act
    With him, and by this man, the easy husband,   40
    Pardoned; whose timeless° bounty makes him now
    Stand here, the most unhappy, innocent person
    That ever man's own goodness made accused.
    For these, not knowing how to owe° a gift
    Of that dear grace but with their shame, being placed

---

frontless: shameless.   close: secret.   timeless: untimely.
owe: own.

So above all powers of their gratitude,
Began to hate the benefit and in place
Of thanks devise t'extirp the memory
Of such an act. Wherein, I pray your fatherhoods,
To observe the malice, yea, the rage of creatures   50
Discovered in their evils, and what heart
Such take even from their crimes. But that anon
Will more appear. This gentleman, the father,
Hearing of this foul fact,* with many others,
Which daily struck at his too tender ears,
And grieved in nothing more than that he could not
Preserve himself a parent (his son's ills
Growing to that strange flood) at last decreed
To disinherit him.

AVOCATORE 1.   These be strange turns!

AVOCATORE 2. The young man's fame was ever fair and
      honest.   60

VOLTORE. So much more full of danger is his vice
That can beguile so under shade of virtue.
But, as I said, my honored sires, his father
Having this settled purpose (by what means
To him betrayed, we know not), and this day
Appointed for the deed, that parricide
(I cannot style him better), by confederacy
Preparing this his paramour to be there,
Entered Volpone's house (who was the man,
Your fatherhoods must understand, designed   70
For the inheritance), there sought his father:
But with what purpose sought he him, my lords?
I tremble to pronounce it, that a son
Unto a father, and to such a father,
Should have so foul, felonious intent!
It was to murder him! When, being prevented
By his more happy absence, what then did he?
Not check his wicked thoughts? No, now new deeds
(Mischief doth ever end where it begins),
An act of horror, fathers! He dragged forth   80
The agèd gentleman, that had there [lain] bed-rid
Three years and more, out off his innocent couch,
Naked, upon the floor, there left him; wounded
His servant in the face; and, with this strumpet,

---

fact: deed; crime.

The stale* to his forged practice, who was glad
To be so active (I shall here desire
Your fatherhoods to note but my collections*
As most remarkable), thought at once to stop
His father's ends, discredit his free choice
In the old gentleman, redeem themselves   90
By laying infamy upon this man,
To whom, with blushing, they should owe their lives.
AVOCATORE 1. What proofs have you of this?
BONARIO.   Most
    honored fathers,
I humbly crave there be no credit given
To this man's mercenary tongue.
AVOCATORE 2.   Forbear.
BONARIO. His soul moves in his fee.
AVOCATORE 3.   O, sir!
BONARIO.   This fel-
    low
For six sols* more would plead against his Maker.
AVOCATORE 1. You do forget yourself.
VOLTORE.   Nay, nay, grave
    fathers,
Let him have scope. Can any man imagine
That he will spare's accuser, that would not   100
Have spared his parent?
AVOCATORE 1.   Well, produce your proofs.
CELIA. I would I could forget I were a creature!
VOLTORE. Signor Corbaccio!
AVOCATORE 4.   What is he?
VOLTORE.   The father.
AVOCATORE 2. Has he had an oath?
NOTARIO.   Yes.
CORBACCIO.   What must
    I do now?
NOTARIO. Your testimony's craved.
CORBACCIO.   Speak to the knave?
I'll ha' my mouth first stopped with earth; my heart
Abhors his knowledge. I disclaim in him.
AVOCATORE 1. But for what cause?

---

stale: decoy; mask.   collections: conclusions, evidences.
sols: small coins.

CORBACCIO. The mere portent *
    of nature.
  He is an utter stranger to my loins.
BONARIO. Have they made you to this?
CORBACCIO. I will not hear
    thee,
  Monster of men, swine, goat, wolf, parricide!
  Speak not, thou viper!
BONARIO. Sir, I will sit down
  And rather wish my innocence should suffer
  Than I resist the authority of a father.
VOLTORE. Signor Corvino!
AVOCATORE 2. This is strange.
AVOCATORE 1. Who's that?
NOTARIO. The husband.
AVOCATORE 4. Is he sworn?
NOTARIO. He is.
AVOCATORE 3. Speak,
    then.
CORVINO. This woman, please your fatherhoods, is a
    whore
  Of most hot exercise, more than a partridge,
  Upon recòrd—
AVOCATORE 1. No more.
CORVINO. Neighs like a jennet.
NOTARIO. Preserve the honor of the court!
CORVINO. I shall,
  And modesty of your most reverend ears.
  And yet I hope that I may say these eyes
  Have seen her glued unto that piece of cedar,
  That fine, well-timbered gallant; and that here
  [*He points to his forehead.*]
  The letters may be read, thorough the horn, *
  That make the story perfect. *
MOSCA. Excellent, sir!
CORVINO [*aside to* MOSCA]. There is no shame in this
    now, is there?
MOSCA [*aside*]. None.

110

120

mere portent: an absolute monster.
horn: hornbook (used as a pun on horns of a cuckold).
perfect: complete.

CORVINO. Or if I said I hoped that she were onward
  To her damnation, if there be a hell
  Greater than whore and woman, a good Catholic   130
  May make the doubt.
AVOCATORE 3.   His grief hath made him fran-
    tic.
AVOCATORE 1. Remove him hence.
  (*She swoons.*)
AVOCATORE 2.   Look to the woman!
CORVINO.   Rare!
  Prettily feigned! Again!
AVOCATORE 4.   Stand from about her!
AVOCATORE 1. Give her the air.
AVOCATORE 3 [*to* MOSCA].   What can you say?
MOSCA.   My wound,
  May't please your wisdoms, speaks for me, received
  In aid of my good patron, when he missed
  His sought-for father, when that well-taught dame
  Had her cue given her to cry out a rape.
BONARIO. O most laid° impudence! Fathers—
AVOCATORE 3.   Sir, be
    silent;
  You had your hearing free, so must they theirs.   140
AVOCATORE 2. I do begin to doubt th'imposture here.
AVOCATORE 4. This woman has too many moods.
VOLTORE.   Grave
    fathers,
  She is a creature of a most professed
  And prostituted lewdness.
CORVINO.   Most impetuous,
  Unsatisfied, grave fathers!
VOLTORE.   May her feignings
  Not take your wisdoms; but, this day, she baited
  A stranger, a grave knight, with her loose eyes
  And more lascivious kisses. This man saw 'hem
  Together on the water in a gondola.
MOSCA. Here is the lady herself that saw 'hem too,   150
  Without, who then had in the open streets
  Pursued them but for saving her knight's honor.

---

laid: well-contrived.

AVOCATORE 1. Produce that lady.
AVOCATORE 2.   Let her come.

                                  [*Exit* MOSCA.]
AVOCATORE 4.   These things,
  They strike with wonder!
AVOCATORE 3.   I am turned a stone!

[IV.vi]

        MOSCA, LADY [WOULD-BE), *Avocatori, etc.*
[MOSCA.] Be resolute, madam.
LADY WOULD-BE.   Ay, this same is she.
  Out, thou chameleon harlot! Now thine eyes
  Vie tears with the hyena. Dar'st thou look
  Upon my wrongèd face?—I cry your pardons.
  I fear I have forgettingly transgressed
  Against the dignity of the court—
AVOCATORE 2.   No, madam.
LADY WOULD-BE. And been exorbitant*—
AVOCATORE [2].   You have not,
  lady.
AVOCATORE 4. These proofs are strong.
LADY WOULD-BE.   Surely, I had
  no purpose
To scandalize your honors or my sex's.
AVOCATORE 3. We do believe it.
LADY WOULD-BE.   Surely, you may be-
  lieve it.   10
AVOCATORE 2. Madam, we do.
LADY WOULD-BE.   Indeed, you may; my
  breeding
Is not so coarse—
AVOCATORE 4.   We know it.
LADY WOULD-BE.   To offend
  With pertinacy*—
AVOCATORE 3.   Lady—
LADY WOULD-BE.   Such a presence.
  No, surely.
AVOCATORE 1. We well think it.
LADY WOULD-BE.   You may think it.

---

  exorbitant: disorderly.   pertinacy: pertinacity.

AVOCATORE 1. Let her o'ercome.—What witnesses have you
  To make good your report?
BONARIO.   Our consciences.
CELIA. And heaven, that never fails the innocent.
AVOCATORE 4. These are no testimonies.
BONARIO.   Not in your courts,
  Where multitude and clamor overcomes.
AVOCATORE 1. Nay, then you do wax insolent.

> VOLPONE *is brought in, as impotent.*
> [LADY WOULD-BE *kisses him.*]

VOLTORE.   Here, here,   20
  The testimony comes that will convince
  And put to utter dumbness their bold tongues.
  See here, grave fathers, here's the ravisher,
  The rider on men's wives, the great impostor,
  The grand voluptuary! Do you not think
  These limbs should affect venery? Or these eyes
  Covet a concubine? Pray you, mark these hands.
  Are they not fit to stroke a lady's breasts?
  Perhaps he doth dissemble!
BONARIO.   So he does.
VOLTORE. Would you ha' him tortured?
BONARIO.   I would have
  him proved.*   30
VOLTORE. Best try him, then, with goads or burning irons;
  Put him to the strappado; I have heard
  The rack hath cured the gout. Faith, give it him,
  And help him of a malady; be courteous.
  I'll undertake, before these honored fathers,
  He shall have yet as many left diseases
  As she has known adulterers, or thou strumpets.
  O, my most equal * hearers, if these deeds,
  Acts of this bold and most exorbitant strain,
  May pass with sufferance, what one citizen   40
  But owes the forfeit of his life, yea, fame,
  To him that dares traduce him? Which of you

-----

proved: tested.   equal: impartial.

Are safe, my honored fathers? I would ask,
With leave of your grave fatherhoods, if their plot
Have any face or color like to truth?
Or if, unto the dullest nostril here,
It smell not rank and most abhorrèd slander?
I crave your care of this good gentleman,
Whose life is much endangered by their fable;
And, as for them, I will conclude with this,   50
That vicious persons, when they are hot and fleshed*
In impious acts, their constancy abounds:
Damned deeds are done with greatest confidence.

AVOCATORE 1. Take 'hem to custody, and sever them.
AVOCATORE 2. 'Tis pity two such prodigies* should live.
AVOCATORE 1. Let the old gentleman be returned with
    care;

> [*Exeunt Commendatori with* VOLPONE.]

I'm sorry our credulity wronged him.
AVOCATORE 4. These are two creatures!
AVOCATORE 3.   I have an
    earthquake in me!
AVOCATORE 2. Their shame, even in their cradles, fled
    their faces.
AVOCATORE 4 [*to* VOLTORE]. You've done a worthy service
    to the state, sir,   60
In their discovery.
AVOCATORE 1.   You shall hear, ere night,
What punishment the court decrees upon 'hem.
VOLTORE. We thank your fatherhoods.

> [*Exeunt Avocatori*, NOTARIO, *and*
> *Commendatori with* BONARIO *and* CELIA.]
>   How like you it?
MOSCA.   Rare!
I'ld ha' your tongue, sir, tipped with gold for this;
I'ld ha' you be the heir to the whole city;
The earth I'ld have want men, ere you want living.
They're bound to erect your statue in Saint Mark's.—
Signor Corvino, I would have you go
And show yourself, that you have conquered.
CORVINO.   Yes.
MOSCA. It was much better that you should profess   70

---

fleshed: confirmed.   prodigies: portents; monsters.

Yourself a cuckold, thus, than that the other
Should have been proved.

CORVINO.   Nay, I considered that;
Now, it is her fault.

MOSCA.   Then, it had been yours.

CORVINO. True, I do doubt this advocate still.

MOSCA.   I'faith,
You need not; I dare ease you of that care.

CORVINO. I trust thee, Mosca.

MOSCA.   As your own soul, sir.

                                        [*Exit* CORVINO.]

CORBACCIO.   Mosca!

MOSCA. Now for your business, sir.

CORBACCIO.   How! Ha' you
     business?

MOSCA. Yes, yours, sir.

CORBACCIO.   O, none else?

MOSCA.   None else, not I.

CORBACCIO. Be careful then.

MOSCA.   Rest you with both your
     eyes, sir.

CORBACCIO. Dispatch it.

MOSCA.   Instantly.

CORBACCIO.   And look that all   80
     Whatever be put in: jewels, plate, moneys,
     Household stuff, bedding, curtains.

MOSCA.   Curtain-rings, sir;
Only the advocate's fee must be deducted.

CORBACCIO. I'll pay him now; you'll be too prodigal.

MOSCA. Sir, I must tender it.

CORBACCIO.   Two chequins is well?

MOSCA. No, six, sir.

CORBACCIO.   'Tis too much.

MOSCA.   He talked a great
     while—
You must consider that, sir.

CORBACCIO.   Well, there's three—

MOSCA. I'll give it him.

CORBACCIO.   Do so, and there's for thee.

                                        [*Exit.*]

MOSCA. Bountiful bones! What horrid, strange offense
Did he commit 'gainst nature in his youth   90

Worthy this age?—[*To* VOLTORE.] You see, sir, how I
   work
Unto your ends; take you no notice.

VOLTORE.   No,
I'll leave you.

                                   [*Exit.*]

MOSCA.   All is yours—the devil and all,
   Good advocate!—Madam, I'll bring you home.
LADY WOULD-BE. No, I'll go see your patron.
MOSCA.   That you
   shall not;
I'll tell you why: my purpose is to urge
My patron to reform his will; and for
The zeal you've shown today, whereas before
You were but third or fourth, you shall be now
Put in the first, which would appear as begged   100
If you were present. Therefore—
LADY WOULD-BE.   You shall sway me.
                              [*Exeunt.*]

ACT V

[V.i.]

VOLPONE.

[VOLPONE.] Well, I am here, and all this brunt is past.
I ne'er was in dislike with my disguise
Till this fled moment; here 'twas good, in private;
But in your public—*cavè,*° whilst I breathe.
'Fore God, my left leg 'gan to have the cramp,
And I apprehended straight some power had struck
   me
With a dead palsy. Well, I must be merry
And shake it off. A many of these fears
Would put me into some villainous disease
Should they come thick upon me. I'll prevent 'hem.   10
Give me a bowl of lusty wine to fright
This humor from my heart.
(*He drinks.*)
                      Hum, hum, hum!
'Tis almost gone already; I shall conquer.

---

cavè: beware.

Any device now of rare, ingenious knavery
That would possess me with a violent laughter
Would make me up again.
(*Drinks again.*)
        So, so, so, so!
This heat is life; 'tis blood by this time!—Mosca!

[V.ii]
   MOSCA, VOLPONE [, NANO, CASTRONE *later*].
[MOSCA.] How now, sir? Does the day look clear again?
 Are we recovered? And wrought out of error
 Into our way to see our path before us?
 Is our trade free once more?
VOLPONE.   Exquisite Mosca!
MOSCA. Was it not carried learnedly?
VOLPONE.   And stoutly.
 Good wits are greatest in extremities.
MOSCA. It were a folly beyond thought to trust
 Any grand act unto a cowardly spirit.
 You are not taken with it enough, methinks?
VOLPONE. O, more than if I had enjoyed the wench: 10
 The pleasure of all womankind's not like it.
MOSCA. Why, now you speak, sir! We must here be fixed;
 Here we must rest. This is our masterpiece:
 We cannot think to go beyond this.
VOLPONE.   True,
 Th'ast played thy prize, my precious Mosca.
MOSCA.   Nay, sir,
 To gull the court—
VOLPONE.   And quite divert the torrent
 Upon the innocent.
MOSCA.   Yes, and to make
 So rare a music out of discords—
VOLPONE.   Right.
 That yet to me's the strangest—how th'ast borne it!—
 That these, being so divided 'mongst themselves,   20
 Should not scent somewhat, or* in me or thee,
 Or doubt their own side.
MOSCA.   True, they will not see't.
 Too much light blinds 'hem, I think. Each of 'hem

---

 or: either.

Is so possessed and stuffed with his own hopes
That anything unto the contrary,
Never so true or never so apparent,
Never so palpable, they will resist it—
VOLPONE. Like a temptation of the devil.
MOSCA.   Right, sir.
Merchants may talk of trade, and your great signors
Of land that yields well; but, if Italy   30
Have any glebe* more fruitful than these fellows,
I am deceived. Did not your advocate rare?
VOLPONE. O—"My most honored fathers, my grave fathers,
Under correction of your fatherhoods,
What face of truth is here? If these strange deeds
May pass, most honored fathers"—I had much ado
To forbear laughing.
MOSCA.   'T seemed to me you sweat, sir.
VOLPONE. In troth, I did a little.
MOSCA.   But confess, sir,
Were you not daunted?
VOLPONE.   In good faith, I was
A little in a mist, but not dejected: 40
Never but still myself.
MOSCA.   I think it, sir.
Now, so truth help me, I must needs say this, sir,
And out of conscience for your advocate:
He's taken pains, in faith, sir, and deserved
(In my poor judgment, I speak it under favor,
Not to contrary you, sir) very richly—
Well—to be cozened.*
VOLPONE.   Troth, and I think so too,
By that I heard him in the latter end.
MOSCA. O, but before, sir, had you heard him first
Draw it to certain heads, then aggravate,   50
Then use his vehement figures—I looked still
When he would shift a shirt;* and doing this
Out of pure love, no hope of gain—
VOLPONE.   'Tis right.
I cannot answer* him, Mosca, as I would,

---

glebe: cultivated land.   cozened: cheated.
shift a shirt: by the violence of his gestures.   answer: repay.

Not yet; but for thy sake, at thy entreaty,
I will begin e'en now to vex 'hem all,
This very instant.

MOSCA.   Good, sir.

VOLPONE.   Call the dwarf
And eunuch forth.

MOSCA.   Castrone! Nano!

                        [*Enter* CASTRONE *and* NANO.]

NANO.   Here.

VOLPONE. Shall we have a jig now?

MOSCA.   What you please,
sir.

VOLPONE.   Go,
Straight give out about the streets, you two,   60
That I am dead; do it with constancy,*
Sadly,* do you hear? Impute it to the grief
Of this late slander.

                              [*Exeunt* CASTRONE *and* NANO.]

MOSCA.   What do you mean, sir?

VOLPONE.   O,
I shall have, instantly, my vulture, crow,
Raven, come flying hither on the news
To peck for carrion, my she-wolf and all,
Greedy and full of expectation—

MOSCA. And then to have it ravished from their mouths?

VOLPONE. 'Tis true. I will ha' thee put on a gown,   70
And take upon thee as thou wert mine heir;
Show 'hem a will. Open that chest, and reach
Forth one of those that has the blanks. I'll straight
Put in thy name.

MOSCA.   It will be rare, sir.

[*He gives him a paper.*]

                                              Ay,
When they e'en gape and find themselves deluded—

MOSCA. Yes.

VOLPONE.   And thou use them scurvily! Dispatch;
Get on thy gown.

MOSCA.   But what, sir, if they ask
After the body?

VOLPONE.   Say it was corrupted.

_____

constancy: boldness.   sadly: seriously, gravely.

MOSCA. I'll say it stunk, sir, and was fain t'have it
    Coffined up instantly and sent away.
VOLPONE. Anything, what thou wilt. Hold, here's my
    will.   80
    Get thee a cap, a count-book, pen and ink,
    Papers afore thee; sit as thou wert taking
    An inventory of parcels. I'll get up
    Behind the curtain, on a stool, and hearken;
    Sometime peep over, see how they do look,
    With what degrees their blood doth leave their faces.
    O, 'twill afford me a rare meal of laughter!
MOSCA. Your advocate will turn stark dull upon it.
VOLPONE. It will take off his oratory's edge.
MOSCA. But your *clarissimo*,° old round-back, he   90
    Will crump you like a hog-louse with the touch.
VOLPONE. And what Corvino?
MOSCA.   O, sir, look for him
    Tomorrow morning with a rope and a dagger
    To visit all the streets; he must run mad.
    My lady, too, that came into the court
    To bear false witness for your worship—
VOLPONE.   Yes,
    And kissed me 'fore the fathers, when my face
    Flowed all with oils—
MOSCA.   And sweat, sir. Why, your
    gold
    Is such another med'cine, it dries up
    All those offensive savors! It transforms   100
    The most deformèd and restores 'hem lovely
    As 'twere the strange poetical girdle.° Jove
    Could not invent t'himself a shroud more subtle
    To pass Acrisius' guards.° It is the thing
    Makes all the world her grace, her youth, her beauty.
VOLPONE. I think she loves me.
MOSCA.   Who? The lady, sir?
    She's jealous of you.

---

clarissimo: a Venetian grandee (here, Corbaccio).

strange poetical girdle: Jonson's marginal note at this point
reads *"cestus"*:—the girdle of Venus, into which were woven all her
seductive powers.

Acrisius' guards: referring to Jove's seduction of Danaë, daughter
of Acrisius, in a shower of gold.

VOLPONE.   Dost thou say so?
MOSCA.   Hark,
There's some already.
VOLPONE.   Look!
MOSCA.   It is the vulture;
He has the quickest scent.
VOLPONE.   I'll to my place,
Thou to thy posture.
MOSCA.   I am set.
VOLPONE.   But, Mosca,   110
Play the artificer now; torture 'hem rarely.

[V.iii]
          VOLTORE, MOSCA [, CORBACCIO, CORVINO,
              LADY WOULD-BE, *later*], VOLPONE.

[VOLTORE.] How now, my Mosca?
MOSCA [*writing*].   Turkey carpets,
    nine—
VOLTORE. Taking an inventory? That is well.
MOSCA. Two suits of bedding, tissue—
VOLTORE.   Where's the
    will?
Let me read that the while.
        [*Enter Servants carrying* CORBACCIO *in a chair.*]
CORBACCIO.   So, set me down,
    And get you home.
                              [*Exeunt Servants.*]
VOLTORE.   Is he come now to trouble us?
MOSCA. Of cloth of gold, two more—
CORBACCIO.   Is it done,
    Mosca?
MOSCA. Of several vellets,* eight—
VOLTORE.   I like his care.
CORBACCIO. Dost thou not hear?
              [*Enter* CORVINO.]
CORVINO.   Ha! Is the hour come,
    Mosca?
    (VOLPONE *peeps from behind a traverse.*)
VOLPONE [*aside*]. Ay, now they muster.
CORVINO.   What does the advocate here?
    Or this Corbaccio?

———

vellets: velvets.

CORBACCIO.   What do these here?
                    [*Enter* LADY WOULD-BE.]
LADY WOULD-BE.   Mosca!   10
  Is his thread spun?
MOSCA.   Eight chests of linen—
VOLPONE [*aside*].   O,
  My fine Dame Would-be, too!
CORVINO.   Mosca, the will,
  That I may show it these and rid 'hem hence.
MOSCA. Six chests of diaper,* four of damask—There!
  [*He hands them the will and continues to write.*]
CORBACCIO. Is that the will?
MOSCA.   Down-beds and bolsters—
VOLPONE [*aside*].   Rare!
  Be busy still. Now they begin to flutter;
  They never think of me. Look, see, see, see!
  How their swift eyes run over the long deed
  Unto the name and to the legacies
  What is bequeathed them there.
MOSCA.   Ten suits of hang-
    ings—   20
VOLPONE [*aside*]. Ay, i'their garters, Mosca! Now their
    hopes
  Are at the gasp.
VOLTORE.   Mosca the heir!
CORBACCIO.   What's that?
VOLPONE [*aside*]. My advocate is dumb. Look to my
    merchant;
  He has heard of some strange storm, a ship is lost,
  He faints. My lady will swoon. Old glazen-eyes,
  He hath not reached his despair yet.
CORBACCIO.   All these
  Are out of hope; I'm sure the man.
CORVINO.   But, Mosca—
MOSCA. Two cabinets—
CORVINO.   Is this in earnest?
MOSCA.   One
  Of ebony—
CORVINO.   Or do you but delude me?
MOSCA. The other, mother of pearl—I am very busy.   30
  Good faith, it is a fortune thrown upon me—

———————————

  diaper: fine patterned linen.

Item, one salt* of agate—not my seeking.

LADY WOULD-BE. Do you hear, sir?

MOSCA.   A perfumed box—

Pray you forbear;

You see I am troubled—made of an onyx—

LADY WOULD-BE.   How?

MOSCA. Tomorrow, or next day, I shall be at leisure

To talk with you all.

CORVINO.   Is this my large hope's issue?

LADY WOULD-BE. Sir, I must have a fairer answer.

MOSCA.   Madam!

Marry, and shall: pray you, fairly quit my house.

Nay, raise no tempest with your looks; but, hark you,

Remember what your ladyship offered me   40

To put you in an heir; go to, think on't.

And what you said e'en your best madams did

For maintenance, and why not you? Enough.

Go home and use the poor Sir Pol, your knight, well,

For fear I tell some riddles. Go, be melancholic.

                              [*Exit* LADY WOULD-BE.]

VOLPONE [*aside*]. O, my fine devil!

CORVINO.   Mosca, pray you

a word.

MOSCA. Lord! Will not you take your dispatch hence yet?

Methinks of all you should have been th'example.

Why should you stay here? With what thought? What

promise?

Hear you, do not you know I know you an ass?   50

And that you would most fain have been a wittol*

If fortune would have let you? That you are

A declared cuckold, on good terms? This pearl,

You'll say, was yours? Right. This diamond?

I'll not deny't, but thank you. Much here else?

It may be so. Why, think that these good works

May help to hide you[r] bad. I'll not betray you,

Although you be but extraordinary,

And have it only in title, it sufficeth.

Go home, be melancholic too, or mad.   60

                                    [*Exit* CORVINO.]

VOLPONE [*aside*]. Rare, Mosca! How his villainy be-

comes him!

_____

salt: saltcellar.   wittol: a willing and contented cuckold.

VOLTORE. Certain he doth delude all these for me.
CORBACCIO. Mosca the heir?
VOLPONE [*aside*]. O, his four eyes have
found it!
CORBACCIO. I'm cozened, cheated, by a parasite slave!
Harlot,° th'ast gulled me!
MOSCA. Yes, sir. Stop your mouth,
Or I shall draw the only tooth is left.
Are not you he, that filthy, covetous wretch,
With the three legs,° that here, in hope of pray,
Have, any time this three year, snuffed about
With your most grov'ling nose and would have hired   70
Me to the pois'ning of my patron, sir?
Are not you he that have today in court
Professed the disinheriting of your son?
Perjured yourself? Go home, and die, and stink.
If you but croak a syllable, all comes out.
Away, and call your porters! Go, go, stink!

[*Exit* CORBACCIO.]

VOLPONE [*aside*]. Excellent varlet!
VOLTORE. Now, my faithful
Mosca,
I find thy constancy—
MOSCA. Sir?
VOLTORE. Sincere.
MOSCA [*writing.*] A table
Of porphyry—I mar'l° you'll be thus troublesome.
VOLTORE. Nay, leave off now; they are gone.
MOSCA. Why,
who are you?   80
What? Who did send for you? O, cry you mercy,
Reverend sir! Good faith, I am grieved for you,
That any chance of mine should thus defeat
Your (I must needs say) most deserving travails;
But I protest, sir, it was cast upon me,
And I could almost wish to be without it,
But that the will o'th' dead must be observed.
Marry, my joy is that you need it not;
You have a gift, sir (thank your education),
Will never let you want while there are men   90

---

harlot: knave.   three legs: that is, with a cane.
mar'l: marvel.

And malice to breed causes.* Would I had
But half the like, for all my fortune, sir.
If I have any suits (as I do hope,
Things being so easy and direct, I shall not),
I will make bold with your obstreperous aid,
Conceive me, for your fee, sir. In meantime,
You that have so much law I know ha' the conscience
Not to be covetous of what is mine.
Good sir, I thank you for my plate; 'twill help
To set up a young man. Good faith, you look   100
As you were costive;* best go home and purge, sir.
                                        [*Exit* VOLTORE.]

VOLPONE [*coming out from hiding*]. Bid him eat lettuce*
          well! My witty mischief,
     Let me embrace thee. O, that I could now
     Transform thee to a Venus—Mosca, go,
     Straight take my habit of *clarissimo*
     And walk the streets. Be seen, torment 'hem more:
     We must pursue as well as plot. Who would
     Have lost this feast?
MOSCA.   I doubt it will lose them.
VOLPONE. O, my recovery shall recover all.
     That I could now but think on some disguise   110
     To meet 'hem in and ask 'hem questions.
     How I would vex 'hem still at every turn!
MOSCA. Sir, I can fit you.
VOLPONE.   Canst thou?
MOSCA.   Yes, I know
     One o' the *commendatori*, sir, so like you;
     Him will I straight make drunk and bring you his
          habit.
VOLPONE. A rare disguise, and answering thy brain!
     O, I will be a sharp disease unto 'hem.
MOSCA. Sir, you must look for curses—
VOLPONE.   Till they burst;
     The fox fares ever best when he is cursed.
                                             [*Exeunt.*]

----

causes: lawsuits.   costive: constipated.   lettuce: a laxative.

[V.iv]

> PEREGRINE, *Mercatori* 3, WOMAN [*later*],
>
> [SIR] POLITIC.

[PEREGRINE.] Am I enough disguised?

MERCATORE 1.   I warrant you.

PEREGRINE. All my ambition is to fright him only.

MERCATORE 2. If you could ship him away, 'twere excellent.

MERCATORE 3. To Zant or to Aleppo?

PEREGRINE.   Yes, and ha' his
Adventures put i'th'*Book of Voyages*,*
And his gulled story registered for truth?
Well, gentlemen, when I am in a while,
And that you think us warm in our discourse,
Know your approaches.

MERCATORE 1.   Trust it to our care.

> [*Exeunt Mercatori.*]
>
> [*Enter* WOMAN.]

PEREGRINE. Save you, fair lady! Is Sir Pol within?   10

WOMAN. I do not know, sir.

PEREGRINE.   Pray you say unto him,
Here is a merchant, upon earnest business,
Desires to speak with him.

WOMAN.   I will see, sir.

PEREGRINE.   Pray you.

> [*Exit* WOMAN.]

I see the family is all female here.

> [*Re-enter* WOMAN.]

WOMAN. He says, sir, he has weighty affairs of state
That now require him whole; some other time
You may possess him.

PEREGRINE.   Pray you say again,
If those require him whole, these will exact* him,
Whereof I bring him tidings.

> [*Exit* WOMAN.]
>
> —What might be

His grave affair of state now? How to make   20

Book of Voyages: such as Hakluyt's.
exact: finish off (completely); force.

Bolognian sausages here in Venice, sparing
One o'th'ingredients?
                                   [*Re-enter* WOMAN.]
WOMAN.   Sir, he says he knows
By your word "tidings" * that you are no statesman,
And therefore wills you stay.
PEREGRINE.   Sweet, pray you return
    him:
I have not read so many proclamations,
And studied them for words, as he has done,
But—Here he deigns to come.
                                                     [*Exit* WOMAN.]
                            [*Enter* SIR POLITIC.]
SIR POLITIC.   Sir, I must crave
Your courteous pardon. There hath chanced today
Unkind disaster 'twixt my lady and me,
And I was penning my apology   30
To give her satisfaction as you came now.
PEREGRINE. Sir, I am grieved I bring you worse disaster:
The gentleman you met at th'port today,
That told you he was newly arrived—
SIR POLITIC.   Ay, was
A fugitive punk?*
PEREGRINE.   No, sir, a spy set on you,
And he has made relation to the Senate
That you professed to him to have a plot
To sell the state of Venice to the Turk.
SIR POLITIC. O me!
PEREGRINE.   For which warrants are signed by
    this time
To apprehend you and to search your study   40
For papers—
SIR POLITIC.   Alas, sir, I have none but notes
Drawn out of play-books—
PEREGRINE.   All the better, sir.
SIR POLITIC. And some essays. What shall I do?
PEREGRINE.   Sir,
    best
Convey yourself into a sugar-chest,
Or, if you could lie round, a frail* were rare,

---

tidings: instead of the statesman's "intelligence."
punk: prostitute.   frail: rush basket.

And I could send you aboard.

SIR POLITIC.   Sir, I but talked so
     For discourse' sake merely.
     (*They knock without.*)

PEREGRINE.   Hark, they are there!

SIR POLITIC. I am a wretch, a wretch!

PEREGRINE.   What will you
     do, sir?
     Ha' you ne'er a curran[t]-butt* to leap into?
     They'll put you to the rack; you must be sudden.   50

SIR POLITIC. Sir, I have an engine*—

MERCATORE 3 [*within*].   Sir Politic
     Would-be?

MERCATORE 2 [*within*]. Where is he?

SIR POLITIC.   That I have
     thought upon beforetime.

PEREGRINE. What is it?

SIR POLITIC [*aside*].   I shall ne'er endure the tor-
     ture!—
     Marry, it is, sir, of a tortoise shell,
     Fitted for these extremities. Pray you, sir, help me.
     [PEREGRINE *helps him into a large tortoise shell.*]
     Here I've a place, sir, to put back my legs;
     Please you to lay it on, sir. With this cap
     And my black gloves, I'll lie, sir, like a tortoise,
     Till they are gone.

PEREGRINE.   And call you this an engine?

SIR POLITIC. Mine own device.—Good sir, bid my wife's
     women   60
     To burn my papers.

                                 [*Exit* PEREGRINE.]

                 They rush in.

MERCATORE 1.   Where's he hid?

MERCATORE 3.   We must,
     And will, sure, find him.

MERCATORE 2.   Which is his study?
            [*Re-enter* PEREGRINE.]

MERCATORE 1.   What
     Are you, sir?

PEREGRINE.   I'm a merchant that came here
     To look upon this tortoise.

---

curran[t]-butt: wine cask.   engine: mechanical contrivance.

MERCATORE 3.   How?

MERCATORE 1.   Saint Mark!
What beast is this?

PEREGRINE.   It is a fish.

MERCATORE 2 [*striking the shell*]. Come out here!

PEREGRINE. Nay, you may strike him, sir, and tread
    upon him;
He'll bear a cart.

MERCATORE 1.   What, to run over him?

PEREGRINE.   Yes.

MERCATORE 3. Let's jump upon him.

MERCATORE 2.   Can he not go?*

PEREGRINE.   He creeps, sir.

MERCATORE 1. Let's see him creep.

PEREGRINE.   No, good sir, you
will hurt him.

MERCATORE 2. Heart! I'll see him creep, or prick his
    guts.   70

MERCATORE 3. Come out here!

PEREGRINE.   Pray you, sir.—(Creep
a little!)

MERCATORE 1.   Forth!

MERCATORE 2. Yet further.

PEREGRINE.   Good sir!—(Creep!)

MERCATORE 2.   We'll see his legs.
(*They pull off the shell and discover him.*)

MERCATORE 3. Godso, he has garters!

MERCATORE 1.   Ay, and gloves!

MERCATORE 2.   Is this
Your fearful tortoise?

PEREGRINE [*discovering himself*].
                            Now, Sir Pol, we are even;
For your next project I shall be prepared.
I am sorry for the funeral of your notes, sir.

MERCATORE 1. 'Twere a rare motion* to be seen in Fleet
    Street!

MERCATORE 2. Ay, i'the term.*

MERCATORE 1.   Or Smithfield,* in the
    fair.

---

go: walk.   motion: spectacle.
term: sitting of the sessions of court.
Smithfield: Bartholomew Fair, with its sideshows.

MERCATORE 3. Methinks 'tis but a melancholic sight.

PEREGRINE. Farewell, most politic tortoise!

[*Exeunt* PEREGRINE *and Merchants.*]
[*Re-enter* WOMAN.]

SIR POLITIC.   Where's my
   lady?   80
   Knows she of this?

WOMAN.   I know not, sir.

SIR POLITIC.   Inquire.—

[*Exit* WOMAN.]

   O, I shall be the fable of all feasts,
   The freight of the *gazetti,*° ship-boys' tale,
   And, which is worst, even talk for ordinaries.

[*Re-enter* WOMAN.]

WOMAN. My lady's come most melancholic home
   And says, sir, she will straight to sea for physic.

SIR POLITIC. And I, to shun this place and clime forever,
   Creeping with house on back, and think it well
   To shrink my poor head in my politic shell.

[*Exeunt.*]

[V.v]

VOLPONE, MOSCA; *the first in
the habit of a commendatore;
the other, of a clarissimo.*

[VOLPONE.] Am I then like him?

MOSCA.   O, sir, you are he;
   No man can sever you.

VOLPONE.   Good.

MOSCA.   But what am I?

VOLPONE. 'Fore heaven, a brave *clarissimo;* thou becom'st
   it!
   Pity thou wert not born one.

MOSCA [*aside*].   If I hold
   My made one, 'twill be well.

VOLPONE.   I'll go and see
   What news first at the court.

[*Exit.*]

MOSCA.   Do so.—My fox
   Is out on his hole; and, ere he shall re-enter,
   I'll make him languish in his borrowed case,°

---

freight . . . *gazetti:* theme of the newspapers.   case: disguise.

Except he come to composition* with me.—
Androgyno, Castrone, Nano!
      [*Enter* ANDROGYNO, CASTRONE, *and* NANO.]
ALL.   Here!   10
MOSCA. Go, recreate yourselves abroad; go, sport.
                                    [*Exeunt the others.*]
So, now I have the keys and am possessed.
Since he will needs be dead afore his time,
I'll bury him or gain by him. I'm his heir,
And so will keep me till he share at least.
To cozen him of all were but a cheat
Well placed; no man would construe it a sin.
Let his sport pay for't: this is called the fox-trap.
                                                [*Exit.*]

[V.vi]
            CORBACCIO, CORVINO, VOLPONE [*later*].
[CORBACCIO.] They say the court is set.
CORVINO.   We must
      maintain
Our first tale good, for both our reputations.
CORBACCIO. Why, mine's no tale! My son would there
      have killed me.
CORVINO. That's true; I had forgot. Mine is, I am sure.
      But for your will, sir—
CORBACCIO.   Ay, I'll come upon him
For that hereafter, now his patron's dead.
                        [*Enter* VOLPONE.]
VOLPONE. Signor Corvino! And Corbaccio! Sir,
      Much joy unto you.
CORVINO.   Of what?
VOLPONE.   The sudden good
      Dropped down upon you—
CORBACCIO.   Where?
VOLPONE [*aside*].   And none
      knows how. —
      From old Volpone, sir.
CORBACCIO.   Out, arrant knave!   10
VOLPONE. Let not your too much wealth, sir, make you
      furious.

———————

      composition; terms, agreement.

CORBACCIO. Away, thou varlet!*

VOLPONE.   Why, sir?

CORBACCIO.   Dost thou
    mock me?

VOLPONE. You mock the world, sir; did not you change
    wills?

CORBACCIO. Out, harlot!

VOLPONE.   O! Belike you are the man,
  Signor Corvino? Faith, you carry it well;
  You grow not mad withal: I love your spirit.
  You are not over-leavened with your fortune.
  You should ha' some would swell now like a wine-fat*
  With such an autumn.—Did he gi' you all, sir?

CORVINO. Avoid, you rascal!

VOLPONE.   Troth, your wife has
    shown   20
  Herself a very woman! But you are well;
  You need not care. You have a good estate
  To bear it out, sir, better by this chance—
  Except Corbaccio have a share?

CORBACCIO.   Hence, varlet!

VOLPONE. You will not be a'known,* sir? Why, 'tis wise.
  Thus do all gamesters, at all games, dissemble.
  No man will seem to win.

              [*Exeunt* CORVINO *and* CORBACCIO.]
              —Here comes my vulture,
  Heaving his beak up i'the air, and snuffing.

[V.vii]

VOLTORE, VOLPONE.

[VOLTORE.] Outstripped thus, by a parasite! A slave,
  Would run on errands, and make legs* for crumbs!
  Well, what I'll do—

VOLPONE.   The court stays for you[r]
    worship.
  I e'en rejoice, sir, at your worship's happiness
  And that it fell into so learned hands,
  That understand the fingering.

---

varlet: base person; but here, also court sergeant.
wine-fat: wine vat.   a'known: acknowledged, recognized.
make legs: bows.

VOLTORE.   What do you mean?
VOLPONE. I mean to be a suitor to your worship
    For the small tenement, out of reparations,°
    That at the end of your long row of houses,
    By the *Pescheria*°—it was, in Volpone's time,   10
    Your predecessor, ere he grew diseased,
    A handsome, pretty, customed° bawdy-house
    As any in Venice (none dispraised)
    But fell with him. His body and that house
    Decayed together.
VOLTORE.   Come, sir, leave your prating.
VOLPONE. Why, if your worship give me but your hand
    That I may ha' the refusal, I have done.
    'Tis a mere toy to you, sir, candle-rents.°
    As your learned worship knows—
VOLTORE.   What do I know?
VOLPONE. Marry, no end of your wealth, sir; God de-
    crease it!   20
VOLTORE. Mistaking knave! What, mock'st thou my mis-
    fortune?
VOLPONE. His blessing on your heart, sir; would 'twere
    more!
                                          [*Exit* VOLTORE.]
    —Now, to my first again, at the next corner.

[V.viii]
    CORBACCIO, CORVINO, (MOSCA, *passant*°), VOLPONE.
[CORBACCIO.] See, in our habit! See the impudent varlet!
CORVINO. That I could shoot mine eyes at him, like gun-
    stones!
VOLPONE. But is this true, sir, of the parasite?
CORBACCIO. Again t'afflict us? Monster!
VOLPONE.   In good faith,
    sir,
    I'm heartily grieved a beard of your grave length
    Should be so over-reached. I never brooked
    That parasite's hair; methought his nose should cozen.

---

reparations: repairs.   *Pescheria:* fish market.
customed: well-frequented.
candle-rents: rents from deteriorating properties.
passant: passing (over the stage).

There still was somewhat in his look did promise
The bane of a *clarissimo*.

CORBACCIO.   Knave—

VOLPONE.   Methinks

Yet you, that are so traded i'the world,   10
A witty merchant, the fine bird Corvino,
That should have such moral emblems on your name,
Should not have sung your shame and dropped your
    cheese
To let the fox laugh at your emptiness.

CORVINO. Sirrah, you think the privilege of the place
And your red, saucy cap, that seems to me
Nailed to your jolt-head with those two chequins*
Can warrant your abuses. Come you hither:
You shall perceive, sir, I dare beat you. Approach!

VOLPONE. No haste, sir. I do know your valor well   20
Since you durst publish what you are, sir.

CORVINO.   Tarry;
I'ld speak with you.

VOLPONE.   Sir, sir, another time—

CORVINO. Nay, now.

VOLPONE.   O God, sir! I were a wise man
Would stand the fury of a distracted cuckold.
  (MOSCA *walks by 'hem.*)

CORBACCIO. What! Come again?

VOLPONE [*aside*].   Upon 'hem, Mosca;
    save me.

CORBACCIO. The air's infected where he breathes.

CORVINO.   Let's
fly him.

                     [*Exeunt* CORVINO *and* CORBACCIO.]

VOLPONE. Excellent basilisk!* Turn upon the vulture.

[V.ix]

           VOLTORE, MOSCA, VOLPONE.

[VOLTORE.] Well, flesh-fly,* it is summer with you now;
Your winter will come on.

MOSCA.   Good advocate,

---

chequins: here, gilt buttons.
basilisk: a fabled serpent whose glance was fatal.
flesh-fly: definition of Mosca's name.

Pray thee not rail nor threaten out of place thus;
Thou'lt make a solecism, as Madam says.
Get you a biggen* more; your brain breaks loose.

                                                            [Exit.]

VOLTORE. Well, sir.
VOLPONE.   Would you ha' me beat the in-
    solent slave?
Throw dirt upon his first good clothes?
VOLTORE.   This same
    Is doubtless some familiar!*
VOLPONE.   Sir, the court,
    In troth, stays for you. I am mad, a mule
    That never read Justinian* should get up   10
    And ride an advocate! Had you no quirk*
    To avoid gullage, sir, by such a creature?
    I hope you do but jest; he has not done't;
    This's but confederacy to blind the rest.
    You are the heir?
VOLTORE.   A strange, officious,
    Troublesome knave! Thou dost torment me.
VOLPONE [aside].   I
    know.——
It cannot be, sir, that you should be cozened;
'Tis not within the wit of man to do it:
You are so wise, so prudent, and 'tis fit
That wealth and wisdom still should go together.   20

                                             [Exeunt.]

[V.x]
    Avocatori 4, NOTARIO, *Commendatori*, BONARIO,
      CELIA, CORBACCIO, CORVINO, VOLTORE, VOLPONE
                [the last two later].
[AVOCATORE 1.] Are all the parties here?
NOTARIO.   All but the
    advocate.
AVOCATORE 2. And here he comes.
                [*Enter* VOLTORE *and* VOLPONE.]

---

    biggen: lawyer's cap.   familiar: attendant spirit.
    Justinian: the 6th-century Byzantine emperor who ordered the
compilation of Roman law.
    quirk: trick.

AVOCATORE [1].   Then bring 'hem
    forth to sentence.
VOLTORE. O, my most honored fathers, let your mercy
    Once win upon your justice to forgive—
    I am distracted—
VOLPONE [*aside*].   What will he do now?
[VOLTORE.]   O,
    I know not what t'address myself to first,
    Whether your fatherhoods or these innocents—
CORVINO [*aside*]. Will   he   betray   himself?
VOLTORE.   Whom
    equally
    I have abused, out of most covetous ends—
CORVINO [*aside*]. The man is mad!
CORBACCIO [*aside*].   What's that?
CORVINO [*aside*].   He
    is possessed.*   10
VOLTORE. For which, now struck in conscience, here I
    prostrate
Myself at your offended feet, for pardon.
AVOCATORI 1, 2. Arise.
CELIA.   O heaven, how just thou art!
VOLPONE [*aside*].   I'm caught
    I'mine own noose—
CORVINO [*to* CORBACCIO].   Be constant, sir; naught now
    Can help but impudence.
AVOCATORE 1.   Speak forward.
COMMENDATORE.   Silence!
VOLTORE. It is not passion in me, reverend fathers,
    But only conscience, conscience, my good sires,
    That makes me now tell truth. That parasite,
    That knave, hath been the instrument of all.
AVOCATORE [1]. Where is that knave? Fetch him.
VOLPONE.   I
    go.
                                 [*Exit.*]
CORVINO.   Grave fathers,   20
    This man's distracted; he confessed it now;
    For, hoping to be old Volpone's heir,
    Who now is dead—
AVOCATORE 3.   How!

---

possessed: i.e., by the devil.

AVOCATORE 2.   Is Volpone dead?
CORVINO. Dead since, grave fathers—
BONARIO.   O sure ven-
    geance!
AVOCATORE 1.   Stay;
                            Then he was no deceiver?
VOLTORE.   O, no, none;
    The parasite, grave fathers.
CORVINO.   He does speak
    Out of mere envy 'cause the servant's made
    The thing he gaped for. Please your fatherhoods,
    This is the truth, though I'll not justify
    The other, but he may be somedeal* faulty.   30
VOLTORE. Ay, to your hopes, as well as mine, Corvino;
    But I'll use modesty.* Pleaseth your wisdoms
    To view these certain notes and but confer* them;
    As I hope favor, they shall speak clear truth.
CORVINO. The devil has entered him!
BONARIO.   Or bides in you.
AVOCATORE 4. We have done ill, by a public officer
    To send for him, if he be heir.
AVOCATORE 2.   By whom?
AVOCATORE 4. Him that they call the parasite.
AVOCATORE 3.   'Tis
    true;
    He is a man of great estate now left.
AVOCATORE 4. Go you, and learn his name; and say the
    court   40
    Entreats his presence here but to the clearing
    Of some few doubts.
                                        [*Exit* NOTARIO.]
AVOCATORE 2.   This same's a labyrinth!
AVOCATORE 1. Stand you unto your first report?
CORVINO.   My
    state,
    My life, my fame—
BONARIO.   Where is't?
CORVINO.   Are at the stake.
AVOCATORE 1. Is yours so, too?
_____

    somedeal: somewhat.   modesty: moderation.
    confer: compare.

CORBACCIO. The advocate's a
    knave,
And has a forkèd tongue—
AVOCATORE 2. Speak to the point.
CORBACCIO. So is the parasite, too.
AVOCATORE 1. This is confusion.
VOLTORE. I do beseech your fatherhoods, read but
    those—
    [He gives them papers.]
CORVINO. And credit nothing the false spirit hath writ;
    It cannot be but he is possessed, grave fathers. 50
                    [Exeunt.]

[V.xi]
    VOLPONE, NANO, ANDROGYNO, CASTRONE, [*the last
            three later*].
[VOLPONE.] To make a snare for mine own neck! And
    run
My head into it wilfully, with laughter!
When I had newly 'scaped, was free and clear!
Out of mere wantonness! O, the dull devil
Was in this brain of mine when I devised it,
And Mosca gave it second; he must now
Help to sear up this vein, or we bleed dead.—
      [Enter NANO, ANDROGYNO, and CASTRONE.]
How now! Who let you loose? Whither go you now?
What, to buy gingerbread or to drown kitlings?° 10
NANO. Sir, Master Mosca called us out of doors,
    And bid us all go play, and took the keys.
ANDROGYNO. Yes.
VOLPONE. Did Master Mosca take the keys? Why, so!
I am farther in. These are my fine conceits!
I must be merry, with a mischief to me!
What a vile wretch was I, that could not bear
My fortune soberly. I must ha' my crotchets
And my conundrums! Well, go you and seek him:
His meaning may be truer than my fear.
Bid him, he straight come to me to the court;
Thither will I and, if't be possible, 20

    kitlings: kittens.

Unscrew my advocate upon new hopes.
When I provoked him, then I lost myself.

[*Exeunt.*]

[V.xii]
               Avocatori, etc.
[AVOCATORE 1.] These things can ne'er be reconciled.
    He, here,
    [*He points to* VOLTORE's *papers.*]
    Professeth that the gentleman was wronged
    And that the gentlewoman was brought thither,
    Forced by her husband, and there left.
VOLTORE.   Most true.
CELIA. How ready is heaven to those that pray!
AVOCATORE 1.   But
    that
    Volpone would have ravished her, he holds
    Utterly false, knowing his impotence.
CORVINO. Grave fathers, he is possessed; again, I say,
    Possessed. Nay, if there be possession
    And obsession,° he has both.
AVOCATORE 3.   Here comes our officer.   10
             [*Enter* VOLPONE, *still disguised.*]
VOLPONE. The parasite will straight be here, grave
    fathers.
AVOCATORE 4. You might invent some other name, sir
    varlet.
AVOCATORE 3. Did not the notary meet him?
VOLPONE.   Not that
    I know.
AVOCATORE 4. His coming will clear all.
AVOCATORE 2.   Yes, it is
    misty.
VOLTORE. May't please your fatherhoods—
    (VOLPONE *whispers to the Advocate.*)
VOLPONE.   Sir, the
    parasite
    Willed me to tell you that his master lives;
    That you are still the man; your hopes the same;
    And this was only a jest—

_____

    possession and obsession: possessed by the devil, from within
the body and from without.

VOLTORE. How?

VOLPONE. Sir, to try
If you were firm and how you stood affected.

VOLTORE. Art sure he lives?

VOLPONE. Do I live, sir?

VOLTORE. O me! 20
I was to[o] violent.

VOLPONE. Sir, you may redeem it:
They said you were possessed; fall down, and seem so.
I'll help to make it good.

(VOLTORE *falls.*)

—God bless the man!—
(Stop your wind hard, and swell.)—See, see, see, see!
He vomits crooked pins! His eyes are set
Like a dead hare's hung in a poulter's shop!
His mouth's running away! Do you see, signor?
Now, 'tis his belly.

CORVINO [*aside*]. Ay, the devil!

VOLPONE. Now in his throat.

CORVINO [*aside*]. Ay, I perceive it plain.

VOLPONE. 'Twill out, 'twill out! Stand clear. See where
it flies! 30
In shape of a blue toad, with a bat's wings!—
Do not you see it, sir?

CORBACCIO. What? I think I do.

CORVINO. 'Tis too manifest.

VOLPONE. Look! He comes t'himself.

VOLTORE. Where am I?

VOLPONE. Take good heart; the worst is
past, sir.
You are dispossessed.

AVOCATORE 1. What accident is this?

AVOCATORE [2]. Sudden, and full of wonder!

AVOCATORE 3. If he
were
Possessed, as it appears, all this is nothing.

CORVINO. He has been often subject to these fits.

AVOCATORE 1. Show him that writing.—Do you know
it, sir?

VOLPONE [*whispering to* VOLTORE]. Deny it, sir; for-
swear it; know it not. 40

VOLTORE. Yes, I do know it well; it is my hand:
But all that it contains is false.

BONARIO.   O, practice!°
AVOCATORE 2. What maze is this!
AVOCATORE 1.   Is he not guilty then,
Whom you, there, name the parasite?
VOLTORE.   Grave fathers,
No more than his good patron, old Volpone.
AVOCATORE 4. Why, he is dead.
VOLTORE.   O, no, my honored
fathers.
He lives—
AVOCATORE 1. How! Lives?
VOLTORE.   Lives.
AVOCATORE 2.   This is subtler yet!
AVOCATORE 3. You said he was dead.
VOLTORE.   Never.
AVOCATORE 3.   You
said so!
CORVINO.   I heard so.
AVOCATORE 4. Here comes the gentleman; make him
way.

                      [*Enter* MOSCA.]

AVOCATORE 3.   A stool!
AVOCATORE 4 [*aside*]. A proper° man and, were Vol-   50
pone dead,
A fit match for my daughter.
AVOCATORE 3.   Give him way.
VOLPONE [*aside to* MOSCA]. Mosca, I was a'most lost;
the advocate
Had betrayed all; but now it is recovered.
All's o'the hinge again.—Say I am living.
MOSCA. What busy knave is this?—Most reverend fa-
thers,
I sooner had attended your grave pleasures,
But that my order for the funeral
Of my dear patron did require me—
VOLPONE [*aside*].   Mosca!
MOSCA. Whom I intend to bury like a gentleman.
VOLPONE [*aside*]. Ay, quick,° and cozen me of all.
AVOCATORE 2.   Still stranger!   60
More intricate!

------

practice: deceit.   proper: handsome.   quick: alive.

AVOCATORE 1.   And come about again!

AVOCATORE 4 [*aside*]. It is a match: my daughter is
    bestowed.

MOSCA [*aside to* VOLPONE]. Will you gi' me half?

VOLPONE [*aside*].   First
    I'll be hanged.

MOSCA [*aside*].   I know
    Your voice is good; cry not so loud.

AVOCATORE 1.   Demand*
    The advocate.—Sir, did not you affirm
    Volpone was alive.

VOLPONE.   Yes, and he is;
    This gent'man told me so.
    [*Aside to* MOSCA.]

                Thou shalt have half.

MOSCA. Whose drunkard is this same? Speak, some that
    know him.
    I never saw his face.—[*Aside to* VOLPONE.] I cannot
    now
    Afford it to you so cheap.

VOLPONE [*aside*].   No?

AVOCATORE 1.   What say you?   70

VOLTORE. The officer told me.

VOLPONE.   I did, grave fathers,
    And will maintain he lives with mine own life,
    And that this creature told me.—
    [*He points to* MOSCA.]

                [*Aside.*] I was
    born
    With all good stars my enemies!

MOSCA.   Most grave fathers,
    If such insolence as this must pass
    Upon me, I am silent; 'twas not this
    For which you sent, I hope.

AVOCATORE 2.   Take him away.

VOLPONE [*aside*]. Mosca!

AVOCATORE 3.   Let him be whipped.

VOLPONE [*aside*].   Wilt
    thou betray me?
    Cozen me?

---

demand: question.

AVOCATORE 3. And taught to bear himself
  Toward a person of his rank.
AVOCATORE 4.   Away!   80
  [*The* COMMENDATORE *seizes* VOLPONE.]
MOSCA. I humbly thank your fatherhoods.
VOLPONE [*aside*].   Soft, soft!
    Whipped?
  And [lose] all that I have? If I confess,
  It cannot be much more.
AVOCATORE 4 [*to* MOSCA]. Sir, are you married?
VOLPONE [*aside*]. They'll be allied anon; I must be
    resolute:
  The fox shall here uncase.
  (*He puts off his disguise.*)
MOSCA.   Patron!
VOLPONE.   Nay, now
  My ruins shall not come alone; your match
  I'll hinder sure. My substance shall not glue you,
  Nor screw you, into a family.
MOSCA.   Why, patron!
VOLPONE. I am Volpone, and this is my knave;
  [*He points to* MOSCA.]
  This [*to* VOLTORE], his own knave; this [*to* CORBACCIO],
    avarice's fool;   90
  This [*to* CORVINO], a chimera* of wittol, fool, and
    knave.
  And, reverend fathers, since we all can hope
  Naught but a sentence, let's not now despair it.
  You hear me brief.
CORVINO.   May it please your fatherhoods—
COMMENDATORE.   Silence!
AVOCATORE 1. The knot is now undone by miracle!
AVOCATORE 2. Nothing can be more clear.
AVOCATORE 3.   Or can
    more prove
  These innocent.
AVOCATORE 1.   Give 'hem their liberty.
BONARIO. Heaven could not long let such gross crimes
    be hid.
AVOCATORE 2. If this be held the highway to get riches,
  May I be poor!

---

  chimera: monster.

AVOCATORE 3.   This's not the gain, but torment. 100

AVOCATORE 1. These possess wealth as sick men possess fevers,

Which trulier may be said to possess them.

AVOCATORE 2. Disrobe that parasite.

CORVINO. }   Most honored
MOSCA. }   fathers—

AVOCATORE 1. Can you plead aught to stay the course of justice?

If you can, speak.

CORVINO. }
VOLTORE. }   We beg favor.

CELIA.   And mercy.

AVOCATORE 1. You hurt your innocence, suing for the guilty.

Stand forth; and, first, the parasite. You appear

T'have been the chiefest minister, if not plotter,

In all these lewd impostures; and now, lastly,

Have, with your impudence, abused the court 110

And habit of a gentleman of Venice,

Being a fellow of no birth or blood:

For which our sentence is, first thou be whipped,

Then live perpetual prisoner in our galleys.

VOLPONE. I thank you for him.

MOSCA.   Bane to thy wolfish nature!

AVOCATORE 1. Deliver him to the *Saffi*.—

[MOSCA *is led out.*]

                            Thou, Volpone,

By blood and rank a gentleman, canst not fall

Under like censure; but our judgment on thee

Is that thy substance all be straight confiscate

To the hospital of the *Incurabili*. 120

And, since the most was gotten by imposture,

By feigning lame, gout, palsy, and such diseases,

Thou art to lie in prison, cramped with irons,

Till thou be'st sick and lame indeed. Remove him!

VOLPONE. This is called mortifying of a fox.

AVOCATORE 1. Thou, Voltore, to take away the scandal

Thou hast giv'n all worthy men of thy profession,

Art banished from their fellowship and our state.—

Corbaccio, bring him near! We here possess

Thy son of all thy state* and confine thee   130
To the monastery of San Spirito,
Where, since thou knew'st not how to live well here,
Thou shalt be learned to die well.

CORBACCIO.   Ha! What said he?

COMMENDATORE. You shall know anon, sir.

AVOCATORE [1].   Thou, Cor-
    vino, shalt
Be straight embarked from thine own house and rowed
Round about Venice, through the Grand Canal,
Wearing a cap with fair long ass's ears
Instead of horns; and so to mount—a paper
Pinned on thy breast—to the *Berlin[a]**—

CORVINO.   Yes,
And have mine eyes beat out with stinking fish,   140
Bruised fruit, and rotten eggs—'Tis well; I'm glad
I shall not see my shame yet.

AVOCATORE 1.   And to expiate
Thy wrongs done to thy wife, thou art to send her
Home to her father, with her dowry trebled:
And these are all your judgments—

ALL.   Honored fathers!

AVOCATORE 1. Which may not be revoked. Now you
    begin,
When crimes are done and past, and to be punished,
To think what your crimes are. Away with them!
Let all that see these vices thus rewarded
Take heart and love to study 'hem. Mischiefs feed   150
Like beasts till they be fat, and then they bleed.

                                                    [*Exeunt.*]

                VOLPONE [*comes forward*].

VOLPONE. The seasoning of a play is the applause.
Now, though the fox be punished by the laws,
He yet doth hope there is no suff'ring due
For any fact* which he hath done 'gainst you.
If there be, censure him: here he doubtful stands.
If not, fare jovially, and clap your hands.

                        THE END.

---

state: estate.   berlina: pillory.   fact: crime.

THE
KNIGHT OF
the Burning Pestle.

————————— Quod si
Iudicium subtile, videndis artibus illud
Ad libros & ad hæc Musarum dona vocares:
Bœotum in crasso iurares.aëre natos.
Horat. in Epist. ad Oct. Aug.

LONDON,
Printed for *Walter Burre*, and are to be sold at the
signe of the Crane in Paules Church-yard.
1613.

Introduction

> NANO. . . . *First, for your dwarf, he's little and witty,*
> *And everything, as it is little, is pretty;*
> *Else, why do men say to a creature of my shape,*
> *So soon as they see him, "It's a pretty little ape"?*
> *And why a pretty ape but for pleasing imitation*
> *Of greater men's action in a ridiculous fashion.*
>
> (Volpone, III. iii.)

The convictions that made possible judgment and the reaffirmation of a moral order in a play like *Volpone* were essentially the traditional Elizabethan ones, shared by a national audience that was disturbed by the disruption of the times. An ominous feature, however, of the theatrical situation at the beginning of the seventeenth century, although it posed no immediate threat, was the division of audience into public and private, foreshadowing the estrangement of classes under the Stuarts that was to culminate in civil war at mid-century. When James I (James VI of Scotland) ascended the English throne in 1603, London was enjoying the intense activity of two rival traditions, in Alfred Harbage's phrase, of theater—public or national and private or coterie. The former consisted of the adult professional actors who performed six days a week throughout most of the year in large open-air amphitheaters to audiences of a thousand to two thousand or more. Their repertoire was popular in the fullest sense—patriotic, romantic, moral, with emphasis on "story," swift action, and expressive dialogue. Episodic plots, with their intermixing of subplots and mingling of comic and tragic scenes, reflected the influence of the medieval morality and cycle plays that covered the entire life of man from childhood to death and the entire biblical story from creation to doomsday—a total view and a total explanation of man. A bare stage and lack of act or scene breaks made possible continuous action, the fluid staging resembling our most popular dramatic medium today—the movies.

Rivals of the adult companies were the boy choristers of Saint Paul's Cathedral and the Children of Her Majesty's Revels (of the Chapel Royal in Elizabeth's reign), who performed at the indoor Blackfriars theater. These theaters were not actually "private," but the prohibitive admission price effectively excluded the working classes. The boys played on an average of six months a year, one day a week only, to audiences, so Professor Harbage estimates, of about four hundred that consisted mainly of the wealthy and fashionably literate, the consciously *avant-garde*—young gentlemen, students at the Inns of Court, country gallants come to London, distinguished foreign visitors. As actors, the boys were never so highly esteemed as their adult rivals; much of their appeal came from the hour's concert that they provided and from their being boys who, in their plays, "aped" adult antics. Most of their repertoire, for this latter reason, consisted of satirical works.

Although many playwrights, like Jonson, wrote for both types of theater, and although the repertoire of each expressed common disillusionment, the patrons of the private houses, seeking in a cult of exclusiveness a form of self-definition, prompted the creation of a drama directed specifically against the citizen or mercantile middle class, to which they conveniently attributed the economic and social unrest of the times. Known as "London" or "City comedies," these plays, usually obvious and gross in their satire, but often hilarious too, chronicled Volpone's world in the specific setting of early seventeenth-century London. The roles of the worthy citizens and their wives, when acted by boys no older than fourteen years of age, were reduced automatically to a child's level of absurdity.

Because of its greater subtlety and interest, *The Knight of the Burning Pestle* (1607), written for the Blackfriars' boys, is an outstanding example of London comedy. Though a failure when it was first performed, *The Knight* has come into its own through the years as possibly the first and greatest dramatic burlesque. Historically, its interest is great for the light that it sheds on the conventions of the private playhouse, which is the setting of the play, and on the rivalry between the two "traditions" that inspires the plot. As a "freeman" of "the noble city," George the Citizen has good reason to fear what the title of the afternoon's fare holds in store:

> . . . you have no good meaning: This seven years there hath been plays at this house, I have observed it, you have still girds at citizens; and now you call your play *The London Merchant*. Down with your title, boy! Down with your title!

In calling for a play about a grocer and his "admirable" deeds, he has in mind the plays with which Heywood was flattering and inspiring his lower middle-class audience at the newly built Red Bull theater—plays such as *The Four Prentices of London* or those based upon the lives of famous citizens such as Sir Thomas Gresham, the founder of the Royal Exchange.

"The privy mark of irony" about *The Knight* that apparently escaped even its sophisticated spectators is that "The London Merchant," despite the Prologue's disclaimer that it intends "no abuse to the city," is a parody of the kind of play that George and Nell normally would enjoy. Basically, as John Doebler has pointed out, the parody is a variation of the Prodigal Son play but with the traditional elements misplaced so that it is not the prodigal (Jasper) who is in need of reclaiming but rather the vested interests that have driven him away by not seeing his true worth. In their naïve and humorless response to a familiar form, George and Nell betray, in Doebler's words, an "easy middle-class morality" that identifies "material and moral values"—the kind of identifying "which created the stock pattern of the Prodigal Son play." Against genuine love and goodness (Jasper and Luce) and against disinterested mirth (Master Merrythought), they side with Venturewell, the rich London merchant who wants his daughter to marry the wealthy Humphrey for socially advantageous reasons, and with the greedy and unhappy Mistress Merrythought. Their moral insensitivity is also their esthetic insensitivity.

The Playwright

FRANCIS BEAUMONT (c. 1584–1616) was born of an ancient family at Grace-Dieu in Leicestershire. He entered Broadgates Hall, Oxford, in 1597, but took no degree; and in 1600 he became a member of the Inner Temple. He published non-dramatic poetry in 1602, and about this time apparently he joined the circle of Jonson's friends. His name is first linked with Fletcher's in 1607, when both contributed commendatory verses to the publication of Jonson's *Volpone*. His collaborative efforts with Fletcher from about 1608 to 1613 or so were so successful that their names became linked together permanently although they wrote possibly only some half-dozen plays jointly. Beaumont seems to have been the leading spirit of the collaboration. In 1613 or 1614 he married and probably retired to Kent. He was buried in Westminster Abbey near Chaucer and Spenser.

JOHN FLETCHER: see *Philaster*, p. 407.

The Play

The present text of *The Knight of the Burning Pestle* is based on copies of the first quarto of 1613 in the Henry E. Huntington and Boston Public libraries, collated with the old-spelling edition of Cyrus Hoy. The quarto is divided into prologue, five acts, and epilogue, with only "scœna prima" of each act designated. The address "To the Readers of This Comedy," "The Prologue" (from Lyly's *Sappho and Phao*), and "The Speakers' Names" are supplied from the second quarto of 1635. The play is usually dated about 1607 as a production for the Children of Her Majesty's Revels at the Blackfriars.

The names of the authors do not appear on the title page until the second quarto; and scholarship has divided itself on the question of authorship, the consensus having been that the evidence for Fletcher's hand is slight, except possibly in the Jasper-Luce-Humphrey scenes; Hoy, however, finds that "the play is quite certainly the unaided work of Beaumont."

SELECTED BIBLIOGRAPHY

See also: *Philaster*, pp. 408–409.

Francis Beaumont, *The Knight of the Burning Pestle,* ed. J. Doebler. Lincoln: University of Nebraska Press, 1967. (Regents Renaissance Drama Series.)

The Knight of the Burning Pestle, ed. B. W. Griffith, Jr. Great Neck, N. Y.: Barron's Educational Series, 1963.

The Knight of the Burning Pestle, ed. C. Hoy, in Volume One of *The Dramatic Works in the Beaumont and Fletcher Canon,* gen. ed. F. Bowers. Cambridge: Cambridge University Press, 1966.

The Knight of the Burning Pestle, ed. H. S. Murch. Yale Studies in English 33. New York: Holt, 1908.

Doebler, J. "Beaumont's *The Knight of the Burning Pestle* and the Prodigal Son Plays," *Studies in English Literature,* V (1965), 333–344.

Fellowes, E. H., ed. *Songs and Lyrics from the Plays of Beaumont and Fletcher with Contemporary Musical Settings.* London: Etchells and MacDonald, 1928.

Gayley, C. M. *Beaumont the Dramatist: A Portrait.* New York: Century, 1914.

Leimberg, I. "Das Spiel mit der dramatischen Illusion in Beaumont's *The Knight of the Burning Pestle,*" *Anglia,* LXXXI (1963), 142–174.

[Dedication of the Publisher, Walter Burre]

To his many ways endeared friend, Master Robert Keysar*
Sir,

This unfortunate child, who in eight days (as lately I
have learned) was begot and born, soon after was by his
parents (perhaps because he was so unlike his brethren)
exposed to the wide world, who, for want of judgment or
not understanding the privy mark of irony about it (which
showed it was no offspring of any vulgar brain), utterly
rejected it, so that for want of acceptance it was even
ready to give up the ghost and was in danger to have   10
been smothered in perpetual oblivion if you out of your
direct antipathy to ingratitude had not been moved both
to relieve and cherish it, wherein I must needs commend
both your judgment, understanding, and singular love to
good wits. You afterwards sent it to me, yet being an infant and somewhat ragged. I have fostered it privately
in my bosom these two years, and now to show my love
return it to you, clad in good, lasting clothes, which
scarce memory will wear out, and able to speak for itself,
and withal, as it telleth me, desirous to try his fortune in   20
the world, where, if yet it be welcome, father, foster-
father, nurse and child, all have their desired end. If it be
slighted or traduced, it hopes his father will beget him a
younger brother who shall revenge his quarrel and challenge the world either of fond* and merely literal interpretation or illiterate misprision.* Perhaps it will be
thought to be of the race of *Don Quixote:* we both may
confidently swear it is his elder above a year,* and therefore may (by virtue of his birthright) challenge the wall
of him. I doubt not but they will meet in their adven-   30
tures, and I hope the breaking of one staff will make
them friends; and perhaps they will combine themselves

Robert Keysar: one of the managers of the children of the
Queen's Revels at the Blackfriars Theater.   fond: foolish.
  misprision: misinterpretation.
  above a year: referring to Shelton's English translation of the
first part in 1612.

and travel through the world to seek their adventures.
So I commit him to his good fortune, and myself to your
love.

Your assured friend,
W. B.

[To the Readers of This Comedy.
Gentlemen,

The world is so nice° in these our times that for apparel there is no fashion; for music, which is a rare art
(though now slighted), no instrument; for diet, none
but the French kickshews° that are delicate; and for
plays, no invention but that which now runneth an invec-
tive way, touching some particular person, or else it is
contemned before it is th[o]roughly understood. This is
all that I have to say: that the author had no intent to   10
wrong anyone in this comedy but, as a merry passage,
here and there interlaced it with delight, which he hopes
will please all and be hurtful to none.]

[The Prologue.
Where the bee can suck no honey, she leaves her sting
behind; and, where the bear cannot find origanum° to heal
his grief, he blasteth all other leaves with his breath. We
fear it is like to fare so with us—that, seeing you cannot
draw from our labors sweet content, you leave behind you
a sour mislike, and with open reproach blame our good
meanings because you cannot reap the wonted mirth.
Our intent was at this time to move inward delight, not
outward lightness, and to breed (if it might be) soft smiling, not loud laughing, knowing it to the wise to be a   10
great pleasure to hear counsel mixed with wit, as to the
foolish to have sport mingled with rudeness. They were
banished the theater of Athens, and from Rome hissed,
that brought parasites on the stage with apish actions, or
fools with uncivil habits, or courtesans with immodest
words. We have endeavored to be as far from unseemly
speeches to make your ears glow as we hope you will be
free from unkind reports or mistaking the author's inten-

---

nice: foolish.   kickshews: kickshaws.   origanum: marjoram.

tion (who never aimed at any one particular in this play) to make our cheeks blush. And thus I leave it, and thee to thine own censure, to like or dislike.—*Vale.**]   20

---

vale: farewell.

[THE SPEAKERS' NAMES

*

The PROLOGUE.

Then a CITIZEN [*George*].

The Citizen's WIFE [*Nell*], *and*

RAFE, *her man, sitting below amidst the spectators.*

[VENTUREWELL,] *a rich merchant.*

JASPER, *his apprentice.*

MASTER HUMPHREY, *a friend to the merchant.*

LUCE, [*the*] *merchant's daughter.*

MISTRESS MERRYTHOUGHT, *Jasper's mother.*

MICHAEL, *a second son of Mistress Merrythought.*

OLD MASTER MERRYTHOUGHT.

[TIM,] *a squire.*

[GEORGE,] *a dwarf.* } [*Apprentices.*]

A Tapster.

A Boy that danceth and singeth.

An Host.

A Barber.

[*Three*] *Knights* [*supposed captives*].

A Sergeant.

Soldiers.

[WILLIAM HAMMERTON, *pewterer.*]

[GEORGE GREENGOOSE, *poulterer.*]

[POMPIONA, *daughter to the King of Moldavia.*]

[*A Woman, supposed captive.*]

[*Gentlemen, Attendants, Servants.*]]

The Famous History of the Knight of the Burning Pestle

[Induction.

*Several Gentlemen sitting on stools on the
stage; the* CITIZEN, *his* WIFE, *and* RAFE
below among the audience.]

Enter PROLOGUE.

[PROLOGUE.] From all that's near the court,* from all
    that's great
  Within the compass of the city walls,*
  We now have brought our scene—

Enter CITIZEN [*, climbing onto the stage*].

CITIZEN. Hold your peace, goodman boy!

PROLOGUE. What do you mean, sir?

CITIZEN. That you have no good meaning: This seven
  years there hath been plays at this house, I have observed it, you have still * girds at citizens; and now
  you call your play *The London Merchant.* Down with
  your title,* boy! Down with your title!   10

PROLOGUE. Are you a member of the noble city?

CITIZEN. I am.

---

    court: at Westminster.
    city walls: the medieval walls that encompassed the business
section of London.   still: always.
    title: sign hung on stage giving name of play to be presented (?).

PROLOGUE. And a freeman?*

CITIZEN. Yea, and a grocer.

PROLOGUE. So, grocer, then, by your sweet favor, we intend no abuse to the city.

CITIZEN. No, sir? Yes, sir! If you were not resolved to play the jacks,* what need you study for new subjects purposely to abuse your betters? Why could not you be contented, as well as others, with *The Legend of Whit-* 20 *tington,* or *The Life and Death of Sir Thomas Gresham, with the Building of the Royal Exchange,* or *The Story of Queen Eleanor, with the Rearing of London Bridge upon Woolsacks?*

PROLOGUE. You seem to be an understanding man. What would you have us do, sir?

CITIZEN. Why, present something notably in honor of the commons of the city.

PROLOGUE. Why, what do you say to *The Life and Death of Fat Drake* or *The Repairing of Fleet-privies?* 30

CITIZEN. I do not like that; but I will have a citizen, and he shall be of my own trade.

PROLOGUE. O, you should have told us your mind a month since; our play is ready to begin now.

CITIZEN. 'Tis all one for that; I will have a grocer, and he shall do admirable things.

PROLOGUE. What will you have him do?

CITIZEN. Marry, I will have him—

WIFE (*below*). Husband, husband!

RAFE (*below*). Peace, mistress! 40

WIFE. Hold thy peace, Rafe; I know what I do, I warrant tee.*—Husband, husband!

CITIZEN. What sayst thou, cony?*

WIFE. Let him kill a lion with a pestle, husband! Let him kill a lion with a pestle!

CITIZEN. So he shall.—I'll have him kill a lion with a pestle.

WIFE. Husband! Shall I come up, husband?

CITIZEN. Ay, cony.—Rafe, help your mistress this way. —Pray, gentlemen, make her a little room.—I pray 50

---

freeman: member of a craft or trade guild.
play the jacks: play tricks; make mischief.   tee: thee.
cony: rabbit (term of endearment).

you, sir, lend me your hand to help up my wife. I
thank you, sir.—So.

[WIFE *is helped onto the stage.*]

WIFE. By your leave, gentlemen all; I'm something
troublesome. I'm a stranger here; I was ne'er at one of
these plays, as they say, before; but I should have seen
Jane Shore once; and my husband hath promised me
any time this twelvemonth to carry me to *The Bold
Beauchamps,* but in truth he did not. I pray you, bear
with me.

CITIZEN. Boy, let my wife and I have a couple stools, and   60
then begin, and let the grocer do rare things.

[*Stools are brought.*]

PROLOGUE. But, sir, we have never a boy to play him;
everyone hath a part already.

WIFE. Husband, husband, for God's sake, let Rafe play
him! Beshrew me if I do not think he will go beyond
them all.

CITIZEN. Well remembered, wife.—Come up, Rafe.—I'll
tell you, gentlemen, let them but lend him a suit of reparel ° and necessaries, and, by gad, if any of them all
blow wind in the tail ° on him, I'll be hanged.   70

[RAFE *leaps onto the stage.*]

WIFE. I pray you, youth, let him have a suit of reparell
—I'll be sworn, gentlemen, my husband tells you true.
He will act you sometimes at our house that all the
neighbors cry out on him; he will fetch you up a
couraging part so in the garret that we are all as
feared, I warrant you, that we quake again. We'll fear
our children with him; if they be never so unruly, do
but cry, "Rafe comes, Rafe comes!" to them, and they'll
be as quiet as lambs.—Hold up thy head, Rafe; show
the gentlemen what thou canst do. Speak a huffing °   80
part; I warrant you, the gentlemen will accept of it.

CITIZEN. Do, Rafe, do.

RAFE. "By heaven, methinks, it were an easy leap
To pluck bright honor from the pale-faced moon,
Or dive into the bottom of the sea,

---

reparel: apparel.
blow . . . tail: come near (are able to perform as well).
huffing: blustering.

Where never fathom line touched any ground,
And pluck up drownèd honor from the lake of hell." *

CITIZEN. How say you, gentlemen? Is it not as I told you?

WIFE. Nay, gentlemen, he hath played before, my husband says, Mucedorus,* before the wardens of our   90
company.

CITIZEN. Ay, and he should have played Jeronimo* with a shoemaker for a wager.

PROLOGUE. He shall have a suit of apparel if he will go in.

CITIZEN. In, Rafe, in, Rafe, and set out the grocery in their kind * if thou lov'st me.

[*Exit* RAFE.]

WIFE. I warrant our Rafe will look finely when he's dressed.

PROLOGUE. But what will you have it called?   100

CITIZEN. *The Grocer's Honor.*

PROLOGUE. Methinks *The Knight of the Burning Pestle* were better.

WIFE. I'll be sworn, husband, that's as good a name as can be.

CITIZEN. Let it be so.—Begin, begin; my wife and I will sit down.

PROLOGUE. I pray you, do.

CITIZEN. What stately music have you? You have shawms? *   110

PROLOGUE. Shawms? No.

CITIZEN. No? I'm a thief if my mind did not give* me so. Rafe plays a stately part, and he must needs have shawms. I'll be at the charge of them myself rather than we'll be without them.

PROLOGUE. So you are like to be.

CITIZEN. Why, and so I will be: there's two shillings. [*He gives money.*] Let's have the waits* of Southwark; they are as rare fellows as any are in England; and that

---

by heaven . . . hell: see *Henry IV* Part I, I. iii.

Mucedorus: titular hero of a very popular comedy anonymously printed in 1589.

Jeronimo: Hieronimo, hero of Kyd's *The Spanish Tragedy* (c. 1589).   kind: nature.   shawms: wind instruments.

give: misgive.   waits: street musicians.

will fetch them o'er the water with a vengeance, as if   120
they were mad.

PROLOGUE. You shall have them. Will you sit down then?

CITIZEN. Ay.—Come, wife.

WIFE. Sit you merry all, gentlemen; I'm bold to sit
amongst you for my ease.

PROLOGUE. From all that's near the court, from all that's
    great,
Within the compass of our city walls,
We now have brought our scene. Fly far from hence
All private taxes,* immodest phrases,
Whate'er may but show like vicious!   130
For wicked mirth never true pleasure brings,
But honest minds are pleased with honest things.—
Thus much for that we do; but for Rafe's part you must
answer for yourself.

CITIZEN. Take you no care for Rafe; he'll discharge himself, I warrant you.

                                        [*Exit* PROLOGUE.]

WIFE. I'faith, gentlemen, I'll give my word for Rafe.

ACTUS PRIM[US]

[I.i]

Enter MERCHANT [VENTUREWELL] *and* JASPER,
                his prentice.

MERCHANT. Sirrah, I'll make you know you are my
    prentice,
And whom my charitable love redeemed
Even from the fall of fortune; gave thee heat
And growth, to be what now thou art; new-cast * thee.
Adding the trust of all I have at home,
In foreign staples* or upon the sea,
To thy direction; tied the good opinions
Both of myself and friends to thy endeavors;
So fair were thy beginnings. But with these,
As I remember, you had never charge   10
To love your master's daughter, and even then
When I had found a wealthy husband for her.

---

private taxes: personal attacks.   new-cast: remade.
staples: markets or business centers.

I take it, sir, you had not; but, however,
I'll break the neck of that commission,
And make you know you are but a merchant's factor.*

JASPER. Sir, I do liberally confess I am yours,
Bound both by love and duty to your service,
In which my labor hath been all my profit;
I have not lost in bargain, nor delighted
To wear your honest gains upon my back;   20
Nor have I given a pension to my blood,*
Or lavishly in play* consumed your stock.
These, and the miseries that do attend them,
I dare with innocence proclaim are strangers
To all my temperate actions. For your daughter,
If there be any love to my deservings
Borne by her virtuous self, I cannot stop it;
Nor am I able to refrain* her wishes.
She's private to herself and best of knowledge
Whom she'll make so happy as to sigh for;   30
Besides, I cannot think you mean to match her
Unto a fellow of so lame a presence,
One that hath little left of nature in him.

MERCHANT. 'Tis very well, sir; I can tell your wisdom
How all this shall be cured.

JASPER.   Your care becomes you.

MERCHANT. And thus it must be, sir: I here discharge you
My house and service; take your liberty,
And when I want a son I'll send for you.

                                      Exit.

JASPER. These be the fair rewards of them that love!
O, you that live in freedom, never prove   40
The travail of a mind led by desire!

              Enter LUCE.

LUCE. Why, how now, friend? Struck with my father's thunder?

JASPER. Struck, and struck dead, unless the remedy
Be full of speed and virtue;* I am now,
What I expected long, no more your father's.

LUCE. But mine.

---

factor: agent.   pension . . . blood: free reign to my passion.
play: gambling.   refrain: restrain.   virtue: efficacy.

JASPER.   But yours, and only yours, I am;
　　That's all I have to keep me from the statute.*
　　You dare be constant still?
LUCE.   O, fear me not!
　　In this I dare be better than a woman.
　　Nor shall his anger nor his offers move me,   50
　　Were they both equal to a prince's power.
JASPER.   You know my rival?
LUCE.   Yes, and love him dearly,
　　Even as I love an ague or foul weather.
　　I prithee, Jasper, fear him not.
JASPER.   O, no!
　　I do not mean to do him so much kindness.
　　But to our own desires: you know the plot
　　We both agreed on?
LUCE.   Yes, and will perform
　　My part exactly.
JASPER.   I desire no more.
　　Farewell, and keep my heart; 'tis yours.
LUCE.   I take it;
　　He must do miracles makes me forsake it.   60

　　　　　　　　　　　　　　　　　　　　　　　　　　　　　　Exeunt.

CITIZEN.   Fie upon 'em, little infidels! What a matter's
　　here now? Well, I'll be hanged for a halfpenny if there
　　be not some abomination knavery in this play. Well,
　　let 'em look to't; Rafe must come, and if there be any
　　tricks a-brewing——
WIFE.   Let 'em brew and bake too, husband, o' God's
　　name! Rafe will find all out, I warrant you, and * they
　　were older than they are.——
　　　　　　　　　　　　　　　[Enter BOY.]
　　I pray, my pretty youth, is Rafe ready?
BOY.   He will be presently.   70
WIFE.   Now, I pray you, make my commendations unto
　　him, and withal carry him this stick of licorice. Tell
　　him his mistress sent it him, and bid him bite a piece;
　　'twill open his pipes the better, say.

　　　　　　　　　　　　　　　　　　　　　　　　　　　[Exit BOY.]

_____

　　statute: referring to the law against apprentices who leave their
masters.   and: if.

MERCHANT. Well, sir, you know my love, and rest, I
    hope,
    Assured of my consent; get but my daughter's,
    And wed her when you please. You must be bold,
    And clap in close unto her; come, I know
    You have language good enough to win a wench.

WIFE. A whoreson* tyrant! H'as been an old stringer*
    in's days, I warrant him.

HUMPHREY. I take your gentle offer and withal
    Yield love again for love reciprocal.
MERCHANT. What, Luce! Within there!
Enter LUCE.
LUCE.   Called you,
    sir?
MERCHANT.   I did.   40
    Give entertainment to this gentleman,
    And see you be not froward.—To her, sir;
    My presence will but be an eyesore to you.
                                  Exit.
HUMPHREY. Fair Mistress Luce, how do you? Are you
    well?
    Give me your hand, and then I pray you tell
    How doth your little sister and your brother,
    And whether you love me or any other.
LUCE. Sir, these are quickly answered.
HUMPHREY.   So they are,
    Where women are not cruel. But how far
    Is it now distant from this place we are in   50
    Unto that blessed place, your father's warren?
LUCE. What makes you think of that, sir?
HUMPHREY.   Even that face;
    For, stealing rabbits whilom in that place,
    God Cupid, or the keeper, I know not whether,*
    Unto my cost and charges brought you thither,
    And there began—
LUCE.   Your game, sir.
HUMPHREY.   Let no game,
    Or anything that tendeth to the same,

---

    whoreson: rascally.   stringer: libertine.   whether: which.

[I.ii]

Enter MERCHANT *and* MASTER HUMPHREY.

MERCHANT. Come, sir, she's yours; upon my faith, she's
    yours.
  You have my hand. For other idle lets*
  Between your hopes and her, thus with a wind
  They are scattered and no more. My wanton prentice,
  That like a bladder blew himself with love,
  I have let out and sent him to discover
  New masters yet unknown.

HUMPHREY.   I thank you, sir;
  Indeed, I thank you, sir; and, ere I stir,
  It shall be known, however you do deem,
  I am of gentle blood and gentle seem.   10

MERCHANT. O, sir, I know it certain.

HUMPHREY.   Sir, my friend,
  Although, as writers say, all things have end,
  And that we call a pudding hath his two,
  O, let it not seem strange, I pray, to you,
  If in this bloody simile I put
  My love, more endless than frail things or gut!

WIFE. Husband, I prithee, sweet lamb, tell me one thing,
  but tell me truly.—Stay, youths, I beseech you till I
  question my husband.

CITIZEN. What is it, mouse?   20

WIFE. Sirrah, didst thou ever see a prettier child? How
  it behaves itself, I warrant ye, and speaks and looks
  and perts up the head!—I pray you, brother, with your
  favor, were you never none of Master Moncaster's*
  scholars?

CITIZEN. Chicken, I prithee heartily, contain thyself; the
  childer* are pretty childer; but, when Rafe comes,
  lamb—

WIFE. Ay, when Rafe comes conv! Well, my youth,
  you may proceed.   30

---

  lets: obstacles, hindrances.
  Master Moncaster: Richard Mulcaster, famed headmaster of
Saint Paul's School; his students often performed in masques, interludes, and plays before Queen Elizabeth and her court.
  childer: children.

Be evermore remembered, thou fair killer,
For whom I sat me down and brake my tiller.*

WIFE. There's a kind gentleman, I warrant you. When 60
will you do as much for me, George?

LUCE. Beshrew me, sir, I am sorry for your losses;
But, as the proverb says, I cannot cry.
I would you had not seen me!
HUMPHREY. So would I,
Unless you had more maw* to do me good.
LUCE. Why, cannot this strange passion be withstood?
Send for a constable and raise the town.
HUMPHREY. O, no! My valiant love will batter down
Millions of constables and put to flight
Even that great watch of Midsummer Day* at night. 70
LUCE. Beshrew me, sir, 'twere good I yielded then;
Weak women cannot hope, where valiant men
Have no resistance.
HUMPHREY. Yield, then; I am full
Of pity, though I say it, and can pull
Out of my pocket thus a pair of gloves.
Look, Lucy, look; the dog's tooth nor the dove's
Are not so white as these; and sweet they be,
And whipped about with silk, as you may see.
If you desire the price, [shoot] from your eye
A beam to this place, and you shall espy 80
F. S.,* which is to say, my sweetest honey,
They cost me three and twopence, or no money.
LUCE. Well, sir, I take them kindly, and I thank you.
What would you more?
HUMPHREY. Nothing.
LUCE. Why, then, farewell.
HUMPHREY. Nor so, nor so; for, lady, I must tell,
Before we part, for what we met together.
God grant me time and patience and fair weather!
LUCE. Speak, and declare your mind in terms so brief.

---

tiller: crossbow.   maw: desire.
that . . . Day: when the citizens of London annually gathered
to form a militia.
F. S.: a trademark or coded price.

HUMPHREY. I shall. Then, first and foremost, for relief 90
  I call to you if that you can afford it;
  I care not at what price; for, on my word, it
  Shall be repaid again although it cost me
  More than I'll speak of now, for love hath tossed me
  In furious blanket like a tennis ball,
  And now I rise aloft, and now I fall.

LUCE. Alas, good gentleman, alas the day!

HUMPHREY. I thank you heartily; and, as I say,
  Thus do I still continue without rest,
  I'th' morning like a man, at night a beast,
  Roaring and bellowing mine own disquiet, 100
  That much I fear forsaking of my diet
  Will bring me presently to that quandary
  I shall bid all adieu.

LUCE.   Now, by Saint Mary,
  That were great pity!

HUMPHREY.   So it were, beshrew me;
  Then, ease me, lusty° Luce, and pity show me.

LUCE. Why, sir, you know my will is nothing worth
  Without my father's grant; get his consent,
  And then you may with assurance try me.

HUMPHREY. The worshipful your sire will not deny me;
  For I have asked him, and he hath replied, 110
  "Sweet Master Humphrey, Luce shall be thy bride."

LUCE. Sweet Master Humphrey, then I am content.

HUMPHREY. And so am I, in truth.

LUCE.   Yet take me with
  you;°
  There is another clause must be annexed,
  And this it is (I swore, and will perform it):
  No man shall ever joy me as his wife
  But he that stole me hence. If you dare venture,
  I am yours (you need not fear—my father loves you);
  If not, farewell forever!

HUMPHREY.   Stay, nymph, stay.
  I have a double gelding, colored bay, 120
  Sprung by his father from Barbarian kind;
  Another for myself, though somewhat blind,
  Yet true as trusty tree.

---

lusty: jolly.   take . . . you: hear what I have to say.

LUCE.   I am satisfied,
  And so I give my hand. Our course must lie
  Through Waltham Forest, where I have a friend
  Will entertain us. So, farewell, Sir Humphrey,
  And think upon your business.

Exit LUCE.

HUMPHREY.   Though I die,
  I am resolved to venture life and limb
  For one so young, so fair, so kind, so trim.

Exit HUMPHREY.

WIFE. By my faith and troth, George, and, as I am vir-   130
  tuous, it is e'en the kindest young man that ever trod
  on shoe leather.—Well, go thy ways; if thou hast her
  not, 'tis not thy fault, faith.
CITIZEN. I prithee, mouse, be patient; 'a° shall have her,
  or I'll make some [of] 'em smoke for't.
WIFE. That's my good lamb, George.—Fie, this stinking
  tobacco kills men! Would there were none in England!
  —Now, I pray, gentlemen, what good does this stinking tobacco do you? Nothing, I warrant; you make
  chimneys o' your faces!—O, husband, husband, now,   140
  now! There's Rafe, there's Rafe!

[I.iii]

Enter RAFE, *like a grocer in's shop, with
two Prentices* [TIM *and* GEORGE], *reading*
Palmerin of England.

CITIZEN. Peace, fool! Let Rafe alone.—Hark you, Rafe;
  do not strain yourself too much at the first.—Peace!—
  Begin, Rafe.
RAFE [*reading*]. "Then Palmerin° and Trineus, snatching
  their lances from their dwarfs, and clasping their helmets, galloped amain after the giant; and Palmerin,
  having gotten a sight of him, came posting amain,
  saying, 'Stay, traiterous thief! For thou mayst not so
  carry away her that is worth the greatest lord in the
  world'; and with these words gave him a blow on the   10
  shoulder that he struck him besides° his elephant. And

'a: he.   then Palmerin, etc.: from Munday's translation of 1588.
besides: off.

Trineus, coming to the knight that had Agricola behind
him, set him soon besides his horse, with his neck
broken in the fall, so that the princess, getting out of
the throng, between joy and grief, said, 'All happy
knight, the mirror of such as follow arms, now may I
be well assured of the love thou bearest me.' "—I
wonder why the kings do not raise an army of fourteen
or fifteen hundred thousand men, as big as the army
that the Prince of Portigo brought against Rosicleer,*   20
and destroy these giants; they do much hurt to
wand'ring damsels that go in quest of their knights.

WIFE. Faith, husband, and Rafe says true; for they say
the King of Portugal cannot sit at his meat but the
giants and the ettins* will come and snatch it from
him.

CITIZEN. Hold thy tongue!—On, Rafe!

RAFE. And certainly those knights are much to be commended, who, neglecting their possessions, wander
with a squire and a dwarf through the deserts to re-   30
lieve poor ladies.

WIFE. Ay, by my faith, are they, Rafe; let 'em say what
they will, they are indeed. Our knights neglect their
possessions well enough, but they do not the rest.

RAFE. There are no such courteous and fair well-spoken
knights in this age; they will call one "the son of a
whore" that Palmerin of England would have called
"fair sir"; and one that Rosicleer would have called
"right beauteous damsel" they will call "damned
bitch."   40

WIFE. I'll be sworn will they, Rafe; they have called me
so an hundred times about a scurvy pipe of tobacco.

RAFE. But what brave spirit could be content to sit in his
shop with a flappet* of wood and a blue apron* before

Rosicleer: hero of *The Mirror of Knighthood*.   ettins: giants.
flappet: counter.
blue apron: traditional garb and color for a tradesman.

him, selling mithridatum and dragon's-water to vis-ited* houses, that might pursue feats of arms and, through his noble achievements, procure such a famous history to be written of his heroic prowess?

CITIZEN. Well said, Rafe; some more of those words, Rafe!

WIFE. They go finely, by my troth.

50

RAFE. Why should not I then pursue this course, both for the credit of myself and our company? For, amongst all the worthy books of achievements, I do not call to mind that I yet read of a grocer-errant. I will be the said knight.—Have you heard of any that hath wan-dered unfurnished of his squire and dwarf? My elder prentice Tim shall be my trusty squire, and little George my dwarf. Hence, my blue apron! Yet, in re-membrance of my former trade, upon my shield shall be portrayed a burning pestle, and I will be called the Knight o'th'Burning Pestle.

60

WIFE. Nay, I dare swear thou wilt not forget thy old trade; thou wert ever meek.

RAFE. Tim!

TIM. Anon.

RAFE. My beloved squire, and George, my dwarf, I charge you that from henceforth you never call me by any other name but "the Right Courteous and Valiant Knight of the Burning Pestle" and that you never call any female by the name of a woman or wench but "fair lady," if she have her desires; if not, "distressed damsel"; that you call all forests and heaths "deserts," and all horses "palfreys."

70

WIFE. This is very fine, faith.—Do the gentlemen like Rafe, think you, husband?

CITIZEN. Ay, I warrant thee; the players would give all the shoes in their shop for him.

---

visited: infected (with the plague).

RAFE. My beloved squire Tim, stand out; admit this
    were a desert, and over it a knight-errant pricking, and   80
    I should bid you inquire of his intents, what would
    you say?

TIM. Sir, my master sent me to know whither you are
    riding?

RAFE. No, thus: "Fair sir, the Right Courteous and
    Valiant Knight of the Burning Pestle commanded me
    to inquire upon what adventure you are bound,
    whether to relieve some distressed damsels, or other-
    wise."

CITIZEN. Whoreson blockhead, cannot remember!   90

WIFE. I'faith, and Rafe told him on't before; all the gen-
    tlemen heard him.—Did he not, gentlemen? Did not
    Rafe tell him on't?

GEORGE. Right Courteous and Valiant Knight of the
    Burning Pestle, here is a distressed damsel to have a
    halfpennyworth of pepper.

WIFE. That's a good boy!—See, the little boy can hit it;
    by my troth, it's a fine child.

RAFE. Relieve her, with all courteous language. Now
    shut up shop; no more my prentice, but my trusty   100
    squire and dwarf. I must bespeak my shield and arm-
    ing* pestle.

                        [*Exeunt* TIM *and* GEORGE.]

CITIZEN. Go thy ways, Rafe! As I'm a true man, thou art
    the best on 'em all.

WIFE. Rafe, Rafe!

RAFE. What say you, mistress?

WIFE. I prithee, come again quickly, sweet Rafe.

RAFE. By and by.

                                  Exit RAFE.

[I.iv]

    Enter JASPER *and his mother,* MISTRESS MERRYTHOUGHT.

MISTRESS MERRYTHOUGHT. Give thee my blessing? No,

---

    arming: armorial.

I'll ne'er give thee my blessing; I'll see thee hanged
first; it shall ne'er be said I gave thee my blessing.
Th'art thy father's own son, of the right blood of the
Merrythoughts. I may curse the time that e'er I knew
thy father—he hath spent all his own, and mine too;
and, when I tell him of it, he laughs and dances and
sings and cries, "A merry heart lives long-a." And thou
art a wastethrift, and art run away from the master
that loved thee well, and art come to me; and I have   10
laid up a little for my younger son Michael, and thou
think'st to bezzle° that; but thou shalt never be able
to do it.—Come hither, Michael!

Enter MICHAEL.

Come, Michael, down on thy knees; thou shalt have
my blessing.

MICHAEL [*kneeling*]. I pray you, mother, pray to God to
bless me.

MISTRESS MERRYTHOUGHT. God bless thee! [MICHAEL
rises.] But Jasper shall never have my blessing; he
shall be hanged first, shall he not, Michael? How sayst   20
thou?

MICHAEL. Yes, forsooth, mother, and grace of God.

MISTRESS MERRYTHOUGHT. That's a good boy.

WIFE. Ay, faith, it's a fine-spoken child.

JASPER. Mother, though you forget a parent's love,
I must preserve the duty of a child.
I ran not from my master, nor return
To have your stock maintain my idleness.

WIFE. Ungracious child, I warrant him; hark, how he
chops logic with his mother!—Thou hadst best tell her   30
she lies; do, tell her she lies.

CITIZEN. If he were my son, I would hang him up by the
heels and flay him and salt him, whoreson haltersack!°

JASPER. My coming only is to beg your love,
Which I must ever, though I never gain it;
And, howsoever you esteem of me,
There is no drop of blood hid in these veins

---

bezzle: squander.   haltersack: gallows-bird.

But I remember well belongs to you
That brought me forth, and would be glad for you
To rip them all again and let it out.   40
MISTRESS MERRYTHOUGHT. Ay, faith, I had sorrow
enough for thee, God knows; but I'll hamper thee well
enough. Get thee in, thou vagabond; get thee in, and
learn of thy brother Michael.

[*Exeunt* JASPER *and* MICHAEL.]
OLD MERRYTHOUGHT ([*singing*] *within*).
        Nose, nose, jolly red nose,
        And who gave thee this jolly red nose?
MISTRESS MERRYTHOUGHT. Hark, my husband! He's singing and hoiting,° and I'm fain to cark and care, and all
little enough.—Husband! Charles! Charles Merry-
thought!   50

Enter OLD MERRYTHOUGHT.
OLD MERRYTHOUGHT [*singing*].
        Nutmegs and ginger, cinnamon and cloves;
        And they gave me this jolly red nose.
MISTRESS MERRYTHOUGHT. If you would consider your
state, you would have little list° to sing, iwis.°
OLD MERRYTHOUGHT. It should never be considered,
while it were an estate, if I thought it would spoil my
singing.
MISTRESS MERRYTHOUGHT. But how wilt thou do,
Charles? Thou art an old man, and thou canst not
work, and thou hast not forty shillings left, and thou   60
eatest good meat, and drinkest good drink, and
laughest!
OLD MERRYTHOUGHT. And will do.
MISTRESS MERRYTHOUGHT. But how wilt thou come by
it, Charles?
OLD MERRYTHOUGHT. How? Why, how have I done
hitherto this forty years? I never came into my dining
room but at eleven and six o'clock I found excellent
meat and drink o'th'table; my clothes were never worn
out but next morning a tailor brought me a new suit;   70
and without question it will be so ever: use makes
perfectness. If all should fail, it is but a little straining
myself extraordinary and laugh myself to death.

_____

hoiting: rejoicing noisily.   list: desire.   iwis: indeed.

WIFE. It's a foolish old man this, is not he, George?

CITIZEN. Yes, cony.

WIFE. Give me a penny i'th'purse while I live, George.

CITIZEN. Ay, by Lady, cony; hold thee there.°

MISTRESS MERRYTHOUGHT. Well, Charles, you promised to provide for Jasper, and I have laid up for Michael. I pray you, pay Jasper his portion. He's come home, and he shall not consume Michael's stock; he says his master turned him away, but, I promise you truly, I think he ran away. 80

WIFE. No, indeed, Mistress Merrythought, though he be a notable gallows,° yet I'll assure you his master did turn him away, even in this place. 'Twas, i'faith, within this half hour, about his daughter; my husband was by.

CITIZEN. Hang him, rogue! He served him well enough. Love his master's daughter! By my troth, cony, if there were a thousand boys, thou wouldst spoil them all 90 with taking their parts; let his mother alone with him.

WIFE. Ay, George, but yet truth is truth.

OLD MERRYTHOUGHT. Where is Jasper? He's welcome, however. Call him in; he shall have his portion. Is he merry?

MISTRESS MERRYTHOUGHT. Ay, foul chive° him, he is too merry!—Jasper! Michael!

Enter JASPER *and* MICHAEL.

OLD MERRYTHOUGHT. Welcome, Jasper! Though thou runn'st away, welcome! God bless thee! 'Tis thy mother's mind thou shouldst receive thy portion. Thou 100 hast been abroad, and I hope hast learned experience enough to govern it; thou art of sufficient years. Hold thy hand—one, two, three, four, five, six, seven, eight, nine, there's ten shillings for thee. [*He gives money.*] Thrust thyself into the world with that, and take some settled course; if fortune cross thee, thou hast a retiring place. Come home to me; I have twenty shillings left. Be a good husband,° that is, wear ordinary clothes, eat the best meat, and drink the best drink; be

---

hold thee there: stick to it. gallows: cheat.
foul chive: ill betide. husband: thrifty person.

merry, and give to the poor; and, believe me, thou hast 110
no end of thy goods.

JASPER. Long may you live free from all thought of ill,
And long have cause to be thus merry still!
But, father—

OLD MERRYTHOUGHT. No more words, Jasper; get thee
gone. Thou hast my blessing; thy father's spirit upon
thee! Farewell, Jasper!
[*He sings.*]
  But yet, or ere you part (O cruel!),
 Kiss me, kiss me, sweeting, mine own dear jewell!
So, now begone! No words. 120

          Exit JASPER.

MISTRESS MERRYTHOUGHT. So, Michael, now get thee
gone, too.

MICHAEL. Yes, forsooth, mother; but I'll have my father's
blessing first.

MISTRESS MERRYTHOUGHT. No, Michael, 'tis [no] matter
for his blessing. Thou hast my blessing; begone! I'll
fetch my money and jewels, and follow thee. I'll stay
no longer with him, I warrant thee.

          [*Exit* MICHAEL.]

—Truly, Charles, I'll be gone, too.

OLD MERRYTHOUGHT. What, you will not? 130

MISTRESS MERRYTHOUGHT. Yes, indeed, will I.

OLD MERRYTHOUGHT [*singing*].
  Heigh-ho, farewell, Nan!
  I'll never trust wench more again, if I can.

MISTRESS MERRYTHOUGHT. You shall not think, when all
your own is gone, to spend that I have been scraping
up for Michael.

OLD MERRYTHOUGHT. Farewell, good wife; I expect it
not. All I have to do in this world is to be merry, which
I shall if the ground be not taken from me; and, if it be,
[*He sings.*]
   When earth and seas from me are reft, 140
   The skies aloft for me are left.

          Exeunt.

    BOY *danceth. Music.*
    FINIS ACTUS PRIMI.

WIFE. I'll be sworn he's a merry old gentleman for all
that. Hark, hark, husband, hark! Fiddles, fiddles! Now

surely they go finely. They say 'tis present death for
these fiddlers to tune their rebecks before the great
Turk's grace, is't not, George? But look, look! Here's
a youth dances!—Now, good youth, do a turn o'th' toe.
—Sweetheart, i'faith, I'll have Rafe come and do some
of his gambols.—He'll ride the wild mare,° gentlemen,
'twould do your hearts good to see him.—I thank you,   150
kind youth; pray, bid Rafe come.

CITIZEN. Peace, cony!—Sirrah, you scurvy boy, bid the
players send Rafe; or, by God's———and they do not,
I'll tear some of their periwigs beside their heads; this
is all riff-raff.

                                                    [*Exit* BOY.]

ACTUS SECUND[US]

[II.i]

Enter MERCHANT *and* HUMPHREY.

MERCHANT. And how, faith, how goes it now, son
Humphrey?

HUMPHREY. Right worshipful, and my beloved friend
And father dear, this matter's at an end.

MERCHANT. 'Tis well; it should be so. I'm glad the girl
Is found so tractable.

HUMPHREY.   Nay, she must whirl
From hence (and you must wink, for so, I say,
The story tells) tomorrow before day.

WIFE. George, dost thou think in thy conscience now
'twill be a match? Tell me but what thou think'st, sweet
rogue. Thou seest the poor gentleman, dear heart, how   10
it labors and throbs, I warrant you, to be at rest! I'll
go move the father for't.

CITIZEN. No, no; I prithee, sit still, honeysuckle; thou'lt
spoil all. If he deny him, I'll bring half a dozen good
fellows myself and in the shutting of an evening
knock't up, and there's an end.

WIFE. I'll buss° thee for that, i'faith, boy. Well, George,
well, you have been a wag in your days, I warrant you;
but God forgive you, and I do with all my heart.

---

wild mare: seesaw.   buss: kiss.

MERCHANT. How was it, son? You told me that tomorrow   20
    Before daybreak you must convey her hence.
HUMPHREY. I must, I must, and thus it is agreed:
    Your daughter rides upon a brown-bay steed,
    I on a sorrel, which I bought of Brian,
    The honest host of the Red Roaring Lion
    In Waltham situate. Then, if you may,
    Consent in seemly sort, lest, by delay,
    The fatal sisters* come and do the office;
    And then you'll sing another song.
MERCHANT.   Alas,
    Why should you be thus full of grief to me,   30
    That do as willing as yourself agree
    To anything so it be good and fair?
    Then, steal her when you will if such a pleasure
    Content you both; I'll sleep and never see it,
    To make your joys more full. But tell me why
    You may not here perform your marriage?

WIFE. God's blessing o'thy soul, old man! I'faith, thou
    art loath to part true hearts.—I see 'a has her, George;
    and I'm glad on't!—Well, go thy ways, Humphrey, for
    a fair-spoken man; I believe thou hast not thy fellow   40
    within the walls of London; and I should say the sub-
    urbs too, I should not lie.—Why dost not rejoice with
    me, George?
CITIZEN. If I could but see Rafe again, I were as merry
    as mine host, i'faith.

HUMPHREY. The cause you seem to ask, I thus declare—
    Help me, O Muses nine! Your daughter sware
    A foolish oath, the more it was the pity;
    Yet none but myself within this city
    Shall dare to say so but a bold defiance   50
    Shall meet him, were he of the noble science.*
    And yet she sware, and yet why did she swear?
    Truly, I cannot tell unless it were
    For her own ease; for, sure, sometimes an oath,
    Being sworn, thereafter is like cordial broth;
    And this it was she swore: never to marry
    But such a one whose mighty arm could carry

---

fatal sisters: three fates.   noble science: fencing.

(As meaning me, for I am such a one)
Her bodily away through stick and stone
Till both of us arrive, at her request,   60
Some ten miles off, in the wild Waltham Forest.

MERCHANT. If this be all, you shall not need to fear
Any denial in your love. Proceed—
I'll neither follow nor repent the deed.

HUMPHREY. Good night, twenty good nights, and twenty
more,
And twenty more good nights—that makes threescore!

Exeunt.

[II.ii]

Enter MISTRESS MERRYTHOUGHT *and her son* MICHAEL.

MISTRESS MERRYTHOUGHT. Come, Michael; art thou not
weary, boy?

MICHAEL. No, forsooth, mother, not I.

MISTRESS MERRYTHOUGHT. Where be we now, child?

MICHAEL. Indeed, forsooth, mother, I cannot tell, unless
we be at Mile End; is not all the world Mile End,
mother?

MISTRESS MERRYTHOUGHT. No, Michael, not all the
world, boy; but I can assure thee, Michael, Mile End is
a goodly matter. There has been a pitchfield, my child,   10
between the naughty Spaniels and the Englishmen;
and the Spaniels ran away, Michael, and the Englishmen followed. My neighbor Coxstone was there, boy,
and killed them all with a birding piece.

MICHAEL. Mother, forsooth—

MISTRESS MERRYTHOUGHT. What says my white* boy?

MICHAEL. Shall not my father go with us too?

MISTRESS MERRYTHOUGHT. No, Michael, let thy father go
snick up;* he shall never come between a pair of sheets
with me again while he lives. Let him stay at home and   20
sing for his supper, boy. Come, child, sit down; and
I'll show my boy fine knacks, indeed. [*They sit down,
and she opens a casket.*] Look here, Michael; here's a
ring, and here's a brooch, and here's a bracelet, and
here's two rings more, and here's money and gold by
th'eye,* my boy.

---

white: dear, favorite.   snick up: be hanged.
by th'eye: unlimited.

MICHAEL. Shall I have all this, mother?

MISTRESS MERRYTHOUGHT. Ay, Michael, thou shalt have
all, Michael.

CITIZEN. How lik'st thou this, wench?   30

WIFE. I cannot tell. I would have Rafe, George; I'll see
no more else, indeed, la; and I pray you, let the youths
understand so much by word of mouth; for, I tell you
truly, I'm afraid o' my boy. Come, come, George, let's
be merry and wise. The child's a fatherless child; and
say they should put him into a straight pair of gaskins,
'twere worse than knotgrass;* he would never grow
after it.

              Enter RAFE, SQUIRE, *and* DWARF.

CITIZEN. Here's Rafe, here's Rafe!

WIFE. How do you, Rafe? You are welcome, Rafe, as I   40
may say. It's a good boy; hold up thy head, and be not
afraid; we are thy friends, Rafe. The gentlemen will
praise thee, Rafe, if thou play'st thy part with audacity.
Begin, Rafe, o' God's name!

RAFE. My trusty squire, unlace my helm; give me my
    hat.
  Where are we, or what desert may this be?

DWARF. Mirror of knighthood, this is, as I take it, the
perilous Waltham Down, in whose bottom stands the
enchanted valley.

MISTRESS MERRYTHOUGHT. O, Michael, we are betrayed,   50
we are betrayed! Here be giants! Fly, boy! Fly, boy,
fly!

          Exeunt MOTHER *and* MICHAEL [*leaving the casket.*]

RAFE. Lace on my helm again. What noise is this?
  A gentle lady, flying the embrace
  Of some uncourteous knight! I will relieve her.
  Go, squire, and say the knight that wears this pestle
  In honor of all ladies swears revenge
  Upon that recreant coward that pursues her.
  Go, comfort her, and that same gentle squire
  That bears her company.

SQUIRE.   I go, brave knight.   60
                                              [*Exit.*]

_____

knotgrass: supposed to retard growth.

RAFE. My trusty dwarf and friend, reach me my shield,
   And hold it while I swear: First, by my knighthood;
   Then by the soul of Amadis de Gaul,
   My famous ancestor; then by my sword
   The beauteous Brionella girt about me;
   By this bright burning pestle, of mine honor
   The living trophy; and by all respect
   Due to distressèd damsels, here I vow
   Never to end the quest of this fair lady
   And that forsaken squire till by my valor   70
   I gain their liberty!
DWARF.   Heaven bless the knight
   That thus relieves poor errant gentlewomen!
                                        Exit [with RAFE].

WIFE. Ay, marry, Rafe, this has some savor in't.—I would
   see the proudest of them all offer to carry his books
   after him. But, George, I will not have him go away so
   soon; I shall be sick if he go away, that I shall. Call
   Rafe again, George, call Rafe again. I prithee, sweetheart, let him come fight before me, and let's ha' some
   drums and some trumpets, and let him kill all that
   comes near him, and thou lov'st me, George.   80
CITIZEN. Peace a little, bird; he shall kill them all and
   they were twenty more on 'em than there are.

                        Enter JASPER.
JASPER. Now, Fortune, if thou be'st not only ill,
   Show me thy better face and bring about
   Thy desperate wheel that I may climb at length
   And stand. This is our place of meeting
   If love have any constancy. O age
   Where only wealthy men are counted happy!
   How shall I please thee? How deserve thy smiles
   When I am only rich in misery?   90
   My father's blessing and this little coin
   Is my inheritance—a strong revenue!
   From earth thou art, and to the earth I give thee;
   [*He throws away the money.*]
   There grow and multiply whilst fresher air
   Breeds me a fresher fortune.
   (*Spies the casket.*)
                                        How! Illusion?

What, hath the devil coined himself before me?
'Tis metal good; it rings well. I am waking,
And taking too. 1 hope. Now, God's dear blessing
Upon his heart that left it here! 'Tis mine;
These pearls, I take it, were not left for swine.   100

                                                                Exit.

WIFE. I do not like that this unthrifty youth should em-
    bezzle away the money; the poor gentlewoman his
    mother will have a heavy heart for it, God knows.
CITIZEN. And reason good, sweetheart.
WIFE. But let him go; I'll tell Rafe a tale in's ear shall
    fetch him again with a wanion,* I warrant him, if he
    be above ground; and besides, George, here are a
    number of sufficient gentlemen can witness, and my-
    self, and yourself, and the musicians, if we be called
    in question. But here comes Rafe, George; thou shalt   110
    hear him speak [as] he were an emperal.*

[II.iii]

                        Enter RAFE *and* DWARF.
RAFE. Comes not Sir Squire again?
DWARF.   Right   courteous
        knight,
    Your squire doth come, and with him comes the lady,
    Enter MISTRESS MERRYTHOUGHT *and* MICHAEL *and* SQUIRE.
    For and * the Squire of Damsels, as I take it.
RAFE. Madam, if any service or devoir
    Of a poor errant knight may right your wrongs,
    Command it. I am pressed* to give you succor,
    For to that holy end I bear my armor.
MISTRESS MERRYTHOUGHT. Alas, sir, I am a poor gentle-
    woman, and I have lost my money in this forest!
RAFE. Desert, you would say, lady; and not lost   10
    Whilst I have sword and lance. Dry up your tears,
    Which ill befits the beauty of that face,
    And tell the story, if I may request it,
    Of your disastrous fortune.
MISTRESS MERRYTHOUGHT. Out, alas! I left a thousand

---

with a wanion: with bad luck or a vengeance.
emperal: emperor.   for and: and also.   pressed: ready.

pound, a thousand pound, e'en all the money I had laid
up for this youth, upon the sight of your mastership—
you looked so grim and, as I may say it, saving your
presence, more like a giant than a mortal man.

RAFE. I am as you are, lady; so are they　　　　　　20
　All mortal. But why weeps this gentle squire?

MISTRESS MERRYTHOUGHT. Has he not cause to weep, do
you think, when he hath lost his inheritance?

RAFE. Young hope of valor, weep not; I am here
　That will confound thy foe and pay it dear
　Upon his coward head that dares deny
　Distressèd squires and ladies equity.
　I have but one horse, on which shall ride
　This lady fair behind me, and before
　This courteous squire. Fortune will give us more　　30
　Upon our next adventure. Fairly speed
　Beside us, squire and dwarf, to do us need!

　　　　　　　　　　　　　　　　　　　Exeunt.

CITIZEN. Did not I tell you, Nell, what your man would
do? By the faith of my body, wench, for clean action
and good delivery they may all cast their caps at him.

WIFE. And so they may, i'faith, for, I dare speak it
boldly, the twelve companies* of London cannot
match him, timber for timber. Well, George, and he
be not inveigled by some of these paltry players, I
ha' much marvel. But, George, we ha' done our parts　　40
if the boy have any grace to be thankful.

CITIZEN. Yes, I warrant thee, duckling.

[II.iv]

　　　　　　　Enter HUMPHREY *and* LUCE.

HUMPHREY. Good Mistress Luce, however I in fault am
　For your lame horse, you're welcome unto Waltham;
　But which way now to go or what to say
　I know not truly till it be broad day.

LUCE. O, fear not, Master Humphrey; I am guide
　For this place good enough.

HUMPHREY. 　　　　　　　　Then up and ride;
　Or, if it please you, walk for your repose;

———————————

twelve companies: London guilds.

Or sit, or, if you will, go pluck a rose:°
Either of which shall be indifferent
To your good friend and Humphrey, whose consent   10
Is so entangled ever to your will
As the poor harmless horse is to the mill.

LUCE. Faith, and you say the word, we'll e'en sit down
And take a nap.

HUMPHREY.   'Tis better in the town,
Where we may nap together; for, believe me,
To sleep without a snatch would mickle° grieve me.

LUCE. You're merry, Master Humphrey.

HUMPHREY.   So I am,
And have been ever merry from my dam.

LUCE. Your nurse had the less labor.

HUMPHREY.   Faith, it may be,
Unless it were by chance I did beray° me.   20

Enter JASPER.

JASPER. Luce! Dear friend, Luce!

LUCE.   Here, Jasper.

JASPER.   You
    are mine.

HUMPHREY. If it be so, my friend, you use me fine.
What do you think I am?

JASPER.   An arrant noddy.

HUMPHREY. A word of obloquy! Now, by God's body,
I'll tell thy master, for I know thee well.

JASPER. Nay, and you be so forward for to tell,
Take that, and that!
[*He beats him.*]
                    And tell him, sir, I gave it,
And say I paid you well.

HUMPHREY.   O, sir, I have it,
And do confess the payment! Pray, be quiet.

JASPER. Go, get you to your nightcap and the diet   30
To cure your beaten bones.

LUCE.   Alas, poor Humphrey!
Get thee some wholesome broth with sage and
    comfrey,
A little oil of roses and a feather

---

go pluck a rose: euphemism for defecate.   mickle: much.
beray: befoul.

To 'noint thy back withal.

HUMPHREY. When I came hither,
Would I had gone to Paris with John Dory!*

LUCE. Farewell, my pretty nump;* I am very sorry
I cannot bear thee company.

HUMPHREY. Farewell!
The devil's dam was ne'er so banged in hell.

Exeunt [LUCE *and* JASPER]; *manet** HUMPHREY.

WIFE. This young Jasper will prove me another [thing],
o' my conscience, and he may be suffered. George, dost   40
not see, George, how 'a swaggers and flies at the very
heads o' folks as he were a dragon? Well, if I do not do
his lesson* for wronging the poor gentleman, I am no
true woman. His friends that brought him up might
have been better occupied, iwis, than ha' taught him
these fegaries;* he's e'en in the highway to the gallows,
God bless him!

CITIZEN. You're too bitter, cony; the young man may do
well enough for all this.

WIFE. Come hither, Master Humphrey. Has he hurt you?   50
Now, beshrew his fingers for't! Here, sweetheart, here's
some green ginger for thee.—Now, beshrew my heart,
but 'a has peppernel * in's head as big as a pullet's
egg!—Alas, sweet lamb, how thy temples beat! Take
the peace on him, sweetheart, take the peace on him.

Enter a BOY.

CITIZEN. No, no; you talk like a foolish woman. I'll ha'
Rafe fight with him and swinge him up well-favoredly.
—Sirrah, boy, come hither! Let Rafe come in and fight
with Jasper.

WIFE. Ay, and beat him well; he's an unhappy* boy.   60

BOY. Sir, you must pardon us; the plot of our play lies
contrary and 'twill hazard the spoiling of our play.

CITIZEN. Plot me no plots! I'll ha' Rafe come out; I'll
make your house too hot for you else.

John Dory: hero of a popular song.
nump: blockhead (also a pun on "Humphrey").
manet: remains.   do his lesson: teach him.
fegaries: vagaries, tricks, pranks.   peppernel: lump.
unhappy: mischievous; good-for-nothing.

BOY. Why, sir, he shall; but, if anything fall out of order,
   the gentlemen must pardon us.
CITIZEN. Go your ways, goodman boy!

                                                  [*Exit* BOY.]

   —I'll hold him a penny he shall have his bellyful of
fighting now. Ho, here comes Rafe! No more!

[II.v]
              Enter RAFE, MISTRESS MERRYTHOUGHT, MICHAEL,
                         SQUIRE, *and* DWARF.
RAFE. What knight is that, squire? Ask him if he keep
   The passage, bound by love of lady fair,
   Or else but prickant.°
HUMPHREY.   Sir, I am no knight,
   But a poor gentleman, that this same night
   Had stolen from me, on yonder green,
   My lovely wife and suffered to be seen
   Yet extant on my shoulders such a greeting
   That, whilst I live, I shall think of that meeting.

WIFE. Ay, Rafe, he beat him unmercifully, Rafe; and
   thou spar'st him, Rafe, I would thou wert hanged.   10
CITIZEN. No more, wife, no more.

RAFE. Where is the caitiff wretch hath done this deed?
   Lady, your pardon, that I may proceed
   Upon the quest of this injurious knight.—
   And thou, fair squire, repute me not the worse
   In leaving the great venture of the purse
   And the rich casket till some better leisure.
                    Enter JASPER *and* LUCE.
HUMPHREY. Here comes the broker° hath purloined my
   treasure.
RAFE. Go, squire, and tell him I am here,
   An errant knight-at-arms, to crave delivery   20
   Of that fair lady to her own knight's arms.
   If he deny, bid him take choice of ground,
   And so defy him.
SQUIRE.   From the knight that bears

_____

prickant: traveling on a knightly quest.
broker: pander (pun).

The golden pestle, I defy thee, knight,
Unless thou make fair restitution
Of that bright lady.
JASPER.   Tell the knight that sent thee
He is an ass, and I will keep the wench
And knock his headpiece.
RAFE.   Knight, thou art but dead
If thou recall not thy uncourteous terms.

WIFE. Break's pate,* Rafe; break's pate, Rafe, soundly!   30

JASPER. Come, knight, I am ready for you. Now your
    pestle
(*Snatches away his pestle.*)
Shall try what temper, sir, your mortar's of.
"With that he stood upright in his stirrups,
And gave the Knight of the Calfskin such a knock
[*He knocks* RAFE *down.*]
That he forsook his horse and down he fell;
And then he leaped upon him, and plucking off his
    helmet—"
HUMPHREY. Nay, and my noble knight be down so soon,
Though I can scarcely go,* I needs must run.
                        [*Exeunt*] HUMPHREY *and* RAFE.

WIFE. Run, Rafe; run, Rafe! Run for thy life, boy!
Jasper comes, Jasper comes!   40

JASPER. Come, Luce, we must have other arms for you.
Humphrey and Golden Pestle, both adieu!
                                        Exeunt.

WIFE. Sure the devil (God bless us!) is in this springald! * Why, George, didst ever see such a firedrake?*
I am afraid my boy's miscarried;* if he be, though he
were Master Merrythought's son a thousand times, if
there be any law in England, I'll make some of them
smart for't.
CITIZEN. No, no; I have found out the matter, sweet-

---

pate: head.   go: walk.   springald: youth, young man.
firedrake: fiery dragon.   miscarried: ruined; perished.

heart. Jasper is enchanted; as sure as we are here, he   50
is enchanted. He could no more have stood in Rafe's
hands than I can stand in my lord mayor's. I'll have a
ring to discover all enchantments, and Rafe shall beat
him yet. Be no more vexed, for it shall be so.

[II.vi]
> *Enter* RAFE, SQUIRE, DWARF, MISTRESS MERRYTHOUGHT,
> *and* MICHAEL.

WIFE. O, husband, here's Rafe again!—Stay, Rafe, let me
speak with thee. How dost thou, Rafe? Art thou not
shrewdly° hurt?—The foul great lungies° laid unmercifully on thee. There's some sugar candy for thee.
Proceed—thou shalt have another bout with him.
CITIZEN. If Rafe had him at the fencing school, if he did
not make a puppy of him, and drive him up and down
the school, he should ne'er come in my shop more.

MISTRESS MERRYTHOUGHT. Truly, Master Knight of the
Burning Pestle, I am weary.   10
MICHAEL. Indeed, la, mother, and I am very hungry.
RAFE. Take comfort, gentle dame, and you, fair squire;
For in this desert there must needs be placed
Many strong castles held by courteous knights;
And, till I bring you safe to one of those,
I swear by this my order ne'er to leave you.

WIFE. Well said, Rafe!—George, Rafe was ever comfortable,° was he not?
CITIZEN. Yes, duck.
WIFE. I shall ne'er forget him. When we had lost our   20
child (you know it was strayed almost alone to Puddle
Wharf, and the criers were abroad for it, and there it
had drowned itself but for a sculler), Rafe was the
most comfortablest to me. "Peace, mistress," says he,
"let it go; I'll get you another as good." Did he not,
George, did he not say so?
CITIZEN. Yes, indeed did he, mouse.

---

shrewdly: shrewdly = severely; seriously.   lungies: tall lout.
comfortable: helpful, comforting.

DWARF. I would we had a mess of pottage and a pot of
  drink, squire, and were going to bed!

SQUIRE. Why, we are at Waltham town's end, and that's   30
  the Bell Inn.

DWARF. Take courage, valiant knight, damsel, and squire!
  I have discovered, not a stonecast off,
  An ancient castle held by the old knight
  Of the most holy Order of the Bell,
  Who gives to all knights-errant entertain:
  There plenty is of food, and all prepared
  By the white hands of his own lady dear.
  He hath three squires that welcome all his guests:
  The first, high[t]* Chamberlino, who will see   40
  Our beds prepared and bring us snowy sheets,
  Where never footman stretched his buttered hams;
  The second, hight Ta[p]stero, who will see
  Our pots filled and no froth therein;
  The third, a gentle squire, Ostlero hight,
  Who will our palfreys slick with wisps of straw,
  And in the manger put them oats enough,
  And never grease their teeth with candle snuff.

WIFE. That same dwarf's a pretty boy, but the squire's
  a groutnoll.*   50

RAFE. Knock at the gates, my squire, with stately lance.
  [SQUIRE *knocks.*]

Enter TAPSTER.

TAPSTER. Who's there?—You're welcome, gentlemen;
  will you see a room?

DWARF. Right courteous and valiant Knight of the Burning Pestle, this is the Squire Tapstero.

RAFE. Fair Squire Tapstero, I a wand'ring knight,
  Hight of the Burning Pestle, in the quest
  Of this fair lady's casket and wrought purse,
  Losing myself in this vast wilderness,
  Am to this castle well by fortune brought,   60
  Where, hearing of the goodly entertain
  Your knight of holy Order of the Bell

---

  hight: called, named.   groutnoll: blockhead.

Gives to all damsels and all errant knights,
I thought to knock, and now am bold to enter.
TAPSTER. An't please you see a chamber, you are very
welcome.

Exeunt.

WIFE. George, I would have something done, and I can-
not tell what it is.
CITIZEN. What is it, Nell?
WIFE. Why, George, shall Rafe beat nobody again?   70
Prithee, sweetheart, let him.
CITIZEN. So he shall, Nell; and, if I join with him, we'll
knock them all.

[II.vii]

Enter HUMPHREY *and* MERCHANT.

WIFE. O, George, here's Master Humphrey again now,
that lost Mistress Luce, and Mistress Lucy's father.
Master Humphrey will do somebody's errant,* I warrant him.

HUMPHREY. Father, it's true in arms I ne'er shall clasp
her,
For she is stol'n away by your man Jasper.

WIFE. I thought he would tell him.

MERCHANT. Unhappy that I am to lose my child!
Now I begin to think on Jasper's words,
Who oft hath urged to me thy foolishness.   10
Why didst thou let her go? Thou lov'st her not,
That wouldst bring home thy life and not bring her.
HUMPHREY. Father, forgive me. Shall I tell you true?
Look on my shoulders; they are black and blue.
Whilst to and fro fair Luce and I were winding,
He came and basted me with a hedge binding.
MERCHANT. Get men and horses straight; we will be there
Within this hour. You know the place again?
HUMPHREY. I know the place where he my loins did
swaddle;*

---

errant: errand.   swaddle: beat.

I'll get six horses, and to each a saddle.   20
MERCHANT. Meantime, I'll go talk with Jasper's father.

Exeunt.

WIFE. George, what wilt thou lay° with me now that
  Master Humphrey has not Mistress Luce yet? Speak,
  George, what wilt thou lay with me?
CITIZEN. No, Nell; I warrant thee, Jasper is at Puckeridge
  with her by this.
WIFE. Nay, George, you must consider Mistress Lucy's
  feet are tender; and besides 'tis dark; and, I promise
  you truly, I do not see how he should get out of
  Waltham Forest with her yet.   30
CITIZEN. Nay, cony, what wilt thou lay with me that
  Rafe has her not yet?
WIFE. I will not lay against Rafe, honey, because I have
  not spoken with him. But look, George, peace! Here
  comes the merry old gentleman again.

[II.viii]

Enter OLD MERRYTHOUGHT.

OLD MERRYTHOUGHT [*singing*].
> *When it was grown to dark midnight,*
> *And all were fast asleep,*
> *In came Margaret's grimly ghost,*
> *And stood at William's feet.*

I have money, and meat and drink beforehand, till
tomorrow at noon; why should I be sad? Methinks I
have half a dozen jovial spirits within me!
[*He sings.*]
> *I am three merry men, and three merry men!*

To what end should any man be sad in this world?
Give me a man that when he goes to hanging cries,   10
"Troll ° the black bowl to me!"—and a woman that
will sing a catch in her travail! I have seen a man
come by my door with a serious face, in a black cloak,
without a hatband, carrying his head as if he looked
for pins in the street; I have looked out of my window
half a year after and have spied that man's head upon
London Bridge.° 'Tis vile. Never trust a tailor that

---

lay: bet.   troll: pass.
London Bridge: where the heads of traitors and heretics were
displayed upon poles.

does not sing at his work; his mind is of nothing but
filching.

WIFE. Mark this, George; 'tis worth noting: Godfrey, my   20
tailor, you know, never sings, and he had fourteen
yards to make this gown; and, I'll be sworn, Mistress
Pennystone, the draper's wife, had one made with
twelve.

OLD MERRYTHOUGHT [*singing*].
      'Tis mirth that fills the veins with blood,
      More than wine, or sleep, or food.
      Let each man keep his heart at ease;
      No man dies of that disease.
      He that would his body keep
      From diseases must not weep;   30
      But whoever laughs and sings
      Never he his body brings
      Into fevers, gouts, or rheums,
      Or ling'ringly his lungs consumes,
      Or meets with achès in the bone,
      Or catarrhs or griping stone,
      But contented lives for aye:
      The more he laughs, the more he may.

WIFE. Look, George; how sayst thou by this, George? Is't
not a fine old man?—Now, God's blessing o' thy sweet   40
lips!—When wilt thou be so merry, George? Faith,
thou art the frowning'st little thing, when thou art
angry, in a country.

Enter MERCHANT.

CITIZEN. Peace, cony; thou shalt see him taken down
too, I warrant thee. Here's Luce's father come now.

OLD MERRYTHOUGHT [*singing*].
      As you came from Walsingham,
        From that holy land,
      There met you not with my true love
        By the way as you came?
MERCHANT. O, Master Merrythought, my daughter's
gone!   50

This mirth becomes you not; my daughter's gone!

OLD MERRYTHOUGHT [*singing*].

> *Why, an if she be, what care I?*
> *Or let her come, or go, or tarry.*

MERCHANT. Mock not my misery; it is your son
(Whom I have made my own, when all forsook him)
Has stol'n my only joy, my child, away.

OLD MERRYTHOUGHT [*singing*].

> *He set her on a milk-white steed,*
> *And himself upon a gray;*
> *He never turned his face again,*
> *But he bore her quite away.*   60

MERCHANT. Unworthy of the kindness I have shown
To thee and thine! Too late I well perceive
Thou art consenting to my daughter's loss.

OLD MERRYTHOUGHT. Your daughter! What a stir's here
wi' your daughter? Let her go, think no more on her,
but sing loud. If both my sons were on the gallows, I
would sing,

> *Down, down, down: they fall*
> *Down, and arise they never shall.*

MERCHANT. O, might I behold her once again,   70
And she once more embrace her aged sire!

OLD MERRYTHOUGHT. Fie, how scurvily this goes! "And
she once more embrace her aged sire!" You'll make a
dog on her, will ye? She cares much for her aged sire,
I warrant you!
[*He sings.*]

> *She cares not for her daddy,*
> *Nor she cares not for her mammy;*
> *For she is, she is, she is, she is*
> *My Lord of Lowgave's lassy.*

MERCHANT. For this thy scorn I will pursue   80
That son of thine to death.

OLD MERRYTHOUGHT. Do; and when you ha' kill'ed him,
[*He sings.*]

> *Give him flowers enow,** palmer, give him flowers*
> *   enow;*
> *Give him red and white, and blue, green, and*
> *   yellow.*

MERCHANT. I'll fetch my daughter—

---

enow: enough.

OLD MERRYTHOUGHT. I'll hear no more o' your daughter;
   it spoils my mirth.
MERCHANT. I say, I'll fetch my daughter.
OLD MERRYTHOUGHT [*singing*].

> *Was never man for lady's sake,*
> *Down, down,*   90
> *Tormented as I, poor Sir Guy,*
> *De derry down,*
> *For Lucy's sake, that lady bright,*
> *Down, down,*
> *As ever men beheld with eye,*
> *De derry down.*

MERCHANT. I'll be revenged, by heaven!

Exeunt.

Music.

FINIS ACTUS SECUNDI.

WIFE. How dost thou like this, George?
CITIZEN. Why, this is well, cony; but, if Rafe were hot
   once, thou shouldst see more.   100
WIFE. The fiddlers go again, husband.
CITIZEN. Ay, Nell; but this is scurvy music. I gave the
   whoreson gallows* money, and I think he has not got
   me the waits of Southwark. If I hear ['em] not anon,
   I'll twinge him by the ears.—You musicians, play
   Baloo!
WIFE. No, good George, let's ha' *Lachrymæ!*
CITIZEN. Why, this is it, cony.
WIFE. It's all the better, George. Now, sweet lamb, what
   story is that painted upon the cloth?* The Confuta-   110
   tion* of Saint Paul?
CITIZEN. No, lamb; that's Rafe and Lucrece.*
WIFE. Rafe and Lucrece? Which Rafe? Our Rafe?
CITIZEN. No, mouse; that was a Tartarian.*
WIFE. A Tartarian! Well, I would the fiddlers had done
   that we might see our Rafe again!

---

gallows: cheats.   cloth; painted backdrop of the stage.
confutation: i.e., conversion.
Rafe and Lucrece: i.e., *The Rape of Lucrece*, who was raped by
Tarquinius, a Tarquin and not a Tartarian.
Tartarian: also cant for thief.

ACTUS TERTIUS

[III.i]

Enter JASPER *and* LUCE.

JASPER. Come, my dear dear; though we have lost our
    way,
  We have not lost ourselves. Are you not weary
  With this night's wand'ring, broken from your rest
  And frighted with the terror that attends
  The darkness of [this] wild, unpeopled place?
LUCE. No, my best friend, I cannot either fear
  Or entertain a weary thought whilst you
  (The end of all my full desires) stand by me.
  Let them that lose their hopes, and live to languish
  Amongst the number of forsaken lovers,   10
  Tell ° the long, weary steps, and number time,
  Start at a shadow, and shrink up their blood
  Whilst I, possessed with all content and quiet,
  Thus take my pretty love and thus embrace him.
  [*She embraces him.*]
JASPER. You have caught me, Luce, so fast that, whilst
    I live,
  I shall become your faithful prisoner
  And [wear] these chains forever. Come, sit down,
  And rest your body, too too delicate
  For these disturbances.
  [*They sit down.*]
               So, will you sleep?
  Come, do not be more able than you are;   20
  I know you are not skillful in these watches,
  For women are no soldiers. Be not nice,°
  But take it;° sleep, I say.
LUCE.   I cannot sleep;
  Indeed, I cannot, friend.
JASPER.   Why, then, we'll sing,
  And try how that will work upon our senses.
LUCE. I'll sing, or say, or anything but sleep.
JASPER. Come, little mermaid, rob me of my heart
  With that enchanting voice.
LUCE.   You mock me, Jasper.

---

  tell: count.   nice: foolish.   take it: yield; acquiesce.

Song.

JASPER.	*Tell me, dearest, what is love?*	
LUCE.	*'Tis a lightning from above;*	30
	'Tis an arrow; 'tis a fire;	
	'Tis a boy they call Desire;	
	* 'Tis a smile*	
	* Doth beguile*	
JASPER.	*The poor hearts of men that prove.*	
	Tell me more, are women true?	
LUCE.	*Some love change, and so do you.*	
JASPER.	*Are they fair and never kind?*	
LUCE.	*Yes, when men turn with the wind.*	
JASPER.	* Are they froward?*	40
LUCE.	* Ever toward*	
	Those that love, to love anew.	

JASPER. Dissemble it no more; I see the god
  Of heavy sleep lay on his heavy mace
  Upon your eyelids.

LUCE.   I am very heavy.

  [*She sleeps.*]

JASPER. Sleep, sleep; and quiet rest crown thy sweet
    thoughts!

  Keep from her fair blood distempers, startings,
  Horrors, and fearful shapes! Let all her dreams
  Be joys and chaste delights, embraces, wishes,
  And such new pleasures as the ravished soul   50
  Gives to the senses!—So, my charms have took.—
  Keep her, you powers divine, whilst I contemplate
  Upon the wealth and beauty of her mind!
  She is only fair and constant, only kind,
  And only to thee, Jasper. O my joys!
  Wither will you transport me? Let not fullness
  Of my poor buried hopes come up together
  And overcharge my spirits! I am weak.
  Some say (however ill) the sea and women
  Are governed by the moon: both ebb and flow,   60
  Both full of changes; yet to them that know,
  And truly judge, these but opinions are,
  And heresies, to bring on pleasing war
  Between our tempers, that without these were

Both void of after-love* and present fear,
Which are the best of Cupid. O thou child
Bred from despair, I dare not entertain thee,
Having a love without the faults of women,
And greater in her perfect goods than men!
Which to make good, and please myself the stronger,   70
Though certainly I am certain of her love,
I'll try her, that the world and memory
May sing to aftertimes her constancy.—
[*He draws his sword.*]
Luce! Luce! Awake!

LUCE.   Why do you fright me, friend,
With those distempered looks? What makes your
     sword
Drawn in your hand? Who hath offended you?
I prithee, Jasper, sleep; thou art wild with watching.

JASPER. Come, make your way to heaven, and bid the
     world,
With all the villainies that stick upon it,
Farewell; you're for another life.

LUCE.   O, Jasper,   80
How have my tender years committed evil,
Especially against the man I love,
Thus to be cropped untimely?

JASPER.   Foolish girl,
Canst thou imagine I could love his daughter
That flung me from my fortune into nothing?
Dischargèd me his service, shut the doors
Upon my poverty, and scorned my prayers,
Sending me, like a boat without a mast,
To sink or swim? Come, by this hand, you die;
I must have life and blood to satisfy   90
Your father's wrongs.

WIFE. Away, George, away! Raise the watch at Ludgate,
and bring a *mittimus** from the justice for this desperate villain!—Now, I charge you, gentlemen, see
the king's peace kept!—O, my heart, what a varlet's

---

after-love: i.e., after the lovers have made up.
mittimus: warrant for arrest.

this to offer manslaughter upon the harmless gentlewoman?

CITIZEN. I warrant thee, sweetheart, we'll have him
hampered.

LUCE. O, Jasper, be not cruel!   100
If thou wilt kill me, smile, and do it quickly,
And let not many deaths appear before me.
I am a woman, made of fear and love,
A weak, weak woman. Kill not with thy eyes;
They shoot me through and through. Strike, I am
ready;
And, dying, still I love thee.
              Enter MERCHANT, HUMPHREY, *and his Men.*
MERCHANT.   Whereabouts?
JASPER [*aside*]. No more of this; now to myself again.
HUMPHREY. There, there he stands with sword, like
martial knight,
Drawn in his hand; therefore, beware the fight,
You that be wise; for, were I good Sir Bevis,*   110
I would not stay his coming, by your leaves.
MERCHANT. Sirrah, restore my daughter!
JASPER.   Sirrah, no!
MERCHANT. Upon him, then!
          [*They set upon* JASPER *and force* LUCE *from him.*]

WIFE. So; down with him, down with him, down with
him! Cut him i'th' leg, boys, cut him i'th' leg!

MERCHANT. Come your ways, minion; I'll provide a cage
For you, you're grown so tame.—Horse her away.
HUMPHREY. Truly, I'm glad your forces have the day.
                              Exeunt; manet JASPER.
JASPER. They are gone, and I am hurt; my love is lost,   120
Never to get again. O, me unhappy!
Bleed, bleed and die! I cannot. O, my folly,
Thou hast betrayed me! Hope, where art thou fled?
Tell me if thou be'st anywhere remaining.
Shall I but see my love again? O, no!
She will not deign to look upon her butcher,

Sir Bevis: of Hampton—hero of a popular metrical romance.

Nor is it fit she should; yet I must venture.
O, Chance, or Fortune, or whate'er thou art
That men adore for powerful, hear my cry,
And let me loving live, or losing die!

Exit.

WIFE. Is 'a gone, George? 130
CITIZEN. Ay, cony.
WIFE. Marry, and let him go, sweetheart. By the faith o'
my body, 'a has put me into such a fright that I tremble
(as they say) as 'twere an aspen-leaf. Look o' my little
finger, George, how it shakes. Now, i'truth, every
member of my body is the worse for't.
CITIZEN. Come, hug in mine arms, sweet mouse; he shall
not fright thee any more. Alas, mine own dear heart,
how it quivers!

[III.ii]
Enter MISTRESS MERRYTHOUGHT, RAFE, MICHAEL,
SQUIRE, DWARF, HOST, *and a* TAPSTER.

WIFE. O, Rafe! How dost thou, Rafe? How hast thou
slept tonight?° Has the knight used thee well?
CITIZEN. Peace, Nell; let Rafe alone.

TAPSTER. Master, the reckoning is not paid.
RAFE. Right courteous knight, who, for the order's sake
Which thou hast ta'en, hang'st out the holy Bell,
As I this flaming pestle bear about,
We render thanks to your puissant self,
Your beauteous lady, and your gentle squires
For thus refreshing of our wearied limbs, 10
Stiffened with hard achievements in wild desert.
TAPSTER. Sir, there is twelve shillings to pay.
RAFE. Thou merry Squire Tapstero, thanks to thee
For comforting our souls with double jug;
And, if advent'rous fortune prick thee forth,
Thou jovial squire, to follow feats of arms,
Take heed thou tender every lady's cause,
Every true knight, and every damsel fair;

―――――――――

tonight: last night.

But spill the blood of treacherous Saracens
And false enchanters that with magic spells   20
Have done to death full many a noble knight.

HOST. Thou valiant Knight of the Burning Pestle, give
ear to me; there is twelve shillings to pay, and, as I am
a true knight, I will not bate a penny.

WIFE. George, I pray thee, tell me, must Rafe pay twelve
shillings now?

CITIZEN. No, Nell, no; nothing but the old knight is
merry with Rafe.

WIFE. O, is't nothing else? Rafe will be as merry as he.

RAFE. Sir knight, this mirth of yours becomes you well;   30
But, to requite this liberal courtesy,
If any of your squires will follow arms,
He shall receive from my heroic hand
A knighthood, by the virtue of this pestle.

HOST. Fair knight, I thank you for [your] noble offer;
Therefore, gentle knight,
Twelve shillings you must pay, or I must cap* you.

WIFE. Look, George! Did not I tell thee as much? The
Knight of the Bell is in earnest. Rafe shall not be beholding to him. Give him his money, George, and let   40
him go snick up.

CITIZEN. Cap Rafe? No.—Hold your hand, Sir Knight of
the Bell; there's your money. [*He gives money.*] Have
you anything to say to Rafe now? Cap Rafe?

WIFE. I would you should know it, Rafe has friends that
will not suffer him to be capped for ten times so much,
and ten times to the end of that.—Now take thy
course, Rafe.

MISTRESS MERRYTHOUGHT. Come, Michael; thou and I
will go home to thy father; he hath enough left to   50
keep up a day or two, and we'll set fellows abroad to
cry our purse and our casket. Shall we, Michael?

MICHAEL. Ay, I pray, mother; in truth, my feet are full
of chilblains with traveling

---

cap: arrest.

WIFE. Faith, and those chilblains are a foul trouble.
Mistress Merrythought, when your youth comes home,
let him rub all the soles of his feet and the heels and
his ankles with a mouse skin; or, if none of your people
can catch a mouse, when he goes to bed, let him roll
his feet in the warm embers, and, I warrant you, he   60
shall be well; and you may make him put his fingers
between his toes and smell to them. It's very sovereign
for his head if he be costive.*

MISTRESS MERRYTHOUGHT. Master Knight of the Burning
Pestle, my son Michael and I bid you farewell. I thank
your worship heartily for your kindness.
RAFE. Farewell, fair lady, and your tender squire.
If, pricking through these deserts, I do hear
Of any traitorous knight who through his guile
Hath light upon your casket and your purse,   70
I will despoil him of them and restore them.
MISTRESS MERRYTHOUGHT. I thank your worship.

Exit with MICHAEL.

RAFE. Dwarf, bear my shield; squire, elevate my lance.
And now farewell, you Knight of holy Bell.

CITIZEN. Ay, ay, Rafe, all is paid.

RAFE. But yet, before I go, speak, worthy knight,
If aught you do of sad * adventures know,
Where errant [knight] may through his prowess win
Eternal fame and free some gentle souls
From endless bonds of steel and ling'ring pain.   80
HOST. Sirrah, go to Nick the barber, and bid him prepare
himself, as I told you before, quickly.
TAPSTER. I am gone, sir.

Exit TAPSTER.

HOST. Sir Knight, this wilderness affordeth none
But the great venture, where full many a knight
Hath tried his prowess and come off with shame,
And where I would not have you lose your life
Against no man but furious fiend of hell.
RAFE. Speak on, sir knight; tell what he is and where,

costive: constipated.   sad: important.

For here I vow, upon my blazing badge,   90
Never to blaze a day in quietness,
But bread and water will I only eat,
And the green herb and rock shall be my couch
Till I have quelled ° that man or beast or fiend
That works such damage to all errant knights.
HOST. Not far from hence, near to a craggy cliff,
At the north end of this distressèd town,
There doth stand a lowly house,
Ruggedly builded, and in it a cave
In which an ugly giant now doth won,°   100
Yclepèd ° Barbaroso. In his hand
He shakes a naked lance of purest steel,
With sleeves turned up; and him before he wears
A motley garment to preserve his clothes
From blood of those knights which he massacres,
And ladies gent.° Without his door doth hang
A copper basin on a prickant° spear,
At which no sooner gentle knights can knock
But the shrill sound fierce Barbaroso hears,
And, rushing forth, brings in the errant knight   110
And sets him down in an enchanted chair.
Then with an engine, which he hath prepared
With forty teeth, he claws his courtly crown,
Next makes him wink,° and underneath his chin
He plants a brazen piece of mighty bord,°
And knocks his bullets° round about his cheeks
Whilst with his fingers and an instrument
With which he snaps his hair off he doth fill
The wretch's ears with a most hideous noise.
Thus every knight adventurer he doth trim,   120
And now no creature dares encounter him.
RAFE. In God's name, I will fight him. Kind sir,
Go but before me to this dismal cave,
Where this huge giant Barbaroso dwells,
And, by that virtue that brave Rosicleer
That damnèd brood of ugly giants slew,

---

quelled: killed.   won: dwell.   yclepèd: called, named.
gent: gentle, noble.
prickant: pointing upwards (referring to the barber's "spear" or
pole).   wink: close eyes tight.
bord: rim (of the barber's bowl).   bullets: pellets of soap.

And Palmerin Frannarco overthrew,
I doubt not but to curb this traitor foul
And to the devil send his guilty soul.

HOST. Brave-sprighted knight, thus far I will perform   130
This your request: I'll bring you within sight
Of this most loathsome place, inhabited
By a more loathsome man, but dare not stay,
For his main force [swoops] all he sees away.

RAFE. Saint George, set on before! March, squire and
page!

Exeunt.

WIFE. George, dost think Rafe will confound the giant?

CITIZEN. I hold my cap to a farthing he does. Why, Nell,
I saw him wrestle with the great Dutchman and hurl
him.

WIFE. Faith, and that Dutchman was a goodly man if   140
all things were answerable to his bigness. And yet they
say there was a Scotchman higher than he, and that
they two and a knight met and saw one another for
nothing. But of all the sights that ever were in London
since I was married, methinks the little child that was
so fair grown about the members was the prettiest;
that, and the hermaphrodite.

CITIZEN. Nay, by your leave, Nell, *Ninivy*° was better.

WIFE. *Ninivy!* O, that was the story of Joan and the
wall,° was it not, George?   150

CITIZEN. Yes, lamb.

[III.iii]

Enter MISTRESS MERRYTHOUGHT.

WIFE. Look, George, here comes Mistress Merrythought
again! And I would have Rafe come and fight with the
giant; I tell you true, I long to see't.

CITIZEN. Good Mistress Merrythought, be gone, I pray
you, for my sake. I pray you, forbear a little; you shall
have audience presently. I have a little business.

WIFE. Mistress Merrythought, if it please you to refrain

Ninivy: a popular puppet show about Nineveh.
Joan . . . wall: Jonah and the whale.

your passion a little till Rafe have dispatch[ed] the
giant out of the way, we shall think ourselves much
bound to you. I thank you, good Mistress Merry-   10
thought.

Exit MISTRESS MERRYTHOUGHT.
Enter a BOY.

CITIZEN. Boy, come hither. Send away Rafe and this
whoreson giant quickly.

BOY. In good faith, sir, we cannot; you'll utterly spoil our
play and make it to be hissed; and it cost money. You
will not suffer us to go on with our plot.—I pray, gentlemen, rule him.

CITIZEN. Let him come now and dispatch this, and I'll
trouble you no more.

BOY. Will you give me your hand of that?   20

WIFE. Give him thy hand, George, do; and I'll kiss him.
I warrant thee, the youth means plainly.*

BOY. I'll send him to you presently.*

WIFE [kissing him]. I thank you, little youth.

(Exit BOY.)

—Faith, the child hath a sweet breath, George; but I
think it be troubled with the worms. *Carduus benedictus** and mare's milk were the only thing in the
world for't.—O, Rafe's here, George!—God send thee
good luck, Rafe!

[III.iv]

Enter RAFE, HOST, SQUIRE, and DWARF.

HOST. Puissant knight, yonder his mansion is;
Lo, where the spear and the copper basin are!
Behold that string on which hangs many a tooth,*
Drawn from the gentle jaw of wand'ring knights!
I dare not stay to sound;* he will appear.

Exit HOST.

RAFE. O, faint not, heart! Susan, my lady dear,
The cobbler's maid in Milk Street, for whose sake
I take these arms, O, let the thought of thee
Carry thy knight through all adventurous deeds;

---

plainly: sincerely.   presently: at once, immediately.
carduus benedictus: the blessed thistle (medicinal); panacea.
tooth: a barber-surgeon also extracted teeth.
sound: blow horn.

And, in the honor of thy beauteous self,   10
May I destroy this monster Barbaroso!—
Knock, squire, upon the basin till it break
With the shrill strokes or till the giant speak.
[TIM *knocks upon the basin.*]
Enter BARBER.

WIFE. O, George, the giant, the giant!—Now, Rafe, for
thy life!

BARBER. What fond * unknowing wight is this that dares
So rudely knock at Barbaroso's cell,
Where no man comes but leaves his fleece behind?
RAFE. I, traitorous caitiff, who am sent by fate
To punish all the sad enormities   20
Thou hast committed against ladies gent
And errant knights. Traitor to God and men,
Prepare thyself! This is the dismal hour
Appointed for thee to give strict account
Of all thy beastly treacherous villainies.
BARBER. Foolhardy knight, full soon thou shalt aby*
This fond reproach; thy body will I bang;
(*He takes down his pole.*)
And, lo, upon that string thy teeth shall hang!
Prepare thyself, for dead soon shalt thou be.
RAFE. Saint George for me!
(*They fight.*)
BARBER.   Gargantua for me!   30

WIFE. To him, Rafe, to him! Hold up the giant; set out
thy leg before, Rafe!
CITIZEN. Falsify a blow, Rafe, falsify a blow! The giant
lies open on the left side.
WIFE. Bear't off, bear't off still! There, boy!—O, Rafe's
almost down, Rafe's almost down!

RAFE. Susan, inspire me!—Now have up again.

WIFE. Up, up, up, up, up! So, Rafe! Down with him,
down with him, Rafe!
CITIZEN. Fetch him o'er the hip, boy!   40

---

fond: foolish.   aby: pay for.

WIFE. There, boy! Kill, kill, kill, kill, kill, Rafe!
CITIZEN. No, Rafe; get all out of him first.

RAFE. Presumptuous man, see to what desperate end
   Thy treachery hath brought thee! The just gods,
   Who never prosper those that do despise them,
   For all the villainies which thou hast done
   To knights and ladies, now have paid thee home
   By my stiff arm, a knight adventurous.
   But say, vile wretch, before I send thy soul
   To sad Avernus,* whither it must go,   50
   What captives hold'st thou in thy sable cave?
BARBER. Go in, and free them all; thou hast the day.
RAFE. Go, squire and dwarf, search in this dreadful cave,
   And free the wretched prisoners from their bonds.
                  [*Exeunt*] SQUIRE *and* DWARF.
BARBER. I crave for mercy, as thou art a knight
   And scorn'st to spill the blood of those that beg.
RAFE. Thou showed'st no mercy, nor shalt thou have any;
   Prepare thyself, for thou shalt surely die.
    Enter SQUIRE, *leading One winking, with a basin*
              under his chin.
SQUIRE. Behold, brave knight, here is one prisoner,
   Whom this wild man hath used as you see.   60

WIFE. This is the first wise word I heard the squire speak.

RAFE. Speak what thou art and how thou hast been used,
   That I may give [him] condign punishment.
1 KNIGHT. I am a knight that took my journey post
   Northward from London; and in courteous wise
   This giant trained * me to his loathsome den
   Under pretense of killing of the itch;
   And all my body with a powder strewed,
   That smarts and stings, and cut away my beard,
   And my curled locks wherein were ribands tied;   70
   And with a water washed my tender eyes
   (Whilst up and down about me still * he skipped),
   Whose virtue is that, till mine eyes be wiped

Avernus: the infernal regions.   trained: lured.
still: continually.

With a dry cloth, for this my foul disgrace
I shall not dare to look a dog i'th' face.

WIFE. Alas, poor knight!—Relieve him, Rafe; relieve
poor knights whilst you live.

RAFE. My trusty squire, convey him to the town,
Where he may find relief.—Adieu, fair knight.

Exit [1] KNIGHT.

Enter DWARF, *leading One with a patch o'er his nose.*

DWARF. Puissant knight, of the Burning Pestle hight,   80
See here another wretch, whom this foul beast
Hath scorched * and scored in this inhuman wise.

RAFE. Speak me thy name, and eke thy place of birth,
And what hath been thy usage in this cave.

2 KNIGHT. I am a knight, Sir Pockhole is my name.
And by my birth I am a Londoner,
Free by my copy; * but my ancestors
Were Frenchmen all; and, riding hard this way
Upon a trotting horse, my bones did ache; *
And I, faint knight, to ease my weary limbs,   90
Light at this cave when straight this furious fiend
With sharpest instrument of purest steel
Did cut the gristle of my nose away,
And in the place this velvet plaster stands.
Relieve me, gentle knight, out of his hands!

WIFE. Good Rafe, relieve Sir Pockhole and send him
away, for in truth his breath stinks.

RAFE. Convey him straight after the other knight.—
Sir Pockhole, fare you well!

2 KNIGHT.   Kind sir, good night.

Exit.

(*Cries within.*)

MAN. Deliver us!   100

WOMAN. Deliver us!

---

scorched: scotched, cut.
copy: certification of citizenship, of being a freeman.
bones did ache: from his bad case of syphilis.

WIFE. Hark, George, what a woeful cry there is! I think
    some woman lies in there.

MAN. Deliver us!
WOMAN. Deliver us!
RAFE. What ghastly noise is this? Speak, Barbaroso,
    Or, by this blazing steel, thy head goes off!
BARBER. Prisoners of mine, whom I in diet* keep.
    Send lower down into the cave,
    And in a tub that's heated smoking hot   110
    There may they find them and deliver them.
RAFE. Run, squire and dwarf; deliver them with speed.
                            Exeunt SQUIRE *and* DWARF.

WIFE. But will not Rafe kill this giant? Surely I am
    afeared, if he let him go, he will do as much hurt as
    ever he did.
CITIZEN. Not so, mouse, neither, if he could convert him.
WIFE. Ay, George, if he could convert him; but a giant
    is not so soon converted as one of us ordinary people.
    There's a pretty tale of a witch that had the devil's
    mark about her (God bless us!), that had a giant to   120
    her son, that was called Lob-lie-by-the-fire. Didst
    never hear it, George?

        Enter SQUIRE, *leading a* MAN *with a glass of lotion
            in his hand, and the* DWARF, *leading a* WOMAN
                with diet-bread and drink.

CITIZEN. Peace, Nell, here comes the prisoners.

DWARF. Here be these pinèd wretches, manful knight,
    That for these six weeks have not seen a wight.
RAFE. Deliver what you are, and how you came
    'To this sad cave, and what your usage was.
MAN. I am an errant knight that followed arms
    With spear and shield; and in my tender years
    I stricken was with Cupid's fiery shaft   130
    And fell in love with this my lady dear
    And stole her from her friends in Turnbull Street *

---

diet: treatment for syphilis.
Turnbull Street: notorious for prostitutes.

And bore her up and down from town to town,
Where we did eat and drink and music hear;
Till at the length at this unhappy town
We did arrive; and, coming to this cave,
This beast us caught and put us in a tub,
Where we this two months sweat, and should have
　done
Another month if you had not relieved us.
WOMAN.　This bread and water hath our diet been,　　140
Together with a rib cut from a neck
Of burnèd mutton; hard hath been our fare.
Release us from this ugly giant's snare.
MAN.　This hath been all the food we have received;
But only twice a day, for novelty,
He gave a spoonful of this hearty broth
(*Pulls out a syringe.*)
To each of us through this same slender quill.
RAFE.　From this infernal monster you shall go,
That useth knights and gentle ladies so!—
Convey them hence.　　150

　　　　　　　　　　　　Exeunt MAN *and* WOMAN.

CITIZEN.　Cony, I can tell thee, the gentlemen like Rafe.
WIFE.　Ay, George, I see it well enough.—Gentlemen, I
　thank you all heartily for gracing my man Rafe; and,
　I promise you, you shall see him oft'ner.

BARBER.　Mercy, great knight! I do recant my ill
And henceforth never gentle blood will spill.
RAFE.　I give thee mercy, but yet shalt thou swear
Upon my burning pestle to perform
Thy promise uttered.
BARBER.　I swear and kiss.
[*He kisses the pestle.*]
RAFE.　　　　　　　　　　Depart then, and amend.—　　160
　　　　　　　　　　　　　[*Exit* BARBER.]
Come, squire and dwarf; the sun grows towards his set,
And we have many more adventures yet.

　　　　　　　　　　　　　　　　Exeunt.

CITIZEN.　Now Rafe is in this humor, I know he would
　ha' beaten all the boys in the house if they had been
　set on him.

WIFE. Ay, George, but it is well as it is. I warrant you,
the gentlemen do consider what it is to overthrow a
giant. But, look, George; here comes Mistress Merrythought and her son Michael.—Now you are welcome,
Mistress Merrythought; now Rafe has done, you may   170
go on.

[III.v]
    Enter MISTRESS MERRYTHOUGHT *and* MICHAEL.
MISTRESS MERRYTHOUGHT. Mick, my boy—
MICHAEL. Ay, forsooth, mother.
MISTRESS MERRYTHOUGHT. Be merry, Mick; we are at
home now, where, I warrant you, you shall find the
house flung out at the windows. [*Music within.*] Hark!
Hey, dogs, hey! This is the old world, i'faith, with my
husband. If I get in among 'em, I'll play 'em such a
lesson that they shall have little list to come scraping
hither again.—Why, Master Merrythought! Husband!
Charles Merrythought!   10
OLD MERRYTHOUGHT (*within* [*singing*]).
    If you will sing and dance and laugh
      And hollo and laugh again,
    And then cry, "There, boys, there!" why, then,
      One, two, three, and four,
      We shall be merry within this hour.
MISTRESS MERRYTHOUGHT. Why, Charles, do you not
know your own natural wife? I say, open the door, and
turn me out those mangy companions; 'tis more than
time that they were fellow and fellowlike with you.
You are a gentleman, Charles, and an old man, and   20
father of two children; and I myself (though I say it)
by my mother's side niece to a worshipful gentleman
and a conductor;* ha* has been three times in his
majesty's service at Chester and is now the fourth time,
God bless him and his charge, upon his journey.
OLD MERRYTHOUGHT [*singing, at the window*].
    Go from my window, love, go;
    Go from my window, my dear!
      The wind and the rain
      Will drive you back again;
    You cannot be lodgèd here.   30

---

conductor: captain.   ha: he.

Hark you, Mistress Merrythought, you that walk upon
adventures and forsake your husband because he sings
with never a penny in his purse—what, shall I think
myself the worse? Faith, no; I'll be merry. You come
not here; here's none but lads of mettle, lives of a hundred years and upwards; care never drunk their bloods,
nor want made 'em warble, "Heigh-ho, my heart is
heavy."

> *[Exit from window.]*

MISTRESS MERRYTHOUGHT. Why, Master Merrythought,
what am I that you should laugh me to scorn thus   40
abruptly? Am I not your fellow-feeler (as we may say)
in all our miseries? Your comforter in health and sickness? Have I not brought you children? Are they not
like you, Charles? Look upon thine own image, hard-
hearted man! And yet for all this—

OLD MERRYTHOUGHT (*within*).

> *Begone, begone, my juggy, my puggy,*
> *Begone, my love, my dear!*
> *The weather is warm;*
> *'Twill do thee no harm;*
> *Thou canst not be lodgèd here.*   50

Be merry, boys! Some light music and more wine!

WIFE. He's not in earnest, I hope, George, is he?

CITIZEN. What if he be, sweetheart?

WIFE. Marry, if he be, George, I'll make bold to tell him
he's an ingrant * old man to use his bedfellow so scurvily.

CITIZEN. What! How does he use her, honey?

WIFE. Marry, come up, Sir Saucebox! I think you'll take
his part, will you not? Lord, how hot you are grown!
You are a fine man, an you had a fine dog; it becomes   60
you sweetly!

CITIZEN. Nay, prithee, Nell, chide not; for, as I am an
honest man and a true Christian grocer, I do not like
his doings.

WIFE. I cry you mercy, then, George! You know we are
all frail and full of infirmities.—D'ye hear, Master
Merrythought? May I crave a word with you?

---

ingrant: ignorant (and ingrate).

OLD MERRYTHOUGHT (*within*). Strike up lively, lads!

WIFE. I had not thought, in truth, Master Merrythought,
that a man of your age and discretion (as I may say),   70
being a gentleman, and therefore known by your gentle conditions, could have used so little respect to the
weakness of his wife; for your wife is your own flesh,
the staff of your age, your yokefellow, with whose help
you draw through the mire of this transitory world;
nay, she's your own rib! And again—

OLD MERRYTHOUGHT [*singing*].
          I come not hither for thee to teach;
          I have no pulpit for thee to preach;
          I would thou hadst kissed me under the breech,
                    As thou art a lady gay.   80

WIFE. Marry, with a vengeance! I am heartily sorry for
the poor gentlewoman; but, if I were thy wife, i'faith,
graybeard, i'faith—

CITIZEN. I prithee, sweet honeysuckle, be content.

WIFE. Give me such words that am a gentlewoman born!
Hang him, hoary rascal! Get me some drink, George;
I am almost molten with fretting. Now, beshrew his
knave's heart for it!

                                        [*Exit* CITIZEN.]

OLD MERRYTHOUGHT. Play me a light lavolta.* Come, be
frolic. Fill the good fellows wine.   90

MISTRESS MERRYTHOUGHT. Why, Master Merrythought,
are you disposed to make me wait here? You'll open, I
hope; I'll fetch them that shall open else.

OLD MERRYTHOUGHT. Good woman, if you will sing, I'll
give you something; if not—
                    Song.
          You are no love for me, Marg'ret;
          I am no love for you.—
Come aloft, boys, aloft!

MISTRESS MERRYTHOUGHT. Now a churl's fart in your
teeth, sir!—Come, Mick, we'll not trouble him; 'a shall 100
not ding us i'th'teeth with his bread and his broth,

---

lavolta: lively French dance for two people.

that he shall not. Come, boy; I'll provide for thee, I warrant thee. We'll go to Master Venturewell's, the merchant. I'll get his letter to mine host of the Bell in Waltham; there I'll place thee with the tapster. Will not that do well for thee, Mick? And let me alone for that old cuckoldly knave, your father; I'll use him in his kind, I warrant ye.

[*Exeunt.*]

[*Re-enter* CITIZEN *with beer.*]

WIFE. Come, George, where's the beer?

CITIZEN. Here, love.   110

WIFE. This old fornicating fellow will not out of my mind yet.—Gentlemen, I'll begin to you all; and I desire more of your acquaintance with all my heart. [*She drinks.*]—Fill the gentlemen some beer, George.

FINIS ACTUS TERTII.
Music.

ACTUS QUARTUS

[IV.i]

BOY *danceth.*

WIFE. Look, George, the little boy's come again. Methinks he looks something like the Prince of Orange in his long stocking if he had a little harness* about his neck. George, I will have him dance *Fading.*—*Fading* is a fine jig, I'll assure you, gentlemen.—Begin, brother. —Now 'a capers, sweetheart!—Now a turn o'th' toe, and then tumble! Cannot you tumble, youth?

BOY. No, indeed, forsooth.

WIFE. Nor eat fire?

BOY. Neither.   10

WIFE. Why, then, I thank you heartily; there's twopence to buy you points * withal.

Enter JASPER *and* BOY.

JASPER. There, boy, deliver this.
[*He gives a letter.*]

But do it well.

---

harness: armor.
points: tagged lace that attaches to hose to fasten clothes.

Hast thou provided me four lusty fellows
Able to carry me? And art thou perfect
In all thy business?

BOY.   Sir, you need not fear;
I have my lesson here and cannot miss it.
The men are ready for you and what else
Pertains to this employment.

JASPER.   There, my boy.
[*He gives money.*]
Take it, but buy no land.

BOY.   Faith, sir, 'twere rare   20
To see so young a purchaser. I fly,
And on my wings carry your destiny.

                                              Exit.

JASPER. Go, and be happy!—Now, my latest hope,
Forsake me not but fling thy anchor out
And let it hold! Stand fixed, thou rolling stone,
Till I enjoy my dearest! Hear me, all
You powers, that rule in men, celestial!

                                              Exit.

WIFE. Go thy ways; thou art as crooked a sprig as ever
grew in London. I warrant him, he'll come to some
naughty end or other, for his looks say no less. Besides,   30
his father (you know, George) is none of the best; you
heard him take me up like a flirt-gill * and sing bawdy
songs upon me. But, i'faith, if I live, George—

CITIZEN. Let me alone, sweetheart. I have a trick in my
head shall lodge him in the Arches* for one year and
make him sing *peccavi** ere I leave him, and yet he
shall never know who hurt him neither.

WIFE. Do, my good George, do!

CITIZEN. What shall we have Rafe do now, boy?

BOY. You shall have what you will, sir.   40

CITIZEN. Why, so, sir; go and fetch me him then, and let
the Sophy of Persia come and christen him a child.

---

flirt-gill: prostitute.
Arches: ecclesiastics court in London (probably with prison attached).   *peccavi:* I have sinned.

BOY. Believe me, sir, that will not do so well; 'tis stale;
it has been had before at the Red Bull.*

WIFE. George, let Rafe travel over great hills, and let
him be very weary, and come to the King of Cracovia's
house, covered with [black] velvet; and there let the
king's daughter stand in her window, all in beaten
gold, combing her golden locks with a comb of ivory;
and let her spy Rafe and fall in love with him and   50
come down to him and carry him into her father's
house; and then let Rafe talk with her.

CITIZEN. Well said, Nell; it shall be so.—Boy, let's ha't
done quickly.

BOY. Sir, if you will imagine all this to be done already,
you shall hear them talk together; but we cannot present a house covered with black velvet and a lady in
beaten gold.

CITIZEN. Sir boy, let's ha't as you can, then.

BOY. Besides, it will show ill-favoredly to have a grocer's   60
prentice to court a king's daughter.

CITIZEN. Will it so, sir? You are well read in histories! I
pray you, what was Sir Dagonet? Was not he prentice
to a grocer in London? Read the play of *The Four
Prentices of London*, where they toss their pikes so. I
pray you, fetch him in, sir, fetch him in.

BOY. It shall be done.—It is not our fault, gentlemen.

                                                        Exit.

WIFE. Now we shall see fine doings, I warrant tee,
George. O, here they come! How prettily the King of
Cracovia's daughter is dressed!   70

[IV.ii]
        Enter RAFE *and the* LADY, SQUIRE, *and* DWARF.

CITIZEN. Ay, Nell, it is the fashion of that country, I
warrant tee.

LADY. Welcome, sir knight, unto my father's court,
King of Moldavia, unto me, Pompiona,

Red Bull: public theater catering particularly to popular taste.
Nell has in mind an incident in *The Travels of the Three English
Brothers* (1607).

His daughter dear! But, sure, you do not like
Your entertainment, that will stay with us
No longer but a night.

RAFE.   Damsel right fair,
I am on many sad adventures bound,
That call me forth into the wilderness;
Besides, my horse's back is something galled,   10
Which will enforce me ride a sober pace.
But many thanks, fair lady, be to you
For using errant knight with courtesy!

LADY. But say, brave knight, what is your name and
    birth?

RAFE. My name is Rafe; I am an Englishman,
As true as steel, a hearty Englishman,
And prentice to a grocer in the Str[a]nd
By deed indent,* of which I have one part.
But, Fortune calling me to follow arms,
On me this holy order I did take   20
Of Burning Pestle, which in all men's eyes
I bear, confounding ladies' enemies.

LADY. Oft have I heard of your brave countrymen
And fertile soil and store of wholesome food;
My father oft will tell me of a drink
In England found, and nippitato* called,
Which driveth all the sorrow from your hearts.

RAFE. Lady, 'tis true; you need not lay your lips
To better nippitato than there is.

LADY. And of a wild fowl he will often speak,   30
Which powdered -beef *-and-mustard callèd is;
For there have been great wars 'twixt us and you.
But truly, Rafe, it was not long* of me.
Tell me then, Rafe, could you contented be
To wear a lady's favor in your shield?

RAFE. I am a knight of religious order,
And will not wear a favor of a lady's
That trusts in Antichrist and false traditions.

CITIZEN. Well said, Rafe! Convert her if thou canst.

---

indent: indenture.   nippitato: strong ale.
powdered-beef: salted beef.   long: because.

RAFE. Besides, I have a lady of my own   40
  In merry England, for whose virtuous sake
  I took these arms; and Susan is her name,
  A cobbler's maid in Milk Street, whom I vow
  Ne'er to forsake whilst life and pestle last.
LADY. Happy that cobbling dame, whoe'er she be,
  That for her own, dear Rafe, hath gotten thee;
  Unhappy I, that ne'er shall see the day
  To see thee more, that bear'st my heart away.
RAFE. Lady, farewell; I needs must take my leave.
LADY. Hard-hearted Rafe, that ladies dost deceive!   50

CITIZEN. Hark thee, Rafe; there's money for thee. [*He
  gives money.*] Give something in the King of Cracovia's
  house; be not beholding to him.

RAFE. Lady, before I go, I must remember
  Your father's officers, who, truth to tell,
  Have been about me very diligent.
  Hold up thy snowy hand, thou princely maid!
  There's twelvepence for your father's chamberlain;
  And another shilling for his cook,
  For, by my troth, the goose was roasted well;   60
  And twelvepence for your father's horse-keeper,
  For 'nointing my horse' back, and for his butter
  There is another shilling; to the maid
  That washed my boothose, there's an English groat,
  And twopence to the boy that wiped my boots;
  And last, fair lady, there is for yourself
  Threepence to buy you pins at Bumbo Fair.
LADY. Full many thanks, and I will keep them safe
  Till all the heads be off, for thy sake, Rafe.
RAFE. Advance, my squire and dwarf! I cannot stay.   70
LADY. Thou kill'st my heart in parting thus away.

Exeunt.

WIFE. I commend Rafe yet, that he will not stoop to a
  Cracovian; there's properer women in London than
  any are there, iwis. But here comes Master Humphrey
  and his love again now, George.
CITIZEN. Ay, cony; peace!

[IV.iii]

Enter MERCHANT, HUMPHREY, LUCE, *and a* BOY.

MERCHANT. Go, get you up;* I will not be entreated.
And, gossip mine, I'll keep you sure hereafter
From gadding out again with boys and unthrifts.
Come, they are women's tears; I know your fashion.—
Go, sirrah, lock her in and keep the key
Safe as you love your life.

                    [*Exeunt*] LUCE *and* BOY.
              —Now, my son Humphrey,
You may both rest assurèd of my love
In this, and reap your own desire.

HUMPHREY. I see this love you speak of, through your
    daughter,
Although the hole be little, and hereafter   10
Will yield the like in all I may or can,
Fitting a Christian and a gentleman.

MERCHANT. I do believe you, my good son, and thank
    you;
For 'twere an impudence to think you flattered.

HUMPHREY. It were, indeed; but shall I tell you why?
I have been beaten twice about the lie.

MERCHANT. Well, son, no more of compliment. My
    daughter
Is yours again; appoint the time, and take her.
We'll have no stealing for it; I myself
And some few of our friends will see you married.   20

HUMPHREY. I would you would, i'faith; for, be it known,
I ever was afraid to lie alone.

MERCHANT. Some three days hence, then.

HUMPHREY.   Three days!
    Let me see;
'Tis somewhat of the most; yet I agree
Because I mean against the appointed day
To visit all my friends in new array.

                 Enter SERVANT.

SERVANT. Sir, there's a gentlewoman without would
speak with your worship.

MERCHANT. What is she?

---

    up: upstairs.

SERVANT. Sir, I asked her not. 30
MERCHANT. Bid her come in.

[*Exit* SERVANT.]
Enter MISTRESS MERRYTHOUGHT *and* MICHAEL.

MISTRESS MERRYTHOUGHT. Peace be to your worship! I come as a poor suitor to you, sir, in the behalf of this child.

MERCHANT. Are you not wife to Merrythought?

MISTRESS MERRYTHOUGHT. Yes, truly. Would I had ne'er seen his eyes! Ha has undone me and himself and his children; and there he lives at home, and sings and hoits* and revels among his drunken companions! But, I warrant you, where to get a penny to put bread in his 40 mouth he knows not; and, therefore, if it like your worship, I would entreat your letter to the honest host of the Bell in Waltham that I may place my child under the protection of his tapster in some settled course of life.

MERCHANT. I'm glad the heavens have heard my prayers.
Thy husband,
When I was ripe in sorrows, laughed at me;
Thy son, like an unthankful wretch, I having
Redeemed him from his fall and made him mine,
To show his love again first stole my daughter, 50
Then wronged this gentleman, and, last of all,
Gave me that grief had almost brought me down
Unto my grave had not a stronger hand
Relieved my sorrows. Go and weep, as I did,
And be unpitied; for I here profess
An everlasting hate to all thy name.

MISTRESS MERRYTHOUGHT. Will you so, sir? How say you by that?—Come, Mick, let him keep his wind to cool his porridge. We'll go to thy nurse's, Mick. She knits silk stockings, boy; and we'll knit too, boy, and be 60 beholding to none of them all.

Exeunt MICHAEL *and* MOTHER.
Enter a BOY *with a letter.*

BOY. Sir, I take it you are the master of this house.
MERCHANT. How then, boy?
BOY. Then to yourself, sir, comes this letter.

---

hoits: has a good time.

MERCHANT. From whom, my pretty boy?
BOY. From him that was your servant; but no more
Shall that name ever be, for he is dead:
Grief of your purchased anger broke his heart.
I saw him die, and from his hand received
This paper, with a charge to bring it hither.   70
Read it, and satisfy yourself in all.

Letter.

MERCHANT. "Sir, that I have wronged your love I must
confess; in which I have purchased to myself, besides
mine own undoing, the ill opinion of friends. Let not
your anger, good sir, outlive me, but suffer me to rest
in peace with your forgiveness. Let my body (if a
dying man may so much prevail with you) be brought
to your daughter, that she may truly know my hot
flames are now buried, and withal receive a testimony
of the zeal I bore her virtue. Farewell forever, and be   80
ever happy!   *Jasper.*"
God's hand is great in this. I do forgive him;
Yet I am glad he's quiet, where I hope
He will not bite again.—Boy, bring the body
And let him have his will if that be all.
BOY. 'Tis here without, sir.
MERCHANT.   So, sir, if you please,
You may conduct it in; I do not fear it.
HUMPHREY. I'll be your usher, boy; for, though I say it,
He owed me something once and well did pay it.

Exeunt.

Enter LUCE, *alone.*

LUCE. If there be any punishment inflicted   90
Upon the miserable more than yet I feel,
Let it together seize me and at once
Press down my soul! I cannot bear the pain
Of these delaying tortures.—Thou that art
The end of all, and the sweet rest of all,
Come, come, O Death! Bring me to thy peace,
And blot out all the memory I nourish
Both of my father and my cruel friend!—
O, wretched maid, still living to be wretched,
To be a say* to Fortune in her changes   100

---

say: material for testing.

And grow to number times and woes together!
How happy had I been if, being born,
My grave had been my cradle!

Enter SERVANT.

SERVANT.   By your leave,
Young mistress, here's a boy hath brought a coffin.
What 'a would say, I know not; but your father
Charged me to give you notice. Here they come.

[*Exit.*]

Enter Two bearing a coffin, JASPER *in it.*

LUCE. For me I [hope] 'tis come, and 'tis most welcome.
BOY. Fair mistress, let me not add greater grief
To that great store you have already. Jasper
(That whilst he lived was yours, now dead   110
And here enclosed) commanded me to bring
His body hither and to crave a tear
From those fair eyes (though he deserved not pity)
To deck his funeral; for so he bid me
Tell her for whom he died.
LUCE.   He shall have many.—
Good friends, depart a little whilst I take
My leave of this dead man that once I loved.

Exeunt Coffin Carrier and BOY.

Hold yet a little, life, and then I give thee
To thy first heavenly being. O, my friend!
Hast thou deceived me thus and got before me?   120
I shall not long be after. But, believe me,
Thou wert too cruel, Jasper, 'gainst thyself,
In punishing the fault I could have pardoned,
With so untimely death. Thou didst not wrong me
But ever wert most kind, most true, most loving,
And I the most unkind, most false, most cruel!
Didst thou but ask a tear? I'll give thee all,
Even all my eyes can pour down, all my sighs,
And all myself. Before thou goest from me
There are but sparing rites; but, if thy soul   130
Be yet about this place, and can behold
And see what I prepare to deck thee with,
It shall go up, borne on the wings of peace,
And satisfied. First will I sing thy dirge,
Then kiss thy pale lips, and then die myself,
And fill one coffin and one grave together.

Song.

Come, you whose loves are dead,
　　And, whiles I sing,
　　　Weep and wring
Every hand, and every head　　　　　　　　140
Bind with cypress and sad yew;
Ribands black and candles blue
For him that was of men most true!

Come with heavy [moaning],
　　And on his grave
　　　Let him have
Sacrifice of sighs and groaning;
Let him have fair flowers enow,
White and purple, green and yellow,
For him that was of men most true!　　　　150

Thou sable cloth, sad cover of my joys,
I lift thee up, and thus I meet with death.
[*She removes the cloth, and* JASPER *rises out of
　the coffin.*]

JASPER. And thus you meet the living!
LUCE.　　　　　　　　　　　　　　Save me,
　heaven!
JASPER. Nay, do not fly me, fair; I am no spirit.
　Look better on me; do you know me yet?
LUCE. O, thou dear shadow of my friend!
JASPER.　　　　　　　　　　　　Dear sub-
　stance,
　I swear I am no shadow. Feel my hand;
It is the same it was. I am your Jasper,
Your Jasper that's yet living and yet loving.
Pardon my rash attempt, my foolish proof　　160
I put in practice of your constancy;
For sooner should my sword have drunk my blood,
And set my soul at liberty, than drawn
The least drop from that body—for which boldness
Doom me to anything. If death, I take it,
And willingly.
LUCE.　　　　　　This death I'll give you for it.
　[*She kisses him.*]
So, now I am satisfied you are no spirit
But my own truest, truest, truest friend.

Why do you come thus to me?

JASPER.   First to see you;
Then to convey you hence.

LUCE.   It cannot be;   170
For I am locked up here and watched at all hours,
That 'tis impossible for me to 'scape.

JASPER. Nothing more possible. Within this coffin
Do you convey yourself. Let me alone;
I have the wits of twenty men about me.
Only I crave the shelter of your closet
A little, and then fear me° not. Creep in,
That they may presently convey you hence.
Fear nothing, dearest love; I'll be your second.

[LUCE *lies down in the coffin, and* JASPER *places the
    cloth over her.*]

Lie close; so. All goes well yet.—Boy!

            [*Re-enter* BOY *with Coffin Carrier.*]

BOY.   At hand, sir.   180

JASPER. Convey away the coffin, and be wary.

BOY. 'Tis done already.

                    [*Exeunt with the coffin.*]

JASPER.   Now must I go conjure.

                                        Exit.

                Enter MERCHANT.

MERCHANT. Boy, boy!

                [*Enter* BOY.]

BOY. Your servant, sir.

MERCHANT. Do me this kindness, boy. Hold, here's a
crown. Before thou bury the body of this fellow, carry
it to his old merry father and salute him from me and
bid him sing; he hath cause.

BOY. I will, sir.

MERCHANT. And then bring me word what tune he is in,   190
and have another crown; but do it truly. I have fitted
him a bargain now will vex him.

BOY. God bless your worship's health, sir!

MERCHANT. Farewell, boy.

                                        Exeunt.

——————

fear me: fear for me.

[IV.iv]

Enter MASTER MERRYTHOUGHT.

WIFE. Ah, old Merrythought, art thou there again? Let's
hear some of thy songs.

OLD MERRYTHOUGHT [*singing*].
>   *Who can sing a merrier note*
>   *Than he that cannot change a groat?*

Not a denier* left, and yet my heart leaps! I do wonder
yet, as old as I am, that any man will follow a trade,
or serve, that may sing and laugh and walk the streets.
My wife and both my sons are I know not where; I
have nothing left, nor know I how to come by meat to
supper, yet am I merry still; for I know I shall find it   10
upon the table at six o'clock; therefore, hang thought!
[*He sings.*]
>   *I would not be a serving-man*
>   *To carry the cloak-bag still,*
>   *Nor would I be a falconer*
>   *The greedy hawks to fill;*
>   *But I would be in a good house,*
>   *And have a good master too;*
>   *But I would eat and drink of the best,*
>   *And no work would I do.*

This is it that keeps life and soul together—mirth; this   20
is the philosopher's stone that they write so much on,
that keeps a man ever young.

Enter BOY.

BOY. Sir, they say they know all your money is gone, and
they will trust you for no more drink.

OLD MERRYTHOUGHT. Will they not? Let '[e]m choose!
The best is, I have mirth at home and need not send
abroad for that. Let them keep their drink to themselves.
[*He sings.*]
>   *For Jillian of Berry, she dwells on a hill,*
>   *And she hath good beer and ale to sell,*   30
>   *And of good fellows she thinks no ill;*

---

denier: penny.

> *And thither will we go now, now, now, now.*
> *And thither will we go now.*
>
> *And, when you have made a little stay,*
> *You need not ask what is to pay,*
> *But kiss your hostess, and go your way;*
> *And thither, etc.*
> *Enter another* BOY.

2 BOY. Sir, I can get no bread for supper.

OLD MERRYTHOUGHT. Hang bread and supper! Let's preserve our mirth, and we shall never feel hunger, I'll   40
warrant you. Let's have a catch. Boy, follow me; come.
([*They*] *sing this catch.*)

> *Ho, ho, nobody at home!*
> *Meat, nor drink, nor money ha' we none.*
> *Fill the pot, Eedy,*
> *Never more need I.*

OLD MERRYTHOUGHT. So, boys, enough. Follow me; let's
change our place, and we shall laugh afresh.

> *Exeunt.*

WIFE. Let him go, George; 'a shall not have any countenance from us, nor a good word from any i'th'company
if I may strike stroke* in't.   50

CITIZEN. No more 'a sha'not, love. But, Nell, I will have
Rafe do a very notable matter now, to the eternal
honor and glory of all grocers.—Sirrah! You there,
boy! Can none of you hear?

> [*Enter* BOY.]

BOY. Sir, your pleasure?

CITIZEN. Let Rafe come out on May Day in the morning
and speak upon a conduit, with all his scarfs about
him, and his feathers and his rings and his knacks.

BOY. Why, sir, you do not think of our plot; what will
become of that, then?   60

CITIZEN. Why, sir, I care not what become on't. I'll have
him come out, or I'll fetch him out myself; I'll have
something done in honor of the city. Besides, he hath
been long enough upon adventures. Bring him out
quickly; or, if I come in amongst you—

---

strike stroke: have a hand.

BOY. Well, sir, he shall come out; but, if our play mis-
carry, sir, you are like to pay for't.

Exit BOY.

CITIZEN. Bring him away, then!

WIFE. This will be brave, i'faith! George, shall not he
dance the morris too, for the credit of the Strand?   70

CITIZEN. No, sweetheart, it will be too much for the boy.
O, there he is, Nell! He's reasonable well in reparel,
but he has not rings enough.

Enter RAFE *[dressed as the Lord of the May].*

RAFE. London, to thee I do present the merry month of
May;

Let each true subject be content to hear me what I say:

For from the top of conduit head, as plainly may
appear,

I will both tell my name to you and wherefore I came
here.

My name is Rafe, by due descent though not ignoble
I,*

Yet far inferior to the flock of gracious grocery;

And by the common counsel of my fellows in the
Strand,   80

With gilded staff and crossèd scarf, the May Lord here
I stand.

Rejoice, O English hearts, rejoice! Rejoice, O lovers
dear!

Rejoice, O city, town and country! Rejoice, eke every
shire!

For now the fragrant flowers do spring and sprout in
seemly sort,

The little birds do sit and sing, the lambs do make fine
sport;

And now the birchen tree doth bud, that makes the
schoolboy cry;

The morris rings while hobbyhorse doth foot it feateously;*

The lords and ladies now abroad, for their disport and
play,

Do kiss sometimes upon the grass, and sometimes in
the hay;

---

ignoble I, etc.: see speech of Don Andrea's Ghost at the beginning of Kyd's *The Spanish Tragedy.*   feateously: nimbly.

Now butter with a leaf of sage is good to purge the
blood; 90
Fly Venus and phlebotomy, for they are neither good;
Now little fish on tender stone begin to cast their
bellies,
And sluggish snails, that erst were mute,* do creep out
of their shellies;
The rumbling rivers now do warm for little boys to
paddle;
The sturdy steed now goes to grass, and up they hang
his saddle;
The heavy hart, the bellowing buck, the rascal,* and
the pricket,*
Are now among the yeoman's peas, and leave the
fearful thicket.
And be like them, O you, I say, of this same noble
town,
And lift aloft your velvet heads, and, slipping off your
gown,
With bells on legs, and napkins clean unto your
shoulders tied, 100
With scarfs and garters as you please, and "Hey for
our town!" cried,
March out and show your willing minds, by twenty
and by twenty,
To Hogsdon or to Newington, where ale and cakes are
plenty;
And let it ne'er be said for shame that we, the youths
of London,
Lay thrumming* of our caps at home and left our custom undone.
Up, then, I say, both young and old, both man and
maid a-maying,
With drums and guns that bounce* aloud, and merry
tabor playing!
Which to prolong, God save our king, and send his
country peace,

---

mute: mewed (?): confined.   rascal: lean young deer.
pricket: a yearling buck.
thrumming: setting tufts on, raising a pile (hence, dawdling).
bounce: bang.

And root out treason from the land! And so, my friends,
  I cease.

[Exit.]

FINIS ACTUS QUARTI.

ACTUS QUINTUS

[V.i]

Enter MERCHANT, solus.*

MERCHANT. I will have no great store of company at the
  wedding—a couple of neighbors and their wives; and
  we will have a capon in stewed broth, with marrow,
  and a good piece of beef stuck with rosemary.

Enter JASPER, his face mealed.*

JASPER. Forbear thy pains, fond man! It is too late.
MERCHANT. Heaven bless me! Jasper?
JASPER.   Ay, I am his
  ghost,
Whom thou hast injured for his constance love,
Fond worldly wretch, who dost not understand
In death that true hearts cannot parted be.
First, know thy daughter is quite borne away   10
On wings of angels, through the liquid air,
To far out of thy reach, and never more
Shalt thou behold her face. But she and I
Will in another world enjoy our loves,
Where neither father's anger, poverty,
Nor any cross that troubles earthly men
Shall make us sever our united hearts.
And never shalt thou sit or be alone
In any place, but I will visit thee
With ghastly looks and put into thy mind   20
The great offenses which thou didst to me.
When thou art at thy table with thy friends,
Merry in heart, and filled with swelling wine,
I'll come in midst of all thy pride and mirth,
Invisible to all men but thyself,
And whisper such a sad tale in thine ear
Shall make thee let the cup fall from thy hand
And stand as mute and pale as Death itself.

---

solus: alone.   mealed: whitened with flour.

MERCHANT. Forgive me, Jasper! O, what might I do,
  Tell me, to satisfy thy troubled ghost? 30
JASPER. There is no means; too late thou think'st of this.
MERCHANT. But tell me what were best for me to do?
JASPER. Repent thy deed, and satisfy my father,
  And beat fond Humphrey out of thy doors.

Exit JASPER.

Enter HUMPHREY.

WIFE. Look, George; his very ghost would have folks
  beaten.

HUMPHREY. Father, my bride is gone, fair Mistress Luce;
  My soul's the fount of vengeance, mischief's sluice.
MERCHANT. Hence, fool, out of my sight with thy fond
    passion!
  Thou hast undone me.
  [*He beats him.*]
HUMPHREY.   Hold, my father dear, 40
  For Luce thy daughter's sake, that had no peer!
MERCHANT. Thy father, fool? There's some blows more;
    begone!—
  [*He beats him again.*]
  Jasper, I hope thy ghost be well appeased
  To see thy will performed. Now will I go
  To satisfy thy father for thy wrongs.

Exit.

HUMPHREY. What shall I do? I have been beaten twice,
  And Mistress Luce is gone. Help me, device! *
  Since my true love is gone, I never more,
  Whilst I do live, upon the sky will pore,
  But in the dark will wear out my shoe soles 50
  In passion in Saint Faith's Church under Paul's.

Exit.

WIFE. George, call Rafe hither; if you love me, call Rafe
  hither. I have the bravest thing for him to do, George;
  prithee, call him quickly.
CITIZEN. Rafe! Why, Rafe, boy!

Enter RAFE.

---

  device: ingenuity.

RAFE. Here, sir.

CITIZEN. Come hither, Rafe; come to thy mistress, boy.

WIFE. Rafe, I would have thee call all the youths together in battle 'ray, with drums and guns and flags, and march to Mile End in pompous fashion, and there 60 exort your soldiers to be merry and wise, and to keep their beards from burning, Rafe; and then skirmish, and let your flags fly, and cry, "Kill, kill, kill!" My husband shall lend you his jerkin, Rafe, and there's a scarf; for the rest, the house shall furnish you, and we'll pay for't. Do it bravely, Rafe; and think before whom you perform and what person you represent.

RAFE. I warrant you, mistress, if I do it not for the honor of the city and the credit of my master, let me never hope for freedom! 70

WIFE. 'Tis well spoken, i'faith. Go thy ways; thou art a spark indeed.

CITIZEN. Rafe, Rafe, double your files bravely, Rafe!

RAFE. I warrant you, sir.

Exit RAFE.

CITIZEN. Let him look narrowly to his service; I shall take him else. I was there myself a pikeman once in the hottest of the day, wench; had my feather shot sheer away, the fringe of my pike burnt off with powder, my pate broken with a scouring-stick,* and yet, I thank God, I am here. 80

(*Drum within.*)

WIFE. Hark, George, the drums!

CITIZEN. Ran, tan, tan, tan; ran, tan! O, wench, an thou hadst but seen little Ned of Algate, Drum Ned, how he made it roar again, and laid on like a tyrant, and then struck softly till the ward * came up, and then thundered again, and together we go! "Sa, sa, sa, bounce!" quoth the guns; "Courage, my hearts!" quoth the captains; "Saint George!" quoth the pikemen; and withal, here they lay, and there they lay. And yet for all this I am here, wench. 90

WIFE. Be thankful for it, George; for, indeed, 'tis wonderful.

---

scouring-stick: ramrod.
ward: defense; guard; militia detachment.

[V.ii]

    Enter RAFE *and his Company with drums and colors.*

RAFE. March fair, my hearts! Lieutenant, beat the rear
up.—Ancient,° let your colors fly; but have a great
care of the butchers' hooks at Whitechapel; they have
been the death of many a fair ancient.—Open your
files that I may take a view both of your persons and
munition.—Sergeant, call a muster.

SERGEANT. A stand!—William Hammerton, pewterer?

HAMMERTON. Here, captain.

RAFE. A corselet and a Spanish pike; 'tis well. Can you
shake it with a terror?   10

HAMMERTON. I hope so, captain.

RAFE. Charge upon me! [*He charges on* RAFE.] 'Tis with
the weakest; put more strength, William Hammerton,
more strength. As you were, again!—Proceed, sergeant.

SERGEANT. George Greengoose, poulterer?

GREENGOOSE. Here.

RAFE. Let me see your piece, neighbor Greengoose.
When was she shot in?

GREENGOOSE. And like you, Master Captain, I made a   20
shot even now, partly to scour her, and partly for
audacity.

RAFE. It should seem so certainly, for her breath is yet
inflamed; besides, there is a main fault in the touchhole—it runs and stinketh; and I tell you, moreover,
and believe it, ten such touchholes would breed the
pox in the army. Get you a feather, neighbor, get you a
feather, sweet oil, and paper; and your piece may do
well enough yet. Where's your powder?

GREENGOOSE. Here.   30

RAFE. What, in a paper? As I am a soldier and a gentleman, it craves a martial court! You ought to die for't.
Where's your horn? Answer me to that.

GREENGOOSE. An't like you, sir, I was oblivious.

RAFE. It likes me not you should be so; 'tis a shame for
you, and a scandal to all our neighbors, being a man
of worth and estimation, to leave your horn behind
you; I am afraid 'twill breed example. But let me tell

---

    ancient: ensign or standard-bearer.

you no more on't.—Stand, till I view you all. What's
become o'th'nose of your flask?   40

1 SOLDIER. Indeed, la, captain, 'twas blown away with
powder.

RAFE. Put on a new one at the city's charge.—Where's
the stone* of this piece?

2 SOLDIER. The drummer took it out to light tobacco.

RAFE. 'Tis a fault, my friend; put it in again.—You want
a nose, and you a stone.—Sergeant, take a note on't,
for I mean to stop it in the pay.—Remove, and march!
[*They march.*] Soft and fair, gentlemen, soft and fair!
Double your files! As you were! Faces about! Now, you   50
with the sodden face, keep it there! Look to your
match, sirrah; it will be in your fellow's flask anon!
So; make a crescent now! Advance your pikes! Stand
and give ear!—Gentlemen, countrymen, friends, and
my fellow soldiers, I have brought you this day from
the shops of security and the counters of content to
measure out in these furious fields honor by the ell and
prowess by the pound. Let it not, O, let it not, I say, be
told hereafter the noble issue of this city fainted; but
bear yourselves in this fair action like men, valiant men   60
and free men! Fear not the face of the enemy nor the
noise of the guns; for, believe me, brethren, the rude
rumbling of a brewer's car is far more terrible, of which
you have a daily experience; neither let the stink of
powder offend you since a more valiant stink is nightly
with you. To a resolved mind, his home is everywhere:
I speak not this to take away the hope of your return,
for you shall see (I do not doubt it), and that very
shortly, your loving wives again and your sweet children, whose care doth bear you company in baskets.   70
Remember, then, whose cause you have in hand and,
like a sort* of true-born scavengers, scour me this
famous realm of enemies. I have no more to say but
this: stand to your tacklings,* lads, and show to the
world you can as well brandish a sword as shake an
apron. Saint George, and on, my hearts!

OMNES.* Saint George, Saint George!

                                                     Exeunt.

_____

stone: flint stone.   sort: pack.
tacklings: clothes; equipment.   omnes: all.

WIFE. 'Twas well done, Rafe; I'll send thee a cold capon
afield and a bottle of March beer, and, it may be, come
myself to see thee.   80
CITIZEN. Nell, the boy has deceived me much; I did
not think it had been in him. He has performed such a
matter, wench, that, if I live, next year I'll have him
captain of the galley-foist* or I'll want my will.

[V.iii]

Enter OLD MERRYTHOUGHT.

OLD MERRYTHOUGHT. Yet, I thank God, I break not a
wrinkle more than I had. Not a stoup,* boys! Care,
live with cats; I defy thee! My heart is as sound as an
oak; and, though I want drink to wet my whistle, I
can sing.
[*He sings.*]
Come no more there, boys, come no more there;
For we shall never, whilst we live, come any more there.
        Enter a BOY [*and a Coffin Carrier*] *with a coffin.*
BOY. God save you, sir!
OLD MERRYTHOUGHT. It's a brave boy. Canst thou sing?
BOY. Yes, sir, I can sing; but 'tis not so necessary at this   10
time.
OLD MERRYTHOUGHT [*singing*].
                Sing we and chant it
                Whilst love doth grant it.
BOY. Sir, sir, if you knew what I have brought you, you
would have little list to sing.
OLD MERRYTHOUGHT [*singing*].
                O, the [*Minion*] *round,*
            Full long, long I have thee sought,
                And now I have thee found,
            And what hast thou here brought?
BOY. A coffin, sir, and your dead son Jasper in it.   20
                            [*Exit with Coffin Carrier.*]
OLD MERRYTHOUGHT. Dead?
[*He sings.*]
                Why, farewell he!
                Thou wast a bonny boy,
                And I did love thee.

---

galley-foist: state barge, such as used in a lord mayor's pageant.
stoup: drinking vessel.

Enter JASPER.

JASPER. Then, I pray you, sir, do so still.

OLD MERRYTHOUGHT. Jasper's ghost!
[*He sings.*]
>   *Thou art welcome from Stygian lake so soon;*
>   *Declare to me what wond'rous things in Pluto's*
>   *court are done.*

JASPER. By my troth, sir, I ne'er came there; 'tis too
hot for me, sir.   30

OLD MERRYTHOUGHT. A merry ghost, a very merry ghost!
[*He sings.*]
>   *And where is your true love? O, where is yours?*

JASPER. Marry, look you, sir!
(*Heaves up the coffin [and helps* LUCE *out*].)

OLD MERRYTHOUGHT. Ah, ha! Art thou good at that,
i'faith?
[*He sings.*]
5 >   *With hey, trixy, terlery-whiskin,*
>   *The world it runs on wheels:*
>   *When the young man's* ——,
>   *Up goes the maiden's heels.*

MISTRESS MERRYTHOUGHT *and* MICHAEL *within.*

MISTRESS MERRYTHOUGHT. What, Master Merrythought,   40
will you not let's in? What do you think shall become
of us?

OLD MERRYTHOUGHT. What voice is that that calleth
at our door?

MISTRESS MERRYTHOUGHT. You know me well enough;
I am sure I have not been such a stranger to you.

OLD MERRYTHOUGHT [*singing*].
>   *And some they whistled, and some they sung,*
>   *"Hey, down, down!"*
>   *And some did loudly say,*
>   *Ever as the Lord Barnet's horn blew,*   50
>   *"Away, Musgrave, away!"*

MISTRESS MERRYTHOUGHT. You will not have us starve
here, will you, Master Merrythought?

JASPER. Nay, good sir, be persuaded; she is my mother.
If her offenses have been great against you, let your
own love remember she is yours, and so forgive her.

LUCE. Good Master Merrythought, let me entreat you; I
will not be denied.

MISTRESS MERRYTHOUGHT. Why, Master Merrythought, will you be a vexed thing still? 60

OLD MERRYTHOUGHT. Woman, I take you to my love again, but you shall sing before you enter; therefore, dispatch your song and so come in.

MISTRESS MERRYTHOUGHT. Well, you must have your will when all's done.—Mick, what song canst thou sing, boy?

MICHAEL [*within*]. I can sing none, forsooth, but *A Lady's Daughter, of Paris* properly.

MISTRESS MERRYTHOUGHT [*and* MICHAEL, *within*].
Song.
It was a lady's daughter, etc.

[OLD MERRYTHOUGHT *opens the door;* MISTRESS MERRYTHOUGHT *and* MICHAEL *enter.*]

OLD MERRYTHOUGHT. Come, you're welcome home 70 again.

[*He sings.*]
If such danger be in playing,
And jest must to earnest turn,
You shall go no more a-maying—

MERCHANT (*within*). Are you within, sir, Master Merrythought?

JASPER. It is my master's voice! Good sir, go hold him in talk whilst we convey ourselves into some inward room.
[*Exit with* LUCE.]

OLD MERRYTHOUGHT. What are you? Are you merry? You must be very merry if you enter. 80

MERCHANT [*within*]. I am, sir.

OLD MERRYTHOUGHT. Sing, then.

MERCHANT [*within*]. Nay, good sir, open to me.

OLD MERRYTHOUGHT. Sing, I say, or, by the merry heart, you come not in!

MERCHANT [*within*]. Well, sir, I'll sing.
[*He sings.*]
Fortune, my foe, etc.

[OLD MERRYTHOUGHT *opens the door for* VENTUREWELL.]

OLD MERRYTHOUGHT. You are welcome, sir; you are welcome. You see your entertainment; pray you, be merry.

MERCHANT. O, Master Merrythought, I am come to ask you 90
Forgiveness for the wrongs I offered you

And your most virtuous son! They're infinite;
Yet my contrition shall be more than they.
I do confess my hardness broke his heart,
For which just heaven hath given me punishment
More than my age can carry. His wand'ring spirit,
Not yet at rest, pursues me everywhere,
Crying, "I'll haunt thee for thy cruelty."
My daughter, she is gone, I know not how,
Taken invisible, and whether living   100
Or in grave, 'tis yet uncertain to me.
O, Master Merrythought, these are the weights
Will sink me to my grave! Forgive me, sir.

OLD MERRYTHOUGHT. Why, sir, I do forgive you; and be
    merry.
And, if the wag in's lifetime played the knave,
Can you forgive him too?

MERCHANT.   With all my heart, sir.

OLD MERRYTHOUGHT. Speak it again, and heartily.

MERCHANT.   I do,
    sir.
Now, by my soul, I do.

OLD MERRYTHOUGHT [*singing*].
            With that came out his paramour;
            She was as white as the lily flower.   110
            Hey, troll, trolly, lolly!

            Enter LUCE *and* JASPER.

            With that came out her own dear knight;
            He was as true as ever did fight, etc.
Sir, if you will forgive 'hem, clap their hands together.
There's no more to be sa[i]d i'th' matter.

MERCHANT. I do, I do.

CITIZEN. I do not like this! Peace, boys! Hear me, one
    of you! Everybody's part is come to an end but Rafe's,
    and he's left out.

BOY. 'Tis long of yourself, sir; we have nothing to do   120
    with his part.

CITIZEN. Rafe, come away!—Make on him as you have
    done of the rest, boys; come.

WIFE. Now, good husband, let him come out and die.

CITIZEN. He shall, Nell.—Rafe, come away quickly and die, boy.

BOY. 'Twill be very unfit he should die, sir, upon no occasion—and in a comedy too.

CITIZEN. Take you no care of that, sir boy. Is not his part at an end, think you, when he's dead?—Come away, 130 Rafe!

Enter RAFE, *with a forked arrow through his head.*

RAFE. When I * was mortal, this my costive corpse
Did lap up figs and raisins in the Strand,
Where, sitting, I espied a lovely dame,
Whose master wrought with lingel * and with awl,
And underground he vampied * many a boot.
Straight did her love prick forth me, tender sprig,
To follow feats of arms in warlike wise
Through Waltham Desert, where I did perform
Many achievements, and did lay on ground   140
Huge Barbaroso, that insulting giant,
And all his captives soon set at liberty.
Then honor pricked me from my native soil
Into Moldavia, where I gained the love
Of Pompiona, his beloved daughter,
But yet proved constant to the black-thumbed maid,
Susan, and scornèd Pompiona's love;
Yet liberal I was and gave her pins
And money for her father's officers.
I then returnèd home and thrust myself   150
In action, and by all men chosen was
Lord of the May, where I did flourish it,
With scarfs and rings, and posy in my hand.
After this action I preferrèd was,
And chosen city captain at Mile End,
With hat and feather and with leading-staff, *
And trained my men, and brought them all off clear,
Save one man that berayed him with the noise.
But all these things I, Rafe, did undertake
Only for my beloved Susan's sake.   160

when I, etc.: compare again with the speech of Don Andrea's
ghost at the beginning of *The Spanish Tragedy.*
lingel: waxed thread.   vampied: vamped, patched.
leading-staff: baton.

Then coming home, and sitting in my shop
With apron blue, Death came into my stall
To cheapen° *aquavitæ;* but, ere I
Could take the bottle down and fill a taste,
Death caught a pound of pepper in his hand
And sprinkled all my face and body o'er
And in an instant vanishèd away.

CITIZEN. 'Tis a pretty fiction, i'faith.

RAFE. Then took I up my bow and shaft in hand,
And walked into Moorfields to cool myself;   170
But there grim cruel Death met me again
And shot this forkèd arrow through my head,
And now I faint. Therefore, be warned by me,
My fellows every one, of forkèd heads! °
Farewell, all you good boys in merry London!
Ne'er shall we more upon Shrove Tuesday° meet
And pluck down houses of iniquity.—
My pain increaseth; I shall never more
Hold open whilst another pumps both legs,
Nor daub a satin gown with rotten eggs;   180
Set up a stake, O, never more I shall!
I die! Fly, fly, my soul, to Grocers' Hall!
O, O, O, *etc.*

WIFE. Well said, Rafe! Do your obeisance to the gentlemen, and go your ways. Well said, Rafe!

                                                   Exit RAFE.

OLD MERRYTHOUGHT. Methinks all we, thus kindly and
unexpectedly reconciled, should not depart without a
song.
MERCHANT. A good motion.
OLD MERRYTHOUGHT. Strike up, then!   190
                        Song.
            Better music ne'er was known
            Than a quire of hearts in one.
            Let each other that hath been

---

cheapen: bargain for.   forkèd heads: cuckolds.
Shrove Tuesday: holiday for apprentices.

> *Troubled with the gall or spleen*
> *Learn of us to keep his brow*
> *Smooth and plain as ours are now.*
> *Sing, though before the hour of dying;*
> *He shall rise and then be crying,*
> *"Hey, ho, 'tis naught but mirth*
> *That keeps the body from the earth."* 200

Exeunt omnes.

Epilogus.

CITIZEN. Come, Nell, shall we go? The play's done.

WIFE. Nay, by my faith, George, I have more manners than so; I'll speak to these gentlemen first.—I thank you all, gentlemen, for your patience and countenance to Rafe, a poor fatherless child; and, if I might see you at my house, it should go hard but I would have a pottle° of wine and a pipe of tobacco for you; for, truly, I hope you do like the youth, but I would be glad to know the truth. I refer it to your own discretions whether you will applaud him or no; for I will 210 wink, and whilst° you shall do what you will. I thank you with all my heart. God give you good night!—Come, George.

[*Exeunt.*]

FINIS.

_____

pottle: bottle; tankard.   whilst: meanwhile.

THE
CHARACTERS

of

Two royall Masques.

The one of BLACKNESSE,
The other of BEAVTIE.

personated

By the most magnificent of Queenes

ANNE

Queene of great Britaine, &c.

With her honorable Ladyes,

1605. and 1608.

at White-hall:

and

Inuented by BEN: IONSON.

Ouid. —*Salue festa dies, meliorq́, reuertere semper.*

Imprinted at London for *Thomas Thorp*, and are to
be sold at the signe of the Tigers head
in Paules Church-yard.

Introduction

Concomitant with the abusive criticism of the middle class in the drama of the private theaters was the increasing alienation of that class from the political life of the nation in the reign of the first two Stuarts. Although she too was an absolute monarch, Elizabeth was astute enough to avoid parading the fact and to allow her subjects to think that they were sharing in the government by their representation in Parliament. James, however, perhaps because as an alien he felt insecure in his new kingdom, kept reminding Parliament that even God Himself called kings gods; and, to prove that its members sat solely by his own divine grace, he ruled without summoning a Parliament for a full decade, from 1611 to 1621. So taken was his son with personal government that Charles also summoned no Parliament from 1629 to 1640. During most of these years political life centered solely at court, and intrigue and favor—no higher standards of merit —became the only ready means of advancement.

To establish the court as a focus of national interest and to enhance their prestige as divine rulers, the first two Stuarts spent lavishly; but with crown revenues inadequate to their needs they resorted to high-handed methods of acquiring wealth—to unpopular, if not illegal, taxation, the creation of crown-sponsored monopolies, and the selling of knighthoods. In the first two months of his reign, James sold as many knighthoods as Elizabeth had conferred in the last ten years of her reign, thereby creating a class of men who outright bought their heritage and rank.

Thus, hostile to the court party that seemed so influential, but as yet still loyal to the crown, the disaffected middle class went its own way in the greater part of the early seventeenth century. Armed with pious faith and confident of its own worth, it was, after all, this class—the class of the literal-minded Citizen and his Wife, of Eyre and his journeymen-apprentices—that was adapting itself to the changing times and was working to establish the city of God on earth in the Massachusetts Bay Colony early in the century and in England itself at mid-century. Its alliance with Puritanism is understandable; for, as Professor Haller explains, Puritan preachers were trying "to adapt Christian morality to the needs of a population which was being steadily driven from its old feudal status into the untried conditions of competition between man and man in an increasingly commercial and industrial society under a money economy." Meanwhile, courtiers, out of touch with the temper of the larger part of the population, danced in unbelievably expensive masques and seemed oblivious or indifferent to the needs of the nation. As the Earl of Clarendon, the Lord Chancellor to both Charles I and Charles II, commented in his *History of the Rebellion:*

> There was in truth a strange absence of understanding in most, and a strange perverseness of understanding in the rest: the court full of excess, idleness, and luxury; and the country full of pride, mutiny, and discontent.

Unlike their immediate predecessors, the Stuarts took an active and genuine interest in the arts; but their particular interest in drama, especially its spectacular elements, ultimately was to lead to the alienation of the middle class from serious theater completely and to influence the coterie course of *important drama* throughout the remainder of the century. From the accession of James, who in one of his first acts conferred the badge of his livery upon the former Lord Chamberlain's Men, now the Company of His Majesty's Servants (or simply the King's Men), the acting profession became socially respectable. James frequently commanded in a year at court as many as four times the number of performances that Elizabeth had; and, although he himself did not perform in the lavish masques that his treasury paid for, his queen and sons did. Later, Charles, as king, joined his French queen, Henrietta Maria, as a dancer in more spectacular masques than his father ever dreamed of or paid for; and he also suggested plots to courtly playwrights. To the honest chagrin of earnest-minded men throughout the realm, Henrietta Maria commissioned plays at court in which she would perform the leading roles. She also became the first monarch to attend public performances of plays, setting a precedent for her royal son in the Restoration.

An indication of the attenuating effect that such exclusive patronage was to have on drama was the rapid elaboration of the masque at court during the first half of the century and Jonson's relationship to the form whose literary and artistic value he did so much to enhance. The masque was primarily an amateur masquerade dance centering around a literary device that explained the setting and costumes and provided for the introduction of formal speeches to explain its purpose and to pay homage to the dancer's hosts (usually the king and queen). Under the Tudors it had served a modest purpose on festive occasions. Bacon had described the masques as "toys" that "should be graced with elegancy, then daubed with cost"; but under James and Charles they developed into a spectacular form, with elaborately constructed sets and rich costumes. So costly did they become, in fact, that they figured as a prime source of contention between Charles and Parliament until finally, in 1640, he had to put an end to them, royally explaining that the smoke from the candles was ruining the paintings on the ceiling in the Whitehall banqueting room where they were being performed.

In 1605 Jonson began his long career as the leading writer of masques for the court with the modest (in terms of what the form was to develop into) *The Masque of Blackness*. The Italian-trained Inigo Jones, destined to be the court's leading scenic designer and for a time Jonson's chief collaborator, designed the "bodily part" for the "invention" that Jonson "derived" from a suggestion of Queen Anne, herself the leading masquer. Significantly, in fulfilling Her Majesty's will to have the masquers disguised as blackamoors, Jonson shocked the old courtiers from Elizabeth's day, who were "sorry," as one put it, "that strangers should see our court so strangely disguised."

To Jonson belongs the credit for having tried to raise the masque into an important literary form whose "soul" would last long after the "body" had died in performance. He deeply resented being forced to share the title pages of his elaborately annotated quartos with Jones, who claimed equal credit for the "inventions." In time his resentment grew into abusive attacks on the designer, and in the quarrel that ensued between the two independently minded artists Charles took Jones' part. In 1631 Jonson gave up his court connection; and thereafter Jones hired such lesser writers as Sir William Davenant to provide him with libretti that were only excuses for the elaboration of spectacle.

With his high ideals concerning form and content, and with his scorn for mere—and costly—show, Jonson revealed himself to be primarily an Elizabethan, out of touch with the formalism of the Stuart court. He could not be sympathetic to the purely spectacular function of the masque that had catapulted Jones into high esteem. Masques had won the day, however, as the repertoire of the King's Men increasingly revealed. Their influence extended to such diverse plays as *Philaster, The Duchess of Malfi, The Changeling, The Broken Heart,* and, of course, *The Tempest.* The King's Men were themselves invited to court frequently to perform in the antimasques, comic interludes of buffoonery before the main masques that Jonson first introduced in *The Masque of Queens* in 1609.

The Playwright

BEN JONSON: see *Volpone,* pp. 162–163.

The Play

The present text of *The Masque of Blackness* is based on the 1616 folio edition (*The Workes of Benjamin Jonson*) in the Henry E. Huntington Library, but it silently incorporates a few corrections suggested by the original quarto of 1608 (THE CHARACTERS *of Two royall Masques. The one of* BLACKNESSE, *The other of* BEAUTIE); Jonson's elaborate marginal notes have been omitted. The bracketed portion in the description of "the attire of the masquers" is taken from a manuscript of the masque, entitled *The Twelvth nights Revells,* in the British Museum (Royal MS. 17. B. xxxi; reproduced in the Herford and Simpson edition, Vol. VII, pp. 195–201) that was submitted to Queen Anne for the performance in Queen Elizabeth's old banqueting house at Whitehall on January 6, 1605.

SELECTED BIBLIOGRAPHY

See also: *Volpone,* pp. 163–164.

Cunningham, D. "The Jonsonian Masque as a Literary Form," *Journal of English Literary History,* XXII (1955), 108–124.

Furniss, W. T. "Ben Jonson's Masques," in *Three Studies in the Renaissance.* Yale University Studies in English 138. New Haven, Conn.: Yale University Press, 1958.

Gilbert, A. H. *The Symbolic Persons in the Masques of Ben Jonson.* Durham, N.C.: Duke University Press, 1948.

Gordon, D. J. "The Imagery of Ben Jonson's *The Masque of Blacknesse* and *The Masque of Beautie,*" *Journal of the Warburg and Courtauld Institutes,* VI (1943), 122–141.

———. "Poet and Architect: The Intellectual Setting of the Quarrel between Ben Jonson and Inigo Jones," *Journal of the Warburg and Courtauld Institutes,* XII (1949), 152–178.

Meagher, J. C. *Method and Meaning in Jonson's Masques.* Notre Dame, Ind.: University of Notre Dame Press, 1966.

Nicoll, A. *Stuart Masques and the Renaissance Stage.* New York: Harcourt, Brace, 1938.

Orgel, S. K. *The Jonsonian Masque.* Berkeley and Los Angeles: University of California Press, 1964.

Reyher, P. *Les masques anglais: étude sur les ballets et la vie de cour en Angleterre (1512–1640).* New York: B. Blom, 1964 (reprinted from 1909 edition).

Welsford, E. *The Court Masque: A Study in the Relationship between Poetry and the Revels.* Cambridge: Cambridge University Press, 1927.

The Masque
of Blackness

The honor and splendor of these spectacles was such
in the performance as, could those hours have lasted, this
of mine now had been a most unprofitable work. But,
when it is the fate even of the greatest and most absolute
births to need and borrow a life of posterity, little had
been done to the study of magnificence in these if, presently with the rage of the people, who (as a part of
greatness) are privileged by custom to deface their carcasses, the spirits had also perished. In duty, therefore,
to that majesty, who gave them their authority and grace,   10
and no less than the most royal of predecessors deserves
eminent celebration for these solemnities, I add this later
hand to redeem them as well from ignorance as envy—
two common evils, the one of censure, the other of oblivion.

Pliny, Solinus, Ptolemy, and, of late, Leo the African
remember unto us a river in Ethiopia, famous by the
name of Niger, of which the people were called Nigritæ,
now Negroes, and are the blackest nation of the world.
This river taketh spring out of a certain lake, eastward,   20
and after a long race falleth into the Western Ocean;
hence (because it was Her Majesty's will to have them
black[a]moors at first) the invention* was derived by me
and presented thus:

First, for the scene was drawn a landscape, consisting
of small woods and here and there a void place filled with

---

invention: plan.

huntings, which, falling, an artificial sea was seen to
shoot forth as if it flowed to the land, raised with waves,
which seemed to move and in some places the billow to
break, as imitating that orderly disorder which is common   30
in nature. In front of this sea were placed six tritons, in
moving and sprightly actions, their upper parts human,
save that their hairs were blue, as partaking of the sea
color; their desinent parts fish, mounted above their
heads and all varied in disposition. From their backs
were borne out certain light pieces of taffeta, as if carried
by the wind, and their music made out of wreathed
shells. Behind these, a pair of sea-maids, for song, were
as conspicuously seated, between which two great sea-
horses (as big as the life) put forth themselves, the one   40
mounting aloft and writhing his head from the other,
which seemed to sink forwards, so intended for variation
and that the figure behind might come off better; upon
their backs Oceanus and Niger were advanced.

Oceanus, presented in a human form, the color of his
flesh blue and shadowed with a robe of sea-green; his
head gray and horned, as he is described by the ancients;
his beard of the like mixed color. He was garlanded with
alga or sea-grass, and in his hand a trident.

Niger, in form and color of an Ethiope; his hair and   50
rare beard curled, shadowed with a blue and bright
mantle; his front, neck, and wrists adorned with pearl and
crowned with an artificial wreath of cane and papyrus.

These induced° the masquers, which were twelve
nymphs, Negroes and the daughters of Niger, attended
by so many of the Oceaniæ, which were their light-
bearers.

The Masquers were placed in a great concave shell,
like mother of pearl, curiously° made to move on those
waters and rise with the billow; the top thereof was stuck   60
with a chevron° of lights, which, indented to the proportion of the shell, struck a glorious beam upon them as
they were seated, one above another, so that they were all
seen—but in an extravagant order.

On sides of the shell did swim six huge sea-monsters,

---

induced: introduced.   curiously: ingeniously.
chevron (of light): beam.

*varied in their shapes and dispositions, bearing on their
backs the twelve torchbearers, who were planted there
in several gr[e]ces,* so as the backs of some were seen,
some in purfle* or side, others in face, and all having
their lights burning out of whelks or murex shells.*   70

   *The attire of the masquers was alike in all, without
difference: the colors, azure and silver; [their hair thick
and curled upright in tresses, like pyramids] but returned
on the top with a scroll and antic dressing of feathers and
jewels interlaced with ropes of pearl. And, for the front,
ear, neck, and wrists, the ornament was of the most
choice and orient pearl, best setting off from the black.
For the light-bearers: sea-green, waved above the skirts
with gold and silver; their hair loose and flowing, garlanded with sea-grass, and that stuck with branches of   80
coral.*

   *These thus presented, the scene behind seemed a vast
sea (and united with this that flowed forth) from the termination or horizon of which (being the level of the
state,* which was placed in the upper end of the hall)
was drawn by the lines of prospective,* the whole work
shooting downwards from the eye: which decorum made
it more conspicuous and caught the eye afar off with a
wand'ring beauty. To which was added an obscure and
cloudy nightpiece that made the whole set off. So much   90
for the bodily part, which was of Master Inigo Jones his
design and act.*

   *By this, one of the tritons, with the two sea-maids,
began to sing to the others' loud music, their voices being
a tenor and two trebles.*

Song.
*Sound, sound aloud
The welcome of the Orient flood
Into the West.
Fair Niger, son to great Oceanus,
New honored thus,*   100
*With all his beautious race,
Who, though but black in face,*

---

greces: steps, stairs.   purfle: profile.
state: throne, canopied chair of state.
prospective: perspective.

> *Yet are they bright*
> *And full of light and light*
> *To prove that beauty best*
> *Which not the color but the feature*
> *Assures unto the creature.*

OCEANUS.

Be silent, now the ceremony's done!
And Niger, say how it comes, lovely son,
That thou, the Ethiope's river, so far east,   110
Art seen to fall into th' extremest west
Of me, the king of floods, Oceanus,
And in mine empire's heart salute me thus?
My ceaseless current now amazèd stands
To see thy labor, through so many lands,
Mix thy fresh billow with my brackish stream
And, in thy sweetness, stretch thy diadem
To these far distant and unequalled skies,
This squarèd circle of celestial bodies.

NIGER.

Divine Oceanus, 'tis not strange at all   120
That (since the immortal souls of creatures mortal
Mix with their bodies, yet reserve forever
A power of separation) that I should sever
My fresh streams from thy brackish (like things fixed)
Though, with thy powerful saltness, thus far mixed.
Virtue, though chained to earth, will still live free;
And hell itself must yield to industry.

OCEANUS.

But what's the end of thy Herculean labors,
Extended to these calm and blessèd shores?

NIGER.

To do a kind and careful father's part   130
In satisfying every pensive heart
Of these my daughters, my most loved birth,
Who, though they were the first formed dames of earth,
And in whose sparkling and refulgent eyes
The glorious Sun did still delight to rise;
Though he—the best judge and most formal cause
Of all dames' beauties—in their firm hues draws
Signs of his fervent'st love and thereby shows
That, in their black, the perfect'st beauty grows
Since the fixed color of their curlèd hair   140

(Which is the highest grace of dames most fair)
No cares, no age can change or there display
The fearful tincture of abhorrèd gray
Since Death herself (herself being pale and blue)
Can never alter their most faithful hue.
All which are arguments to prove how far
Their beauties conquer in great beauties' war
And, more, how near divinity they be
That stand from passion or decay so free.
Yet, since the fabulous voices of some few   150
Poor brainsick men, styled poets, here with you
Have, with such envy of their graces, sung
The painted beauties, other empires sprung,
Letting their loose and wingèd fictions fly
To infect all climates, yea, our purity,
As of one Phaëton,° that fired the world,
And that, before his heedless flames were hurled
About the globe, the Ethiopes were as fair
As other dames; now black, with black despair,
And in respect of their complexions changed   160
Are eachwhere since for luckless creatures ranged.
Which, when my daughters heard (as women are
Most jealous of their beauties), fear and care
Possessed them whole; yet, and believing them,
They wept such ceaseless tears into my stream
That it hath, thus far, overflowed his shore
To seek them patience who have since, e'ermore
As the Sun riseth, charged his burning throne
With volleys of revilings' cause he shone
On their scorched cheeks with such intemperate fires   170
And other dames made queens of all desires.
To frustrate which strange error, oft I sought
(Though most in vain against a settled thought,
As women's are) till they confirmed at length
By miracle what I with so much strength
Of argument resisted; else they feigned;
For in the lake, where their first spring they gained,
As they sat cooling their soft limbs one night,

Phaëton: permitted by his father Helios (the Sun) to drive his
chariot for one day, he came perilously close to scorching the earth
until Zeus struck him with a thunderbolt.

Appeared a face, all circumfused with light
(And sure they saw't, for Ethiopes never dream),   180
Wherein they might decipher through the stream
These words:
   That they a land must forthwith seek
   Whose termination (of the Greek)
   Sounds *Tannia;* where bright Sol, that heat
   Their bloods, doth never rise or set
   But in his journey passeth by
   And leaves the climate of the sky
   To comfort of a greater light,
   Who forms all beauty with his sight.   190
In search of this have we three princedoms past
That speak out *Tannia* in their accents last:
Black Mauritania, first; and, secondly,
Swarth Lusitania; next, we did descry
Rich Aquitania; and yet cannot find
The place unto these longing nymphs designed.
Instruct and aid me, great Oceanus,
What land is this that now appears to us?
OCEANUS.
This land, that lifts into the temperate air
His snowy cliff, is Albion the fair,   200
So called of Neptune's son, who ruleth here:
For whose dear guard myself (four thousand year
Since old Deucalion's days) have walked the round
About his empire, proud to see him crowned
Above my waves.

   *At this, the Moon was discovered in the upper part of
the house, triumphant in a silver throne made in figure
of a pyramis;*° *her garments white and silver, the dressing of her head antic and crowned with a luminary or
sphere of light, which, striking on the clouds and height-*   210
*ened with silver, reflected as natural clouds do by the
splendor of the moon. The heaven about her was vaulted
with blue silk and set with stars of silver, which had in
them their several lights burning, the sudden sight of
which made Niger to interrupt Oceanus with this present
passion:*

---

   pyramis: pyramid.

NIGER.

—O, see our silver star,
Whose pure, auspicious light greets us thus far!
Great Ethiopia, goddess of our shore,
Since with particular worship we adore   220
Thy general brightness, let particular grace
Shine on my zealous daughters. Show the place,
Which, long, their longings urged their eyes to see;
Beautify them, which long have deified thee.

ETHIOPIA.

Niger, be glad: resume thy native cheer;
Thy daughters' labors have their period here,
And so thy errors. I was that bright face
Reflected by the lake, in which thy race
Read mystic lines (which skill Pythagoras
First taught to men by a reverberate glass).   230
This blessèd isle doth with that *Tannia* end,
Which there they saw inscribed, and shall extend
Wished satisfaction to their best desires.
Britannia, which the triple world admires,
This isle hath now recovered for her name,
Where reign those beauties that with so much fame
The sacred Muses' sons have honorèd
And from bright Hesperus to Eos spread.
With that great name *Britannia,* this blessèd isle
Hath won her ancient dignity and style,   240
A world divided from the world and tried
The abstract* of it in his general pride.
For were the world, with all his wealth, a ring,
Britannia, whose new name makes all tongues sing,
Might be a diamond worthy to enchase it,
Ruled by a Sun that to this height doth grace it,
Whose beams shine day and night, and are of force
To blanch an Ethiope and revive a corse.*
His light sciential is and (past mere nature)
Can salve the rude defects of every creature.   250
    Call forth thy honored daughters, then,
    And let them, 'fore the Britain men,
    Indent* the land with those pure traces
    They flow with in their native graces.

---

tried the abstract: experienced the perfection (of it).
corse: corpse.   indent: leave a mark on.

Invite them boldly to the shore;
Their beauties shall be scorched no more:
This sun is temperate and refines
All things on which his radiance shines.

Here the tritons sounded; and they danced on shore, every couple, as they advanced, severally presenting their 260 *fans, in one of which were inscribed their mixed names, in the other a mute hieroglyphic,* expressing their mixed qualities. Which manner of symbol I rather chose than impress,* as well for strangeness as relishing of antiquity, and more applying to that original doctrine of sculpture which the Egyptians are said first to have brought from the Ethiopians.*

	*The Names.**		*The Symbols.*
The Queen. Countess of Bedford.	1. { EUPHORIS. AGLAIA.	1. {	A golden tree, laden with fruit. 270
Lady Herbert. Countess of Derby.	2. { DIAPHANE. EUCAMPSE.	2. {	The figure Icosahedron, of crystal.
Lady Rich. Countess of Suffolk.	3. { OCYTE. KATHARE.	3. {	A pair of naked feet, in a river.
Lady Bevil. Lady Effingham.	4. { NOTIS. PSYCHROTE.	4. {	The salamander simple.*
Lady Eleanor Howard. Lady Susan Vere.	5. { GLYCYTE. MALACIA.	5. {	A cloud full of rain, dropping. 280

hieroglyphic: symbolic character.
impress: an emblematic figure or design.
The Names: "Euphoris–abundance   Notis–moisture
            Aglaia–splendor   Psychrote–coldness
            Diaphane–transparent   Glycyte–sweetness
            Eucampse–flexibility   Malacia–delicacy
            Ocyte–swiftness   Baryte–weight
            Kathare–spotless   Periphere–revolving"
simple: alone.

Lady Wroth.
Lady Walsing-   6. { BARYTE.   6. { An urn, sphered
  ham.   { PERIPHERE.   {   with wine.

The names of the Oceaniæ were:

DORIS.		CYDIPPE.		BEROE.		IANTHE.
PETRÆA.	}	CLAUCE.	}	ACASTE.	}	LYCORIS.
OCYRHOE.		TYCHE.		CLYTIA.		PLEXAURE.

*Their own single dance ended, as they were about to
make choice of their men, one from the sea was heard to
call 'hem with this charm, sung by a tenor voice:*   290
                      Song.
              Come away, come away;
              We grow jealous of your stay.
              If you do not stop your ear,
              We shall have more cause to fear
              Sirens of the land than they
              To doubt ° the sirens of the sea.
*Here they danced with their men several measures°
and corantos;° all which ended, they were again accited ° to sea with a song of two trebles, whose cadences
were iterated by a double Echo from several parts of the*   300
land.

                      Song.
          Daughters of the subtle flood,
              Do not let earth longer entertain you;
          1 ECHO. Let earth longer entertain you.
              2 ECHO. Longer entertain you.

          'Tis to them enough of good
          That you give this little hope to gain you.
              1 ECHO. Give this little hope to gain you.
              2 ECHO. Little hope to gain you.

              If they love,   310
                  You shall quickly see;
              For, when to flight you move,

---
doubt: fear.
measures: formal, stately dances.
corantos: French dance with fast-moving steps.
accited: summoned.

They'll follow you the more you flee.
1 ECHO. *Follow you the more you flee.*
2 ECHO. *The more you flee.*

If not, impute it each to others' matter;
They are but earth,   and what you vowed was water.

                             1 ECHO. *And what you vowed*
                               was water.
1 ECHO. *But earth,*   ⎫
  2 ECHO. *Earth.* ⎬   2 ECHO. *You vowed was* 320
              ⎭   *water.*

ETHIOPIA.

Enough, bright nymphs, the night grows old;
And we are grieved we cannot hold
You longer light. But comfort take:
Your father only to the lake
Shall make return; yourselves, with feasts,
Must here remain the Ocean's guests.
Nor shall this veil the sun hath cast
Above your blood more summers last,
For which you shall observe these rites: 330
Thirteen times thrice on thirteen nights
(So often as I fill my sphere
With glorious light throughout the year),
You shall (when all things else do sleep,
Save your chaste thoughts) with reverence steep
Your bodies in that purer brine
And wholesome dew called rose-marine;
Then, with that soft and gentler foam,
Of which the Ocean yet yields some,
Whereof bright Venus, Beauty's queen,   340
Is said to have begotten been,
You shall your gentler limbs o'erlave
And for your pains perfection have.
So that this night, the year gone round,
You do again salute this ground;
And, in the beams of yond bright sun,
Your faces dry, and all is done.

At which, in a dance, they returned to the sea, where
they took their shell and, with this full song, went out:

Song.

Now Diane, with her burning face,   350
    Declines apace:

By which our waters know
To ebb that late did flow.
Back seas, back nymphs; but, with a forward grace,
Keep still * your reverence to the place,
And shout with joy of favor you have won
In sight of Albion, Neptune's son.

So ended the first masque, which (beside the singular
grace of music and dances) had that success in the nobility of as nothing needs to the illustration but the   360
memory by whom it was personated.

---

still: forever.

PHILASTER.

OR,

Loue lies a Bleeding.

As it hath beene diuerse times Acted,
at the Globe, and Blacke-Friers, by
his *Maiesties Seruants.*

Written by {*Francis Beaumont.*
and {Gent.
Iohn Fletcher.

The second Impression, corrected, and
amended.

LONDON,

Printed for THOMAS WALKLEY, and are to
be solde at his shoppe, at the signe of the
Eagle and Childe, in *Brittaines Burße.*
1622.

Introduction

With their elevation to the status of "the premier company of London," as G. E. Bentley describes them, the King's Men had the business acumen to realize that their real future resided in the court circle, which, along with the gentry and professional and educated classes, supported the private theaters. Thus, when the lease of the Blackfriars reverted in 1608 to the company's leading actor, Richard Burbage, whose father had originally built the theater in 1596 for the company's use, they knew a good thing when they saw it. Twelve years earlier the tenants of the modish neighborhood where the Blackfriars was located objected to the quartering of actors there, and James Burbage subsequently was forced to lease the building to the managers of the Chapel children.* Court patronage in the meantime, however, had changed that attitude; and by the end of 1609, for the first time in English theatrical history, a professional company was acting simultaneously at both a public and a private theater. Their realistic awareness of the importance of privileged patronage was to pay off for the King's Men—at the start of the Caroline period, Blackfriars receipts were averaging about two and a half times as much as the Globe's.

Although they successfully operated both the Globe and the Blackfriars for many years after 1608, even going to the enormous expense of rebuilding a larger and more elegant Globe after the original had burned down in 1613, the King's

---

Chapel children: see Introduction to *The Knight of the Burning Pestle*, p. 292.

Men shifted their major interest to their new concern. For the former theater they had built up a solid repertoire that they could use over and over. In contrast, the sophisticated clientele at the Blackfriars demanded frequent changes of plays, and plays that catered to their special tastes. Thus, newer playwrights for the company wrote particularly with the private theater in mind. In a prefatory note to the reader published with *The White Devil* in 1612, Webster laments that the play was first performed "in so dull a time of winter, presented in so open and black a theater [the Globe], that it wanted (that which is the only grace and setting out of a tragedy) a full and understanding auditory."

Replacing Shakespeare as the leading playwright for the King's Men in the second decade was the aristocratically born John Fletcher. For a greater part of the century he was to outrank both his predecessor and Ben Jonson in popularity. That he worked mainly as a collaborator indicates that he was primarily a dramatic craftsman rather than a poet with an integrated vision. The Fletcherian mode in drama could be described as a formula successfully repeated. Fletcher's name from the beginning of his career became linked with that of Francis Beaumont, also nobly born. Although, in fact, they wrote no more than a handful of plays together, as a team they became preeminent purveyors to an exclusive audience. Their major contribution was a new tragicomic form of drama ideally suited to their patrons.

In the preface to his first solo dramatic venture, *The Faithful Shepherdess* (1608–1609), Fletcher defined what he meant by "tragicomedy":

> A tragicomedy is not so called in respect of mirth and killing, but in respect it wants deaths, which is enough to make it no tragedy, yet brings some near it, which is enough to make it no comedy . . .

As the definition indicates, Fletcherian tragicomedy is an entirely different matter from the "mongrel tragicomedy" denounced by Sir Philip Sidney in the 1580s—that mixture of tragic and comic scenes in one play whose tradition in English drama extended from medieval times to the Renaissance. It is, rather, what A. H. Thorndike has called "either/or drama" and Una Ellis-Fermor "the middle mood"—"this creation of an imagined world neither tragic nor comic which yet, taking something from each, resulted in something different again from either." Instead of revealing how close the worlds of comedy and tragedy could be, as "mongrel tragicomedy" was capable of doing, the plays of Beaumont and Fletcher evade the clarity of vision and the honesty of judgment that tragedy and comedy demand, with the creation of a world of refined sensationalism where only the given moment counts because no overall pattern of meaning exists. Their characters speak in blank verse, but the dialogue might almost be prose; for the metaphoric quality of poetry vanishes in a world without tension.

Philaster; or, Love Lies a-Bleeding (1608–1610) is the first major collaboration of Beaumont and Fletcher. Unlike *The Knight of the Burning Pestle* this play was immediately successful and enjoyed numerous performances throughout the Restoration. Many have read in it a serious topical "message," a warning to James against his idea of personal monarchy. Lines like Dion's "he [the king] articles with the gods" have been interpreted as gibes against James' frequent assertions of his divine right; and the aphoristic couplet at the conclusion has, one might think, the ring of summarizing the play:

> *Let princes learn*
> *By this to rule the passions of their blood,*
> *For what heaven wills can never be withstood.*

Yet, as a warning to James and as a summation of the play's meaning, or even of the king's role, the couplet seems irrelevant. At the end the king has learned nothing; he is as authoritative and as arbitrary as ever. Philaster, like Hamlet, is a man beloved by the people; but in the final scene his influence over them means nothing as he wretchedly and self-pityingly submits to the royal order for the punishment of his faithful Bellario. He even promises to forgive the murder of his father as merely "a fault" if the king will restore his own daughter, whom Philaster loves, to parental favor. The play touches on certain political and social issues, but they dissolve in a mist of romantic situation and melodrama; the emphasis is on "love lies a-bleeding." If it was meant in any way as a warning to James, it is remarkable that he seems not to have noticed, particularly since he saw the play twice when the King's Men performed it at court in the winter of 1613.

Like the "well-made" plays of the nineteenth century, and with as little meaning, *Philaster* has a surface logic that determines the unfolding of the plot; but the deeper and more rigorous logic of comedy and tragedy it eschews. In the final scene, as in the formulaic *scêne à faire* of the "well-made" play, when dire consequences threaten, the page Bellario, slanderously accused of being the lover of the king's daughter, saves the situation by throwing off his disguise to reveal that he is in reality the Lord Dion's daughter Euphrasia. But where has Euphrasia suddenly come from? An alert spectator, more detective than playgoer, might have caught in Act I the significance of Philaster's asking Dion about the latter's missing daughter and his being told that she has gone on a pilgrimage. No more is said of her until she reveals herself in Act V and explains her disguise as a ruse to keep her near her beloved Philaster. When one recalls that a real boy acted the part of the disguised Euphrasia, the deception is that more believable. Thus the *dénouement* does have a certain logic—but a logic that hardly pertains to any conception of reality.

Perfectly suited to their romantic world is the "easy" language of Beaumont and Fletcher. Although he recognized Shakespeare as the greater dramatist, Dryden condemned his "use of metaphors from passions," preferring—as the early Restoration apparently did—the "quickness and easiness" of Fletcher's rhetoric. Rhetoric in form, however, makes for melodrama in content; and the immediate situation becomes important only for the rhetorical pose that it permits—in Philaster's embellished description of his discovery of Bellario (I.ii), in Arethusa's legalistic protestation of her virginity (III.ii), in the king's unintentionally vulgar protestation of his daughter's virginity (I.i), and in Philaster's self-pitying sentimentality (IV.ii). When Arethusa pleads for Bellario's innocence, and Philaster mistakes the cause of her defense, the scene (III.ii) exists to permit the display of Philaster's reactions, but not for any meaning it may have for the play itself.

Shaw recognized the skill of Beaumont and Fletcher, but he described their plays as having "no depth, no conviction, no religious or philosophical basis, no real power or seriousness." Yet where Shaw understandably was repelled by these characteristics, the well-meaning but irresponsible coterie audience of Beaumont and Fletcher's day was drawn by them. When it became increasingly difficult to make up one's mind, this type of tragicomedy offered the allure of a world of momentary repose in the quiet sentiment of rhetoric. But, despite the absence of any significant dramatic tension in the play, *Philaster,* even with its happy ending, is a melancholy work, most of the major characters at one point or another wishing that they could escape from life altogether. Philaster wishes that "this had been a life/ Free from vexation," that he could sleep forever; he finds a "recreation" and a "joy" in dying. Bellario, too, wishes to sleep forever. Arethusa craves "peace in death." Oblivion seems almost a blessing. This is drama of the death wish.

The Playwrights

FRANCIS BEAUMONT: see *The Knight of the Burning Pestle*, p. 294.

JOHN FLETCHER (1579–1625), the successor to Shakespeare as the chief playwright for the King's Men, is surprisingly obscure biographically. He was born at Rye, in Sussex, the benefice of his father, Richard Fletcher, who became Bishop of Bristol, Worcester, and (in 1594) London. The bishop's second marriage incurred the displeasure of Queen Elizabeth, and at his death in 1596 he left behind an impoverished family of nine children. The playwright may have attended Bene't (Corpus Christi) College, Cambridge, of which his father had been president. From about 1608 to 1613 or so he engaged with Beaumont in the most successful collaboration of the period, at first for the boy companies, later almost entirely for the King's Men; *Philaster* was the first of their joint successes. Although most of his plays are collaborative efforts with many playwrights, Fletcher was sole author of not less than sixteen plays. He died of the plague and was buried at Saint Saviour's, Southwark. His cousins were the Spenserian poets Giles and Phineas Fletcher.

The Play

The present text of *Philaster; or, Love Lies a-Bleeding* is based on copies of the 1622 quarto ("The second Impression, corrected, and amended") in the Henry E. Huntington and the

Folger Shakespeare libraries that have been collated with the old-spelling edition of Robert K. Turner. Much of the bracketed material derives from the first quarto of 1620 and from later quartos. The *dramatis personæ* is supplied from the third quarto of 1628 in the Beinecke Rare Book and Manuscript Library of Yale University. The play is divided into acts, with only "Scœna 1" of each designated. General agreement places the date of the first performance between 1608 and 1610, and scholarship gives Beaumont credit for the greater share in the collaboration. The King's Men performed the play "diverse times" at both the Globe and Blackfriars theaters.

SELECTED BIBLIOGRAPHY

See also: *The Knight of the Burning Pestle*, p. 295.

Philaster, ed. R. K. Turner, in Volume One of *The Dramatic Works in the Beaumont and Fletcher Canon*, gen. ed. F. Bowers. Cambridge: Cambridge University Press, 1966.
Works, ed. A. H. Bullen *et al.* 4 vols. London: Bell and Bullen, 1904–1912. "Variorum Edition" (incomplete).
Works, ed. A. Glover and A. R. Waller. 10 vols. Cambridge: Cambridge University Press, 1905–1912.

Adkins, M. G. M. "The Citizens in *Philaster:* Their Function and Significance," *Studies in Philology*, XLIII (1946), 203–212.
Appleton, W. W. *Beaumont and Fletcher: A Critical Study*. London: Allen and Unwin, 1956.
Danby, J. *Poets on Fortune's Hill: Studies in Sidney, Shakespeare, Beaumont and Fletcher*. London: Faber and Faber, 1952.
Davison, P. "The Serious Concerns of *Philaster*," *Journal of English Literary History*, XXX (1963), 1–15.
Hoy, C. "The Shares of Fletcher and His Collaborators in the Beaumont and Fletcher Canon," *Studies in Bibliography*, VIII (1956)–XV (1962). See especially Vol. XI (1958), 85–99.
Leech, C. *The John Fletcher Plays*. London: Chatto and Windus, 1962.
Maxwell, B. *Studies in Beaumont, Fletcher, and Massinger*. Chapel Hill: University of North Carolina Press, 1939.
Shaw, B. *Plays and Players: Essays on the Theatre*. London: Oxford University Press, 1952. (The World's Classics.)

Waith, E. M. *The Pattern of Tragicomedy in Beaumont and Fletcher.* Yale Studies in English 120. New Haven, Conn.: Yale University Press, 1952.

Wallis, L. B. *Fletcher, Beaumont and Company: Entertainers to the Jacobean Gentry.* New York: King's Crown Press, 1947.

Wilson, H. S. *"Philaster* and *Cymbeline,"* in *English Institute Essays, 1951,* ed. A. S. Downer. New York: Columbia University Press, 1952.

To the Reader.

Courteous Reader:

Philaster and Arethusa his love have lain so long a-bleeding, by reason of some dangerous and gaping wounds which they received in the first impression, that it is wondered how they could go abroad so long or travel so far as they have done. Although they were hurt neither by me nor the printer, yet I, knowing and finding by experience how many well-wishers they have abroad, have adventured to bind up their wounds and to enable them to visit upon better terms such friends of theirs as were pleased to take knowledge of them, so mai[m]ed and deformed as they at the first were; and, if they were then gracious in your sight, assuredly they will now find double favor, being reformed and set forth suitable to their birth and breeding,

By your serviceable friend,
Thomas Walkley.

[THE SCENE BEING IN SICILY

THE PERSONS PRESENTED ARE
THESE, *viz.:*

*

The KING.
PHILASTER, *heir to the crown.*
PHARAMOND, *Prince of Spain.*
DION, *a lord.*
CLEREMONT } *noble gentlemen, his associates.*
THRASILINE
ARETHUSA, *the King's daughter.*
GALATEA, *a wise, modest lady attending the Princess.*
MEGRA, *a lascivious lady.*
An Old Wanton Lady, or Crone.
Another Lady attending the Princess.
EUPHRASIA, *daughter of Dion, but disguised like a page, and*
   called BELLARIO.
An Old Captain.
Five Citizens.
A Country Fellow.
Two Woodmen.
The King's Guard and Train.]

Philaster;
or, Love Lies
a-Bleeding

ACTUS I

[I.i]

Enter DION, CLEREMONT, *and* THRASILINE.

CLEREMONT. Here's nor lords nor ladies.

DION. Credit me, gentlemen, I wonder at it. They received strict charge from the king to attend here; besides, it was boldly published that no officer should forbid any gentlemen that desired to attend and hear.

CLEREMONT. Can you guess the cause?

DION. Sir, it is plain—about the Spanish prince that's come to marry our kingdom's heir and be our sovereign.

THRASILINE. Many that will seem to know much say she looks not on him like a maid in love.

DION. Faith, sir, the multitude (that seldom know anything but their own opinions) speak that they would have; but the prince, before his own approach, received so many confident messages from the state that I think she's resolved to be ruled.

CLEREMONT. Sir, it is thought with her he shall enjoy both these kingdoms of Sicily and Calabria.

DION. Sir, it is without controversy so meant. But 'twill be a troublesome labor for him to enjoy both these kingdoms with safety, the right heir to one of them

living, and living so virtuously—especially, the people
admiring the bravery of his mind and lamenting his
injuries.

CLEREMONT. Who? Philaster?

DION. Yes; whose father, we all know, was by our late
King of Calabria unrighteously deposed from his fruitful Sicily. Myself drew some blood in those wars,
which I would give my hand to be washed from.

CLEREMONT. Sir, my ignorance in state policy will not   30
let me know why, Philaster being heir to one of these
kingdoms, the king should suffer him to walk abroad
with such free liberty.

DION. Sir, it seems your nature is more constant than to
inquire after state news. But the king, of late, made
a hazard of both the kingdoms, of Sicily and his own,
with offering but to imprison Philaster, at which the
city was in arms, not to be charmed down by any
state order or proclamation till they saw Philaster ride
through the streets pleased and without a guard, at   40
which they threw their hats and their arms from them,
some to make bonfires, some to drink, all for his de-
liverance—which, wise men say, is the cause the king
labors to bring in the power of a foreign nation to awe
his own with.

Enter GALATEA, MEGRA, *and a Lady.*

THRASILINE. See, the ladies! What's the first?

DION. A wise and modest gentlewoman that attends the
princess.

CLEREMONT. The second?

DION. She is one that may stand still discreetly enough and   50
ill-favoredly dance her measure,° simper when she is
courted by her friend,° and slight her husband.

CLEREMONT. The last?

DION. Faith, I think she is one whom the state keeps for
the agents of our confederate princes: she'll cog° and
lie with a whole army before the league shall break.
Her name is common through the kingdom, and the
trophies of her dishonor advanced beyond Hercules'
Pillars. She loves to try the several constitutions of

---

measure: formal, stately dance.   friend: lover.
cog: cajole, cheat.

men's bodies and, indeed, has destroyed the worth of   60
her own body by making experiment upon it for the
good of the commonwealth.

CLEREMONT. She's a profitable member.

LADY. Peace, if you love me! You shall see these gentlemen stand their ground and not court us.

GALATEA. What if they should?

MEGRA. What if they should!

LADY [to GALATEA]. Nay, let her alone.—What if they
should? Why, if they should, I say they were never
abroad. What foreigner would do so? It writes them   70
directly untraveled.

GALATEA. Why, what if they be?

MEGRA. What if they be!

LADY. Good madam, let her go on.—What if they be?
Why, if they be, I will justify they cannot maintain
discourse with a judicious lady, nor make a leg,* nor
say, "Excuse me."

GALATEA. Ha, ha, ha!

LADY. Do you laugh, madam?

DION. Your desires upon you, ladies!   80

LADY. Then you must sit beside us.

DION. I shall sit near you then, lady.

LADY. Near me, perhaps; but there's a lady endures no
stranger, and to me you appear a very strange fellow.

MEGRA. Methinks he's not so strange; he would quickly
to be acquainted.

THRASILINE. Peace, the king!

        Enter KING, PHARAMOND, ARETHUSA, and Train.

KING. To give a stronger testimony of love
    Than sickly promises (which commonly
    In princes find both birth and burial   90
    In one breath), we have drawn you, worthy sir,
    To make your fair endearments to our daughter,
    And worthy services known to our subjects,
    Now loved and wondered at; next, our intent
    To plant you deeply our immediate heir
    Both to our blood and kingdoms. For this lady
    (The best part of your life, as you confirm me,
    And I believe), though her few years and sex

---

make a leg: bow.

Yet teach her nothing but her fears and blushes,
Desires without desire, discourse and knowledge   100
Only of what herself is to herself,
Make her feel moderate health; and, when she sleeps,
In making no ill day, knows no ill dreams.
Think not, dear sir, these undivided parts,
That must mold up a virgin, are put on
To show her so, as borrowed ornaments
To talk of her perfect love to you or add
An artificial shadow to her nature.
No, sir; I boldly dare proclaim her yet
No woman. But woo her still, and think her modesty   110
A sweeter mistress than the offered language
Of any dame, were she a queen, whose eye
Speaks common loves and comforts to her servants.*
Last, noble son (for so I now must call you),
What I have done thus public is not only
To add comfort in particular
To you or me, but all, and to confirm
The nobles and the gentry of these kingdoms
By oath to your succession, which shall be
Within this month at most   120

THRASILINE [*aside*]. This will be hardly done.

CLEREMONT. [*aside*]. It must be ill done if it be done.

DION [*aside*]. When 'tis at best, 'twill be but half done whilst

So brave a gentleman is wronged and flung off.

THRASILINE [*aside*]. I fear.

CLEREMONT [*aside*]. Who does not?

DION [*aside*]. I fear not for myself, and yet I fear too.
Well, we shall see, we shall see. No more.

PHARAMOND. Kissing your white hand, mistress, I take leave

To thank your royal father and thus far   130
To be my own free trumpet. Understand,
Great king, and these your subjects, mine that must be
(For so deserving you have spoke me, sir,
And so deserving I dare speak myself),
To what a person, of what eminence,
Ripe expectation, of what faculties,

---

servants: lovers; suitors.

Manners, and virtues, you would wed your kingdoms;
You in me have you[r] wishes. O, this country!
By more than all the gods, I hold it happy—
Happy in their dear memories that have been   140
Kings great and good; happy in yours that is;
And from you (as a chronicle to keep
Your noble name from eating age) do I
Open myself most happy. Gentlemen,
Believe me in a word, a prince's word,
There shall be nothing to make up a kingdom
Mighty and flourishing, defensèd, feared,
Equal to be commanded and obeyed,
But through the travails of my life I'll find it
And tie it to this country. By all the gods,   150
My reign shall be so easy to the subject
That every man shall be his prince himself
And his own law: yet I his prince and law.
And, dearest lady, to your dearest self
(Dear in the choice of him whose name and luster
Must make you more and mightier), let me say
You are the blessed'st living; for, sweet princess,
You shall enjoy a man of men to be
Your servant; you shall make him yours, for whom
Great queens must die.   160

THRASILINE. [aside]. Miraculous!

CLEREMONT [aside]. This speech calls him Spaniard,
being nothing but a large inventory of his own commendations.

Enter PHILASTER.

DION [aside]. I wonder what's his price, for certainly
he'll sell himself, he has so praised his shape.—But
here comes one more worthy those large speeches than
the large speaker of them. Let me be swallowed quick*
if I can find, in all the anatomy of yon man's virtues,
one sinew sound enough to promise for him he shall   170
be constable. By this sun, he'll ne'er make king, unless
it be of trifles, in my poor judgment.

PHILASTER [kneeling]. Right noble sir, as low as my obe-
dience,
And with a heart as loyal as my knee,
I beg your favor.

---

quick: alive.

KING.   Rise; you have it, sir.
  [PHILASTER *rises*.]
DION [*aside*]. Mark but the king, how pale he looks!
    He fears!
  O, this same whoreson* conscience, how it jades us!
KING. Speak your intent, sir.
PHILASTER.   Shall I speak um* freely?
  Be still my royal sovereign.
KING.   As a subject,
  We give you freedom.
DION [*aside*].   Now it heats.
PHILASTER.   Then thus I
    turn   180
  My language to you, prince—you, foreign man!
  Ne'er stare nor put on wonder, for you must
  Endure me, and you shall. This earth you tread upon
  (A dowry, as you hope, with this fair princess),
  [By my dead father (O, I had a father,
  Whose memory I bow to!) was not left]
  To your inheritance, and I up and living—
  Having myself about me and my sword,
  The souls of all my name and memories,
  These arms and some few friends beside the gods—   190
  To part so calmly with it, and sit still
  And say, "I might have been." I tell thee, Pharamond,
  When thou art king, look I be dead and rotten,
  And my name ashes, as I; for, hear me, Pharamond,
  This very ground thou goest on, this fat earth
  My father's friends made fertile with their faiths,
  Before that day of shame shall gape and swallow
  Thee and thy nation, like a hungry grave,
  Into her hidden bowels. Prince, it shall;
  By the just gods it shall!
PHARAMOND.   He's mad—beyond cure,
    mad.   200
DION [*aside*]. Here's a fellow has some fire in's veins;
  The outlandish* prince looks like a tooth-drawer.
PHILASTER. Sir Prince of Popinjays, I'll make it well
    appear
  To you I am not mad.

———

whoreson: rascally.   um: them ('em).   outlandish: foreign.

KING.   You displease us;
  You are too bold.
PHILASTER.   No, sir, I am too tame,
  Too much a turtle,* a thing born without passion,
  A faint shadow that every drunken cloud
  Sails over and makes nothing.
KING.   I do not fancy this.
  Call our physicians! Sure he's somewhat tainted.
THRASILINE [aside]. I do not think 'twill prove so.   210
DION [aside]. H'as given him a general purge already,
  for all the right he has; and now he means to let him
  blood. Be constant, gentlemen; by heaven, I'll run his
  hazard* although I run my name out of the kingdom!
CLEREMONT [aside]. Peace, we are all one soul.
PHARAMOND. What you have seen in me to stir offense
  I cannot find, unless it be this lady,
  Offered into mine arms with the succession,
  Which I must keep (though it hath pleased your fury
  To mutiny within you) without disputing   220
  Your genealogies or taking knowledge
  Whose branch you are. The king will leave it me,
  And I dare make it mine. You have your answer.
PHILASTER. If thou wert sole inheritor to him
  That made the world his,* and couldst see no sun
  Shine upon anything but thine; were Pharamond
  As truly valiant as I feel him cold,
  And ringed amongst the choicest of his friends,
  Such as would blush to talk such serious follies
  Or back such belied commendations,   230
  And from this presence, spite of [all] these bugs,*
  You should hear further from me.
KING. Sir, you wrong the prince:
  I gave you not this freedom to brave our best friends.
  You deserve our frown. Go to; be better tempered!
PHILASTER. It must be, sir, when I am nobler used.
GALATEA [aside]. Ladies,
  This would have been a pattern of succession
  Had he ne'er met this mischief. By my life,

---

  turtle: turtledove.   hazard: risk.
  him/ That . . . world his: Alexander the Great.
  bugs: bugbears.

He is the worthiest the true name of man   240
This day within my knowledge.

MEGRA [*aside*]. I cannot tell what you may call your
  knowledge,
But th'other is the man set in my eye:
O, 'tis a prince of wax!*

GALATEA [*aside*].   A dog it is!

KING. Philaster, tell me
The injuries you aim at in your riddles.

PHILASTER. If you had my eyes, sir, and sufferance,*
My griefs upon you, and my broken fortunes,
My wants great, and now-nothing hopes and fears,
My wrongs would make ill riddles to be laughed at.   250
Dare you be still my king and right me [not]?

KING. Give me your wrongs in private.

PHILASTER.   Take them,
And ease me of a load would bow strong Atlas.
(*They whisper.*)

CLEREMONT [*aside*]. He dares not stand the shock.

DION [*aside*]. I cannot blame him; there's danger in't.
Every man in this age has not a soul of crystal for all
men to read their actions through: men's hearts and
faces are so far asunder that they hold no intelligence.
Do but view yon stranger well, and you shall see a
fever through all his bravery,* and feel him shake like   260
a true tenant.* If he give not back his crown again
upon the report of an elder-gun,* I have no augury.

KING. Go to;
Be more yourself as you respect our favor;
You'll stir us else. Sir, I must have you know
That y'are and shall be, at our pleasure, what fashion
  we
Will put upon you. Smooth your brow, or by the
  gods—

PHILASTER. I am dead, sir; y'are my fate. It was not I
Said I was wronged: I carry all about me
My weak stars lead me to, all my weak fortunes.   270
Who dares in all this presence speak (that is,

---

of wax: incomparable; model.   sufferance: pain.
bravery: bravado, insolence.   tenant: temporary possessor.
elder-gun: popgun.

But m[a]n of flesh, and may be mortal), tell me
I do not most entirely love this prince
And honor his full virtues!

KING.   Sure, he's possessed!

PHILASTER. Yes, with my father's spirit. It's here, O king,
A dangerous spirit! Now he tells me, king,
I was a king's heir, bids me be a king,
And whispers to me these are all my subjects.
'Tis strange he will not let me sleep but dives
Into my fancy, and there gives me shapes   280
That kneel and do me service, cry me king.
But I'll suppress him; he's a factious spirit,
And will undo me.—[*To* PHARAMOND.] Noble sir, your
   hand;
I am your servant.

KING.   Away! I do not like this;
I'll make you tamer, or I'll dispossess you
Both of life and spirit. For this time
I pardon your wild speech, without so much
As your imprisonment.

            [*Exeunt*] KING, PHARAMOND, ARETHUSA [, *and Train*].

DION. I thank you, sir; you dare not for the people.

GALATEA. Ladies, what think you now of this brave   290
fellow?

MEGRA. A pretty talking fellow, hot at hand. But eye yon
stranger; is he not a fine complete gentleman? O, these
strangers, I do affect ° them strangely! They do the
rarest home-things and please the fullest. As I live, I
could love all the nation over and over for his sake!

GALATEA. Gods comfort your poor headpiece, lady; 'tis a
weak one and had need of a nightcap.

            [*Exeunt*] *Ladies*.

DION [*aside*]. See how his fancy labors! Has he not spoke
Home, and bravely? What a dangerous train   300
Did he give fire to! How he shook the king,
Made his soul melt within him, and his blood
Run into whey! It stood upon his brow
Like a cold winter dew.

PHILASTER.   Gentlemen,
You have no suit to me? I am no minion.

---

affect: admire, like.

You stand, methinks, like men that would be courtiers,
If* you could well be flattered at a price
Not to undo your children. Y'are all honest;
Go, get you home again, and make your country
A virtuous court, to which your great ones may   310
In their diseasèd age retire and live recluse.

CLEREMONT. How do you, worthy sir?

PHILASTER.   Well, very well;
And so well that, if the king please, I find
I may live many years.

DION.   The king must please
Whilst we know what you are and who you are,
Your wrongs and injuries. Shrink not, worthy sir,
But add your father to you, in whose name
We'll waken all the gods and conjure up
The rods of vengeance, the abusèd people,
Who, like to raging torrents, shall swell high   320
And so begirt the dens of these male dragons
That, through the strongest safety, they shall beg
For mercy at your sword's point.

PHILASTER.   Friends, no more;
Our ears may be corrupted: 'tis an age
We dare not trust our wills to. Do you love me?

THRASILINE. Do we love heaven and honor?

PHILASTER.   My Lord
Dion, you had
A virtuous gentlewoman, called you father;
Is she yet alive?

DION.   Most honored sir, she is,
And for the penance but of an idle dream
Has undertook a tedious pilgrimage.   330

Enter a LADY.

PHILASTER. Is it to me, or any of these gentlemen, you
    come?

LADY. To you, brave lord; the princess would entreat
    Your present company.

PHILASTER. The princess send for me! Y'are mistaken.

LADY. If you be called Philaster, 'tis to you.

PHILASTER. Kiss her fair hand, and say I will attend her.
                                              [*Exit* LADY.]

---

if: as if.

DION. Do you know what you do?

PHILASTER. Yes, go to see a woman.

CLEREMONT. But do you weigh the danger you are in?

PHILASTER. Danger in a sweet face?   340
    By Jupiter, I must not fear a woman!

THRASILINE. But are you sure it was the princess sent?
    It may be some foul train* to catch your life.

PHILASTER. I do not think it, gentlemen; she's noble.
    Her eye may shoot me dead, or those true red
    And white friends in her face may steal my soul out:
    There's all the danger in't; but, be what may,
    Her single* name hath armed me.

                                            Exit PHILASTER.

DION.   Go on,
    And be as truly happy as th'art fearless!—
    Come, gentlemen, let's make our friends acquainted,   350
    Lest the king prove false.

                                        [*Exeunt*] *Gentlemen.*

[I.ii]

                    Enter ARETHUSA *and a* LADY.

ARETHUSA. Comes he not?

LADY.   Madam?

ARETHUSA.   Will Philaster
        come?

LADY. Dear madam, you were wont
    To credit me at first.

ARETHUSA. But didst thou tell me so?
    I am forgetful, and my woman's strength
    Is so o'ercharged with dangers like to grow
    About my marriage that these underthings
    Dare not abide in such a troubled sea.
    How looked he when he told thee he would come?

LADY. Why, well.   10

ARETHUSA. And not a little fearful?

LADY. Fear, madam? Sure he knows not what it is.

ARETHUSA. You all are of his faction; the whole court
    Is bold in praise of him whilst I
    May live neglected and do noble things,
    As fools in strife throw gold into the sea,

---

    train: stratagem, trick, plot.   single: mere.

Drowned in the doing. But I know he fears!
LADY. Fear, madam! Methought his looks hid more
   Of love than fear.
ARETHUSA.   Of love? To whom? To you?
   Did you deliver those plain words I sent   20
   With such a winning gesture and quick look
   That you have caught him?
LADY.   Madam, I mean to you.
ARETHUSA. Of love to me! Alas, thy ignorance
   Lets thee not see the crosses of our births!
   Nature, that loves not to be questionèd
   Why she did this or that, but has her ends,
   And knows she does well, never gave the world
   Two things so opposite, so contrary,
   As he and I am. If a bowl of blood
   Drawn from this arm of mine would poison thee,   30
   A draught of his would cure thee. Of love to me!
LADY. Madam, I think I hear him.
ARETHUSA.   Bring him in.—

                            [*Exit* LADY.]

   You gods, that would not have your dooms withstood,
   Whose holy wisdoms at this time it is
   To make the passions of a feeble maid
   The way unto your justice, I obey.

        Enter PHILASTER [*with* LADY]

LADY. Here is my Lord Philaster.
ARETHUSA.   O, it is well;
   Withdraw yourself.

                            [*Exit* LADY.]

PHILASTER.   Madam, your messenger
   Made me believe you wished to speak with me.
ARETHUSA. 'Tis true, Philaster; but the words are such   40
   I have to say, and do so ill beseem
   The mouth of woman, that I wish them said
   And yet am loath to speak them. Have you known
   That I have aught detracted from your worth?
   Have I in person wronged you? or have set
   My baser instruments to throw disgrace
   Upon your virtue?
PHILASTER.   Never, madam, you.
ARETHUSA. Why, then, should you, in such a public
    place,

Injure a princess and a scandal lay
Upon my fortunes, famed to be so great,   50
Calling a great part of my dowry in question?
PHILASTER. Madam, this truth which I shall speak will be
Foolish; but, for your fair and virtuous self,
I could afford myself to have no right
To anything you wished.
ARETHUSA.   Philaster, know
I must enjoy these kingdoms.
PHILASTER.   Madam, both?
ARETHUSA. Both, or I die; by heaven, I die, Philaster,
If I not calmly may enjoy them both.
PHILASTER. I would do much to save that noble life,
Yet would be loath to have posterity   60
Find in our stories that Philaster gave
His right unto a scepter and a crown
To save a lady's longing.
ARETHUSA.   Nay, then, hear:
I must and will have them, and more—
PHILASTER.   What more?
ARETHUSA. Or lose that little life the gods prepared
To trouble this poor piece of earth withal.
PHILASTER. Madam, what more?
ARETHUSA.   Turn then away thy
    face.
PHILASTER. No.
ARETHUSA. Do.
PHILASTER. I can endure it. Turn away my face?   70
I never yet saw enemy that looked
So dreadfully but that I thought myself
As great a basilisk* as he, or spake
So horrible but that I thought my tongue
Bore thunder underneath as much as his,
Nor beast that I could turn from. Shall I, then,
Begin to fear sweet sounds? A lady's voice,
Whom I do love? Say you would have my life—
Why, I will give it you; for it is of me
A thing so loathed, and unto you that ask   80
Of so poor use, that I shall make no price.
If you entreat, I will unmov'dly hear.

---

basilisk: a fabled serpent whose glance was fatal.

ARETHUSA. Yet, for my sake, a little bend thy looks.
PHILASTER. I do.
ARETHUSA.   Then know I must have them and
      thee.
PHILASTER. And me?
ARETHUSA.   Thy love, without which all the
      land
   Discovered yet will serve me for no use
   But to be buried in.
PHILASTER.   Is't possible?
ARETHUSA. With it, it were too little to bestow
   On thee. Now, though my breath do strike me dead
   (Which, know, it may), I have unripped my breast.   90
PHILASTER. Madam, you are too full of noble thoughts
   To lay a train for this contemnèd life,
   Which you may have for asking. To suspect
   Were base, where I deserve no ill. Love you!
   By all my hopes I do, above my life!
   But how this passion should proceed from you
   So violently would amaze a man
   That would be jealous.°
ARETHUSA. Another soul into my body shot
   Could not have filled me with more strength and spirit   100
   Than this thy breath; but spend not hasty time
   In seeking how I came thus: 'tis the gods,
   The gods, that make me so; and sure our love
   Will be the nobler and the better blessed,
   In that the secret justice of the gods
   Is mingled with it. Let us leave and kiss,
   Lest some unwelcome guest should fall betwixt us,
   And we should part without it.
PHILASTER.   'Twill be ill
   I should abide here long.
ARETHUSA.   'Tis true; and worse
   You should come often. How shall we devise   110
   To hold intelligence,° that our true loves
   On any new occasion may agree
   What path is best to tread?
PHILASTER.   I have a boy,
   Sent by the gods, I hope, to this intent,

---

jealous: suspicious.   intelligence: communication.

Not yet seen in the court. Hunting the buck,
I found him sitting by a fountain's side,
Of which he borrowed some to quench his thirst,
And paid the nymph again as much in tears.
A garland lay him by, made by himself
Of many several flowers bred in the bay,   120
Stuck in that mystic order that the rareness
Delighted me; but, ever when he turned
His tender eyes upon um, he would weep
As if he meant to make um grow again.
Seeing such pretty, helpless innocence
Dwell in his face, I asked him all his story.
He told me that his parents gentle died,
Leaving him to the mercy of the fields,
Which gave him roots, and of the crystal springs,
Which did not stop their courses; and the sun,   130
Which still,° he thanked him, yielded him his light.
Then took he up his garland and did show
What every flower, as country people hold,
Did signify, and how all, ordered thus,
Expressed his grief, and, to my thoughts, did read
The prettiest lecture of his country art
That could be wished, so that methought I could
Have studied it. I gladly entertained °
Him, who was glad to follow, and have got
The trustiest, loving'st, and the gentlest boy   140
That ever master kept. Him will I send
To wait on you and bear our hidden love.

ARETHUSA. 'Tis well; no more.

Enter LADY.

LADY. Madam, the prince is come to do his service.

ARETHUSA. What will you do, Philaster, with yourself?

PHILASTER. Why, that which all the gods have appointed
   out for me.

ARETHUSA. Dear, hide thyself!—
Bring in the prince.

[*Exit* LADY.]

PHILASTER.   Hide me from Pharamond!
When thunder speaks, which is the voice of God,
Though I do reverence, yet I hide me not;   150

---

still: continually, constantly.   entertained: employed.

And shall a stranger prince have leave to brag
Unto a foreign nation that he made
Philaster hide himself?

ARETHUSA.   He cannot know it.

PHILASTER. Though it should sleep forever to the world,
It is a simple sin to hide myself,
Which will forever on my conscience lie.

ARETHUSA. Then, good Philaster, give him scope and way
In what he says; for he is apt to speak
What you are loath to hear. For my sake, do.

PHILASTER. I will.   160

Enter PHARAMOND [*with* LADY].

PHARAMOND. My princely mistress, as true lovers ought,
I come to kiss these fair hands and to show,

[*Exit* LADY.]

In outward ceremonies, the dear love
Writ i[n] my heart.

PHILASTER. If I shall have an answer no directlier,
I am gone.

PHARAMOND.   To what would he have answer?

ARETHUSA. To his claim unto the kingdom.

PHARAMOND. Sirrah, I forbare° you before the king—

PHILASTER. Good sir, do so still; I would not talk with
you.

PHARAMOND. But now the time is fitter; do but offer   170
To make mention of right to any kingdom,
Though it be scarce habitable—

PHILASTER.   Good sir, let me go.

PHARAMOND. And, by the gods—

PHILASTER.   Peace, Pharamond!
If thou—

ARETHUSA. Leave us, Philaster.

PHILASTER. I have done.

PHARAMOND. You are gone! By heaven, I'll fetch you
back!

PHILASTER. You shall not need.

PHARAMOND.   What now?

PHILASTER.   Know,
Pharamond,
I loathe to brawl with such a blast as thou,

---

forbare: forbore.

Who are naught but a valiant voice; but, if
Thou shalt provoke me further, men shall say   180
Thou wert—and not lament it.
PHARAMOND.   Do you slight
  My greatness so? And in the chamber of the princess?
PHILASTER. It is a place to which, I must confess,
  I owe a reverence; but, were't the church,
  Ay, at the altar, there's no place so safe
  Where thou dar'st injure me, but I dare kill thee.
  And for your greatness, know, sir, I can grasp
  You and your greatness thus, thus into nothing.
  Give not a word, not a word back! Farewell.

                                                    Exit.
PHARAMOND. 'Tis an odd fellow, madam; we must stop   190
  His mouth with some office when we are married.
ARETHUSA. You were best make him your controller.
[PHARAMOND.] I think he would discharge it well. But,
      madam,
  I hope our hearts are knit; but yet so slow
  The ceremonies of state are that 'twill be long
  Before our hands be so. If, then, you please,
  Being agreed in heart, let us not wait
  For dreaming form but take a little stol'n
  Delights, and so prevent ° our joys to come.
ARETHUSA. If you dare speak such thoughts,   200
  I must withdraw in honor.
                                        Exit ARETHUSA.
PHARAMOND. The constitution of my body will never
  hold out till the wedding: I must seek elsewhere.
                                        Exit PHARAMOND.

ACTUS II

[II.i]
                    Enter PHILASTER *and* BELLARIO.
PHILASTER. And thou shalt find her honorable, boy,
  Full of regard unto thy tender youth,
  For thine own modesty, and, for my sake,
  Apter to give than thou wilt be to ask,
  Ay, or deserve.

———————————————
  prevent: anticipate.

BELLARIO.   Sir, you did take me up
  When I was nothing, and only yet am something
  By being yours. You trusted me unknown,
  And that which you were apt to co[n]ster*
  A simple innocence in me perhaps
  Might have been craft, the cunning of a boy   10
  Hardened in lies and theft, yet ventured you
  To part my miseries and me—for which
  I never can expect to serve a lady
  That bears more honor in her breast than you.
PHILASTER. But, boy, it will prefer* thee. Thou art young
  And bearest a childish, overflowing love
  To them that clap thy cheeks and speak thee fair yet;
  But when thy judgment comes to rule those passions,
  Thou wilt remember best those careful friends
  That placed thee in the noblest way of life.   20
  She is a princess I prefer thee to.
BELLARIO. In that small time that I have seen the world,
  I never knew a man hasty to part
  With a servant he thought trusty. I remember
  My father would prefer the boys he kept
  To greater men than he, but did it not
  Till they were grown too saucy for himself.
PHILASTER. Why, gentle boy, I find no fault at all
  In thy behavior.
BELLARIO.   Sir, if I have made
  A fault of ignorance, instruct my youth: 30
  I shall be willing, if not apt, to learn;
  Age and experience will adorn my mind
  With larger knowledge. And, if I have done
  A willful fault, think me not past all hope
  For once. What master holds so strict a hand
  Over his boy that he will part with him
  Without one warning? Let me be corrected
  To break my stubbornness, if it be so,
  Rather than turn me off; and I shall mend.
PHILASTER. Thy love doth plead so prettily to stay   40
  That, trust me, I could weep to part with thee.
  Alas, I do not turn thee off: thou knowest
  It is my business that doth call thee hence;

---

    conster: interpret, construe.   prefer: advance.

And, when thou art with her, thou dwellest with me.
Think so, and 'tis so: and, when time is full,
That thou hast well discharged this heavy trust,
Laid on so weak a one, I will again
With joy receive thee. As I live, I will!
Nay, weep not, gentle boy. 'Tis more than time
Thou didst attend the princess.

BELLARIO.   I am gone;   50
But, since I am to part with you, my lord,
And none knows whether I shall live to do
More service for you, take this little prayer:
Heaven bless your loves, your fights, all your designs!
May sick men, if they have your wish, be well,
And heaven hate those you curse, though I be one!

Exit.

PHILASTER. The love of boys unto their lords is strange.
I have read wonders of it; yet this boy
For my sake (if a man may judge by looks
And speech) would outdo story. I may see   60
A day to pay him for his loyalty.

Exit PHILASTER.

[II.ii]
Enter PHARAMOND.

PHARAMOND. Why should these ladies stay so long?
They must come this way; I know the queen employs
um not, for the reverend mother° sent me word they
would all be for the garden. If they should all prove
honest ° now, I were in a fair taking;° I was never so
long without sport in my life, and, in my conscience,
'tis not my fault. O, for our country ladies!
Enter GALATEA.
—Here's one bolted; I'll hound at her.—[Madam!]
GALATEA. Your grace!
PHARAMOND. Shall I not be a trouble?   10
GALATEA. Not to me, sir.
PHARAMOND. Nay, nay, you are too quick. By this sweet
hand—
GALATEA. You'll be forsworn, sir; 'tis but an old glove. If

---

mother: chaperon.   honest: chaste.
taking: dilemma, predicament, quandary.

you will talk at a distance, I am for you; but, good
prince, be not bawdy, nor do not brag: these two I
bar; and then, I think, I shall have sense enough to
answer all the weighty apothegms your royal blood
shall manage.

PHARAMOND. Dear lady, can you love?   20

GALATEA. "Dear," prince! How dear? I ne'er cost you a
coach yet, nor put you to the dear repentance of a
banquet. Here's no scarlet, sir, to blush the sin out it
was given for. This wire° mine own hair covers, and
this face has been so far from being dear to any that it
ne'er cost penny painting; and, for the rest of my poor
wardrobe, such as you see, it leaves no hand ° behind
it to make the jealous mercer's wife curse our good
doings.

PHARAMOND. You mistake me, lady.   30

GALATEA. Lord, I do so: would you or I could help it!

PHARAMOND. Do ladies of this country use to give no
more respect to men of my full being?

GALATEA. Full being! I understand you not, unless your
grace means growing to fatness; and then your only
remedy (upon my knowledge, prince) is, in a morning,
a cup of neat white wine, brewed with carduus,° then
fast till supper—about eight you may eat; use exercise,
and keep a sparrow-hawk; you can shoot in a tiller;°
but, of all, your grace must fly phlebotomy, fresh pork,   40
conger, and clarified whey: they are all dullers of the
vital spirits.

PHARAMOND. Lady, you talk of nothing all this while.

GALATEA. 'Tis very true, sir; I talk of you.

[PHARAMOND (*aside*).] This is a crafty wench; I like her
wit well; 'twill be rare to stir up a leaden appetite.
She's a Danaë, and must be courted in a show'r of
gold.—[*He shows her money.*] Madam, look here; all
these, and more than—

GALATEA. What have you there, my lord? Gold? Now, as   50
I live, 'tis fair gold! You would have silver for it to
play with the pages. You could not have taken me in

---

wire: wire support for headdress.   hand: note of indebtedness.
carduus: thistle (used medicinally).
in a tiller: with a crossbow.

a worse time; but, if you have present use, my lord,
I'll send my man with silver and keep your gold for
you.

PHARAMOND. Lady, lady!

GALATEA. She's coming, sir, behind, will take white
money.*—[*Aside.*] Yet for all this I'll match ye.

                Exit GALATEA *behind the hangings.*

PHARAMOND. If there be but two such more in this
   kingdom, and near the court, we may even hang up   60
   our harps. Ten such camphire* constitutions as this
   would call the golden age again in question and teach
   the old way for every ill-faced husband to get his own
   children; and what a mischief that will breed, let all
   consider!—

                Enter MEGRA.

Here's another; if she be of the same last, the devil
shall pluck her on.—Many fair mornings, lady!

MEGRA. As many mornings bring as many days,
Fair, sweet, and hopeful to your grace!

PHARAMOND [*aside*]. She gives good words yet; sure this
   wench is free.—   70
If your more serious business do not call you,
Let me hold quarter* with you; we'll [talk]
An hour quickly.

MEGRA.   What would your grace talk of?

PHARAMOND. Of some such pretty subject as yourself.
I'll go no further than your eye or lip;
There's theme enough for one man for an age.

MEGRA. Sir, they stand right, and my lips are yet even,
Smooth, young enough, ripe enough, and red enough,
Or my glass wrongs me.

PHARAMOND. O, they are two twinned cherries died in
   blushes,   80
Which those fair suns above, with their bright beams,
Reflect upon and ripen. Sweetest beauty,
Bow down those branches, that the longing taste
Of the faint looker-on may meet those blessings,
And taste and live.

[*They kiss.*]

---

white money: silver.   camphire: cold.
quarter: friendly conversation.

MEGRA [*aside*].   O, delicate, sweet prince!
   She that hath snow enough about her heart
   To take the wanton spring of ten such lines off
   May be a nun without probation.—Sir,
   You have in such neat poetry gathered a kiss
   That, if I had but five lines of that number,   90
   Such pretty, begging blanks,* I should commend
   Your forehead or your cheeks, and kiss you too.
PHARAMOND. Do it in prose; you cannot miss it, madam.
MEGRA. I shall, I shall.
PHARAMOND.   By my life, you shall not:
   I'll prompt you first.
   [*He kisses her.*]
                        Can you do it now?
MEGRA. Methinks 'tis easy, now I ha' done 't before;
   But yet I should stick at it.
   [*She kisses him.*]
PHARAMOND.   Stick till tomorrow;
   I'll ne'er part you, sweetest. But we lose time;
   Can you love me?
MEGRA. Love you, my lord? How would you have me   100
   love you?
PHARAMOND. I'll teach you in a short sentence 'cause I
   will not load your memory. This is all: love me, and lie
   with me.
MEGRA. Was it "lie with you" that you said? 'Tis im-
   possible.
PHARAMOND. Not to a willing mind that will endeavor. If
   I do not teach you to do it as easily in one night as
   you'll go to bed, I'll lose my royal blood for't.
MEGRA. Why, prince, you have a lady of your own that   110
   yet wants teaching.
PHARAMOND. I'll sooner teach a mare the old measures
   than teach her anything belonging to the function:
   she's afraid to lie with herself if she have but any
   masculine imaginations about her. I know when we are
   married I must ravish her.
MEGRA. By mine honor, that's a foul fault, indeed; but
   time and your good help will wear it out, sir.
PHARAMOND. And for any other I see, excepting your

blanks: blank verses.

dear self, dearest lady, I had rather be Sir Tim the   120
school-master and leap a dairymaid, madam.

MEGRA. Has your grace seen the court star, Galatea?

PHARAMOND. Out upon her! She's as cold of her favor as
an apoplex; she sailed by but now.

MEGRA. And how do you hold her wit, sir?

PHARAMOND. I hold her wit? The strength of all the
guard cannot hold it if they were tied to it; she would
blow um out of the kingdom. They talk of Jupiter; he's
but a squib-cracker to her. Look well about you, and
you may find a tongue-bolt. But speak, sweet lady,   130
shall I be freely welcome?

MEGRA. Whither?

PHARAMOND. To your bed. If you mistrust my faith, you
do me the unnoblest wrong.

MEGRA. I dare not, prince, I dare not.

PHARAMOND. Make your own conditions; my purse shall
seal um; and, what you dare imagine you can want, I'll
furnish you withal. Give two hours to your thoughts
every morning about it. Come, I know you are bashful;
speak in my ear—will you be mine? [*He gives her*   140
money.] Keep this and, with it, me. Soon I will visit
you.

MEGRA. My lord, my chamber's most unsafe; but, when
'tis night, I'll find some means to slip into your lodging;
till when—

PHARAMOND. Till when, this and my heart go with thee!

Exeunt.

Enter GALATEA *from behind the hangings.*

GALATEA. O, thou pernicious petticoat prince, are these
thy virtues? Well, if I do not lay a train to blow your
sport up, I am no woman; and, Lady Towsabel,° I'll
fit you for't.   150

Exit GALATEA.

[II.iii]

Enter ARETHUSA *and a* LADY.

ARETHUSA. Where's the boy?

LADY. Within, madam.

ARETHUSA. Gave you him gold to buy him clothes?

Lady Towsabel: contemptuous form of "Dowsabel," a sweetheart.

LADY. I did.

ARETHUSA. And has he done't?

LADY. Yes, madam.

ARETHUSA. 'Tis a pretty, sad*-talking boy, is it not? Asked you his name?

LADY. No, madam.

Enter GALATEA.

ARETHUSA. O, you are welcome. What good news?   10

GALATEA. As good as anyone can tell your grace, That says she has done that you would have wished.

ARETHUSA. Hast thou discovered?

GALATEA. I have strained a point of modesty for you.

ARETHUSA. I prithee, how?

GALATEA. In list'ning after bawdry. I see, let a lady live never so modestly, she shall be sure to find a lawful time to harken after bawdry. Your prince, brave Phara- mond, was so hot on't!

ARETHUSA. With whom?   20

GALATEA. Why, with the lady I suspected: I can tell the time and place.

ARETHUSA. O, when, and where?

GALATEA. Tonight, his lodging.

ARETHUSA. Run thyself into the presence;* mingle there again With other ladies; leave the rest to me. —

[*Exit* GALATEA.]

If destiny (to whom we dare not say, Why thou didst this) have not decreed it so, In lasting leaves (whose smallest characters Was never altered), yet this match shall break. —   30 Where's the boy?

LADY. Here, madam.

Enter BELLARIO.

ARETHUSA. Sir, you are sad to change your service, is't not so?

BELLARIO. Madam, I have not changed: I wait on you, To do him service.

ARETHUSA.   Thou disclaim'st* in me. Tell me thy name.

BELLARIO. Bellario.

---

sad: serious.   presence: presence-chamber.
disclaim'st: give up all share.

ARETHUSA.   Thou canst sing and play?
BELLARIO. If grief will give me leave, madam, I can.
ARETHUSA. Alas, what kind of grief can thy years know?
    Hadst thou a curst* master when thou went'st to
    school?   40
    Thou art not capable of other grief;
    Thy brows and cheeks are smooth as waters be
    When no breath troubles them. Believe me, boy,
    Care seeks out wrinkled brows and hollow eyes,
    And builds himself caves to abide in them.
    Come, sir, tell me truly, doth your lord love me?
BELLARIO. Love, madam? I know not what it is.
ARETHUSA. Canst thou know grief, and never yet knewest
    love?
    Thou art deceived, boy. Does he speak of me
    As if he wished me well?
BELLARIO.   If it be love   50
    To forget all respect to his own friends
    With thinking of your face; if it be love
    To sit cross-armed and think away the day,
    Mingled with starts, crying your name as loud
    And hastily as men i'the streets do fire;
    If it be love to weep himself away
    When he but hears of any lady dead
    Or killed because it might have been your chance;
    If, when he goes to rest (which will not be),
    'Twixt every prayer he says, to name you once,   60
    As others drop a [bead], be to be in love,
    Then, madam, I dare swear he loves you.
ARETHUSA. O, y'are a cunning boy, and taught to lie
    For your lord's credit! But thou knowest a lie
    That bears this sound is welcomer to me
    Than any truth that says he loves me not.
    Lead the way, boy.—[To LADY.] Do you attend me
    too.—
    'Tis thy lord's business hastes me thus. Away!
                               Exeunt.

[II.iv]
    Enter DION, CLEREMONT, THRASILINE, MEGRA, GALATEA.
_____

    curst: mean, ill-tempered.

DION. Come, ladies, shall we talk a round? As men
　Do walk a mile, women should talk an hour
　After supper: 'tis their exercise.
GALATEA. 'Tis late.
MEGRA. 'Tis all
　My eyes will do to lead me to my bed.
GALATEA. I fear they are so heavy they'll scarce find
　The way to your own lodging with um tonight.
　　　　　Enter PHARAMOND.
THRASILINE. The prince!
PHARAMOND. Not abed, ladies? Y'are good sitters-up.　　10
　What think you of a pleasant dream to last
　Till morning?
MEGRA. I should choose, my lord, a pleasing wake before
　it.
　　　　Enter ARETHUSA *and* BELLARIO.
ARETHUSA. 'Tis well, my lord; y'are courting of these
　ladies.—
　Is't not late, gentlemen?
CLEREMONT.　　　　　　　Yes, madam.
ARETHUSA.
　　　　　　　　　　　　　　　Wait you
　there.
　　　　　　　　　　　　　Exit ARETHUSA.
MEGRA [*aside*]. She's jealous, as I live.—Look you, my
　lord,
　The princess has a Hylas, an Adonis.
PHARAMOND. His form is angel-like.
MEGRA. Why, this is he must, when you are wed,
　Sit by your pillow, like young Apollo, with　　20
　His hand and voice binding your thoughts in sleep:
　The princess does provide him for you and for herself.
PHARAMOND. I find no music in these boys.
MEGRA.　　　　　　　　　　Nor I.
　They can do little, and that small they do
　They have not wit to hide.
DION.　　　　　　　Serves he the princess?
THRASILINE. Yes.
DION.　　　　　'Tis a sweet boy; how brave° she
　keeps him!
PHARAMOND. Ladies all, good rest; I mean to kill a buck

---

　brave: richly dressed.

Tomorrow morning ere y'have done your dreams.

MEGRA. All happiness attend your grace!

> [*Exit* PHARAMOND.]
>
> Gentlemen,

good rest.—

Come, shall we to bed?

GALATEA.   Yes.—All, good night.   30

> *Exit* GALATEA [, *with*] MEGRA.

DION. May your dreams be true to you!—

What shall we do, gallants? 'Tis late; the king

Is still up; see, he comes, a guard along

With him.

> *Enter* KING, ARETHUSA, *and Guard.*

KING.   Look your intelligence be true.

ARETHUSA. Upon my life, it is; and I do hope

Your highness will not tie me to a man

That in the heat of wooing throws me off

And takes another.

DION. What should this mean?

KING.   If it be true,

That lady had been better have embraced   40

Cureless diseases. Get you to your rest;

> *Exeunt* ARETHUSA, BELLARIO.

You shall be righted.—Gentlemen, draw near;

We shall employ you. Is young Pharamond

Come to his lodging?

DION.   I saw him enter there.

KING. Haste, some of you, and cunningly discover

If Megra be in her lodging.

> [*Exit* DION.]

CLEREMONT.   Sir,

She parted hence but now with other ladies.

KING. If she be there, we shall not need to make

A vain discovery of our suspicion.—

[*Aside.*] You gods, I see that who unrighteously   50

Holds wealth or state from others shall be cursed

In that which meaner men are blessed withal:

Ages to come shall know no male of him

Left to inherit, and his name shall be

Blotted from earth; if he have any child,

It shall be crossly matched; the gods themselves

Shall sow wild strife betwixt her lord and her.

Yet, if it be your wills, forgive the sin

I have committed; let it not fall
Upon this understanding child of mine!   60
She has not broke your laws. But how can I
Look to be heard of gods that must be just,
Praying upon ground I hold by wrong?

Enter DION.

DION. Sir, I have asked, and her women swear she is
within; but they, I think, are bawds. I told um I must
speak with her; they laughed and said their lady lay
speechless. I said my business was important; they
said their lady was about it. I grew hot and cried my
business was a matter that concerned life and death;
they answered, so was sleeping, at which their lady   70
was. I urged again, she had scarce time to be so since
last I saw her. They smiled again and seemed to instruct me that sleeping was nothing but lying down
and winking.° Answers more direct I could not get;
in short, sir, I think she is not there.

KING. 'Tis then no time to dally.—You, o'th' guard,
Wait at the back door of the prince's lodging
And see that none pass thence, upon your lives.—

                                          [*Exeunt Guards.*]

Knock, gentlemen; knock loud; louder yet.
[*They knock.*]
What, has their pleasure taken off their hearing?—   80
I'll break your meditations.—Knock again!—
Not yet? I do not think he sleeps, having his
'Larum° by him.—Once more.—Pharamond! Prince!
[*Re-enter*] PHARAMOND *above.*

PHARAMOND. What saucy groom knocks at this dead of
    night?
Where be our waiters?° By my vexèd soul,
He meets his death that meets me, for this boldness.

KING. Prince, you wrong your thoughts; we are your
    friends.
Come down.

PHARAMOND.   The king?

KING.   The same, sir. Come down;
We have cause of present counsel with you.

_____

winking: closing eyes tight.   'larum: alarum.
waiters: servants, attendants.

PHARAMOND. If your grace please to use me,   90
    I'll attend you to your chamber.
               [*Re-enter*] PHARAMOND *below.*
KING. No, 'tis too late, prince; I'll make bold with yours.
PHARAMOND. I have some private reasons to myself
    Makes me unmannerly, and say you cannot.—
    Nay, press not forward, gentlemen; he must come
    Through my life that comes here.
KING. Sir, be resolved I must and will come.—Enter!
PHARAMOND. I will not be dishonored:
    He that enters, enters upon his death.
    Sir, 'tis a sign you make no stranger of me   100
    To bring these renegadoes to my chamber
    At these unseasoned hours.
KING.   Why do you
    Chafe yourself so? You are not wronged, nor shall be;
    Only I'll search your lodging for some cause
    To ourself known.—Enter, I say.
PHARAMOND.   I say, no.
             [*Re-enter*] MEGRA *above.*
MEGRA. Let um enter, prince, let um enter;
    I am up and ready.* I know their business;
    'Tis the poor breaking of a lady's honor
    They hunt so hotly after: let um enjoy it.—
    You have your business, gentlemen. I lay here.   110
    O, my lord the king, this is not noble in you
    To make public the weakness of a woman!
KING. Come down.
MEGRA. I dare, my lord. Your whootings and your
    clamors,
    Your private whispers and your broad fleerings,
    Can no more vex my soul than this base carriage;*
    But I have vengeance yet in store for some
    Shall, in the most contempt you can have of me,
    Be joy and nourishment.
KING.   Will you come down?
MEGRA. Yes, to laugh at your worst; but I shall wring you   120
    If my skill fail me not.
                      [*Exit above.*]
KING. Sir, I must dearly chide you for this looseness;

---

    ready: dressed.   carriage: behavior.

You have wronged a worthy lady; but no more.—
Conduct him to my lodging and to bed.

                    [Exeunt PHARAMOND *and Attendants.]*

CLEREMONT [*aside*]. Get him another wench, and you
    bring him to bed indeed.
DION [*aside*]. 'Tis strange a man cannot ride a stag°
    Or two, to breathe himself, without a warrant.
    If this gear° hold, that lodgings be searched thus,
    Pray God we may lie with our own wives in safety,
    That they be not by some trick of state mistaken!   130

            Enter [Attendants] with MEGRA.

KING. Now, lady of honor, where's your honor now?
    No man can fit your palate but the prince.
    Thou most ill-shrouded rottenness, thou piece
    Made by a painter and a pothecary,
    Thou troubled sea of lust, thou wilderness
    Inhabited by wild thoughts, thou swoll'n cloud
    Of infection, thou ripe mine of all diseases,
    Thou all-sin, all-hell, and, last, all-devils, tell me,
    Had you none to pull on with your courtesies
    But he that must be mine, and wrong my daughter?   140
    By all the gods, all these, and all the pages,
    And all the court shall hoot thee through the court,
    Fling rotten oranges, make ribald rhymes,
    And sear thy name with candles upon walls!
    Do ye laugh, Lady Venus?
MEGRA. Faith, sir, you must pardon me;
    I cannot choose but laugh to see you merry.
    If you do this, O king, nay, if you dare do it,
    By all those gods you swore by, and as many
    More of my own, I will have fellows, and such   150
    Fellows in it, as shall make noble mirth!
    The princess, your dear daughter, shall stand by me
    On walls, and sung in ballads, anything.
    Urge me no more; I know her and her haunts,
    Her lays,° leaps, and outlays, and will discover all,
    Nay, will dishonor her. I know the boy
    She keeps, a handsome boy, about eighteen,
    Know what she does with him, where, and when.

---

stag: boisterous or romping girl.   gear: matter, business.
lays: lairs, hiding places.

Come, sir, you put me to a woman's madness,
The glory of a fury; and, if I do not   160
Do it to the height—

KING.   What boy is this she raves at?

MEGRA. Alas, good-minded prince, you know not these
    things?
I am loath to reveal um. Keep this fault
As you would keep your health from the hot air
Of the corrupted people, or, by heaven,
I will not fall alone. What I have known
Shall be as public as a print; all tongues
Shall speak it as they do the language they
Are born in, as free and commonly; I'll set it,
Like a prodigious° star, for all to gaze at,   170
And so high and glowing that other kingdoms far and
    foreign
Shall read it there, nay, travel with it, till they find
No tongue to make it more, nor no more people;
And then behold the fall of your fair princess!

KING. Has she a boy?

CLEREMONT. So please your grace, I have seen a boy wait
On her, a fair boy.

KING.   Go, get you to your quarter;
For this time I'll study to forget you.

                                   Exeunt KING, MEGRA, *Guard*.

CLEREMONT. Why, here's a male spirit fit for Hercules. If
ever there be Nine Worthies of women, this wench   180
shall ride astride and be their captain.

DION. Sure, she has a garrison of devils in her tongue,
she uttered such balls of wild-fire. She has so [n]ettled
the king that all the doctors in the country will scarce
cure him. That boy was a strange-found-out antidote
to cure her infections; that boy, that princess' boy;
that brave, chaste, virtuous lady's boy! And a fair boy,
a well-spoken boy, all these considered, can make nothing else—but there I leave you, gentlemen.

THRASILINE. Nay, we'll go wander with you.   190

                                              Exeunt.

---

prodigious: portentous (as of a comet).

ACTUS III

[III.i]

Enter CLEREMONT, DION, THRASILINE.

CLEREMONT. Nay, doubtless 'tis true.

DION.   Ay, and 'tis the
    gods
  That raised this punishment to scourge the king
  With his own issue. Is it not a shame
  For us that should write noble in the land,
  For us that should be free men, to behold
  A man that is the bravery of his age,
  Philaster, pressed down from his royal right
  By this regardless king, and only look
  And see the scepter ready to be cast
  Into the hands of that lascivious lady   10
  That lives in lust with a smooth boy, now to be
  Married to yon strange prince, who, but that people
  Please to let him be a prince, is born a slave
  In that which should be his most noble part,
  His mind?

THRASILINE.   That man that would not stir with you
  To aid Philaster, let the gods forget
  That such a creature walks upon the earth!

CLEREMONT. Philaster is too backward in't himself.
  The gentry do await it; and the people
  Against their nature are all bent for him;   20
  And like a field of standing corn, that's moved
  With a stiff gale, their heads bow all one way.

DION. The only cause that draws Philaster back
  From this attempt is the fair princess' love,
  Which he admires, and we can now confute.

THRASILINE. Perhaps he'll not believe it.

DION. Why, gentlemen, 'tis without question so.

CLEREMONT. Ay, 'tis past speech she lives dishonestly.
  But how shall we, if he be curious,* work
  Upon his faith?   30

THRASILINE. We all are satisfied within ourselves.

DION. Since it is true and tends to his own good,
  I'll make this new report to be my knowledge;

---

curious: skeptical.

I'll say I know it; nay, I'll swear I saw it.

CLEREMONT. It will be best.

THRASILINE.   'Twill move him.

Enter PHILASTER.

DION.   Here
  he comes.—
  Good morrow to your honor; we have spent
  Some time in seeking you.

PHILASTER.   My worthy friends,
  You that can keep your memories to know
  Your friend in miseries and cannot frown
  On men disgraced for virtue, a good day   40
  Attend you all! What service may I do
  Worthy your acceptation?

DION.   My good lord,
  We come to urge that virtue, which we know
  Lives in your breast, forth. Rise, and make a head;°
  The nobles and the people are all dulled
  With this usurping king, and not a man
  That ever heard the word, or known such a thing
  As virtue, but will second your attempts.

PHILASTER. How honorable is this love in you
  To me that have deserved none! Know, my friends   50
  (You that were born to shame your poor Philaster
  With too much courtesy), I could afford
  To melt myself to thanks; but my designs
  Are not yet ripe. Suffice it that ere long
  I shall employ your loves, but yet the time
  Is short of what I would.

DION. The time is fuller, sir, than you expect:
  That which hereafter will not, perhaps, be reached
  By violence may now be caught. As for the king,
  You know the people have long hated him;   60
  But now the princess, whom they loved—

PHILASTER. Why, what of her?

DION.   Is loathed as much as
  he.

PHILASTER. By what strange means?

DION.   She's known a
                                                whore.

_____

  make a head: force or raise an army.

[PHILASTER.]   Thou liest!
DION. My lord—
PHILASTER. Thou liest,
  (*Offers to draw and is held.*)
  And thou shalt feel it! I had thought thy mind
  Had been of honor. Thus to rob a lady
  Of her good name is an infectious sin
  Not to be pardoned; be it false as hell,
  'Twill never be redeemed if it be sown   70
  Amongst the people, faithful to increase
  All evil they shall hear. Let me alone
  That I may cut off falsehood whilst it springs!
  Set hills on hills betwixt me and the man
  That utters this, and I will scale them all
  And from the utmost top fall on his neck,
  Like thunder from a cloud.
DION.   This is most strange;
  Sure, he does love her.
PHILASTER.   I do love fair truth:
  She is my mistress, and who injures her
  Draws vengeance from me. Sirs, let go my arms.   80
THRASILINE. Nay, good my lord, be patient.
CLEREMONT. Sir, remember this is your honored friend
  That comes to do his service and will show you
  Why he uttered this.
PHILASTER.   I ask you pardon, sir;
  My zeal to truth made me unmannerly.
  Should I have heard dishonor spoke of you
  Behind your back untruly, I had been
  As much distempered and enraged as now.
DION. But this, my lord, is truth.
PHILASTER.   O, say not so!
  Good sir, forbear to say so. 'Tis then truth   90
  That womankind is false. Urge it no more;
  It is impossible. Why should you think
  The princess light?
DION.   Why, she was taken at it.
PHILASTER. 'Tis false, by heaven, 'tis false! It cannot be,
  Can it? Speak, gentlemen, for God's love, speak!
  Is't possible? Can women all be damned?
DION. Why, no, my lord.
PHILASTER.   Why, then, it cannot be.

DION. And she was taken with her boy.

PHILASTER. What boy?

DION. A page, a boy that serves her.

PHILASTER. O, good gods!
A little boy?

DION. Ay; know you him, my lord? 100

PHILASTER. [aside]. Hell and sin know him!—Sir, you
are deceived;
I'll reason it a little coldly with you.
If she were lustful, would she take a boy,
That knows not yet desire? She would have one
Should meet her thoughts and know the sin he acts,
Which is the great delight of wickedness.
You are abused,* and so is she, and I.

DION. How you, my lord?

PHILASTER. Why, all the world's abused
In an unjust report.

DION. O, noble sir, your virtues
Cannot look into the subtle thoughts of woman! 110
In short, my lord, I took them—I myself.

PHILASTER. Now, all the devils, thou didst! Fly from my
rage!
Would thou hadst ta'en devils engend'ring plagues
When thou didst take them! Hide thee from mine eyes!
Would thou hadst ta'en thunder on thy breast
When thou didst take them, or been strucken dumb
Forever, that this foul deed might have slept
In silence!

THRASILINE [aside]. Have you known him so ill-tempered?

CLEREMONT [aside]. Never before.

PHILASTER. The winds that are
let loose
From the four several corners of the earth, 120
And spread themselves all over sea and land,
Kiss not a chaste one! What friend bears a sword
To run me through?

DION. Why, my lord, are you
So moved at this?

PHILASTER. When any fall from virtue,
I am distracted; I have an interest in't.

---

abused: deceived.

DION. But, good my lord, recall yourself, and think
    What's best to be done.

PHILASTER.   I thank you; I will do it.
    Please you to leave me; I'll consider of it.
    Tomorrow I will find your lodging forth
    And give you answer.

DION.   All the gods direct you   130
    The readiest way!

THRASILINE [*aside*].   He was extreme impatient.

CLEREMONT [*aside*].   It was his virtue and his noble
    mind.

              Exit DION, [*with*]CLEREMONT, THRASILINE.

PHILASTER. I had forgot to ask him where he took them;
    I'll follow him. O, that I had a sea
    Within my breast to quench the fire I feel!
    More circumstances will but fan this fire:
    It more afflicts me now to know by whom
    This deed is done than simply that 'tis done;
    And he that tells me this is honorable,
    As far from lies as she is far from truth.   140
    O, that like beasts we could not grieve ourselves
    With that we see not! Bulls and rams will fight
    To keep their females, standing in their sight;
    But take um from them, and you take at once
    Their spleens away; and they will fall again
    Unto their pastures, growing fresh and fat,
    And taste the waters of the springs as sweet
    As 'twas before, finding no start in sleep.
    But miserable man—

               Enter BELLARIO.

              See, see, you gods,
    He walks still; and the face you let him wear   150
    When he was innocent is still the same,
    Not blasted! Is this justice? Do you mean
    To entrap mortality, that you allow
    Treason so smooth a brow? I cannot now
    Think he is guilty.

BELLARIO.   Health to you, my lord!
    The princess doth commend her love, her life,
    And this unto you.
    [*He gives him a letter.*]

PHILASTER.   O, Bellario,

Now I perceive she loves me; she does show it
In loving thee, my boy; she has made thee brave.
BELLARIO. My lord, she has attired me past my wish,   160
  Past my desert, more fit for her attendant,
  Though far unfit for me who do attend.
PHILASTER. Thou art grown courtly, boy.—[*Aside.*] O,
    let all women
  That love black deeds learn to dissemble here,
  Here, by this paper! She does write to me
  As if her heart were mines of adamant
  To all the world besides, but unto me
  A maiden snow that melted with my looks.—
  Tell me, my boy, how doth the princess use thee?
  For I shall guess her love to me by that.   170
BELLARIO. Scarce like her servant, but as if I were
  Something allied to her or had preserved
  Her life three times by my fidelity;
  As mothers fond do use their only sons,
  As I'd use one that's left unto my trust,
  For whom my life should pay if he met harm,
  So she does use me.
PHILASTER.   Why, this is wondrous well.
  But what kind language does she feed thee with?
BELLARIO. Why, she does tell me she will trust my youth
  With all her loving secrets and does call me   180
  Her pretty servant, bids me weep no more
  For leaving you; she'll see my services
  Regarded, and such words of that soft strain
  That I am nearer weeping when she ends
  Then ere she spake.
PHILASTER.   This is much better still.
BELLARIO. Are you not ill, my lord?
PHILASTER.   Ill? No, Bellario.
BELLARIO. Methinks your words
  Fall not from off your tongue so evenly,
  Nor is there in your looks that quietness
  That I was wont to see.
PHILASTER.   Thou art deceived, boy.   190
  And she strokes thy head?
BELLARIO. Yes.
PHILASTER. And she does clap thy cheeks?
BELLARIO.   She does,
    my lord.

PHILASTER. And she does kiss thee, boy? Ha!

BELLARIO.　　　　　　　　　　　　　　How, my
　　lord?

PHILASTER. She kisses thee?

BELLARIO.　　　　　　　　　　Never, my lord, by heaven!

PHILASTER. That's strange; I know she does.

BELLARIO.　　　　　　　　　　　　　No, by my
　　life.

PHILASTER. Why, then she does not love me. Come, she
　　does;
　　I bade her do it; I charged her, by all charms
　　Of love between us, by the hope of peace
　　We should enjoy, to yield thee all delights　　　　　　200
　　Naked as to her bed. I took her oath
　　Thou shouldst enjoy her. Tell me, gentle boy,
　　Is she not parralle[lle]ss? Is not her breath
　　Sweet as Arabian winds when fruits are ripe?
　　Are not her breasts two liquid ivory balls?
　　Is she not all a lasting mine of joy?

BELLARIO. Ay, now I see why my disturbèd thoughts
　　Were so perplexed. When first I went to her,
　　My heart held augury. You are abused;
　　Some villain has abused you: I do see　　　　　　210
　　Whereto you tend. Fall rocks upon his head
　　That put this to you! 'Tis some subtle train
　　To bring that noble frame of yours to naught.

PHILASTER. Thou think'st I will be angry with thee.
　　Come,
　　Thou shalt know all my drift. I hate her more
　　Than I love happiness and placed thee there
　　To pry with narrow eyes into her deeds.
　　Hast thou discovered? Is she fall'n to lust
　　As I would wish her? Speak some comfort to me.

BELLARIO. My lord, you did mistake the boy you sent:　　220
　　Had she the lust of sparrows or of goats,
　　Had she a sin that way, hid from the world,
　　Beyond the name of lust, I would not aid
　　Her base desires; but what I came to know
　　As servant to her I would not reveal
　　To make my life last ages.

PHILASTER [*aside*].　　　　　　O, my heart!
　　This is a salve worse than the main disease.—
　　Tell me thy thoughts, for I will know the least

That dwells within thee, or will rip thy heart
To know it; I will see thy thoughts as plain   230
As I do now thy face.

BELLARIO.   Why, so you do.
She is (for aught I know), by all the gods,
As chaste as ice; but, were she foul as hell,
And I did know it thus, the breath of kings,
The point of swords, tortures, nor bulls of brass
Should draw it from me.

PHILASTER.   Then 'tis no time
To dally with thee; I will take thy life,
For I do hate thee. I could curse thee now.

BELLARIO. If you do hate, you could not curse me worse:
The gods have not a punishment in store   240
Greater for me than is your hate.

PHILASTER.   Fie, fie,
So young and so dissembling! Tell me when
And where thou didst enjoy her, or let plagues
Fall on me if I destroy thee not!
[*He draws his sword.*]

BELLARIO. By heaven, I never did; and, when I lie
To save my life, may I live long and loathed!
Hew me asunder; and, whilst I can think,
I'll love those pieces you have cut away
Better than those that grow, and kiss those limbs
Because you made um so.

PHILASTER.   Fear'st thou not death?   250
Can boys contemn that?

BELLARIO.   O, what boy is he
Can be content to live to be a man
That sees the best of men thus passionate,
Thus without reason?

PHILASTER.   O, but thou dost not know
What 'tis to die.

BELLARIO.   Yes, I do know, my lord:
'Tis less than to be born, a lasting sleep,
A quiet resting from all jealousy,
A thing we all pursue. I know, besides,
It is but giving over of a game
That must be lost.

PHILASTER.   But there are pains, false boy,   260
For perjured souls. Think but on those, and then

Thy heart will melt and thou wilt utter all.

BELLARIO. May they fall all upon me whilst I live
  If I be perjured or have ever thought
  Of that you charge me with! If I be false,
  Send me to suffer in those punishments
  You speak of: kill me!

[PHILASTER.]   O, what should I do?
  Why, who can but believe him? He does swear
  So earnestly that, if it were not true,
  The gods would not endure him.—Rise, Bellario;   270
  Thy protestations are so deep, and thou
  Dost look so truly when thou utter'st them
  That, though I know um false as were my hopes,
  I cannot urge thee further. But thou wert
  To blame to injure me, for I must love
  Thy honest looks and take no revenge upon
  Thy tender youth. A love from me to thee
  Is firm, whate'er thou doest; it troubles me
  That I have called the blood out of thy cheeks,
  That did so well become thee. But, good boy,   280
  Let me not see thee more; something is done
  That will distract me, that will make me mad
  If I behold thee. If thou tender'st * me,
  Let me not see thee.

BELLARIO.   I will fly as far
  As there is morning ere I give distaste
  To that most honored mind. But through these tears
  Shed at my hopeless parting I can see
  A world of treason practiced upon you,
  And her, and me. Farewell forevermore!
  If you shall hear that sorrow struck me dead,   290
  And after find me loyal, let there be
  A tear shed from you in my memory,
  And I shall rest.

                        Exit BELLARIO.

PHILASTER.   Blessing be with thee,
  Whatever thou deservest! O, where shall I
  Go bathe this body? Nature too unkind,
  That made no medicine for a troubled mind!

                        Exit PHILASTER.

---

tender'st: regard, like.

[III.ii]

Enter ARETHUSA.

ARETHUSA. I marvel my boy comes not back again;
But that I know my love will question him
Over and over—how I slept, waked, talked,
How I remembered him when his dear name
Was last spoke, and how, when I sighed, wept, sung,
And ten thousand such—I should be angry at his stay.

Enter KING.

KING. What, at your meditations? Who attends you?
ARETHUSA. None but my single self; I need no guard:
I do no wrong, nor fear none.
KING. Tell me, have you not a boy?
ARETHUSA.   Yes, sir.   10
KING. What kind of boy?
ARETHUSA.   A page, a waiting-boy.
KING. A handsome boy?
ARETHUSA.   I think he be not ugly:
Well qualified and dutiful I know him;
I took him not for beauty.
KING. He speaks and sings and plays?
ARETHUSA.   Yes, sir.
KING. About eighteen?
ARETHUSA.   I never asked his age.
KING. Is he full of service?
ARETHUSA. By your pardon, why do you ask?
KING. Put him away.
ARETHUSA.   Sir?
KING.   Put him away, I say.
H'as done you that good service shames me to speak of.   20
ARETHUSA. Good sir, let me understand you.
KING.   If you
fear me,
Show it in duty; put away that boy.
ARETHUSA. Let me have reason for it, sir, and then
Your will is my command.
KING. Do not you blush to ask it? Cast him off,
Or I shall do the same to you. Y'are one
Shame with me, and so near unto myself
That, by my life, I dare not tell myself
What you, myself, have done.

ARETHUSA. What have I done, my lord? 30
KING. 'Tis a new language, that all love to learn;
  The common people speak it well already;
  They need no grammar. Understand me well;
  There be foul whispers stirring. Cast him off,
  And suddenly. Do it! Farewell.

Exit KING.

ARETHUSA. Where may a maiden live securely free,
  Keeping her honor fair? Not with the living;
  They feed upon opinions, errors, dreams,
  And make um truths; they draw a nourishment
  Out of defamings, grow upon disgraces, 40
  And, when they see a virtue fortified
  Strongly above the batt'ry of their tongues,
  O, how they cast * to sink it and, defeated
  (Soul-sick with poison), strike the monuments
  Where noble names lie sleeping till they sweat
  And the cold marble melt.

Enter PHILASTER.

PHILASTER. Peace to your fairest thoughts, dearest mistress!
ARETHUSA. O, my dearest servant, I have a war within me!
PHILASTER. He must be more than man that makes these crystals
  Run into rivers. Sweetest fair, the cause? 50
  And, as I am your slave, tied to your goodness,
  Your creature, made again from what I was
  And newly-spirited, I'll right your honor.
ARETHUSA. O, my best love, that boy!
PHILASTER.   What boy?
ARETHUSA. The pretty boy you gave me—
PHILASTER.   What of him?
ARETHUSA. Must be no more mine.
PHILASTER.   Why?
ARETHUSA.   They are jealous of him.
PHILASTER. Jealous! Who?
ARETHUSA.   The king.

---

cast: cast about, plan.

PHILASTER [*aside*].   O, my misfortune!
Then 'tis no idle jealousy.—Let him go.
ARETHUSA. O, cruel!
  Are you hard-hearted too? Who shall now tell you   60
  How much I loved you? Who shall swear it to you
  And weep the tears I send? Who shall now bring you
  Letters, rings, bracelets? Lose his health in service?
  Wake tedious nights in stories of your praise?
  Who shall sing your crying elegies
  And strike a sad soul into senseless pictures
  And make them mourn? Who shall take up his lute
  And touch it till he crown a silent sleep
  Upon my eyelids, making me dream, and cry,
  "O, my dear, dear Philaster!"
PHILASTER [*aside*].   O, my heart!   70
  Would he had broken thee that made thee know
  This lady was not loyal!—Mistress,
  Forget the boy; I'll get thee a far better.
ARETHUSA. O, never, never such a boy again
  As my Bellario!
[PHILASTER.]   'Tis but your fond affection.
ARETHUSA. With thee, my boy, farewell forever
  All secrecy in servants! Farewell, faith,
  And all desire to do well for itself!
  Let all that shall succeed thee for thy wrongs
  Sell and betray chaste love!   80
PHILASTER. And all this passion for a boy?
ARETHUSA. He was your boy, and you put him to me;
  And the loss of such must have a mourning for.
PHILASTER. O, thou forgetful woman!
ARETHUSA.   How, my lord?
PHILASTER. False Arethusa!
  Hast thou a medicine to restore my wits
  When I have lost um? If not, leave to talk
  And do thus.
ARETHUSA.   Do what, sir? Would you sleep?
PHILASTER. Forever, Arethusa. O, you gods,
  Give me a worthy patience! Have I stood   90
  Naked, alone, the shock of many fortunes?
  Have I seen mischiefs numberless and mighty
  Grow like a sea upon me? Have I taken
  Danger as stern as death into my bosom

And laughed upon it, made it but a mirth
And flung it by? Do I live now like him,
Under this tyrant king, that languishing
Hears his sad bell and sees his mourners? Do I
Bear all this bravely and must sink at length
Under a woman's falsehood? O, that boy,   100
That cursed boy! None but a villain boy
To ease your lust?

ARETHUSA.   Nay, then, I am betrayed;
I feel the plot cast for my overthrow.
O, I am wretched!

PHILASTER. Now you may take that little right I have
To this poor kingdom: give it to your joy,
For I have no joy in it. Some far place,
Where never womankind durst set her foot
For° bursting with her poisons, must I seek
And live to curse you.   110
There dig a cave and preach to birds and beasts
What woman is, and help to save them from you:
How heaven is in your eyes, but in your hearts
More hell than hell has; how your tongues, like
    scorpions,
Both heal and poison; how your thoughts are woven
With thousand changes in one subtle web,
And worn so by you; how that foolish man,
That reads the story of a woman's face
And dies believing it, is lost forever;
How all the good you have is but a shadow,   120
I'th' morning with you and at night behind you,
Past and forgotten; how your vows are frosts,
Fast for a night and with the next sun gone;
How you are, being taken all together,
A mere confusion and so dead a chaos
That love cannot distinguish. These sad texts,
Till my last hour, I am bound to utter of you.
So, farewell all my woe, all my delight!

Exit PHILASTER.

ARETHUSA. Be merciful, ye gods, and strike me dead!
What way have I deserved this? Make my breast   130
Transparent as pure crystal, that the world,
Jealous of me, may see the foulest thought

for: for fear of.

My heart holds. Where shall a woman turn her eyes
To find out constancy?
Enter BELLARIO.
                          Save me, how black
And guiltily, methinks, that boy looks now!—
O, thou dissembler, that, before thou spak'st,
Wert in thy cradle false, sent to make lies
And betray innocents! Thy lord and thou
May glory in the ashes of a maid
Fooled by her passion, but the conquest is   140
Nothing so great as wicked. Fly away!
Let my command force thee to that which shame
Would do without it. If thou understood'st
The loathèd office thou hast undergone,
Why, thou wouldst hide thee under heaps of hills,
Lest men should dig and find thee.

BELLARIO.   O, what god,
Angry with men, hath sent this strange disease
Into the noblest minds? Madam, this grief
You add unto me is no more than drops
To seas, for which they are not seen to swell.   150
My lord hath struck his anger through my heart
And let out all the hope of future joys.
You need not bid me fly; I came to part,
To take my latest leave. Farewell forever!
I durst not run away in honesty
From such a lady, like a boy that stole
Or made some grievous fault. The power of gods
Assist you in your sufferings! Hasty time
Reveal the truth to your abusèd lord
And mine, that he may know your worth, whilst I   160
Go seek out some forgotten place to die!
                                    Exit BELLARIO.

ARETHUSA. Peace guide thee! Th'ast overth[r]own me
      once;
Yet, if I had another Troy to lose,
Thou, or another villain with thy looks,
Might talk me out of it and send me naked,
My hair disheveled, through the fiery streets.
                  Enter a LADY.
LADY. Madam, the king would hunt, and calls for you
      With earnestness.

ARETHUSA.   I am in tune to hunt!
   Diana, if thou canst rage with a maid
   As with a man, let me discover thee   170
   Bathing, and turn me to a fearful hind,
   That I may die pursued by cruel hounds°
   And have my story written in my wounds!

                                                        Exeunt.

ACTUS IV

[IV.i]
            Enter KING, PHARAMOND, ARETHUSA, GALATEA,
                  MEGRA, DION, CLEREMONT, THRASILINE,
                        and Attendants.

KING. What, are the hounds before and all the woodmen?
   Our horses ready and our bows bent?
DION.   All, sir.
KING [*to* PHARAMOND]. Y'are cloudy, sir. Come, we have
      forgotten
   Your venial trespass; let not that sit heavy
   Upon your spirit; here's none dare utter it.
DION [*aside*]. He looks like an old surfeited stallion after
   his leaping, dull as a dormouse. See how he sinks! The
   wench has shot him between wind and water, and, I
   hope, sprung a leak.
THRASILINE [*aside*]. He needs no teaching; he strikes   10
   sure enough. His greatest fault is he hunts too much in
   the purlieus;° would he would leave off poaching!
DION [*aside*]. And, for his horn, h'as left it at the lodge
   where he lay late. O, he's a precious limehound!° Turn
   him loose upon the pursue of a lady, and, if he lose
   her, hang him up i'th' slip.° When my fox-bitch,
   Beauty, grows proud,° I'll borrow him.
KING. Is your boy turned away?
ARETHUSA. You did command, sir, and I obeyed you.
KING. 'Tis well done. Hark ye further.   20
   [*They talk apart.*]

─────────────────────

   die . . . hounds: as was Actaeon.
   purlieus: suburbs, where, in London at this time, the brothels
were located.   limehound: bloodhound.
   slip: noose, leash.   proud: sexually aroused.

CLEREMONT. Is't possible this fellow should repent? Methinks that were not noble in him; and yet he looks like a mortified member, as if he had a sick man's salve in's mouth. If a worse man had done this fault now, some physical justice° or other would presently (without the help of an almanac°) have opened the [o]bstructions of his liver and let him blood with a dog whip.

DION. See, see, how modestly yon lady looks, as if she came from churching with her neighbors! Why, what a   30 devil can a man see in her face but that she's honest?

THRASILINE. Faith, no great matter to speak of—a foolish twinkling with the eye that spoils her coat;° but he must be a cunning herald that finds it.

DION. See how they muster° one another! O, there's a rank regiment where the devil carries the colors, and his dam drum major! Now the world and the flesh come behind with the carriage.

CLEREMONT. Sure this lady has a good turn done her against her will: before, she was common talk; now   40 none dare say cantharides° can stir her. Her face looks like a warrant, willing and commanding all tongues, as they will answer it, to be tied up and bolted when this lady means to let herself loose. As I live, she has got her a goodly protection and a gracious, and may use her body discreetly for her health' sake once a week, excepting Lent and dog days. O, if they were to be got for money, what a large sum would come out of the city for these licenses!

KING. To horse, to horse! We lose the morning, gentle-   50
men.

Exeunt.

[IV.ii]

Enter two Woodmen.

1 WOODMAN. What, have you lodged the deer?
2 WOODMAN. Yes, they are ready for the bow.

---

physical justice: a judge or justice also acting as a physician.
help of an almanac: in which instructions for bloodletting were
found.   coat: coat of arms.   muster: set off.
cantharides: Spanish flies (an aphrodisiac).

1 WOODMAN. Who shoots?

2 WOODMAN. The princess.

1 WOODMAN. No, she'll hunt.

2 WOODMAN. She'll take a stand, I say.

1 WOODMAN. Who else?

2 WOODMAN. Why, the young stranger prince.

1 WOODMAN. He shall shoot in a stone-bow for me. I
never loved his beyond-sea-ship since he forsook the   10
say° for paying ten shillings. He was there at the fall
of a deer and would needs (out of his mightiness) give
ten groats for the dowcets;° marry, [his] steward
would have the velvet head into the bargain to turf °
his hat withal. I think he should love venery; he is an
old Sir Tristram:° for, if you be remembered, he forsook the stag once to strike a rascal ° milking in a
meadow, and her he killed in the eye. Who shoots else?

2 WOODMAN. The Lady Galatea.

1 WOODMAN. That's a good wench and ° she would not   20
chide us for tumbling of her women in the brakes.
She's liberal, and, by the gods, they say she's honest;
and whether that be a fault, I have nothing to do.
There's all?

2 WOODMAN. No, one more—Megra.

1 WOODMAN. That's a firker,° i'faith, boy. There's a
wench will ride her haunches as hard after a kennel of
hounds as a hunting saddle and, when she comes
home, get um clapped, and all is well again. I have
known her lose herself three times in one afternoon   30
(if the woods have been answerable),° and it has been
work enough for one man to find her, and he has sweat
for it. She rides well, and she pays well. Hark! Let's go.

Exeunt.

Enter PHILASTER.

PHILASTER. O, that I had been nourished in these woods
With milk of goats and acorns, and not known

---

say: assay, or slitting of the deer (for which Pharamond wished
to avoid paying the fee).   dowcets: testicles (of the deer).
turf: re-cover.
Sir Tristram: referring to an excellent huntsman.
rascal: lean young deer.   and: if.
firker: lively one; prankster.
answerable: suitable, convenient.

The right of crowns nor the dissembling trains
Of women's looks, but digged myself a cave
Where I, my fire, my cattle, and my bed
Might have been shut together in one shed,
And then had taken me some mountain girl,   40
Beaten with winds, chaste as the hardened rocks
Whereon she dwells, that might have strewed my bed
With leaves and reeds and with the skins of beasts,
Our neighbors, and have borne at her big breasts
My large, coarse issue! This had been a life
Free from vexation.

Enter BELLARIO.

BELLARIO [*to himself*].   O, wicked men!
An innocent may walk safe among beasts;
Nothing assaults me here. See, my grieved lord
Sits as his soul were searching out a way
To leave his body.—Pardon me, that must   50
Break thy last commandment, for I must speak.
You that are grieved can pity; hear, my lord!

PHILASTER. Is there a creature yet so miserable
That I can pity?

BELLARIO.   O, my noble lord,
View my strange fortune and bestow on me,
According to your bounty (if my service
Can merit nothing), so much as may serve
To keep that little piece I hold of life
From cold and hunger!

PHILASTER.   Is it thou? Begone!
Go sell those misbeseeming clothes thou wear'st   60
And feed thyself with them.

BELLARIO. Alas, my lord, I can get nothing for them:
The silly country people think 'tis treason
To touch such gay things.

PHILASTER.   Now, by the gods, this is
Unkindly done, to vex me with thy sight;
Th'art fall'n again to thy dissembling trade.
How shouldst thou think to cozen me again?
Remains there yet a plague untried for me?
Even so thou wep[t]'st and look[ed]'st and spok'st
    when first
I took thee up. Curse on the time! If thy   70
Commanding tears can work on any other,

Use thy art; I'll not betray it. Which way
Wilt thou take, that I may shun thee;
For thine eyes are poison to mine, and I
Am loath to grow in rage? This way, or that way?
BELLARIO. Any will serve, but I will choose to have
That path in chase that leads unto my grave.

        [Exeunt] PHILASTER, BELLARIO, *severally.*
        Enter DION *and the Woodmen.*

DION. This is the strangest sudden chance!—You, woodman!

1 WOODMAN. My lord Dion?   80

DION. Saw you a lady come this way on a sable horse
studded with stars of white?

2 WOODMAN. Was she not young and tall?

DION. Yes. Rode she to the wood or to the plain?

2 WOODMAN. Faith, my lord, we saw none.

        [Exeunt] Woodmen.

DION. Pox of you[r] questions then!—
        Enter CLEREMONT.

                 What, is she
  found?

CLEREMONT. Nor will be, I think.

DION. Let him seek his daughter himself; she cannot stray
about a little necessary natural business but the whole
court must be in arms. When she has done, we shall   90
have peace.

CLEREMONT. There's already a thousand fatherless tales
amongst us. Some say her horse ran away with her;
some, a wolf pursued her; others, 'twas a plot to kill
her, and that armed men were seen in the wood; but,
questionless, she rode away willingly.

        Enter KING *and* THRASILINE.

KING. Where is she?

CLEREMONT.   Sir, I cannot tell.

KING.   How's that?
  Answer me so again!

CLEREMONT.   Sir, shall I lie?

KING. Yes, lie and damn, rather than tell me that.
I say again, where is she? Mutter not!—   100
  Sir, speak you; where is she?

DION.   Sir, I do not know.

KING. Speak that again so boldly, and, by heaven,

It is thy last!—You fellows, answer me;
Where is she? Mark me, all: I am your king;
I wish to see my daughter; show her me.
I do command you all, as you are subjects,
To show her me! What, am I not your king?
If ay, then am I not to be obeyed?

DION. Yes, if you command things possible and honest.

KING. Things possible and honest! Hear me, thou,   110
Thou traitor, that dar'st confine thy king to things
Possible and honest! Show her me,
Or let me perish if I cover not
All Sicily with blood!

DION.   Faith, I cannot
Unless you tell me where she is.

KING. You have betrayed me; y' have let me lose
The jewel of my life. Go, bring her me,
And set her here before me. 'Tis the king
Will have it so, whose breath can still the winds,
Uncloud the sun, charm down the swelling sea,   120
And stop the floods of heaven. Speak, can it not?

DION. No.

KING.   No? Cannot the breath of kings do this?

DION. No, nor smell sweet itself if once the lungs
Be but corrupted.

KING.   Is it so? Take heed!

DION. Sir, take you heed how you dare the powers
That must be just.

KING.   Alas! What are we kings?
Why do you gods place us above the rest,
To be served, flattered, and adored till we
Believe we hold within our hands your thunder?
And, when we come to try the power we have,   130
There's not a leaf shakes at our threat'nings.
I have sinned, 'tis true, and here stand to be punished;
Yet would not thus be punished. Let me choose
My way, and lay it on!

DION [aside]. He articles with the gods. Would somebody would draw bonds for the performance of cove-
nants betwixt them!

              Enter PHARAMOND, GALATEA, and MEGRA.

KING. What, is she found?

PHARAMOND. No; we have ta'en her horse;

He galloped empty by. There's some treason. 140
You, Galatea, rode with her into the wood.
Why left you her?

GALATEA.   She did command me.

KING. Command! You should not.

GALATEA. 'Twould ill become my fortunes and my birth
To disobey the daughter of my king.

KING. Y'are all cunning to obey us for our hurts,
But I will have her.

PHARAMOND.   If I have her not,
By this hand, there shall be no more Sicily.

DION [*aside*]. What, will he carry it to Spain in's pocket?

PHARAMOND. I will not leave one man alive but the king, 150
A cook, and a tailor.

DION [*aside*]. Yes; you may do well to spare your lady-
bedfellow, and her you may keep for a spawner.

KING [*aside*]. I see the injuries I have done must be
revenged.

DION. Sir, this is not the way to find her out.

KING. Run all; disperse yourselves. The man that finds
her,
Or (if she be killed) the traitor, I'll make him great.

DION [*aside*]. I know some would give five thousand
pounds to find her.

PHARAMOND. Come, let us seek.

KING. Each man a several way; here I myself. 160

DION. Come, gentlemen, we here.

CLEREMONT. Lady, you must go search too.

MEGRA. I had rather be searched myself.

                    [*Exeunt*] *omnes.*

[IV.iii]

                    Enter ARETHUSA.

ARETHUSA. Where am I now? Feet, find me out a way
Without the counsel of my troubled head;
I'll follow you boldly about these woods,
O'er mountains, through brambles, pits, and floods.
Heaven, I hope, will ease me; I am sick.
[*She sits down.*]

                    Enter BELLARIO.

BELLARIO [*aside*]. Yonder's my lady. God knows I want
nothing

Because I do not wish to live; yet I
Will try her charity.—O, hear, you that have plenty!
From that flowing store, drop some on dry ground.—
    See,
The lively red is gone to guard her heart!   10
I fear she faints.—Madam, look up!—She breathes
    not.—
Open once more those rosy twins, and send
Unto my lord your latest farewell!—O, she stirs.—
How is it, madam? Speak comfort.

ARETHUSA. 'Tis not gently done,
To put me in a miserable life
And hold me there: I prithee, let me go.
I shall do best without thee; I am well.

                    Enter PHILASTER.

PHILASTER [*aside*]. I am to blame to be so much in rage;
I'll tell her coolly when and where I heard   20
This killing truth. I will be temperate
In speaking and as just in hearing.—
O, monstrous! Tempt me not, you gods! Good gods,
Tempt not a frail man! What's he that has a heart
But he must ease it here!

BELLARIO. My lord, help! Help the princess!

ARETHUSA. I am well; forbear.

PHILASTER [*aside*]. Let me love lightning; let me be em-
    braced
And kissed by scorpions, or adore the eyes
Of basilisks, rather than trust the tongues   30
Of hell-bred woman! Some good god look down
And shrink these veins up! Stick me here a stone,
Lasting to ages in the memory
Of this damned act!—Hear me, you wicked ones!
You have put hills of fire into this breast,
Not to be quenched with tears, for which may guilt
Sit on your bosoms! At your meals and beds
Despair await you! What, before my face?
Poison of asps between your lips! Diseases
Be your best issues! Nature make a curse   40
And throw it on you!

ARETHUSA.   Dear Philaster, leave
To be enraged and hear me.

PHILASTER.   I have done;

Forgive my passion. Not the calmèd sea,
When Aeolus locks up his windy brood,
Is less disturbed than I. I'll make you know't.
Dear Arethusa, do but take this sword,
[*He offers his drawn sword.*]
And search how temperate a heart I have;
Then you and this your boy may live and reign
In lust without control.—Wilt thou, Bellario?
I prithee, kill me; thou art poor, and mayst   50
Nourish ambitious thoughts: when I am dead,
This way were freer. Am I raging now?
If I were mad, I should desire to live.
Sirs,* feel my pulse, whether have you known
A man in a more equal tune to die?

BELLARIO. Alas, my lord, your pulse keeps madman's
  time!
So does your tongue!
PHILASTER.   You will not kill me, then?
ARETHUSA. Kill you?
BELLARIO.   Not for the world.
PHILASTER.   I blame not
  thee,
Bellario: thou hast done but that which gods
Would have transformed themselves to do. Begone;   60
Leave me without reply. This is the last
Of all our meeting.

                              (*Exit* BELLARIO.)
          —Kill me with this sword.
Be wise, or worse will follow; we are two
Earth cannot bear at once. Resolve to do,
Or suffer.

ARETHUSA. If my fortune be so good to let me fall
Upon thy hand, I shall have peace in death.
You tell me this: [will there] be no slanders,
No jealousy in the other world, no ill there?
PHILASTER. No.   70
ARETHUSA. Show me then the way.
PHILASTER. Then guide my feeble hand,
  You that have power to do it, for I must

---

sirs: applied to both sexes at this time.

Perform a piece of justice!—If your youth
Have any way offended heaven, let prayers
Short and effectual reconcile you to it.

ARETHUSA. I am prepared.

Enter a COUNTRY FELLOW.

COUNTRY FELLOW [*aside*]. I'll see the king if he be in the
forest; I have hunted him these two hours. If I should
come home and not see him, my sisters would laugh at   80
me. I can see nothing but people better horsed than
myself that outride me; I can hear nothing but shout-
ing. These kings had need of good brains; this whooping is able to put a mean man out of his wits.—There's
a courtier with his sword drawn; by this hand, upon a
woman, I think!

PHILASTER. Are you at peace?

ARETHUSA.   With heaven and earth.

PHILASTER. May they divide thy soul and body.
    [*He wounds her.*]

COUNTRY FELLOW. Hold, dastard! Strike a woman! Th'art
a craven, I warrant thee; thou wouldst be loath to play   90
half a dozen venies at wasters* with a good fellow
for a broken head.

PHILASTER. Leave us, good friend.

ARETHUSA. What ill-bred man art thou, to intrude thyself
Upon our private sports, our recreations?

COUNTRY FELLOW. God 'uds* me, I understand you not;
but I know the rogue has hurt you.

PHILASTER. Pursue thy own affairs; it will be ill
To multiply blood upon my head, which thou
Wilt force me to.   100

COUNTRY FELLOW. I know not your rhetoric, but I can lay
it on if you touch the woman.
    (*They fight.*)

PHILASTER. Slave, take what thou deservest!

ARETHUSA.   Heaven
    guard my lord!

COUNTRY FELLOW. O, do you breathe?

PHILASTER. I hear the tread of people. I am hurt;
The gods take part against me. Could this boor
Have held me thus else? I must shift for life

---

venies at wasters: bouts at cudgels.   'uds: judges (?).

Though I do loathe it. I would find a course
To lose it rather by my will than force.

Exit PHILASTER.

COUNTRY FELLOW. I cannot follow the rogue. I pray thee, 110
wench, come and kiss me now.

Enter PHARAMOND, DION, CLEREMONT, THRASILINE,
and Woodmen.

PHARAMOND. What art thou?

COUNTRY FELLOW. Almost killed I am for a foolish
woman; a knave has hurt her.

PHARAMOND. The princess, gentlemen!—Where's the
wound, madam? Is it dangerous?

ARETHUSA. He has not hurt me.

COUNTRY FELLOW. By God, she lies; h'as hurt her in the
breast; look else.

PHARAMOND. O sacred spring of innocent blood! 120

DION. 'Tis above wonder! Who should dare this?

ARETHUSA. I felt it not.

PHARAMOND. Speak, villain, who has hurt the princess?

COUNTRY FELLOW. Is it the princess?

DION. Ay!

COUNTRY FELLOW. Then I have seen something yet.

PHARAMOND. But who has hurt her?

COUNTRY FELLOW. I told you, a rogue; I ne'er saw him
before, I.

PHARAMOND. Madam, who did it?

ARETHUSA. Some dishonest
wretch; 130
Alas, I know him not, and do forgive him!

COUNTRY FELLOW. He's hurt too; he cannot go far; I
made my father's old fox* fly about his ears.

PHARAMOND. How will you have me kill him?

ARETHUSA. Not at all; 'tis some distracted fellow.

PHARAMOND. By this hand, I'll leave never a piece of
him bigger than a nut and bring him all to you in my
hat.

ARETHUSA. Nay, good sir,
If you do take him, bring him quick* to me, 140
And I will study for a punishment
Great as his fault.

---

fox: broad sword.   quick: living, alive.

PHARAMOND. I will.
ARETHUSA. But swear.
PHARAMOND. By all my love, I
    will.—
  Woodman, conduct the princess to the king,
  And bear that wounded fellow to dressing.—
  Come, gentlemen, we'll follow the chase close.
        [*Exeunt*] ARETHUSA, PHARAMOND, DION, CLEREMONT,
                              THRASILINE, *and* 1 WOODMAN.
COUNTRY FELLOW. I pray you, friend, let me see the king.
2 WOODMAN. That you shall, and receive thanks.
COUNTRY FELLOW. If I get clear of this, I'll go to see no
  more gay sights.   150
                                                     Exeunt.

[IV.iv]
                      Enter BELLARIO.
BELLARIO. A heaviness near death sits on my brow,
  And I must sleep. Bear me, thou gentle bank,
  Forever if thou wilt. You sweet ones all,
  [*He lies down.*]
  Let me unworthy press you: I could wish
  I rather were a corse* strewed o'er with you
  Than quick above you. Dullness shuts mine eyes,
  And I am giddy. O, that I could take
  So sound a sleep that I might never wake!
  [*He sleeps.*]
                      Enter PHILASTER.
PHILASTER. I have done ill; my conscience calls me false
  To strike at her that would not strike at me: 10
  When I did fight, methought I heard her pray
  The gods to guard me. She may be abused,
  And I a loathèd villain; if she be,
  She will conceal who hurt her. He has wounds
  And cannot follow; neither knows he me.
  Who's this? Bellario sleeping? If thou beest
  Guilty, there is no justice that thy sleep
  (*Cry within.*)
  Should be so sound and mine, whom thou hast
    wronged,

---

corse: corpse.

So broken. Hark! I am pursued. You gods,
I'll take this offered means of my escape.   20
They have no mark to know me but my wounds
If she be true; if false, let mischief light
On all the world at once! Sword, print my wounds
Upon this sleeping boy! I ha' none, I think,
Are mortal, nor would I lay greater on thee.
      (*Wounds him.*)
BELLARIO. O, death, I hope, is come: blessed be that
      hand!
It meant me well. Again, for pity's sake!
PHILASTER. I have caught myself;
      (PHILASTER *falls.*)
The loss of blood hath stayed my light. Here, here
Is he that struck thee. Take thy full revenge;   30
Use me, as I did mean thee, worse than death;
I'll teach thee to revenge. This luckless hand
Wounded the princess; tell my followers
Thou didst receive these hurts in staying me,
And I will second thee. Get a reward.
BELLARIO. Fly, fly, my lord, and save yourself!
PHILASTER.   How's
      this?
Wouldst thou I should be safe?
BELLARIO.   Else were it vain
For me to live. These little wounds I have
Ha' not bled much. Reach me that noble hand;
I'll help to cover you.
PHILASTER.   Art thou true to me?   40
BELLARIO. Or let me perish loathed! Come, my good lord,
Creep in among those bushes. Who does know
But that the gods may save your much-loved breath?
PHILASTER. Then I shall die for grief, if not for this,
That I have wounded thee. What wilt thou do?
BELLARIO. Shift for myself well. Peace! I hear um come.
      [PHILASTER *conceals himself.*]
WITHIN. Follow, follow, follow! That way they went.
BELLARIO. With my own wounds, I'll bloody my own
      sword.
I need not counterfeit to fall; heaven knows
That I can stand no longer.   50
      [*He falls.*]

Enter PHARAMOND, DION, CLEREMONT, THRASILINE.

PHARAMOND. To this place we have tracked him by his
   blood.

CLEREMONT. Yonder, my lord, creeps one away.

DION. Stay, sir; what are you?

BELLARIO. A wretched creature, wounded in these woods
   By beasts; relieve me, if your names be men,
   Or I shall perish.

DION.   This is he, my lord,
   Upon my soul, that hurt her; 'tis the boy,
   That wicked boy that served her.

PHARAMOND.   O, thou damned
   In thy creation! What cause couldst thou shape
   To strike the princess?

BELLARIO.   Then I am betrayed.   60

DION. Betrayed! No, apprehended.

BELLARIO.   I confess
   (Urge it no more) that, big with evil thoughts,
   I set upon her and did make my aim
   Her death. For charity, let fall at once
   The punishment you mean and do not load
   This weary flesh with tortures.

PHARAMOND.   I will know
   Who hired thee to this deed.

BELLARIO.   Mine own revenge.

PHARAMOND. Revenge! For what?

BELLARIO.   It pleased her to
   receive
   Me as her page; and, when my fortunes ebbed,
   That men strid o'er them careless, she did show'r   70
   Her welcome graces on me and did swell
   My fortunes till they overflowed their banks,
   Threat'ning the men that crossed um, when, as swift
   As storms arise at sea, she turned her eyes
   To burning suns upon me and did dry
   The streams she had bestowed, leaving me worse
   And more contemned than other little brooks
   Because I had been great. In short, I knew
   I could not live and, therefore, did desire
   To die revenged.

PHARAMOND.   If tortures can be found   80
   Long as thy natural life, resolve to feel
   The utmost rigor.

(PHILASTER *creeps out of a bush.*)

CLEREMONT.   Help to lead him hence.

PHILASTER. Turn back, you ravishers of innocence!
Know ye the price of that you bear away
So rudely?

PHARAMOND.   Who's that?

DION.   'Tis the Lord Philaster.

PHILASTER. 'Tis not the treasure of all kings in one,
The wealth of Tagus, nor the rocks of pearl
That pave the court of Neptune, can weigh down
That virtue. It was I that hurt the princess.
Place me, some god, upon a pyramis*   90
Higher than hills of earth and lend a voice
Loud as your thunder to me, that from thence
I may discourse to all the underworld
The worth that dwells in him!

PHARAMOND.   How's this?

BELLARIO.   My lord,
     some man,
Weary of life, that would be glad to die.

PHILASTER. Leave these untimely courtesies, Bellario.

BELLARIO. Alas, he's mad! Come, will you lead me on?

PHILASTER. By all the oaths that men ought most to keep,
And gods do punish most when men do break,
He touched her not.—Take heed, Bellario,   100
How thou dost drown the virtues thou hast shown
With perjury.—By all the gods, 'twas I!
You know she stood betwixt me and my right.

PHARAMOND. Thy own tongue be thy judge!

CLEREMONT.   It was
     Philaster.

DION. Is't not a brave boy?
Well, sirs, I fear me we were all deceived.

PHILASTER. Have I no friend here?

DION.   Yes.

PHILASTER.   Then show
     it: Some
Good body lend a hand to draw us nearer.
Would you have tears shed for you when you die?
Then lay me gently on his neck, that there   110
I may weep floods and breathe forth my spirit.

---

pyramis: pyramid.

'Tis not the wealth of Plutus, nor the gold
Locked in the heart of earth, can buy away
This armful from me; this had been a ransom
To have redeemed the great Augustus Cæsar
Had he been taken. You hard-hearted men,
More stony than these mountains, can you see
Such clear, pure blood drop and not cut your flesh
To stop his life, to bind whose bitter wounds
Queens ought to tear their hair and with their tears   120
Bathe um?——Forgive me, thou that art the wealth
Of poor Philaster!

       Enter KING, ARETHUSA, *and a Guard.*

KING.   Is the villain ta'en?

PHARAMOND. Sir, here be two confess the deed; but
    [sure]
It was Philaster.

PHILASTER.   Question it no more;
    It was.

KING.   The fellow that did fight with him
    Will tell us that.

ARETHUSA.   Ay me, I know he will.

KING. Did not you know him?

ARETHUSA.   Sir, if it was he,
    He was disguised.

PHILASTER.   I was so.——O, my stars,
    That I should live still!

KING.   Thou ambitious fool,
    Thou that hast laid a train for thy own life!——   130
    Now I do mean to do, I'll leave to talk.
    Bear him to prison.

ARETHUSA. Sir, they did plot together to take hence
    This harmless life; should it pass unrevenged,
    I should to earth go weeping. Grant me, then,
    By all the love a father bears his child,
    Their custodies and that I may appoint
    Their tortures and their deaths.

DION. Death? Soft! Our law will not reach that for this
    fault.

KING. 'Tis granted; take um to you with a guard.——   140
    Come, princely Pharamond, this business past,
    We may with more security go on
    To your intended match.

CLEREMONT [*aside*]. I pray that this action lose not
  Philaster the hearts of the people.
DION [*aside*]. Fear it not; their overwise heads will think
  it but a trick.

Exeunt omnes.

Finis actus quarti.

ACTUS V

[V.i]

Enter DION, CLEREMONT, *and* THRASILINE.

THRASILINE. Has the king sent for him to death?
DION. Yes, but the king must know 'tis not in his power
  to war with heaven.
CLEREMONT. We linger time; the king sent for Philaster
  and the headsman an hour ago.
THRASILINE. Are all his wounds well?
DION. All they were but scratches, but the loss of blood
  made him faint.
CLEREMONT. We dally, gentlemen.
THRASILINE. Away!   10
DION. We'll scuffle hard before he perish.

Exeunt.

[V.ii]

Enter PHILASTER, ARETHUSA, BELLARIO.

ARETHUSA. Nay, faith, Philaster, grieve not; we are well.
BELLARIO. Nay, good my lord, forbear; we're wondrous
  well.
PHILASTER. O, Arethusa! O, Bellario!
  Leave to be kind!
  I shall be shot° from heaven, as now from earth,
  If you continue so. I am a man,
  False to a pair of the most trusty ones
  That ever earth bore; can it bear us all?
  Forgive and leave. But the king hath sent
  To call me to my death. O, show it me,   10
  And then forget me! And for thee, my boy,
  I shall deliver words will mollify
  The hearts of beasts to spare thy innocence.

---

shot: expelled.

BELLARIO. Alas, my lord, my life is not a thing
　　Worthy your noble thoughts! 'Tis not a life;
　　'Tis but a piece of childhood thrown away.
　　Should I outlive you, I should then outlive
　　Virtue and honor; and, when that day comes,
　　If ever I shall close these eyes but once,
　　May I live spotted for my perjury　　　　　　　　20
　　And waste [m]y limbs to nothing!
ARETHUSA. And I (the woeful'st maid that ever was,
　　Forced with my hands to bring my lord to death)
　　Do by the honor of a virgin swear
　　To tell no hours beyond it!
PHILASTER. 　　　　　　　　　Make me not hated so.
ARETHUSA. Come from this prison all joyful to our deaths!
PHILASTER. People will tear me when they find you true
　　To such a wretch as I; I shall die loathed.
　　Enjoy your kingdoms peaceably whilst I
　　Forever sleep, forgotten with my faults.　　　　　　30
　　Every just servant, every maid in love,
　　Will have a piece of me if you be not true.
ARETHUSA. My dear lord, say not so.
BELLARIO. 　　　　　　　　　A piece of you?
　　He was not born of women that can cut
　　It and look on.
PHILASTER. Take me in tears betwixt you, for my heart
　　Will break with shame and sorrow.
ARETHUSA. 　　　　　　　　　Why, 'tis well.
BELLARIO. Lament no more.
PHILASTER. 　　　　　　　　　What would you have
　　done
　　If you had wronged me basely, and had found
　　[Your] life no price compared to [mine]? For love, sirs,　　40
　　Deal with me truly.
BELLARIO. 　　　　　　　　　'Twas mistaken, sir.
PHILASTER. Why, if it were?
BELLARIO. 　　　　　　　　　Then, sir, we would have
　　asked
　　Your pardon.
PHILASTER. 　　　And have hope to enjoy it?
ARETHUSA. Enjoy it? Ay.
PHILASTER. 　　　　　　　　　Would you indeed? Be plain.
BELLARIO. We would, my lord.

PHILASTER. Forgive me, then.
ARETHUSA. So,
so.
BELLARIO. 'Tis as it should be now.
PHILASTER. Lead me to my
death.

Exeunt.

[V.iii]

Enter KING, DION, CLEREMONT, THRASILINE [, *and a Guard*].

KING. Gentlemen, who saw the prince?
CLEREMONT. So please you, sir, he's gone to see the city
And the new platform, with some gentlemen
Attending on him.
KING. Is the princess ready
To bring her prisoner out?
THRASILINE. She waits your grace.
KING. Tell her we stay.

[*Exit* THRASILINE.]

DION [*aside*]. King, you may be deceived
yet;
The head you aim at cost more setting on
Than to be lost so lightly. If it must off,
Like a wild overflow, that soops° before him
A golden stack, and with it shakes down bridges, 10
Cracks the strong hearts of pines, whose cable-roots
Held out a thousand storms, a thousand thunders,
And, so made mightier, takes whole villages
Upon his back, and in that heat of pride
Charges strong towns, towers, castles, palaces,
And lays them desolate, so shall thy head,
Thy noble head, bury the lives of thousands
That must bleed with thee like a sacrifice
In thy red ruins.

Enter PHILASTER, ARETHUSA, BELLARIO *in a
robe and garland* [, *and* THRASILINE].

KING. How now? What masque is this?
BELLARIO. Right royal sir, I should 20
Sing you an epithalamion of these lovers;
But, having lost my best airs with my fortunes,

---

soops: swoops, sweeps.

And wanting a celestial harp to strike
This blessed union on, thus in glad story
I give you all. These two fair cedar branches,
The noblest of the mountain where they grew,
Straightest and tallest, under whose still shades
The worthier beasts have made their lairs, and slept
Free from [the fervor of] the Sirian star
And the fell thunderstroke, free from the clouds   30
When they were big with humor,° and deliver[ed]
In thousand spouts their issues to the earth—
O, there was none but silent quiet there!—
Till never-pleasèd Fortune shot up shrubs,
 Base underbrambles, to divorce these branches;
And for a while they did so, and did reign
Over the mountain and choke up his beauty
With brakes, rude thorns, and thistles till the sun
Scorched them even to the roots and dried them there.
And now a gentler gale hath blown again,   40
That made these branches meet and twine together,
Never to be divided. The god that sings
His holy number[s]° over marriage beds
Hath knit their noble hearts; and here they stand,
Your children, mighty king; and I have done.

KING. How, how?

ARETHUSA.   Sir, if you love it in plain truth,
For now there is no masquing in't, this gentleman,
The prisoner that you gave me, is become
My keeper; and, through all the bitter throes
Your jealousies and his ill fate have wrought him,   50
Thus nobly hath he struggled and at length
Arrived here my dear husband.

KING.   Your dear husband!—
Call in the Captain of the Citadel—
There you shall keep your wedding: I'll provide
A masque shall make your Hymen° turn his saffron
Into a sullen coat and sing sad requiems
To your departing souls.
Blood shall put out your torches; and, instead
Of gaudy flowers about your wanton necks,

---

humor: moisture.   numbers: verses.
Hymen: god of marriage.

An ax shall hang, like a prodigious meteor, 60
Ready to crop your loves' sweets. Hear, you gods!
From this time do I shake all title off
Of father to this woman, this base woman;
And what there is of vengeance in a lion
Chased among dogs, or robbed of his dear young,
The same, enforced more terrible, more mighty,
Expect from me!

ARETHUSA. Sir, by that little life I have left to swear by,
There's nothing that can stir me from myself.
What I have done, I have done without repentance; 70
For death can be no bugbear unto me
So long as Pharamond is not my headsman.

DION [*aside*]. Sweet peace upon thy soul, thou worthy
maid,
Whene'er thou diest! For this time I'll excuse thee,
Or be thy prologue.*

PHILASTER. Sir, let me speak next,
And let my dying words be better with you
Than my dull, living actions. If you aim
At the dear life of this sweet innocent,
Y'are a tyrant and a savage monster
[That feeds upon the blood you gave life to];* 80
Your memory shall be as foul behind you
As you are living; all your better deeds
Shall be in water writ, but this in marble;
No chronicle shall speak you, though your own,
But for the shame of men; no monument
(Though high and big as Pelion) shall be able
To cover this base murder, make it rich
With brass, with purest gold, and shining jasper,
Like the pyramids; lay on epitaphs
Such as make great men gods; my little marble 90
(That only clothes my ashes, not my faults)
Shall far outshine it. And for after-issues*
Think not so madly of the heavenly wisdoms
That they will give you more for your mad rage
To cut off, unless it be some snake or something

---

prologue: that is, in death.
that feeds . . . to: from Quarto One (1620).
after-issues: offspring, future descendants.

Like yourself, that in his birth shall strangle you.
Remember my father, king! There was a fault,
But I forgive it: let that sin persuade you
To love this lady. If you have a soul,
Think, save her, and be savèd. For myself,   100
I have so long expected this glad hour,
So languished under you and daily withered
That, by the gods, it is a joy to die;
I find a recreation in't.

                Enter a MESSENGER.

MESSENGER. Where's the king?
KING.   Here.
MESSENGER.   Get you to your
    strength,*
And rescue the Prince Pharamond from danger;
He's taken prisoner by the citizens,
Fearing* the Lord Philaster.
DION [*aside*].   O, brave followers!
Mutiny, my fine, dear countrymen, mutiny!
Now, my brave, valiant foremen, show your weapons   110
In honor of your mistresses!

              Enter another MESSENGER.

[2] MESSENGER. Arm, arm, arm, arm!
KING. A thousand devils take um!
DION [*aside*]. A thousand blessings on um!
[2] MESSENGER. Arm, O king! The city is in mutiny,
Led by an old gray ruffian, who comes on
In rescue of the Lord Philaster.
KING. Away to the Citadel!—

    [*Exeunt the Guard,*] *with* ARETHUSA, PHILASTER, BELLARIO.
                    I'll see them safe,
And then cope with these burghers. Let the guard
And all the gentlemen give strong attendance.   120

    Exit KING; *manent** DION, CLEREMONT, THRASILENE.

CLEREMONT. The city up! This was above our wishes.
DION. Ay, and the marriage too. By my life, this noble
    lady has deceived us all. A plague upon myself, a
    thousand plagues, for having such unworthy thoughts
    of her dear honor! O, I could beat myself! Or do you

---

    strength: fortress.   fearing: concerned, anxious about.
    manent: remain.

beat me, and I'll beat you, for we had all one thought.

CLEREMONT. No, no, 'twill but lose time.

DION. You say true. Are your swords sharp?—Well, my dear countrymen What-ye-lacks,* if you continue and fall not back upon the first broken shin, I'll have ye 130 chronicled and chronicled, and cut and chronicled, and all to be praised and sung in sonnets, and bathed in new, brave ballads, that all tongues shall trouble you *in sæcula sæculorum,* my kind can-carriers.

THRASILINE. What if a toy* take um i'th' heels now, and they run all away and cry, "The devil take the hindmost?"

DION. Then the same devil take the foremost too, and souse him for his breakfast! If they all prove cowards, my curses fly among them, and be speeding! May they 140 have murrains* reign to keep the gentlemen at home unbound in easy frieze! May the moths branch* their velvets, and their silks only be worn before sore eyes! May their false lights undo um, and discover presses,* holes, stains, and oldness in their stuffs, and make them shoprid! May they keep whores and horses, and break,* and live mewed up with necks of beef and turnips! May they have many children, and none like the father! May they know no language but that gibberish they prattle to their parcels,* unless it be the 150 goatish Latin they write in their bonds—and may they write that false and lose their debts!

Enter the KING.

KING. Now the vengeance of all the gods confound them! How they swarm together! What a hum they raise!— Devils choke your wild throats!—If a man had need to use their valors, he must pay a brokage for it, and then bring um on, and they will fight like sheep. 'Tis Philaster, none but Philaster, must allay this heat. They will not hear me speak, but fling dirt at me, and call me tyrant. O, run, dear friend, and bring the Lord 160

what-ye-lacks: shopkeeper's cry.
in sæcula sæculorum: forever.   toy: whim, trifle.
murrains: plagues.   branch: eat patterns on.
presses: creases.   break: "go broke" or bankrupt.
parcels: conveyances.

Philaster: speak him fair, call him prince, do him all
the courtesy you can; commend me to him. O, my wits,
my wits!

Exit CLEREMONT.

DION [*aside*]. O, my brave countrymen! As I live, I will
not buy a pin out of your walls for this. Nay, you shall
cozen me, and I'll thank you, and send you brawn and
bacon, and soil* you ever[y] long vacation a brace of
foremen,* that at Michælmas shall come up fat and
kicking.

KING. What will they do with this poor prince, the gods   170
know, and I fear.

DION [*aside*]. Why, sir, they'll flay him and make church
buckets on's skin to quench rebellion, then clap a rivet
in's sconce, and hang him up for [a] sign.

Enter CLEREMONT *with* PHILASTER.

KING. O, worthy sir, forgive me! Do not make
Your miseries and my faults meet together
To bring a greater danger. Be yourself,
Still sound amongst diseases. I have wronged you;
And, though I find it last, and beaten to it,
Let first your goodness know it. Calm the people,   180
And be what you were born to. Take your love,
And with her my repentance, all my wishes,
And all my prayers. By the gods, my heart speaks this;
And, if the least fall from me not performed,
May I be strook with thunder!

PHILASTER.   Mighty sir,
I will not do you[r] greatness so much wrong
As not to make your word truth. Free the princess
And the poor boy, and let me stand the shock
Of this mad sea-breach, which I'll either turn
Or perish with it.

KING.   Let your own word free them.   190

PHILASTER. Then thus I take my leave, kissing your hand,
And hanging on your royal word. Be kingly,
And be not moved, sir. I shall bring [you] peace
Or never bring myself back.

Exeunt omnes.

---

soil: feed; fatten.   brace of foremen: geese.

[V.iv]

Enter an old CAPTAIN *and Citizens with* PHARAMOND.

CAPTAIN. Come, my brave Myrmidons,* let's fall on; let
[y]our caps swarm, my boys, and your nimble tongues
forget your mother-gibberish of "what do you lack?"
And set your mouths [ope'], children, till your palates
fall frightened half a fathom past the cure of bay salt
and gross pepper, and then cry, "Philaster, brave Philaster!" Let Philaster be deeper in request, my ding-
dongs, my pairs of dear indentures, kings of clubs, than
your cold water-chamblets* or your paintings spitted
with copper. Let not your hasty* silks, or your   10
branched cloth of bodkin, or your tissues, dearly beloved of spiced cake and custards, [you] Robin Hoods,
Scarlets, and Johns, tie your affections in darkness to
your shops. No, dainty duckers, up with your three-
piled spirits, your wrought valors;* and let your uncut
cholers* make the king feel the measure of your mightiness. Philaster! Cry, my rose-nobles,* cry!

ALL. Philaster! Philaster!

CAPTAIN. How do you like this, my lord prince? These
are mad boys, I tell you; these are things that will not   20
strike their topsails to a foist* and let a man of war, an
argosy, hull and cry "cockles." *

PHARAMOND. Why, you rude slave, do you know what
you do?

CAPTAIN. My pretty prince of puppets, we do know
And give your greatness warning that you talk
No more such bug's* words, or that soldered crown
Shall be scratched with a musket. Dear Prince Pippin,
Down with your noble blood, or, as I live,
I'll have you coddled.— Let [h]im loose, my spirits;
Make us a round ring with your bills, my Hectors,   30
And let me see what this trim man dares do.—
Now, sir, have at you! Here I lie,

Myrmidons: followers of Achilles in the Trojan War.
water-chamblet: a costly watered cloth.   hasty: shoddy.
valors: punning on "velours."   cholers: punning on "collars."
rose-nobles: coins.   foist: a barge.   cry "cockles": lie idle.
bug's: bugbear's; swaggering.

And with this washing* blow (do you see, sweet
   prince?)
I could hulk* your grace and hang you up cross-
   legged,
Like a hare at a poulter's, and do this with this wiper.

PHARAMOND. You will not see me murdered, wicked villains?

1 CITIZEN. Yes, indeed, will we, sir; we have not seen
   one fo[r] a great while.

CAPTAIN. He would have weapons, would he? Give him a
   broadside, my brave boys, with your pikes; branch me   40
   his skin in flowers like a satin, and between every
   flower a mortal cut.—Your royalty shall ravel!—Jag
   him, gentlemen; I'll have him cut to the kell,* then
   down the seams. O, for a whip to make him galloon-
   laces!* I'll have a coach-whip.

PHARAMOND. O, spare me, gentlemen!

CAPTAIN. Hold, hold! The man begins to fear and know
   himself; he shall for this time only be seeled up with
   a feather through his nose, that he may only see heaven
   and think whither he's going. Nay, my good beyond-   50
   sea sir, we will proclaim you. You would be king! Thou
   tender heir apparent to a church ale,* thou slight
   prince of single sarcenet,* thou royal ringtail,* fit to
   fly at nothing but poor men's poultry, and have every
   boy beat thee from that too with his bread and butter!

PHARAMOND. Gods keep me from these hellhounds!

1 CITIZEN. Shall's geld him, captain?

CAPTAIN. No, you shall spare his dowcets, my dear
   donsels;*
   As you respect the ladies, let them flourish;
   The curses of a longing woman kills   60
   As speedy as a plague, boys.

1 CITIZEN. I'll have a leg, that's certain.

2 CITIZEN. I'll have an arm.

---

washing: swashing, slashing.   hulk: disembowel.
kell: caul.   galloon-laces: binding tapes.
church ale: bastard child conceived at a church social function.
sarcenet: fine, soft silk.   ringtail: kind of kite; buzzard.
donsels: young dons (?), fellows.

3 CITIZEN. I'll have his nose, and at mine own charge
build a college and clap't upon the gate.*

4 CITIZEN. I'll have his little gut to string a kit* with,
for certainly a royal gut will sound like silver.

PHARAMOND. Would they were in thy belly, and I past
my pain once!

5 CITIZEN. Good captain, let me have his liver to feed   70
ferrets.

CAPTAIN. Who will have parcels else? Speak.

PHARAMOND. Good gods, consider me! I shall be tortured.

1 CITIZEN. Captain, I'll give you the trimming of your
two-hand sword, and let me have his skin to make
false scabbards.

2 CITIZEN. He had no horns, sir, had he?

CAPTAIN. No, sir, he's a pollard.* What wouldst thou do
with horns?

2 CITIZEN. O, if he had had, I would have made rare   80
hafts and whistles of um; but his shin bones, if they
be sound, shall serve me.

Enter PHILASTER.

ALL. Long live Philaster, the brave Prince Philaster!

PHILASTER. I thank you, gentlemen; but why are these
Rude weapons brought abroad to teach your hands
Uncivil trades?

CAPTAIN.   My royal Rosicleer,
We are thy Myrmidons, thy guard, thy roarers;
And, when thy noble body is in durance,
Thus do we clap our musty murrions* on,
And trace the streets in terror. Is it peace,   90
Thou Mars of men? Is the king sociable,
And bids thee live? Art thou above thy foemen
And free as Phœbus? Speak. If not, this stand*
Of royal blood shall be abroach, atilt,
And run even to the lees of honor.

PHILASTER. Hold and be satisfied; I am myself,
Free as my thoughts are. By the gods, I am!

---

college . . . gate: as at Brasenose College, Oxford.
kit: cithern (a lute-like instrument).
pollard: unhorned animal.   murrions: helmets.
stand: wine cask.

CAPTAIN. Art thou the dainty darling of the king?
Art thou the Hylas to our Hercules?
Do the lords bow, and the regarded scarlets*   100
Kiss their gummed golls,* and cry, "We are your
    servants"?
Is the court navigable and the presence stuck
With flags of friendship? If not, we are thy castle,
And this man sleeps.
PHILASTER. I am what I do desire to be, your friend;
I am what I was born to be, your prince.
PHARAMOND. Sir, there is some humanity in you;
You have a noble soul. Forget my name,
And know my misery; set me safe aboard
From these wild cannibals, and, as I live,   110
I'll quit this land forever. There is nothing—
Perpetual prisonment, cold, hunger, sickness
Of all sorts, of all dangers, and altogether
The worst company of the worst men, madness, age,
To be as many creatures as a woman,
And do as all they do, nay, to despair—
But I would rather make it a new nature
And live with all these than endure one hour
Amongst these wild dogs.
PHILASTER. I do pity you.—Friends, discharge your
    fears;   120
Deliver me the prince; I'll warrant you
I shall be old enough to find my safety.
3 CITIZEN. Good sir, take heed he does not hurt you;
He's a fierce man, I can tell you, sir.
CAPTAIN. Prince, by your leave, I'll have a surcingle*
And make you like a hawk.
    ([PHARAMOND] strives.)
PHILASTER. Away, away, there is no danger in him!
Alas, he had rather sleep to shake his fit off!
Look you, friends, how gently he leads; upon my word,
He's tame enough; he need[s] no further watching.   130
Good my friends, go to your houses,
And by me have your pardons and my love;
And know there shall be nothing in my power

scarlets: scarlet-clad courtiers.
gummed golls: perfumed hands.   surcingle: band.

You may deserve but you shall have your wishes.
To give you more thanks were to flatter you;
Continue still your love, and for an earnest
Drink this.
[*He gives money.*]

ALL. Long mayst thou live, brave prince, brave prince,
    brave prince!

       [*Exeunt*] PHILASTER *and* PHARAMOND.

CAPTAIN. Go thy ways, thou art the king of courtesy!—
Fall off again, my sweet youths. Come,   140
And every man trace to his house again
And hang his pewter up; then to the tavern,
And bring your wives in muffs. We will have music,
And the red grape shall make us dance and rise, boys.

              Exeunt.

[V.v]

    Enter KING, ARETHUSA, GALATEA, MEGRA,
   CLEREMONT, DION, THRASILINE, BELLARIO,
       and Attendants.

KING. Is it appeased?

DION. Sir, all is quiet as this dead of night,
As peaceable as sleep. My Lord Philaster
Brings on the prince himself.

KING.   Kind gentlemen,
I will not break the least word I have given
In promise to him; I have heaped a world
Of grief upon his head, which yet I hope
To wash away.

     Enter PHILASTER *and* PHARAMOND.

CLEREMONT.   My lord is come.

KING.   My son!
Blessed be the time that I have leave to call
Such virtue mine! Now thou art in mine arms,   10
Methinks I have a salve unto my breast
For all the stings that dwell there. Streams of grief
That I have [wronged] thee, and as much of joy
That I repent it, issue from mine eyes;
Let them appease thee. Take thy right. Take her
(She is thy right too), and forget to urge
My vexèd soul with that I did before.

PHILASTER. Sir, it is blotted from my memory,

Past and forgotten.—For you, Prince of Spain,
Whom I have thus redeemed, you have full leave   20
To make an honorable voyage home.
And, if you would go furnished to your realm
With fair provision, I do see a lady,
Methinks, would gladly bear you company.
How like you this piece?

MEGRA.   Sir, he likes it well,
For he hath tried it and hath found it worth
His princely liking. We were ta'en abed;
I know your meaning. I am not the first
That nature taught to seek a fellow forth:
Can shame remain perpetually in me   30
And not in others? Or have princes salves
To cure ill names that meaner people want?

PHILASTER. What mean you?

MEGRA.   You must get another ship
To bear the princess and her boy together.

DION. How now!

MEGRA. Others took me, and I took her and him
At that all women may be ta'en sometime.
Ship us all four, my lord; we can endure
Weather and wind alike.

KING. Clear thou thyself, or know not me for father.   40

ARETHUSA. This earth, how false it is! What means is left
    for me
To clear myself? It lies in your belief.
My lords, believe me, and let all things else
Struggle together to dishonor me.

BELLARIO. O, stop your ears, great king, that I may speak
As freedom would! Then I will call this lady
As base as are her actions. Hear me, sir;
Believe your heated blood when it rebels
Against your reason sooner than this lady.

MEGRA. By this good light, he bears it handsomely.   50

PHILASTER. This lady! I will sooner trust the wind
With feathers, or the troubled sea with pearl,
Than her with anything. Believe her not!
Why, think you, if I did believe her words,
I would outlive 'em? Honor cannot take
Revenge on you. Then what were to be known
But death?

KING.   Forget her, sir, since all is knit
  Between us; but I must request of you
  One favor and will sadly be denied.
PHILASTER. Command, whate'er it be.
KING.   Swear to be true   60
  To what you promise.
PHILASTER.   By the powers above,
  Let it not be the death of her or him,
  And it is granted!
KING.   Bear away that boy
  To torture; I will have her cleared or buried.
PHILASTER. O, let me call my word back, worthy sir!
  Ask something else; bury my life and right
  In one poor grave, but do not take away
  My life and fame at once.
KING. Away with him! It stands irrevocable.
PHILASTER. Turn all your eyes on me; here stands a man,   70
  The falsest and basest of this world.
  Set swords against this breast, some honest man,
  For I have lived till I am pitièd!
  My former deeds were hateful, but this last
  Is pitiful; for I unwillingly
  Have given the dear preserver of my life
  Unto his torture. Is it in the power
  Of flesh and blood to carry this and live?
  (*Offers to kill himself.*)
ARETHUSA. Dear sir, be patient yet! O, stay that hand!
KING. Sirs, strip that boy.
DION.   Come, sir, your tender flesh   80
  Will [try] your constancy.
BELLARIO.   O, kill me, gentlemen.
DION. No.—Help, sirs!
BELLARIO.   Will you torture me?
KING.   Haste
  there;
  Why stay you?
BELLARIO.   Then I shall not break my vow,
  You know, just gods, though I discover all.
KING. How's that? Will he confess?
DION.   Sir, so he says.
KING. Speak then.
BELLARIO.   Great king, if you command

This lord to talk with me alone, my tongue,
Urged by my heart, shall utter all the thoughts
My youth hath known; and stranger thing[s] than these
You hear not often.

KING.   Walk aside with him.   90

[DION *and* BELLARIO *walk apart.*]

DION. Why speak'[s]t thou not?

BELLARIO.   Know you this face,
  my lord?

DION. No.

BELLARIO.   Have you not seen it, nor the like?

DION. Yes, I have seen the like, but readily
  I know not where.

BELLARIO.   I have been often told
  In court of one Euphrasia, a lady
  And daughter to you, betwixt whom and me
  They that would flatter my bad face would swear
  There was such strange resemblance that we two
  Could not be known asunder, dressed alike.

DION. By heaven, and so there is!

BELLARIO.   For her fair sake,   100
  Who now doth spend the springtime of her life
  In holy pilgrimage, move to the king
  That I may 'scape this torture.

DION.   But thou speak'st
  As like Euphrasia as thou dost look.
  How came it to thy knowledge that she lives
  In pilgrimage?

BELLARIO.   I know it not, my lord,
  But I have heard it and do scarce believe it.

DION. O, my shame, is't possible? Draw near
  That I may gaze upon thee. Art thou she,
  Or else her murderer? Where wert thou born?   110

BELLARIO. In Syracusa.

DION.   What's thy name?

BELLARIO.   Euphrasia.

DION. O, 'tis just, 'tis she!
  Now I do know thee. O, that thou hadst died
  And I had never seen thee nor thy shame!
  How shall I own thee? Shall this tongue of mine
  E'er call thee daughter more?

BELLARIO. Would I had died indeed! I wish it too,

And so [I] must have done by vow, ere published
What I have told, but that there was no means
To hide it longer. Yet I joy in this,   120
The princess is all clear.

KING.   What, have you done?

DION. All's discovered.

PHILASTER.   Why then hold you me?
All is discovered! Pray you, let me go.
(*He offers to stab himself.*)

KING. Stay him!

ARETHUSA.   What is discovered?

DION.   Why, my shame.
It is a woman; let her speak the rest.

PHILASTER. How? That again!

DION. It is a woman.

PHILASTER. Blessed be you powers that favor innocence!

KING. Lay hold upon that lady.
[MEGRA *is seized.*]

PHILASTER. It is a woman, sir!—Hark, gentlemen,   130
It is a woman!—Arethusa, take
My soul into thy breast, that would be gone
With joy. It is a woman! Thou art fair
And virtuous still to ages, in despite of malice.

KING. Speak you, where lies his shame?

BELLARIO.   I am his
daughter.

PHILASTER. The gods are just.

DION. I dare accuse none; but, before you two,
The virtue of our age, I bend my knee
For mercy.
[*He kneels.*]

PHILASTER [*raising him*].   Take it freely; for I know,
Though what thou didst were undiscreetly done,   140
'Twas meant well.

ARETHUSA. And, for me,
I have a power to pardon sins as oft
As any man has power to wrong me.

CLEREMONT. Noble and worthy!

PHILASTER.   But, Bellario
(For I must call thee still so), tell me why
Thou didst conceal thy sex; it was a fault,
A fault, Bellario, though thy other deeds

Of truth outweighed it. All these jealousies
Had flown to nothing if thou hadst discovered   150
What now we know.

BELLARIO.   My father oft would speak
Your worth and virtue; and, as I did grow
More and more apprehensive,* I did thirst
To see the man so raised. But yet all this
Was but a maiden longing, to be lost
As soon as found, till, sitting in my window,
Printing my thoughts in lawn, I saw a god,
I thought (but it was you), enter our gates.
My blood flew out and back again as fast
As I had puffed it forth and sucked it in   160
Like breath. Then was I called away in haste
To entertain you. Never was a man,
Heaved from a sheepcote to a scepter, raised
So high in thoughts as I. You left a kiss
Upon these lips then, which I mean to keep
From you forever. I did hear you talk,
Far above singing. After you were gone,
I grew acquainted with my heart and searched
What stirred it so. Alas, I found it love,
Yet far from lust; for, [could I] but have lived   170
In presence of you, I had had my end.
For this I did delude my noble father
With a feigned pilgrimage and dressed myself
In habit of a boy; and, for I knew
My birth no match for you, I was past hope
Of having you. And, understanding well
That when I made discovery of my sex
I could not stay with you, I made a vow,
By all the most religious things a maid
Could call together, never to be known   180
Whilst there was hope to hide me from men's eyes,
For other than I seemed, that I might ever
Abide with you. Then sat I by the fount,
Where first you took me up.

KING.   Search out a match
Within our kingdom, where and when thou wilt,
And I will pay thy dowry; and thyself

---

apprehensive: quick to understand.

Wilt well deserve him.

BELLARIO.   Never, sir, will I
Marry; it is a thing within my vow.
But, if I may have leave to serve the princess,
To see the virtues of her lord and her,   190
I shall have hope to live.

ARETHUSA.   I, Philaster,
Cannot be jealous though you had a lady
Dressed like a page to serve you; nor will I
Suspect her living here.—Come, live with me;
Live free as I do. She that loves my lord,
Cursed be the wife that hates her!

PHILASTER. I grieve such virtue should be laid in earth
Without an heir.—Hear me, my royal father:
Wrong not the freedom of our souls so much
To think to take revenge of that base woman;   200
Her malice cannot hurt us. Set her free
As she was born, saving from shame and sin.

KING. Set her at liberty.—But leave the court;
There is no place for such.—You, Pharamond,
Shall have free passage and a conduct home
Worthy so great a prince. When you come there,
Remember 'twas your faults that lost you her
And not my purposed will.

PHARAMOND.   I do confess,
Renownèd sir.

KING. Last, join your hands in one. Enjoy, Philaster,   210
This kingdom, which is yours, and, after me,
Whatever I call mine. My blessing on you!
All happy hours be at your marriage joys,
That you may grow yourselves over all lands
And li[v]e to see your plenteous branches spring
Wherever there is sun! Let princes learn
By this to rule the passions of their blood,
For what heaven wills can never be withstood.

Exeunt omnes.

FINIS.

THE
TRAGEDY
OF THE DVTCHESSE
Of Malfy.

As it was Presented priuatly, at the Black-Friers; and publiquely at the Globe, By the Kings Maiesties Seruants.

The perfect and exact Coppy, with diuerse things Printed, that the length of the Play would not beare in the Presentment.

VVritten by *John Webster.*

Hora.—— *Si quid*——
——*Candidus Imperti si non his vtere mecum.*

LONDON:

Printed by NICHOLAS OKES, for IOHN
WATERSON, and are to be sold at the
signe of the Crowne, in *Paules*
Church-yard, 1 6 2 3.

Introduction

In Webster's world, death does not merely end the burden of living as it does in Beaumont and Fletcher's; it is, paradoxically, that which makes life meaningful. In *The Duchess of Malfi* (1613–1614), the good Antonio observes near the end of his life: "But all things have their end:/ Churches and cities, which have diseases like to men,/ Must have like death that we have." In a life described as a "mist," death is life's one certainty, and in the face of it an individual sums up the quality of his being. If the concluding couplet of *Philaster* has little to do with that play, that of *The Duchess of Malfi* summarizes its meaning perfectly:

> "Integrity of life is fame's best friend,
> Which nobly, beyond death, shall crown the end."

Thus, to assert one's integrity in the face of the corrupting process of death—to say, "I am Duchess of Malfi still," and then to approach death with calm dignity and generous concern for others—is the only bulwark against meaninglessness.

As early as the second decade of the seventeenth century Webster foreshadows the difficulty that later playwrights would face in writing tragedy. In *The Duchess of Malfi* a moral universe that frames men's actions and makes possible the perception of great tragedy is tenuous: Both the metaphysical and social worlds are wildernesses, "where," says the Duchess, "I shall find nor path nor friendly clue/ To be my guide." Men prey upon men for no understandable reason (the play suggests baffling and contradictory reasons for Ferdinand's insane pursuit of his sister, and the Cardinal's evil is innate). Nature itself is indifferent to man: "Look you, the stars shine still."

In wooing below her rank and in marrying outside the church, the Duchess is breaking a social code; but after what happens to her she can say more honestly than Lear that she is more sinned against than sinning. The anonymous pilgrims at the beginning of Act III, scene iv, realize as much. In a sense her actions proceed from a knowledge that Lear himself must attain: that where men live in a "rank pasture" of their own creating, social laws are arbitrary and absurd. In her world the Elizabethan ideal of the city of God on earth is remote. Antonio's description of a foreign court that opens the play is the opposite of what Malfi is—an almost paradisal vision set against the demonic one of Malfi.

If the Duchess breaks social laws, she does so because they have no validity; they do not reflect the laws of God's universe. That such a good person should have two such titanically evil brothers like Ferdinand and the Cardinal is itself a reflection of the preponderance of evil in the world—Goneril and Regan as against Cordelia. In the play's second scene, when her brothers warn her with threats not to marry, she observes that the speech between them "was studied,/ It came so roundly off." Evil here is rehearsed, even ritualized, coded, and formalized; and the Duchess' only recourse is Cordelia's "Love, and be silent." If the world gives evil form, she wants to be free of form, to live happy like the birds "i'th' field/ On the wild benefit of nature." If her marriage breaks social custom, its genuine goodness belies her being, as people think, a strumpet. Men may part the lovers, but "In the eternal church, sir,/ I do hope we shall not part thus." Significantly, the Duchess of Malfi is addressed by no more personal name in the play, tragically indicating her failure to achieve a private, sheltered world of her own within the larger one of corruption and death. In her unconventional marriage she asks to be only a woman, not a duchess, responding to her heart and not to hollow form. When Antonio fears the worst from her brothers, she comforts him by saying:

> Do not think of them.
> All discord without this circumference
> [She puts her arms about him.]
> Is only to be pitied and not feared;
> Yet, should they know it, time will easily
> Scatter the tempest.

Like the lovers of Donne's early poems, she defies the larger world to make the smaller one of personal love her entire universe. Time, however, brings the tempest instead, as it does to all things, and her social identity is the only one that remains.

That she does attempt to assert her identity amid moral chaos, and thus to re-establish a kind of order in her personal universe, that she meets her death with dignity and without despair makes the Duchess of Malfi a tragic figure. But, unlike the usual hero of tragedy, she *becomes* rather than *is* tragic. Of the great tragic heroes it has been said that they pursue their tragedy, that they seek it out and identify themselves with it; it would never dawn upon them merely to walk away from it. "I will know who I am," says Oedipus for all who actively defy their flawed human condition but who nevertheless assume responsibility for their defiance. The Duchess' tragedy, however, is one of passive suffering; it is thrust upon her. Her role begins as an ordinary one; she wants to be simply a woman. Hers is no metaphysical questioning, no "articling" with the gods. Just before her death she is in the humanly believable state of self-pity and despair, but that she manages to keep faith with herself is her heroism. Because she *finally* does not walk away from her tragedy, she has come to live as a heroic type who retains her personal integrity through self-definition even if to say "I am Duchess of Malfi still" has no ultimate meaning. From her integrity "a terrible beauty is born": the "penitent fountains" of Bosola's eyes are frozen no longer, "the sun shines" again, and evil—like diamonds cut with their own dust—consumes itself.

That the center of Webster's tragic action is a woman, who craves only to be a woman, and a role acted—it must be remembered—by a boy, not by one of the great tragedians of the Company of His Majesty's Servants, is indicative of the shift in tragic mood, more restrained and soft, that comes at the end of the first decade of the new century and coincides with the move of adult drama indoors. The new mood seemed to require a setting different from the outdoor, sunlit stage of the Globe. The title page of the first quarto of *The Duchess of Malfi* observes that the play was performed "privately at the Blackfriars, and publicly at the Globe, by the King's Majesty's Servants"; but, as John Russell Brown points out in his recent edition, Webster surely wrote the play with the former theater in mind. Scenes such as Act IV, scene i, where the Duchess cries out for light when she touches the dead hand that Ferdinand has given her, would seem absurd even in the symbolic setting of the Globe stage. Indeed, the atmosphere of the whole play suggests indoors, an oppressive darkness except for the light that the Duchess sheds. The stage is not a heath where Lear rages against the elements but a prison suffocating an innocent woman.

The Playwright

JOHN WEBSTER (1580?–1634?) is a dramatist about whom we know almost nothing. A Lord Mayor's pageant, *Monuments of Honour,* written and published in 1624, records on the title page: "*Invented and Written* by John Webster Merchant-Taylor," and in the dedicatory epistle the author speaks of himself as "one born free of your Company." He appears generally in collaboration with other playwrights, and his major creative period seems to date before 1616.

The Play

The present text of *The Duchess of Malfi* is based on copies of the first quarto of 1623, published with two casts of the King's Men, in the Henry E. Huntington and Harvard University libraries. The original quarto is divided carefully into acts and scenes, with the character-names from an entire scene listed at the beginning. Sententious passages, in quotation marks in the present edition, were set off originally in italics or in quotation marks; and all prose passages were printed as irregular verse. A number of the stage directions introduced into the present text first appeared in the edition of 1708. Commendatory verses by Middleton, Rowley, and Ford have been omitted. The play has been dated 1613–1614, possibly revised in the period 1617–1623.

SELECTED BIBLIOGRAPHY

Complete Works, ed. F. L. Lucas. 4 vols. London: Chatto and Windus, 1927.

The Duchess of Malfi, ed. E. M. Brennan. New York: Hill and Wang, 1966. (The New Mermaids.)

The Duchess of Malfi, ed. J. R. Brown. London: Methuen; Cambridge, Mass.: Harvard University Press, 1964. (The Revels Plays.)

The Duchess of Malfi, ed. F. L. Lucas. London: Chatto and Windus, 1958. (Revision of 1927 edition.)

Allison, A. W. "Ethical Themes in *The Duchess of Malfi,*" *Studies in English Literature,* IV (1964), 263–273.

Bogard, T. *The Tragic Satire of John Webster.* Berkeley and Los Angeles: University of California Press, 1955.

Boklund, G. *"The Duchess of Malfi": Sources, Themes, Characters.* Cambridge, Mass.: Harvard University Press, 1962.

Brooke, R. *John Webster and the Elizabethan Drama.* London: Sidgwick and Jackson, 1916.

Calderwood, J. L. "The Structure of *The Duchess of Malfi:* An Approach," *English,* XII (1958), 89–93.

Dent, R. W. *John Webster's Borrowing.* Berkeley and Los Angeles: University of California Press, 1960.

Driscoll, J. P. "Integrity of Life in *The Duchess of Malfi,*" *Drama Survey,* VI (1967), 42–53.

Ekeblad, I-S. "The 'Impure Art' of John Webster," *Review of English Studies,* new series IX (1958), 253–267.

Emslie, M. "Motives in *Malfi,*" *Essays in Criticism,* IX (1959), 391–405.

Fieler, F. B. "The Eight Madmen in *The Duchess of Malfi,*" *Studies in English Literature,* VII (1967), 343–350.

Leech, C. *John Webster: A Critical Study.* London: Hogarth, 1951.
———. *Webster: "The Duchess of Malfi."* Studies in English Literature 8. London: Edward Arnold, 1963.

Moore, D. D. *John Webster and His Critics 1617–1964.* Baton Rouge: Louisiana State University Press, 1966.

Price, H. T. "The Function of Imagery in Webster," *Publications of the Modern Language Association of America,* LXX (1955), 717–739.

To the Right Honorable George Harding, Baron Berkeley of Berkeley Castle, and Knight of the Order of the Bath to the Illustrious Prince Charles.

My Noble Lord,

That I may present my excuse why, being a stranger to your lordship, I offer this poem to your patronage, I plead this warrant: men who never saw the sea, yet desire to behold that regiment of waters, choose some eminent river to guide them thither and make that, as it were, their conduct or postilion;° by the like ingenious means has your fame arrived at my knowledge, receiving it from some of worth who, both in contemplation and practice, owe to your honor their clearest service. I do not altogether look up at your title, the ancient'st nobility being but a relic of time past, and the truest honor indeed being for a man to confer honor on himself, which your learning strives to propagate and shall make you arrive at the dignity of a great example. I am confident this work is not unworthy your honor's perusal; for by such poems as this poets have kissed the hands of great princes and drawn their gentle eyes to look down upon their sheets of paper when the poets themselves were bound up in their winding sheets. The like courtesy from your lordship shall make you live in your grave and laurel spring out of it when the ignorant scorners of the Muses (that like worms in libraries seem to live only to destroy learning) shall wither, neglected and forgotten. This work and myself I humbly present to your approved censure, it being the utmost of my wishes to have your honorable self my weighty and perspicuous comment: which grace so done me, shall ever be acknowledged

> By your Lordship's
> in all duty and observance,
> *John Webster.*

° conduct or postilion: escort or guide.

THE ACTORS' NAMES

*

BOSOLA [, *gentleman of the horse to the Duchess*], *J. Lowin.*
FERDINAND [, *Duke of Calabria*], 1 *R. Burbage.* 2 *J. Taylor.*
CARDINAL [, *his brother*], 1 *H. Condell.* 2 *R. Robinson.*
ANTONIO [, *steward to the Duchess' household*], 1 *W. Ostler.*
    2 *R. Benfield.*
DELIO [, *his friend*], *J. Underwood.*
FOROBOSCO* [, *an attendant*], *N. Tooley.*
MALATESTE [, *a count*].
THE MARQUIS OF PESCARA, *J. Rice.*
SILVIO [, *a lord*], *T. Pollard.*
[CASTRUCHIO
 RODERIGO   } *lords.*
 GRISOLAN]
The Several Madmen, *N. Tooley, J. Underwood, etc.*
THE DUCHESS, *R. Sharp.*
The Cardinal's Mistress [, *Julia*], *J. Thompson.*
THE DOCTOR }
CARIOLA   } *R. Pallant.*
Court Officers.
[OLD LADY.]
Three young Children.
Two Pilgrims.
[*Ladies-in-Waiting, Servants, Attendants, Guards, Executioners,*
    and Churchmen.]

Forobosco: a "ghost" role.

The Duchess of Malfi

ACTUS PRIMUS

[I.i]

[*Enter* ANTONIO *and*] DELIO.

DELIO. You are welcome to your country, dear Antonio;
    You have been long in France, and you return
    A very formal Frenchman in your habit.*
    How do you like the French court?

ANTONIO.   I admire it.
    In seeking to reduce both state and people
    To a fixed order, their judicious king
    Begins at home: quits first his royal palace
    Of flatt'ring sycophants, of dissolute
    And infamous persons—which he sweetly terms
    His Master's masterpiece, the work of heaven,   10
    Consid'ring duly that a prince's court
    Is like a common fountain, whence should flow
    Pure silver drops in general;* but, if't chance
    Some curs'd example poison't near the head,
    "Death and diseases through the whole land spread."
    And what is't makes this blessèd government
    But a most provident council, who dare freely
    Inform him the corruption of the times?
    Though some o'th' court hold it presumption
    To instruct princes what they ought to do,   20

---

habit: dress.
in general: everywhere, without exception.

It is a noble duty to inform them
What they ought to foresee.—Here comes Bosola,
The only court-gall.

                [*Enter* BOSOLA.]
                    Yet I observe his railing
Is not for simple love of piety;
Indeed, he rails at those things which he wants,
Would be as lecherous, covetous, or proud,
Bloody, or envious as any man
If he had means to be so.—Here's the cardinal.

                [*Enter* CARDINAL.]

BOSOLA. I do haunt you still.

CARDINAL. So.   30

BOSOLA. I have done you better service than to be slighted thus. Miserable age, where only the reward of doing well is the doing of it!

CARDINAL. You enforce your merit too much.

BOSOLA. I fell into the galleys in your service, where, for two years together, I wore two towels instead of a shirt, with a knot on the shoulder, after the fashion of a Roman mantle. Slighted thus! I will thrive some way. Blackbirds fatten best in hard weather; why not I in these dog days?   40

CARDINAL. Would you could become honest!

BOSOLA. With all your divinity, do but direct me the way to it; I have known many travel far for it and yet return as arrant knaves as they went forth because they carried themselves always along with them. [*Exit* CARDINAL.] Are you gone? Some fellows, they say, are possessed with the devil, but this great fellow were able to possess the greatest devil and make him worse.

ANTONIO. He hath denied thee some suit?

BOSOLA. He and his brother are like plum trees that grow   50 crooked over standing* pools; they are rich and o'er-laden with fruit, but none but crows, pies,* and cater-pillars feed on them. Could I be one of their flatt'ring panders, I would hang on their ears like a horseleech till I were full and then drop off. I pray leave me. Who would not rely upon these miserable dependences, in expectation to be advanced tomorrow? What crea-

---

standing: stagnant.   pies: magpies.

ture ever fed worse than hoping Tantalus?* Nor ever
died any man more fearfully than he that hoped for a
pardon. There are rewards for hawks and dogs when   60
they have done us service; but, for a soldier that haz-
ards his limbs in a battle, nothing but a kind of geometry is his last supportation.

DELIO. Geometry?

BOSOLA. Ay, to hang in a fair pair of slings, take his
latter swing in the world upon an honorable pair of
crutches, from hospital to hospital. Fare ye well, sir.
And yet do not you scorn us, for places in the court
are but like beds in the hospital, where this man's
head lies at that man's foot, and so lower and lower.   70

[*Exit.*]

DELIO. I knew this fellow seven years in the galleys
For a notorious murder, and 'twas thought
The cardinal suborned it. He was released
By the French general, Gaston de Fo[i]x,
When he recovered Naples.

ANTONIO.   'Tis a great pity
He should be thus neglected; I have heard
He's very valiant. This foul melancholy
Will poison all his goodness; for (I'll tell you),
If too immoderate sleep be truly said
To be an inward rust unto the soul,   80
It then doth follow want of action
Breeds all black malcontents; and their close rearing,
Like moths in cloth, do hurt for want of wearing.

[I.ii]

[ANTONIO, DELIO, CASTRUCHIO,
SILVIO, RODERIGO, GRISOLAN.]

DELIO. The presence* 'gins to fill. You promised me
To make me the partaker of the natures
Of some of your great courtiers.

ANTONIO.   The lord cardinal's
And other strangers', that are now in court?
I shall.—Here comes the great Calabrian duke.

[*Enter* FERDINAND *and Attendants.*]

---

hoping Tantalus: condemned in Hades to hope eternally for the
water and fruit just beyond his reach.
presence: presence-chamber.

FERDINAND. Who took the ring* oft'nest?

SILVIO. Antonio Bologna, my lord.

FERDINAND. Our sister duchess' great master of her household? Give him the jewel.—When shall we leave this sportive action and fall to action indeed? 10

CASTRUCHIO. Methinks, my lord, you should not desire to go to war in person.

FERDINAND [*aside*]. Now for some gravity!—Why, my lord?

CASTRUCHIO. It is fitting a soldier arise to be a prince, but not necessary a prince descend to be a captain.

FERDINAND. No.

CASTRUCHIO. No, my lord; he were far better do it by a deputy.

FERDINAND. Why should he not as well sleep, or eat, by 20 a deputy? This might take idle, offensive, and base office from him, whereas the other deprives him of honor.

CASTRUCHIO. Believe my experience: that realm is never long in quiet where the ruler is a soldier.

FERDINAND. Thou told'st me thy wife could not endure fighting.

CASTRUCHIO. True, my lord.

FERDINAND. And of a jest she broke of a captain she met full of wounds—I have forgot it.

CASTRUCHIO. She told him, my lord, he was a pitiful 30 fellow to lie, like the children of Ishmael, all in tents.*

FERDINAND. Why, there's a wit were able to undo all the chirurgeons* o'the City; for, although gallants should quarrel, and had drawn their weapons, and were ready to go to it, yet her persuasions would make them put up.

CASTRUCHIO. That she would, my lord.

[FERDINAND.] How do you like my Spanish jennet?

RODERIGO. He is all fire.

FERDINAND. I am of Pliny's* opinion; I think he was be- 40 got by the wind; he runs as if he were ballassed* with quicksilver.

---

took the ring: tilting at the ring or target.
tents: rolls of linen for dressing or searching wounds (with pun).
chirurgeons: surgeons.
Pliny: Roman author of a *Natural History*.
ballassed: ballasted.

SILVIO. True, my lord, he reels from the tilt often.

RODERIGO. ⎫
GRISOLAN. ⎬   Ha, ha, ha!

FERDINAND. Why do you laugh? Methinks you that are
courtiers should be my touchwood—take fire when I
give fire; that is, laugh when I laugh, were the subject
never so witty.

CASTRUCHIO. True, my lord; I myself have heard a very
good jest and have scorned to seem to have so silly a   50
wit as to understand it.

FERDINAND. But I can laugh at your fool, my lord.

CASTRUCHIO. He cannot speak, you know; but he makes
faces. My lady cannot abide him.

FERDINAND. No?

CASTRUCHIO. Nor endure to be in merry company; for she
says too much laughing, and too much company, fills
her too full of the wrinkle.

FERDINAND. I would then have a mathematical instrument made for her face, that she might not laugh out   60
of compass.—I shall shortly visit you at Milan, Lord
Silvio.

SILVIO. Your grace shall arrive most welcome.

FERDINAND. You are a good horseman, Antonio; you have
excellent riders in France. What do you think of good
horsemanship?

ANTONIO. Nobly, my lord. As out of the Grecian horse*
issued many famous princes, so out of brave horsemanship arise the first sparks of growing resolution that
raise the mind to noble action.   70

FERDINAND. You have bespoke it worthily.

SILVIO. Your brother, the lord cardinal, and sister
duchess.

[*Enter* CARDINAL, DUCHESS, CARIOLA, *and* JULIA.]

CARDINAL. Are the galleys come about?

GRISOLAN.   They are, my
lord.

FERDINAND. Here's the Lord Silvio, is come to take his
leave.

DELIO [*aside to* ANTONIO]. Now,   sir,   your   promise:
what's that cardinal?

Grecian horse: the wooden horse in which the Greek soldiers
concealed themselves as a ruse to gain entry into Troy.

I mean his temper? They say he's a brave fellow,
Will play his five thousand crowns at tennis, dance,
Court ladies, and one that hath fought single combats.

ANTONIO. Some such flashes superficially hang on him for   80
form, but observe his inward character: He is a melancholy churchman; the spring in his face is nothing but
the engend'ring of toads; where he is jealous* of any
man, he lays worse plots for them than ever was imposed on Hercules, for he strews in his way flatter[er]s, intelligencers,* atheists, and a thousand such
political monsters. He should have been Pope; but,
instead of coming to it by the primitive decency of
the church, he did bestow bribes so largely, and so
impudently, as if he would have carried it away with-   90
out heaven's knowledge. Some good he hath done.

DELIO. You have given too much of him; what's his
brother?

ANTONIO. The duke there? A most perverse and turbu-
lent nature.
What appears in him mirth is merely outside;
If he laugh heartily, it is to laugh
All honesty out of fashion.

DELIO.   Twins?

ANTONIO.   In quality:
He speaks with others' tongues and hears men's suits
With others' ears; will seem to sleep o'th' bench
Only to entrap offenders in their answers;
Dooms men to death by information,*   100
Rewards by hearsay.

DELIO.   Then the law to him
Is like a foul black cobweb to a spider—
He makes it his dwelling and a prison
To entangle those shall feed him.

ANTONIO.   Most true:
He ne'er pays debts unless they be [shrewd]* turns,
And those he will confess that he doth owe.
Last: for his brother there, the cardinal,
They that do flatter him most say oracles
Hang at his lips; and verily I believe them,
For the devil speaks in them.   110

---

jealous: suspicious.   intelligencers: spies.
information: evidence of informers.   shrewd: ill; injurious.

But for their sister, the right noble duchess,
You never fixed your eye on three fair medals,
Cast in one figure, of so different temper.
For her discourse, it is so full of rapture
You only will begin then to be sorry
When she doth end her speech, and wish, in wonder,
She held it less vainglory to talk much
Than your penance to hear her. Whilst she speaks,
She throws upon a man so sweet a look
That it were able raise one to a galliard*   120
That lay in a dead palsy, and to dote
On that sweet countenance; but in that look
There speaketh so divine a continence
As cuts off all lascivious and vain hope.
Her days are practiced in such noble virtue
That sure her nights (nay, more, her very sleeps)
Are more in heaven than other ladies' shrifts.
Let all sweet ladies break their flatt'ring glasses,
And dress themselves in her.

DELIO.   Fie, Antonio,
You play the wire-drawer with her commendations.*   130
ANTONIO. I'll case* the picture up only thus much—
All her particular worth grows to this sum:
She stains the time past, lights the time to come.
CARIOLA. You must attend my lady in the gallery
Some half an hour hence.
ANTONIO. I shall.

                                [*Exeunt* ANTONIO *and* DELIO.]
FERDINAND. Sister, I have a suit to you.
DUCHESS.   To me, sir?
FERDINAND. A gentleman here, Daniel de Bosola,
One that was in the galleys—
DUCHESS.   Yes, I know him.
FERDINAND. A worthy fellow h'is; pray let me entreat for   140
The provisorship of your horse.
DUCHESS.   Your knowledge of
    him
Commends him and prefers him.
FERDINAND.   Call him hither.
                                        [*Exit Attendant.*]

_____

galliard: a lively dance.
play . . . commendations: spin out her praises.   case: close.

We [are] now upon parting. Good Lord Silvio,
Do us commend to all our noble friends
At the leaguer.*

SILVIO. Sir, I shall.

FERDINAND. You are for Milan?

SILVIO. I am.

DUCHESS. Bring the caroches.—We'll bring you down to
the haven.

[*Exeunt all except* CARDINAL *and* FERDINAND.]

CARDINAL. Be sure you entertain that Bosola
For your intelligence: I would not be seen in't;
And, therefore, many times I have slighted him   150
When he did court our furtherance, as this morning.

FERDINAND. Antonio, the great master of her household,
Had been far fitter.

CARDINAL. You are deceived in him.
His nature is too honest for such business.—
He comes; I'll leave you.

[*Exit.*]

[*Enter* BOSOLA.]

BOSOLA. I was lured to you.

FERDINAND. My brother here, the cardinal, could never
Abide you.

BOSOLA. Never since he was in my debt.

FERDINAND. May be some oblique character in your face
Made him suspect you!

BOSOLA. Doth he study physiognomy?
There's no more credit to be given to th' face   160
Than to a sick man's urine, which some call
The physician's whore because she cozens* him.
He did suspect me wrongfully.

FERDINAND. For that
You must give great men leave to take their times.
Distrust doth cause us seldom be deceived.
You see, the oft shaking of the cedar tree
Fastens it more at root.

BOSOLA. Yet take heed:
For to suspect a friend unworthily
Instructs him the next way to suspect you
And prompts him to deceive you.

FERDINAND. There's gold.

---

leaguer: military camp.   cozens: cheats.

BOSOLA.   So! 170
    What follows? Never rained such show'rs as these
    Without thunderbolts i'th' tail of them.
    Whose throat must I cut?

FERDINAND. Your inclination to shed blood rides post*
    Before my occasion to use you: I give you that
    To live i'th' court here and observe the duchess,
    To note all the particulars of her 'havior,
    What suitors do solicit her for marriage,
    And whom she best affects.* She's a young widow;
    I would not have her marry again.

BOSOLA.   No, sir?   180

FERDINAND. Do not you ask the reason but be satisfied:
    I say I would not.

BOSOLA.   It seems you would create me
    One of your familiars.*

FERDINAND.   Familiar! What's that?

BOSOLA. Why, a very quaint* invisible devil in flesh—
    An intelligencer.

FERDINAND.   Such a kind of thriving thing
    I would wish thee, and ere long thou mayst arrive
    At a higher place by't.

BOSOLA.   Take your devils,
    Which hell calls angels! * These curs'd gifts would
        make
    You a corrupter, me an impudent traitor;
    And, should I take these, they'ld take me [to] hell.   190

FERDINAND. Sir, I'll take nothing from you that I have
        given.
    There is a place that I procured for you
    This morning—the provisorship o'th' horse.
    Have you heard on't?

BOSOLA.   No.

FERDINAND.   'Tis yours; is't not worth
        thanks?

BOSOLA. I would have you curse yourself now, that your
        bounty
    (Which makes men truly noble) e'er should make

---

    post: in haste.   affects: admires, likes; loves.
    familiars: 1) evil spirits; 2) intimate friends.   quaint: cunning.
    angels: gold coins (often used punningly).

Me a villain. O, that to avoid ingratitude
For the good deed you have done me, I must do
All the ill man can invent! Thus the devil
Candies all sins o'er; and what heaven terms vile,   200
That names he complimental.

FERDINAND.   Be yourself:
Keep your old garb of melancholy; 'twill express
You envy those that stand above your reach,
Yet strive not to come near 'em. This will gain
Access to private lodgings, where yourself
May, like a politic dormouse—

BOSOLA.   As I have seen some
Feed in a lord's dish, half asleep, not seeming
To listen to any talk; and yet these rogues
Have cut his throat in a dream. What's my place?
The provisorship o'th' horse? Say, then, my corruption   210
Grew out of horse dung: I am your creature.

FERDINAND.   Away!

BOSOLA. Let good men, for good deeds, covet good fame
Since place and riches oft are bribes of shame.
Sometimes the devil doth preach.

                                              (*Exit* BOSOLA.)

            [*Enter* CARDINAL, DUCHESS, *and* CARIOLA.]

CARDINAL. We are to part from you, and your own
            discretion
Must now be your director.

FERDINAND.   You are a widow:
You know already what man is; and, therefore,
Let not youth, high promotion, eloquence—

CARDINAL. No, nor anything without the addition, honor,
Sway your high blood.

FERDINAND.   Marry! They are most luxu-
            rious*   220
Will wed twice.

CARDINAL.   O, fie!

FERDINAND.   Their livers* are more
            spotted
Than Laban's sheep.*

DUCHESS.   Diamonds are of most value,

---

luxurious: lecherous.   livers: regarded as the seat of love.
Laban's sheep: *Genesis*, xxx, 31–43.

They say, that have past through most jewelers' hands.

FERDINAND. Whores, by that rule, are precious.

DUCHESS.   Will
    you hear me?
I'll never marry.

CARDINAL.   So most widows say;
But commonly that motion lasts no longer
Than the turning of an hourglass—the funeral sermon
And it end both together.

FERDINAND.   Now hear me:
You live in a rank pasture here, i'th' court—
There is a kind of honeydew that's deadly: 230
'Twill poison your fame; look to't. Be not cunning,
For they whose faces do belie their hearts
Are witches ere they arrive at twenty years—
Ay, and give the devil suck.

DUCHESS. This is terrible good counsel!

FERDINAND. Hypocrisy is woven of a fine small thread,
Subtler than Vulcan's engine;° yet, believe't,
Your darkest actions—nay, your privat'st thoughts—
Will come to light.

CARDINAL.   You may flatter yourself
And take your own choice: privately be married   240
Under the eaves of night—

FERDINAND.   Think't the best voyage
That e'er you made, like the irregular crab,
Which, though't goes backward, thinks that it goes
    right
Because it goes its own way; but observe,
Such weddings may more properly be said
To be executed than celebrated.

CARDINAL.   The marriage night
Is the entrance into some prison.

FERDINAND.   And those joys,
Those lustful pleasures, are like heavy sleeps
Which do forerun man's mischief.

CARDINAL.   Fare you well.
Wisdom begins at the end: remember it.   250
                                       [*Exit.*]

Vulcan's engine: a net also "woven of a fine small thread" that
Vulcan used to catch Mars and Venus in the act of adultery.

DUCHESS. I think this speech between you both was studied,
It came so roundly off.
FERDINAND.   You are my sister.
This was my father's poniard, do you see?
I'ld be loath to see't look rusty 'cause 'twas his.
I would have you to give o'er these chargeable° revels;
A visor and a mask are whispering rooms
That were nev'r built for goodness—fare ye well—
And women like that part which, like the lamprey,
Hath nev'r a bone in 't.
DUCHESS.   Fie, sir!
FERDINAND.   Nay,
I mean the tongue—variety of courtship.   260
What cannot a neat knave with a smooth tale
Make a woman believe? Farewell, lusty widow.

                                              [*Exit.*]

DUCHESS. Shall this move me? If all my royal kindred
Lay in my way unto this marriage,
I'ld make them my low footsteps. And even now,
Even in this hate, as men in some great battles,
By apprehending danger, have achieved
Almost impossible actions (I have heard soldiers say
    so),
So I, through frights and threat'nings, will assay
This dangerous venture. Let old wives report   270
I winked° and chose a husband.—Cariola,
To thy known secrecy I have given up
More than my life—my fame.
CARIOLA.   Both shall be safe,
For I'll conceal this secret from the world
As warily as those that trade in poison
Keep poison from their children.
DUCHESS.   Thy protestation
Is ingenious° and hearty;° I believe it.
Is Antonio come?
CARIOLA.   He attends you.
DUCHESS.   Good dear soul,

---

chargeable: costly.   winked: closed eyes tight.
ingenious: intelligent and also ingenuous or sincere.
hearty: from the heart.

Leave me; but place thyself behind the arras,
Where thou mayst overhear us. Wish me good speed,   280
For I am going into a wilderness
Where I shall find nor path nor friendly clew
To be my guide.
[CARIOLA *hides behind the arras.*]
                    [*Enter* ANTONIO.]
                    —I sent for you; sit down.
Take pen and ink, and write. Are you ready?
ANTONIO. Yes.
DUCHESS. What did I say?
ANTONIO. That I should write somewhat.
DUCHESS.   O, I remem-
    ber:
After [these] triumphs* and this large expense,
It's fit (like thrifty husbands)* we inquire
What's laid up for tomorrow.   290
ANTONIO. So please your beauteous excellence.
DUCHESS.   Beau-
    teous?
Indeed, I thank you: I look young for your sake.
You have ta'en my cares upon you.
ANTONIO.   I'll fetch your
    grace
The particulars of your revenue and expense.
DUCHESS. O, you are an upright treasurer, but you mis-
    took;
For when I said I meant to make inquiry
What's laid up for tomorrow, I did mean
What's laid up yonder for me.
ANTONIO.   Where?
DUCHESS.   In heaven.
I am making my will (as 'tis fit princes should,
In perfect memory); and I pray, sir, tell me   300
Were not one better make it smiling, thus,
Than in deep groans and terrible ghastly looks,
As if the gifts we parted with procured
That violent distr[a]ction?
ANTONIO.   O, much better.
DUCHESS. If I had a husband now, this care were quit.

---

triumphs: festivities.   husbands: housekeepers.

But I intend to make you overseer;°
What good deed shall we first remember? Say.

ANTONIO. Begin with that first good deed began i'th'
world
After a man's creation, the sacrament of marriage.
I'ld have you first provide for a good husband;   310
Give him all.

DUCHESS.   All?

ANTONIO.   Yes, your excellent self.

DUCHESS. In a winding sheet?

ANTONIO.   In a couple.°

DUCHESS. Saint Winfred,° that were a strange will!

ANTONIO.   'Twere strange
If there were no will in you to marry again.

DUCHESS. What do you think of marriage?

ANTONIO. I take't as those that deny purgatory—
It locally contains or° heaven or hell;
There's no third place in't.

DUCHESS.   How do you affect° it?

ANTONIO. My banishment, feeding my melancholy,
Would often reason thus—

DUCHESS.   Pray let's hear it.   320

ANTONIO. Say a man never marry, nor have children,
What takes that from him? Only the bare name
Of being a father, or the weak delight
To see the little wanton ride a cockhorse
Upon a painted stick or hear him chatter
Like a taught starling.

DUCHESS.   Fie, fie, what's all this?
One of your eyes is bloodshot. Use my ring to't;
They say 'tis very sovereign. 'Twas my wedding ring,
And I did vow never to part with it,
But to my second husband.   330

ANTONIO. You have parted with it now.

DUCHESS. Yes, to help your eyesight.

ANTONIO. You have made me stark blind.

DUCHESS. How?

---

overseer: executor of a will.
in a couple: pair of sheets (with pun on "to couple" or copulate).
Saint Winfred: 7th-century Welsh virgin saint.   or: either.
affect: fancy.

ANTONIO. There is a saucy and ambitious devil
    Is dancing in this circle.°
DUCHESS.   Remove him.
ANTONIO.   How?
DUCHESS. There needs small conjuration when your
    finger
    May do it—thus.
    [*She puts the ring upon his finger.*]
                        Is it fit?
ANTONIO.   What said you?
(*He kneels.*)
DUCHESS.   Sir,
    This goodly roof of yours is too low built;
    I cannot stand upright in't, nor discourse,   340
    Without I raise it higher. Raise yourself;
    Or, if you please, my hand to help you—so.
    [*She raises him.*]
ANTONIO. Ambition, madam, is a great man's madness,
    That is not kept in chains and close-pent rooms
    But in fair lightsome lodgings, and is girt
    With the wild noise of prattling visitants,
    Which makes it lunatic beyond all cure.
    Conceive not I am so stupid but I aim
    Whereto your favors tend; but he's a fool
    That, being a-cold, would thrust his hands i'th' fire   350
    To warm them.
DUCHESS.   So, now the ground's broke,
    You may discover what a wealthy mine
    I make you lord of.
ANTONIO.   O, my unworthiness!
DUCHESS. You were ill to sell yourself.
    This dark'ning of your worth is not like that
    Which tradesmen use i'th' city; their false lights
    Are to rid bad wares off. And I must tell you,
    If you will know where breathes a complete man
    (I speak it without flattery), turn your eyes
    And progress through yourself.   360
ANTONIO. Were there nor heaven nor hell,
    I should be honest: I have long served virtue
    And nev'r ta'en wages of her.

───────────

    this circle: the ring, but referring to the magic circle or ring in
which magicians raised spirits.

DUCHESS.   Now she pays it!
This misery of us that are born great!
We are forced to woo because none dare woo us.
And as a tyrant doubles with his words,
And fearfully equivocates, so we
Are forced to express our violent passions
In riddles and in dreams, and leave the path
Of simple virtue, which was never made   370
To seem the thing it is not. Go, go brag
You have left me heartless—mine is in your bosom;
I hope 'twill multiply love there. You do tremble:
Make not your heart so dead a piece of flesh
To fear more than to love me. Sir, be confident;
What is't distracts you? This is flesh and blood, sir;
'Tis not the figure cut in alabaster
Kneels at my husband's tomb. Awake, awake, man!
I do here put off all vain ceremony,
And only do appear to you a young widow   380
That claims you for her husband; and, like a widow,
I use but half a blush in't.

ANTONIO.   Truth speak for me:
I will remain the constant sanctuary
Of your good name.

DUCHESS.   I thank you, gentle love,
And 'cause you shall not come to me in debt
(Being now my steward), here upon your lips
I sign your *Quietus est.*°
[*She kisses him.*]

                                    This you should have
        begged now.
I have seen children oft eat sweetmeats thus,
As fearful to devour them too soon.

ANTONIO. But for your brothers?

DUCHESS.   Do not think of them.   390
All discord without this circumference
[*She puts her arms about him.*]
Is only to be pitied and not feared;
Yet, should they know it, time will easily
Scatter the tempest.

ANTONIO.   These words should be mine,

---

quietus est: an accountant's term indicating acquittal of obligation.

And all the parts you have spoke, if some part of it
Would not have savored flattery.

DUCHESS.   Kneel!

[CARIOLA *reveals herself.*]

ANTONIO.   Hah!

DUCHESS. Be not amazed; this woman's of my counsel.
I have heard lawyers say a contract in a chamber
Per verba [*de*] *presenti** is absolute marriage.—
Bless, heaven, this sacred Gordian,* which let violence   400
Never untwine.

ANTONIO. And may our sweet affections (like the
    spheres)
Be still * in motion.

DUCHESS.   Quick'ning, and make
The like soft music!

ANTONIO. That we may imitate the loving palms,
Best emblem of a peaceful marriage,
That nev'r bore fruit divided!

DUCHESS. What can the church force more?

ANTONIO. That Fortune may not know an accident
Either of joy or sorrow to divide   410
Our fixèd wishes!

DUCHESS.   How can the church build faster?*
We now are man and wife, and 'tis the church
That must but echo this.—Maid, stand apart.—
I now am blind.

ANTONIO.   What's your conceit in this?

DUCHESS. I would have you lead your fortune by the hand
Unto your marriage bed.
(You speak in me this, for we now are one.)
We'll only lie and talk together, and plot
T'appease my humorous* kindred; and, if you please,
Like the old tale in *Alexander and Lodowick,**   420
Lay a naked sword between us, keep us chaste.

---

per . . . presenti: making vows or using words in the present
tense (as, "I take thee," etc.).   Gordian: knot.
still: always, forever.   faster: more firmly.
humorous: ill-humored.
Alexander and Lodowick: in this ballad the two friends looked
so alike that when one of them married a princess in the other's
name he "lay a naked sword between" them so as not to wrong his
absent friend.

O, let me shroud my blushes in your bosom
Since 'tis the treasury of all my secrets.

[Exeunt DUCHESS *and* ANTONIO.*]*

CARIOLA. Whether the spirit of greatness or of woman
Reign most in her, I know not; but it shows
A fearful madness. I owe her much of pity.

[Exit.]

ACTUS II

[II.i]

[Enter BOSOLA *and* CASTRUCHIO.*]*

BOSOLA. You say you would fain be taken for an eminent
courtier?*

CASTRUCHIO. 'Tis the very main* of my ambition.

BOSOLA. Let me see; you have a reasonable face for't
already, and your nightcap* expresses your ears sufficient largely. I would have you learn to twirl the
strings of your band with a good grace, and in a set
speech (at th'end of every sentence) to hum three
or four times, or blow your nose till it smart again, to
recover your memory. When you come to be a presi-   10
dent in criminal causes, if you smile upon a prisoner,
hang him; but, if you frown upon him and threaten
him, let him be sure to 'scape the gallows.

CASTRUCHIO. I would be a very merry president.

BOSOLA. Do not sup o' nights; 'twill beget you an admirable wit.

CASTRUCHIO. Rather it would make me have a good
stomach to quarrel, for they say your roaring boys* eat
meat seldom, and that makes them so valiant. But how
shall I know whether the people take me for an emi-   20
nent fellow?

BOSOLA. I will teach a trick to know it: give out you lie
a-dying; and, if you hear the common people curse
you, be sure you are taken for one of the prime night-
caps.—

[Enter an OLD LADY.*]*

You come from painting now?

---

courtier: member of a law court.   main: goal.
nightcap: lawyer's coif.   roaring boys: rowdies.

OLD LADY. From what?

BOSOLA. Why, from your scurvy face-physic. To behold
thee not painted inclines somewhat near a miracle.
These in thy face here were deep ruts and foul sloughs   30
the last progress.° There was a lady in France that,
having had the smallpox, flayed the skin off her face to
make it more level; and, whereas before she looked like
a nutmeg-grater, after she resembled an abortive
hedgehog.

OLD LADY. Do you call this painting?

BOSOLA. No, no, but you call [it] careening° of an old
morphewed ° lady, to make her disembogue° again—
there's rough-cast phrase to your plastic.°

OLD LADY. It seems you are well acquainted with my   40
closet!

BOSOLA. One would suspect it for a shop of witchcraft, to
find in it the fat of serpents, spawn of snakes, Jews'
spittle, and their young children's ordure—and all
these for the face. I would sooner eat a dead pigeon
taken from the soles of the feet of one sick of the
plague than kiss one of you fasting. Here are two of
you whose sin of your youth is the very patrimony of
the physician, makes him renew his footcloth with the
spring and change his high-prized courtesan with the   50
fall of the leaf. I do wonder you do not loathe yourselves. Observe my meditation now:
What thing is in this outward form of man
To be beloved? We account it ominous
If nature do produce a colt, or lamb,
A fawn, or goat, in any limb resembling
A man, and fly from't as a prodigy.
Man stands amazed to see his deformity
In any other creature but himself.
But in our own flesh, though we bear diseases   60
Which have their true names only ta'en from beasts,
As the most ulcerous wolf ° and swinish measle;

---

progress: term for a royal journey.
careening: caulking, cleaning.
morphewed: covered with scabs.   disembogue: put to sea.
plastic: plastic-modeling.
wolf: translation of *lupus,* medicinal term for ulcer.

Though we are eaten up of lice and worms,
And though continually we bear about us
A rotten and dead body, we delight
To hide it in rich tissue: all our fear
(Nay, all our terror) is lest our physician
Should put us in the ground to be made sweet.—
Your wife's gone to Rome; you two couple and get you
To the wells at Lucca to recover your aches.   70
I have other work on foot.

> [*Exeunt* CASTRUCHIO *and* OLD LADY.]
>   I observe our duchess

Is sick o' days; she pukes, her stomach seethes,
The fins of her eyelids look most teeming blue;°
She wanes i'th' cheek, and waxes fat i'th' flank,
And, contrary to our Italian fashion,
Wears a loose-bodied gown—there's somewhat in't!
I have a trick may chance discover it,
A pretty one: I have bought some apricocks,°
The first our spring yields.

> [*Enter* ANTONIO *and* DELIO.]

DELIO [*aside to* ANTONIO]   And so long since married?
You amaze me.

ANTONIO [*aside to* DELIO].   Let me seal your lips forever;   80
For, did I think that anything but th'air
Could carry these words from you, I should wish
You had no breath at all.—[*To* BOSOLA.] Now, sir, in
  your contemplation?
You are studying to become a great wise fellow?

BOSOLA. O, sir, the opinion of wisdom is a foul tetter that
runs all over a man's body. If simplicity direct us to
have no evil, it directs us to a happy being; for the
subtlest folly proceeds from the subtlest wisdom: let
me be simply honest.

ANTONIO. I do understand your inside.

BOSOLA.   Do you so?   90

ANTONIO. Because you would not seem to appear to
th' world puffed up with your preferment, you continue this out-of-fashion melancholy. Leave it, leave it!

BOSOLA. Give me leave to be honest in any phrase, in any

---

teeming blue: the color of a pregnant woman's eyes.
apricocks: Elizabethan spelling of "apricots."

compliment whatsoever. Shall I confess myself to you?
I look no higher than I can reach. They are the gods
that must ride on winged horses; a lawyer's mule of a
slow pace will both suit my disposition and business;
for, mark me, when a man's mind rides faster than his
horse can gallop, they quickly both tire.   100

ANTONIO. You would look up to heaven; but I think
The devil, that rules i'th' air, stands in your light.

BOSOLA. O, sir, you are lord of the ascendant,* chief man
with the duchess; a duke was your cousin-german* removed. Say you were lineally descended from King
Pepin,* or he himself, what of this? Search the heads
of the greatest rivers in the world, you shall find them
but bubbles of water. Some would think the souls of
princes were brought forth by some more weighty
cause than those of meaner persons. They are de-   110
ceived; there's the same hand to them: the like passions sway them; the same reason that makes a vicar
go to law for a tithe-pig and undo his neighbors makes
them spoil a whole province and batter down goodly
cities with the cannon.

[*Enter* DUCHESS *and Ladies.*]

DUCHESS. Your arm, Antonio. Do I not grow fat?
I am exceeding short-winded.—Bosola,
I would have you, sir, provide for me a litter,
Such a one as the Duchess of Florence rode in.

BOSOLA. The duchess used one when she was great with
      child.   120

DUCHESS. I think she did.—Come hither; mend my ruff.
Here, when? Thou art such a tedious lady, and
Thy breath smells of lemon p[ee]ls. Would thou hadst
      done!
Shall I sound * under thy fingers? I am
So troubled with the mother.*

BOSOLA [*aside*].   I fear too much.

DUCHESS. I have heard you say that the French courtiers
Wear their hats on 'fore the king.

ANTONIO. I have seen it.

---

lord of the ascendant: astrologically favored.
cousin-german: first cousin.
King Pepin: king of the Franks in the 8th century.
sound: swoon.   mother: hysteria (with pun intended).

DUCHESS.   In the presence?
ANTONIO.   Yes.
[DUCHESS.] Why should not we bring up that
    fashion?
'Tis ceremony more than duty that consists   130
In the removing of a piece of felt.
Be you the example to the rest o'th' court;
Put on your hat first.
ANTONIO.   You must pardon me.
I have seen, in colder countries than in France,
Nobles stand bare to th' prince; and the distinction
Methought showed reverently.
BOSOLA. I have a present for your grace.
DUCHESS.   For me, sir?
BOSOLA. Apricocks, madam.
DUCHESS.   O, sir, where are they?
I have heard of none to-year.*
BOSOLA [*aside*].   Good; her color rises.
DUCHESS. Indeed, I thank you; they are wondrous fair
    ones.   140
What an unskillful fellow is our gardener!
We shall have none this month.
BOSOLA. Will not your grace pare them?
DUCHESS. No, they taste of musk, methinks; indeed, they
    do.
BOSOLA. I know not; yet I wish your grace had pared 'em.
DUCHESS. Why?
BOSOLA.   I forgot to tell you, the knave gardener,
Only to raise his profit by them the sooner,
Did ripen them in horse dung.
DUCHESS.   O, you jest!
You shall judge; pray taste one.
ANTONIO.   Indeed, madam,
I do not love the fruit.
DUCHESS.   Sir, you are loath   150
To rob us of our dainties. 'Tis a delicate fruit;
They say they are restorative.
BOSOLA.   'Tis a pretty art,
This grafting.
DUCHESS.   'Tis so; a bett'ring of nature.
BOSOLA. To make a pippin grow upon a crab,

---

to-year: this year.

A damson on a blackthorn.—[*Aside*.] How greedily
   she eats them!
A whirlwind strike off these bawd farthingales!
For, but for that and the loose-bodied gown,
I should have discovered apparently°
The young springal ° cutting a caper in her belly.

DUCHESS. I thank you, Bosola; they were right good
   ones—   160
   If they do not make me sick.

ANTONIO.   How now, madam?

DUCHESS. This green fruit and my stomach are not
   friends.
   How they swell me!

BOSOLA [*aside*].   Nay, you are too much swelled
   already.

DUCHESS. O, I am in an extreme cold sweat!

BOSOLA. I am very sorry.

                                              [*Exit*.]

DUCHESS. Lights to my chamber! O, good Antonio,
   I fear I am undone!

                           Exit DUCHESS [*with Ladies*].

DELIO.   Lights there, lights!

ANTONIO. O my most trusty Delio, we are lost!
   I fear she's fall'n in labor, and there's left
   No time for her remove.

DELIO.   Have you prepared   170
   Those ladies to attend her? And procured
   That politic safe conveyance for the midwife
   Your duchess plotted?

ANTONIO. I have.

DELIO. Make use, then, of this forced occasion:
   Give out that Bosola hath poisoned her
   With these apricocks; that will give some color°
   For her keeping close.

ANTONIO.   Fie, fie, the physicians
   Will then flock to her.

DELIO.   For that you may pretend
   She'll use some prepared antidote of her own,   180
   Lest the physicians should repoison her.

---

apparently: obviously; clearly.   springal: stripling.
color: pretense, pretext.

ANTONIO. I am lost in amazement: I know not what to
think on't.

Exeunt.

[II.ii]

[*Enter* BOSOLA.]

BOSOLA. So, so, there's no question but her tetchiness and
most vulturous eating of the apricocks are apparent
signs of breeding.—

[*Enter* OLD LADY.]

Now?

OLD LADY. I am in haste, sir.

BOSOLA. There was a young waiting-woman had a monstrous desire to see the glass-house*—

OLD LADY. Nay, pray let me go.

BOSOLA. And it was only to know what strange instrument it was should swell up a glass to the fashion of a   10
woman's belly.

OLD LADY. I will hear no more of the glass-house; you are
still abusing women!

BOSOLA. Who? I? No, only, by the way now and then,
mention your frailties. The orange tree bear[s] ripe
and green fruit and blossoms all together: and some
of you give entertainment for pure love, but more for
more precious reward. The lusty spring smells well,
but dropping autumn tastes well. If we have the same
golden showers that rained in the time of Jupiter the   20
Thunderer, you have the same Dan[ä]es* still, to hold
up their laps to receive them. Didst thou never study
the mathematics?

OLD LADY. What's that, sir?

BOSOLA. Why, to know the trick how to make a many
lines meet in one center. Go, go, give your foster-
daughters good counsel: tell them that the devil takes
delight to hang at a woman's girdle, like a false rusty
watch, that she cannot discern how the time passes.

[*Exit* OLD LADY.]

[*Enter* ANTONIO, DELIO, RODERIGO, *and* GRISOLAN.]

---

glass-house: glass factory.
Jupiter . . . Danäes: Jupiter, disguised as a shower of gold,
courted Danäe.

ANTONIO. Shut up the court gates!

RODERIGO.   Why, sir? What's
   the danger?   30

ANTONIO.. Shut up the posterns presently* and call
   All the officers o'th' court.

GRISOLAN.   I shall instantly.

                                        [Exit.]

ANTONIO. Who keeps the key o'th' park gate?

RODERIGO.   Forobosco.

ANTONIO. Let him bring't presently.

         [Re-enter GRISOLAN with Servants.*]

[1] SERVANT. O, gentlemen o'th' court, the foulest treason!

BOSOLA [aside]. If that these apricocks should be poisoned now,
   Without my knowledge!

[1] SERVANT. There was taken even now a Switzer* in
   the duchess' bedchamber.

2 SERVANT. A Switzer?   40

[1] SERVANT. With a pistol in his great codpiece.

BOSOLA. Ha, ha, ha!

[1] SERVANT. The codpiece was the case for't.

2 SERVANT. There was a cunning traitor. Who would
   have searched his codpiece?

[1] SERVANT. True, if he had kept out of the ladies'
   chambers. And all the molds of his buttons were leaden
   bullets.

2 SERVANT. O, wicked cannibal! A firelock in's codpiece!

[1] SERVANT. 'Twas a French plot, upon my life.   50

2 SERVANT. To see what the devil can do!

ANTONIO. All the officers here?

[1] SERVANT. We are.

ANTONIO. Gentlemen,
   We have lost much plate, you know; and but this
     evening
   Jewels, to the value of four thousand ducats,
   Are missing in the duchess' cabinet.
   Are the gates shut?

[1] SERVANT.   Yes.

---

presently: at once, immediately.
servants: officers.
Switzer: a hired Swiss soldier.

ANTONIO.   'Tis the duchess' pleasure
  Each officer be locked into his chamber
  Till the sun-rising, and to send the keys   60
  Of all their chests and of their outward doors
  Into her bedchamber. She is very sick.

RODERIGO. At her pleasure.

ANTONIO. She entreats you take't not ill: the innocent
  Shall be the more approved by it.

BOSOLA. Gentleman o'th' woodyard, where's your Switzer
  now?

[1] SERVANT. By this hand, 'twas credibly reported by
  one o'th' black-guard.*

                      [*Exeunt all except* ANTONIO *and* DELIO.]

DELIO. How fares it with the duchess?

ANTONIO.   She's exposed   70
  Unto the worst of torture, pain, and fear.

DELIO. Speak to her all happy comfort.

ANTONIO. How I do play the fool with mine own danger!
  You are this night, dear friend, to post to Rome;
  My life lies in your service.

DELIO.   Do not doubt me.

ANTONIO. O, 'tis far from me; and yet fear presents me
  Somewhat that looks like danger.

DELIO.   Believe it,
  'Tis but the shadow of your fear, no more:
  How superstitiously we mind our evils!
  The throwing down salt, or crossing of a hare,   80
  Bleeding at nose, the stumbling of a horse,
  Or singing of a cricket are of pow'r
  To daunt whole man in us. Sir, fare you well;
  I wish you all the joys of a blessed father;
  And, for my faith, lay this unto your breast—
  Old friends, like old swords, still are trusted best.

                            [*Exit.*]

              [*Enter* CARIOLA.]

CARIOLA. Sir, you are the happy father of a son;
  Your wife commends him to you.

ANTONIO.   Blessèd comfort!—
  For heaven-sake tend her well; I'll presently
  Go set a figure for's nativity.*

                          [*Exeunt.*]

---

black-guard: scullion; kitchen-hand.   nativity: horoscope.

[II.iii]

           [*Enter* BOSOLA, *with a dark lantern.*]

BOSOLA. Sure I did hear a woman shriek. List, hah!
  And the sound came (if I received it right)
  From the duchess' lodgings: there's some stratagem
  In the confining all our courtiers
  To their several wards. I must have part of it;
  My intelligence will freeze else.—List, again!
  It may be 'twas the melancholy bird
  (Best friend of silence and of solitariness),
  The owl, that screamed so.—Hah! Antonio?

       [*Enter* ANTONIO *with a candle, his sword drawn.*]

ANTONIO. I heard some noise.—Who's there? What art
  thou? Speak.   10

BOSOLA. Antonio? Put not your face nor body
  To such a forced expression of fear—
  I am Bosola, your friend.

ANTONIO.   Bosola!—
  [*Aside.*] This mole does undermine me.—Heard you
    not
  A noise even now?

BOSOLA.   From whence?

ANTONIO.   From the
  duchess' lodging.

BOSOLA. Not I; did you?

ANTONIO.   I did, or else I dreamed.

BOSOLA. Let's walk towards it.

ANTONIO.   No; it may be 'twas
  But the rising of the wind.

BOSOLA.   Very likely.
  Methinks 'tis very cold, and yet you sweat:
  You look wildly.

ANTONIO.   I have been setting a figure   20
  For the duchess' jewels.

BOSOLA.   Ah, and how falls your question?
  Do you find it radical?°

ANTONIO.   What's that to you?
  'Tis rather to be questioned what design,

---

  radical: fit to be decided (astrological term).

When all men were commanded to their lodgings,
Makes you a night-walker.

BOSOLA.   In sooth, I'll tell you:
Now all the court's asleep, I thought the devil
Had least to do here. I came to say my prayers;
And, if it do offend you I do so,
You are a fine courtier.

ANTONIO [*aside*].   This fellow will undo me.—
You gave the duchess apricocks today;   30
Pray heaven they were not poisoned!

BOSOLA.   Poisoned? A
    Spanish fig
For the imputation!

ANTONIO.   Traitors are ever confident
Till they are discovered. There were jewels stol'n too—
In my conceit, none are to be suspected
More than yourself.

BOSOLA.   You are a false steward.

ANTONIO. Saucy slave! I'll pull thee up by the roots.

BOSOLA. May be the ruin will crush you to pieces.

ANTONIO. You are an impudent snake indeed, sir.
Are you scarce warm, and do you show your sting?

. . .*

ANTONIO. You libel * well, sir.

BOSOLA.   No, sir; copy it out,   40
And I will set my hand to't.

ANTONIO [*aside, and accidently dropping a paper as he
takes out his handkerchief*].
               My nose bleeds:
One that were superstitious would count
This ominous when it merely comes by chance.
Two letters, that are wrought here for my name,
Are drowned in blood!
Mere accident!—For you, sir, I'll take order:
I'th' morn you shall be safe.—[*Aside.*] 'Tis that must
    color
Her lying-in.—Sir, this door you pass not;
I do not hold it fit that you come near
The duchess' lodgings till you have [quit] * yourself.—   50

---

ellipses: there may be a speech by Bosola missing here.
libel: draw up charges (with pun?).   quit: acquitted.

[*Aside.*] "The great are like the base, nay, they are
   the same,
When they seek shameful ways to avoid shame."

                                                        [*Exit.*]

BOSOLA. Antonio hereabout did drop a paper.
   Some of your help, false friend.*—O, here it is.
   What's here? A child's nativity calculated!
   [*He reads*]
      *The duchess was delivered of a son, 'tween the hours
      twelve and one in the night: Anno Dom. 1504—*
      that's this year—*decimo nono Decembris*—that's
      this night—*taken according to the meridian of
      Malfi*—that's our duchess. Happy discovery!—*The   60
      lord of the first house, being combust in the ascen-
      dant, signifies short life; and Mars being in a human
      sign, joined to the tail of the Dragon, in the eight[h]
      house, doth threaten a violent death; cætera non
      scrutantur.*
   Why, now 'tis most apparent: this precise* fellow
   Is the duchess' bawd—I have it to my wish!
   This is a parcel of intelligency
   Our courtiers were cased up for! It needs must follow
   That I must be committed on pretence   70
   Of poisoning her, which I'll endure and laugh at.
   If one could find the father now! But that
   Time will discover. Old Castruchio
   I'th'morning posts to Rome; by him I'll send
   A letter that shall make her brothers' galls
   O'erflow their livers. This was a thrifty way!
   "Though lust do mask in nev'r so strange disguise,
   She's oft found witty but is never wise."

                                                        [*Exit.*]

[II.iv]
                     [*Enter* CARDINAL *and* JULIA.]
CARDINAL. Sit; thou art my best of wishes. Prithee, tell
   me

-----

false friend: the dark lantern.
decimo nono Decembris: December 19th.
cætera non scrutantur: other things are not investigated.
precise: puritanical.

What trick didst thou invent to come to Rome
Without thy husband?
JULIA.   Why, my lord, I told him
I came to visit an old anchorite
Here, for devotion.
CARDINAL.   Thou art a witty false one—
I mean, to him.
JULIA.   You have prevailed with me
Beyond my strongest thoughts: I would not now
Find you inconstant.
CARDINAL.   Do not put thyself
To such a voluntary torture, which proceeds
Out of your own guilt.
JULIA.   How, my lord?
CARDINAL.   You fear   10
My constancy because you have approved
Those giddy and wild turning[s] in yourself.
JULIA. Did you e'er find them?
CARDINAL.   Sooth, generally for
      women;
A man might strive to make glass malleable
Ere he should make them fix'd.
JULIA.   So, my lord!
CARDINAL. We had need go borrow that fantastic glass
Invented by Galileo the Florentine
To view another spacious world i'th' moon
And look to find a constant woman there.
JULIA [*weeping*]. This is very well, my lord.
CARDINAL.   Why do   20
      you weep?
Are tears your justification? The selfsame tears
Will fall into your husband's bosom, lady,
With a loud protestation that you love him
Above the world. Come, I'll love you wisely,
That's jealously,* since I am very certain
You cannot me make a cuckold.
JULIA.   I'll go home
To my husband.
CARDINAL.   You may thank me, lady,
I have taken you off your melancholy perch,

---

jealously: ardently.

Bore you upon my fist, and showed you game,
And let you fly at it. I pray thee, kiss me.   30
When thou wast with thy husband, thou wast watched
Like a tame elephant—still you are to thank me;
Thou hadst only kisses from him and high feeding;
But what delight was that? 'Twas just like one
That hath a little fing'ring on the lute,
Yet cannot tune it—still you are to thank me.
JULIA. You told me of a piteous wound i'th' heart
And a sick liver when you wooed me first,
And spake like one in physic.*
CARDINAL.   Who's that?—
                    [*Enter* SERVANT.]
Rest firm; for my affection to thee,   40
Lightning moves slow to't.
SERVANT.   Madam, a gentleman
That's come post from Malfi desires to see you.
CARDINAL. Let him enter; I'll withdraw.
                                                            [*Exit.*]
SERVANT.   He says
Your husband, old Castruchio, is come to Rome,
Most pitifully tired with riding post.
                                                            [*Exit.*]
                    [*Enter* DELIO.]
JULIA. Signor Delio!—[*Aside.*] 'Tis one of my old suitors.
DELIO. I was bold to come and see you.
JULIA.   Sir, you are
  welcome.
DELIO. Do you lie here?
JULIA.   Sure, your own experience
Will satisfy you no—our Roman prelates
Do not keep lodging for ladies.
DELIO.   Very well.   50
I have brought you no commendations from your hus-
  band,
For I know none by him.
JULIA.   I hear he's come to Rome!
DELIO. I never knew man and beast, of a horse and a
  knight,
So weary of each other; if he had a good back,

_____

in physic: undergoing treatment for illness.

He would have undertook to have borne his horse,
His breach was so pitifully sore.

JULIA.   Your laughter
Is my pity.

DELIO.   Lady, I know not whether
You want money, but I have brought you some.

JULIA. From my husband?

DELIO.   No, from mine own allowance.

JULIA. I must hear the condition ere I be bound to take
it.   60

DELIO. Look on't; 'tis gold—hath it not a fine color?

JULIA. I have a bird more beautiful.

DELIO. Try the sound on't.

JULIA.   A lute-string far exceeds it;
It hath no smell, like cassia or civet,
Nor is it physical,* though some fond* doctors
Persuade us seethe['t] in cullises*—I'll tell you,
This is a creature bred by—

                     [*Enter* SERVANT.]

SERVANT.   Your husband's come,
Hath delivered a letter to the Duke of Calabria
That, to my thinking, hath put him out of his wits.

                                                      [*Exit.*]

JULIA. Sir, you hear—   70
Pray let me know your business and your suit
As briefly as can be.

DELIO.   With good speed.
I would wish you
(At such time as you are non-resident
With your husband) my mistress.

JULIA. Sir, I'll go ask my husband if I shall
And straight return your answer.

                                                                 Exit.

DELIO.   Very fine!
Is this her wit or honesty that speaks thus?
I heard one say the duke was highly moved
With a letter sent from Malfi: I do fear   80
Antonio is betrayed. How fearfully
Shows his ambition now! Unfortunate fortune!

---

physical: medicinal.   fond: foolish.   cullises: strong broths.

"They pass through whirlpools and deep woes do shun,
Who the event weigh ere the action's done."

Exit.

[II.v]

[*Enter*] CARDINAL *and* FERDINAND, *with a letter.*

FERDINAND. I have this night digged up a mandrake.*

CARDINAL.   Say you?

FERDINAND. And I am grown mad with't.

CARDINAL.   What's the
  prodigy?

FERDINAND. Read there—a sister damned! She's loose
  i'th' hilts,*
  Grown a notorious strumpet.

CARDINAL.   Speak lower.

FERDINAND.   Lower?
  Rogues do not whisper't now, but seek to publish't
  (As servants do the bounty of their lords)
  Aloud, and with a covetous, searching eye,
  To mark who note them. O, confusion seize her!
  She hath had most cunning bawds to serve her turn
  And more secure conveyances for lust   10
  Than towns of garrison for service.

CARDINAL.   Is't possible?
  Can this be certain?

FERDINAND.   Rhubarb, O, for rhubarb
  To purge this choler!
  [*He points to the horoscope.*]
                                    Here's the cursèd day
  To prompt my memory, and here't shall stick
  Till of her bleeding heart I make a sponge
  To wipe it out.

CARDINAL.   Why do you make yourself
  So wild a tempest?

FERDINAND.   Would I could be one,
  That I might toss her palace 'bout her ears,
  Root up her goodly forests, blast her meads,
  And lay her general territory as waste   20
  As she hath done her honors.

---

mandrake: a plant whose forked root was thought to resemble
the human form and which, when dug up, supposedly gave forth
shrieks that drove its hearers mad.   loose i'th' hilts: unchaste.

CARDINAL.   Shall our blood,
  The royal blood of Arragon and Castile,
  Be thus attainted?
FERDINAND.   Apply desperate physic.
  We must not now use balsamum, but fire—
  The smarting cupping-glass, for that's the mean
  To purge infected blood (such blood as hers).
  There is a kind of pity in mine eye;
  I'll give it to my handkercher; and, now 'tis here,
  I'll bequeath this to her bastard.
CARDINAL.   What to do?
FERDINAND. Why, to make most soft lint for his mother's
    wounds   30
  When I have hewed her to pieces.
CARDINAL.   Cursèd creature!
  Unequal nature, to place women's hearts
  So far upon the left side!
FERDINAND.   Foolish men,
  That e'er will trust their honor in a bark
  Made of so slight, weak bulrush as is woman,
  Apt every minute to sink it!
CARDINAL.   Thus
  Ignorance, when it hath purchased honor,
  It cannot wield it.
FERDINAND.   Methinks I see her laughing—
  Excellent hyena! Talk to me somewhat, quickly,
  Or my imagination will carry me   40
  To see her in the shameful act of sin.
CARDINAL. With whom?
FERDINAND.   Happily* with some strong-
    thighed bargeman,
  Or one [o']th' woodyard that can quoit the sledge,*
  Or toss the bar, or else some lovely squire
  That carries coals up to her privy lodgings.
CARDINAL. You fly beyond your reason.
FERDINAND.   Go to, mistress!
  'Tis not your whore's milk that shall quench my wild
    fire,
  But your whore's blood.
CARDINAL. How idly shows this rage, which carries you,
  As men conveyed by witches through the air,   50

---

happily: haply; perhaps.   quoit the sledge: throw the hammer.

On violent whirlwinds! This intemperate noise
Fitly resembles deaf men's shrill discourse,
Who talk aloud, thinking all other men
To have their imperfection.

FERDINAND.   Have not you
My palsy?

CARDINAL.   Yes, I can be angry
Without this rupture; there is not in nature
A thing that makes man so deformed, so beastly,
As doth intemperate anger. Chide yourself.
You have divers men who never yet expressed
Their strong desire of rest but by unrest,   60
By vexing of themselves. Come, put yourself
In tune.

FERDINAND.   So! I will only study to seem
The thing I am not. I could kill her now,
In you, or in myself; for I do think
It is some sin in us heaven doth revenge
By her.

CARDINAL.   Are you stark mad?

FERDINAND.   I would have their
    bodies
Burnt in a coal-pit with the ventage stopped,
That their cursed smoke might not ascend to heaven;
Or dip the sheets they lie in in pitch or sulphur,
Wrap them in't, and then light them like a match;   70
Or else to boil their bastard to a cullis,
And give't his lecherous father to renew
The sin of his back.

CARDINAL.   I'll leave you.

FERDINAND.   Nay, I have done.
I am confident, had I been damned in hell,
And should have heard of this, it would have put me
Into a cold sweat. In, in! I'll go sleep;
Till I know who leaps my sister, I'll not stir:
That known, I'll find scorpions to string my whips
And fix her in a general eclipse.*

                                                        Exeunt.

_____

general eclipse: death.

ACTUS III

[III.i]

[Enter ANTONIO *and* DELIO.]

ANTONIO. Our noble friend, my most beloved Delio!
  O, you have been a stranger long at court;
  Came you along with the Lord Ferdinand?

DELIO. I did, sir; and how fares your noble duchess?

ANTONIO. Right fortunately well: she's an excellent
  Feeder of pedigrees; since you last saw her,
  She hath had two children more, a son and daughter.

DELIO. Methinks 'twas yesterday: let me but wink
  And not behold your face, which to mine eye
  Is somewhat leaner, verily I should dream   10
  It were within this half hour.

ANTONIO. You have not been in law, friend Delio,
  Nor in prison, nor a suitor at the court,
  Nor begged the reversion of some great man's place,
  Nor troubled with an old wife, which doth make
  Your time so insensibly hasten.

DELIO.   Pray, sir, tell me,
  Hath not this news arrived yet to the ear
  Of the lord cardinal?

ANTONIO.   I fear it hath;
  The Lord Ferdinand, that's newly come to court,
  Doth bear himself right dangerously.

DELIO.   Pray, why?   20

ANTONIO. He is so quiet that he seems to sleep
  The tempest out, as dormice do in winter;
  Those houses that are haunted are most still
  Till the devil be up.

DELIO.   What say the common people?

ANTONIO. The common rabble do directly say
  She is a strumpet.

DELIO.   And your graver heads,
  Which would be politic, what censure they?

ANTONIO. They do observe I grow to infinite purchase°
  The left-hand way, and all suppose the duchess
  Would amend it if she could; for, say they,   30
  Great princes, though they grudge their officers

----

  purchase: wealth.

Should have such large and unconfinèd means
To get wealth under them, will not complain,
Lest thereby they should make them odious
Unto the people; for other obligation
Of love or marriage between her and me
They never dream of.

       [*Enter* DUCHESS, FERDINAND, *and* BOSOLA.]

DELIO.   The Lord Ferdinand
  Is going to bed.

FERDINAND.   I'll instantly to bed,
  For I am weary.—I am to bespeak
  A husband for you.

DUCHESS.   For me, sir? Pray who is't?   40

FERDINAND. The great Count Malateste.

DUCHESS.   Fie upon him!
  A count? He's a mere stick of sugar candy
  (You may look quite thorough him); when I choose
  A husband, I will marry for your honor.

FERDINAND. You shall do well in't.—How is't, worthy
    Antonio?

DUCHESS. But, sir, I am to have private conference with
    you
  About a scandalous report is spread
  Touching mine honor.

FERDINAND.   Let me be ever deaf to't:
  One of Pasquil's paper bullets,* court calumny,
  A pestilent air which princes' palaces   50
  Are seldom purged of. Yet, say that it were true,
  I pour it in your bosom, my fixed love
  Would strongly excuse, extenuate, nay, deny
  Faults, [were] they apparent in you. Go, be safe
  In your own innocency.

DUCHESS.   O blessed comfort!
  This deadly air is purged.

        Exeunt [*except* FERDINAND *and* BOSOLA].

FERDINAND.   Her guilt treads on
  Hot-burning colters.*Now, Bosola,
  How thrives our intelligence?

Pasquil's paper bullets: lampoons (particularly in the manner of
Pasquil, the censorious 15th-century schoolmaster or cobbler).

colters: ploughshares, which, when red hot, were instruments in
medieval tests of chastity.

BOSOLA.   Sir, uncertainly;
'Tis rumored she hath had three bastards, but
By whom we may go read i'th' stars.
FERDINAND.   Why, some   60
Hold opinion all things are written there.
BOSOLA. Yes, if we could find spectacles to read them.
I do suspect there hath been some sorcery
Used on the duchess.
FERDINAND.   Sorcery! To what purpose?
BOSOLA. To make her dote on some desertless fellow
She shames to acknowledge.
FERDINAND.   Can your faith give way
To think there's pow'r in potions or in charms
To make us love whether we will or no?
BOSOLA. Most certainly.
FERDINAND. Away! These are mere gulleries.* horrid
    things   70
Invented by some cheating mountebanks
To abuse us. Do you think that herbs or charms
Can force the will? Some trials have been made
In this foolish practice; but the ingredients
Were lenitive* poisons, such as are of force
To make the patient mad; and straight the witch
Swears (by equivocation) they are in love.
The witchcraft lies in her rank blood. This night
I will force confession from her. You told me
You had got, within these two days, a false key   80
Into her bedchamber.
BOSOLA.   I have.
FERDINAND.   As I would wish.
BOSOLA. What do you intend to do?
FERDINAND.   Can you guess?
BOSOLA.   No.
FERDINAND. Do not ask, then:
He that can compass me and know my drifts
May say he hath put a girdle 'bout the world
And sounded all her quicksands.
BOSOLA.   I do not
Think so.
FERDINAND.   What do you think, then, pray?

---

gulleries: deceptions.   lenitive: soothing.

BOSOLA.   That you
 are
 Your own chronicle too much and grossly
 Flatter yourself.
FERDINAND.   Give me thy hand; I thank thee.
 I never gave pension but to flatterers   90
 Till I entertained thee. Farewell.
 "That friend a great man's ruin strongly checks
 Who rails into his belief all his defects."

            Exeunt.

[III.ii]
   [*Enter* DUCHESS, ANTONIO, *and* CARIOLA.]
DUCHESS. Bring me the casket hither, and the glass.—
 You get no lodging here tonight, my lord.
ANTONIO. Indeed, I must persuade one.
DUCHESS.   Very good:
 I hope in time 'twill grow into a custom
 That noblemen shall come with cap and knee
 To purchase a night's lodging of their wives.
ANTONIO. I must lie here.
DUCHESS.   Must? You are a lord of
 misrule.*
ANTONIO. Indeed, my rule is only in the night.
DUCHESS. To what use will you put me?
ANTONIO.   We'll sleep
 together.
DUCHESS. Alas, what pleasure can two lovers find in
 sleep?   10
CARIOLA. My lord, I lie with her often; and I know
 She'll much disquiet you—
ANTONIO.   See, you are complained
 of.
CARIOLA. For she's the sprawling'st bedfellow.
ANTONIO. I shall like her the better for that.
CARIOLA. Sir, shall I ask you a question?
ANTONIO. I pray thee, Cariola.
CARIOLA. Wherefore still* when you lie with my lady
 Do you rise so early?

   lord of misrule: who presided over holiday revels at court, in
the homes of the nobility, or at universities. still: always.

ANTONIO.   Laboring men
　　Count the clock oft'nest, Cariola,
　　Are glad when their task's ended.
DUCHESS.   I'll stop your
　　mouth.   20
　　[*She kisses him.*]
ANTONIO. Nay, that's but one; Venus had two soft doves
　　To draw her chariot: I must have another.—
　　[*He kisses her.*]
　　When wilt thou marry, Cariola?
CARIOLA.   Never, my lord.
ANTONIO. O, fie upon this single life! Forgo it!
　　We read how Daphne, for her peevish slight,
　　Became a fruitless bay tree; Syrinx turned
　　To the pale empty reed; Anaxarete
　　Was frozen into marble; whereas those
　　Which married, or proved kind unto their friends,*
　　Were, by a gracious influence, transshaped   30
　　Into the olive, pomegranate, mulberry,
　　Became flow'rs, precious stones, or eminent stars.
CARIOLA. This is a vain poetry; but I pray you tell me,
　　If there were proposed me wisdom, riches, and
　　　beauty
　　In three several young men, which should I choose?
ANTONIO. 'Tis a hard question. This was Paris' case,*
　　And he was blind in't; and there was great cause:
　　For how was't possible he could judge right,
　　Having three amorous goddesses in view,
　　And they stark naked? 'Twas a motion*   40
　　Were able to benight the apprehension
　　Of the severest counsellor of Europe.
　　Now I look on both your faces so well formed,
　　It puts me in mind of a question I would ask.
CARIOLA. What is't?
ANTONIO.   I do wonder why hard-favored
　　ladies
　　For the most part keep worse-favored waiting-women

---

friends: lovers.
Paris' case: the son of King Priam of Troy whose choice of
Aphrodite, rather than Hera or Pallas Athene, as the most beautiful
goddess precipitated the Trojan War.   motion: spectacle.

To attend them and cannot endure fair ones.
DUCHESS. O, that's soon answered.
　　Did you ever in your life know an ill painter
　　Desire to have his dwelling next door to the shop　　　　50
　　Of an excellent picture-maker? 'Twould disgrace
　　His face-making and undo him. I prithee,
　　When were we so merry?—My hair tangles.
ANTONIO [aside]. Pray thee, Cariola, let's steal forth the
　　　　room
　　And let her talk to herself. I have divers times
　　Served her the like when she hath chafed extremely.
　　I love to see her angry. Softly, Cariola.
　　　　　　　　　　　　Exeunt [ANTONIO and CARIOLA].
DUCHESS. Doth not the color of my hair 'gin to change?
　　When I wax gray, I shall have all the court
　　Powder their hair with arras* to be like me.　　　　　　60
　　You have cause to love me; I entered you into my heart
　　Before you would vouchsafe to call for the keys.
　　　　　　　　　　[Enter FERDINAND unseen.]
　　We shall one day have my brothers take you napping.
　　Methinks his presence, being now in court,
　　Should make you keep your own bed; but you'll say
　　Love mixed with fear is sweetest. I'll assure you
　　You shall get no more children till my brothers
　　Consent to be your gossips.* Have you lost your
　　　　tongue?—
　　[She sees FERDINAND with a poniard.]
　　'Tis welcome:
　　For know, whether I am doomed to live or die,　　　　　70
　　I can do both like a prince.
　　(FERDINAND gives her a poniard.)
FERDINAND.　　　　　　　　　Die, then, quickly!
　　Virtue, where art thou hid? What hideous thing
　　Is it that doth eclipse thee?
DUCHESS.　　　　　　　　　Pray, sir, hear me!
FERDINAND. Or is it true thou art but a bare name
　　And no essential thing?
DUCHESS.　　　　　　　Sir—
FERDINAND.　　　　　　　　　Do not speak.

————————

arras: powder of orris root.
gossips: those related by the sacrament of baptism; godfathers.

DUCHESS. No, sir!
  I will plant my soul in mine ears to hear you.
FERDINAND. O most imperfect light of human reason,
  That mak'st [us] so unhappy to foresee
  What we can least prevent! Pursue thy wishes,   80
  And glory in them; there's in shame no comfort
  But to be past all bounds and sense of shame.
DUCHESS. I pray, sir, hear me: I am married.
FERDINAND.   So!
DUCHESS. Happily,* not to your liking; but for that,
  Alas, your shears do come untimely now
  To clip the bird's wings that's already flown!
  Will you see my husband?
FERDINAND.   Yes, if I could change
  Eyes with a basilisk.*
DUCHESS.   Sure, you came hither
  By his con[fe]deracy.
FERDINAND.   The howling of a wolf
  Is music to the[e],* screech owl! Prithee, peace.—   90
  Whate'er thou art that hast enjoyed my sister
  (For I am sure thou hear'st me), for thine own sake
  Let me not know thee. I came hither prepared
  To work thy discovery, yet am now persuaded
  It would beget such violent effects
  As would damn us both. I would not for ten millions
  I had beheld thee; therefore, use all means
  I never may have knowledge of thy name;
  Enjoy thy lust still, and a wretched life,
  On that condition.—And for thee, vile woman,   100
  If thou do wish thy lecher may grow old
  In thy embracements, I would have thee build
  Such a room for him as our anchorites
  To holier use inhabit. Let not the sun
  Shine on him till he's dead; let dogs and monkeys
  Only converse with him, and such dumb things
  To whom nature denies use to sound his name.
  Do not keep a paraquito, lest she learn it.
  If thou do love him, cut out thine own tongue,
  Lest it bewray him.

---

happily: haply, perhaps.
basilisk: a fabled serpent whose glance was fatal.
to thee: compared to thee.

DUCHESS.   Why might not I marry?   110
　I have not gone about in this to create
　Any new world or custom.
FERDINAND.   Thou art undone;
　And thou hast ta'en that massy sheet of lead
　That hid thy husband's bones and folded it
　About my heart.
DUCHESS.   Mine bleeds for't.
FERDINAND.   Thine? Thy
　heart?
　What should I name't, unless a hollow bullet
　Filled with unquenchable wild-fire?
DUCHESS.   You are in this
　Too strict; and, were you not my princely brother,
　I would say too willful. My reputation
　Is safe.
FERDINAND.   Dost thou know what reputation is?   120
　I'll tell thee—to small purpose since th'instruction
　Comes now too late:
　Upon a time Reputation, Love, and Death
　Would travel o'er the world; and it was concluded
　That they should part and take three several ways.
　Death told them they should find him in great battles
　Or cities plagued with plagues. Love gives them
　　counsel
　To inquire for him 'mongst unambitious shepherds,
　Where dowries were not talked of, and sometimes
　'Mongst quiet kindred that had nothing left   130
　By their dead parents. "Stay," quoth Reputation,
　"Do not forsake me; for it is my nature,
　If once I part from any man I meet,
　I am never found again." And so, for you.
　You have shook hands with Reputation
　And made him invisible. So, fare you well.
　I will never see you more.
DUCHESS.   Why should only I,
　Of all the other princes of the world,
　Be caśed up, like a holy relic? I have youth
　And a little beauty.
FERDINAND.   So you have some virgins   140
　That are witches. I will never see thee more.

Exit.

Enter ANTONIO *with a pistol* [*, and* CARIOLA].

DUCHESS. You saw this apparition?

ANTONIO.   Yes; we are
Betrayed. How came he hither?
[*He points the pistol at* CARIOLA.]
                             I should turn
This to thee for that.

CARIOLA.   Pray, sir, do; and, when
That you have cleft my heart, you shall read there
Mine innocence.

DUCHESS.   That gallery gave him entrance.

ANTONIO. I would this terrible thing would come again
That, standing on my guard, I might relate
My warrantable love.
(*She shows the poniard.*)
                  Ha! what means this?

DUCHESS. He left this with me.

ANTONIO.   And it seems did wish   150
You would use it on yourself?

DUCHESS.   His action seemed
To intend so much.

ANTONIO.   This hath a handle to't,
As well as a point—turn it towards him,
And so fasten the keen edge in his rank gall.—
[*Knocking within.*]
How now? Who knocks? More earthquakes?

DUCHESS.   I stand
As if a mine beneath my feet were ready
To be blown up.

CARIOLA.   'Tis Bosola.

DUCHESS.   Away!
O misery! Methinks unjust* actions
Should wear these masks and curtains, and not we.
You must instantly part hence; I have fashioned it
    already.   160
                                  Exit ANTONIO.

[*Enter* BOSOLA.]

BOSOLA. The duke your brother is ta'en up in a whirl-
    wind,
Hath took horse, and's rid post to Rome.

---

unjust: dishonest.

DUCHESS.   So late?
BOSOLA. He told me, as he mounted into th' saddle,
   You were undone.
DUCHESS.   Indeed, I am very near it.
BOSOLA. What's the matter?
DUCHESS. Antonio, the master of our household,
   Hath dealt so falsely with me in's accounts;
   My brother stood engaged with me for money
   Ta'en up of certain Neapolitan Jews,
   And Antonio lets the bonds be forfeit.   170
BOSOLA. Strange!—[*Aside*.] This is cunning.
DUCHESS.   And here-
   upon
   My brother's bills at Naples are protested
   Against.—Call up our officers.
BOSOLA.   I shall.

                                                              Exit.

                          [*Enter* ANTONIO.]
DUCHESS. The place that you must fly to is Ancona.
   Hire a house there; I'll send after you
   My treasure and my jewels. Our weak safety
   Runs upon enginous* wheels: short syllables
   Must stand for periods.* I must now accuse you
   Of such a feignèd crime as Tasso calls
   Magnanima menzogna, "a noble lie,"   180
   'Cause it must shield our honors.—Hark! they are
      coming.
                    [*Enter* BOSOLA *and Officers*.]
ANTONIO. Will your grace hear me?
DUCHESS. I have got well by you: you have yielded me
   A million of loss; I am like to inherit
   The people's curses for your stewardship.
   You had the trick in audit-time to be sick
   Till I had signed your *quietus**; and that cured you
   Without help of a doctor.—Gentlemen,
   I would have this man be an example to you all:
   So shall you hold my favor. I pray, let him;   190
   For h'as done that, alas, you would not think of,
   And (because I intend to be rid of him)

-----

enginous: ingenious.   periods: sentences.
quietus: see I. ii. 387.

I mean not to publish.—Use your fortune elsewhere.

ANTONIO. I am strongly armed to brook my overthrow,
As commonly men bear with a hard year:
I will not blame the cause on't but do think
The necessity of my malevolent star
Procures this, not her humor. O, the inconstant
And rotten ground of service, you may see!
'Tis ev'n like him, that in a winter night   200
Takes a long slumber o'er a dying fire,
As loath to part from't, yet parts thence as cold
As when he first sat down.

DUCHESS.   We do confiscate,
Towards the satisfying of your accounts,
All that you have.

ANTONIO.   I am all yours, and 'tis very fit
All mine should be so.

DUCHESS.   So, sir; you have your pass.

ANTONIO. You may see, gentlemen, what 'tis to serve
A prince with body and soul.

                                              Exit.

BOSOLA. Here's an example for extortion: what moisture
is drawn out of the sea, when foul weather comes,   210
pours down, and runs into the sea again.

DUCHESS. I would know what are your opinions of this
Antonio.

2 OFFICER. He could not abide to see a pig's head
gaping—I thought your grace would find him a Jew.

3 OFFICER. I would you had been his officer, for your
own sake.

4 OFFICER. You would have had more money.

1 OFFICER. He stopped his ears with black wool, and
to those came to him for money said he was thick of   220
hearing.

2 OFFICER. Some said he was an hermaphrodite, for he
could not abide a woman.

4 OFFICER. How scurvy proud he would look when the
treasury was full! Well, let him go.

1 OFFICER. Yes, and the chippings of the butt'ry* fly
after him to scour his gold chain.*

---

chippings of the butt'ry: bread crumbs.
gold chain: steward's badge of office.

DUCHESS. Leave us.—

[Exeunt Officers.]

What do you think of these?

BOSOLA. That these are rogues that, in's prosperity,
    But to have waited on his fortune could have wished   230
    His dirty stirrup riveted through their noses
    And followed after's mule, like a bear in a ring;
    Would have prostituted their daughters to his lust;
    Made their first-born intelligencers; thought none
       happy
    But such as were born under his blessed planet
    And wore his livery—and do these lice drop off now?
    Well, never look to have the like again:
    He hath left a sort* of flatt'ring rogues behind him;
    Their doom must follow. Princes pay flatterers
    In their own money: flatterers dissemble their vices,   240
    And they dissemble their lies. That's justice.
    Alas, poor gentleman!
DUCHESS. Poor? He hath amply filled his coffers.
BOSOLA. Sure he was too honest. Pluto, the god of riches,
    When he's sent by Jupiter to any man,
    He goes limping to signify that wealth
    That comes on God's name comes slowly; but, when
      he's sent
    [On] the devil's errand, he rides post and comes in by
      scuttles.*
    Let me show you what a most unvalued * jewel
    You have, in a wanton humor, thrown away,   250
    To bless the man shall find him: He was an excellent
    Courtier, and most faithful; a soldier that thought it
    As beastly to know his own value too little
    As devilish to acknowledge it too much.
    Both his virtue and form deserved a far better fortune.
    His discourse rather delighted to judge itself than show
      itself;
    His breast was filled with all perfection,
    And yet it seemed a private whisp'ring room,
    It made so little noise of't.

---

sort: gang, pack.   scuttles: short, quick steps.
unvalued: 1) invaluable; 2) thought to have no value.

DUCHESS. But he was basely descended.   260
 BOSOLA. Will you make yourself a mercenary herald,
 Rather to examine men's pedigrees than virtues?
 You shall want him,
 For know an honest statesman to a prince
 Is like a cedar planted by a spring;
 The spring bathes the tree's root; the grateful tree
 Rewards it with his shadow: you have not done so.
 I would sooner swim to the Bermoothes* on two
  politicians'
 Rotten bladders, tied together with an intelligencer's
  heart-string,
 Than depend on so changeable a prince's favor.— 270
 Fare thee well, Antonio; since the malice of the world
 Would needs down with thee, it cannot be said yet
 That any ill happened unto thee, considering thy fall
 Was accompanied with virtue.
DUCHESS. O, you render me excellent music.
BOSOLA.   Say you?
DUCHESS. This good one that you speak of is my husband.
BOSOLA. Do I not dream? Can this ambitious age
 Have so much goodness in't as to prefer
 A man merely for worth, without these shadows
 Of wealth and painted honors? Possible?   280
DUCHESS. I have had three children by him.
BOSOLA.   Fortunate
 lady!
 For you have made your private nuptial bed
 The humble and fair seminary* of peace.
 No question but many an unbeneficed scholar
 Shall pray for you for this deed and rejoice
 That some preferment in the world can yet
 Arise from merit. The virgins of your land
 That have no dowries shall hope your example
 Will raise them to rich husbands. Should you want
 Soldiers, 'twould make the very Turks and Moors 290
 Turn Christians and serve you for this act.
 Last, the neglected poets of your time,
 In honor of this trophy of a man,

Bermoothes: Bermuda.   seminary: nursery.

Raised by that curious* engine, your white hand,
Shall thank you in your grave for't and make that
More reverend than all the cabinets
Of living princes. For Antonio,
His fame shall likewise flow from many a pen
When heralds shall want coats to sell to men.
DUCHESS. As I taste comfort in this friendly speech,   300
  So would I find concealment.
BOSOLA. O, the secret of my prince,
  Which I will wear on th'inside of my heart.
DUCHESS. You shall take charge of all my coin and jewels,
  And follow him; for he retires himself
  To Ancona.
BOSOLA.   So.
DUCHESS.   Whither, within few days,
  I mean to follow thee.
BOSOLA.   Let me think:
  I would wish your grace to feign a pilgrimage
  To our Lady of Loretto (scarce seven leagues
  From fair Ancona); so may you depart   310
  Your country with more honor, and your flight
  Will seem a princely progress, retaining
  Your usual train about you.
DUCHESS.   Sir, your direction
  Shall lead me by the hand.
CARIOLA.   In my opinion,
  She were better progress to the baths
  At Lucca or go visit the Spa
  In Germany; for, if you will believe me,
  I do not like this jesting with religion,
  This feignèd pilgrimage.
DUCHESS. Thou art a superstitious fool!—   320
  Prepare us instantly for our departure.
  Past sorrows, let us moderately lament them;
  For those to come, seek wisely to prevent them.
                                        Exit [*with* CARIOLA].
BOSOLA. A politician is the devil's quilted anvil:
  He fashions all sins on him, and the blows
  Are never heard; he may work in a lady's chamber,
  As here for proof. What rests, but I reveal

---

curious: exquisite.

All to my lord? O, this base quality°
Of intelligencer! Why, every quality i'th' world
Prefers but gain or commendation: 330
Now, for this act I am certain to be raised,
"And men that paint weeds to the life are praised."

                                                            Exit.

[III.iii]
    [*Enter*] CARDINAL, FERDINAND, MALATESTE, PESCARA,
                  SILVIO, DELIO.

CARDINAL. Must we turn soldier, then?
MALATESTE.   The emperor,°
  Hearing your worth that way, ere you attained
  This reverend garment, joins you in commission
  With the right fortunate soldier, the Marquis of
    Pescara,
  And the famous Lannoy.
CARDINAL.   He that had the honor
  Of taking the French king prisoner?
MALATESTE.   The same.
  Here's a plot drawn for a new fortification
  At Naples.
    [CARDINAL *and* MALATESTE *talk apart.*]
FERDINAND.   This great Count Malateste, I perceive,
  Hath got employment?
DELIO.   No employment, my lord;
  A marginal note in the muster-book that he is   10
  A voluntary° lord.
FERDINAND.   He's no soldier?
DELIO. He has worn gunpowder in's hollow tooth for the
    toothache.
SILVIO. He comes to the leaguer with a full intent
  To eat fresh beef and garlic, means to stay
  Till the scent be gone, and straight return to court.
DELIO. He hath read all the late service
  As the city chronicle relates it,
  And keep[s] two painters going, only to express
  Battles in model.

---

  quality: profession.   emperor: Charles V.
  voluntary: volunteer.

SILVIO.   Then he'll fight by the book.

DELIO. By the almanac, I think,   20
  To choose good days and shun the critical.
  That's his mistress' scarf.

SILVIO.   Yes, he protests
  He would do much for that taffeta.

DELIO. I think he would run away from a battle
  To save it from taking prisoner.

SILVIO.   He is horribly afraid
  Gunpowder will spoil the perfume on't.

DELIO. I saw a Dutchman break his pate once
  For calling him potgun;* he made his head
  Have a bore in't, like a musket.

SILVIO. I would he had made a touchhole to't.   30
  He is indeed a guarded * sumpter-cloth,*
  Only for the remove of the court.

                    [*Enter* BOSOLA.]

PESCARA. Bosola arrived! What should be the business?
  Some falling out amongst the cardinals.
  These factions amongst great men, they are like
  Foxes: when their heads are divided,
  They carry fire in their tails, and all the country
  About them goes to wrack for't.

SILVIO.   What's that Bosola?

DELIO. I knew him in Padua—a fantastical scholar, like
  such who study to know how many knots was in   40
  Hercules' club, of what color Achilles' beard was, or
  whether Hector were not troubled with the toothache.
  He hath studied himself half blear-eyed to know the
  true symmetry of Caesar's nose by a shoeing-horn, and
  this he did to gain the name of a speculative man.

PESCARA. Mark Prince Ferdinand:
  A very salamander lives in's eye
  To mock the eager violence of fire.

SILVIO. That cardinal hath made more bad faces with
  his oppression than ever Michael Angelo made good   50
  ones; he lifts up's nose like a foul porpoise before a
  storm.

PESCARA. The Lord Ferdinand laughs.

---

  potgun: popgun.   guarded: decorated, ornamented.
  sumpter-cloth: horse cloth.

DELIO.   Like a deadly
    cannon
  That lightens ere it smokes.
PESCARA. These are your true pangs of death,
  The pangs of life that struggle with great statesmen.
DELIO. In such a deformed silence, witches whisper
  Their charms.
            [SILVIO, PESCARA, *and* DELIO *stand aside.*]
CARDINAL. Doth she make religion her riding-hood
  To keep her from the sun and tempest?
FERDINAND.   That!   60
  That damns her. Methinks her fault and beauty,
  Blended together, show like leprosy—
  The whiter, the fouler. I make it a question
  Whether her beggarly brats were ever christened.
CARDINAL. I will instantly solicit the state of Ancona
  To have them banished.
FERDINAND.   You are for Loretto?
  I shall not be at your ceremony. Fare you well.—
  Write to the Duke of Malfi, my young nephew
  She had by her first husband, and acquaint him
  With's mother's honesty.°
BOSOLA.   I will.
FERDINAND.   Antonio!   70
  A slave that only smelled of ink and compters,°
  And nev'r in's life looked like a gentleman
  But in the audit-time.—Go, go presently;°
  Draw me out an hundredth and fifty of our horse,
  And meet me at the fort-bridge.

                                                    Exeunt.

[III.iv]
                [*Enter*] *Two* PILGRIMS *to the Shrine of
                      Our Lady of Loretto.*
1 PILGRIM. I have not seen a goodlier shrine than this;
  Yet I have visited many.
2 PILGRIM.   The Cardinal of Arragon
  Is this day to resign his cardinal's hat;
  His sister duchess likewise is arrived

---

  honesty: chastity.   compters: counters.
  presently: immediately.

To pay her vow of pilgrimage. I expect
A noble ceremony.

1 PILGRIM.   No question.—They come.

Here the ceremony of the CARDINAL'*s installment in
the habit of a soldier, performed in delivering up his
cross, hat, robes, and ring at the shrine, and invest-
ing him with sword, helmet, shield, and spurs. Then*
ANTONIO, *the* DUCHESS, *and their Children, having
presented themselves at the shrine, are (by a form
of banishment in dumb-show expressed towards
them by the* CARDINAL *and the state of Ancona)
banished: during all which ceremony, this ditty is
sung (to very solemn music) by divers Churchmen;
and then exeunt [except the Two Pilgrims].*

> Arms and honors deck thy story,   The author
> To thy fame's eternal glory!   disclaims
> Adverse fortune ever fly thee;   this ditty to
> No disastrous fate come nigh thee!   be his.   10
>
> I alone will sing thy praises,
> Whom to honor virtue raises,
> And thy study, that divine is,
> Bent to martial discipline is:
> Lay aside all those robes lie by thee;
> Crown thy arts with arms; they'll beautify thee.
>
> O worthy of worthiest name, adorned in this
>   manner,
> Lead bravely thy forces on under war's warlike
>   banner!
> O, mayst thou prove fortunate in all martial
>   courses!*
> Guide thou still, by skill, in arts and forces!   20
> Victory attend thee nigh whilst fame sings loud thy
>   pow'rs;
> Triumphant conquest crown thy head, and blessings
>   pour down show'rs!

1 PILGRIM. Here's a strange turn of state! Who would
have thought

---

courses: encounters.

So great a lady would have matched herself
Unto so mean a person? Yet the cardinal
Bears himself much too cruel.

2 PILGRIM.   They are banished.

1 PILGRIM. But I would ask what power hath this state
Of Ancona to determine of a free prince?

2 PILGRIM. They are a free state, sir; and her brother
showed
How that the Pope, forehearing of her looseness,   30
Hath seized into th' protection of the church
The dukedom, which she held as dowager.

1 PILGRIM. But by what justice?

2 PILGRIM.   Sure, I think by none,
Only her brother's instigation.

1 PILGRIM. What was it with such violence he took
Off from her finger?

2 PILGRIM.   'Twas her wedding ring,
Which he vowed shortly he would sacrifice
To his revenge.

1 PILGRIM.   Alas, Antonio!
If that a man be thrust into a well,
No matter who sets hand to't, his own weight   40
Will bring him sooner to th' bottom.—Come, let's
hence.
Fortune makes this conclusion general:
"All things do help th' unhappy man to fall."

                                        Exeunt.

[III.v]

[*Enter*] ANTONIO, DUCHESS, *Children*, CARIOLA, *Servants.*

DUCHESS. Banished Ancona!

ANTONIO.   Yes, you see what pow'r
Lightens in great men's breath.

DUCHESS.   Is all our train
Shrunk to this poor remainder?

ANTONIO.   These poor men,
Which have got little in your service, vow
To take your fortune: but your wiser buntings,
Now they are fledged, are gone.

DUCHESS.   They have done
wisely.
This puts me in mind of death; physicians thus,

With their hands full of money, use to give o'er
Their patients.

ANTONIO.   Right° the fashion of the world—
From decayed fortunes every flatterer shrinks;   10
Men cease to build where the foundation sinks.

DUCHESS. I had a very strange dream tonight.°

ANTONIO.   What
was't?

DUCHESS. Methought I wore my coronet of state,
And on a sudden all the diamonds
Were changed to pearls.

ANTONIO.   My interpretation
Is you'll weep shortly, for to me the pearls
Do signify your tears.

DUCHESS.   The birds that live i'th' field
On the wild benefit of nature live
Happier than we; for they may choose their mates
And carol their sweet pleasures to the spring.   20

[*Enter* BOSOLA *with a letter.*]

BOSOLA. You are happily o'erta'en.

DUCHESS.   From my brother?

BOSOLA. Yes, from the Lord Ferdinand your brother
All love and safety.

DUCHESS.   Thou dost blanch° mischief,
Wouldst make it white. See, see, like to calm weather
At sea before a tempest, false hearts speak fair
To those they intend most mischief.

([*She reads*] *a letter.*)
Send Antonio to me; I want his head in a business.
A politic equivocation!
He doth not want your counsel but your head;
That is, he cannot sleep till you be dead.   30
And here's another pitfall that's strewed o'er
With roses. Mark it; 'tis a cunning one:
I stand engaged for your husband for several debts at
Naples. Let not that trouble him; I had rather have his
heart than his money.
And I believe so too.

BOSOLA.   What do you believe?

DUCHESS. That he so much distrusts my husband's love,

---

right: exactly.   tonight: last night.   blanch: whitewash.

He will by no means believe his heart is with him
Until he see it: the devil is not cunning enough
To circumvent us in riddles.   40

BOSOLA. Will you reject that noble and free league
Of amity and love which I present you?

DUCHESS. Their league is like that of some politic kings,
Only to make themselves of strength and pow'r
To be our after-ruin. Tell them so.

BOSOLA. And what from you?

ANTONIO.   Thus tell him: I will not
come.

BOSOLA. And what of this?

ANTONIO.   My brothers have dispersed
Bloodhounds abroad, which, till I hear are muzzled,
No truce, though hatched with ne'er such politic skill,
Is safe that hangs upon our enemies' will.   50
I'll not come at them.

BOSOLA.   This proclaims your breeding.
Every small thing draws a base mind to fear
As the adamant° draws iron. Fare you well, sir;
You shall shortly hear from's.

                                                          Exit.

DUCHESS.   I suspect some ambush;
Therefore, by all my love, I do conjure you
To take your eldest son and fly towards Milan.
Let us not venture all this poor remainder
In one unlucky bottom.°

ANTONIO.   , You counsel safely.
Best of my life, farewell. Since we must part,
Heaven hath a hand in't; but no otherwise   60
Than as some curious artist takes in sunder
A clock or watch, when it is out of frame,
To bring't in better order.

DUCHESS. I know not which is best,
To see you dead or part with you.—Farewell, boy.
Thou art happy that thou hast not understanding
To know thy misery, for all our wit
And reading brings us to a truer sense
Of sorrow.—In the eternal church, sir,
I do hope we shall not part thus.

---

adamant: magnet.   bottom: the hold of a ship.

ANTONIO.   O, be of comfort!   70
    Make patience a noble fortitude,
    And think not how unkindly* we are used:
    "Man, like to cassia, is proved best, being bruised."
DUCHESS. Must I, like to a slave-born Russian,
    Account it praise to suffer tyranny?
    And yet, O heaven, thy heavy hand is in't.
    I have seen my little boy oft scourge his top
    And compared myself to 't: naught made me e'er
    Go right but heaven's scourge-stick.
ANTONIO.   Do not weep: 80
    Heaven fashioned us of nothing, and we strive
    To bring ourselves to nothing.—Farewell, Cariola,
    And thy sweet armful. If I do never see thee more,
    Be a good mother to your little ones
    And save them from the tiger. Fare you well.
DUCHESS. Let me look upon you once more, for that
        speech
    Came from a dying father. Your kiss is colder
    Than that I have seen an holy anchorite
    Give to a dead man's skull.
ANTONIO. My heart is turned to a heavy lump of lead,
    With which I sound my danger. Fare you well.   90
                                    Exit [with elder Son].
DUCHESS. My laurel is all withered.
CARIOLA. Look, madam, what a troop of armèd men
    Make toward us!
                Enter BOSOLA [masked,] with a Guard.
DUCHESS.   O, they are very welcome.
    When Fortune's wheel is overcharged with princes,
    The weight makes it move swift. I would have my ruin
    Be sudden.—I am your adventure,* am I not?
BOSOLA. You are; you must see your husband no more.
DUCHESS. What devil art thou that counterfeits heaven's
        thunder?
BOSOLA. Is that terrible? I would have you tell me
        whether
    Is that note worse that frights the silly* birds   100
    Out of the corn, or that which doth allure them

---

unkindly: unnaturally; monstrously.
adventure: object of quest.   silly: ignorant; defenseless.

To the nets? You have hearkened to the last too much.
DUCHESS. O misery! Like to a rusty o'erchar[g]ed cannon,
Shall I never fly in pieces? Come, to what prison?
BOSOLA. To none.
DUCHESS.   Whither, then?
BOSOLA.   To your palace.
DUCHESS.   I
    have heard
That Charon's° boat serves to convey all o'er
The dismal lake but brings none back again.
BOSOLA. Your brothers mean you safety and pity.
DUCHESS.   Pity!
With such a pity men preserve alive
Pheasants and quails when they are not fat enough   110
To be eaten.
BOSOLA.   These are your children?
DUCHESS.   Yes.
BOSOLA.   Can
    they prattle?
DUCHESS.   No.
But I intend, since they were born accursed,
Curses shall be their first language.
BOSOLA.   Fie, madam!
Forget this base, low fellow!
DUCHESS.   Were I a man,
I'ld beat that counterfeit face° into thy other.
BOSOLA. One of no birth—
DUCHESS.   Say that he was born mean,
Man is most happy when's own actions
Be arguments and examples of his virtue.
BOSOLA. A barren, beggarly virtue.
DUCHESS. I prithee, who is greatest? Can you tell?   120
Sad tales befit my woe; I'll tell you one.
A salmon, as she swam unto the sea,
Met with a dog-fish, who encounters her
With this rough language: "Why art thou so bold
To mix thyself with our high state of floods,
Being no eminent courtier but one
That for the calmest and fresh time o'th' year

Charon: the ferryman who conveyed the dead over the river
Styx to Hades.   counterfeit face: mask (see stage direction).

Dost live in shallow rivers, rank'st thyself
Will silly smelts and shrimps? And darest thou
Pass by our dog-ship without reverence?"   130
"O," quoth the salmon, "sister, be at peace;
Thank Jupiter we both have passed the net!
Our value never can be truly known
Till in the fisher's basket we be shown;
I'th' market then my price may be the higher,
Even when I am nearest to the cook and fire."
So to great men the moral may be stretchèd:
"Men oft are valued high when th'are most wretched."
But come, whither you please: I am armed 'gainst
    misery,
Bent to all sways of the oppressor's will.   140
"There's no deep valley but near some great hill."

                                                    Exeunt.

ACTUS IV

[IV.i]

            [Enter FERDINAND *and* BOSOLA.*]*

FERDINAND. How doth our sister duchess bear herself
  In her imprisonment?
BOSOLA.   Nobly; I'll describe her:
  She's sad, as one long used to it; and she seems
  Rather to welcome the end of misery
  Than shun it—a behavior so noble
  As gives a majesty to adversity.
  You may discern the shape of loveliness
  More perfect in her tears than in her smiles;
  She will muse four hours together, and her silence,
  Methinks, expresseth more than if she spake.   10
FERDINAND. Her melancholy seems to be fortified
  With a strange disdain.
BOSOLA.   'Tis so; and this restraint,
  Like English mastiffs that grow fierce with tying,
  Makes her too passionately apprehend
  Those pleasures she's kept from.
FERDINAND.   Curse upon her!
  I will no longer study in the book
  Of another's heart. Inform her what I told you.

                                                     Exit.

[*Enter* DUCHESS *and Attendants.*]

BOSOLA. All comfort to your grace!

DUCHESS. I will have none
Pray thee, why dost thou wrap thy poisoned pills
In gold and sugar? 20

BOSOLA. Your elder brother, the Lord Ferdinand,
Is come to visit you, and sends you word,
'Cause once he rashly made a solemn vow
Never to see you more, he comes i'th' night;
And prays you gently neither torch nor taper
Shine in your chamber. He will kiss your hand
And reconcile himself; but, for his vow,
He dares not see you.

DUCHESS. At his pleasure.—
Take hence the lights.—He's come.

[*Exeunt Attendants with lights.*]
[*Enter* FERDINAND.]

FERDINAND. Where are you?

DUCHESS. Here, sir.

FERDINAND. This darkness suits you well. 30

DUCHESS. I would ask you pardon.

FERDINAND. You have it;
For I account it the honorabl'st revenge,
Where I may kill, to pardon.—Where are your cubs?

DUCHESS. Whom?

FERDINAND. Call them your children;
For, though our national law distinguish bastards
From true legitimate issue, compassionate nature
Makes them all equal.

DUCHESS. Do you visit me for this?
You violate a sacrament o'th' church
Shall make you howl in hell for't.

FERDINAND. It had been well 40
Could you have lived thus always; for, indeed,
You were too much i'th' light. But no more—
I come to seal my peace with you. Here's a hand
(*Gives her a dead man's hand.*)
To which you have vowed much love; the ring upon't
You gave.

DUCHESS. I affectionately kiss it.

FERDINAND. Pray do, and bury the print of it in your
heart.

I will leave this ring with you for a love-token,
And the hand as sure as the ring; and do not doubt
But you shall have the heart too. When you need a
   friend,
Send it to him that owed * it: you shall see   50
Whether he can aid you.
DUCHESS.   You are very cold.
I fear you are not well after your travel.—
Hah! Lights!—O, horrible!
FERDINAND.   Let her have lights
   enough.

                                       Exit.

DUCHESS. What witchcraft doth he practice that he hath
   left
A dead man's hand here?
   [*By Servants who enter,*] *here is discovered* (*behind
   a traverse*) *the artificial figures of* ANTONIO *and his
   Children, appearing as if they were dead.*
BOSOLA. Look you, here's the piece from which 'twas
   ta'en.
He doth present you this sad spectacle
That, now you know directly they are dead,
Hereafter you may wisely cease to grieve
For that which cannot be recoverèd.   60
DUCHESS. There is not between heaven and earth one
   wish
I stay for after this: it wastes me more
Than were't my picture, fashioned out of wax,
Stuck with a magical needle, and then buried
In some foul dunghill; and yond's an excellent property
For a tyrant, which I would account mercy.
BOSOLA.   What's
   that?
DUCHESS. If they would bind me to that lifeless trunk,
And let me freeze to death.
BOSOLA.   Come, you must live.
DUCHESS. That's the greatest torture souls feel in hell—
In hell, that they must live and cannot die.   70
Portia,* I'll new-kindle thy coals again

———————

owed: owned.
Portia: Brutus' faithful wife, who, after his death, killed herself
by swallowing hot coals.

And revive the rare and almost dead example
Of a loving wife.
BOSOLA.   O, fie! Despair? Remember
You are a Christian.
DUCHESS.   The church enjoins fasting:
I'll starve myself to death.
BOSOLA.   Leave this vain sorrow;
Things being at the worst begin to mend:
The bee, when he hath shot his sting into your hand,
May then play with your eyelid.
DUCHESS.   Good comfortable
    fellow,
Persuade a wretch that's broke upon the wheel
To have all his bones new set; entreat him live   80
To be executed again. Who must dispatch me?
I account this world a tedious theater,
For I do play a part in't 'gainst my will.
BOSOLA. Come, be of comfort; I will save your life.
DUCHESS. Indeed, I have not leisure to tend so small a
    business.
BOSOLA. Now, by my life, I pity you.
DUCHESS.   Thou art a fool,
    then,
To waste thy pity on a thing so wretched
As cannot pity it[self]. I am full of daggers.
Puff! let me blow these vipers from me.—
[*To a* SERVANT.]
What are you?
SERVANT.   One that wishes you long life.   90
DUCHESS. I would thou wert hanged for the horrible curse
Thou hast given me. I shall shortly grow one
Of the miracles of pity. I'll go pray—No,
I'll go curse!
BOSOLA.   O, fie!
DUCHESS.   I could curse the stars—
BOSOLA.   O,
    fearful!
DUCHESS. And those three smiling seasons of the year
Into a Russian winter—nay, the world
To its first chaos.
BOSOLA.   Look you, the stars shine still.
DUCHESS. O, but you must remember my curse hath a
    great way to go.—

Plagues, that make lanes through largest families,
Consume them!

BOSOLA.   Fie, lady!

DUCHESS.   Let them, like tyrants,   100
Never be remembered but for the ill they have done;
Let all the zealous prayers of mortified
Churchmen forget them!

BOSOLA.   O, uncharitable!

DUCHESS. Let heaven a little while cease crowning martyrs
To punish them!
Go, howl them this, and say I long to bleed:
"It is some mercy when men kill with speed."

                                                  Exit [with Servants].
                              [*Re-enter* FERDINAND.]

FERDINAND. Excellent, as I would wish; she's plagued in
          art.
These presentations are but framed in wax
By the curious° master in that quality,°   110
Vincentio Lauriola, and she takes them
For true substantial bodies.

BOSOLA.   Why do you do this?

FERDINAND. To bring her to despair.

BOSOLA.   Faith, end here,
And go no farther in your cruelty.
Send her a penitential garment to put on
Next to her delicate skin, and furnish her
With beads and prayer books.

FERDINAND.   Damn her! That body
          of hers,
While that my blood ran pure in't, was more worth
Than that which thou wouldst comfort (called a soul).
I will send her masques of common courtesans,   120
Have her meat served up by bawds and ruffians,
And, 'cause she'll needs be mad, I am resolved
To remove forth° the common hospital
All the mad folk and place them near her lodging;
There let them practice together, sing, and dance,
And act their gambols to the full o'th' moon:
If she can sleep the better for it, let her.
Your work is almost ended.

BOSOLA.   Must I see her again?

---

curious: expert.   quality: profession.   forth: from.

FERDINAND. Yes.

BOSOLA.   Never.

FERDINAND.   You must.

BOSOLA.   Never in mine
    own shape;
    That's forfeited by my intelligence*   130
    And this last cruel lie. When you send me next,
    The business shall be comfort.

FERDINAND.   Very likely!
    Thy pity is nothing of kin to thee. Antonio
    Lurks about Milan; thou shalt shortly thither
    To feed a fire as great as my revenge,
    Which nev'r will slack till it have spent his fuel:
    "Intemperate agues make physicians cruel."

Exeunt.

[IV.ii]

[*Enter* DUCHESS *and* CARIOLA.]

DUCHESS. What hideous noise was that?

CARIOLA.   'Tis the wild
    consort*
    Of madmen, lady, which your tyrant brother
    Hath placed about your lodging. This tyranny,
    I think, was never practiced till this hour.

DUCHESS. Indeed, I thank him: nothing but noise and
    folly
    Can keep me in my right wits, whereas reason
    And silence make me stark mad. Sit down;
    Discourse to me some dismal tragedy.

CARIOLA. O, 'twill increase your melancholy.

DUCHESS.   Thou art
    deceived;
    To hear of greater grief would lessen mine.   10
    This is a prison?

CARIOLA.   Yes, but you shall live
    To shake this durance off.

DUCHESS.   Thou art a fool;
    The robin redbreast and the nightingale
    Never live long in cages.

---

intelligence: work as an "intelligencer" or spy.
consort: company.

CARIOLA.   Pray, dry your eyes.
  What think you of, madam?
DUCHESS.   Of nothing;
  When I muse thus, I sleep.
CARIOLA. Like a madman, with your eyes open?
DUCHESS. Dost thou think we shall know one another
  In th'other world?
CARIOLA.   Yes, out of question.
DUCHESS. O, that it were possible we might   20
  But hold some two days' conference with the dead!
  From them I should learn somewhat, I am sure,
  I never shall know here. I'll tell thee a miracle:
  I am not mad yet, to my cause of sorrow.
  Th' heaven o'er my head seems made of molten brass,
  The earth of flaming sulphur, yet I am not mad.
  I am acquainted with sad misery
  As the tanned galley-slave is with his oar;
  Necessity makes me suffer constantly,
  And custom makes it easy. Who do I look like now?   30
CARIOLA. Like to your picture in the gallery,
  A deal of life in show, but none in practice;
  Or rather like some reverend monument
  Whose ruins are even pitied.
DUCHESS.   Very proper;
  And Fortune seems only to have her eyesight
  To behold my tragedy.—How now!
  What noise is that?
                    [*Enter* SERVANT.]
SERVANT.   I am come to tell you
  Your brother hath intended you some sport.
  A great physician, when the Pope was sick
  Of a deep melancholy, presented him   40
  With several sorts* of madmen, which wild object
  (Being full of change and sport) forced him to laugh,
  And so th'imposthume* broke. The selfsame cure
  The duke intends on you.
DUCHESS.   Let them come in.
SERVANT. There's a mad lawyer and a secular priest;
  A doctor that hath forfeited his wits
  By jealousy; an astrologian
  That in his works said such a day o'th' month

  _____

  sorts: groups.   imposthume: abscess.

Should be the day of doom, and, failing of't,
Ran mad; an English tailor crazed i' the brain   50
With the study of new fashion; a gentleman usher
Quite beside himself with care to keep in mind
The number of his lady's salutations
(Or "How do you") she employed him in each morn-
   ing;
A farmer, too, an excellent knave in grain,*
Mad 'cause he was hindered transportation;
And let one broker* that's mad loose to these,
You'ld think the devil were among them.
DUCHESS. Sit, Cariola.—Let them loose when you please,
For I am chained to endure all your tyranny.   60
                   [*Enter* MADMEN.]
          (*Here, by a* MADMAN, *this song is sung to a
                dismal kind of music.*)

          *O, let us howl some heavy note,
               Some deadly dogged howl,
          Sounding as from the threat'ning throat
               Of beasts and fatal fowl!
          As ravens, screech-owls, bulls, and bears,
               We'll b[e]ll * and bawl our parts
          Till irksome noise have cloyed your ears
               And corrosived * your hearts.
          At last, whenas our choir wants breath,
               Our bodies being blessed,*   70
          We'll sing like swans, to welcome death,
               And die in love and rest.*

1 MADMAN [ASTROLOGER]. Doomsday not come yet? I'll
   draw it nearer by a perspective,* or make a glass
   that shall set all the world on fire upon an instant. I
   cannot sleep; my pillow is stuffed with a litter of
   porcupines.
2 MADMAN [LAWYER]. Hell is a mere glass-house, where
   the devils are continually blowing up women's souls on
   hollow irons, and the fire never goes out.   80
3 MADMAN [PRIEST]. I will lie with every woman in my

---

in grain: also pun on "ingrained."
broker: pawnbroker (?); procurer (?).   bell: bellow.
corrosived: corroded.   perspective: telescope.

parish the tenth night: I will tithe them over like
haycocks.

4 MADMAN [DOCTOR]. Shall my pothecary outgo me because I am cuckold? I have found out his roguery: he
makes alum of his wife's urine and sells it to Puritans
that have sore throats with overstraining.

1 MADMAN. I have skill in heraldry.

2 [MADMAN]. Hast?

1 [MADMAN]. You do give for your crest a woodcock's   90
head with the brains picked out on't: you are a very
ancient gentleman.

3 [MADMAN]. Greek is turned Turk; we are only to be
saved by the Helvetian° translation.

1 [MADMAN]. Come on, sir, I will lay the law to you.

2 [MADMAN]. O, rather lay a corrosive; the law will eat
to the bone.

3 [MADMAN]. He that drinks but to satisfy nature is
damned.

4 [MADMAN]. If I had my glass here, I would show a   100
sight should make all the women here call me mad
doctor.

1 [MADMAN, *pointing to* 3 MADMAN]. What's he? A
rope-maker?

2 [MADMAN]. No, no, no; a snuffling knave that, while
he shows the tombs, will have his hand in a wench's
placket.

3 [MADMAN]. Woe to the caroche that brought home my
wife from the masque at three o'clock in the morning;
it has a large featherbed in it.   110

4 [MADMAN]. I have pared the devil's nails forty times,
roasted them in raven's eggs, and cured agues with
them.

3 [MADMAN]. Get me three hundred milch-bats to make
possets to procure sleep.

4 [MADMAN]. All the college may throw their caps at
me: I have made a soap-boiler costive; it was my
masterpiece.

> *Here the dance, consisting of Eight Madmen,
> with music answerable thereunto, after
> which* BOSOLA, *like an old man, enters.*

Helvetian: Genevan; referring to the Geneva Bible, prohibited
in England because of its Puritan tone.

DUCHESS. Is he mad too?

SERVANT.   Pray, question him. I'll leave
   you.

   [*Exeunt* SERVANT *and Madmen.*]

BOSOLA. I am come to make thy tomb.

DUCHESS.   Hah! my tomb?   120
   Thou speak'st as if I lay upon my death-bed,
   Gasping for breath. Dost thou perceive me sick?

BOSOLA. Yes, and the more dangerously since thy sickness is insensible.

DUCHESS. Thou art not mad, sure: dost know me?

BOSOLA.   Yes.

DUCHESS.   Who am I?

BOSOLA. Thou art a box of worm-seed, at best but a
   salvatory of green mummy.* What's this flesh? A
   little crudded* milk, fantastical puff-paste. Our bodies
   are weaker than those paper prisons boys use to keep
   flies in; more contemptible, since ours is to preserve   130
   earthworms. Didst thou ever see a lark in a cage? Such
   is the soul in the body: this world is like her little turf
   of grass; and the heaven o'er our heads, like her look-
   ing-glass, only gives us a miserable knowledge of the
   small compass of our prison.

DUCHESS. Am not I thy duchess?

BOSOLA. Thou art some great woman, sure, for riot begins
   to sit on thy forehead (clad in gray hairs) twenty
   years sooner than on a merry milkmaid's. Thou sleep'st
   worse than if a mouse should be forced to take up her   140
   lodging in a cat's ear; a little infant that breeds its
   teeth, should it lie with thee, would cry out as if thou
   wert the more unquiet bedfellow.

DUCHESS. I am Duchess of Malfi still.

BOSOLA. That makes thy sleep so broken:
   "Glories, like glow-worms, afar off shine bright
   But, looked to near, have neither heat nor light."

DUCHESS. Thou art very plain.

BOSOLA. My trade is to flatter the dead, not the living—
   I am a tomb-maker.   150

DUCHESS. And thou com'st to make my tomb?

BOSOLA. Yes.

---

green mummy: ointment of dried flesh, used medicinally.
crudded: curdled.

DUCHESS. Let me be a little merry. Of what stuff wilt thou
  make it?

BOSOLA. Nay, resolve me first, of what fashion?

DUCHESS. Why, do we grow fantastical in our death-bed?
  Do we affect fashion in the grave?

BOSOLA. Most ambitiously. Princes' images on their tombs
  do not lie, as they were wont, seeming to pray up to
  heaven, but with their hands under their cheeks (as   160
  if they died of the toothache); they are not carved
  with their eyes fixed upon the stars, but, as their minds
  were wholly bent upon the world, the selfsame way
  they seem to turn their faces.

DUCHESS. Let me know fully, therefore, the effect *
  Of this thy dismal preparation,
  This talk fit for a charnel.

BOSOLA.   Now I shall.—
  [*Enter Executioners, with*] *a coffin, cords, and a bell.*
  Here is a present from your princely brothers;
  And may it arrive welcome, for it brings
  Last benefit, last sorrow.

DUCHESS.   Let me see it.   170
  I have so much obedience in my blood,
  I wish it in their veins to do them good.

BOSOLA. This is your last presence-chamber.

CARIOLA. O my sweet lady!

DUCHESS.   Peace! It affrights me not.

BOSOLA. I am the common bellman
  That usually is sent to condemned persons
  The night before they suffer.

DUCHESS.   Even now thou said'st
  Thou was a tomb-maker!

BOSOLA.   'Twas to bring you
  By degrees to mortification. Listen:
  [*He rings his bell.*]
          Hark, now everything is still;   180
          The screech-owl and the whistler shrill
          Call upon our dame aloud
          And bid her quickly don her shroud!
          Much you had of land and rent;
          Your length in clay's now competent. *

---

effect: purpose.   competent: appropriate.

> *A long war disturbed your mind;*
> *Here your perfect peace is signed.*
> *Of what is't fools make such vain keeping?*
> *Sin their conception, their birth weeping,*
> *Their life a general mist of error,* 190
> *Their death a hideous storm of terror.*
> *Strew your hair with powders sweet,*
> *Don clean linen, bathe your feet.*
> *And (the foul fiend more to check)*
> *A crucifix let bless your neck.*
> *'Tis now full tide 'tween night and day;*
> *End your groan, and come away.*

CARIOLA. Hence, villains, tyrants, murderers! Alas!
  What will you do with my lady?—Call for help!

DUCHESS. To whom? To our next neighbors? They are
  madfolks. 200

BOSOLA. Remove that noise!

DUCHESS.   Farewell, Cariola.
  In my last will I have not much to give—
  A many hungry guests have fed upon me;
  Thine will be a poor reversion.*

CARIOLA.   I will die with her.

DUCHESS. I pray thee, look thou giv'st my little boy
  Some syrup for his cold, and let the girl
  Say her prayers ere she sleep.
  [CARIOLA *is forced off.*]

                   —Now what you please;
  What death?

BOSOLA.   Strangling; here are your executioners.

DUCHESS. I forgive them:
  The apoplexy, catarrh, or cough o'th' lungs 210
  Would do as much as they do.

BOSOLA. Doth not death fright you?

DUCHESS.   Who would be
  afraid on't,
  Knowing to meet such excellent company
  In th'other world?

BOSOLA.   Yet, methinks,
  The manner of your death should much afflict you;
  This cord should terrify you!

---

reversion: right guaranteeing future possession.

DUCHESS.   Not a whit:
  What would it pleasure me to have my throat cut
  With diamonds? Or to be smothered
  With cassia? Or to be shot to death with pearls?
  I know death hath ten thousand several doors   220
  For men to take their exits; and 'tis found
  They go on such strange geometrical hinges,
  You may open them both ways—any way (for heaven
    sake)
  So I were out of your whispering. Tell my brothers
  That I perceive death, now I am well awake,
  Best gift is they can give or I can take.
  I would fain put off my last woman's fault:
  I'ld not be tedious to you.
[1] EXECUTIONER.   We are ready.
DUCHESS. Dispose my breath how please you; but my
    body
  Bestow upon my women, will you?
[1] EXECUTIONER.   Yes.   230
DUCHESS. Pull, and pull strongly, for your able strength
  Must pull down heaven upon me.—
  Yet stay. Heaven-gates are not so highly arched
  As princes' palaces; they that enter there
  Must go upon their knees.
  [*She kneels.*]
               —Come, violent death;
  Serve for mandragora to make me sleep!
  Go tell my brothers, when I am laid out,
  They then may feed in quiet.
  (*They strangle her.*)
BOSOLA. Where's the waiting-woman?
  Fetch her.

                   [*Exeunt Executioners.*]
      Some other strangle the children.   240
    [*Re-enter Executioners with* CARIOLA.]
  Look you, there sleeps your mistress.
CARIOLA.   O, you are
    damned
  Perpetually for this! My turn is next;
  Is't not so ordered?
BOSOLA.   Yes, and I am glad
  You are so well prepared for't.

CARIOLA. You are deceived, sir;
I am not prepared for't. I will not die;
I will first come to my answer° and know
How I have offended.
BOSOLA. Come, dispatch her.—
You kept her counsel; now you shall keep ours.
CARIOLA. I will not die; I must not! I am contracted
To a young gentleman.
[1] EXECUTIONER. Here's your wedding ring. 250
CARIOLA. Let me but speak with the duke; I'll discover
Treason to his person.
BOSOLA. Delays!—Throttle her!
[1] EXECUTIONER. She bites and scratches.
CARIOLA. If you kill
me now,
I am damned; I have not been at confession
This two years.
BOSOLA [*impatiently, to Executioners*]. When!.
CARIOLA. I am
quick with child.
BOSOLA. Why, then,
Your credit's saved.
[*They strangle her and bear her body away.*]
—Bear her into th'next room.
Let this lie still.

[*Enter* FERDINAND.]
FERDINAND. Is she dead?
BOSOLA. She is what
You'ld have her. But here begin your pity!
(*Shows the children strangled.*)
Alas, how have these offended?
FERDINAND. The death
Of young wolves is never to be pitied. 260
BOSOLA. Fix your eye here.
FERDINAND. Constantly.
BOSOLA. Do you not
weep?
Other sins only speak; murder shrieks out.
The element of water moistens the earth,
But blood flies upwards and bedews the heavens.

---

answer: legal trial.

FERDINAND. Cover her face! Mine eyes dazzle; she died
    young.
BOSOLA. I think not so: her infelicity
    Seemed to have years too many.
FERDINAND. She and I were twins;
    And, should I die this instant, I had lived
    Her time to a minute.
BOSOLA.   It seems she was born first.   270
    You have bloodily approved the ancient truth
    That kindred commonly do worse agree
    Than remote strangers.
FERDINAND.   Let me see her face again.
    Why didst not thou pity her? What an excellent
    Honest man mightst thou have been
    If thou hadst borne her to some sanctuary!
    Or, bold in a good cause, opposed thyself
    With thy advancèd sword above thy head
    Between her innocence and my revenge!
    I bade thee, when I was distracted of my wits,   280
    Go kill my dearest friend; and thou hast done't.
    For let me but examine well the cause:
    What was the meanness of her match to me?
    Only I must confess, I had a hope
    (Had she continued widow) to have gained
    An infinite mass of treasure by her death—
    And that was the main cause. Her marriage—
    That drew a stream of gall quite through my heart.
    For thee (as we observe in tragedies
    That a good actor many times is cursed   290
    For playing a villain's part), I hate thee for't;
    And, for my sake, say thou hast done much ill well.
BOSOLA. Let me quicken your memory, for I perceive
    You are falling into ingratitude: I challenge
    The reward due to my service.
FERDINAND.   I'll tell thee
    What I'll give thee.
BOSOLA.   Do.
FERDINAND.   I'll give thee a pardon
    For this murder.
BOSOLA.   Hah!
FERDINAND.   Yes, and 'tis
    The largest bounty I can study to do thee.

By what authority didst thou execute
This bloody sentence?

BOSOLA.   By yours.

FERDINAND.   Mine? Was I her
   judge?   300
Did any ceremonial form of law
Doom her to not-being? Did a complete jury
Deliver her conviction up i'th' court?
Where shalt thou find this judgment registered
Unless in hell? See, like a bloody fool
Th' hast forfeited thy life, and thou shalt die for't.

BOSOLA. The office of justice is perverted quite
When one thief hangs another. Who shall dare
Reveal this?

FERDINAND.   O, I'll tell thee:
The wolf shall find her grave and scrape it up,   310
Not to devour the corpse but to discover
The horrid murder.

BOSOLA.   You, not I, shall quake for't.

FERDINAND. Leave me.

BOSOLA.   I will first receive my pension.

FERDINAND. You are a villain!

BOSOLA.   When your ingratitude
Is judge, I am so.

FERDINAND.   O horror!
That not the fear of him which binds the devils
Can prescribe man obedience!—
Never look upon me more.

BOSOLA.   Why, fare thee well.
Your brother and yourself are worthy men;
You have a pair of hearts are hollow graves,   320
Rotten and rotting others; and your vengeance
(Like two chained bullets) still goes arm in arm.
You may be brothers; for treason, like the plague,
Doth take much in a blood.* I stand like one
That long hath ta'en a sweet and golden dream:
I am angry with myself, now that I wake.

FERDINAND. Get thee into some unknown part o'th' world
That I may never see thee.

BOSOLA.   Let me know

---

take . . . blood: "catch a strong hold on a family" (Brown).

Wherefore I should be thus neglected. Sir,
I served your tyranny and rather strove   330
To satisfy yourself than all the world;
And, though I loathed the evil, yet I loved
You that did counsel it and rather sought
To appear a true servant than an honest man.

FERDINAND. I'll go hunt the badger by owl-light:
'Tis a deed of darkness.

Exit.

BOSOLA. He's much distracted.—Off my painted honor!
While with vain hopes our faculties we tire,
We seem to sweat in ice and freeze in fire.
What would I do, were this to do again?   340
I would not change my peace of conscience
For all the wealth of Europe.—She stirs; here's life!
Return, fair soul, from darkness and lead mine
Out of this sensible hell!—She's warm; she breathes!—
Upon thy pale lips I will melt my heart
To store them with fresh color.—Who's there?
Some cordial drink!—Alas! I dare not call.
So pity would destroy pity. Her eye opes;
And heaven in it seems to ope, that late was shut,
To take me up to mercy.   350

DUCHESS. Antonio!

BOSOLA.   Yes, madam, he is living;
The dead bodies you saw were but feigned statues.
He's reconciled to your brothers; the Pope hath
   wrought
The atonement.*

DUCHESS.   Mercy!
   (*She dies.*)

BOSOLA. O, she's gone again! There the cords of life
   broke.
O sacred innocence, that sweetly sleeps
On turtles' * feathers, whilst a guilty conscience
Is a black register, wherein is writ
All our good deeds and bad, a perspective*
That shows us hell! That we cannot be suffered   360
To do good when we have a mind to it!
This is manly sorrow:

---

atonement: reconciliation.   turtles: turtledoves.
perspective: telescope.

These tears, I am very certain, never grew
In my mother's milk. My estate is sunk
Below the degree of fear. Where were
These penitent fountains while she was living?
O, they were frozen up! Here is a sight
As direful to my soul as is the sword
Unto a wretch hath slain his father. Come,
I'll bear thee hence   370
And execute thy last will—that's deliver
Thy body to the reverent dispose
Of some good women: that the cruel tyrant
Shall not deny me. Then I'll post to Milan,
Where somewhat I will speedily enact
Worth my dejection.°

Exit [with the body].

ACTUS V

[V.i]

[Enter ANTONIO *and* DELIO.]

ANTONIO. What think you of my hope of reconcilement
　To the Arragonian brethren?
DELIO.　　　　　　　　　 I misdoubt it;
　For, though they have sent their letters of safe conduct
　For your repair to Milan, they appear
　But nets to entrap you. The Marquis of Pescara,
　Under whom you hold certain land in cheat,°
　Much 'gainst his noble nature hath been moved
　To seize those lands; and some of his dependants
　Are at this instant making it their suit
　To be invested in your revenues.   10
　I cannot think they mean well to your life
　That do deprive you of your means of life,
　Your living.
ANTONIO.　　　 You are still an heretic
　To any safety I can shape myself.
DELIO. Here comes the marquis. I will make myself
　Petitioner for some part of your land,
　To know whither it is flying.
ANTONIO.　　　　　　　　　　 I pray do.
　[He withdraws.]

———

dejection: overthrow.　　cheat: escheat.

[*Enter* PESCARA.]

DELIO. Sir, I have a suit to you.

PESCARA.   To me?

DELIO.   An easy one:
  There is the Citadel of Saint Bennet,*
  With some demesnes, of late in the possession   20
  Of Antonio Bologna—please you bestow them on me?

PESCARA. You are my friend; but this is such a suit
  Nor fit for me to give, nor you to take.

DELIO. No, sir?

PESCARA.   I will give you ample reason for't
  Soon in private.—Here's the cardinal's mistress.

[*Enter* JULIA.]

JULIA. My lord, I am grown your poor petitioner,
  And should be an ill beggar had I not
  A great man's letter here, the cardinal's,
  To court you in my favor.
  [*She gives him a letter.*]

PESCARA [*after reading*].   He entreats for you
  The Citadel of Saint Bennet, that belonged   30
  To the banished Bologna.

JULIA.   Yes.

PESCARA. I could not have thought of a friend I could
  Rather pleasure with it: 'tis yours.

JULIA.   Sir, I thank you;
  And he shall know how doubly I am engaged
  Both in your gift and speediness of giving,
  Which makes your grant the greater.

                                                         Exit.

ANTONIO [*aside*].   How they
  fortify
  Themselves with my ruin!

DELIO.   Sir, I am
  Little bound to you.

PESCARA.   Why?

DELIO. Because you denied this suit to me and gave't
  To such a creature.

PESCARA.   Do you know what it was?   40
  It was Antonio's land, not forfeited
  By course of law, but ravished from his throat
  By the cardinal's entreaty. It were not fit

Bennet: Benedict.

I should bestow so main a piece of wrong
Upon my friend; 'tis a gratification
Only due to a strumpet, for it is injustice.
Shall I sprinkle the pure blood of innocents
To make those followers I call my friends
Look ruddier* upon me? I am glad
This land (ta'en from the owner by such wrong)   50
Returns again unto so foul an use
As salary for his lust. Learn, good Delio,
To ask noble things of me; and you shall find
I'll be a noble giver.

DELIO.   You instruct me well.

ANTONIO [*aside*]. Why, here's a man now would fright
    impudence
From sauciest beggars.

PESCARA.   Prince Ferdinand's come to
    Milan
Sick, as they give out, of an apoplexy;
But some say 'tis a frenzy. I am going
To visit him.

                                                                 Exit.

ANTONIO [*coming forward*].   'Tis a noble old fellow.
DELIO. What course do you mean to take, Antonio?   60
ANTONIO. This night I mean to venture all my fortune
    (Which is no more than a poor ling'ring life)
    To the cardinal's worst of malice. I have got
    Private access to his chamber and intend
    To visit him about the mid of night
    As once his brother did our noble duchess.
    It may be that the sudden apprehension
    Of danger (for I'll go in mine own shape),
    When he shall see it fraight* with love and duty,
    May draw the poison out of him and work   70
    A friendly reconcilement; if it fail,
    Yet it shall rid me of this infamous calling;
    For better fall once than be ever falling.
DELIO. I'll second you in all danger; and, howe'er,*
    My life keeps rank with yours.
ANTONIO. You are still my loved and best friend.

                                                               Exeunt.

---

ruddier: more favorably.   fraight: fraught.
howe'er: whatever happens.

[V.ii]
                    [*Enter* PESCARA *and a* DOCTOR.]
PESCARA. Now, doctor, may I visit your patient?
DOCTOR. If't please your lordship; but he's instantly
    To take the air here in the gallery
    By my direction.
PESCARA.   Pray thee, what's his disease?
DOCTOR. A very pestilent disease, my lord,
    They call lycanthropia.
PESCARA.   What's that?
    I need a dictionary to't.
DOCTOR.   I'll tell you:
    In those that are possessed with't there o'erflows
    Such melancholy humor they imagine
    Themselves to be transformèd into wolves,   10
    Steal forth to churchyards in the dead of night,
    And dig dead bodies up; as two nights since
    One met the duke, 'bout midnight in a lane
    Behind Saint Mark's church, with the leg of a man
    Upon his shoulder; and he howled fearfully;
    Said he was a wolf, only the difference
    Was, a wolf's skin was hairy on the outside,
    His on the inside; bade them take their swords,
    Rip up his flesh, and try. Straight I was sent for
    And, having ministered to him, found his grace   20
    Very well recovered.
PESCARA.   I am glad on't.
DOCTOR. Yet not without some fear
    Of a relapse. If he grow to his fit again,
    I'll go a nearer way to work with him
    Than ever Paracelsus* dreamed of; if
    They'll give me leave, I'll buffet his madness out of
        him.
    Stand aside; he comes.
        [*Enter* FERDINAND, CARDINAL, MALATESTE, *and* BOSOLA.]
FERDINAND. Leave me.
MALATESTE. Why doth your lordship love this solitari-
    ness?   30
FERDINAND. Eagles commonly fly alone; they are crows,

_____

    Paracelsus: 16th-century German physician-magician.

daws, and starlings that flock together. Look, what's that follows me?

MALATESTE. Nothing, my lord.

FERDINAND. Yes.

MALATESTE. 'Tis your shadow.

FERDINAND. Stay it; let it not haunt me.

MALATESTE. Impossible, if you move, and the sun shine.

FERDINAND. I will throttle it.

[*He throws himself down on his shadow.*]

MALATESTE. O, my lord, you are angry with nothing.   40

FERDINAND. You are a fool. How is't possible I should catch my shadow unless I fall upon't? When I go to hell, I mean to carry a bribe; for, look you, good gifts evermore make way for the worst persons.

PESCARA. Rise, good my lord.

FERDINAND. I am studying the art of patience.

PESCARA. 'Tis a noble virtue.

FERDINAND. To drive six snails before me from this town to Moscow; neither use goad nor whip to them but let them take their own time (the patient'st man i'th'   50 world match me for an experiment!), and I'll crawl after like a sheepbiter.°

CARDINAL. Force him up.

[*They raise him.*]

FERDINAND. Use me well, you were best. What I have done, I have done; I'll confess nothing.

DOCTOR. Now let me come to him.—Are you mad, my lord? Are you out of your princely wits?

FERDINAND. What's he?

PESCARA. Your doctor.

FERDINAND. Let me have his beard sawed off and his eye-   60 brows filed more civil.

DOCTOR. I must do mad tricks with him, for that's the only way on't.—I have brought your grace a sala-mander's skin to keep you from sunburning.

FERDINAND. I have cruel sore eyes.

DOCTOR. The white of a cockatrix's° egg is present° remedy.

---

sheepbiter: sheep stealer; thief.
cockatrix: a poisonous serpent.   present: instant.

FERDINAND. Let it be a new-laid one, you were best.
    Hide me from him! Physicians are like kings:
    They brook no contradiction.   70

DOCTOR. Now he begins to fear me, now let me alone
    with him.
    [*He takes off his gown.*]

CARDINAL. How now! Put off your gown?

DOCTOR. Let me have some forty urinals filled with rose-
    water. He and I'll go pelt one another with them.—
    Now he begins to fear me.—Can you fetch a frisk,*
    sir?—Let him go, let him go, upon my peril! I find by
    his eye he stands in awe of me; I'll make him as tame
    as a dormouse.

FERDINAND. Can you fetch your frisks, sir?—I will stamp   80
    him into a cullis, flay off his skin to cover one of the
    anatomies* this rogue hath set i'th' cold yonder in
    Barber-Chirurgeons'* Hall.—Hence, hence! You are
    all of you like beasts for sacrifice. [*He throws the
    DOCTOR down and beats him.*] There's nothing left of
    you but tongue and belly, flattery and lechery.

                                                   [*Exit.*]

PESCARA. Doctor, he did not fear you throughly!*

DOCTOR. True, I was somewhat too forward.

BOSOLA. Mercy upon me, what a fatal judgment
    Hath fall'n upon this Ferdinand!

PESCARA.   Knows your grace   90
    What accident hath brought unto the prince
    This strange distraction?

CARDINAL [*aside*]. I must feign somewhat.—Thus they
    say it grew:
    You have heard it rumored, for these many years,
    None of our family dies but there is seen
    The shape of an old woman, which is given
    By tradition to us to have been murdered
    By her nephews for her riches. Such a figure
    One night, as the prince sat up late at's book,
    Appeared to him when, crying out for help,   100
    The gentlemen of's chamber found his grace
    All on a cold sweat, altered much in face

---

fetch a frisk: cut a caper.   anatomies: skeletons, cadavers.
barber-chirurgeons: barber-surgeons.   throughly: thoroughly.

And language; since which apparition
He hath grown worse and worse, and I much fear
He cannot live.

BOSOLA.   Sir, I would speak with you.

PESCARA. We'll leave your grace,
  Wishing to the sick prince, our noble lord,
  All health of mind and body.

CARDINAL.   You are most welcome.
          [Exeunt all except CARDINAL *and* BOSOLA.]
  Are you come? So.—*[Aside.]* This fellow must not
    know
  By any means I had intelligence   110
  In our duchess' death; for, though I counselled it,
  The full of all th'engagement seemed to grow
  From Ferdinand.—Now, sir, how fares our sister?
  I do not think but sorrow makes her look
  Like to an oft-dyed garment. She shall now
  Taste comfort from me. Why do you look so wildly?
  O, the fortune of your master here, the prince,
  Dejects you; but be you of happy comfort.
  If you'll do one thing for me, I'll entreat,
  Though he had a cold tombstone o'er his bones,   120
  I'ld make you what you would be.

BOSOLA.   Anything;
  Give it me in a breath, and let me fly to't:
  They that think long small expedition win,
  For musing much o'th'end cannot begin.
          [Enter JULIA.]

JULIA. Sir, will you come in to supper?

CARDINAL. I am busy; leave me.

JULIA *[aside]*. What an excellent shape hath that fellow!
                          Exit.

CARDINAL. 'Tis thus: Antonio lurks here in Milan;
  Inquire him out, and kill him. While he lives,
  Our sister cannot marry; and I have thought   130
  Of an excellent match for her. Do this, and style me
  Thy advancement.

BOSOLA. But by what means shall I find him out?

CARDINAL. There is a gentleman called Delio
  Here in the camp, that hath been long approved
  His loyal friend. Set eye upon that fellow;
  Follow him to Mass—may be Antonio,

Although he do account religion
But a school-name, for fashion of the world
May accompany him; or else go inquire out   140
Delio's confessor and see if you can bribe
Him to reveal it. There are a thousand ways
A man might find to trace him—as to know
What fellows haunt the Jews for taking up
Great sums of money, for sure he's in want;
Or else to go to th' picture-makers and learn
Who [bought] her picture lately. Some of these
Happily may take.

BOSOLA.   Well, I'll not freeze i'th' business;
I would see that wretched thing, Antonio,
Above all the sights i'th' world.

CARDINAL.   Do, and be happy.   150

Exit.

BOSOLA. This fellow doth breed basilisks in's eyes;
He's nothing else but murder; yet he seems
Not to have notice of the duchess' death.
'Tis his cunning: I must follow his example.
There cannot be a surer way to trace
Than that of an old fox.

[*Re-enter* JULIA, *pointing a pistol at him.*]

JULIA.   So, sir, you are well met.

BOSOLA. How now?

JULIA.   Nay, the doors are fast enough.
Now, sir,
I will make you confess your treachery.

BOSOLA. Treachery?

JULIA.   Yes, confess to me
Which of my women 'twas you hired to put   160
Love powder into my drink.

BOSOLA.   Love powder!

JULIA.   Yes,
When I was at Malfi—
Why should I fall in love with such a face else?
I have already suffered for thee so much pain,
The only remedy to do me good
Is to kill my longing.

BOSOLA.   Sure your pistol holds
Nothing but perfumes or kissing-comfits.°

---

kissing-comfits: sweetmeats for the breath.

Excellent lady,
You have a pretty way on't to discover
Your longing. Come, come, I'll disarm you,
And arm you thus.
[*He embraces her.*]
      —Yet this is wondrous strange.   170
JULIA. Compare thy form and my eyes together,
 You'll find my love no such great miracle.
 Now you'll say
 I am wanton: this nice modesty in ladies
 Is but a troublesome familiar*
 That haunts them.
BOSOLA. Know you me; I am a blunt soldier.
JULIA.   The
 better;
 Sure, there wants fire where there are no lively sparks
 Of roughness.
BOSOLA.   And I want* compliment.
JULIA.   Why,
 ignorance
 In courtship cannot make you do amiss   180
 If you have a heart to do well.
BOSOLA.   You are very fair.
JULIA. Nay, if you lay beauty to my charge,
 I must plead unguilty.
BOSOLA.   Your bright eyes
 Carry a quiver of darts in them, sharper
 Than sunbeams.
JULIA.   You will mar me with commenda-
 tion;
 Put yourself to the charge of courting me,
 Whereas now I woo you.
BOSOLA [*aside*]. I have it; I will work upon this crea-
 ture.—
 Let us grow most amorously familiar:
 If the great cardinal now should see me thus,   190
 Would he not count me a villain?
JULIA. No; he might count me a wanton,
 Not lay a scruple of offense on you;
 For, if I see and steal a diamond,
 The fault is not i'th' stone but in me, the thief

---

familiar: attendant spirit.   want: lack the ability to.

That purloins it. I am sudden with you—
We that are great women of pleasure use to cut off
These uncertain wishes and unquiet longings
And in an instant join the sweet delight
And the pretty excuse together. Had you been i'th'
    street,   200
Under my chamber window, even there
I should have courted you.
BOSOLA. O, you are an excellent lady!
JULIA. Bid me do somewhat for you presently*
    To express I love you.
BOSOLA.   I will;
    And, if you love me, fail not to effect it:
The cardinal is grown wondrous melancholy;
Demand the cause; let him not put you off
With feigned excuse; discover the main ground on't.
JULIA. Why would you know this?
BOSOLA.   I have depended on
    him,   210
And I hear that he is fall'n in some disgrace
With the Emperor. If he be, like the mice
That forsake falling houses, I would shift
To other dependence.
JULIA. You shall not need follow the wars;
    I'll be your maintenance.
BOSOLA.   And I your loyal servant;
    But I cannot leave my calling.
JULIA.   Not leave
An ungrateful general for the love of a sweet lady?
You are like some cannot sleep in feather beds
But must have blocks for their pillows.
BOSOLA.   Will you do
    this?   220
JULIA. Cunningly.
BOSOLA.   Tomorrow I'll expect th'intelligence.
JULIA. Tomorrow? Get you into my cabinet;
You shall have it with you. Do not delay me,
No more than I do you. I am like one
That is condemned: I have my pardon promised,
But I would see it sealed. Go, get you in;

----

presently: at once, immediately.

You shall see me wind my tongue about his heart
Like a skein of silk.

> [*Exit* BOSOLA, *into her cabinet.*]
> [*Enter* CARDINAL.]

CARDINAL. Where are you?

> [*Enter Servants.*]

SERVANTS. Here.

CARDINAL. Let none, upon your lives,
Have conference with the Prince Ferdinand   230
Unless I know it.—

> [*Exeunt Servants.*]
> [*Aside.*] In this distraction

He may reveal the murder.
Yond's my ling'ring consumption:
I am weary of her, and by any means
Would be quit of.

JULIA. How now, my lord?
What ails you?

CARDINAL. Nothing.

JULIA. O, you are much altered.
Come, I must be your secretary,* and remove
This lead from off your bosom. What's the matter?

CARDINAL. I may not tell you.

JULIA. Are you so far in love with sorrow   240
You cannot part with part of it? Or think you
I cannot love your grace when you are sad
As well as merry? Or do you suspect
I, that have been a secret to your heart
These many winters, cannot be the same
Unto your tongue?

CARDINAL. Satisfy thy longing—
The only way to make thee keep my counsel
Is not to tell thee.

JULIA. Tell your echo this,
Or flatterers that, like echoes, still report
What they hear, though most imperfect, and not me; 250
For, if that you be true unto yourself,
I'll know.

CARDINAL. Will you rack me?

---

secretary: sharer of secrets; confidant.

JULIA.   No, judgment shall
　Draw it from you. It is an equal fault
　To tell one's secrets unto all or none.
CARDINAL. The first argues folly.
JULIA.   But the last tyranny.
CARDINAL. Very well; why, imagine I have committed
　Some secret deed, which I desire the world
　May never hear of.
JULIA.   Therefore may not I know it?
　You have concealed for me as great a sin
　As adultery. Sir, never was occasion   260
　For perfect trial of my constancy
　Till now. Sir, I beseech you—
CARDINAL.   You'll repent it.
JULIA. Never.
CARDINAL. It hurries thee to ruin: I'll not tell thee.
　Be well advised and think what danger 'tis
　To receive a prince's secrets: they that do
　Had need have their breasts hooped with adamant
　To contain them. I pray thee yet be satisfied;
　Examine thine own frailty; 'tis more easy
　To tie knots than unloose them. 'Tis a secret   270
　That, like a ling'ring poison, may chance lie
　Spread in thy veins and kill thee seven year hence.
JULIA. Now you dally with me.
CARDINAL.   No more; thou shalt
　　know it.
　By my appointment, the great Duchess of Malfi
　And two of her young children four nights since
　Were strangled.
JULIA.   O heaven! Sir, what have you done?
CARDINAL. How now? How settles this? Think you your
　　bosom
　Will be a grave, dark and obscure enough,
　For such a secret?
JULIA.   You have undone yourself, sir.
CARDINAL. Why?
JULIA.   It lies not in me to conceal it.
CARDINAL.   No?   280
　Come, I will swear you to't upon this book.
JULIA. Most religiously.
CARDINAL.   Kiss it.

[*She kisses the book.*]
Now you shall never utter it; thy curiosity
Hath undone thee: thou'rt poisoned with that book.
Because I knew thou couldst not keep my counsel,
I have bound thee to't by death.

[*Enter* BOSOLA.]

BOSOLA. For pity sake, hold!

CARDINAL. Ha, Bosola!

JULIA. I forgive you
This equal piece of justice you have done;
For I betrayed your counsel to that fellow:
He overheard it—that was the cause I said 290
It lay not in me to conceal it.

BOSOLA. O foolish woman,
Couldst not thou have poisoned him?

JULIA. 'Tis weakness
Too much to think what should have been done;
I go, I know not whither.

[*She dies.*]

CARDINAL. Wherefore com'st thou
hither?

BOSOLA. That I might find a great man, like yourself,
Not out of his wits as the Lord Ferdinand,
To remember my service.

CARDINAL. I'll have thee hewed in
pieces.

BOSOLA. Make not yourself such a promise of that life
Which is not yours to dispose of.

CARDINAL. Who placed thee
here? 300

BOSOLA. Her lust, as she intended.

CARDINAL. Very well;
Now you know me for your fellow murderer.

BOSOLA. And wherefore should you lay fair marble
colors*
Upon your rotten purposes to me
Unless you imitate some that do plot great treasons
And, when they have done, go hide themselves i'th'
graves
Of those were actors in't?

---

fair marble colors: as applied to rotten wood (see next line).

CARDINAL.   No more; there is
   A fortune attends thee.
BOSOLA. Shall I go sue to Fortune any longer?
   'Tis the fool's pilgrimage.   310
CARDINAL. I have honors in store for thee.
BOSOLA. There are a many ways that conduct to seeming
   Honor, and some of them very dirty ones.
CARDINAL. Throw to the devil
   Thy melancholy; the fire burns well—
   What needs we keep a stirring of't and make
   A greater smother? Thou wilt kill Antonio?
BOSOLA. Yes.
CARDINAL.   Take up that body.
BOSOLA.   I think I shall
   Shortly grow the common bier for churchyards!
CARDINAL. I will allow thee some dozen of attendants   320
   To aid thee in the murder.
BOSOLA. O, by no means. Physicians that apply horse-
   leeches to any rank swelling use to cut off their tails,
   that the blood may run through them the faster. Let
   me have no train when I go to shed blood, lest it make
   me have a greater when I ride to the gallows.
CARDINAL. Come to me after midnight, to help to remove
   that body to her own lodging. I'll give out she died
   o'th' plague; 'twill breed the less inquiry after her
   death.   330
BOSOLA. Where's Castruchio, her husband?
CARDINAL. He's rode to Naples to take possession
   Of Antonio's citadel.
BOSOLA. Believe me, you have done a very happy turn.
CARDINAL. Fail not to come. There is the master-key
   Of our lodgings, and by that you may conceive
   What trust I plant in you.
BOSOLA.   You shall find me ready.—
                                    Exit [CARDINAL].
   O poor Antonio, though nothing be so needful
   To thy estate as pity, yet I find
   Nothing so dangerous! I must look to my footing;   340
   In such slippery ice-pavements men had need
   To be frost-nailed well: they may break their necks
     else.
   The precedent's here afore me. How this man

Bears up in blood! Seems fearless! Why, 'tis well:
Security some men call the suburbs of hell,
Only a dead wall between. Well, good Antonio,
I'll seek thee out; and all my care shall be
To put thee into safety from the reach
Of these most cruel biters* that have got
Some of thy blood already. It may be   350
I'll join with thee in a most just revenge.
The weakest arm is strong enough that strikes
With the sword of justice. Still, methinks the duchess
Haunts me. There, there! 'Tis nothing but my melan-
    choly.
O Penitence, let me truly taste thy cup,
That throws men down only to raise them up!

                                                                 Exit.

[V.iii]
    [*Enter*] ANTONIO, DELIO, ECHO (*from the* DUCHESS' *grave*).
DELIO. Yond's the cardinal's window. This fortification
    Grew from the ruins of an ancient abbey;
    And to yond side o'th' river lies a wall,
    Piece of a cloister, which in my opinion
    Gives the best echo that you ever heard—
    So hollow, and so dismal, and withal
    So plain in the distinction of our words
    That many have supposed it is a spirit
    That answers.
ANTONIO.   I do love these ancient ruins:
    We never tread upon them but we set   10
    Our foot upon some reverend history;
    And, questionless, here in this open court
    (Which now lies naked to the injuries
    Of stormy weather) some men lie interred
    Loved the church so well, and gave so largely to't,
    They thought it should have canopied their bones
    Till doomsday. But all things have their end:
    Churches and cities, which have diseases like to men,
    Must have like death that we have.
ECHO.   *Like death that*
        we have.

―――――――――
    biters: deceivers.

DELIO. Now the echo hath caught you.

ANTONIO.   It groaned, me-   20
    thought, and gave
  A very deadly accent.

ECHO.   *Deadly accent.*

DELIO. I told you 'twas a pretty one. You may make it
  A huntsman, or a falconer, a musician,
  Or a thing of sorrow.

ECHO.   *A thing of sorrow.*

ANTONIO. Ay, sure, that suits it best.

ECHO.   *That suits it best.*

ANTONIO. 'Tis very like my wife's voice.

ECHO.   *Ay, wife's*
  voice.

DELIO. Come, let's walk farther from't.
  I would not have you go to th' cardinal's tonight;
  Do not.

ECHO.   *Do not.*

DELIO. Wisdom doth not more moderate wasting sorrow   30
  Than time. Take time for't; be mindful of thy safety.

ECHO. *Be mindful of thy safety.*

ANTONIO.   Necessity compels me:
  Make scrutiny throughout the passes
  Of your own life, you'll find it impossible
  To fly your fate.

[ECHO.]   *O, fly your fate!*

DELIO. Hark! The dead stones seem to have pity on you
  And give you good counsel.

ANTONIO. Echo, I will not talk with thee,
  For thou art a dead thing.

ECHO.   *Thou art a dead thing.*

ANTONIO. My duchess is asleep now,   40
  And her little ones, I hope sweetly. O heaven,
  Shall I never see her more?

ECHO.   *Never see her more.*

ANTONIO. I marked not one repetition of the echo
  But that, and on the sudden a clear light
  Presented me a face folded in sorrow.

DELIO. Your fancy, merely.

ANTONIO.   Come, I'll be out of this
  ague;
  For to live thus is not, indeed, to live:
  It is a mockery and abuse of life.

I will not henceforth save myself by halves;
Lose all, or nothing.

DELIO.   Your own virtue save you!   50
I'll fetch your eldest son and second you:
It may be that the sight of his own blood
Spread in so sweet a figure may beget
The more compassion.

[ANTONIO.]   How ever, fare you well.
Though in our miseries Fortune have a part,
Yet in our noble suff'rings she hath none:
Contempt of pain, that we may call our own.

[V.iv]
     [*Enter* CARDINAL, PESCARA, MALATESTE, RODERIGO,
              and GRISOLAN.]

CARDINAL. You shall not watch tonight by the sick prince;
His grace is very well recovered.

MALATESTE. Good my lord, suffer* us.

CARDINAL.   O, by no means;
The noise and change of object in his eye
Doth more distract him. I pray, all to bed;
And, though you hear him in his violent fit,
Do not rise, I entreat you.

PESCARA. So, sir, we shall not.

CARDINAL.   Nay, I must have you
    promise
Upon your honors, for I was enjoined to't
By himself; and he seemed to urge it sensibly.   10

PESCARA. Let our honors bind this trifle.

CARDINAL. Nor any of your followers.

MALATESTE.   Neither.

CARDINAL. It may be, to make trial of your promise
When he's asleep, myself will rise and feign
Some of his mad tricks and cry out for help
And feign myself in danger.

MALATESTE.   If your throat were
    cutting,
I'ld not come at you, now I have protested against it.

CARDINAL. Why, I thank you.
    [*He withdraws.*]

---

suffer: permit, allow.

GRISOLAN.   'Twas a foul storm tonight.

RODERIGO. The Lord Ferdinand's chamber shook like an
   osier.

MALATESTE. 'Twas nothing but pure kindness in the devil   20
   To rock his own child.

                            Exeunt [*except* CARDINAL].

CARDINAL. The reason why I would not suffer these
   About my brother is because at midnight
   I may with better privacy convey
   Julia's body to her own lodging.
   O, my conscience!
   I would pray now, but the devil takes away my heart
   For having any confidence in prayer.
   About this hour I appointed Bosola
   To fetch the body: when he hath served my turn,   30
   He dies.

                                          Exit.

              [*Enter* BOSOLA.]

BOSOLA. Hah! 'Twas the cardinal's voice. I heard him
   name
   Bosola and my death. Listen; I hear one's footing.

            [*Enter* FERDINAND.]

FERDINAND. Strangling is a very quiet death.

BOSOLA [*aside*]. Nay, then, I see I must stand upon my
   guard.

FERDINAND. What say to that? Whisper softly. Do you
   agree to't?
   So—it must be done i'th' dark: the cardinal
   Would not for a thousand pounds the doctor should
   see it.

                                          Exit.

BOSOLA. My death is plotted; here's the consequence of
   murder:
   "We value not desert, nor Christian breath,   40
   When we know black deeds must be cured with death."

        [*Enter* ANTONIO *and* SERVANT.]

SERVANT. Here stay, sir, and be confident, I pray;
   I'll fetch you a dark lantern.

                                          Exit.

ANTONIO. Could I take him at his prayers,
   There were hope of pardon.

BOSOLA.   Fall right, my sword!—
[*He stabs him.*]
  I'll not give thee so much leisure as to pray.
ANTONIO. O, I am gone! Thou hast ended a long suit
  In a minute.
BOSOLA.   What art thou?
ANTONIO.   A most wretched
    thing,
  That only have thy benefit in death,
  To appear myself.
                  [*Re-enter* SERVANT *with lantern.*]
SERVANT.   Where are you, sir?   50
ANTONIO. Very near my home.—Bosola!
SERVANT.   O, misfortune!
BOSOLA. [*to* SERVANT]. Smother thy pity; thou art dead
    else.—Antonio!
  The man I would have saved 'bove mine own life!
  We are merely the stars' tennis balls, struck and
    banded *
  Which way please them.—O good Antonio,
  I'll whisper one thing in thy dying ear
  Shall make thy heart break quickly: Thy fair duchess
  And two sweet children—
ANTONIO.   Their very names
  Kindle a little life in me.
BOSOLA.   Are murdered!
ANTONIO. Some men have wished to die   60
  At the hearing of sad tidings: I am glad
  That I shall do't in sadness.* I would not now
  Wish my wounds balmed nor healed, for I have no use
  To put my life to. In all our quest of greatness,
  Like wanton boys, whose pastime is their care,
  We follow after bubbles blown in th'air.
  Pleasure of life, what is't? Only the good hours
  Of an ague; merely a preparative to rest,
  To endure vexation. I do not ask
  The process* of my death; only commend me   70
  To Delio.
BOSOLA. Break, heart!

---

  banded: bandied.   in sadness: in earnest.   process: account.

ANTONIO.   And let my son fly the courts of
    princes.
    [*He dies.*]
BOSOLA. Thou seem'st to have loved Antonio?
SERVANT.   I brought
    him hither
    To have reconciled him to the cardinal.
BOSOLA. I do not ask thee that.
    Take him up, if thou tender thine own life,
    And bear him where the Lady Julia
    Was wont to lodge.—O, my fate moves swift!
    I have this cardinal in the forge already;
    Now I'll bring him to th' hammer. O direful mis-
      prision!*   80
    I will not imitate things glorious,
    No more than base: I'll be mine own example.—
    On, on, and look thou represent, for silence,
    The thing thou bear'st.

                                Exeunt.

[V.v]
           [*Enter*] CARDINAL (*with a book*).
CARDINAL. I am puzzled in a question about hell:
    He says, in hell there's one material fire,
    And yet it shall not burn all men alike.
    Lay him by. How tedious is a guilty conscience!
    When I look into the fish-ponds in my garden,
    Methinks I see a thing armed with a rake
    That seems to strike at me.
      [*Enter* BOSOLA *and Servant bearing* ANTONIO'S *body.*]
    Now, art thou come? Thou look'st ghastly:
    There sits in thy face some great determination,
    Mixed with some fear.
BOSOLA.   Thus it lightens into action;   10
    I am come to kill thee.
CARDINAL.   Hah!—Help! Our guard!
BOSOLA. Thou art deceived; they are out of thy howling.
CARDINAL. Hold, and I will faithfully divide
    Revenues with thee.
BOSOLA.   Thy prayers and proffers
    Are both unseasonable.

---

    misprision: mistake, error.

CARDINAL.   Raise the watch!
We are betrayed!
BOSOLA.   I have confined your flight;
I'll suffer your retreat to Julia's chamber,
But no further.
CARDINAL.   Help! We are betrayed!
    [*Enter* MALATESTE, RODERIGO, PESCARA, *and*
              GRISOLAN, *above.*]
MALATESTE.   Listen!
CARDINAL. My dukedom for rescue!
RODERIGO.   Fie upon his coun-
terfeiting!
MALATESTE. Why, 'tis not the cardinal.
RODERIGO.   Yes, yes, 'tis he;   20
But I'll see him hanged ere I'll go down to him.
CARDINAL. Here's a plot upon me; I am assaulted! I am
lost
Unless some rescue!
GRISOLAN.   He doth this pretty well,
But it will not serve to laugh me out of mine honor.
CARDINAL. The sword's at my throat!
RODERIGO.   You would not
bawl so loud then.
MALATESTE. Come, come, let's go to bed; he told us
thus much aforehand.
PESCARA. He wished you should not come at him; but,
believe't,
The accent of the voice sounds not in jest.
I'll down to him, howsoever, and with engines
Force ope the doors.
                          [*Exit above.*]
RODERIGO.   Let's follow him aloof,   30
And note how the cardinal will laugh at him.
                         [*Exeunt above.*]
BOSOLA. There's for you first
'Cause you shall not unbarricade the door
To let in rescue.
    (*He kills the Servant.*)
CARDINAL. What cause hast thou to pursue my life?
BOSOLA.   Look there.
CARDINAL. Antonio!
BOSOLA.   Slain by my hand unwittingly.
Pray, and be sudden; when thou kill'dst thy sister,

Thou took'st from Justice her most equal balance
And left her naught but her sword.

CARDINAL.   O, mercy!

BOSOLA. Now it seems thy greatness was only outward,   40
For thou fall'st faster of thyself than calamity
Can drive thee. I'll not waste longer time. There!
[*He stabs him.*]

CARDINAL. Thou hast hurt me!

BOSOLA.   Again!
[*He stabs him again.*]

CARDINAL.   Shall I die like
a leveret*
Without any resistance?—Help, help, help!
I am slain!
                        [*Enter* FERDINAND.]

FERDINAND.   Th'alarum! Give me a fresh horse;
Rally the vaunt-guard,* or the day is lost.
Yield, yield! I give you the honor of arms,
Shake my sword over you. Will you yield?

CARDINAL. Help me; I am your brother!

FERDINAND.   The devil!   50
My brother fight upon the adverse party?
(*He wounds the* CARDINAL, *and in the scuffle gives*
    BOSOLA *his death-wound.*)
There flies your ransom.

CARDINAL.   O Justice!
I suffer now for what hath former been:
"Sorrow is held the eldest child of sin."

FERDINAND. Now you're brave fellows. Caesar's fortune
was harder than Pompey's: Caesar died in the arms of
prosperity; Pompey, at the feet of disgrace. You both
died in the field. The pain's nothing: pain many times
is taken away with the apprehension of greater, as the
toothache with the sight of a barber that comes to pull   60
it out. There's philosophy for you.

BOSOLA. Now my revenge is perfect.—Sink, thou main
cause
Of my undoing!—The last part of my life
Hath done me best service.
(*He kills* FERDINAND.)

---

leveret: young hare.   vaunt-guard: vanguard.

FERDINAND. Give me some wet hay; I am broken-winded.
  I do account this world but a dog-kennel:
  I will vault credit* and affect high pleasures
  Beyond death.
BOSOLA.   He seems to come to himself,
  Now he's so near the bottom.
FERDINAND. My sister, O my sister! There's the cause on't.   70
  "Whether we fall by ambition, blood, or lust,
  Like diamonds, we are cut with our own dust."
  [*He dies.*]
CARDINAL. Thou hast thy payment too.
BOSOLA. Yes, I hold my weary soul in my teeth;
  'Tis ready to part from me. I do glory
  That thou, which stood'st like a huge pyramid
  Begun upon a large and ample base,
  Shalt end in a little point, a kind of nothing.
  [*Enter* PESCARA, MALATESTE, RODERIGO, *and* GRISOLAN.]
PESCARA. How now, my lord!
MALATESTE.   O, sad disaster!
RODERIGO.   How
  comes this?
BOSOLA. Revenge for the Duchess of Malfi, murdered   80
  By th'Arragonian brethren; for Antonio,
  Slain by [t]his hand; for lustful Julia,
  Poisoned by this man; and, lastly, for myself,
  That was an actor in the main of all
  Much 'gainst mine own good nature, yet i'th'end
  Neglected.
PESCARA.   How now, my lord?
CARDINAL.   Look to my brother.
  He gave us these large wounds as we were struggling
  Here i'th' rushes. And now, I pray, let me
  Be laid by and never thought of.
  [*He dies.*]
PESCARA. How fatally, it seems, he did withstand   90
  His own rescue!
MALATESTE.   Thou wretched thing of blood,
  How came Antonio by his death?
BOSOLA. In a mist: I know not how;
  Such a mistake as I have often seen

---

vault credit: overcome belief.

In a play. O, I am gone!
We are only like dead walls or vaulted graves,
That, ruined, yields no echo. Fare you well!
It may be pain, but no harm, to me to die
In so good a quarrel. O, this gloomy world!
In what a shadow or deep pit of darkness   100
Doth womanish and fearful mankind live!
Let worthy minds ne'er stagger in distrust
To suffer death or shame for what is just—
Mine is another voyage.
[*He dies.*]

PESCARA. The noble Delio, as I came to th' palace,
Told me of Antonio's being here and showed me
A pretty gentleman, his son and heir.
                    [*Enter* DELIO *and* ANTONIO's *Son.*]

MALATESTE. O, sir, you come too late!

DELIO.   I heard so, and
Was armed for't ere I came. Let us make noble use
Of this great ruin and join all our force   110
To establish this young hopeful gentleman
In's mother's right. These wretched eminent things
Leave no more fame behind 'em than should one
Fall in a frost and leave his print in snow:
As soon as the sun shines, it ever melts
Both form and matter. I have ever thought
Nature doth nothing so great for great men
As when she's pleased to make them lords of truth:
"Integrity of life is fame's best friend,
Which nobly, beyond death, shall crown the end."   120
                                                                    Exeunt.

FINIS.

THE
CHANGELING:

As it was Acted (with great Applause)
at the Privat house in D R U R Y ʃ L A N E,
and *Salisbury Court.*

Written by
$\left\{\begin{array}{c} \textit{THOMAS MIDLETON,} \\ \text{and} \\ \textit{WILLIAM ROWLEY.} \end{array}\right\}$ Gent^s.

Never Printed before.

LONDON,
Printed for H U M P H R E Y M O S E L E Y, and are to
be sold at his shop at the sign of the *Princes-Arms*
in St *Pauls* Church-yard, 1653.

Art No. 8 for Changeling

Introduction

The area of tragedy is circumscribed even further in Middleton and Rowley's *The Changeling* (1622), a play of the late Jacobean period, than it is in *The Duchess of Malfi*. The final summation of the play—"Man and his sorrow at the grave must part"—resembles Webster's. Middleton (to whom the major and more serious portion of the play is usually attributed), however, states the theme with the most clinical dispassion, without a hint of melancholy. Life may be, as Walpole said, a comedy to those who think and a tragedy to those who feel; but in *The Changeling* the distinction is gone. Indeed, the grotesque comic subplot of "fools and madmen," as it interweaves with, and ironically comments on, the main plot turns the latter into a sort of *comédie noire*. Isabella, the virtuous wife of the subplot, at one point observes, "Why, here's none but fools and madmen"; to which the keeper of the asylum answers, "Very well; and where will you find any other if you should go abroad?"

More like a study of sin than a tragedy of sinners, *The Changeling* is in the end a frightening play because of its dispassionate tone. Though they are consummate sinners, Middleton neither condemns Beatrice-Joanna and De Flores (they damn themselves, of course) nor admires them (as Webster implicitly seems to admire certain of his titanic sinners—like Bosola). He seems rather to be saying, "This is the way it is." The grave parts man and his sorrow, but there is no beyond for judgment; there is no passionate probing of a universal flaw, no criticism of society, no outrage or indignation. By the conclusion of the play the evil has undone itself, the characters recognize their personal evil and simply accept it or glory in it, a crisis is resolved, and society—neither good nor bad—resumes its normal tenor. An individual's sinning does not, as it does in Macbeth's case, shake the fabric of the universe.

The title of the play comes from the subplot (seemingly more popular than the main plot in the seventeenth century), but it applies as well to Beatrice-Joanna, so changeable in her love; and by extension it applies to the whole world of the play where appearances, attitudes, desires, attractions, even reasons keep changing, where nothing seems authentically real or certain. In the opening scene, for example, Alsemero, a "stoic" in matters of love, suddenly changes when he sees Beatrice-Joanna; and the latter, engaged to be married, changes her mind at first sight of him.

Physically beautiful but morally ugly, Beatrice-Joanna is, of course, the greatest changeling. Whatever she looks upon she desires, so she claims, with "the eyes of judgment"; but in reality her judgment is no more than the reflection of an unbridled appetite. Her tragedy, if it can be called that, lies in her failure to assume responsibility for her thoughts and actions and to understand her rationalizations. When in Act II, scene ii, she turns to De Flores to murder Piracquo because "blood-guiltiness becomes a fouler visage" than her beloved Alsemero's, she is totally unaware of the irony of what she is saying: At this moment she has become, without realizing it, "the deed's creature" that De Flores later calls her. In time she discovers her inner rottenness, that her eyes are not "sentinels unto [her] judgments." But even when she finally becomes aware of her basic degradation, she disavows personal responsibility for her condition:

> Beneath the stars, upon yon meteor
> [She points to DE FLORES.]
> Ever h[u]ng my fate, 'mongst things corruptible.

The lines echo De Flores' "Can you weep fate from its determined purpose?/ So soon may [you] weep me" [III.iv]. Ugly De Flores *is* her fate: In the last act she finds that "the east is not more beauteous than his service."

Perhaps the play's greatest irony is that "honest" De Flores is, indeed, honest De Flores. The only clear-sighted character in the main plot, he *knows* what he *wants*, does not rationalize his desires, and is true to his will:

> *I know she hates me,*
> *Yet cannot choose but love her.*
> *No matter, if but to vex her, I'll haunt her still;*
> *Though I get nothing else, I'll have my will.*

(I.i)

At the beginning of Act II, Beatrice-Joanna, having changed her love from Piracquo to Alsemero, claims to "love now with the eyes of judgment. . . . With intellectual eyesight"; but De Flores pretends to no such distinctions: "I can as well be hanged as refrain seeing her." All he knows is that he must possess Beatrice-Joanna, and her very changeableness is a hopeful sign to him. Alsemero's courtly idealization of her is to him mere wasteful nonsense. If she can change so quickly from one man to another, he has reason to be optimistic:

>   *I'm sure both*
> *Cannot be served unless she transgress. Happily*
> *Then I'll put in for one: for, if a woman*
> *Fly from one point, from him she makes a husband,*
> *She spreads and mounts then like arithmetic,*
> *One, ten, a hundred, a thousand, ten thousand,*
> *Proves in time sutler to an army royal.*

(II.ii)

In De Flores, Middleton anticipated the Hobbesian man of Restoration drama whose passions are his fate—passions that have no divine sanction but are rooted in the material and animal nature of man, for which man will do anything, even rationalize as Beatrice-Joanna does. But whereas she, by attributing her fate to "things corruptible," does not recognize herself as a creature made moral—as human beings are—by her deeds, De Flores at least retains his inner consistency to the end of the play. Like Webster's best villains, he glories in the pleasures that he has limned for himself and then kills himself unrepentantly:

>   *. . . her honor's prize*
> *Was my reward. I thank life for nothing*
> *But that pleasure; it was so sweet to me*
> *That I have drunk up all, left none behind*
> *For any man to pledge me.*

Middleton's vision does not preclude the possibility of reason and control. Isabella, in the subplot of "fools and madmen," is as clear-eyed as De Flores and maintains her integral goodness as a result. But the play as a whole suggests an irresponsible universe. We remember not Isabella but the solitary egos who find meaning only in the private world of the fulfillment of their anarchic wills.

The Playwrights

THOMAS MIDDLETON (1580–1627) was the son of a London bricklayer. He matriculated at Queen's College, Oxford, in 1598, but probably returned to London to earn a living before graduation. In 1602 he was associated with the Admiral's company, and sometime before 1604 he had married the sister of one of its actors. From about 1602 to 1608 he wrote a successful series of plays, at the rate of almost one a year and mostly "London comedies," for the boy companies. After 1615 he began writing for the King's company, though never exclusively for them. In 1620 he became City Chronologer (the official historian of the City of London), and in that office he prepared a number of Lord Mayors' pageants and other civic "entertainments." He wrote successfully, alone and in collaboration, both comedy and serious drama; and he continued to write plays until his death.

WILLIAM ROWLEY (c. 1585–1626) left behind few records about himself; almost nothing is known of his early life. He probably began his career as an actor in Queen Anne's company, and after 1609 he was a leading comedian in Prince Charles' (I) company. After August, 1623, he was a member of the King's company. He wrote most of his plays in collaboration. The comic scenes of *The Changeling* (which give the play its title) are usually attributed to him; most of the scenes of the main plot, to Middleton.

The Play

The present text of *The Changeling* is based on copies of the first quarto of 1653 in the Henry E. Huntington and the

Folger Shakespeare libraries; these divide the play into acts only. The play had been licensed for performance by the Lady Elizabeth's company on May 7, 1622, presumably the approximate date of the first performance.

SELECTED BIBLIOGRAPHY

The Changeling, ed. N. W. Bawcutt. London: Methuen; Cambridge, Mass.: Harvard University Press, 1958. (The Revels Plays.)

The Changeling, ed. M. W. Black. Philadelphia: University of Pennsylvania Press, 1966.

The Changeling, ed. P. Thomson. New York: Hill and Wang, 1964 (The New Mermaids).

The Changeling, ed. G. W. Williams. Lincoln: University of Nebraska Press, 1966. (Regents Renaissance Drama Series.)

Works, ed. A. H. Bullen. 8 vols. London: Nimmo, 1885–1886.

Barker, R. H. *Thomas Middleton*. New York: Columbia University Press, 1958.

Dunkel, W. D. "Did Not Rowley Merely Revise Middleton?" *Publications of the Modern Language Association of America*, XLVIII (1933), 799–805.

Engelberg, E. "Tragic Blindness in *The Changeling* and *Women Beware Women*," *Modern Language Quarterly*, XXIII (1962), 20–28.

Farr, D. M. "*The Changeling*," *Modern Language Review*, LXII (1967), 586–597.

Gardner, H. "Milton's 'Satan' and the Theme of Damnation in Elizabethan Tradgedy," *English Studies*, new series I (1948), pp. 55–58.

Hibbard, G. R. "The Tragedies of Thomas Middleton and the Decadence of Drama," *Renaissance and Modern Studies* (University of Nottingham Press), I (1957), 35–64.

Holtzknecht, K. J. "The Dramatic Structure of *The Changeling*," in *Renaissance Papers: A Selection of Papers Presented at the Renaissance Meeting in the Southeastern States*, ed. A. H. Gilbert (Orangeburg: University of South Carolina Press, 1954), pp. 77–87.

Ricks, C. "The Moral and Poetical Structure of *The Changeling*," *Essays in Criticism*, X (1960), 290–306.

Schoenbaum, S. *Middleton's Tragedies: A Critical Study*. New York: Columbia University Press, 1955.

Tomlinson, T. B. "Poetic Naturalism—*The Changeling*," *Journal of English and Germanic Philology*, LXIII (1964), 648–659.

Wiggin, P. G. *An Inquiry into the Authorship of the Middleton-Rowley Plays*. Radcliffe Monographs 9. Boston: Ginn, 1897.

DRAMATIS PERSONAE

*

VERMANDERO, *father to Beatrice.*
TOMAZO DE PIRACQUO, *a noble lord.*
ALONZO DE PIRACQUO, *his brother, suitor to Beatrice.*
ALSEMERO, *a nobleman, afterwards married to Beatrice.*
JASPERINO, *his friend.*
ALIBIUS, *a jealous doctor.*
LOLLIO, *his man.*
PEDRO, *friend to Antonio.*
ANTONIO, *the changeling.*
FRANCISCUS, *the counterfeit madman.*
DE FLORES, *servant to Vermandero.*
Madmen.
Servants.

BEATRICE [JOANNA], *daughter to Vermandero.*
DIAPHANTA, *her waiting-woman.*
ISABELLA, *wife to Alibius.*

The Scene: *Alicant.*

The Changeling

ACTUS PRIMUS

[I.i]

Enter ALSEMERO.

[ALSEMERO.] 'Twas in the temple where I first beheld her,
  And now again the same; what omen yet
  Follows of that? None but imaginary.
  Why should my hopes or fate be timorous?
  The place is holy; so is my intent:
  I love her beauties to the holy purpose;*
  And that, methinks, admits comparison
  With man's first creation, the place blessed,
  And is his right home back (if he achieve it).
  The church hath first begun our interview,   10
  And that's the place must join us into one;
  So there's beginning and perfection too.

Enter JASPERINO.

JASPERINO. O, sir, are you here? Come, the wind's fair with you;
  Y'are like to have a swift and pleasant passage.

ALSEMERO. Sure y'are deceived, friend; 'tis contrary
  In my best judgment.

JASPERINO.   What, for Malta?
  If you could buy a gale amongst the witches,
  They could not serve you such a lucky pennyworth
  As comes o' God's name.

---

holy purpose: marriage.

ALSEMERO.   Even now I observed
   The temple's vane to turn full in my face;   20
   I know 'tis against me.
JASPERINO.   Against you?
   Then you know not where you are.
ALSEMERO.   Not well, indeed.
JASPERINO. Are you not well, sir?
ALSEMERO.   Yes, Jasperino,
   Unless there be some hidden malady
   Within me that I understand not.
JASPERINO.   And that
   I begin to doubt,* sir; I never knew
   Your inclinations to travels at a pause
   With any cause to hinder it till now.
   Ashore you were wont to call your servants up
   And help to trap your horses for the speed;   30
   At sea I have seen you weigh the anchor with 'em,
   Hoist sails for fear to lose the foremost breath,
   Be in continual prayers for fair winds;
   And have you changed your orisons?
ALSEMERO.   No, friend;
   I keep the same church, same devotion.
JASPERINO. Lover I'm sure y'are none; the stoic
   Was found in you long ago. Your mother
   Nor best friends, who have set snares of beauty, ay,
   And choice ones too, could never trap you that way.
   What might be the cause?
ALSEMERO.   Lord, how violent   40
   Thou art! I was but meditating of
   Somewhat I heard within the temple.
JASPERINO. Is this violence? 'Tis but idleness
   Compared with your haste yesterday.
ALSEMERO. I'm all this while a-going, man.
                Enter SERVANTS.
JASPERINO. Backwards, I think, sir. Look, your servants.
1 SERVANT. The seamen call; shall we board your trunks?
ALSEMERO. No, not today.
JASPERINO. 'Tis the critical day, it seems, and the sign
   in Aquarius.*   50
2 SERVANT. We must not to sea today; this smoke will
   bring forth fire.

---

doubt: fear.   sign in Aquarius: favorable for traveling by water.

ALSEMERO. Keep all on shore; I do not know the end
(Which needs I must do) of an affair in hand
Ere I can go to sea.

1 SERVANT. Well, your pleasure.

2 SERVANT. Let him e'en take his leisure too; we are
safer on land.

Exeunt Servants.

Enter BEATRICE JOANNA, DIAPHANTA, *and Servants.*

[ALSEMERO *greets and kisses* BEATRICE.]

JASPERINO. [*aside*]. How now! The laws of the Medes*
are changed sure. Salute a woman! He kisses too!   60
Wonderful! Where learnt he this? And does it perfectly too; in my conscience he ne'er rehearsed it before. Nay, go on; this will be stranger and better news
at Valencia than if he had ransomed half Greece from
the Turk.

BEATRICE. You are a scholar, sir.

ALSEMERO.   A weak one, lady.

BEATRICE. Which of the sciences is this love you speak of.

ALSEMERO. From your tongue I take it to be music.

BEATRICE. You are skillful in't, can sing at first sight.

ALSEMERO. And I have showed you all my skill at once.   70
I want more words to express me further
And must be forced to repetition:
I love you dearly.

BEATRICE.   Be better advised, sir.
Our eyes are sentinels unto our judgments
And should give certain judgment what they see;
But they are rash sometimes and tell us wonders
Of common things, which, when our judgments find,
They can then check the eyes and call them blind.

ALSEMERO. But I am further, lady; yesterday
Was mine eyes' employment, and hither now   80
They brought my judgment where are both agreed.
Both houses* then consenting, 'tis agreed;
Only there wants the confirmation
By the hand royal; that's your part, lady.

BEATRICE. O, there's one above me, sir.—[*Aside.*] For
five days past

---

laws of the Medes: see Daniel 6:8; known to be unchangeable.
both houses: i.e., of the eyes and of judgment.

To be recalled! Sure, mine eyes were mistaken;
This was the man was meant for me. That he should come
So near his time and miss it!

JASPERINO [*aside*]. We might have come by the carriers
from Valencia, I see, and saved all our sea-provision; 90
we are at farthest sure. Methinks I should do something too; I meant to be a venturer in this voyage.
Yonder's another vessel; I'll board her. If she be lawful
prize, down goes her topsail.

[*He greets* DIAPHANTA.]

Enter DE FLORES.

DE FLORES. Lady, your father—

BEATRICE.   Is in health, I hope.

DE FLORES. Your eye shall instantly instruct you, lady;
He's coming hitherward.

BEATRICE.   What needed then
Your duteous preface? I had rather
He had come unexpected; you must stall°
A good presence with unnecessary blabbing;   100
And how welcome for your part you are,
I'm sure you know.

DE FLORES [*aside*].   Will't never mend, this scorn,
One side nor other? Must I be enjoined
To follow still° whilst she flies from me? Well,
Fates do your worst, I'll please myself with sight
Of her at all opportunities
If but to spite her anger. I know she had
Rather see me dead than living, and yet
She knows no cause for't but a peevish will.

ALSEMERO. You seemed displeased, lady, on the sudden. 110

BEATRICE. Your pardon, sir; 'tis my infirmity;
Nor can I other reason render you
Than his or hers, [of] some particular thing
They must abandon as a deadly poison,
Which to a thousand other tastes were wholesome.
Such to mine eyes is that same fellow there,
The same that report speaks of the basilisk.°

ALSEMERO. This is a frequent frailty in our nature;

---

stall: forestall.   still: always.
basilisk: a fabled serpent whose glance was fatal.

There's scarce a man amongst a thousand sound
But hath his imperfection: one distastes   120
The scent of roses, which to infinites°
Most pleasing is and odoriferous;
One oil, the enemy of poison;
Another wine, the cheerer of the heart
And lively refresher of the countenance.
Indeed, this fault (if so it be) is general;
There's scarce a thing but is both loved and loathed.
Myself, I must confess, have the same frailty.
BEATRICE. And what may be your poison, sir? I am bold
     with you.
ALSEMERO What might be your desire, perhaps—a   130
     cherry.
BEATRICE. I am no enemy to any creature
My memory has but yon gentleman.
ALSEMERO. He does ill to tempt your sight if he knew it.
BEATRICE. He cannot be ignorant of that, sir.
I have not spared to tell him so, and I want
To help myself since he's a gentleman
In good respect with my father and follows him.
ALSEMERO. He's out of his place then now.
     [*They talk apart.*]
JASPERINO. I am a mad wag, wench.
DIAPHANTA. So methinks; but for your comfort I can tell   140
     you we have a doctor in the city that undertakes the
     cure of such.
JASPERINO. Tush, I know what physic is best for the state
     of mine own body.
DIAPHANTA. 'Tis scarce a well-governed state, I believe.
JASPERINO. I could show thee such a thing with an in-
     gredien[t] that we two would compound together;
     and, if it did not tame the maddest blood i'th' town
     for two hours after, I'll ne'er profess physic again.
DIAPHANTA. A little poppy, sir, were good to cause you   150
     sleep.
JASPERINO. Poppy! I'll give thee a pop i'th' lips for that
     first and begin there. [*He kisses her.*] Poppy is one
     simple indeed, and cuckoo° (what you call't) another.

---

infinites: infinite number of people.
cuckoo: wake-robin, a plant that grows to a great length.

I'll discover no more now; another time I'll show thee
all.

BEATRICE. My father, sir.

Enter VERMANDERO *and Servants.*

VERMANDERO.   O, Joanna, I came to meet
thee.
Your devotion's ended?

BEATRICE.   For this time, sir.—
[*Aside.*] I shall change my saint, I fear me; I find
A giddy turning in me.—Sir, this while   160
I am beholding to this gentleman,
Who left his own way to keep me company,
And in discourse I find him much desirous
To see your castle. He hath deserved it, sir,
If ye please to grant it.

VERMANDERO.   With all my heart, sir.
Yet there's an article between; I must know
Your country. We use° not to give survey
Of our chief strengths to strangers; our citadels
Are placed conspicuous to outward view
On promonts' tops, but within are secrets.   170

ALSEMERO. A Valencian, sir.

VERMANDERO.   A Valencian?
That's native, sir; of what name, I beseech you?

ALSEMERO. Alsemero, sir.

VERMANDERO.   Alsemero? Not the son
Of John de Alsemero?

ALSEMERO.   The same, sir.

VERMANDERO. My best love bids you welcome.

BEATRICE [*aside*].   He was wont
To call me so, and then he speaks a most
Unfeignèd truth.

VERMANDERO.   O, sir, I knew your father.
We two were in acquaintance long ago
Before our chins were worth Iulan° down
And so continued till the stamp of time   180
Had coined us into silver. Well, he's gone;
A good soldier went with him.

ALSEMERO. You went together in that, sir.

---

use: are accustomed.
Iulan (down): youthful (applied to first growth of beard).

VERMANDERO. No, by Saint Jacques,* I came behind
    him;
  Yet I have done somewhat too. An unhappy day
  Swallowed him at last at Gibraltar*
  In fight with those rebellious Hollanders,
  Was it not so?
ALSEMERO.   Whose death I had revenged
  Or followed him in fate had not the late league*
  Prevented me.
VERMANDERO.   Ay, ay, 'twas time to breathe.—   190
  O, Joanna, I should ha'told thee news;
  I saw Piracquo lately.
BEATRICE [aside].   That's ill news.
VERMANDERO. He's hot preparing for this day of triumph;
  Thou must be a bride within this sevennight.
ALSEMERO [aside].   Ha!
BEATRICE. Nay, good sir, be not so violent; with speed
  I cannot render satisfaction
  Unto the dear companion of my soul,
  Virginity, whom I thus long have lived with,
  And part with it so rude and suddenly.
  Can such friends divide never to meet again   200
  Without a solemn farewell?
VERMANDERO.   Tush, tush, there's a toy.
ALSEMERO [aside]. I must now part and never meet
    again
  With any joy on earth.—Sir, your pardon;
  My affairs call on me.
VERMANDERO.   How, sir? By no means;
  Not changed so soon, I hope? You must see my castle
  And her best entertainment ere we part;
  I shall think myself unkindly used else.
  Come, come, let's on; I had good hope your stay
  Had been a while with us in Alicant;
  I might have bid you to my daughter's wedding.   210
ALSEMERO. [aside]. He means to feast me and poisons
  me beforehand.—

Saint Jacques: Saint James the Greater, the patron saint of Spain.
Gibraltar: where the Dutch defeated the Spanish in a naval
battle on April 25, 1607.
late league: treaty between Spain and the Netherlands, signed
on April 9, 1609.

I should be dearly glad to be there, sir,
Did my occasions suit as I could wish.

BEATRICE. I shall be sorry if you be not there
When it is done, sir—but not so suddenly.

VERMANDERO. I tell you, sir, the gentleman's complete,
A courtier and a gallant, enriched
With many fair and noble ornaments;
I would not change him for a son-in-law
For any he in Spain, the proudest he,   220
And we have great ones, that you know.

ALSEMERO.   He's much
Bound to you, sir.

VERMANDERO.   He shall be bound to me
As fast as this tie can hold; I'll want
My will else.

BEATRICE [*aside*].   I shall want mine if you do it.

VERMANDERO. But come; by the way I'll tell you more of
him.

ALSEMERO [*aside*]. How shall I dare to venture in his
castle
When he discharges murderers° at the gate?
But I must on, for back I cannot go.

BEATRICE [*aside*]. Not this serpent gone yet?
[*She drops her glove.*]

VERMANDERO.   Look,
girl, thy glove's fallen;
Stay, stay.—De Flores, help a little.

                    [*Exeunt* VERMANDERO, ALSEMERO, JASPERINO,
                                and Servants.]

DE FLORES [*offering her the glove*].   Here, lady.   230

BEATRICE. Mischief on your officious forwardness!
Who bade you stoop? They touch my hand no more;
There, for t'other's sake I part with this.
[*She throws down her other glove.*]
Take 'em and draw thine own skin off with 'em.

                            Exeunt [*all but* DE FLORES.]

DE FLORES. Here's a favor come with a mischief! Now
I know she had rather wear my pelt tanned in a pair
Of dancing pumps than I should thrust my fingers
Into her sockets here. I know she hates me,
Yet cannot choose but love her.

_____

murderers: small cannons.

No matter, if but to vex her, I'll haunt her still;   240
Though I get nothing else, I'll have my will.

Exit.

[I.ii]
                    Enter ALIBIUS *and* LOLLIO.
ALIBIUS. Lollio, I must trust thee with a secret,
  But thou must keep it.
LOLLIO. I was ever close to a secret, sir.
ALIBIUS. The diligence that I have found in thee,
  The care and industry already past,
  Assures me of thy good continuance.
  Lollio, I have a wife.
LOLLIO. Fie, sir, 'tis too late to keep her secret; she's
  known to be married all the town and country over.
ALIBIUS. Thou goest too fast, my Lollio. That knowledge   10
  I allow no man can be barred it;
  But there is a knowledge which is nearer,
  Deeper, and sweeter, Lollio.
LOLLIO. Well, sir, let us handle that between you and I.
ALIBIUS. 'Tis that I go about, man; Lollio,
  My wife is young.
LOLLIO. So much the worse to be kept secret, sir.
ALIBIUS. Why, now thou meet'st the substance of the
  point;
  I am old, Lollio.
LOLLIO. No, sir, 'tis I am old Lollio.   20
ALIBIUS. Yet why may not this concord and sympathize?
  Old trees and young plants often grow together,
  Well enough agreeing.
LOLLIO. Ay, sir, but the old trees raise themselves higher
  and broader than the young plants.
ALIBIUS. Shrewd application! There's the fear, man;
  I would wear my ring on my own finger;
  Whilst it is borrowed, it is none of mine
  But his that useth it.
LOLLIO. You must keep it on still then; if it but lie by,   30
  one or other will be thrusting into't.
ALIBIUS. Thou conceiv'st me, Lollio. Here thy watchful
  eye
  Must have employment; I cannot always be
  At home.

LOLLIO. I dare swear you cannot.

ALIBIUS. I must look out.

LOLLIO. I know't, you must look out; 'tis every man's case.

ALIBIUS. Here I do say must thy employment be
To watch her treadings and in my absence   40
Supply my place.

LOLLIO. I'll do my best, sir; yet surely I cannot see who
you should have cause to be jealous of.

ALIBIUS. Thy reason for that, Lollio? 'Tis a comfortable
question.

LOLLIO. We have but two sorts of people in the house,
and both under the whip—that's fools and madmen;
the one has not wit enough to be knaves, and the other
not knavery enough to be fools.

ALIBIUS. Ay, those are all my patients, Lollio.   50
I do profess the cure of either sort:
My trade, my living 'tis; I thrive by it.
But here's the care that mixes with my thrift:
The daily visitants, that come to see
My brainsick patients, I would not have
To see my wife. Gallants I do observe
Of quick, enticing eyes, rich in habits,°
Of stature and proportion very comely:
These are most shrewd temptations, Lollio.

LOLLIO. They may be easily answered, sir. If they come   60
to see the fools and madmen, you and I may serve the
turn, and let my mistress alone; she's of neither sort.

ALIBIUS. 'Tis a good ward;° indeed, come they to see
Our madmen or our fools, let 'em see no more
Than what they come for. By that consequent
They must not see her; I'm sure she's no fool.

LOLLIO. And I'm sure she's no madman.

ALIBIUS. Hold that buckler fast, Lollio; my trust
Is on thee, and I account it firm and strong.
What hour is't, Lollio?   70

LOLLIO. Towards belly hour, sir.

ALIBIUS. Dinner time? Thou mean'st twelve o'clock.

LOLLIO. Yes, sir, for every part has his hour. We wake at
six and look about us, that's eye hour; at seven we

---

habits: dress.   ward: defense.

should pray, that's knee hour; at eight walk, that's leg
hour; at nine gather flowers and pluck a rose,* that's
nose hour; at ten we drink, that's mouth hour; at eleven
lay about us for victuals, that's hand hour; at twelve go
to dinner, that's belly hour.

ALIBIUS. Profoundly, Lollio! It will be long　　　　　　80
Ere all thy scholars learn this lesson, and
I did look to have a new one entered. Stay,
I think my expectation is come home.

　　　　Enter PEDRO, *and* ANTONIO *like an idiot.*

PEDRO. Save you, sir. My business speaks itself;
This sight takes off the labor of my tongue.

ALIBIUS. Ay, ay, sir, 'tis plain enough you mean him for
my patient.

PEDRO. And if your pains prove but commodious, to give
but some little strength to his sick and weak part of
nature in him, these are [*He gives him money.*] but　　90
patterns to show you of the whole pieces that will follow to you, beside the charge of diet, washing, and
other necessaries fully defrayed.

ALIBIUS. Believe it, sir, there shall no care be wanting.

LOLLIO. Sir, an officer in this place may deserve something; the trouble will pass through my hands.

PEDRO. 'Tis fit something should come to your hands
then, sir.
[*He gives him money.*]

LOLLIO. Yes, sir, 'tis I must keep him sweet* and read to
him. What is his name?　　　　　　　　　　100

PEDRO. His name is Antonio; marry, we use but half to
him, only Tony.

LOLLIO. Tony, Tony, 'tis enough and a very good name
for a fool. What's your name, Tony? *

ANTONIO. He, he, he! Well, I thank you, cousin. He, he,
he!

LOLLIO. Good boy! Hold up your head.—He can laugh; I
perceive by that he is no beast.

PEDRO. Well, sir,
If you can raise him but to any height,　　　　　　110
Any degree of wit, might he attain
(As I might say) to creep but on all four

---

pluck a rose: euphemism for defecate.　　　sweet: clean.
Tony: fool, simpleton (pun on "Antonio").

Towards the chair of wit or walk on crutches,
'Twould add an honor to your worthy pains;
And a great family might pray for you
To which he should be heir had he discretion
To claim and guide his own. Assure you, sir,
He is a gentleman.

LOLLIO. Nay, there's nobody doubted that. At first sight I
knew him for a gentleman; he looks no other yet.   120

PEDRO. Let him have good attendance and sweet lodging.

LOLLIO. As good as my mistress lies in, sir; and, as you
allow us time and means, we can raise him to the
higher degree of discretion.

PEDRO. Nay, there shall no cost want, sir.

LOLLIO. He will hardly be stretched up to the wit of a
magnifico.*

PEDRO. O, no, that's not to be expected; far shorter will
be enough.   130

LOLLIO. I'll warrant you [I'll] make him fit to bear office
in five weeks; I'll undertake to wind him up to the wit
of constable.

PEDRO. If it be lower than that, it might serve turn.

LOLLIO. No, fie; to level him with a headborough,*
beadle, or watchman were but little better than he is.
Constable I'll able him: if he do come to be a justice
afterwards, let him thank the keeper. Or I'll go further
with you. Say I do bring him up to my own pitch; say
I make him as wise as myself.   140

PEDRO. Why, there I would have it.

LOLLIO. Well, go to; either I'll be as arrant a fool as he,
or he shall be as wise as I, and then I think 'twill
serve his turn.

PEDRO. Nay, I do like thy wit passing well.

LOLLIO. Yes, you may; yet if I had not been a fool, I had
had more wit than I have too. Remember what state*
you find me in.

PEDRO. I will, and so leave you. Your best cares, I beseech you.   150

ALIBIUS. Take you none with you; leave 'em all with us.

Exit PEDRO.

---

magnifico: magistrate.   headborough: constable.
state: position of authority.

ANTONIO. O, my cousin's gone! Cousin, cousin, O!

LOLLIO. Peace, peace, Tony! You must not cry, child;
you must be whipped if you do. Your cousin is here
still; I am your cousin, Tony.

ANTONIO. He, he! Then I'll not cry if thou be'st my
cousin. He, he, he!

LOLLIO. I were best try his wit a little, that I may know
what form* to place him in.

ALIBIUS. Ay, do, Lollio, do.   160

LOLLIO. I must ask him easy questions at first.—Tony,
how many true* fingers has a tailor on his right hand?

ANTONIO. As many as on his left, cousin.

LOLLIO. Good; and how many on both?

ANTONIO. Two less than a deuce, cousin.

LOLLIO. Very well answered. I come to you again, cousin
Tony: how many fools goes to* a wise man?

ANTONIO. Forty in a day sometimes, cousin.

LOLLIO. Forty in a day? How prove you that?

ANTONIO. All that fall out amongst themselves and go to   170
a lawyer to be made friends.

LOLLIO. A parlous fool! He must sit in the fourth form at
least, I perceive that.—I come again, Tony: how many
knaves make an honest man?

ANTONIO. I know not that, cousin.

LOLLIO. No, the question is too hard for you: I'll tell you,
cousin. There's three knaves may make an honest man
—a sergeant, a jailor, and a beadle; the sergeant
catches him, the jailor holds him, and the beadle lashes
him; and, if he be not honest then, the hangman must   180
cure him.

ANTONIO. Ha, ha, ha! That's fine sport, cousin.

ALIBIUS. This was too deep a question for the fool,
Lollio.

LOLLIO. Yes, this might have served yourself, though I
say't.—Once more and you shall go play, Tony.

ANTONIO. Ay, play at push-pin, cousin. Ha, he!

LOLLIO. So thou shalt; say how many fools are here.

ANTONIO. Two, cousin; thou and I.

LOLLIO. Nay, y'are too forward there, Tony; mark my   190

----

form: school class.   true: honest.
goes to: 1) make up (Lollio's meaning); 2) visit (Antonio's
meaning).

question: how many fools and knaves are here? A fool before a knave, a fool behind a knave, between every two fools a knave—how many fools, how many knaves?

ANTONIO. I never learnt so far, cousin.

ALIBIUS. Thou putt'st too hard questions to him, Lollio.

LOLLIO. I'll make him understand it easily.—Cousin, stand there.

ANTONIO. Ay, cousin.

LOLLIO. Master, stand you next the fool.   200

ALIBIUS. Well, Lollio.

LOLLIO. Here's my place. Mark now, Tony, there a fool before a knave.

ANTONIO. That's I, cousin.

LOLLIO. Here's a fool behind a knave, that's I; and between us two fools there is a knave, that's my master; 'tis but we three, that's all.

ANTONIO. We three, we three, cousin.

(*Madmen within.*)

1 WITHIN. Put's head i'th' pillory; the bread's too little.

2 WITHIN. Fly, fly, and he catches the swallow.   210

3 WITHIN. Give her more onion, or the devil put the rope about her crag.*

LOLLIO. You may hear what time of day it is; the chimes of Bedlam* goes.

ALIBIUS. Peace, peace, or the wire* comes!

3 WITHIN. Cat whore, cat whore, her parmasant,* her parmasant!

ALIBIUS. Peace, I say!—Their hour's come; they must be fed, Lollio.

LOLLIO. There's no hope of recovery of that Welsh mad-   220
man; was undone by a mouse that spoiled him a parmasant; lost his wits for't.

ALIBIUS. Go to your charge, Lollio; I'll to mine.

LOLLIO. Go to your madmen's ward; let me alone with
your fools.

ALIBIUS. And remember my last charge, Lollio.

---

crag: neck.

Bedlam: Bethlehem Hospital, a London asylum for the insane. Citizens visited it daily as a place of entertainment. (The "chimes" are the inmates clamoring for food.)   wire: whip.

parmasant: Parmesan cheese.

LOLLIO. Of which your patients do you think I am?—

Exit [ALIBIUS.]

Come, Tony, you must amongst your schoolfellows
now; there's pretty scholars amongst 'em, I can tell
you. There's some of 'em at *stultus, stulta, stultum.** 230
ANTONIO. I would see the madmen, cousin, if they would
not bite me.
LOLLIO. No, they shall not bite thee, Tony.
ANTONIO. They bite when they are at dinner, do they not,
coz?
LOLLIO. They bite at dinner, indeed, Tony. Well, I hope
to get credit by thee; I like thee the best of all the
scholars that ever I brought up, and thou shalt prove
a wise man, or I'll prove a fool myself.

Exeunt.

ACTUS SECUNDUS

[II.i]

Enter BEATRICE *and* JASPERINO *severally.*

BEATRICE. O, sir, I'm ready now for that fair service
Which makes the name of friend sit glorious on you.
Good angels and this conduct be your guide!
[*She gives him a paper.*]
Fitness of time and place is there set down, sir.
JASPERINO. The joy I shall return rewards my service.

Exit.

BEATRICE. How wise is Alsemero in his friend!
It is a sign he makes his choice with judgment.
Then I appear in nothing more approved
Than making choice of him;
For 'tis a principle, he that can choose   10
That bosom well, who of his thoughts partakes,
Proves most discreet in every choice he makes.
Methinks I love now with the eyes of judgment
And see the way to merit, clearly see it.
A true deserver like a diamond sparkles;
In darkness you may see him that's in absence,
Which is the greatest darkness falls on love;
Yet is he best discerned then

---

stultus, stulta, stultum: beginning of Latin declension of "stupid."

With intellectual eyesight. What's Piracquo
My father spends his breath for? And his blessing   20
Is only mine as I regard his name;
Else it goes from me and turns head against me,
Transformed into a curse. Some speedy way
Must be remembered; he's so forward too,
So urgent that way, scarce allows me breath
To speak to my new comforts.

Enter DE FLORES.

DE FLORES [*aside*].   Yonder's she.
Whatever ails me, now a-late especially,
I can as well be hanged as refrain seeing her;
Some twenty times a day, nay, not so little,
Do I force errands, frame ways and excuses   30
To come into her sight, and I have small reason for't
And less encouragement; for she baits me still
Every time worse than other, does profess herself
The cruelest enemy to my face in town,
At no hand can abide the sight of me,
As if danger or ill luck hung in my looks.
I must confess my face is bad enough,
But I know far worse has better fortune
And not endured alone, but doted on;
And yet such pick-haired* faces, chins like witches',   40
Here and there five hairs, whispering in a corner
As if they grew in fear one of another,
Wrinkles like troughs where swine-deformity swills
The tears of perjury that lie there like wash
Fallen from the slimy and dishonest eye—
Yet such a one pluck[s] sweets without restraint
And has the grace of beauty to his sweet.
Though my hard fate has thrust me out to servitude,
I tumbled into th' world a gentleman.
She turns her blessèd eye upon me now,   50
And I'll endure all storms before I part with't.
BEATRICE [*aside*]. Again!
This ominous ill-faced fellow more disturbs me
Than all my other passions.
DE FLORES [*aside*].   Now't begins again;
I'll stand this storm of hail though the stones pelt me.

---

pick-haired: hard-bristled (?); thin-bearded (?).

BEATRICE. Thy business? What's thy business?
DE FLORES [aside].   Soft and
    fair,
I cannot part so soon now.
BEATRICE [aside].   The villain's fixed.—
    Thou standing toad-pool!
DE FLORES [aside].   The shower falls amain
    now.
BEATRICE. Who sent thee? What's thy errand? Leave my
    sight.
DE FLORES. My lord your father charged me to deliver   60
    A message to you.
BEATRICE.   What, another since?
    Do't and be hanged then; let me be rid of thee.
DE FLORES. True service merits mercy.
BEATRICE.   What's thy
    message?
DE FLORES. Let beauty settle but in patience,
    You shall hear all.
BEATRICE.   A dallying, trifling torment!
DE FLORES. Signor Alonzo de Piracquo, lady,
    Sole brother to Tomazo de Piracquo—
BEATRICE. Slave, when wilt make an end?
DE FLORES.   Too soon I
    shall.
BEATRICE. What all this while of him?
DE FLORES.   The said Alonzo,
    With the foresaid Tomazo—
BEATRICE.   Yet again?   70
DE FLORES. Is new alighted.
BEATRICE.   Vengeance strike the news!
    Thou thing most loathed, what cause was there in this
    To bring thee to my sight?
DE FLORES.   My lord your father
    Charged me to seek you out.
BEATRICE.   Is there no other
    To send his errand by?
DE FLORES.   It seems 'tis my luck
    To be i'th' way still.
BEATRICE.   Get thee from me.
DE FLORES.   So.—
    [Aside.] Why, am not I an ass to devise ways
    Thus to be railed at? I must see her still!

I shall have a mad qualm within this hour again,
I know't, and like a common Garden-bull*   80
I do but take breath to be lugged* again.
What this may bode I know not; I'll despair the less
Because there's daily precedents of bad faces
Beloved beyond all reason. These foul chops
May come into favor one day 'mongst his fellows.
Wrangling has proved the mistress of good pastime;
As children cry themselves asleep, I ha' seen
Women have chid themselves abed to men.

Exit DE FLORES.

BEATRICE. I never see this fellow but I think
  Of some harm towards me; danger's in my mind still;   90
  I scarce leave trembling of an hour after.
  The next good mood I find my father in,
  I'll get him quite discarded. O, I was
  Lost in this small disturbance and forgot
  Affliction's fiercer torrent that now comes
  To bear down all my comforts.

Enter VERMANDERO, ALONZO, TOMAZO.

VERMANDERO.   Y'are both welcome,
  But an especial one belongs to you, sir,
  To whose most noble name our love presents
  The addition of a son, our son Alonzo.
ALONZO. The treasury of honor cannot bring forth   100
  A title I should more rejoice in, sir.
VERMANDERO. You have improved it well.—Daughter,
  prepare;
  The day will steal upon thee suddenly.
BEATRICE [*aside*]. Howe'er, I will be sure to keep* the
  night
  If it should come so near me.
  [BEATRICE *and* VERMANDERO *talk apart.*]
TOMAZO.   Alonzo!
ALONZO.   Brother?
TOMAZO. In troth I see small welcome in her eye.
ALONZO. Fie, you are too severe a censurer
  Of love in all points; there's no bringing on you.*
  If lovers should mark everything a fault,

Garden-bull: like one of the bulls baited in the Paris Garden in
Southwark.   lugged: baited, harassed.   keep: watch.
bringing on you: making you realize; persuading you.

Affection would be like an ill-set book,   110
Whose faults might prove as big as half the volume.
BEATRICE. That's all I do entreat.
VERMANDERO.   It is but reasonable;
   I'll see what my son says to't.—Son Alonzo,
   Here's a motion made but to reprieve
   A maidenhead three days longer; the request
   Is not far out of reason, for indeed
   The former time is pinching.
ALONZO.   Though my joys
   Be set back so much time as I could wish
   They had been forward, yet, since she desires it,
   The time is set as pleasing as before;   120
   I find no gladness wanting.
VERMANDERO. May I ever meet it in that point still!°
   Y'are nobly welcome, sirs.
                  Exeunt VERMANDERO *and* BEATRICE.
TOMAZO. So, did you mark the dullness of her parting
     now?
ALONZO. What dullness? Thou art so exceptious still.
TOMAZO. Why, let it go then; I am but a fool
   To mark your harms so heedfully.
ALONZO.   Where's the over-
     sight?
TOMAZO. Come, your faith's cozened° in her, strongly
     cozened.
   Unsettle your affection with all speed
   Wisdom can bring it to; your peace is ruined else.   130
   Think what a torment 'tis to marry one
   Whose heart is leaped into another's bosom:
   If ever pleasure she receive from thee,
   It comes not in thy name or of thy gift;
   She lies but with another in thine arms,
   He the half-father unto all thy children
   In the conception; if he get 'em not,
   She helps to get 'em for him . . . ;°
   And how dangerous
   And shameful her restraint may go in time to,   140
   It is not to be thought on without sufferings.

---

still: always.   cozened: cheated.
ellipses: the troublesome phrase "in his passion" is omitted.

ALONZO. You speak as if she loved some other then.
TOMAZO. Do you apprehend so slowly?
ALONZO.   Nay, and* that
  Be your fear only, I am safe enough.
  Preserve your friendship and your counsel, brother,
  For times of more distress. I should depart
  An enemy, a dangerous, deadly one
  To any but thyself that should but think
  She knew the meaning of inconstancy
  Much less the use and practice; yet w'are friends.   150
  Pray let no more be urged; I can endure
  Much till I meet an injury to her;
  Then I am not myself. Farewell, sweet brother;
  How much w'are bound to heaven to depart lovingly!

                                                   Exit.

TOMAZO. Why, here is love's tame madness; thus a man
  Quickly steals into his vexation.

                                                   Exit.

[II.ii]
                    Enter DIAPHANTA *and* ALSEMERO.
DIAPHANTA. The place is my charge; you have kept your
    hour,
  And the reward of a just meeting bless you.
  I hear my lady coming. Complete gentleman,
  I dare not be too busy with my praises;
  Th'are dangerous* things to deal with.

                                                   Exit.

ALSEMERO.   This goes
    well;
  These women are the ladies' cabinets;
  Things of most precious trust are lock[ed] into 'em.
                    Enter BEATRICE.
BEATRICE. I have within mine eye all my desires;
  Requests that holy prayers ascend heaven for
  And brings 'em down to furnish our defects   10
  Come not more sweet to our necessities
  Than thou unto my wishes.

_____

  and: if.
  dangerous: because Diaphanta unwittingly may arouse Beatrice's
jealousy.

ALSEMERO.   W'are so like
   In our expressions, lady, that unless I borrow
   The same words I shall never find their equals.
   [*He kisses her.*]
BEATRICE. How happy were this meeting, this embrace,
   If it were free from envy! This poor kiss,
   It has an enemy, a hateful one,
   That wishes poison to't. How well were I now
   If there were none such name known as Piracquo
   Nor no such tie as the command of parents!   20
   I should be but too much blessed.
ALSEMERO.   One good service
   Would strike off both your fears, and I'll go near it too
   Since you are so distressed. Remove the cause,
   The command ceases; so there's two fears blown out
   With one and the same blast.
BEATRICE.   Pray let me find * you,
   sir.
   What might that service be so strangely happy?
ALSEMERO. The honorablest piece 'bout man, valor.
   I'll send a challenge to Piracquo instantly.
BEATRICE. How? Call you that extinguishing of fear
   When 'tis the only way to keep it flaming?   30
   Are not you ventured in the action
   That's all my joys and comforts? Pray, no more, sir.
   Say you prevailed, [you're] danger's and not mine then;
   The law would claim you from me, or obscurity
   Be made the grave to bury you alive.
   I'm glad these thoughts come forth. O, keep not one
   Of this condition, sir. Here was a course
   Found to bring sorrow on her way to death;
   The tears would ne'er 'a' dried till dust had choked 'em.
   Blood-guiltiness becomes a fouler visage.—   40
   [*Aside.*] And now I think on one! I was to blame
   I ha' marred so good a market with my scorn.
   'T had been done questionless; the ugliest creature
   Creation framed for some use, yet to see
   I could not mark so much where it should be!
ALSEMERO. Lady—
BEATRICE [*aside*].   Why, men of art make much of
   poison,

---

find: understand.

Keep one to expel another. Where was my art?

ALSEMERO. Lady, you hear not me.

BEATRICE.   I do especially, sir;
  The present times are not so sure of our side
  As those hereafter may be; we must use 'em then   50
  As thrifty folks their wealth, sparingly now
  Till the time opens.

ALSEMERO.   You teach wisdom, lady.

BEATRICE. Within there, Diaphanta!

                Enter DIAPHANTA.

DIAPHANTA.   Do you call,
  madam?

BEATRICE. Perfect your service, and conduct this gentleman
  The private way you brought him.

DIAPHANTA.   I shall, madam.

ALSEMERO. My love's as firm as love e'er built upon.

            Exeunt DIAPHANTA *and* ALSEMERO.

             Enter DE FLORES.

DE FLORES [*aside*]. I have watched this meeting and do
  wonder much
  What shall become of t'other; I'm sure both
  Cannot be served unless she transgress. Happily*
  Then I'll put in for one: for, if a woman   60
  Fly from one point, from him she makes a husband,
  She spreads and mounts then like arithmetic,
  One, ten, a hundred, a thousand, ten thousand,
  Proves in time sutler* to an army royal.
  Now do I look to be most richly railed at,
  Yet I must see her.

BEATRICE [*aside*].   Why, put case I loathed him
  As much as youth and beauty hates a sepulcher,
  Must I needs show it? Cannot I keep that secret
  And serve my turn upon him? See, he's here.—
  De Flores!

DE FLORES [*aside*]. Ha, I shall run mad with joy!   70
  She called me fairly by my name, De Flores,
  And neither rogue nor rascal.

BEATRICE.   What ha' you done
  To your face a-late? Y'ave met with some good physician;

---

happily: haply; perhaps.   sutler: provisioner to an army.

Y'ave pruned yourself, methinks; you were not wont
To look so amorously.

DE FLORES [*aside*].   Not I;
'Tis the same physnomy° to a hair and pimple
Which she called scurvy scarce an hour ago.
How is this?

BEATRICE.   Come hither; nearer, man.

DE FLORES [*aside*]. I'm up to the chin in heaven!

BEATRICE.   Turn,
   let me see.
Vaugh! 'Tis but the heat of the liver, I perceive't.   80
I thought it had been worse.

DE FLORES [*aside*].   Her fingers touched me!
She smells all amber.

BEATRICE. I'll make a water for you shall cleanse this
Within a fortnight.

DE FLORES.   With your own hands, lady?

BEATRICE. Yes, mine own, sir; in a work of cure,
I'll trust no other.

DE FLORES [*aside*].   'Tis half an act of pleasure
To hear her talk thus to me.

BEATRICE.   When w'are used
To a hard face, 'tis not so unpleasing;
It mends still in opinion, hourly mends;
I see it bv experience.

DE FLORES [*aside*].   I was blessed   90
To light upon this minute; I'll make use on't.

BEATRICE. Hardness becomes the visage of a man well;
It argues service, resolution, manhood,
If cause were of employment.

DE FLORES.   'Twould be soon seen
If e'er your ladyship had cause to use it.
I would but wish the honor of a service
So happy as that mounts to.

BEATRICE.   We shall try you.
O, my De Flores!

DE FLORES [*aside*]. How's that?
She calls me hers already, "my De Flores!"—
You were about to sigh out somewhat, madam.   100

BEATRICE. No, was I? I forgot—O!

---

physnomy: physiognomy.

DE FLORES. There 'tis again,
The very fellow on't.
BEATRICE. You are too quick, sir.
DE FLORES. There's no excuse for't now; I heard it twice,
madam;
That sigh would fain have utterance; take pity on't
And lend it a free word. 'Las, how it labors
For liberty! I hear the murmur yet
Beat at your bosom.
BEATRICE. Would creation—
DE FLORES. Ay, well said, that's it.
BEATRICE. Had formed me
man.
DE FLORES. Nay, that's not it.
BEATRICE. O, 'tis the soul of freedom!
I should not then be forced to marry one 110
I hate beyond all depths; I should have power
Then to oppose my loathings, nay, remove 'em
Forever from my sight.
DE FLORES. O blessed occasion!
Without change to your sex you have your wishes.
Claim so much man in me.
BEATRICE. In thee, De Flores?
There's small cause for that.
DE FLORES. Put it not from me;
It's a service that I kneel for to you.
[*He kneels.*]
BEATRICE. You are too violent to mean faithfully;
There's horror in my service, blood and danger.
Can those be things to sue for?
DE FLORES. If you knew 120
How sweet it were to me to be employed
In any act of yours, you would say then
I failed and used not reverence enough
When I received the charge on't.
BEATRICE [*aside*]. This is much,
methinks;
Belike his wants are greedy, and to such
Gold tastes like angels' food.—Rise!
DE FLORES. I'll have the work first.
BEATRICE [*aside*]. Possible his need
Is strong upon him.—There's to encourage thee.

[*She gives him money.*]
As thou art forward and thy service dangerous,
Thy reward shall be precious.
DE FLORES.   That I have thought
   on;   130
I have assured myself of that beforehand
And know it will be precious; the thought ravishes.
BEATRICE. Then take him to thy fury.
DE FLORES.   I thirst for him.
BEATRICE. Alonzo de Piracquo.
DE FLORES [*rising*].   His end's upon him;
He shall be seen no more.
BEATRICE.   How lovely now
Dost thou appear to me! Never was man
Dearlier rewarded.
DE FLORES.   I do think of that.
BEATRICE. Be wondrous careful in the execution.
DE FLORES. Why, are not both our lives upon the cast?
BEATRICE. Then I throw all my fears upon thy service.   140
DE FLORES. They ne'er shall rise to hurt you.
BEATRICE.   When
   the deed's done,
I'll furnish thee with all things for thy flight;
Thou mayst live bravely in another country.
DE FLORES. Ay, ay, we'll talk of that hereafter.
BEATRICE [*aside*].   I shall
   rid myself
Of two inveterate loathings at one time:
Piracquo and his dog-face.
                              Exit.

DE FLORES.   O my blood!°
Methinks I feel her in mine arms already,
Her wanton fingers combing out this beard
And, being pleased, praising this bad face;
Hunger and pleasure, they'll commend sometimes   150
Slovenly dishes and feed heartily on 'em,
Nay, which is stranger, refuse daintier for 'em.
Some women are odd feeders.—I'm too loud.
Here comes the man goes supperless to bed,
Yet shall not rise tomorrow to his dinner.

———

blood: passion.

Enter ALONZO.

ALONZO. De Flores.
DE FLORES.   My kind, honorable lord.
ALONZO. I am glad I ha' met with thee.
DE FLORES.   Sir.
ALONZO.   Thou
    canst show me
  The full strength of the castle?
DE FLORES.   That I can, sir.
ALONZO. I much desire it.
DE FLORES.   And, if the ways and straits
  Of some of the passages be not too tedious for you,   160
  I will assure you, worth your time and sight, my lord.
ALONZO. Puh! That shall be no hindrance.
DE FLORES.   I'm your
    servant, then.
  'Tis now near dinner time; 'gainst* your lordship's
    rising
  I'll have the keys about me.
ALONZO.   Thanks, kind De Flores.
DE FLORES [*aside*]. He's safely thrust upon me beyond
    hopes.

                                              Exeunt.

ACTUS TERTIUS

[III.i]

Enter ALONZO *and* DE FLORES.
(*In the act-time** DE FLORES *hides a naked rapier.*)

DE FLORES. Yes, here are all the keys; I was afraid, my
    lord,
  I'd wanted for the postern—this is it.
  I've all, I've all, my lord. This for the sconce.*
ALONZO. 'Tis a most spacious and impregnable fort.
DE FLORES. You'll tell me more, my lord. This descent
  Is somewhat narrow; we shall never pass
  Well with our weapons; they'll but trouble us.
ALONZO. Thou sayst true.

—————————

'gainst: before.   act-time: interval between acts of a play.
sconce: small fortress.

DE FLORES.   Pray let me help your lordship.

ALONZO. 'Tis done. Thanks, kind De Flores.

DE FLORES.   Here are
  hooks, my lord,
  To hang such things on purpose.
  [*He hangs up the two swords.*]

ALONZO.   Lead; I'll follow
  thee.   10

  Exeunt at one door and enter at the other.

[III.ii]

DE FLORES. All this is nothing; you shall see anon
  A place you little dream on.

ALONZO.   I am glad
  I have this leisure; all your master's house
  Imagine I ha' taken a gondola.

DE FLORES. All but myself, sir—[*Aside.*] which makes
  up my safety.—
  My lord, I'll place you at a casement here
  Will show you the full strength of the castle.
  Look, spend your eye awhile upon that object.

ALONZO. Here's rich variety, De Flores.

DE FLORES.   Yes, sir.

ALONZO. Goodly munition.

DE FLORES.   Ay, there's ordnance, sir,   10
  No bastard metal, will ring you a peal like bells
  At great men's funerals. Keep your eye straight, my
    lord;
  Take special notice of that sconce before you;
  There you may dwell awhile.
  [*He takes the rapier that he has hidden.*]

ALONZO.   I am upon't.

DE FLORES. And so am I.
  [*He stabs him.*]

ALONZO.   De Flores! O, De Flores,
  Whose malice hast thou put on?

DE FLORES.   Do you question
  A work of secrecy? I must silence you.
  [*He stabs him.*]

ALONZO. O, O, O!

DE FLORES. I must silence you.

[*He stabs him again;* ANTONIO *dies.*]
So, here's an undertaking well accomplished.
This vault serves to good use now. Ha! What's that   20
Threw sparkles in my eye? O, 'tis a diamond
He wears upon his finger. It was well found;
This will approve* the work. What, so fast on?
Not part in death? I'll take a speedy course then;
Finger and all shall off.
[*He cuts off the finger.*]
                                So, now I'll clear
The passages from all suspect or fear.

                                        Exit with body.

[III.iii]

                    Enter ISABELLA *and* LOLLIO.

ISABELLA. Why, sirrah? Whence have you commission
    To fetter the doors against me? If you
    Keep me in a cage, pray whistle to me;
    Let me be doing something.

LOLLIO. You shall be doing if it please you; I'll whistle
    to you if you'll pipe after.

ISABELLA. Is it your master's pleasure or your own
    To keep me in this pinfold?

LOLLIO. 'Tis for my master's pleasure, lest, being taken
    in another man's corn, you might be pounded in an-   10
    other place.

ISABELLA. 'Tis very well, and he'll prove very wise.

LOLLIO. He says you have company enough in the house,
    if you please to be sociable, of all sorts of people.

ISABELLA. Of all sorts? Why, here's none but fools and
    madmen.

LOLLIO. Very well; and where will you find any other if
    you should go abroad? There's my master and I to
    boot, too.

ISABELLA. Of either sort one, a madman and a fool.   20

LOLLIO. I would ev'n participate of both then if I were
    as you. I know y'are half mad already; be half foolish,
    too.

ISABELLA. Y'are a brave saucy rascal! Come on, sir;
    Afford me then the pleasure of your bedlam;

─────────────

approve: verify.

You were commending once today to me
Your last-come lunatic: what a proper°
Body there was without brains to guide it,
And what a pitiful delight appeared
In that defect, as if your wisdom had found   30
A mirth in madness. Pray, sir, let me partake
If there be such a pleasure.

LOLLIO. If I do show you the handsomest, discreetest
madman, one that I may call the understanding madman, then say I am a fool.

ISABELLA. Well, a match, I will say so.

LOLLIO. When you have a taste of the madman, you
shall, if you please, see Fool's College, o' th' side. I
seldom lock there; 'tis but shooting a bolt or two, and
you are amongst 'em. (*Exit. Enter presently.*)—Come   40
on, sir; let me see how handsomely you'll behave yourself now.

Enter FRANCISCUS.

FRANCISCUS. How sweetly she looks! O, but there's a
wrinkle in her brow as deep as philosophy. Anacreon,°
drink to my mistress' health; I'll pledge it. Stay, stay,
there's a spider in the cup—no, 'tis but a grapestone;
swallow it, fear nothing, poet; so, so, lift higher.

ISABELLA. Alack, alack, 'tis too full of pity
To be laughed at. How fell he mad? Canst thou tell?

LOLLIO. For love, mistress. He was a pretty poet, too,   50
and that set him forwards first; the muses then forsook
him; he ran mad for a chambermaid, yet she was but
a dwarf neither.

FRANCISCUS. Hail, bright Titania!
Why stand'st thou idle on these flow'ry banks?
Oberon° is dancing with his Dryades;
I'll gather daisies, primrose, violets,
And bind them in a verse of poesy.

LOLLIO [*showing a whip*]. Not too near; you see your
danger.   60

---

proper: handsome.
Anacreon: who, while drinking wine, choked to death on a
grapestone.
Titania . . . Oberon: queen and king of fairies (see *A Midsummer Night's Dream*).

FRANCISCUS. O, hold thy hand, great Diomede!*
    Thou feed'st thy horses well; they shall obey thee.
    Get up! Bucephalus* kneels.
    [*He kneels.*]

LOLLIO. You see how I awe my flock? A shepherd has
    not his dog at more obedience.

ISABELLA. His conscience is unquiet; sure that was
    The cause of this. A proper gentleman.

FRANCISCUS. Come hither, Aesculapius;* hide the poison.

LOLLIO [*hiding the whip*]. Well, 'tis hid.

FRANCISCUS. Didst thou never hear of one Tiresias,*   70
    A famous poet?

LOLLIO. Yes, that kept tame wild geese.

FRANCISCUS. That's he; I am the man.

LOLLIO. No!

FRANCISCUS. Yes; but make no words on't; I was a man
    Seven years ago.

LOLLIO. A stripling, I think you might.

FRANCISCUS. Now I'm a woman, all feminine.

LOLLIO. I would I might see that.

FRANCISCUS. Juno struck me blind.

LOLLIO. I'll ne'er believe that; for a woman, they say,
    has an eye more than a man.

FRANCISCUS. I say she struck me blind.   80

LOLLIO. And Luna* made you mad; you have two trades
    to beg with.

FRANCISCUS. Luna is now big-bellied, and there's room
    For both of us to ride with Hecate.*
    I'll drag thee up into her silver sphere,
    And there we'll kick the dog and beat the bush
    That barks against the witches of the night;   90
    The swift lycanthropi* that walks the round,

Diomede: king of the Bistonians in Thrace who fed the flesh of humans to his horses.

Bucephalus: the wild war horse of Alexander the Great.

Aesculapius: Greek god of medicine and healing.

Tiresias: actually the Theban soothsayer who was changed to a woman and seven years later back to a man. Juno struck him blind when he agreed with Jupiter that women derived more pleasure from love than men did.   Luna: the moon.

Hecate: goddess of witchcraft; another name for the moon.

lycanthropi: werewolves.

We'll tear their wolvish skins and save the sheep.
[*He tries to seize* LOLLIO.]

LOLLIO. Is't come to this? Nay, then, my poison comes
forth again. [*He shows the whip.*] Mad slave, indeed,
abuse your keeper!

ISABELLA. I prithee hence with him, now he grows dangerous.

FRANCISCUS [*sings*].   *Sweet love, pity me;*
                        Give me leave to lie with thee.

LOLLIO. No, I'll see you wiser first. To your own kennel!

FRANCISCUS. No noise; she sleeps. Draw all the curtains   100
round;
Let no soft sound molest the pretty soul
But love, and love creeps in at a mouse-hole.

LOLLIO. I would you would get into your hole.—

                                   Exit FRANCISCUS.

Now, mistress, I will bring you another sort; you shall
be fooled another while.—Tony, come hither, Tony!
Look who's yonder, Tony.

                Enter ANTONIO.

ANTONIO. Cousin, is it not my aunt?*

LOLLIO. Yes, 'tis one of 'em, Tony.

ANTONIO. He, he! How do you do, uncle?

LOLLIO. Fear him not, mistress; 'tis a gentle nidget.*   110
You may play with him, as safely with him as with his
bauble.

ISABELLA. How long hast thou been a fool?

ANTONIO. Ever since I came hither, cousin.

ISABELLA. Cousin? I'm none of thy cousins, fool.

LOLLIO. O, mistress, fools have always so much wit as
to claim their kindred.

MADMAN (*within*). Bounce, bounce! He falls, he falls!

ISABELLA. Hark you, your scholars in the upper room
Are out of order.   120

LOLLIO. Must I come amongst you there? Keep you the
fool, mistress; I'll go up and play left-handed Orlando*
amongst the madmen.

                                          Exit.

ISABELLA. Well, sir.

----

aunt: prostitute.   nidget: idiot.
play . . . Orlando: imitate the hero of Ariosto's *Orlando Furioso.*

ANTONIO [*revealing his identity*]. 'Tis opportuneful now,
    sweet lady! Nay,
Cast no amazing eye upon this change.
ISABELLA. Ha!
ANTONIO. This shape of folly shrouds your dearest love,
    The truest servant to your powerful beauties,
    Whose magic had this force thus to transform me.   130
ISABELLA. You are a fine fool, indeed.
ANTONIO.   O, 'tis not strange:
    Love has an intellect that runs through all
    The scrutinous sciences and, like
    A cunning poet, catches a quantity
    Of every knowledge, yet brings all home
    Into one mystery, into one secret
    That he proceeds in.
ISABELLA.   Y'are a parlous* fool.
ANTONIO. No danger in me: I bring naught but love
    And his soft-wounding shafts to strike you with.
    Try but one arrow; if it hurt you,   140
    I'll stand you twenty back in recompense.
    [*He kisses her.*]
ISABELLA. A forward fool, too!
ANTONIO.   This was love's teach-
    ing:
    A thousand ways [he] fashioned out my way,
    And this I found the safest and nearest
    To tread the galaxia* to my star.
ISABELLA. Profound withal! Certain, you dreamed of this;
    Love never taught it waking.
ANTONIO.   Take no acquaintance
    Of these outward follies; there is within
    A gentleman that loves you.
ISABELLA.   When I see him,
    I'll speak with him; so in the meantime keep   150
    Your habit;* it becomes you well enough.
    As you are a gentleman, I'll not discover you;
    That's all the favor that you must expect.
    When you are weary, you may leave the school;
    For all this while you have but played the fool.

---

parlous: perilous.   galaxia: Milky Way.   habit: disguise.

Enter LOLLIO.

ANTONIO. And must again.—He, he! I thank you, cousin;
   I'll be your valentine tomorrow morning.

LOLLIO. How do you like the fool, mistress?

ISABELLA. Passing well, sir.

LOLLIO. Is he not witty, pretty well, for a fool?   160

ISABELLA. If he hold on as he begins, he is like
   To come to something.

LOLLIO. Ay, thank a good tutor. You may put him to't;
   he begins to answer pretty hard questions.—Tony,
   how many is five times six?

ANTONIO. Five times six is six times five.

LOLLIO. What arithmetician could have answered better?
   How many is one hundred and seven?

ANTONIO. One hundred and seven is seven hundred and
   one, cousin.   170

LOLLIO. This is no wit to speak on. Will you be rid of
   the fool now?

ISABELLA. By no means; let him stay a little.

MADMAN (*within*). Catch there, catch the last couple
   in hell!

LOLLIO. Again must I come amongst you? Would my
   master were come home! I am not able to govern both
   these wards together.

                                                   Exit.

ANTONIO. Why should a minute of love's hour be lost?

ISABELLA. Fie, out again! I had rather you kept   180
   Your other posture: you become not your tongue
   When you speak from your clothes.

ANTONIO.   How can he
      freeze
   Lives near so sweet a warmth? Shall I alone
   Walk through the orchard of the Hesperides
   And cowardly not dare to pull an apple?*
   This with the red cheeks I must venture for.
   [*He tries to kiss her.*]

              Enter LOLLIO *above.*

ISABELLA. Take heed; there's giants keep 'em.

LOLLIO [*aside*]. How now, fool, are you good at that?

---

   pull an apple: the golden apples of the Hesperides were guarded
by a hundred-headed dragon.

Have you read Lipsius?* He's past *Ars Amandi;* I
believe I must put harder questions to him, I perceive   190
that—

ISABELLA. You are bold without fear, too.

ANTONIO.   What should
        I fear,
Having all joys about me? Do you smile,
And love shall play the wanton on your lip,
Meet and retire, retire and meet again;
Look you but cheerfully, and in your eyes
I shall behold mine own deformity
And dress myself up fairer. I know this shape
Becomes me not, but in those bright mirrors
I shall array me handsomely.   200

LOLLIO [*aside*]. Cuckoo, cuckoo!*

                                                          Exit.

[Enter] Madmen above, some as birds, others as beasts.

ANTONIO. What are these?

ISABELLA.   Of fear enough to part us;
Yet are they but our schools of lunatics,
That act their fantasies in any shapes
Suiting their present thoughts; if sad, they cry;
If mirth be their conceit, they laugh again.
Sometimes they imitate the beasts and birds,
Singing or howling, braying, barking—all
As their wild fancies prompt 'em.

                                    [Exeunt Madmen.]

                Enter LOLLIO.

ANTONIO.   These are no fears.

ISABELLA. But here's a large one, my man.   210

ANTONIO. Ha, he! That's fine sport, indeed, cousin.

LOLLIO. I would my master were come home; 'tis too
    much for one shepherd to govern two of these flocks;
    nor can I believe that one churchman can instruct two
    benefices at once. There will be some incurable mad

Lipsius: Justus Lipsius, famous 16th-century jurist, whose name
here is introduced, as the Reverend Alexander Dyce pointed out in
his edition of the play (1840), "merely for the sake of its first
syllable."

Ars Amandi: Ovid's *The Art of Loving.*

cuckoo: Lollio hints that Isabella is about to make her husband
a cuckold.

of the one side, and very fools on the other.—Come,
Tony.

ANTONIO. Prithee, cousin, let me stay here still.

LOLLIO. No, you must to your book now you have played
sufficiently.   220

ISABELLA. Your fool is grown wondrous witty.

LOLLIO. Well, I'll say nothing; but I do not think but he
will put you down one of these days.

Exeunt LOLLIO *and* ANTONIO.

ISABELLA. Here the restrained current might make
breach,
Spite of the watchful bankers. Would a woman stray,
She need not gad abroad to seek her sin;
It would be brought home one ways or other:
The needle's point will to the fixèd north;
Such drawing arctics women's beauties are.

Enter LOLLIO.

LOLLIO. How dost thou, sweet rogue?   230

ISABELLA. How now?

LOLLIO. Come, there are degrees; one fool may be better
than another.

ISABELLA. What's the matter?

LOLLIO. Nay, if thou giv'st thy mind to fool's flesh,
have at thee!

[*He tries to kiss her.*]

ISABELLA. You bold slave, you!

LOLLIO. I could follow now as t'other fool did:
"What should I fear,
Having all joys about me? Do you but smile,   240
And love shall play the wanton on your lip,
Meet and retire, retire and meet again;
Look you but cheerfully, and in your eyes
I shall behold my own deformity
And dress myself up fairer. I know this shape
Becomes me not—"
And so as it follows. But is not this the more foolish
way? Come, sweet rogue, kiss me, my little Lacedæ-
monian.* Let me feel how thy pulses beat. Thou hast
a thing about thee would do a man pleasure; I'll lay   250
my hand on't.

Lacedæmonian: prostitute.

ISABELLA. Sirrah, no more! I see you have discovered
    This love's knight errant, who hath made adventure
    For purchase of my love. Be silent, mute,
    Mute as a statue; or his injunction
    For me enjoying shall be to cut thy throat.
    I'll do it though for no other purpose,
    And be sure he'll not refuse it.
LOLLIO. My share, that's all; I'll have my fool's part
    with you.
ISABELLA. No more! Your master.   260
                Enter ALIBIUS.
ALIBIUS.   Sweet, how dost
    thou?
ISABELLA. Your bounden servant, sir.
ALIBIUS.   Fie, fie, sweet-
    heart,
    No more of that.
ISABELLA.   You were best lock me up.
ALIBIUS. In my arms and bosom, my sweet Isabella,
    I'll lock thee up most nearly.—Lollio,
    We have employment, we have task in hand.
    At noble Vermandero's, our castle captain,
    There is a nuptial to be solemnized—
    Beatrice Joanna his fair daughter, bride—
    For which the gentleman hath bespoke our pains: 270
    A mixture of our madmen and our fools
    To finish, as it were, and make the fag°
    Of all the revels the third night from the first;
    Only an unexpected passage over
    To make a frightful pleasure, that is all,
    But not the all I aim at. Could we so act it,
    To teach it in a wild, distracted measure,
    Though out of form and figure, breaking time's head,
    It were no matter; 'twould be healed again
    In one age or other if not in this;   280
    This, this, Lollio, there's a good reward begun
    And will beget a bounty, be it known.
LOLLIO. This is easy, sir, I'll warrant you. You have about
    you fools and madmen that can dance very well; and,
    'tis no wonder, your best dancers are not the wisest

---

fag: end.

men; the reason is, with often jumping they jolt their
brains down into their feet, that their wits lie more in
their heels than in their heads.

ALIBIUS. Honest Lollio, thou giv'st me a good reason
And a comfort in it.

ISABELLA.   Y'ave a fine trade on't: 290
Madmen and fools are a staple commodity.

ALIBIUS. O, wife, we must eat, wear clothes, and live;
Just at the lawyer's haven we arrive,
By madmen and by fools we both do thrive.

                                                            Exeunt.

[III.iv]
              Enter VERMANDERO, ALSEMERO, JASPERINO,
                        and BEATRICE.

VERMANDERO. Valencia speaks so nobly of you, sir,
I wish I had a daughter now for you.

ALSEMERO. The fellow of this creature were a partner
For a king's love.

VERMANDERO.   I had her fellow once, sir,
But heaven has married her to joys eternal;
'Twere sin to wish her in this vale again.
Come, sir, your friend and you shall see the pleasures
Which my health chiefly joys in.

ALSEMERO. I hear the beauty of this seat largely.*

VERMANDERO. It falls much short of that.
                              *Exeunt. Manet** BEATRICE.

BEATRICE.   So, here's   10
     one step
Into my father's favor; time will fix him.
I have got him now the liberty of the house;
So wisdom by degrees works out her freedom.
And if that eye be dark'ned that offends me—
I wait but that eclipse—this gentleman
Shall soon shine glorious in my father's liking
Through the refulgent virtue of my love.
                        Enter DE FLORES.

DE FLORES [*aside*]. My thoughts are at a banquet for
     the deed;
I feel no weight in't—'tis but light and cheap

————————

largely: widely (praised).   *manet:* remains.

For the sweet recompense that I set down for't.   20
BEATRICE. De Flores!
DE FLORES.   Lady?
BEATRICE.   Thy looks promise cheer-
    fully.
DE FLORES. All things are answerable: time, circum-
    stance,
Your wishes, and my service.
BEATRICE.   Is it done, then?
DE FLORES. Piracquo is no more.
BEATRICE. My joys start at mine eyes; our sweet'st de-
    lights
Are evermore born weeping.
DE FLORES.   I've a token for you.
BEATRICE. For me?
DE FLORES.   But it was sent somewhat unwill-
    ingly;
I could not get the ring without the finger.
[He shows her the finger.]
BEATRICE. Bless me! What hast thou done?
DE FLORES.   Why, is
    that more
Than killing the whole man? I cut his heartstrings;   30
A greedy hand thrust in a dish at court
In a mistake hath had as much as this.
BEATRICE. 'Tis the first token my father made me send
    him.
DE FLORES. And I made him send it back again
For his last token; I was loath to leave it,
And I'm sure dead men have no use of jewels.
He was as loath to part with't, for it stuck
As if the flesh and it were both one substance.
BEATRICE. At the stag's fall the keeper has his fees.
'Tis soon applied: all dead men's fees are yours, sir.   40
I pray bury the finger, but the stone
You may make use on shortly; the true value,
Take't of my truth, is near three hundred ducats.
DE FLORES. 'Twill hardly buy a capcase° for one's con-
    science, though,
To keep it from the worm, as fine as 'tis.

---

capcase: wallet; traveling case.

Well, being my fees I'll take it;
Great men have taught me that, or else my merit
Would scorn the way on't.

BEATRICE.   It might justly, sir.
Why, thou mistak'st, De Flores; 'tis not given
In state of recompense.

DE FLORES.   No, I hope so, lady;   50
You should soon witness my contempt to't then!

BEATRICE. Prithee, thou look'st as if thou wert offended.

DE FLORES. That were strange, lady; 'tis not possible
My service should draw such a cause from you.
Offended? Could you think so? That were much
For one of my performance and so warm
Yet in my service.

BEATRICE. 'Twere misery in me to give you cause, sir.

DE FLORES. I know so much, it were so—misery
In her most sharp condition.

BEATRICE.   'Tis resolved then.   60
Look you, sir, here's three thousand golden florins;
I have not meanly thought upon thy merit.

DE FLORES. What! Salary? Now you move me.

BEATRICE.   How,
  De Flores?

DE FLORES. Do you place me in the rank of verminous
  fellows
To destroy things for wages? Offer gold?
The life blood of man! Is anything
Valued too precious for my recompense?

BEATRICE. I understand thee not.

DE FLORES.   I could ha' hired
A journeyman in murder at this rate,
And mine own conscience might have [slept at ease] 70
And have had the work brought home.

BEATRICE [aside].   I'm in a lab-
  yrinth;
What will content him? I would fain be rid of him.—
I'll double the sum, sir.

DE FLORES.   You take a course
To double my vexation, that's the good you do.

BEATRICE [aside]. Bless me! I am now in worse plight
  than I was;
I know not what will please him.—For my fear's sake
I prithee make away with all speed possible.

And if thou be'st so modest not to name
The sum that will content thee, paper blushes not;
Send thy demand in writing, it shall follow thee.   80
But prithee take thy flight.

DE FLORES.   You must fly too, then.

BEATRICE. I?

DE FLORES.   I'll not stir a foot else.

BEATRICE.   What's your
    meaning?

DE FLORES. Why, are not you as guilty? In, I'm sure,
As deep as I? And we should stick together.
Come, your fears counsel you but ill; my absence
Would draw suspect upon you instantly;
There were no rescue for you.

BEATRICE [*aside*].   He speaks home.

DE FLORES. Nor is it fit we two, engaged so jointly,
    Should part and live asunder.
    [*He tries to kiss her.*]

BEATRICE.   How now, sir?
    This shows not well.

DE FLORES.   What makes your lip so strange?   90
    This must not be betwixt us.

BEATRICE [*aside*].   The man talks wildly.

DE FLORES. Come, kiss me with a zeal now.

BEATRICE [*aside*].   Heaven,
    I doubt° him!

DE FLORES. I will not stand so long to beg 'em shortly.

BEATRICE. Take heed, De Flores, of forgetfulness;
    'Twill soon betray us.

DE FLORES.   Take you heed first;
    Faith, y'are grown much forgetful; y'are to blame in't.

BEATRICE [*aside*]. He's bold, and I am blamed for't!

DE FLORES.   I
    have eased you
Of your trouble, think on't! I'm in pain
And must be eased of you; 'tis a charity.
Justice invites your blood to understand me.   100

BEATRICE. I dare not.

DE FLORES.   Quickly!

BEATRICE.   O, I never shall!

---

doubt: fear.

Speak it yet further off that I may lose
What has been spoken and no sound remain on't.
I would not hear so much offense again
For such another deed.
DE FLORES.   Soft, lady, soft!
  The last is not yet paid for. O, this act
  Has put me into spirit; I was as greedy on't
  As the parched earth of moisture when the clouds
      weep.
  Did you not mark I wrought myself into't,
  Nay, sued and kneeled for't? Why was all that pains
      took?   110
  You see I have thrown contempt upon your gold;
  Not that I want it [not], for I do piteously;
  In order I will come unto't and make use on't,
  But 'twas not held so precious to begin with,
  For I place wealth after the heels of pleasure;
  And were I not resolved in my belief
  That thy virginity were perfect in thee,
  I should but take my recompense with grudging
  As if I had but half my hopes I agreed for.
BEATRICE. Why, 'tis impossible thou canst be so wicked   120
  Or shelter such a cunning cruelty,
  To make his death the murderer of my honor!
  Thy language is so bold and vicious
  I cannot see which way I can forgive it
  With any modesty.
DE FLORES.   Push, you forget yourself!
  A woman dipped in blood and talk of modesty!
BEATRICE. O misery of sin! Would I had been bound
  Perpetually unto my living hate
  In that Piracquo than to hear these words.
  Think but upon the distance that creation   130
  Set 'twixt thy blood and mine, and keep thee there.
DE FLORES. Look but into your conscience, read me
      there;
  'Tis a true book; you'll find me there your equal.
  Push! Fly not to your birth, but settle you
  In what the act has made you; y'are no more now.
  You must forget your parentage to* me:
  Y'are the deed's creature; by that name

---

parentage to: relationship with.

You lost your first condition, and I challenge you
As peace and innocency has turned you out
And made you one with me.

BEATRICE.   With thee, foul villain? 140

DE FLORES. Yes, my fair murd'ress. Do you urge me?
Though thou writ'st maid, thou whore in thy affection,
'Twas changed from thy first love, and that's a kind
Of whoredom in thy heart; and he's changed now
To bring thy second on, thy Alsemero,
Whom (by all sweets that ever darkness tasted),
If I enjoy thee not, thou ne'er enjoy'st!
I'll blast the hopes and joys of marriage;
I'll confess all; my life I rate at nothing.

BEATRICE. De Flores!   150

DE FLORES. I shall rest from all lovers' plagues then;
I live in pain now: that shooting eye
Will burn my heart to cinders.

BEATRICE.   O, sir, hear me.

DE FLORES. She that in life and love refuses me,
In death and shame my partner she shall be.

BEATRICE [*kneeling*]. Stay, hear me once for all. I make
   thee master
Of all the wealth I have in gold and jewels;
Let me go poor unto my bed with honor,
And I am rich in all things.

DE FLORES.   Let this silence thee:
The wealth of all Valencia shall not buy   160
My pleasure from me.
Can you weep fate from its determined purpose?
So soon may [you] weep me.

BEATRICE.   Vengeance begins;
Murder, I see, is followed by more sins.
Was my creation in the womb so cursed
It must engender with a viper first?

DE FLORES [*raising her*]. Come, rise, and shroud your
   blushes in my bosom;
Silence is one of pleasure's best receipts:°
Thy peace is wrought forever in this yielding.
'Las, how the turtle° pants! Thou'lt love anon   170
What thou so fear'st and faint'st to venture on.

                                        Exeunt.

---

receipts: recipes.   turtle: turtledove.

ACTUS QUARTUS

[IV.i]
[Dumb Show.]

Enter Gentlemen, VERMANDERO *meeting them with action of wonderment at the flight of* PIRACQUO. *Enter* ALSEMERO, *with* JASPERINO *and Gallants.* VERMANDERO *points to him, the Gentlemen seeming to applaud the choice.* [Exeunt in procession VERMANDERO,] ALSEMERO, JASPERINO, *and Gentlemen;* BEATRICE *the bride following in great state, accompanied with* DIAPHANTA, ISABELLA, *and other Gentlewomen;* DE FLORES *after All, smiling at the accident.*° ALONZO's *Ghost appears to* DE FLORES *in the midst of his smile, startles him, showing him the hand whose finger he had cut off. They pass over in great solemnity.*

Enter BEATRICE.

BEATRICE. This fellow has undone me endlessly;
Never was bride so fearfully distressed.
The more I think upon th'ensuing night
And whom I am to cope with in embraces—
One [who's] ennobled both in blood and mind,
So clear in understanding (that's my plague now),
Before whose judgment will my fault appear
Like malefactors' crimes before tribunals,
There is no hiding on't—the more I dive
Into my own distress. How a wise man   10
Stands for° a great calamity! There's no venturing
Into his bed, what course soe'er I light upon,
Without my shame, which may grow up to danger.
He cannot but in justice strangle me
As I lie by him, as a cheater use me.
'Tis a precious craft to play with a false die
Before a cunning gamester. Here's his closet,
The key left in't, and he abroad i'th' park;
Sure, 'twas forgot; I'll be so bold as look in't.
[*She opens the closet.*]
Bless me! A right physician's closet 'tis,   20
Set round with vials, every one her mark, too.
Sure, he does practice physic° for his own use,

---

accident: event, occurrence.
stands for: stands uprightly to (?).   physic: medicine.

Which may be safely called your great man's wisdom.
What manuscript lies here? *The Book of Experiment,
Called Secrets in Nature.* So 'tis, 'tis so.
"How to know whether a woman be with child or no."
I hope J am not yet; if he should try though!
Let me see: "Folio forty-five." Here 'tis,
The leaf tucked down upon't, the place suspicious.
"If you would know whether a woman be with child   30
or not, give her two spoonfuls of the white water in
glass C—"
Where's that glass C? O, yonder I see't now—
"and if she be with child, she sleeps full twelve hours
after; if not, not."
None of that water comes into my belly;
I'll know you from a hundred. I could break you now
Or turn you into milk and so beguile
The master of the mystery, but I'll look to you.
Ha! That which is next is ten times worse: 40
"How to know whether a woman be a maid or not."
If that should be applied, what would become of me?
Belike he has a strong faith of my purity
That never yet made proof. But this he calls
"A merry sleight, but true experiment, the author An-
tonius Mizaldus. Give the party you suspect the quan-
tity of a spoonful of the water in the glass M, which
upon her that is a maid makes three several effects:
'twill make her incontinently° gape, then fall into a
sudden sneezing, last into a violent laughing; else dull,   50
heavy, and lumpish."
Where had I been?
I fear it; yet 'tis seven hours to bedtime.

Enter DIAPHANTA.

DIAPHANTA. Cuds,° madam, are you here?
BEATRICE [*aside*].   Seeing that
    wench now,
A trick comes in my mind; 'tis a nice piece
Gold cannot purchase.—I come hither, wench,
To look my lord.
DIAPHANTA [*aside*]. Would I had such a cause to look
    him, too!—
Why, he's i'th' park, madam.

---

incontinently: immediately.   Cuds: God's (mild oath).

BEATRICE. There let him be.

DIAPHANTA.   Ay, madam, let him compass   60
    Whole parks and forests as great rangers do;
    At roosting time a little lodge can hold 'em.
    Earth-conquering Alexander, that thought the world
    Too narrow for him, in the end had but his pit-hole.

BEATRICE. I fear thou art not modest, Diaphanta.

DIAPHANTA. Your thoughts are so unwilling to be known, madam;
    'Tis ever the bride's fashion towards bedtime
    To set light by her joys as if she owed* 'em not.

BEATRICE. Her joys? Her fears, thou would'st say.

DIAPHANTA.   Fear of what?

BEATRICE. Art thou a maid and talk'st so to a maid?   70
    You leave a blushing business behind,
    Beshrew your heart for't!

DIAPHANTA.   Do you mean good sooth, madam?

BEATRICE. Well, if I'd thought upon the fear at first,
    Man should have been unknown.

DIAPHANTA.   Is't possible?

BEATRICE. I will give a thousand ducats to that woman
    Would try what my fear were and tell me true
    Tomorrow when she gets from't; as she likes,
    I might perhaps be drawn to't.

DIAPHANTA.   Are you in earnest?

BEATRICE. Do you get the woman, then challenge me,
    And see if I'll fly away from't; but I must tell you   80
    This by the way: she must be a true maid,*
    Else there's no trial; my fears are not hers else.

DIAPHANTA. Nay, she that I would put into your hands, madam,
    Shall be a maid.

BEATRICE.   You know I should be shamed else
    Because she lies for me.

DIAPHANTA.   'Tis a strange humor;
    But are you serious still? Would you resign
    Your first night's pleasure and give money, too?

---

owed: owned.   true maid: a virgin.

BEATRICE. As willingly as live.—[*Aside.*] Alas, the gold
Is but a by-bet to wedge in the honor.

DIAPHANTA. I do not know how the world goes abroad   90
For faith or honesty; there's both required in this.
Madam, what say you to me, and stray no further?
I've a good mind, in troth, to earn your money.

BEATRICE. Y'are too quick,* I fear, to be a maid.

DIAPHANTA. How? Not a maid? Nay, then you urge me,
madam;
Your honorable self is not a truer
With all your fears upon you—

BEATRICE [*aside*].   Bad enough then.

DIAPHANTA. Than I with all my lightsome joys about me.

BEATRICE. I'm glad to hear't; then you dare put your
honesty*
Upon an easy trial?

DIAPHANTA.   Easy? Anything.   100

BEATRICE. I'll come to you straight.
[*She goes to the closet.*]

DIAPHANTA [*aside*].   She will not search
me, will she,
Like the forewoman of a female jury?

BEATRICE. Glass M—ay, this is it.—Look, Diaphanta,
You take no worse than I do.
[*She drinks.*]

DIAPHANTA.   And in so doing
I will not question what 'tis, but take it.
[*She drinks.*]

BEATRICE [*aside*]. Now if the experiment be true, 'twill
praise itself
And give me noble ease. Begins already!
[DIAPHANTA *gapes.*]
There's the first symptom; and what haste it makes
To fall into the second, there by this time!
[DIAPHANTA *sneezes.*]
Most admirable secret! On the contrary,   110
It stirs not me a whit, which most concerns it.

DIAPHANTA. Ha, ha, ha!

BEATRICE [*aside*].   Just in all things and in order

---

quick: lively; wanton.   honesty: chastity.

As if 'twere circumscribed: one accident°
Gives way unto another.

DIAPHANTA.　　　　　　　　　Ha, ha, ha!

BEATRICE.　　　　　　　　　　　　　　How now,
wench?

DIAPHANTA. Ha, ha, ha! I am so, so light at heart—ha,
ha, ha!—so pleasurable.
But one more swig, sweet madam.

BEATRICE.　　　　　　　　　　　Ay, tomorrow;
We shall have time to sit by't.

DIAPHANTA.　　　　　　　　　Now I'm sad again.

BEATRICE [aside]. It lays itself so gently, too.—Come,
wench;
Most honest Diaphanta I dare call thee now.

DIAPHANTA. Pray tell me, madam, what trick call you
this?　　　　　　　　　　　　　　　　　　　　　120

BEATRICE.　I'll tell thee all hereafter; we must study
The carriage of this business.

DIAPHANTA.　　　　　　　I shall carry't well
Because I love the burden.

BEATRICE.　　　　　　About midnight
You must not fail to steal forth gently
That I may use the place.

DIAPHANTA.　　　　　　O, fear not, madam;
I shall be cool by that time. The bride's place
And with a thousand ducats! I'm for a justice now:
I bring a portion° with me; I scorn small fools.

　　　　　　　　　　　　　　　　　　　　Exeunt.

[IV.ii]
　　　　　　　Enter VERMANDERO *and* SERVANT.

VERMANDERO. I tell thee, knave, mine honor is in ques-
tion,
A thing till now free from suspicion,
Nor ever was there cause. Who of my gentlemen
Are absent? Tell me, and truly, how many and who.

SERVANT. Antonio, sir, and Franciscus.

VERMANDERO.　When did they leave the castle?

SERVANT. Some ten days since, sir, the one intending to
Briamata, th'other for Valencia.

――――――――

accident: symptom.　　portion: dowry.

VERMANDERO. The time accuses 'em. A charge of murder
  Is brought within my castle gate, Piracquo's murder;   10
  I dare not answer faithfully their absence.
  A strict command of apprehension
  Shall pursue 'em suddenly and either wipe
  The stain off clear or openly discover it.
  Provide me wingèd warrants for the purpose.

                          Exit SERVANT.
  See, I am set on again.

            Enter TOMAZO.

TOMAZO. I claim a brother of you.
VERMANDERO.   Y'are too hot;
  Seek him not here.
TOMAZO.   Yes, 'mongst your dearest bloods
  If my peace find no fairer satisfaction;
  This is the place must yield account for him,   20
  For here I left him; and the hasty tie
  Of this snatched marriage gives strong testimony
  Of his most certain ruin.
VERMANDERO.   Certain falsehood!
  This is the place indeed; his breach of faith
  Has too much marred both my abusèd love,
  The honorable love I reserved for him,
  And mocked my daughter's joy. The prepared morning
  Blushed at his infidelity; he left
  Contempt and scorn to throw upon those friends
  Whose belief* hurt 'em. O, 'twas most ignoble   30
  To take his flight so unexpectedly
  And throw such public wrongs on those that loved
    him.
TOMAZO. Then this is all your answer?
VERMANDERO.   'Tis too fair
  For one of his alliance, and I warn you
  That this place no more see you.

                           Exit.

           Enter DE FLORES.

TOMAZO.   The best is
  There is more ground to meet a man's revenge on.—
  Honest De Flores!
DE FLORES.   That's my name, indeed.

---

  belief: i.e., in him; confidence (in him).

Saw you the bride? Good, sweet sir, which way took
    she?
TOMAZO. I have blessed mine eyes from seeing such a
    false one.
DE FLORES [*aside*]. I'd fain get off; this man's not for
    my company;   40
    I smell his brother's blood when I come near him.
TOMAZO. Come hither, kind and true one; I remember
    My brother loved thee well.
DE FLORES.   O, purely, dear sir.—
    [*Aside.*] Methinks I am now again a-killing on him,
    He brings it so fresh to me.
TOMAZO.   Thou canst guess, sirrah
    (One honest friend has an instinct of jealousy),
    At some foul guilty person.
DE FLORES. 'Las, sir, I am so charitable, I think none
    Worse than myself.—You did not see the bride, then?
TOMAZO. I prithee name her not. Is she not wicked?   50
DE FLORES. No, no; a pretty, easy, round-packed sinner
    As your most ladies are, else you might think
    I flattered her; but, sir, at no hand wicked
    Till th'are so old their sins and vices meet
    And they salute witches. I am called, I think, sir.—
    [*Aside.*] His company ev'n o'erlays my conscience.
                                                        Exit.

TOMAZO. That De Flores has a wondrous honest heart;
    He'll bring it out in time, I'm assured on't.
    O, here's the glorious master of the day's joy.
    ['Twill] not be long till he and I do reckon.   60
                    Enter ALSEMERO.
    Sir!
ALSEMERO. You are most welcome.
TOMAZO.   You may call that
    word back;
    I do not think I am, nor wish to be.
ALSEMERO. 'Tis strange you found the way to this house,
    then.
TOMAZO. Would I'd ne'er known the cause! I'm none of
    those, sir,
    That come to give you joy and swill your wine;
    'Tis a more precious liquor that must lay
    The fiery thirst I bring.

ALSEMERO.   Your words and you
  Appear to me great strangers.
TOMAZO.   Time and our swords
  May make us more acquainted. This the business:
  I should have a brother in your place;   70
  How treachery and malice have disposed of him
  I'm bound to inquire of him which holds his right,
  Which never could come fairly.
ALSEMERO.   You must look
  To answer for that word, sir.
TOMAZO.   Fear you not;
  I'll have it* ready drawn at our next meeting.
  Keep your day solemn. Farewell, I disturb it not;
  I'll bear the smart with patience for a time.

                                        Exit.

ALSEMERO. 'Tis somewhat ominous, this, a quarrel en-
    tered
  Upon this day! My innocence relieves me;
               Enter JASPERINO.
  I should be wondrous sad else.—Jasperino,   80
  I have news to tell thee, strange news.
JASPERINO.   I ha' some, too,
  I think as strange as yours; would I might keep
  Mine, so my faith and friendship might be kept in't!
  Faith, sir, dispense a little with my zeal
  And let it cool in this.
ALSEMERO.   This puts me on
  And blames thee for thy slowness.
JASPERINO.   All may prove
    nothing,
  Only a friendly fear that leaped from me, sir.
ALSEMERO.   No question it may prove nothing; let's par-
    take it, though.
JASPERINO. 'Twas Diaphanta's chance (for to that wench
  I pretend* honest love, and she deserves it)   90
  To leave me in a back part of the house,
  A place we chose for private conference;
  She was no sooner gone, but instantly
  I heard your bride's voice in the next room to me

---

  it: a sword (Tomazo's "answer").   pretend: offer.

And, lending more attention, found De Flores
Louder than she.

ALSEMERO.   De Flores? Thou art out now.

JASPERINO. You'll tell me more anon.

ALSEMERO.   Still I'll prevent°
thee:
The very sight of him is poison to her.

JASPERINO. That made me stagger, too; but Diaphanta
At her return confirmed it.

ALSEMERO.   Diaphanta!   100

JASPERINO. Then fell we both to listen, and words passed
Like those that challenge interest in a woman.

ALSEMERO. Peace, quench thy zeal; 'tis dangerous to thy
bosom.

JASPERINO. Then truth is full of peril.

ALSEMERO.   Such truths are.
O, were she the sole glory of the earth,
Had eyes that could shoot fire into kings' breasts,
And touched,° she sleeps not here! Yet I have time,
Though night be near, to be resolved hereof;
And prithee do not weigh me by my passions.

JASPERINO. I never weighed friend so.

ALSEMERO.   Done charita-
bly!   110
That key will lead thee to a pretty secret
[*He gives him a key.*]
By a Chaldean taught me, and I've [made]
My study upon some. Bring from my closet
A glass inscribed there with the letter M,
And question not my purpose.

JASPERINO.   It shall be done, sir.
                                                              Exit.

ALSEMERO. How can this hang together? Not an hour
since
Her woman came pleading her lady's fears,
Delivered her for the most timorous virgin
That ever shrunk at man's name, and so modest
She charged her weep out her request to me   120
That she might come obscurely° to my bosom.

---

prevent: anticipate.   touched: corrupted.
obscurely: in darkness.

Enter BEATRICE.

BEATRICE [*aside*]. All things go well; my woman's preparing yonder

For her sweet voyage, which grieves me to lose;

Necessity compels it—I lose all, else.

ALSEMERO [*aside*]. Push! Modesty's shrine is set in yonder
forehead.

I cannot be too sure, though.—My Joanna!

BEATRICE. Sir, I was bold to weep a message to you;

Pardon my modest fears.

ALSEMERO [*aside*]. The dove's not meeker;

She's abused, questionless.

Enter JASPERINO [*with a glass*].

—O, are you come, sir?

BEATRICE [*aside.*] The glass, upon my life! I see the
letter.   130

JASPERINO. Sir, this is M.

ALSEMERO. 'Tis it.

BEATRICE [*aside*]. I am suspected.

ALSEMERO. How fitly our bride comes to partake with us!

BEATRICE. What is't, my lord?

ALSEMERO. No hurt.

BEATRICE. Sir, pardon
me,

I seldom taste of any composition.

ALSEMERO. But this upon my warrant you shall venture
on.

BEATRICE. I fear 'twill make me ill.

ALSEMERO. Heaven forbid
that!

BEATRICE [*aside*]. I'm put now to my cunning; th'effects
I know

If I can now but feign 'em handsomely.

[*She drinks.*]

ALSEMERO [*aside to* JASPERINO]. It has that secret virtue, it ne'er missed, sir,

Upon a virgin.

JASPERINO. Treble qualitied?   140

[BEATRICE *gapes and then sneezes.*]

ALSEMERO. By all that's virtuous, it takes there, proceeds!

JASPERINO. This is the strangest trick to know a maid by.

BEATRICE. Ha, ha, ha!
  You have given me joy of heart to drink, my lord.
ALSEMERO. No, thou hast given me such joy of heart
  That never can be blasted.
BEATRICE.   What's the matter, sir?
ALSEMERO [aside to JASPERINO]. See, now 'tis settled in
    a melancholy
  Keep[s] both the time and method.—My Joanna!
  Chaste as the breath of heaven or morning's womb
  That brings the day forth, thus my love encloses thee.   150
  [He embraces her.]

                                                    Exeunt.

[IV.iii]
                  Enter ISABELLA and LOLLIO.
ISABELLA. O, heaven! Is this the waiting* moon?
  Does love turn fool, run mad, and all [at] once?
  Sirrah, here's a madman, akin to the fool, too,
  A lunatic lover.
LOLLIO. No, no, not he I brought the letter from?
ISABELLA. Compare his inside with his out, and tell me.
LOLLIO. The out's mad, I'm sure of that; I had a taste
  on't. [He reads the letter.] "To the bright Andromeda,
  chief chambermaid to the Knight of the Sun, at the
  sign of Scorpio, in the Middle Region, sent by the   10
  bellows-mender of Æolus.* Pay the post." This is
  stark madness.
ISABELLA. Now mark the inside. [She takes the letter
  and reads.] "Sweet lady, having now cast off this

---

waiting: meaning uncertain (Williams suggests "waxing").
Andromeda . . . Æolus: "Isabella is addressed as Andromeda
presumably because Franciscus is the Perseus who is to rescue her
from the dragon Alibius. In his character of 'A Chamber-Mayde'
(whom he describes as being extremely lascivious), Overbury says
of her that 'Shee . . . is so carried away with the *Myrrour of
Knighthood*, she is many times resolv'd to . . . become a Ladie
Errant. . . .' The Knight of the Sun is one of the heroes of the
work Overbury mentions, *The Mirrour of Princely deedes and
Knighthood*. . . . Scorpio was the sign governing the privy parts
of the body, and this turns 'middle region,' an astronomical term,
into an obvious pun. . . . The remaining references appear to be
simple jokes." (Bawcutt.) Æolus: god of the winds.

counterfeit cover of a madman, I appear to your best
judgment a true and faithful lover of your beauty."

LOLLIO. He is mad still.

ISABELLA. "If any fault you find, chide those perfections
in you which have made me imperfect; 'tis the same
sun that causeth to grow and enforceth to wither—" 20

LOLLIO. O, rogue!

ISABELLA. "Shapes and transshapes, destroys and builds
again. I come in winter to you dismantled of my proper
ornaments; by the sweet splendor of your cheerful
smiles, I spring and live a lover."

LOLLIO. Mad rascal still!

ISABELLA. "Tread him not under foot, that shall appear
an honor to your bounties. I remain—mad till I speak
with you, from whom I expect my cure. Yours all, or
one beside himself, Franciscus." 30

LOLLIO. You are like to have a fine time on't. My master
and I may give over our professions; I do not think but
you can cure fools and madmen faster than we, with
little pains, too.

ISABELLA. Very likely.

LOLLIO. One thing I must tell you, mistress: you perceive
that I am privy to your skill; if I find you minister
once and set up the trade, I put in for my thirds—I
shall be mad or fool else.

ISABELLA. The first place is thine, believe it, Lollio; 40
If I do fall—

LOLLIO. I fall upon you.

ISABELLA. So.

LOLLIO. Well, I stand to my venture.

ISABELLA. But thy counsel now: how shall I deal with
'em?

LOLLIO. [Why,] do you mean to deal with 'em?

ISABELLA. Nay, the fair understanding: how to use 'em.

LOLLIO. Abuse 'em! That's the way to mad the fool and
make a fool of the madman, and then you use 'em 50
kindly.*

ISABELLA. 'Tis easy; I'll practice. Do thou observe it.
The key of the wardrobe.

LOLLIO [*giving her the key*]. There. Fit yourself for 'em,
and I'll fit 'em both for you.

---

kindly: naturally; as their nature warrants.

ISABELLA. Take thou no further notice than the outside.

Exit.

LOLLIO. Not an inch; I'll put you to the inside.

Enter ALIBIUS.

ALIBIUS. Lollio, art there? Will all be perfect, think'st
thou?
Tomorrow night, as if to close up the solemnity,
Vermandero expects us.   60

LOLLIO. I mistrust the madmen most; the fools will do
well enough: I have taken pains with them.

ALIBIUS. Tush! They cannot miss: the more absurdity,
The more commends it, so no rough behaviors
Affright the ladies; they are nice° things, thou know'st.

LOLLIO. You need not fear, sir; so long as we are there
with our commanding pizzles,° they'll be as tame as
the ladies themselves.

ALIBIUS. I will see them once more rehearse before they
go.   70

LOLLIO. I was about it, sir; look you to the madmen's
morris, and let me alone with the other. There is one or
two that I mistrust their fooling; I'll instruct them, and
then they shall rehearse the whole measure.

ALIBIUS. Do so; I'll see the music prepared. But, Lollio,
By the way, how does my wife brook her restraint?
Does she not grudge at it?

LOLLIO. So, so; she takes some pleasure in the house; she
would abroad else. You must allow her a little more
length; she's kept too short.   80

ALIBIUS. She shall along to Vermandero's with us;
That will serve her for a month's liberty.

LOLLIO. What's that on your face, sir?

ALIBIUS. Where, Lollio? I see nothing.

LOLLIO. Cry you mercy, sir, 'tis your nose; it showed like
the trunk of a young elephant.°

ALIBIUS. Away, rascal! I'll prepare the music, Lollio.

LOLLIO. Do, sir, and I'll dance the whilst.—

Exit ALIBIUS.

---

nice: sensitive.
pizzles: whips (literally, dried penises of animals, often bulls,
generally used for flogging).
nose . . . elephant: suggestive of the cuckold's horns (?).

Tony, where art thou, Tony?

                Enter ANTONIO.

ANTONIO. Here, cousin; where art thou?   90

LOLLIO. Come, Tony, the footmanship I taught you.

ANTONIO. I had rather ride, cousin.

LOLLIO. Ay, a whip take you! But I'll keep you out.
    Vault in; look you, Tony, fa, la, la, la, la.
    [*He dances.*]

ANTONIO. Fa la, la, la, la.
    [*He dances.*]

LOLLIO. There, an honor.*

ANTONIO. Is this an honor, coz?
    [*He bows.*]

LOLLIO. Yes, and it please your worship.

ANTONIO. Does honor bend in the hams, coz?

LOLLIO. Marry does it; as low as worship, squireship,   100
    nay, yeomanry itself sometimes, from whence it first
    stiffened. There, rise—a caper!

ANTONIO. Caper after an honor, coz?

LOLLIO. Very proper; for honor is but a caper, rise[s] as
    fast and high, has a knee or two, and falls to th' ground
    again. You can remember your figure,* Tony?

                                   Exit.

ANTONIO. Yes, cousin; when I see thy figure, I can re-
    member mine.

        Enter ISABELLA [*dressed like a madwoman*].

ISABELLA. Hey, how [he] treads the air! Shoo, shoo,
    t'other way! He burns his wings else; here's wax*   110
    enough below, Icarus, more than will be canceled these
    eighteen moons.
    [ANTONIO *falls.*]
    He's down, he's down! What a terrible fall he had!
    Stand up, thou son of Cretan Dædalus,
    And let us tread the lower labyrinth;

---

honor: bow.

figure: dance pattern (with pun on its meaning of "face" below).

wax: with which Dædalus attached feathers to the wings that
carried him and his son Icarus from their imprisonment in the
Cretan labyrinth. Not heeding his father's injunction to keep away
from the sun, Icarus fell into the sea below and drowned (the
"terrible fall" of 1. 113) when the heat melted the wax. Isabella
facetiously thinks of the wax used to seal legal documents.

I'll bring thee to the clue.*

[ANTONIO *rises.*]

ANTONIO. Prithee, coz, let me alone.

ISABELLA. Art thou not drowned?
    About thy head I saw a heap of clouds
    Wrapped like a Turkish turban; on thy back   120
    A crook'd, chameleon-colored rainbow hung
    Like a tiara down unto thy hams.
    Let me suck out those billows in the belly;
    Hark, how they roar and rumble in the [straits]!
    Bless thee from the pirates!

ANTONIO. Pox upon you, let me alone!

ISABELLA. Why shouldst thou mount so high as Mercury*
    Unless thou hadst reversion* of his place?
    Stay in the moon with me, Endymion,*
    And we will rule these wild rebellious waves   130
    That would have drowned my love.

ANTONIO. I'll kick thee if again thou touch me,
    Thou wild, unshapen antic;* I am no fool,
    You bedlam!

ISABELLA.   But you are, as sure as I am, mad.
    Have I put on this habit of a frantic,
    With love as full of fury to beguile
    The nimble eye of watchful jealousy,
    And am I thus rewarded?

    [*She reveals herself.*]

ANTONIO. Ha! Dearest beauty!

ISABELLA.   No, I have no beauty
    now,
    Nor never had but what was in my garments.   140
    You a quick-sighted lover? Come not near me!
    Keep your caparisons, y'are aptly clad;
    I came a feigner to return stark mad.

                                  Exit.

Enter LOLLIO.

---

clue: presumably the thread that Ariadne had given Theseus
when he "treaded" the labyrinth to slay Minotaur.

Mercury: messenger of the gods.

reversion: right guaranteeing future possession.

Endymion: handsome shepherd youth with whom Luna (or the
Moon) fell in love.   antic: clown, fool.

ANTONIO. Stay, or I shall change condition
  And become as you are.

LOLLIO. Why, Tony, whither now? Why, fool—

ANTONIO. Whose fool, usher of idiots? You coxcomb!
  I have fooled too much.

LOLLIO. You were best be mad another while then.

ANTONIO. So I am, stark mad; I have cause enough,   150
  And I could throw the full effects on thee
  And beat thee like a fury.

LOLLIO. Do not, do not; I shall not forbear the gentleman
  under the fool if you do. Alas, I saw through your fox-
  skin before now. Come, I can give you comfort: my
  mistress loves you, and there is as arrant a madman
  i'th' house as you are a fool—your rival, whom she
  loves not. If after the masque we can rid her of him,
  you earn her love, she says, and the fool shall ride her.

ANTONIO. May I believe thee?   160

LOLLIO. Yes, or you may choose whether you will or no.

ANTONIO. She's eased of him; I have a good quarrel on't.

LOLLIO. Well, keep your old station yet, and be quiet.

ANTONIO. Tell her I will deserve her love.

LOLLIO. And you are like to have your desire.

[*Exit* ANTONIO.]

Enter FRANCISCUS.

FRANCISCUS [*singing*]. *Down, down, down a-down a-down,*
  and then with a horse-trick
  To kick Latona's° forehead and break her bowstring.

LOLLIO. This is t'other counterfeit; I'll put him out of his
  humor. [*He reads* FRANCISCUS's *letter.*] "Sweet lady,
  having now cast this counterfeit cover of a madman,   170
  I appear to your best judgment a true and faithful
  lover of your beauty."—This is pretty well for a madman.

FRANCISCUS. Ha! What's that?

LOLLIO. "Chide those perfections in you which [have]
  made me imperfect."

FRANCISCUS. I am discovered to the fool.

LOLLIO. I hope to discover the fool in you ere I have
  done with you. "Yours all, or one beside himself, Franciscus." This madman will mend, sure.   180

Latona: mother of Artemis, goddess of the hunt.

FRANCISCUS. What do you read, sirrah?

LOLLIO. Your destiny, sir: you'll be hanged for this trick and another that I know.

FRANCISCUS. Art thou of counsel with thy mistress?

LOLLIO. Next her apron strings?

FRANCISCUS. Give me thy hand.

LOLLIO. Stay, let me put yours in my pocket first. [*He puts away the letter.*] Your hand is true, is it not? It will not pick? I partly fear it because I think it does lie.

FRANCISCUS. Not in a syllable.   190

LOLLIO. So, if you love my mistress so well as you have handled the matter here, you are like to be cured of your madness.

FRANCISCUS. And none but she can cure it:

LOLLIO. Well, I'll give you over then, and she shall cast* your water next.

FRANCISCUS [*giving him money*]. Take for thy pains past.

LOLLIO. I shall deserve more, sir, I hope; my mistress loves you but must have some proof of your love to her.

FRANCISCUS. There I meet my wishes.   200

LOLLIO. That will not serve; you must meet her enemy and yours.

FRANCISCUS. He's dead already!

LOLLIO. Will you tell me that, and I parted but now with him?

FRANCISCUS. Show me the man.

LOLLIO. Ay, that's a right course now; see him before you kill him in any case. And yet it needs not go so far neither; 'tis but a fool that haunts the house and my mistress in the shape of an idiot. Bang but his fool's   210 coat well-favoredly, and 'tis well.

FRANCISCUS. Soundly, soundly!

LOLLIO. Only reserve him till the masque be past; and, if you find him not now in the dance yourself, I'll show you. In, in! My master!

FRANCISCUS. He handles him like a feather. Hey!

[*Exit dancing.*]

Enter ALIBIUS.

ALIBIUS. Well said;* in a readiness, Lollio?

LOLLIO. Yes, sir.

---

cast: analyze.   said: done.

ALIBIUS. Away then, and guide them in, Lollio;
Entreat your mistress to see this sight.—   220

                                                     [*Exit* LOLLIO.]

Hark, is there not one incurable fool
That might be begged?* I have friends.
LOLLIO [*within*]. I have him for you, one that shall de-
serve it, too.
ALIBIUS. Good boy, Lollio.
    [*Re-enter* ISABELLA, *then* LOLLIO *with Madmen and
         Fools.*] *The Madmen and Fools dance.*
'Tis perfect; well, fit but once these strains,
We shall have coin and credit for our pains.

                                                  Exeunt.

ACTUS QUINTUS

[V.i]

            Enter BEATRICE. *A clock strikes one.*
BEATRICE. One struck, and yet she lies by't. O, my fears!
This strumpet serves her own ends, 'tis apparent now,
Devours the pleasure with a greedy appetite,
And never minds my honor or my peace,
Makes havoc of my right; but she pays dearly for't:
No trusting of her life with such a secret
That cannot rule her blood to keep her promise.
Beside, I have some suspicion of her faith to me
Because I was suspected of my lord,
And it must come from her.
    (*Strike two.*)

                            Hark, by my horrors,   10
Another clock strikes two.
               Enter DE FLORES.
DE FLORES.   Pist! Where are you?
BEATRICE. De Flores?
DE FLORES.   Ay. Is she not come from him yet?
BEATRICE. As I am a living soul, not!
DE FLORES.   Sure the devil
Hath sowed his itch within her; who'd trust
A waiting-woman?
BEATRICE.   I must trust somebody.

---

begged: assigned a guardian to control his estate.

DE FLORES. Push! They are termagants.
  Especially when they fall upon their masters
  And have their ladies' first fruits, th'are mad whelps;
  You cannot stave 'em off from game royal. Then
  You are so harsh and hardy, ask no counsel;   20
  And I could have helped you to a[n] apothecary's
    daughter
  Would have fall'n off before eleven and thank[ed] you,
    too.
BEATRICE. O me, not yet? This whore forgets herself.
DE FLORES. The rascal fares so well; look, y'are undone—
  The day-star, by this hand! See [Ph]osphorus* plain
    yonder.
BEATRICE. Advise me now to fall upon some ruin;*
  There is no counsel safe else.
DE FLORES.   Peace! I ha't now,
  For we must force a rising; there's no remedy.
BEATRICE. How? Take heed of that.
DE FLORES.   Tush! Be you
  quiet,
  Or else give over all.
BEATRICE.   Prithee, I ha' done then.   30
DE FLORES. This is my reach:* I'll set some part afire
  Of Diaphanta's chamber.
BEATRICE.   How? Fire, sir?
  That may endanger the whole house.
DE FLORES. You talk of danger when your fame's* on
  fire?
BEATRICE. That's true; do what thou wilt now.
DE FLORES.   Push!
  I aim
  At a most rich success strikes all dead sure.
  The chimney being afire, and some light parcels
  Of the least danger in her chamber only,
  If Diaphanta should be met by chance then
  Far from her lodging, which is now suspicious,   40
  It would be thought her fears and affrights then
  Drove her to seek for succor; if not seen

Phosphorous: the morning star.
ruin: i.e., plan to destroy Diaphanta.   reach: scheme.
fame: reputation.

Or met at all, as that's the likeliest,
For her own shame she'll hasten towards her lodging.
I will be ready with a piece° high-charged
As 'twere to cleanse the chimney. There, 'tis proper
    now;
But she shall be the mark.

BEATRICE.   I'm forced to love thee
    now
'Cause thou provid'st so carefully for my honor.

DE FLORES. 'Slid,° it concerns the safety of us both,
Our pleasure and continuance.

BEATRICE.   One word now, prithee: 50
How for the servants?

DE FLORES.   I'll dispatch them,
Some one way, some another in the hurry,
For buckets, hooks, ladders; fear you not;
The deed shall find its time, and I've thought since
Upon a safe conveyance for the body, too.
How this fire purifies wit! Watch you your minute.

BEATRICE. Fear keeps my soul upon't; I cannot stray
    from't.

                Enter ALONZO's *Ghost.*

DE FLORES. Ha! What art thou that tak'st away the light
'Twixt that star and me? I dread thee not;
'Twas but a mist of conscience.—All's clear again.   60
                                                    Exit.

BEATRICE. Who's that, De Flores? Bless me! It slides by;
                                        [*Exit Ghost.*]
Some ill thing haunts the house; 't has left behind it
A shivering sweat upon me. I'm afraid now.
This night hath been so tedious. O, this strumpet!
Had she a thousand lives, he should not leave her
Till he had destroyed the last.—List! O my terrors!
(*Struck three o'clock.*)
Three struck by Saint Sebastian's!

WITHIN.   Fire, fire, fire!

BEATRICE. Already! How rare is that man's speed!
How heartily he serves me! His face loathes one,
But look upon his care, who would not love him?   70
The east is not more beauteous than his service.

---

piece: gun.   'slid: contraction of "by God's eyelid!"

WITHIN. Fire, fire, fire!
> *Enter* DE FLORES. *Servants pass over, ring a bell.*

DE FLORES. Away, dispatch! Hooks, buckets, ladders;
  that's well said.
The fire bell rings, the chimney works. My charge!
The piece is ready.

                                                          Exit.

BEATRICE.   Here's a man worth loving!
> *Enter* DIAPHANTA.

O, y'are a jewel!
DIAPHANTA.   Pardon frailty, madam;
In troth I was so well I ev'n forgot myself.
BEATRICE. Y'have made trim work!
DIAPHANTA.   What?
BEATRICE.   Hie quickly
  to your chamber;
Your reward follows you.
DIAPHANTA.   I never made
So sweet a bargain.

                                                          Exit.

> *Enter* ALSEMERO.

ALSEMERO.   O my dear Joanna,   80
Alas, art thou risen, too? I was coming,
My absolute treasure.
BEATRICE.   When I missed you,
I could not choose but follow.
ALSEMERO.   Th'art all sweetness!
The fire is not so dangerous.
BEATRICE.   Think you so, sir?
ALSEMERO. I prithee tremble not; believe me, 'tis not.
> *Enter* VERMANDERO, JASPERINO.

VERMANDERO. O, bless my house and me!
ALSEMERO.   My lord your
  father.
> *Enter* DE FLORES *with a piece.*

VERMANDERO. Knave, whither goes that piece?
DE FLORES.   To scour
  the chimney.

                                                          Exit.

VERMANDERO. O, well said, well said!
That fellow's good on all occasions.
BEATRICE. A wondrous necessary man, my lord.   90

VERMANDERO. He hath a ready wit; he's worth 'em all, sir:

Dog* at a house of fire; I ha' seen him singed ere now.—
(*The piece goes off.*)

Ha, there he goes!

BEATRICE. 'Tis done.

ALSEMERO. Come, sweet, to bed now;

Alas, thou wilt get cold.

BEATRICE. Alas, the fear keeps that out!

My heart will find no quiet till I hear

How Diaphanta, my poor woman, fares;

It is her chamber, sir, her lodging chamber.

VERMANDERO. How should the fire come there?

BEATRICE. As good a soul as ever lady countenanced,

But in her chamber negligent and heavy. 100

She 'scaped a mine* twice.

VERMANDERO. Twice?

BEATRICE. Strangely twice, sir.

VERMANDERO. Those sleepy sluts are dangerous in a house,

And they be ne'er so good.

Enter DE FLORES.

DE FLORES. O, poor virginity!

Thou hast paid dearly for't.

VERMANDERO. Bless us! What's that?

DE FLORES. A thing you all knew once—Diaphanta's burnt.

BEATRICE. My woman, O, my woman!

DE FLORES. Now the flames

Are greedy of her; burnt, burnt, burnt to death, sir!

BEATRICE. O, my presaging soul!

ALSEMERO. Not a tear more,

I charge you by the last embrace I gave you

In bed before this raised us.

BEATRICE. Now you tie me; 110

Were it my sister, now she gets no more.

Enter SERVANT.

VERMANDERO. How now?

---

dog: expert, proficient.   mine: accident.

SERVANT.   All danger's past; you may
   now take
  Your rests, my lords; the fire is throughly quenched.
  Ah, poor gentlewoman, how soon she was stifled!
BEATRICE. De Flores, what is left of her inter,
  And we as mourners all will follow her:
  I will entreat that honor to my servant
  Ev'n of my lord himself.
ALSEMERO.   Command it, sweetness.
BEATRICE. Which of you spied the fire first?
DE FLORES.   'Twas I,
  madam.
BEATRICE. And took such pains in't, too? A double good-
  ness!   120
  'Twere well he were rewarded.
VERMANDERO.   He shall be;
  De Flores, call upon me.
ALSEMERO.   And upon me, sir.
                            Exeunt [all but DE FLORES].
DE FLORES. Rewarded? Precious! Here's a trick beyond
  me!
  I see in all bouts, both of sport and wit,
  Always a woman strives for the last hit.

                                             Exit.

[V.ii]
                Enter TOMAZO.
TOMAZO. I cannot taste the benefits of life
  With the same relish I was wont to do.
  Man I grow weary of and hold his fellowship
  A treacherous bloody friendship; and, because
  I am ignorant in whom my wrath should settle,
  I must think all men villains, and the next
  I meet, whoe'er he be, the murderer
  Of my most worthy brother.—Ha! What's he?
      Enter DE FLORES, *passes over the stage.*
  O, the fellow that some call honest De Flores;
  But methinks honesty was hard bested   10
  To come there for a lodging: as if a queen
  Should make her palace of a pesthouse.
  I find a contrariety in nature
  Betwixt that face and me; the least occasion

Would give me game upon him; yet he's so foul
One would scarce touch [him] with a sword he loved
And made account of; so most deadly venomous
He would go near to poison any weapon
That should draw blood on him; one must resolve
Never to use that sword again in fight   20
In way of honest manhood that strikes him;
Some river must devour't; 'twere not fit
That any man should find it.—What, again?

              Enter DE FLORES.

He walks o'purpose by, sure, to choke me up,
To infect my blood.

DE FLORES.   My worthy noble lord!

TOMAZO. Dost offer to come near and breathe upon me?
    [*He strikes him.*]

DE FLORES. A blow!
    [*He draws his sword.*]

TOMAZO.   Yea; are you so prepared?
I'll rather like a soldier die by th' sword
Than like a politician by thy poison.
    [*He draws.*]

DE FLORES. Hold, my lord, as you are honorable.   30

TOMAZO. All slaves that kill by poison are still cowards.

DE FLORES [*aside*]. I cannot strike; I see his brother's
    wounds
Fresh bleeding in his eye as in a crystal.—
I will not question this; I know y'are noble;
I take my injury with thanks given, sir,
Like a wise lawyer, and as a favor
Will wear it for the worthy hand that gave it.—
[*Aside.*] Why this from him that yesterday appeared
So strangely loving to me?
O, but instinct is of a subtler strain.   40
Guilt must not walk so near his lodge again;
He came near me now.

                               Exit.

TOMAZO. All league with mankind I renounce forever
Till I find this murderer. Not so much
As common courtesy but I'll lock up,
For in the state of ignorance I live in
A brother may salute his brother's murderer
And wish good speed to th' villain in a greeting.

Enter VERMANDERO, ALIBIUS, *and* ISABELLA.

VERMANDERO. Noble Piracquo!

TOMAZO.   Pray keep on your way,
   sir;
  I've nothing to say to you.

VERMANDERO.   Comforts bless you, sir.   50

TOMAZO. I have forsworn compliment, in troth I have, sir;
  As you are merely man, I have not left
  A good wish for you nor any here.

VERMANDERO. Unless you be so far in love with grief
  You will not part from't upon any terms,
  We bring that news will make a welcome for us.

TOMAZO. What news can that be?

VERMANDERO.   Throw no scornful
   smile
  Upon the zeal I bring you; 'tis worth more, sir.
  Two of the chiefest men I kept about me
  I hide not from the law or your just vengeance.   60

TOMAZO. Ha!

VERMANDERO. To give your peace more ample satisfaction,
  Thank these discoverers.

TOMAZO.   If you bring that calm,
  Name but the manner I shall ask forgiveness in
  For that contemptuous smile upon you;
  I'll perfect it with reverence that belongs
  Unto a sacred altar.
  [*He kneels.*]

VERMANDERO [*raising him*].   Good sir, rise;
  Why, now you overdo as much o'this hand
  As you fell short o't'other.—Speak, Alibius.

ALIBIUS. 'Twas my wife's fortune, as she is most lucky   70
  At a discovery, to find out lately
  Within our hospital of fools and madmen
  Two counterfeits slipped into these disguises:
  Their names, Franciscus and Antonio.

VERMANDERO. Both mine, sir, and I ask no favor for 'em.

ALIBIUS. Now that which draws suspicion to their habits,
  The time of their disguisings agrees justly
  With the day of the murder.

TOMAZO.   O, blessed revelation!

VERMANDERO. Nay more, nay more, sir—I'll not spare
   mine own

In way of justice: they both feigned a journey   80
To Br[i]amata and so wrought out their leaves;
My love was so abused in't.
TOMAZO.   Time's too precious
To run in waste now. You have brought a peace
The riches of five kingdoms could not purchase.
Be my most happy conduct; I thirst for 'em;
Like subtle lightning will I wind about 'em
And melt their marrow in 'em.

                                                              Exeunt.

[V.iii]
                    Enter ALSEMERO *and* JASPERINO.
JASPERINO. Your confidence, I'm sure, is now of proof;°
The prospect from the garden has showed
Enough for deep suspicion.
ALSEMERO.   The black mask
That so continually was worn upon't
Condemns the face for ugly ere't be seen—
Her despite to him, and so seeming bottomless.
JASPERINO. Touch it home then; 'tis not a shallow probe
Can search this ulcer soundly; I fear you'll find it
Full of corruption. 'Tis fit I leave you.
She meets you opportunely from that walk;   10
She took the back door at his parting with her.

                                                    Exit JASPERINO.

ALSEMERO. Did my fate wait for this unhappy stroke
At my first sight of woman? She's here.
                              Enter BEATRICE.
BEATRICE. Alsemero!
ALSEMERO.   How do you?
BEATRICE.   How do I?
Alas! How do you? You look not well.
ALSEMERO. You read me well enough: I am not well.
BEATRICE. Not well, sir? Is't in my power to better you?
ALSEMERO. Yes.
BEATRICE.   Nay, then y'are cured again.
ALSEMERO. Pray resolve me one question, lady.
BEATRICE.   If I can.
ALSEMERO. None can so sure. Are you honest? °   20

___

proof: i.e., against attack.   honest: chaste.

BEATRICE. Ha, ha, ha! That's a broad question, my lord.

ALSEMERO. But that's not a modest answer, my lady.
Do you laugh? My doubts are strong upon me.

BEATRICE. 'Tis innocence that smiles, and no rough brow
Can take away the dimple in her cheek.
Say I should strain a tear to fill the vault,*
Which would you give the better faith to?

ALSEMERO. 'Twere but hypocrisy of a sadder color
But the same stuff; neither your smiles nor tears
Shall move or flatter me from my belief: 30
You are a whore!

BEATRICE.   What a horrid sound it hath!
It blasts a beauty to deformity;
Upon what face soever that breath falls,
It strikes it ugly. O, you have ruined
What you can ne'er repair again.

ALSEMERO.   I'll all
Demolish and seek out truth within you
If there be any left. Let your sweet tongue
Prevent your heart's rifling; there I'll ransack
And tear out my suspicion.

BEATRICE.   You may, sir;
'Tis an easy passage. Yet, if you please,   40
Show me the ground whereon you lost your love;
My spotless virtue may but tread on that
Before I perish.

ALSEMERO.   Unanswerable!
A ground you cannot stand on; you fall down
Beneath all grace and goodness when you set
Your ticklish* heel on't. There was a visor*
O'er that cunning face, and that became you;
Now impudence in triumph rides upon't.
How comes this tender reconcilement else
'Twixt you and your despite, your rancorous loathing,   50
De Flores? He that your eye was sore at sight of,
He's now become your arms' supporter, your
Lip's saint.

BEATRICE.   Is this the cause?

---

vault: arch of the sky.   ticklish: lewd, lascivious.
visor: compare l. 3 above.

ALSEMERO.   Worse; your lust's
    devil,
  Your adultery!
BEATRICE.   Would any but yourself say that,
  'Twould turn him to a villain.
ALSEMERO.   'Twas witnessed
  By the counsel of your bosom, Diaphanta.
BEATRICE. Is your witness dead, then?
ALSEMERO.   'Tis to be feared
  It was the wages of her knowledge; poor soul,
  She lived not long after the discovery.
BEATRICE. Then hear a story of not much less horror   60
  Than this your false suspicion is beguiled with.
  To your bed's scandal I stand up innocence,
  Which even the guilt of one black other deed
  Will stand for proof of: your love has made me
  A cruel murd'ress.
ALSEMERO.   Ha!
BEATRICE.   A bloody one.
  I have kissed poison for't, stroked a serpent,
  That thing of hate, worthy in my esteem
  Of no better employment; and him most worthy
  To be so employed, I caused to murder
  That innocent Piracquo, having no   70
  Better means than that worst to assure
  Yourself to me.
ALSEMERO.   O, the place itself e'er since
  Has crying been for vengeance, the temple
  Where blood and beauty first unlawfully
  Fired their devotion and quenched the right one.
  'Twas in my fears at first; 'twill have it now.
  O, thou art all deformed!
BEATRICE.   Forget not, sir,
  It for your sake was done; shall greater dangers
  Make the less welcome?
ALSEMERO.   O, thou shouldst have gone
  A thousand leagues about to have avoided   80
  This dangerous bridge of blood; here we are lost.
BEATRICE. Remember I am true unto your bed.
ALSEMERO. The bed itself's a charnel, the sheets shrouds
  For murdered carcasses; it must ask pause

What I must do in this; meantime you shall
Be my prisoner only. Enter my closet.

Exit BEATRICE.

I'll be your keeper yet.—O, in what part
Of this sad story shall I first begin?

Enter DE FLORES.

Ha!

This same fellow has put me in.°—De Flores!

DE FLORES. Noble Alsemero!

ALSEMERO.   I can tell you   90
News, sir; my wife has her commended to you.

DE FLORES. That's news indeed, my lord; I think she
    would
Commend me to the gallows if she could,
She ever loved me so well; I thank her.

ALSEMERO. What's this blood upon your band,° De
    Flores?

DE FLORES. Blood? No, sure 'twas washed since.

ALSEMERO.   Since
    when, man?

DE FLORES. Since t'other day I got a knock
In a sword and dagger school; I think 'tis out.

ALSEMERO. Yes, 'tis almost out; but 'tis perceived, though.
I had forgot my message; this it is: 100
What price goes murder?

DE FLORES.   How, sir?

ALSEMERO.   I ask you, sir.
My wife's behindhand with you, she tells me,
For a brave, bloody blow you gave for her sake
Upon Piracquo.

DE FLORES.   Upon?°'Twas quite through him,
    sure.
Has she confessed it?

ALSEMERO.   As sure as death to both of you,
And much more than that.

DE FLORES.   It could not be much
    more;
'Twas but one thing, and that she's a whore.

ALSEMERO. I[t] could not choose but follow. O, cunning
    devils!

---

put me in: given me my cue.   band: collar.

How should blind men know you from fair-faced
  saints?

BEATRICE (*within*). He lies! The villain does belie me! 110

DE FLORES. Let me go to her, sir.

ALSEMERO.   Nay, you shall to
  her.—
Peace, crying crocodile, your sounds are heard.
Take your prey to you.—Get you in to her, sir.

                                    Exit DE FLORES.

I'll be your pander now; rehearse again
Your scene of lust, that you may be perfect
When you shall come to act it to the black audience
Where howls and gnashings shall be music to you.
Clip° your adult'ress freely; 'tis the pilot
Will guide you to the *Mare Mortuum,*°
Where you shall sink to fathoms bottomless. 120

      Enter VERMANDERO, ALIBIUS, ISABELLA, TOMAZO,
            FRANCISCUS, *and* ANTONIO.

VERMANDERO. O, Alsemero, I have a wonder for you.

ALSEMERO. No, sir, 'tis I; I have a wonder for you.

VERMANDERO. I have suspicion near as proof itself
  For Piracquo's murder.

ALSEMERO.   Sir, I have proof
  Beyond suspicion for Piracquo's murder.

VERMANDERO. Beseech you, hear me; these two have
  been disguised
E'er since the deed was done.

ALSEMERO.   I have two other
  That were more close disguised than your two could
  be
E'er since the deed was done.

VERMANDERO. You'll hear me! These mine own servants— 130

ALSEMERO. Hear me—those nearer than your servants
  That shall acquit them and prove them guiltless.

FRANCISCUS. That may be done with easy truth, sir.

TOMAZO. How is my cause bandied through your delays!
  'Tis urgent in blood and calls for haste;
  Give me a brother alive or dead:

---

clip: embrace.
Mare Mortuum: the Dead Sea (here Hell?).

Alive, a wife with him; if dead, for both
A recompense for murder and adultery.
BEATRICE (*within*). O, O, O!
ALSEMERO.   Hark! 'Tis coming to
   you.
DE FLORES (*within*). Nay, I'll along for company.
BEATRICE (*within*).   O,
   O!   140
VERMANDERO. What horrid sounds are these?
ALSEMERO. Come forth, you twins of mischief.
    Enter DE FLORES *bringing in* BEATRICE [*wounded*].
DE FLORES. Here we are; if you have any more
To say to us, speak quickly; I shall not
Give you hearing else; I am so stout yet,
And so, I think, that broken rib of mankind.
VERMANDERO. An host of enemies entered my citadel
Could not amaze like this!—Joanna! Beatrice Joanna!
BEATRICE. O, come not near me, sir; I shall defile you.
I am that of your blood was taken from you   150
For your better health; look no more upon't,
But cast it to the ground regardlessly;
Let the common [sewer] take it from distinction.
Beneath the stars, upon yon meteor
[*She points to* DE FLORES.]
Ever h[u]ng my fate, 'mongst things corruptible;
I ne'er could pluck it from him. My loathing
Was prophet to the rest but ne'er believed;
Mine honor fell with him, and now my life.—
Alsemero, I am a stranger to your bed;
Your bed was cozened° on the nuptial night,   160
For which your false bride died.
ALSEMERO.   Diaphanta!
DE FLORES. Yes; and the while I coupled with your mate
At barley-break; now we are left in hell.
VERMANDERO. We are all there; it circumscribes here.
DE FLORES. I loved this woman in spite of her heart;
Her love I earned out of Piracquo's murder.
TOMAZO. Ha! My brother's murderer!
DE FLORES.   Yes; and her
   honor's prize

———————

cozened: cheated.

Was my reward. I thank life for nothing
But that pleasure; it was so sweet to me
That I have drunk up all, left none behind   170
For any man to pledge me.
VERMANDERO.   Horrid villain!
Keep life in him for further tortures.
DE FLORES.   No!
I can prevent you; here's my penknife still.
It is but one thread more,
[*He stabs himself.*]

                                    and now 'tis cut.
—Make haste, Joanna, by that token* to thee
Canst not forget so lately put in mind;
I would not go to leave thee far behind.
(*Dies.*)
BEATRICE. Forgive me, Alsemero, all forgive!
'Tis time to die when 'tis a shame to live.
(*Dies.*)
VERMANDERO. O, my name is entered now in that record   180
Where till this fatal hour 'twas never read.
ALSEMERO. Let it be blotted out; let your heart lose it,
And it can never look you in the face
Nor tell a tale behind the back of life
To your dishonor. Justice hath so right
The guilty hit that innocence is quit*
By proclamation and may joy again.—
Sir, you are sensible of what truth hath done;
'Tis the best comfort that your grief can find.
TOMAZO. Sir, I am satisfied; my injuries   190
Lie dead before me. I can exact no more
Unless my soul were loose and could o'ertake
Those black fugitives, that are fled from thence,
To take a second vengeance; but there are wraths
Deeper than mine ('tis to be feared) about 'em.
ALSEMERO. What an opacous body had that moon
That last changed on us! Here's beauty changed
To ugly whoredom; here servant obedience
To a master sin, imperious murder;
I, a supposed husband, changed embraces   200
With wantonness, but that was paid before.—

---

token: wound.   quit: acquitted.

[*To* TOMAZO.] Your change is come, too, from an igno-
    rant wrath
To knowing friendship.—Are there any more on's?

ANTONIO. Yes, sir; I was changed, too, from a little ass
    as I was to a great fool as I am, and had like to ha'been
    changed to the gallows but that you know my inno-
    cence° always excuses me.

FRANCISCUS. I was changed from a little wit to be stark
    mad, almost for the same purpose.

ISABELLA [*to* ALIBIUS]. Your change is still behind,°   210
But deserve best your transformation.
You are a jealous coxcomb, keep schools of folly,
And teach your scholars how to break your own head.

ALIBIUS. I see all apparent, wife, and will change now
Into a better husband and never keep
Scholars that shall be wiser than myself.

ALSEMERO. Sir, you have yet a son's duty living;
Please you, accept it; let that your sorrow,
As it goes from your eye, go from your heart;
Man and his sorrow at the grave must part.   220

Epilogue

ALSEMERO. All we can do to comfort one another,
To stay a brother's sorrow for a brother,
To dry a child from the kind father's eyes,
Is to no purpose: it rather multiplies.
Your only smiles° have power to cause relive
The dead again or in their rooms to give
Brother a new brother, father a child;
If these appear, all griefs are reconciled.

                                      Exeunt omnes.

FINIS.

---

innocence: idiocy, as well as guiltlessness.
behind: to come.   your only smiles: only your smiles.

THE BROKEN HEART.

A Tragedy.

ACTED
By the KINGS Majesties Seruants
at the priuate House in the
BLACK-FRIERS.

Fide Honor.

LONDON,
Printed by I. B. for HVGH BEESTON, and are to
be sold at his Shop, neere the Castle in
Corne-hill. 1633.

Art No. 9 for Broken Heart

Introduction

Ford's *The Broken Heart* (c. 1627–1631?), performed early in Charles' reign "By the King's Majesty's Servants at the private house in the Blackfriars," as the original title page indicates, culminates the dramatic tradition that began with the movement of the professional companies indoors and the concomitant patronage of serious drama by an exclusive audience, including royalty itself. The softening of tone, the lessening of tragic tension and of comic assurance, the emphasis on private sensibility, the increasing reliance on fate to absolve responsibility, the strong underlying wish for peace, the development of the heroine and with her the theme of passive suffering—all gather force and come to fulfillment, as it were, in this model Caroline play of quiet dignity, restrained diction, and chiseled effect. Sparta is properly the setting of a play written to provide a world of divided loyalties and ambiguous responsibilities with Spartan examples of nobility in living and in dying.

Missing almost completely from *The Broken Heart* is the authentic tragic note; instead, the Prologue appeals to an aristocratic audience to "partake a pity with delight" and thus to indulge its sensibilities to the fullest. More than in the tragicomic world of Beaumont and Fletcher, the heart has come to rest in Ford. Disturbing tensions and conflicts ultimately mean nothing in a world where "Mortality/ Creeps on the dung of earth and cannot reach/ The riddles which are purposed by the gods" (I.iii). As the unfortunate Penthea concludes in what one character calls "perfect philosophy":

> *In vain we labor in this course of life*
> *To piece our journey out at length or crave*
> *Respite of breath; our home is in the grave.*
>
> (II.iii)

In the face of so defeatist a view of existence—"all ways/
Are alike pleasant to me," Penthea ironically observes—
Ford's heroes and, even more, his heroines self-consciously
seek identity; and they succeed by gracefully adhering to a
code of noble gestures that in effect becomes a principle en-
abling them to assert continually their personal reality. Where
nothing is certain, the assertion of the ego's image in conscious
poses is at least something to believe in. "He cannot fear/
Who builds on noble grounds" or "They die too basely who
outlive their glories."

Such assertion of the ego, however, as the only meaningful
response to existence, no matter how beautiful the gesture is,
is itself a confession of anarchy and failure. The two songs
by which the broken-hearted Penthea and Calantha die sug-
gest the impasse that must result when the individual ego
takes an absolute stand in a socially relative world. Penthea
dies to the tune of "Love's martyrs must be ever, ever dying,"
and the only comfort for Calantha's broken heart—which no
"art" can find—is: "Love only reigns in death."

To some, *The Broken Heart* has seemed more like a "problem play" than a true tragedy, posing dilemmas for its characters to escape from rather than indicating the fate that they
must embrace. Because, the reasoning goes, it considered
premarital contracts as binding, Ford's audience would have
understood Penthea's dilemma. Morally, as well as emotion-
ally, Penthea considers herself married to Orgilus, as he does
to her; nevertheless, she is legally, though unwillingly, married
to the jealous old fool Bassanes. Courtly love conventions of
her society would have sympathized with her remaining
loyal to Orgilus even under the present circumstances; indeed,
he expects her loyalty. She is aware, of course, of this permis-
sive code; but, still, she will not violate her social and religious
contract of marriage. Whether faithfully married to Bassanes
and thus faithless to Orgilus, or faithful to Orgilus and faithless to Bassanes, she is, in her own eyes, a whore.

The same conventions of courtly love call upon Orgilus to
revenge his and Penthea's situation by killing Ithocles, her

brother, who caused their separation. As Tecnicus the philosopher points out (III.i), however, "real honor/ Is the reward of virtue and acquired/ By justice or by valor," not by taking revenge. Orgilus concurs; but the dying (and demented) Penthea, so scrupulous, it would seem, about her moral code, seems to demand vengeance from Orgilus in her final words: "O, cruel Ithocles and injured Orgilus!" But by this point Orgilus is reconciled in friendship to Ithocles, so that to avenge Penthea, as one kind of "honor" would demand, means violating the "honor" of friendship. Thus, Orgilus' knowing the code and concurring with it does not necessarily mean that he is able to follow it: The code compels contradictory responses in complex situations. In such an impasse he calmly makes the grand gesture; he takes vengeance upon Ithocles, satisfying thereby his personal honor, and then nobly submits to his own death, gracefully adhering to his own apothegm: "They die too basely who outlive their glories." What dilemmas his and Penthea's deaths have solved are not clear. He dies with a mist hanging over his eyes—a mist that hangs over all the casuistries of the play.

The Broken Heart is not, however, a tract on the miseries of enforced marriage although the theme is prominent in the play and although the happy and socially viable marriage of Prophilus and Euphranea would seem to supply an alternative. Ford is not really concerned with living but with dying, and Calantha—not Penthea or Orgilus or Ithocles—is the central figure of the play. Her death is the climax, and even the festivities for the wedding of Prophilus and Euphranea become part of its ritual. All struggles seem vain where love's martyrs are ever dying—and where, as Calantha says, "Those that are dead/ Are dead; had they not now died, of necessity/ They must have paid the debt they owed to nature/ One time or other." The beauty of life, it would seem, is to know how to "die smiling," without struggle and without complaint. As in Webster, the truly heroic person is the woman of quiet suffering. Calantha dies with "a masculine spirit." Other characters in Ford's aristocratic world die well, too; but she is the pattern for all: Her life is chaste and exemplary as befits a princess; her death, an elaborate work of art, a final and beautiful gesture to defy the fact of corruption. The gesture is not mere pose. The silence that attends it is her recognition that "They are the silent griefs which cut the

heartstrings," and to speak of them is to cheapen and to senti-
mentalize them.

The silence, the restraint, and the magnificent gesture of
Calantha's death are the keys to the tone of the entire play,
reflecting the silence, the restraint, and the magnificent gestures of characters who, in effect, have ceased to struggle
against uncertainties. Ford does not ask "Why does one act?"
but rather "How will one act?" This question appeals to a
world of manners and form; for, although they are a part of
assured and ordered societies, manners and form are essential to the maintenance of a character's integrity in a world
of no recognizable meaning. That is why his characters, even
if they at moments utter the poetry of passionate suffering,
seem most of the time to be coolly analyzing their thoughts
and actions as a means of disciplining themselves. They become to themselves and to one another "fair example[s] of
nobility," such as Ford found in Lord Craven, to whom he
dedicated the play. Significantly, Ford's name is missing from
the title page of the original quarto; in its stead appears his
anagram: *Fide Honor*. "Trust in Honor," appropriately, when
one's own identity means so little.

The Playwright

JOHN FORD (1586–1639?) was born in Devonshire,
and he may have entered Exeter College, Oxford, in March
1601; in November 1602, he was admitted to the Middle
Temple, where his grand-uncle, Lord Chief Justice Popham,
was a member. Evidence indicates that he performed some
legal work in his life but that he never actually practiced as
a barrister. In 1606 he published an elegy, *Fame's Memorial*,
on the death of the Earl of Devonshire and a pamphlet, *Honour Triumphant, or The Peers' Challenge*, which defends
certain amorous propositions in the manner of a court-of-love
disciple. Monetary difficulties appear to have beset him all his
life, and very likely he depended for his living on writing
plays. From 1621 to 1624 he collaborated on five plays (only
two of which are extant), chiefly with Thomas Dekker; thereafter, he wrote independently. No record of him exists after

1639, when he may have left London, possibly to return to Devonshire, or when he may have died. A contemporary couplet characterizes him thus: "Deep in a dump Jack Ford alone was got,/ With folded arms and melancholy hat."

The Play

The present text of *The Broken Heart* is based on copies of the first quarto of 1633 in the Henry E. Huntington and the Folger Shakespeare libraries. The entry of the play in the Stationers' Register also is dated 1633. The best conjectural dates for the first performance range from 1627 to 1631. The original quarto divides the play into acts; an attempt at scene division breaks down by the third act.

SELECTED BIBLIOGRAPHY

Dramatic Works, ed. W. Bang and H. de Vocht, in *Materials for the Study of Old English Drama*, XXIII (1908) and New Series I (1927). Louvain: Librairie Universitaire, Uystpruyst.

The Broken Heart, ed. D. K. Anderson, Jr. Lincoln: University of Nebraska Press, 1968. (Regents Renaissance Drama Series.)

The Broken Heart, ed. B. Morris. New York: Hill and Wang, 1966. (The New Mermaids.)

"*'Tis Pity She's a Whore*" and "*The Broken Heart*," ed. S. P. Sherman. Boston and London: Heath, 1915. (Belles-Lettres Series.)

Works, ed. W. Gifford and A. Dyce. 3 vols. London: Toovey, 1869.

Anderson, D. K., Jr. "The Heart and the Banquet: Imagery in Ford's *'Tis Pity* and *The Broken Heart*," *Studies in English Literature*, II (1962), 209–217.

Blayney, G. L. "Convention, Plot, and Structure in *The Broken Heart*," *Modern Philology*, LVI (1958), 1–9.

Carsaniga, G. M. "The Truth in John Ford's *The Broken Heart*," *Comparative Literature*, X (1958), 344–348.

Davril, R. *Le Drame de John Ford*. Paris: Didier, 1954.

Leech, C. *John Ford and the Drama of His Time*. London: Chatto and Windus, 1957.

McDonald, C. O. "The Design of John Ford's *The Broken Heart*: A Study in the Development of Caroline Sensibility," *Studies in Philology*, LIX (1962), 141–161.

Oliver, H. J. *The Problem of John Ford*. Melbourne, Australia: University Press, 1955.

Sargeaunt, M. J. *John Ford*. Oxford: Blackwell, 1935.

Sensabaugh, G. F. "John Ford Revisited," *Studies in English Literature*, IV (1964), 195–216.

———. *The Tragic Muse of John Ford*. Palo Alto, Calif.: Stanford University Press, 1944.

Sherman, S. P. "Stella and *The Broken Heart*," *Publications of the Modern Language Association of America*, XXIV (1909), 274–285.

Stavig, M. *John Ford and the Traditional Moral Order*, Madison, Milwaukee, and London: University of Wisconsin Press, 1968.

Ure, P. "Marriage and the Domestic Drama in Heywood and Ford," *English Studies*, XXXII (1951), 200–216.

To the Most Worthy Deserver
of the Noblest Titles in Honor,
William, Lord Craven, Baron of Hampstead-Marshall.

My Lord:
The glory of a great name, acquired by a greater glory
of action, hath in all ages lived the truest chronicle to
his own memory. In the practice of which argument,
your growth to perfection (even in youth) hath appeared
so sincere, so unflattering a penman, that posterity cannot with more delight read the merit of noble endeavors
than noble endeavors merit thanks from posterity to be
read with delight. Many nations, many eyes, have been
witnesses of your deserts and loved them; be pleased,   10
then, with the freedom of your own nature to admit
one amongst all, particularly into the list of such as honor
a fair example of nobility. There is a kind of humble
ambition, not uncommendable, when the silence of study
breaks forth into discourse, coveting rather encouragement than applause; yet herein censure commonly is too
severe an auditor without the moderation of an able
patronage. I have ever been slow in courtship of greatness, not ignorant of such defects as are frequent to
opinion; but the justice of your inclination to industry   20
emboldens my weakness of confidence to relish an experience of your mercy as many brave dangers have
tasted of your courage. Your lordship strove to be known
to the world (when the world knew you least) by voluntary but excellent attempts: like allowance I plead of
being known to your lordship (in this low presumption)
by tend'ring to a favorable entertai[n]ment, a devotion
offered from a heart that can be as truly sensible of any
least respect as ever profess the owner in my best, my
readiest services,   30

        a lover of your natural love to virtue,
               John Ford.

THE SCENE: SPARTA

THE SPEAKERS' NAMES, FITTED TO THEIR QUALITIES.

*

AMYCLAS, *common to the kings of Laconia.*
ITHOCLES, *Honor of Loveliness: a favorite.*
ORGILUS, *Angry: son to Crotolon.*
BASSANES, *Vexation: a jealous nobleman.*
ARMOSTES, *an Appeaser: a counselor of state.*
CROTOLON, *Noise: another counselor.*
PROPHILUS, *Dear: friend to Ithocles.*
NEARCHUS, *Young Prince: Prince of Argos.*
TECNICUS, *Artist: a philosopher.*
LEMOPHIL, *Glutton* ⎫
GRONEAS, *Tavern-haunter* ⎭ *two courtiers.*
AMELUS, *Trusty: friend to Nearchus.*
PHULAS, *Watchful: servant to Bassanes.*

CALANTHA, *Flower of Beauty: the king's daughter.*
PENTHEA, *Complaint: sister to Ithocles [and wife to Bassanes].*
EUPHRANEA, *Joy: a maid of honor [and daughter of Crotolon].*
CHRISTALLA, *Crystal* ⎫
PHILEMA, *a Kiss* ⎭ *maids of honor.*
GRA[U]SIS, *Old Beldam: overseer of Penthea.*
[*Courtiers, Officers, Attendants, etc.*]

Persons Included.
THRASUS, *Fierceness: father of Ithocles.*
APLOTES, *Simplicity: Orgilus so disguised.*

The Prologue

Our scene is Sparta. He whose best of art
Hath drawn this piece calls it *The Broken Heart*.
The title lends no expectation here
Of apish laughter or of some lame jeer
At place or persons; no pretended clause
Of jests,° fit for a brothel, courts applause
From vulgar admiration; such low songs,
Tuned to unchaste ears, suit not modest tongues.
The Virgin Sisters° then deserved fresh bays
When Innocence and Sweetness crowned their lays;   10
Then vices gasped for breath, whose whole commerce
Was whipped to exile by unblushing verse.
This law we keep in our presentment now,
Not to take freedom more than we allow;
What may be here thought a fiction, when Time's youth
Wanted some riper years, was known a truth:
In which, if words have clothed the subject right,
You may partake a pity with delight.

---

pretended . . . jests: group of stories offered (Morris).
Virgin Sisters: the Muses.

The
Broken Heart

ACTUS PRIMUS

[I.i]

Enter CROTOLON *and* ORGILUS.

CROTOLON. Dally not further; I will know the reason
  That speeds thee to this journey.

ORGILUS.　　　　　　　Reason? Good sir,
  I can yield many.

CROTOLON.　　　　Give me one, a good one;
  Such I expect and ere we part must have.
  Athens? Pray, why to Athens? You intend not
  To kick against the world, turn cynic, stoic,
  Or read the logic lecture, or become
  An Areopagite° and judge in causes
  Touching the commonwealth? For, as I take it,
  The budding of your chin cannot prognosticate 　　10
  So grave an honor.

ORGILUS.　　　　All this I acknowledge.

CROTOLON. You do! Then, son, if books and love of knowledge
  Inflame you to this travel, here in Sparta
  You may as freely study.

ORGILUS.　　　　　　'Tis not that, sir.

CROTOLON. Not that, sir! As a father, I command thee
  To acquaint me with the truth.

ORGILUS.　　　　　　　Thus I obey 'ee:

Areopagite: member of the Athenian court of justice.

After so many quarrels as dissension,
Fury, and rage had broached in blood, and sometimes
With death to such confederates as sided
With now dead Thrasus and yourself, my lord,   20
Our present king, Amyclas, reconciled
Your eager swords and sealed a gentle peace.
Friends you professed yourselves, which to confirm,
A resolution for a lasting league
Betwixt your families was entertained
By joining in a Hymenean° bond
Me and the fair Penthea, only daughter
To Thrasus.

CROTOLON.   What of this?

ORGILUS.   Much, much, dear sir.
A freedom of converse, an interchange
Of holy and chaste love, so fixed our souls   30
In a firm growth of holy union that no time
Can eat into the pledge; we had enjoyed
The sweets our vows expected had not cruelty
Prevented all those triumphs° we prepared for
By Thrasus his untimely death.

CROTOLON.   Most certain.

ORGILUS. From this time sprouted up that poisonous stalk
Of aconite, whose ripened fruit hath ravished
All health, all comfort of a happy life:
For Ithocles, her brother, proud of youth,
And prouder in his power, nourished closely   40
The memory of former discontents.
To glory in revenge, by cunning partly,
Partly by threats, 'a° woos at once and forces
His virtuous sister to admit a marriage
With Bassanes, a nobleman, in honor
And riches, I confess, beyond my fortunes.

CROTOLON. All this is no sound reason to importune
My leave for thy departure.

ORGILUS.   Now it follows.
Beauteous Penthea, wedded to this torture
By an insulting brother, being secretly   50
Compelled to yield her virgin freedom up
To him who never can usurp her heart,

---

hymenean: marital.   triumphs: festivities.   'a: he.

Before contracted mine, is now so yoked
To a most barbarous thralldom, misery,
Affliction, that he savors not humanity
Whose sorrow melts not into more than pity
In hearing but her name.

CROTOLON.   As how, pray?

ORGILUS.   Bassanes,
The man that calls her wife, considers truly
What heaven of perfections he is lord of
By thinking fair Penthea his. This thought   60
Begets a kind of monster-love, which love
Is nurse unto a fear so strong and servile
As brands all dotage with a jealousy.
All eyes who gaze upon that shrine of beauty,
He doth resolve,° do homage to the miracle;
Someone, he is assured, may now or then
(If opportunity but sort°) prevail.
So much, out of a self-unworthiness,
His fears transport him—not that he finds cause
In her obedience, but his own distrust.   70

CROTOLON. You spin out your discourse.

ORGILUS.   My griefs are
    violent;
For, knowing how the maid was heretofore
Courted by me, his jealousies grow wild
That I should steal again into her favors
And undermine her virtues, which the gods
Know I nor dare nor dream of. Hence, from hence
I undertake a voluntary exile;
First, by my absence to take off the cares
Of jealous Bassanes; but chiefly, sir,
To free Penthea from a hell on earth;   80
Lastly, to lose the memory of something
Her presence makes to live in me afresh.

CROTOLON. Enough, my Orgilus, enough. To Athens
I give full consent.—Alas, good lady!—
We shall hear from thee often?

ORGILUS.   Often.

CROTOLON.   See,
Thy sister comes to give a farewell.

                        Enter EUPHRANEA.

------

resolve: conclude.   sort: occur, take place.

EUPHRANEA.   Brother!
ORGILUS. Euphranea, thus upon thy cheeks I print
  A brother's kiss, more careful of thine honor,
  Thy health, and thy well-doing than my life.
  Before we part, in presence of our father,   90
  I must prefer a suit to 'ee.
EUPHRANEA.   You may style it,
  My brother, a command.
ORGILUS.   That you will promise
  To pass never to any man, however
  Worthy, your faith till with our father's leave
  I give a free consent.
CROTOLON.   An easy motion!°
  I'll promise for her, Orgilus.
ORGILUS.   Your pardon;
  Euphranea's oath must yield me satisfaction.
EUPHRANEA. By Vesta's sacred fires I swear.
CROTOLON.   And I
  By great Apollo's beams join in the vow,
  Not without thy allowance to bestow her   100
  On any living.
ORGILUS.   Dear Euphranea,
  Mistake me not; far, far 'tis from my thought,
  As far from any wish of mine, to hinder
  Preferment to an honorable bed
  Or fitting fortune. Thou art young and handsome,
  And 'twere injustice—more, a tyranny—
  Not to advance thy merit. Trust me, sister,
  It shall be my first care to see thee matched
  As may become thy choice and our contents.
  I have your oath.
EUPHRANEA.   You have. But mean you, brother,   110
  To leave us as you say?
CROTOLON.   Ay, ay, Euphranea;
  He has just grounds direct him. I will prove
  A father and a brother to thee.
EUPHRANEA.   Heaven
  Does look into the secrets of all hearts.
  Gods, you have mercy with 'ee, else—
CROTOLON.   Doubt° noth-
    ing;

---

  motion: proposal.   doubt: fear.

Thy brother will return in safety to us.
ORGILUS. Souls sunk in sorrows never are without 'em;
   They change fresh airs but bear their briefs about 'em.
                                                    Exeunt omnes.°

[I.ii]
            Flourish. Enter AMYCLAS *the King,* ARMOSTES,
                    PROPHILUS, *and Attendants.*
AMYCLAS. The Spartan gods are gracious; our humility
   Shall bend before their altars and perfume
   Their temples with abundant sacrifice.
   See, lords, Amyclas, your old king, is ent'ring
   Into his youth again. I shall shake off
   This silver badge of age and change this snow
   For hairs as gay as are Apollo's locks;
   Our heart leaps in new vigor.
ARMOSTES.   May old time
   Run back to double your long life, great sir!
AMYCLAS. It will, it must, Armostes; thy bold nephew,   10
   Death-braving Ithocles, brings to our gates
   Triumphs and peace upon his conquering sword.
   Laconia is a monarchy at length,
   Hath in this latter war trod underfoot
   Messene's pride; Messene bows her neck
   To Lacedemon's royalty. O, 'twas
   A glorious victory and doth deserve
   More than a chronicle—a temple, lords,
   A temple to the name of Ithocles!—
   Where didst thou leave him, Prophilus?
PROPHILUS.   At Pephon,   20
   Most gracious sovereign; twenty of the noblest
   Of the Messenians there attend your pleasure
   For such conditions as you shall propose
   In settling peace and liberty of life.
AMYCLAS. When comes your friend the general?
PROPHILUS.   He
      promised
   To follow with all speed convenient.
            Enter CROTOLON, CALANTHA, CHRISTALLA,
            PHILEMA [*with a garland*], *and* EUPHRANEA.

---

   omnes: all.

AMYCLAS. Our daughter!—Dear Calantha, the happy news,
The conquest of Messene, hath already
Enriched thy knowledge.

CALANTHA.   With the circumstance
And manner of the fight, related faithfully   30
By Prophilus himself.—But pray, sir, tell me
How doth the youthful general demean
His actions in these fortunes?

PROPHILUS.   Excellent princess,
Your own fair eyes may soon report a truth
Unto your judgment, with what moderation,
Calmness of nature, measure, bounds, and limits
Of thankfulness and joy 'a doth digest
Such amplitude of his success as would
In others, molded of a spirit less clear,
Advance 'em to comparison with heaven.   40
But Ithocles—

CALANTHA.   Your friend.

PROPHILUS.   He is so, madam,
In which the period of my fate consists:
He, in this firmament of honor, stands
Like a star fixed, not moved with any thunder
Of popular applause or sudden lightning
Of self-opinion; he hath served his country
And thinks 'twas but his duty.

CROTOLON.   You describe
A miracle of man.

AMYCLAS.   Such, Crotolon,
On forfeit of a king's word, thou wilt find him.—
(*Flourish.*)
Hark, warning of his coming! All attend him.   50

          Enter ITHOCLES, LEMOPHIL, *and* GRONEAS:
          the rest of the Lords ushering him in.
Return into these arms, thy home, thy sanctuary,
Delight of Sparta, treasure of my bosom,
Mine own, own Ithocles!

ITHOCLES.   Your humblest subject.

ARMOSTES. Proud of the blood I claim an interest in,
As brother to thy mother, I embrace thee,
Right noble nephew.

ITHOCLES.   Sir, your love's too partial.

CROTOLON. Our country speaks by me, who by thy valor,
    Wisdom, and service shares in this great action,
    Returning thee, in part of thy due merits,
    A general welcome.
ITHOCLES.   You exceed in bounty.   60
CALANTHA. Christalla, Philema, the chaplet.—Ithocles,
    Upon the wings of Fame the singular
    And chosen fortune of an high attempt
    Is borne so past the view of common sight
    That I myself with mine own hands have wrought
    To crown thy temples, this provincial garland: °
    Accept, wear, and enjoy it as our gift
    Deserved, not purchased.
ITHOCLES.   Y'are a royal maid.
AMYCLAS. She is in all our daughter.
ITHOCLES.   Let me blush,
    Acknowledging how poorly I have served,   70
    What nothings I have done, compared with th' honors
    Heaped on this issue of a willing mind;
    In that lay mine ability, that only.
    For who is he so sluggish from his birth,
    So little worthy of a name or country,
    That owes not out of gratitude for life
    A debt of service, in what kind soever
    Safety or counsel of the commonwealth
    Requires, for payment?
CALANTHA.   'A speaks truth.
ITHOCLES.   Whom
    heaven
    Is pleased to style victorious, there, to such,   80
    Applause runs madding, like the drunken priests
    In Bacchus' ° sacrifices, without reason,
    Voicing the leader-on a demi-god;
    Whenas, indeed, each common soldier's blood
    Drops down as current coin in that hard purchase
    As his whose much more delicate condition
    Hath sucked the milk of ease. Judgment commands,
    But resolution executes. I use not,
    Before this royal presence, these fit slights

---

    provincial garland: conferred upon Ithocles for adding a province
to the realm.   Bacchus: Greek god of wine.

As in contempt of such as can direct; 90
My speech hath other end, not to attribute
All praise to one man's fortune, which is strengthed
By many hands. For instance, here is Prophilus,
A gentleman (I cannot flatter truth)
Of much desert; and, though in other rank,
Both Lemophil and Groneas were not missing
To wish their country's peace; for, in a word,
All there did strive their best, and 'twas our duty.

AMYCLAS. Courtiers turn soldiers! We vouchsafe our hand.

[LEMOPHIL *and* GRONEAS *kiss his hand.*]
Observe your great example.

LEMOPHIL. With all diligence. 100

GRONEAS. Obsequiously and hourly.

AMYCLAS. Some repose
After these toils are needful. We must think on
Conditions for the conquered; they expect 'em.
On!—Come, my Ithocles.

[PROPHILUS *offers to escort* EUPHRANEA.]

EUPHRANEA. Sir, with your favor,
I need not a supporter.

PROPHILUS. Fate instructs me.

*Exeunt. Manent** LEMOPHIL, GRONEAS, CHRISTALLA,
et PHILEMA. LEMOPHIL *stays**
CHRISTALLA; GRONEAS, PHILEMA.

CHRISTALLA. With me?

PHILEMA. Indeed, I dare not stay.

LEMOPHIL. Sweet
lady,
Soldiers are blunt—your lip.

CHRISTALLA. Fie, this is rudeness;
You went not hence such creatures.

GRONEAS. Spirit of valor
Is of a mounting nature.

PHILEMA. It appears so.
Pray, in earnest, how many men apiece 110
Have yo[u] two been the death of?

GRONEAS. Faith, not many;
We were composed of mercy.

---

manent: remain.   stays: detains.

LEMOPHIL.   For our daring
  You heard the general's approbation
  Before the king.
CHRISTALLA.   You "wished your country's peace";
  That showed your charity. Where are your spoils,
  Such as the soldier fights for?
PHILEMA.   They are coming.
CHRISTALLA. By the next carrier, are they not?
GRONEAS.   Sweet
  Philema,
  When I was in the thickest of mine enemies,
  Slashing off one man's head, another's nose,
  Another's arms and legs—
PHILEMA.   And [all together].   120
GRONEAS. Then would I with a sigh remember thee
  And cry, "Dear Philema, 'tis for thy sake
  I do these deeds of wonder!"—Dost not love me
  With all thy heart now?
PHILEMA.   Now as heretofore.
  I have not put my love to use;* the principal
  Will hardly yield an interest.
GRONEAS.   By Mars,
  I'll marry thee!
PHILEMA.   By Vulcan,* y'are forsworn,
  Except my mind do alter strangely.
GRONEAS.   One word.
CHRISTALLA. You lie beyond all modesty. Forbear me!
LEMOPHIL. I'll make thee mistress of a city; 'tis   130
  Mine own by conquest.
CHRISTALLA.   By petition; sue for't
  In forma pauperis.* City? Kennel!* Gallants;
  Off with your f[e]athers; put on aprons, gallants;
  Learn to reel,* thrum,* or trim a lady's dog,
  And be good, quiet souls of peace, hobgoblins!
LEMOPHIL. Christalla!
CHRISTALLA.   Practice to drill hogs, in hope
  To share in the acorns. Soldiers? Corncutters,

---

put . . . use: lent my love out for profit.
Vulcan: who caught his wife Venus in adultery with Mars.
in forma pauperis: status as a pauper.   kennel: gutter.
reel: wind (thread).   thrum: make fringe.

But not so valiant: they ofttimes draw blood,
Which you durst never do. When you have practiced
More wit or more civility, we'll rank 'ee 140
I'th' list of men; till then, brave things-at-arms,
Dare not to speak to us—most potent Groneas!

PHILEMA. And Lemophil the hardy!—at your services.

　　　　　　　　Exeunt CHRISTALLA *et* PHILEMA.

GRONEAS. They scorn us as they did before we went.

LEMOPHIL. Hang 'em! Let us scorn them and be revenged.

GRONEAS. Shall we?

LEMOPHIL. 　　　　We will; and, when we slight them thus,
Instead of following them, they'll follow us;
It is a woman's nature.

GRONEAS. 　　　　　'Tis a scurvy one.

　　　　　　　　　　　　Exeunt omnes.

[I.iii]

　　Enter TECNICUS, *a philosopher, and* ORGILUS
　　　　disguised like a scholar of his.

TECNICUS. Tempt not the stars, young man; thou canst not play
With the severity of fate. This change
Of habit° and disguise in outward view
Hides not the secrets of thy soul within thee
From their quick-piercing eyes, which dive at all times
Down to thy thoughts: in thy aspect I note
A consequence of danger.

ORGILUS. 　　　　　Give me leave,
Grave Tecnicus, without foredooming destiny,
Under thy roof to ease my silent griefs
By applying to my hidden wounds the balm 10
Of thy oraculous lectures. If my fortune
Run such a crooked byway as to wrest
My steps to ruin, yet thy learned precepts
Shall call me back and set my footings straight.
I will not court the world.

TECNICUS. 　　　　　Ah, Orgilus,

――――――――

habit: dress.

Neglects in young men of delights and life
Run often to extremities; they care not
For harms to others who contemn their own.
ORGILUS. But I, most learned artist,° am not so much
    At odds with nature that I grutch° the thrift°   20
Of any true deserver; nor doth malice
Of present hopes so check them with despair
As that I yield to thought of more affliction
Than what is incident to frailty. Wherefore
Impute not this retired course of living
Some little time to any other cause
Than what I justly render: the information
Of an unsettled mind as the effect
Must clearly witness.
TECNICUS.   Spirit of truth inspire thee!
    On these conditions I conceal thy change   30
And willingly admit thee for an auditor.
I'll to my study.
ORGILUS.   I to contemplations
In these delightful walks.—

                          [*Exit* TECNICUS.]
                   Thus metamorph[o]sed,
I may without suspicion hearken after
Penthea's usage and Euphranea's faith.
Love, thou art full of mystery! The deities
Themselves are not secure in searching out
The secrets of those flames, which, hidden, waste
A breast made tributary to the laws
Of beauty; physic° yet hath never found   40
A remedy to cure a lover's wound.
Ha! Who are those that cross yon private walk
Into the shadowing grove in amorous foldings?
(PROPHILUS *passeth over, supporting* EUPHRANEA, *and*
    whispering.)
My sister, O, my sister! 'Tis Euphranea
With Prophilus! Supported too! I would
It were an apparition! Prophilus
Is Ithocles his friend. It strangely puzzles me.
Again? Help me, my book; this scholar's habit

---

artist: scholar.   grutch: grudge.   thrift: success; reward.
physic: medicine.

Must stand my privilege; my mind is busy,
Mine eyes and ears are open.
(*Walk[s] by, reading.*)

        Enter again PROPHILUS *and* EUPHRANEA.

PROPHILUS.   Do not waste   50
The span of this stol'n time (lent by the gods
For precious use) in niceness.° Bright Euphranea,
Should I repeat old vows or study new
For purchase of belief to my desires—
ORGILUS [*aside*]. Desires!
PROPHILUS.   My service, my integrity—
ORGILUS [*aside*]. That's better.
PROPHILUS.   I should but repeat a
    lesson
Oft conned without a prompter but thine eyes.
My love is honorable—
ORGILUS [*aside*].   So was mine
To my Penthea—chastely honorable.
PROPHILUS. Nor wants there more addition to my wish   60
Of happiness than having thee a wife,
Already sure of Ithocles, a friend
Firm and unalterable.
ORGILUS [*aside*].   But a brother
More cruel than the grave.
EUPHRANEA.   What can you look for
In answer to your noble protestations,
From an unskillful° maid, but language suited
To a divided mind?
ORGILUS [*aside*].   Hold out, Euphranea!
EUPHRANEA. Know, Prophilus, I never undervalued,
From the first time you mentioned worthy love,
Your merit, means, or person: it had been   70
A fault of judgment in me and a dullness
In my affections not to weigh and thank
My better stars that offerèd me the grace
Of so much blissfulness. For, to speak truth,
The law of my desires kept equal pace
With yours, nor have I left that resolution;
But only, in a word, whatever choice
Lives nearest in my heart must first procure

---

niceness: coyness; scrupulous modesty.   unskillful: innocent.

Consent both from my father and my brother
Ere he can own me his.

ORGILUS [*aside*].   She is forsworn else.   80

PROPHILUS. Leave me that task.

EUPHRANEA.   My brother, ere he
    parted
To Athens, had my oath.

ORGILUS [*aside*].   Yes, yes, 'a had, sure.

PROPHILUS. I doubt not, with the means the court sup-
    plies,
But to prevail at pleasure.

ORGILUS [*aside*].   Very likely!

PROPHILUS. Meantime, best, dearest, I may build my
    hopes
On the foundation of thy constant suff'rance
In any opposition.

EUPHRANEA.   Death shall sooner
Divorce life and the joys I have in living
Than my chaste vows from truth.

PROPHILUS.   On thy fair hand
I seal the like.

ORGILUS [*aside*]. There is no faith in woman.   90
Passion, O, be contained! My very heartstrings
Are on the tenters.°

EUPHRANEA.   Sir, we are overheard.
Cupid protect us! 'Twas a stirring, sir,
Of someone near.

PROPHILUS.   Your fears are needless, lady;
None have access into these private pleasures
Except some near in court or bosom student
From Tecnicus his oratory,° granted
By special favor lately from the king
Unto the grave philosopher.

EUPHRANEA.   Methinks
I hear one talking to himself—I see him.   100

PROPHILUS. 'Tis a poor scholar, as I told you, lady.

ORGILUS [*aside*]. I am discovered.—
[*He pretends to think aloud.*]
                        Say it: is it possi-
    ble,

---

tenters: tenterhooks (to stretch cloth).
oratory: lecture hall; study.

With a smooth tongue, a leering countenance,
Flattery, or force of reason—I come t'ee, sir—
To turn or to appease the raging sea?
Answer to that.—Your art? What art to catch
And hold fast in a net the sun's small atoms?
No, no; they'll out, they'll out; ye may as easily
Outrun a cloud driven by a northern blast
As fiddle-faddle so. Peace, or speak sense. 110

EUPHRANEA. Call you this thing a scholar? 'Las, he's
lunatic.

PROPHILUS. Observe him, sweet; 'tis but his recreation.

ORGILUS. But will you hear a little! You are so tetchy.
You keep no rule in argument. Philosophy
Works not upon impossibilities
But natural conclusions.—Mew!—Absurd!
The metaphysics are but speculations
Of the celestial bodies or such accidents
As, not mixed perfectly, in the air engendered
Appear to us unnatural; that's all. 120
Prove it; yet, with a reverence to your gravity,
I'll balk illiterate sauciness, submitting
My sole opinion to the touch of writers.

PROPHILUS. Now let us fall in with him.

[*They come forward.*]

ORGILUS. Ha, ha, ha!
These apish boys, when they but taste the grammates°
And principles of theory, imagine
They can oppose their teachers. Confidence
Leads many into errors.

PROPHILUS. By your leave, sir.

EUPHRANEA. Are you a scholar, friend?

ORGILUS. I am, gay crea-
ture,
With pardon of your deities, a mushroom 130
On whom the dew of heaven drops now and then;
The sun shines on me too, I thank his beams!
Sometime I feel their warmth, and eat, and sleep.

PROPHILUS. Does Tecnicus read° to thee?

ORGILUS. Yes, forsooth;
He is my master surely; yonder door
Opens upon his study.

---

grammates: rudiments, fundamentals.   read: lecture.

PROPHILUS.   Happy creatures!
   Such people toil not, sweet, in heats of state
   Nor sink in thaws of greatness; their affections
   Keep order with the limits of their modesty;
   Their love is love of virtue.—What's thy name?   140
ORGILUS. Aplotes, sumptuous master, a poor wretch.
EUPHRANEA. Dost thou want anything?
ORGILUS.   Books, Venus,
   books.
PROPHILUS. Lady, a new conceit° comes in my thought,
   And most available for both our comforts.
EUPHRANEA. My lord—
PROPHILUS.   Whiles I endeavor to deserve
   Your father's blessing to our loves, this scholar
   May daily at some certain hours attend
   What notice I can write of my success,
   Here in this grove, and give it to your hands;
   The like from you to me: so can we never,   150
   Barred of our mutual speech, want sure intelligence;
   And thus our hearts may talk when our tongues cannot.
EUPHRANEA. Occasion is most favorable; use it.
PROPHILUS. Aplotes, wilt thou wait us twice a day,
   At nine i'th' morning and at four at night,
   Here in this bower, to convey such letters
   As each shall send to other? Do it willingly,
   Safely, and secretly; and I will furnish
   Thy study or what else thou canst desire.
ORGILUS. Jove, make me thankful, thankful, I beseech   160
   thee,
   Propitious Jove! I will prove sure and trusty.
   You will not fail me books?
PROPHILUS.   Nor aught besides
   Thy heart can wish. This lady's name's Euphranea,
   Mine Prophilus.
ORGILUS.   I have a pretty memory;
   It must prove my best friend. I will not miss
   One minute of the hours appointed.
PROPHILUS.   Write
   The books thou wouldst have bought thee in a note,
   Or take thyself some money.

---

conceit: idea, thought.

ORGILUS.   No, no money;
   Money to scholars is a spirit invisible;
   We dare not finger it: or° books or nothing.   170
PROPHILUS. Books of what sort thou wilt. Do not forget
   Our names.
ORGILUS.   I warrant 'ee, I warrant 'ee.
PROPHILUS. Smile, Hymen,° on the growth of our desires;
   We'll feed thy torches with eternal fires.

      Exeunt [PROPHILUS *and* EUPHRANEA]. *Manet* ORGILUS.

ORGILUS. Put out thy torches, Hymen, or their light
   Shall meet a darkness of eternal night!
   Inspire me, Mercury,° with swift deceits!
   Ingenious Fate has leapt into mine arms
   Beyond the compass of my brain. Mortality
   Creeps on the dung of earth and cannot reach   180
   The riddles which are purposed by the gods.
     Great arts best write themselves in their own stories;
     They die too basely who outlive their glories.

                                    Exit.

ACTUS SECUNDUS

[II.i]

        Enter BASSANES *and* PHULAS.

BASSANES. I'll have that window next the street dammed
     up;
   It gives too full a prospect to temptation
   And courts a gazer's glances. There's a lust
   Committed by the eye that sweats and travails,
   Plots, wakes, contrives, till the deformed bear-whelp
   Adultery be licked into the act,
   The very act. That light shall be dammed up;
   D'ee hear, sir?
PHULAS.   I do hear, my lord; a mason
   Shall be provided suddenly.°
BASSANES.   Some rogue,
   Some rogue of your confederacy (factor°   10

---

   or: either.   Hymen: god of marriage.
   Mercury: not only the messenger of the gods but also the god of
luck and of thieves.   suddenly: immediately.
   factor: agent.

For slaves and strumpets) to convey close* packets
From this spruce springal* and the tother youngster,
That gaudy earwrig;* or my lord your patron,
Whose pensioner you are! I'll tear thy throat out,
Son of a cat, ill-looking hound's head, rip up
Thy ulcerous maw, if I but scent a paper,
A scroll but half as big as what can cover
A wart upon thy nose, a spot, a pimple,
Directed to my lady; it may prove
A mystical preparative to lewdness.   20

PHULAS. Care shall be had. I will turn every thread
About me to an eye.—[*Aside.*] Here's a sweet life!

BASSANES. The city housewives, cunning in the traffic
Of chamber merchandise, set all at price
By wholesale; yet they wipe their mouths and simper,
Cull,* kiss, and cry "sweetheart," and stroke the head
Which they have branched,* and all is well again!
Dull clods of dirt, who dare not feel the rubs
Stuck on the foreheads!

PHULAS.   'Tis a villainous world;
One cannot hold his own in't.

BASSANES.   Dames at court,   30
Who flaunt in riots, run another bias:*
Their pleasure heaves the patient ass that suffers
Upon the stilts of office, titles, incomes;
Promotion justifies the shame and sues for't.
Poor Honor, thou art stabbed and bleed'st to death
By such unlawful hire! The country mistress
Is yet more wary and in blushes hides
Whatever trespass draws her troth to guilt;
But all are false. On this truth I am bold:
No woman but can fall, and doth, or would.—   40
Now for the newest news about the city;
What blab the voices, sirrah?

PHULAS.   O, my lord,
The rarest, quaintest, strangest, tickling news
That ever—

---

close: secret.   springal: youth; young man.
earwrig: earwig, flatterer.   cull: embrace.
branched: caused horns to sprout from; i.e., cuckolded.
bias: direction, course.

BASSANES.   Heyda[y]! Up and ride me, rascal!
  What is't?

PHULAS.   Forsooth, they say the king has mewed*
  All his gray beard, instead of which is budded
  Another of a pure carnation color,
  Speckled with green and russet.

BASSANES.   Ignorant block!

PHULAS. Yes, truly; and 'tis talked about the streets
  That, since Lord Ithocles came home, the lions   50
  Never left roaring, at which noise the bears
  Have danced their very hearts out.

BASSANES.   Dance out thine,
  too.

PHULAS. Besides, Lord Orgilus is fled to Athens
  Upon a fiery dragon, and 'tis thought
  'A never can return.

BASSANES.   Grant it, Apollo!

PHULAS. Moreover, please your lordship, 'tis reported
  For certain that whoever is found jealous
  Without apparent proof that's wife is wanton
  Shall be divorced; but this is but she-news—
  I had it from a midwife. I have more yet.   60

BASSANES. Antic,* no more! Idiots and stupid fools
  Grate my calamities. Why, to be fair
  Should yield presumption of a faulty soul!—
  Look to the doors.

PHULAS [*aside*].   The horn of plenty crest him!

                              Exit PHULAS.

BASSANES. Swarms of confusion huddle in my thoughts
  In rare distemper. Beauty! O, it is
  An unmatched blessing or a horrid curse.
       Enter PENTHEA *and* GRAUSIS, *an old lady.*
  She comes, she comes! So shoots the morning forth,
  Spangled with pearls of transparent dew.
  The way to poverty is to be rich   70
  As I in her am wealthy; but for her,
  In all contents a bankrupt.—Loved Penthea,
  How fares my heart's best joy?

GRAUSIS.   In sooth, not well;
  She is so oversad.

---

mewed: lost, moulted.   antic: clown, fool.

BASSANES.   Leave chattering, magpie.—
Thy brother is returned, sweet, safe, and honored
With a triumphant victory; thou shalt visit him.
We will to court, where, if it be thy pleasure,
Thou shalt appear in such a ravishing luster
Of jewels above value that the dames
Who brave it there, in rage to be outshined,   80
Shall hide them in their closets and unseen
Fret in their tears whiles every wond'ring eye
Shall crave none other brightness but thy presence.
Choose thine own recreations; be a queen
Of what delights thou fanciest best, what company,
What place, what times; do anything, do all things
Youth can command, so thou wilt chase these clouds
From the pure firmament of thy fair looks.
GRAUSIS. Now 'tis well said, my lord.—What, lady!
    Laugh,
Be merry! Time is precious.
BASSANES [aside].   Furies whip thee!   90
PENTHEA. Alas, my lord, this language to your handmaid
Sounds as would music to the deaf: I need
No braveries* nor cost of art to draw
The whiteness of my name into offense;
Let such (if any such there are) who covet
A curiosity of admiration,
By laying out their plenty to full view,
Appear in gaudy outsides; my attires
Shall suit the inward* fashion of my mind,
From which, if your opinion, nobly placed,   100
Change not the livery your words bestow,
My fortunes with my hopes are at the highest.
BASSANES. This house, methinks, stands somewhat too
    much inward;
It is too melancholy. We'll remove
Nearer the court. Or what thinks my Penthea
Of the delightful island we command?
Rule me as thou canst wish.
PENTHEA.   I am no mistress.
Whither you please, I must attend; all ways
Are alike pleasant to me.

---

braveries: expensive dress, fineries   inward: secluded.

GRAUSIS. Island? Prison! 110
A prison is as gaysome; we'll no islands.
Marry, out upon 'em! Whom shall we see there?
Seagulls, and porpoises, and water rats,
And crabs, and mews, and dogfish—goodly gear*
For a young lady's dealing—or an old one's!
On no terms islands; I'll be stewed first.

BASSANES [*aside*]. Grausis,
You are a juggling bawd.—This sadness, sweetest,
Becomes not youthful blood.—
[*Aside to* GRAUSIS.] I'll have you pounded.*—
For my sake put on a more cheerful mirth;
Thou't mar thy cheeks and make me old in griefs.—
[*Aside to* GRAUSIS.] Damnable bitch-fox!

GRAUSIS. I am thick
of hearing 120
Still* when the wind blows southerly.—What think 'ee
If your fresh lady breed young bones, my lord?
Would not a chopping* boy d'ee good at heart?
But, as you said—

BASSANES [*aside*]. I'll spit thee on a stake,
Or chop thee into collops.*

GRAUSIS. Pray, speak louder.
Sure, sure, the wind blows south still.

PENTHEA. Thou prat'st
madly.

BASSANES. 'Tis very hot; I sweat extremely.—

Enter PHULAS.

Now?

PHULAS. A herd of lords, sir.

BASSANES. Ha?

PHULAS. A flock of ladies.

BASSANES. Where?

PHULAS. Shoals of horses.

BASSANES. Peasant, how?

PHULAS. Caroches*
In drifts—th'one enter, th'other stand without, sir. 130
And now I vanish.

Exit PHULAS.

---

gear: matter.   pounded: impounded.   still: always.
chopping: strapping, vigorous.   collops: strips of flesh.
caroches: coaches.

Enter PROPHILUS, LEMOPHIL, GRONEAS,
CHRISTALLA, *and* PHILEMA.

PROPHILUS.   Noble Bassanes!

BASSANES. Most welcome, Prophilus. Ladies, gentlemen,
To all my heart is open; you all honor me.—
[*Aside.*] A tympany° swells in my head already.—
Honor me bountifully.—[*Aside.*] How they flutter,
Wagtails and jays together!

PROPHILUS.   From your brother,
By virtue of your love to him, I require
Your instant presence, fairest.

PENTHEA.   He is well, sir?

PROPHILUS. The gods preserve him ever! Yet, dear beauty,
I find some alteration in him lately   140
Since his return to Sparta.—My good lord,
I pray, use no delay.

BASSANES.   We had not needed
An invitation if his sister's health
Had not fallen into question.—Haste, Penthea;
Slack not a minute.—Lead the way, good Prophilus;
I'll follow step by step.

PROPHILUS.   Your arm, fair madam.
                          Exeunt omnes sed° BASSANES *et* GRAUSIS.

BASSANES. One word with your old bawdship: th' hadst
     been better
Railed at the sins thou worshipp'st than have thwarted
My will. I'll use thee cursedly.

GRAUSIS.   You dote;
You are beside yourself. A politician   150
In jealousy? No, y'are too gross, too vulgar.
Pish! Teach not me my trade; I know my cue.
My crossing you sinks me into her trust,
By which I shall know all; my trade's a sure one.

BASSANES. Forgive me, Grausis; 'twas consideration
I relished° not; but have a care now.

GRAUSIS.   Fear not,
I am no new-come-to't.

BASSANES.   Thy life's upon it,
And so is mine. My agonies are infinite.
                                    Exeunt omnes.

-----

tympany: tumor.   *omnes sed:* all but.
relished: considered, understood.

[II.ii]

Enter ITHOCLES *alone.*

ITHOCLES. Ambition! 'Tis of vipers' breed; it gnaws
  A passage through the womb that gave it motion.
  Ambition, like a seelèd° dove, mounts upward,
  Higher and higher still, to perch on clouds
  But tumbles headlong down with heavier ruin.
  So squibs and crackers fly into the air;
  Then, only breaking with a noise, they vanish
  In stench and smoke. Morality, applied
  To timely practice, keeps the soul in tune,
  At whose sweet music all our actions dance.   10
  But this is form of books and school-tradition;
  It physics not the sickness of a mind
  Broken with griefs: strong fevers are not eased
  With counsel but with best receipts and means—
  Means, speedy means and certain; that's the cure.

Enter ARMOSTES *and* CROTOLON.

ARMOSTES. You stick, Lord Crotolon, upon a point
  Too nice° and too unnecessary; Prophilus
  Is every way desertful. I am confident
  Your wisdom is too ripe to need instruction
  From your son's tutelage.

CROTOLON.   Yet not so ripe,   20
  My Lord Armostes, that it dares to dote
  Upon the painted meat of smooth persuasion,
  Which tempts me to a breach of faith.

ITHOCLES.   Not yet
  Resolved, my lord? Why, if your son's consent
  Be so available, we'll write to Athens
  For his repair° to Sparta. The king's hand
  Will join with our desires; he has been moved to't.

ARMOSTES. Yes, and the king himself importuned Crotolon
  For a dispatch.

CROTOLON.   Kings may command; their wills
  Are laws not to be questioned.

ITHOCLES.   By this marriage   30
  You knot an union so devout, so hearty,
  Between your loves to me and mine to yours

---

seelèd: with eyelids sewn together.   nice: precise.
repair: return.

As if mine own blood had an interest in it;
For Prophilus is mine, and I am his.
CROTOLON. My lord, my lord!
ITHOCLES.   What, good sir? Speak
your thought.
CROTOLON. Had this sincerity been real once,
My Orgilus had not been now unwived,
Nor your lost sister buried in a bride-bed.
Your uncle here, Armostes, knows this truth;
For, had your father Thrasus lived—but peace   40
Dwell in his grave! I have done.
ARMOSTES.   Y'are bold and bitter.
ITHOCLES [*aside.*] 'A presses home the injury; it smarts.—
No reprehensions, uncle; I deserve 'em.
Yet, gentle sir, consider what the heat
Of an unsteady youth, a giddy brain,
Green indiscretion, flattery of greatness,
Rawness of judgment, willfulness in folly,
Thoughts vagrant as the wind and as uncertain,
Might lead a boy in years to. 'Twas a fault,
A capital fault; for then I could not dive   50
Into the secrets of commanding love;
Since when, experience, by the extremities in others,
Hath forced me to collect.* And, trust me, Crotolon,
I will redeem those wrongs with any service
Your satisfaction can require for current.
ARMOSTES. Thy acknowledgment is satisfaction.
What would you more?
CROTOLON.   I'm conquered; if Euphranea
Herself admit the motion, let it be so.
I doubt not my son's liking.
ITHOCLES.   Use my fortunes,
Life, power, sword, and heart—all are your own.   60
        Enter BASSANES, PROPHILUS, CALANTHA, PENTHEA,
        EUPHRANEA, CHRISTALLA, PHILEMA, *and* GRAUSIS.
ARMOSTES. The princess, with your sister.
CALANTHA.   I present 'ee
A stranger here in court, my lord; for, did not
Desire of seeing you draw her abroad,
We had not been made happy in her company.

---

collect: understand.

ITHOCLES. You are a gracious princess.—Sister, wedlock
  Holds too severe a passion in your nature,
  Which can engross all duty to your husband
  Without attendance on so dear a mistress.—
  [*To* BASSANES.] 'Tis not my brother's pleasure, I pre-
    sume,
  T'immure her in a chamber.
BASSANES.   'Tis her will;   70
  She governs her own hours. Noble Ithocles,
  We thank the gods for your success and welfare.
  Our lady has of late been indisposed,
  Else we had waited on you with the first.
ITHOCLES. How does Penthea now?
PENTHEA.   You best know,
  brother,
  From whom my health and comforts are derived.
BASSANES [*aside*]. I like the answer well; 'tis sad° and
  modest.
  There may be tricks yet, tricks.—Have an eye, Grausis.
CALANTHA. Now, Crotolon, the suit we joined in must not
  Fall by too long demur.
CROTOLON.   'Tis granted, princess,   80
  For my part.
ARMOSTES.   With condition that his son
  Favor the contract.
CALANTHA.   Such delay is easy.—
  The joys of marriage make thee, Prophilus,
  A proud deserver of Euphranea's love,
  And her of thy desert!
PROPHILUS.   Most sweetly gracious.
BASSANES. The joys of marriage are the heaven on earth,
  Life's paradise, great princess, the soul's quiet,
  Sinews of concord, earthly immortality,
  Eternity of pleasures—no restoratives
  Like to a constant woman.—[*Aside*.] But where is she?   90
  'Twould puzzle all the gods but to create
  Such a new monster.—I can speak by proof,
  For I rest in Elysium; 'tis my happiness.
CROTOLON. Euphranea, how are you resolved, speak
  freely,

---

  sad: serious, earnest.

In your affections to this gentleman?

EUPHRANEA. Nor more nor less than as his love assures
   me,
  Which (if your liking with my brother's warrants)
  I cannot but approve in all points worthy.

CROTOLON. So, so!—[*To* PROPHILUS.] I know your answer.

ITHOCLES.   'T had been pity
  To sunder hearts so equally consented.   100

Enter LEMOPHIL.

LEMOPHIL. The king, Lord Ithocles, commands your
  presence—
  And, fairest princess, yours.

CALANTHA.   We will attend him.

Enter GRONEAS.

GRONEAS. Where are the lords? All must unto the king
  Without delay; the Prince of Argos—

CALANTHA.   Well, sir?

GRONEAS. Is coming to the court, sweet lady.

CALANTHA.   How!
  The Prince of Argos?

GRONEAS.   'Twas my fortune, madam,
  T'enjoy the honor of these happy tidings.

ITHOCLES. Penthea!

PENTHEA.   Brother?

ITHOCLES.   Let me an hour hence
  Meet you alone within the palace grove;
  I have some secret with you.—Prithee, friend,   110
  Conduct her thither, and have special care
  The walks be cleared of any to disturb us.

PROPHILUS. I shall

BASSANES [*aside*].   How's that?

ITHOCLES.   Alone, pray be alone.—
  I am your creature, princess.—On, my lords!

Exeunt [All but] BASSANES.

BASSANES. Alone, alone! What means that word "alone"?
  Why might not I be there?—Hum!—He's her brother.
  Brothers and sisters are but flesh and blood,
  And this same whoreson* court-ease is temptation
  To a rebellion in the veins; besides,

---

whoreson: rascally.

His fine friend Prophilus must be her guardian.   120
Why may not he dispatch a business nimbly
Before the other come? Or pand'ring—pand'ring
For one another (be't to sister, mother,
Wife, cousin, anything) 'mongst youths of mettle
Is in request. It is so—stubborn fate!
But if I be a cuckold and can know it,
I will be fell,° and fell.

Enter GRONEAS.

GRONEAS.   My lord, y'are called for.
BASSANES. Most heartily I thank ye. Where's my wife,
   pray?
GRONEAS. Retired amongst the ladies.
BASSANES.   Still I thank 'ee.
   There's an old waiter° with her; saw you her, too?   130
GRONEAS. She sits i'th' presence-lobby fast asleep, sir.
BASSANES. Asleep? 'Sleep, sir?
GRONEAS.   Is your lordship trou-
   bled?
   You will not to the king?
BASSANES.   Your humblest vassal.
GRONEAS. Your servant, my good lord.
BASSANES.   I wait your
   footsteps.

Exeunt.

[II.iii]

Enter PROPHILUS, PENTHEA.

PROPHILUS. In this walk, lady, will your brother find you;
And, with your favor, give me leave a little
To work a preparation. In his fashion
I have observed of late some kind of slackness
To such alacrity as nature [once]
And custom took delight in. Sadness grows
Upon his recreations, which he hoards
In such a willing silence that to question
The grounds will argue [little] skill in friendship
And less good manners.
PENTHEA.   Sir, I'm not inquisitive   10
Of secrecies without an invitation.

---

   fell: ruthless, cruel.   waiter: servant, attendant.

PROPHILUS. With pardon, lady, not a syllable
　　Of mine implies so rude a sense; the drift—
　　　　　　Enter ORGILUS [*disguised as before*].
　　[*To* ORGILUS.] Do thy best
　　To make this lady merry for an hour.

　　　　　　　　　　　　　　　　　　　　　　　　　　　　Exit.

ORGILUS. Your will shall be law, sir.
PENTHEA.　　　　　　　　　　Prithee, leave me;
　　I have some private thoughts I would account with;
　　Use thou thine own.
ORGILUS.　　　　　　　　Speak on, fair nymph; our souls
　　Can dance as well to music of the spheres
　　As any's who have feasted with the gods.　　　　　　　　　20
PENTHEA. Your school° terms are too troublesome.
ORGILUS.　　　　　　　　　　　What heaven
　　Refines mortality from dross of earth
　　But such as uncompounded beauty hallows
　　With glorified perfection?
PENTHEA.　　　　　　　　　Set thy wits
　　In a less wild proportion.
ORGILUS.　　　　　　　　　　Time can never
　　On the white table of unguilty faith
　　Write counterfeit dishonor; turn those eyes
　　(The arrows of pure love) upon that fire
　　Which once rose to a flame, perfumed with vows
　　As sweetly scented as the incense smoking　　　　　　30
　　[On Vesta's altars—virgin tears (the
　　Holiest odors)] sprinkled [like] dews to feed 'em
　　And to increase their fervor.
PENTHEA.　　　　　　　　　Be not frantic!
ORGILUS. All pleasures are but mere imagination,
　　Feeding the hungry appetite with steam
　　And sight of banquet whilst the body pines,
　　Not relishing the real taste of food;
　　Such is the leanness of a heart divided
　　From intercourse of troth-contracted loves;
　　No horror should deface that precious figure　　　　40
　　Sealed with the lively stamp of equal souls.
PENTHEA. Away! Some fury hath bewitched thy tongue.
　　The breath of ignorance that flies from thence
　　Ripens a knowledge in me of afflictions

　　────────

　　school: scholastic; rhetorical.

Above all suff'rance.—Thing of talk, begone,
Begone, without reply!

ORGILUS.   Be just, Penthea,
In thy commands; when thou send'st forth a doom
Of banishment, know first on whom it lights.
Thus I take off the shroud, in which my cares
Are folded up from view of common eyes.   50
[*He reveals himself.*]
What is thy sentence next?

PENTHEA.   Rash man, thou layest
A blemish on mine honor, with the hazard
Of thy too desperate life; yet I profess,
By all the laws of ceremonious wedlock,
I have not given admittance to one thought
Of female change since cruelty enforced
Divorce betwixt my body and my heart.
Why would you fall from goodness thus?

ORGILUS.   O, rather
Examine me how I could live to say
I have been much, much wronged. 'Tis for thy sake   60
I put on this imposture. Dear Penthea,
If thy soft bosom be not turned to marble,
Thou't pity our calamities; my interest
Confirms me thou art mine still.

PENTHEA.   Lend me your hand;
With both of mine I clasp it thus, thus kiss it,
Thus kneel before ye.

ORGILUS.   You instruct my duty.

PENTHEA. We may stand up. Have you aught else to
    urge
Of new demand? As for the old, forget it;
'Tis buried in an everlasting silence
And shall be, shall be ever. What more would ye?   70

ORGILUS. I would possess my wife; the equity
Of very reason bids me.

PENTHEA.   Is that all?

ORGILUS. Why, 'tis the all of me, myself.

PENTHEA.   Remove
Your steps some distance from me.—At this space
A few words I dare change; but first put on
Your borrowed shape.
[*He dons his disguise.*]

ORGILUS.   You are obeyed; 'tis done.

PENTHEA. How, Orgilus, by promise I was thine
    The heavens do witness; they can witness, too,
    A rape done on my truth.° How I do love thee
    Yet, Orgilus, and yet must best appear   80
    In tendering thy freedom; for I find
    The constant preservation of thy merit,
    By thy not daring to attempt my fame
    With injury of any loose conceit,
    Which might give deeper wounds to discontents.
    Continue this fair race;° then, though I cannot
    Add to thy comfort, yet I shall more often
    Remember from what fortune I am fallen
    And pity mine own ruin. Live, live happy,
    Happy in thy next choice, that thou mayst people   90
    This barren age with virtues in thy issue!
    And, O, when thou art married, think on me
    With mercy, not contempt. I hope thy wife,
    Hearing my story, will not scorn my fall.
    Now let us part.
ORGILUS.   Part! Yet advise thee better:
    Penthea is the wife to Orgilus
    And ever shall be.
PENTHEA.   Never shall nor will.
ORGILUS. How!
PENTHEA.   Hear me; in a word I'll tell thee why:
    The virgin dowry which my birth bestowed
    Is ravished by another; my true love   100
    Abhors to think that Orgilus deserved
    No better favors than a second bed.
ORGILUS. I must not take this reason.
PENTHEA.   To confirm it,
    Should I outlive my bondage, let me meet
    Another worse than this, and less desired,
    If of all the men alive thou shouldst but touch
    My lip or hand again.
ORGILUS.   Penthea, now
    I tell 'ee, you grow wanton in my sufferance;
    Come, sweet, th'art mine.
PENTHEA.   Uncivil sir, forbear,
    Or I can turn affection into vengeance!   110

---

    truth: troth.   race: course of behavior.

Your reputation (if you value any)
Lies bleeding at my feet. Unworthy man,
If ever henceforth thou appear in language,
Message, or letter to betray my frailty,
I'll call thy former protestations lust
And curse my stars for forfeit of my judgment.
Go thou, fit only for disguise and walks,
To hide thy shame. This once I spare thy life.
I laugh at mine own confidence; my sorrows
By thee are made inferior to my fortunes.   120
If ever thou didst harbor worthy love,
Dare not to answer. My good genius guide me
That I may never see thee more!—Go from me!

ORGILUS. I'll tear my veil of politic French off
And stand up like a man resolved to do;
Action, not words, shall show me. O, Penthea!

                        Exit ORGILUS.

PENTHEA. 'A sighed my name, sure, as he parted from
   me;
I fear I was too rough. Alas, poor gentleman,
'A looked not like the ruins of his youth
But like the ruins of those ruins. Honor,   130
How much we fight with weakness to preserve thee!

         Enter BASSANES *and* GRAUSIS.

BASSANES. Fie on thee! Damn thee, rotten maggot, damn
   thee!
 Sleep? Sleep at court? And now? Aches,° convulsions,
Imposthumes, rhe[u]ms, gouts, palsies clog thy bones
A dozen years more yet!

GRAUSIS.   Now y'are in humors.

BASSANES. She's by herself; there's hope of that. She's
   sad, too;
She's in strong contemplation; yes, and fixed.
The signs are wholesome.

GRAUSIS.   Very wholesome, truly.

BASSANES. Hold your chops,° nightmare!—Lady, come;
   your brother
Is carried to his closet; you must thither.   140

PENTHEA. Not well, my lord?

BASSANES.   A sudden fit; 'twill off;

---

aches: pronounced "aitches."   chops: jaws.

Some surfeit or disorder.—How dost, dearest?

PENTHEA. Your news is none o'th' best.

              Enter PROPHILUS.

PROPHILUS.   The chief of
  men,

  The excellentest Ithocles, desires

  Your presence, madam.

BASSANES.   We are hasting to him.

PENTHEA. In vain we labor in this course of life

  To piece our journey out at length or crave

  Respite of breath; our home is in the grave.

BASSANES. Perfect philosophy.

[PENTHEA.] °   Then let us care

  To live so that our reckonings may fall even   150

  When w'are to make account.

PROPHILUS.   He cannot fear

  Who builds on noble grounds; sickness or pain

  Is the deserver's exercise, and such

  Your virtuous brother to the world is known.

  Speak comfort to him, lady; be all gentle.

      Stars fall but in the grossness of our sight;

      A good man dying, th'earth doth lose a light.

                      Exeunt omnes.

ACTUS TERTIUS

[III.i]

    Enter TECNICUS, *and* ORGILUS *in his own shape.*

TECNICUS. Be well advised; let not a resolution

  Of giddy rashness choke the breath of reason.

ORGILUS. It shall not, most sage master.

TECNICUS.   I am jealous;°

  For, if the borrowed shape so late put on

  Inferred a consequence, we must conclude

  Some violent design of sudden nature

  Hath shook that shadow off to fly upon

  A new-hatched execution.° Orgilus,

  Take heed thou hast not, under our integrity,

  Shrouded unlawful plots. Our mortal eyes   10

     [PENTHEA]: speech ascribed to Bassanes in Quarto.
    jealous: suspicious.   execution: enterprise.

Pierce not the secrets of your hearts; the gods
Are only privy to them.
ORGILUS.   Learned Tecnicus,
Such doubts are causeless; and, to clear the truth
From misconceit,° the present state commands me.
The Prince of Argos comes himself in person
In quest of great Calantha for his bride,
Our kingdom's heir; besides, mine only sister,
Euphranea, is disposed to Prophilus;
Lastly, the king is sending letters for me
To Athens for my quick repair to court.   20
Please to accept these reasons.
TECNICUS.   Just ones, Orgilus,
Not to be contradicted; yet beware
Of an unsure foundation; no fair colors
Can fortify a building faintly jointed.
I have observed a growth in thy aspect
Of dangerous extent, sudden, and (look to't)
I might add, certain—
ORGILUS.   My aspect? Could art
Run through mine inmost thoughts, it should not sift
An inclination there more than what suited
With justice of mine honor.
TECNICUS.   I believe it.   30
But know then, Orgilus, what honor is:
Honor consists not in a bare opinion
By doing any act that feeds content,
Brave in appearance because we think it brave;
Such honor comes by accident, not nature,
Proceeding from the vices of our passion,
Which makes our reason drunk. But real honor
Is the reward of virtue and acquired
By justice or by valor, which for basis
Hath justice to uphold it. He then fails   40
In honor, who for lucre o[r] revenge
Commits thefts, murders, treasons, and adulteries,
With suchlike, by intrenching on just laws,
Whose sovereignty is best preserved by justice.
Thus, as you see how honor must be grounded
On knowledge, not opinion—for opinion

_____

misconceit: misconception.

Relies on probability and accident,
But knowledge on necessity and truth—
I leave thee to the fit consideration
Of what becomes the grace of real honor,   50
Wishing success to all thy virtuous meanings.

ORGILUS. The gods increase thy wisdom, reverend oracle,
And in thy precepts make me ever thrifty!*

TECNICUS. I thank thy wish.

                                        Exit ORGILUS.
                            —Much mystery of fate
Lies hid in that man's fortunes; curiosity
May lead his actions into rare attempts.
But let the gods be moderators still,
No human power can prevent their will.

                    Enter ARMOSTES [*with a box*].
From whence come 'e?

ARMOSTES.   From King
    Amyclas—pardon
My interruption of your studies. Here,   60
In this sealed box, he sends a treasure dear
To him as his crown. 'A prays your gravity
You would examine, ponder, sift, and bolt
The pith and circumstance of every tittle
The scroll within contains.

TECNICUS.   What is't, Armostes?

ARMOSTES. It is the health of Sparta, the king's life,
    Sinews and safety of the commonwealth,
    The sum of what the oracle delivered
    When last he visited the prophetic temple
    At Delphos. What his reasons are, for which   70
    After so long a silence he requires
    You[r] counsel now, grave man, his majesty
    Will soon himself acquaint you with.

TECNICUS [*taking the box*].   Apollo
    Inspire my intellect!—The Prince of Argos
    Is entertained?

ARMOSTES.   He is, and has demanded
    Our princess for his wife, which I conceive
    One special cause the king importunes you
    For resolution of the oracle.

---

thrifty: careful to observe.

TECNICUS. My duty to the kíng, good peace to Sparta,
    And fair day to Armostes!
ARMOSTES.   Like to Tecnicus!   80
                                              Exeunt.

[III.ii]

Soft music. A song.
Can you paint a thought? Or number
Every fancy in a slumber?
Can you count soft minutes roving
From a dial's point by moving?
Can you grasp a sigh? Or, lastly,
Rob a virgin's honor chastely?
    No, O, no! Yet you may
Sooner do both that and this,
This and that, and never miss,
    Than by any praise display   10
Beauty's beauty—such a glory,
As beyond all fate, all story,
    All arms, all arts,
    All loves, all hearts,
Greater than those or they,
Do, shall, and must obey.

During which time enters PROPHILUS, BASSANES,
    PENTHEA, GRAUSIS, *passing over the stage.*
    BASSANES *and* GRAUSIS *enter again softly,*
        stealing to several stands,° and listen.
BASSANES. All silent, calm, secure.—Grausis, no creaking?
    No noise? Dost hear nothing?
GRAUSIS.   Not a mouse
    Or whisper of the wind.
BASSANES.   The floor is matted;
    The bedposts sure are steel or marble.—Soldiers   20
    Should not affect, methinks, strains so effeminate;
    Sounds of such delicacy are but fawnings
    Upon the sloth of luxury:° they heighten
    Cinders of covert lust up to a flame.
GRAUSIS. What do you mean, my lord? Speak low; that
    gabbling
_____

    stands: positions.   luxury: lechery.

Of yours will but undo us.
BASSANES.   Chamber combats
Are felt, not h[e]ard.
PROPHILUS [*within*].   'A wakes.
BASSANES.   What's that?
ITHOCLES [*within*].   Who's
    there?
Sister?—All quit the room else.
BASSANES.   'Tis consented.

                    Enter PROPHILUS.

PROPHILUS. Lord Bassanes, your brother would be pri-
    vate;
We must forbear; his sleep hath newly left him.   30
Please 'ee, withdraw.
BASSANES.   By any means, 'tis fit.
PROPHILUS. Pray, gentlewoman, walk too.
GRAUSIS.   Yes, I will,
    sir.

                                        Exeunt omnes.
    ITHOCLES *discovered in a chair, and* PENTHEA.
ITHOCLES. Sit nearer, sister, to me; nearer yet.
We had one father, in one womb took life,
Were brought up twins together, yet have lived
At distance like two strangers. I could wish
That the first pillow whereon I was cradled
Had proved to me a grave.
PENTHEA.   You had been happy;
Then had you never known that sin of life
Which blots all following glories with a vengeance   40
For forfeiting the last will of the dead,
From whom you had your being.
ITHOCLES.   Sad Penthea,
Thou canst not be too cruel; my rash spleen
Hath with a violent hand plucked from thy bosom
A lover-blessed heart, to grind it into dust,
For which mine's now a-breaking.
PENTHEA.   Not yet, heaven,
I do beseech thee! First let some wild fires
Scorch, not consume, it! May the heat be cherished
With desires infinite, but hopes impossible!
ITHOCLES. Wronged soul, thy prayers are heard.
PENTHEA.   Here,
    lo, I breathe,   50

A miserable creature led to ruin
By an unnatural brother.
ITHOCLES.   I consume
In languishing affections° for that trespass,
Yet cannot die.
PENTHEA.   The handmaid to the wages
[Of country toil drinks the untroubled streams]
With leaping kids and with the bleating lambs
And so allays her thirst secure whiles I
Quench my hot sighs with fleetings° of my tears.
ITHOCLES. The laborer doth eat his coarsest bread,
Earned with his sweat, and lies him down to sleep,   60
[While] every bit I touch turns in digestion
To gall as bitter as Penthea's curse.
Put me to any penance for my tyranny,
And I will call thee merciful.
PENTHEA.   Pray, kill me;
Rid me from living with a jealous husband.
Then we will join in friendship, be again
Brother and sister. Kill me, pray; nay, will 'e?
ITHOCLES. How does thy lord esteem thee?
PENTHEA.   Such an
one
As only you have made me: a faith-breaker,
A spotted whore. Forgive me; I am one   70
In art,° not desires, the gods must witness.
ITHOCLES. Thou dost belie thy friend.
PENTHEA.   I do not, Ithocles;
For she that's wife to Orgilus and lives
In known adultery with Bassanes
Is at the best a whore. Wilt kill me now?
The ashes of our parents will assume
Some dreadful figure and appear to charge
Thy bloody guilt, that hast betrayed their name
To infamy in this reproachful match.
ITHOCLES. After my victories abroad, at home   80
I meet despair; ingratitude of nature
Hath made my actions monstrous. Thou shalt stand
A deity, my sister, and be worshipped
For thy resolvèd martyrdom; wronged maids

---

affections: emotions, passions.   fleetings: flowings.
art: act (?).

And married wives shall to thy hallowed shrine
Offer their orisons and sacrifice
Pure turtles,° crowned with myrtle, if thy pity
Unto a yielding brother's pressure lend
One finger but to ease it.

PENTHEA.   O, no more!

ITHOCLES. Death waits to waft me to thy Stygian banks   90
And free me from this chaos of my bondage;
And, till thou wilt forgive, I must endure.

PENTHEA. Who is the saint you serve?

ITHOCLES.   Friendship, or
  [nearness]
Of birth to any but my sister, durst not
Have moved that question; ['tis] a secret, sister,
I dare not murmur to myself.

PENTHEA.   Let me,
By your new protestations I conjure 'ee,
Partake her name.

ITHOCLES.   Her name—'tis—'tis—I dare not.

PENTHEA. All your respects are forged.

ITHOCLES.   They are not.
  —Peace!
Calantha is—the princess, the king's daughter,   100
Sole heir of Sparta.—Me most miserable!
Do I now love thee? For my injuries
Revenge thyself with bravery,° and gossip
My treasons to the king's ears. Do! Calantha
Knows it not yet, nor Prophilus, my nearest.

PENTHEA. Suppose you were contracted to her, would
  it not
Split even your very soul to see her father
Snatch her out of your arms against her will
And force her on the Prince of Argos?

ITHOCLES.   Trouble not
The fountains of mine eyes with thine own story;   110
I sweat in blood for't.

PENTHEA.   We are reconciled.
Alas, sir, being children, but two branches
Of one stock, 'tis not fit we should divide.
Have comfort; you may find it.

ITHOCLES.   Yes, in thee;

---

turtles: turtledoves.   bravery: boasting.

Only in thee, Penthea mine.

PENTHEA.   If sorrows
Have not too much dulled my infected brain,
I'll cheer invention for an active strain.°

ITHOCLES. Mad man! Why have I wronged a maid so
excellent?

    Enter BASSANES *with a poniard;* PROPHILUS,
      CRONEAS, LEMOPHIL, *and* GRAUSIS.

BASSANES. I can forbear no longer; more, I will not.
Keep off your hands, or fall upon my point.   120
Patience is tired; for, like a slow-paced ass,
Ye ride my easy nature and proclaim
My sloth to vengeance a reproach and property.°

ITHOCLES. The meaning of this rudeness?

PROPHILUS.   He's distracted.

PENTHEA. O, my grieved lord!

GRAUSIS.   Sweet lady, come not
near him;
He holds his perilous weapon in his hand
To prick 'a cares not whom nor where—see, see, see!

BASSANES. My birth is noble. Though the popular blast
Of vanity, as giddy as thy youth,
Hath reared thy name up to bestride a cloud   130
Or progress in the chariot of the sun,
I am no clod of trade to lackey pride,
Nor like your slave of expectation wait
The bawdy hinges of your doors, or whistle
For mystical conveyance to your bed-sports.

GRAUSIS. Fine humors! They become him.

LEMOPHIL.   How 'a
stares,
Struts, puffs, and sweats. Most admirable° lunacy!

ITHOCLES. But that I may conceive the spirit of wine
Has took possession of your soberer custom,
I'd say you were unmannerly.

PENTHEA.   Dear brother—   140

BASSANES. Unmannerly!—Mew, kitling!°—smooth Formal'ty

---

an active strain: some workable plot.
property: personal characteristic.   admirable: unbelievable.
kitling: kitten.

Is usher to the rankness of the blood,
But Impudence bears up the train. Indeed, sir,
Your fiery mettle, or your springal ° blaze
Of huge renown, is no sufficient royalty
To print upon my forehead the scorn "cuckold."
ITHOCLES. His jealousy has robbed him of his wits;
'A talks 'a knows not what.
BASSANES.   Yes, and 'a knows
To whom 'a talks—to one that franks° his lust
In swine-security of bestial incest.   150
ITHOCLES. Hah, devil!
BASSANES.   I will halloo't though I blush
    more
To name the filthiness than thou to act it.
ITHOCLES. Monster!
PROPHILUS.   Sir, by our friendship—
PENTHEA.   By our
    bloods,
Will you quite undo us, brother?
GRAUSIS.   Out on him!
These are his megrims,° firks,° and melancholies.
LEMOPHIL. Well said, old touchhole!
GRONEAS.   Kick him out at
    doors!
PENTHEA. With favor, let me speak.—My lord, what
    slackness
In my obedience hath deserved this rage?
Except humility and [silent] duty
Have drawn on your unquiet, my simplicity   160
Ne'er studied your vexation.
BASSANES.   Light of beauty,
Deal not ungently with a desperate wound!
No breach of reason dares make war with her
Whose looks are sovereignty, whose breath is balm.
O, that I could preserve thee in fruition
As in devotion!
PENTHEA.   Sir, may every evil
Locked in Pandora's box shower, in your presence,
On my unhappy head if, since you made me
A partner in your bed, I have been faulty

---

springal: youthful.   franks: fattens.
megrims: fancies.   firks: whims.

In one unseemly thought against your honor. 170
ITHOCLES. Purge not his griefs, Penthea.
BASSANES.   Yes, say on,
Excellent creature.—[*To* ITHOCLES.] Good, be not a
    hinderance
To peace and praise of virtue.—O, my senses
Are charmed with sounds celestial!—On, dear, on;
I never gave you one ill word; say, did I?
Indeed, I did not.
PENTHEA.   Nor, by Juno's forehead,
Was I e'er guilty of a wanton error.
BASSANES. A goddess! Let me kneel.
GRAUSIS.   Alas, kind animal!
ITHOCLES. No; but for penance—
BASSANES.   Noble sir, what is it?
With gladness I embrace it; yet, pray, let not 180
My rashness teach you to be too unmerciful.
ITHOCLES. When you shall show good proof that manly
    wisdom,
Not overswayed by passion or opinion,
Knows how to lead judgment, then this lady,
Your wife, my sister, shall return in safety
Home, to be guided by you; but, till first
I can out of clear evidence approve* it,
She shall be my care.
BASSANES.   Rip my bosom up!
I'll stand the execution with a constancy;
This torture is unsufferable.
ITHOCLES.   Well, sir, 190
I dare not trust her to your fury.
BASSANES.   But
Penthea says not so.
PENTHEA.   She needs no tongue
To plead excuse who never purposed wrong.
LEMOPHIL [*to* GRAUSIS]. Virgin of reverence and antiq-
    uity,
Stay you behind.
GRONEAS.   The court wants not your diligence.
                    Exeunt omnes sed BASSANES *et* GRAUSIS.
GRAUSIS. What will you do, my lord? My lady's gone;
I am denied to follow.

---

approve: verify.

BASSANES.   I may see her
  Or speak to her once more?
GRAUSIS.   And feel her too, man.
  Be of good cheer, she's your own flesh and bone.
BASSANES. Diseases desperate must find cures alike.   200
  She swore she has been true.
GRAUSIS.   True, on my modesty.
BASSANES. Let him want truth who credits not her vows!
  Much wrong I did her, but to her brother infinite;
  Rumor will voice me the contempt of manhood
  Should I run on thus. Some way I must try
  To outdo art and cry* a jealousy.

                                Exeunt omnes.

[III.iii]
    Flourish. Enter AMYCLAS, NEARCHUS *leading*
    CALANTHA, ARMOSTES, CROTOLON, EUPHRANEA,
      CHRISTALLA, PHILEMA, *and* AMELUS.
AMYCLAS. Cousin of Argos, what the heavens have
    pleased
  In their unchanging counsels to conclude
  For both our kingdoms' weal, we must submit to;
  Nor can we be unthankful to their bounties,
  Who, when we were even creeping to our graves,
  Sent us a daughter, in whose birth our hope
  Continues of succession. As you are
  In title next, being grandchild to our aunt,
  So we in heart desire you may sit nearest
  Calantha's love since we have ever vowed   10
  Not to enforce affection by our will
  But by her own choice to confirm it gladly.
NEARCHUS. You speak the nature of a right just father.
  I come not hither roughly to demand
  My cousin's thralldom but to free mine own.
  Report of great Calantha's beauty, virtue,
  Sweetness, and singular perfections courted
  All ears to credit what I find was published
  By constant truth, from which, if any service
  Of my desert can purchase fair construction,   20
  This lady must command it.

----

  cry: decry.

CALANTHA. Princely sir,
So well you know how to profess observance*
That you instruct your hearers to become
Practitioners in duty, of which number
I'll study to be chief.

NEARCHUS. Chief, glorious virgin,
In my devotions as in all men's wonder.

AMYCLAS. Excellent cousin, we deny no liberty;
Use thine own opportunities.—Armostes,
We must consult with the philosophers;
The business is of weight.

ARMOSTES. Sir, at your pleasure. 30

AMYCLAS. You told me, Crotolon, your son's returned
From Athens. Wherefore comes 'a not to court
As we commanded?

CROTOLON. He shall soon attend
Your royal will, great sir.

AMYCLAS. The marriage
Between young Prophilus and Euphranea
Tastes of too much delay.

CROTOLON. My lord—

AMYCLAS. Some pleasures
At celebration of it would give life
To th'entertainment of the prince our kinsman;
Our court wears gravity more than we relish.

ARMOSTES. Yet the heavens smile on all your high attempts 40
Without a cloud.

CROTOLON. So may the gods protect us.

CALANTHA. A prince a subject?

NEARCHUS. Yes, to beauty's scepter;
As all hearts kneel, so mine.

CALANTHA. You are too courtly.

[*Enter*] *to them* ITHOCLES, ORGILUS, PROPHILUS.

ITHOCLES. Your safe return to Sparta is most welcome;
I joy to meet you here and, as occasion
Shall grant us privacy, will yield you reasons
Why I should covet to deserve the title
Of your respected friend; for, without compliment,
Believe it, Orgilus, 'tis my ambition.

---

observance: courtship; (courtly) service.

ORGILUS. Your lordship may command me your poor
    servant.   50
ITHOCLES [*aside*]. So amorously close? Close so soon?
    My heart!
PROPHILUS. What sudden change is next?
ITHOCLES.   Life to the
    king,
  To whom I here present this noble gentleman,
  New come from Athens. Royal sir, vouchsafe
  Your gracious hand in favor of his merit.
CROTOLON [*aside*]. My son preferred* by Ithocles!
AMYCLAS.   Our
    bounties
  Shall open to thee, Orgilus; for instance—
  Hark in thine ear—if out of those inventions
  Which flow in Athens thou hast there engrossed*
  Some rarity of wit to grace the nuptials   60
  Of thy fair sister and renown our court
  In th'eyes of this young prince, we shall be debtor
  To thy conceit; think on't.
ORGILUS.   Your highness honors me.
NEARCHUS. My tongue and heart are twins.
CALANTHA.   A noble
    birth,
  Becoming such a father.—Worthy Orgilus,
  You are a guest most wished for.
ORGILUS.   May my duty
  Still* rise in your opinion, sacred princess.
ITHOCLES. Euphranea's brother, sir, a gentleman
  Well worthy of your knowledge.
NEARCHUS.   We embrace him,
  Proud of so dear acquaintance.
AMYCLAS.   All prepare   70
  For revels and disport; the joys of Hymen,
  Like Phoebus in his luster, puts to flight
  All mists of dullness. Crown the hours with gladness;
  No sounds but music, no discourse but mirth!
CALANTHA. Thine arm, I prithee, Ithocles.—Nay, good
  My lord, keep on your way; I am provided.

---

preferred: presented for advancement.
engrossed: acquired; learned.   still: always.

NEARCHUS. I dare not disobey.
ITHOCLES.   Most heavenly lady!
                                                    Exeunt.

[III.iv]
                    Enter CROTOLON, ORGILUS.
CROTOLON. The king hath spoke his mind.
ORGILUS.   His will he
     hath;
     But, were it lawful to hold plea against
     The power of greatness, not the reason, haply
     Such undershrubs as subjects sometimes might
     Borrow of nature justice, to inform
     That license* sovereignty holds without check
     Over a meek obedience.
CROTOLON.   How resolve you
     Touching your sister's marriage? Prophilus
     Is a deserving and a hopeful youth.
ORGILUS. I envy not her merit but applaud it;   10
     Could [wish] him thrift* in all his best desires,
     And with a willingness inleague our blood
     With his for purchase of full growth in friendship.
     He never touched on any wrong that maliced
     The honor of our house nor stirred our peace;
     Yet, with your favor, let me not forget
     Under whose wing he gathers warmth and comfort,
     Whose creature he is bound, made, and must live so.
CROTOLON. Son, son, I find in thee a harsh condition;
     No courtesy can win it; 'tis too rancorous.   20
ORGILUS. Good sir, be not severe in your construction;
     I am no stranger to such easy calms
     As sit in tender bosoms. Lordly Ithocles
     Hath graced my entertainment in abundance,
     Too humbly hath descended from that height
     Of arrogance and spleen which wrought the rape
     On grieved Penthea's purity; his scorn
     Of my untoward fortunes is reclaimed
     Unto a courtship, almost to a fawning.
     I'll kiss his foot since you will have it so.   30

-----

     license: authority.   thrift: success.

CROTOLON. Since I will have it so? Friend, I will have it
    so
Without our ruin by your politic plots
Or wolf of hatred snarling in your breast.
You have a spirit, sir, have ye? A familiar*
That posts i'th'air for your intelligence?*
Some such hobgoblin hurried you from Athens,
For yet you come unsent for.
ORGILUS.   If unwelcome,
I might have found a grave there.
CROTOLON.   Sure your business
Was soon dispatched or your mind altered quickly.
ORGILUS. 'Twas care, sir, of my health cut short my
    journey;   40
For there a general infection
Threatens a desolation.
CROTOLON.   And I fear
Thou hast brought back a worse infection with thee—
Infection of thy mind, which, as thou sayst,
Threatens the desolation of our family.
ORGILUS. Forbid it, our dear genius!* I will rather
Be made a sacrifice on Thrasus' monument
Or kneel to Ithocles, his son, in dust
Than woo a father's curse! My sister's marriage
With Prophilus is from my heart confirmed.   50
May I live hated, may I die despised,
If I omit to further it in all
That can concern me!
CROTOLON.   I have been too rough.
My duty to my king made me so earnest;
Excuse it, Orgilus.
ORGILUS.   Dear sir—
    Enter to them PROPHILUS, EUPHRANEA, ITHOCLES,
                GRONEAS, LEMOPHIL.
CROTOLON.   Here comes
Euphranea with Prophilus and Ithocles.
ORGILUS. Most honored! Ever famous!
ITHOCLES.   Your true friend;
On earth not any truer.—With smooth* eyes

---

  familiar: spirit.   intelligence: communication.
  genius: tutelary or attendant spirit.   smooth: kindly.

Look on this worthy couple; your consent
Can only make them one.

ORGILUS.   They have it.—Sister,   60
Thou pawn'dst to me an oath, of which engagement
I never will release thee, if thou aim'st
At any other choice than this.

EUPHRANEA.   Dear brother,
At him or none.

CROTOLON.   To which my blessing's added.

ORGILUS. Which, till a greater ceremony perfect,
Euphranea, lend thy hand.—Here, take her, Prophilus.
Live long a happy man and wife; and further,
That these in presence may conclude an omen,
Thus for a bridal song I close my wishes:

> *Comforts lasting, loves increasing,*   70
> *Like soft hours never ceasing;*
> *Plenty's pleasure, peace complying,*
> *Without jars or tongues envying;*
> *Hearts by holy union wedded*
> *More than theirs by custom bedded;*
> *Fruitful issues; life so gracèd,*
> *Not by age to be defacèd;*
> *Budding, as the year ensu'th,*
> *Every spring another youth:*
> *All what thought can add beside*   80
> *Crown this bridegroom and this bride!*

PROPHILUS. You have sealed joy close to my soul.—
Euphranea,
Now I may call thee mine.

ITHOCLES.   I but exchange
One good friend for another.

ORGILUS.   If these gallants
Will please to grace a poor invention
By joining with me in some slight device,
I'll venture on a strain my younger days
Have studied for delight.

LEMOPHIL.   With thankful willingness
I offer my attendance.

GRONEAS.   No endeavor
Of mine shall fail to show itself.

ITHOCLES.   We will   90
All join to wait on thy directions, Orgilus.

ORGILUS. O, my good lord, your favors flow towards
    A too unworthy worm; but, as you please,
    I am what you will shape me.
ITHOCLES.   A fast friend.
CROTOLON. I thank thee, son, for this acknowledgment;
    It is a sight of gladness.
ORGILUS.   But my duty.

                                    Exeunt omnes.

[III.v]
    Enter CALANTHA, PENTHEA, CHRISTALLA, PHILEMA.
CALANTHA. Whoe'er would speak with us, deny his en-
    trance;
    Be careful of our charge.
CHRISTALLA.   We shall, madam.
CALANTHA. Except the king himself, give none admit-
    tance;
    Not any.
PHILEMA.   Madam, it shall be our care.
                 Exeunt [CHRISTALLA *and* PHILEMA].
CALANTHA. Being alone, Penthea, you have granted
    The opportunity you sought and might
    At all times have commanded.
PENTHEA.   'Tis a benefit
    Which I shall owe your goodness even in death for.
    My glass° of life, sweet princess, hath few minutes
    Remaining to run down; the sands are spent,   10
    For by an inward messenger I feel
    The summons of departure short and certain.
CALANTHA. You feed too much your melancholy.
PENTHEA.   Glories
    Of human greatness are but pleasing dreams
    And shadows soon decaying; on the stage
    Of my mortality, my youth hath acted
    Some scenes of vanity, drawn out at length
    By varied pleasures, sweetened in the mixture,
    But tragical in issue. Beauty, pomp,
    With every sensuality our giddiness   20
    Doth frame an idol, are unconstant friends
    When any troubled passion makes assault

---

glass: hourglass.

On the unguarded castle of the mind.
CALANTHA. Contemn not your condition for the proof
  Of bare opinion only. To what end
  Reach all these moral texts?
PENTHEA.   To place before 'ee
  A perfect mirror, wherein you may see
  How weary I am of a ling'ring life,
  Who count the best a misery.
CALANTHA.   Indeed
  You have no little cause, yet none so great   30
  As to distrust a remedy.
PENTHEA.   That remedy
  Must be a winding sheet, a fold of lead,
  And some untrod-on corner in the earth.
  Not to detain your expectation, princess,
  I have an humble suit.
CALANTHA.   Speak; I enjoy it.
[PENTHEA.] Vouchsafe, then, to be my executrix
  And take that trouble on 'ee to dispose
  Such legacies as I bequeath impartially.
  I have not much to give; the pains are easy.
  Heaven will reward your piety and thank it   40
  When I am dead; for sure I must not live—
  I hope I cannot.
CALANTHA.   Now, beshrew thy sadness;
  Thou turn'st me too much woman.
  [*She weeps.*]
PENTHEA [*aside*].   Her fair eyes
  Melt into passion. Then I have assurance
  Encouraging my boldness.—In this paper
  My will was charactered, which you, with pardon,
  Shall now know from mine own mouth.
CALANTHA.   Talk on,
  prithee;
  It is a pretty earnest.*
PENTHEA.   I have left me
  But three poor jewels to bequeath. The first is
  My youth; for, though I am much old in griefs,   50
  In years I am a child.
CALANTHA.   To whom that?

---

earnest: foretaste; anticipation.

PENTHEA. To virgin wives, such as abuse not wedlock
　By freedom of desires but covet chiefly
　The pledges of chaste beds for ties of love
　Rather than ranging of their blood; and next
　To married maids, such as prefer the number
　Of honorable issue in their virtues
　Before the flattery of delights by marriage—
　May those be ever young!
CALANTHA.　　　　　　　　A second jewel
　You mean to part with?
PENTHEA.　　　　　　　　'Tis my fame, I trust　　　　60
　By scandal yet untouched; this I bequeath
　To Memory and Time's old daughter, Truth.
　If ever my unhappy name find mention
　When I am fall'n to dust, may it deserve
　Beseeming charity without dishonor.
CALANTHA. How handsomely thou play'st with harmless
　　　sport
　Of mere* imagination! Speak the last;
　I strangely like thy will.
PENTHEA.　　　　　　　　This jewel, madam,
　Is dearly precious to me; you must use
　The best of your discretion to employ　　　　70
　This gift as I intend it.
CALANTHA.　　　　　　Do not doubt me.
PENTHEA. 'Tis long agone since first I lost my heart;
　Long I have lived without it, else for certain
　I should have given that too; but, instead
　Of it, to great Calantha, Sparta's heir,
　By service bound and by affection vowed,
　I do bequeath in holiest rites of love
　Mine only brother, Ithocles.
CALANTHA.　　　　　　　　What saidst thou?
PENTHEA. Impute not, heaven-blessed lady, to ambition
　A faith as humbly perfect as the prayers　　　　80
　Of a devoted suppliant can endow it.
　Look on him, princess, with an eye of pity.
　How like the ghost of what he late appeared
　'A moves before you!
CALANTHA [aside].　　　　Shall I answer here,
　Or lend my ear too grossly?

---

mere: sheer, pure.

PENTHEA.   First, his heart
 Shall fall in cinders, scorched by your disdain,
 Ere he will dare, poor man, to ope an eye
 On these divine looks, but with low-bent thoughts
 Accusing such presumption; as for words,
 'A dares not utter any but of service.   90
 Yet this lost creature loves 'ee. Be a princess
 In sweetness as in blood; give him his doom,
 Or raise him up to comfort.
CALANTHA.   What new change
 Appears in my behavior that thou dar'st
 Tempt my displeasure?
PENTHEA.   I must leave the world
 To revel [in] Elysium, and 'tis just
 To wish my brother some advantage here;
 Yet, by my best hopes, Ithocles is ignorant
 Of this pursuit. But, if you please to kill him,
 Lend him one angry look or one harsh word;   100
 And you shall soon conclude how strong a power
 Your absolute authority holds over
 His life and end.
CALANTHA.   You have forgot, Penthea,
 How still I have a father.
PENTHEA.   But remember
 I am a sister though to me this brother
 Hath been, you know, unkind, O, most unkind!
CALANTHA. Christalla, Philema, where are 'e?—Lady,
 Your check lies in my silence.
      Enter CHRISTALLA *and* PHILEMA.
BOTH.   Madam, here.
CALANTHA. I think 'e sleep, 'e drones! Wait on Penthea
 Unto her lodging.—[*Aside*.] Ithocles? Wronged lady!   110
PENTHEA. My reckonings are made even; death or fate
 Can now nor strike too soon nor force too late,

            Exeunt.

ACTUS QUARTUS

[IV.i]
      Enter ITHOCLES *and* ARMOSTES.
ITHOCLES. Forbear your inquisition; curiosity
 Is of too subtle and too searching nature,

In fears of love too quick, too slow of credit.
I am not what you doubt me.*
ARMOSTES.   Nephew, be then
As I would wish.—[*Aside.*] All is not right.—Good
    heaven
Confirm your resolutions for dependence
On worthy ends which may advance your quiet!
ITHOCLES. I did the noble Orgilus much injury,
But grieved Penthea more; I now repent it.
Now, uncle, now; this "now" is now too late.   10
So provident* is folly in sad issue
That after-wit, like bankrupts' debts, stand tallied
Without all possibility of payment.
Sure, he's an honest, very honest gentleman,
A man of single* meaning.
ARMOSTES.   I believe it;
Yet, nephew, 'tis the tongue informs our ears;
Our eyes can never pierce into the thoughts,
For they are lodged too inward. But I question
No truth in Orgilus.—The princess, sir.
ITHOCLES. The princess? Ha!
ARMOSTES.   With her the Prince of
    Argos.   20

        Enter NEARCHUS, *leading* CALANTHA; AMELUS,
                    CHRISTALLA, PHILEMA.

NEARCHUS. Great fair one, grace my hopes with any
    instance
Of livery* from the allowance of your favor.
This little spark—
    [*He attempts to take a ring from her finger.*]
CALANTHA.   A toy!
NEARCHUS.   Love feasts on toys,
For Cupid is a child. Vouchsafe this bounty;
It cannot be [de]nied.
CALANTHA.   You shall not value,
Sweet cousin, at a price, what I count cheap,
So cheap that let him take it who dares stoop for't
And give it at next meeting to a mistress;

---

doubt me: fear me (to be).   provident: productive.
single: direct, honest.   instance/ of livery: token of favor.

She'll thank him for't, perhaps.
  (*Casts it to* ITHOCLES.)
AMELUS.   The ring, sir, is
  The princess's; I could have took it up.   30
ITHOCLES. Learn manners, prithee.—To the blessed
    owner,
  Upon my knees—
  [*He kneels and offers it to* CALANTHA.]
NEARCHUS.   Y'are saucy.
CALANTHA.   This is pretty!
  I am, belike, "a mistress." Wondrous pretty!
  Let the man keep his fortune since he found it;
  He's worthy on't.—On, cousin!
ITHOCLES [*to* AMELUS].   Follow, spaniel;
  I'll force 'ee to a fawning else.
AMELUS.   You dare not.
            Exeunt. Manent ITHOCLES *and* ARMOSTES.
ARMOSTES. My lord, you were too forward.
ITHOCLES.   Look 'ee,
    uncle:
  Some such there are whose liberal contents
  Swarm without care in every sort of plenty,
  Who, after full repasts, can lay them down   40
  To sleep; and they sleep, uncle—in which silence
  Their very dreams present 'em choice of pleasures,
  Pleasures (observe me, uncle) of rare object:
  Here heaps of gold, there increments of honors,
  Now change of garments, then the votes of people,
  Anon varieties of beauties, courting
  In flatteries of the night, exchange of dalliance;
  Yet these are still but dreams. Give me felicity
  Of which my senses waking are partakers,
  A real, visible, material happiness;   50
  And then, too, when I stagger in expectance
  Of the least comfort that can cherish life—
  I saw it, sir, I saw it; for it came
  From her own hand.
ARMOSTES.   The princess threw it t'ee.
ITHOCLES. True, and she said—well I remember what.
  Her cousin prince would beg it.
ARMOSTES.   Yes, and parted
  In anger at your taking on't.

ITHOCLES.   Penthea!
  O, thou hast pleaded with a powerful language!
  I want a fee to gratify thy merit,
  But I will do——
ARMOSTES.   What is't you say?
ITHOCLES.   In anger,   60
  In anger let him part; for, could his breath,
  Like whirlwinds, toss such servile slaves as lick
  The dust his footsteps print into a vapor,
  It durst not stir a hair of mine. It should not;
  I'd rend it up by th' roots first. To be anything
  Calantha smiles on is to be a blessing
  More sacred than a petty prince of Argos
  Can wish to equal or in worth or title.
ARMOSTES. Contain yourself, my lord. Ixion, aiming
  To embrace Juno, bosomed but a cloud   70
  And begat Centaurs: 'tis an useful moral.
  Ambition hatched in clouds of mere opinion
  Proves but in birth a prodigy.*
ITHOCLES.   I thank 'ee;
  Yet, with your license, I should seem uncharitable
  To gentler fate if, relishing the dainties
  Of a soul's settled peace, I were so feeble
  Not to digest it.
ARMOSTES.   He deserves small trust
  Who is not privy counselor to himself.
      Enter NEARCHUS, ORGILUS, *and* AMELUS.
NEARCHUS. Brave me?
ORGILUS.   Your excellence mistakes his
    temper;
  For Ithocles in fashion of his mind   80
  Is beautiful, soft, gentle, the clear mirror
  Of absolute perfection.
AMELUS.   Was't your modesty
  Termed any of the prince his servants "spaniel"?
  Your nurse, sure, taught you other language.
ITHOCLES.   Lan-
    guage!
NEARCHUS. A gallant man-at-arms is here, a doctor
  In feats of chivalry, blunt and rough-spoken,

----

  prodigy: monster.

Vouchsafing not the fustian of civility,
Which [less] rash spirits style good manners!

ITHOCLES.   Manners!

ORGILUS. No more, illustrious sir; 'tis matchless Ithocles.

NEARCHUS. You might have understood who I am.

ITHOCLES.   Yes,   90
I did; else—but the presence calmed th'affront;
Y'are cousin to the princess.

NEARCHUS.   To the king, too;
A certain instrument that lent supportance
To your colossic greatness—to that king, too,
You might have added.

ITHOCLES.   There is more divinity
In beauty than in majesty.

ARMOSTES.   O, fie, fie!

NEARCHUS. This odd youth's pride turns heretic in loy-
    alty.
Sirrah! Low mushrooms never rival cedars.

                              Exeunt NEARCHUS *et* AMELUS.

ITHOCLES. Come back!—What pitiful dull thing am I
So to be tamely scolded at?—Come back!—   100
Let him come back and echo once again
That scornful sound of "mushroom"! Painted colts,
Like heralds' coats gilt o'er with crowns and scepters,
May bait a muzzled lion.

ARMOSTES.   Cousin, cousin,
Thy tongue is not thy friend.

ORGILUS.   In point of honor
Discretion knows no bounds. Amelus told me
'Twas all about a little ring.

ITHOCLES.   A ring
The princess threw away, and I took up.
Admit she threw't to me, what arm of brass
Can snatch it hence? No, could 'a grind the hoop   110
To powder, 'a might sooner reach my heart
Than steal and wear one dust* on't.—Orgilus,
I am extremely wronged.

ORGILUS.   A lady's favor
Is not to be so slighted.

ITHOCLES.   Slighted!

---

dust: speck or particle.

ARMOSTES.   Quiet
  These vain unruly passions, which will render ye
  Into a madness.
ORGILUS.   Griefs will have their vent.
        Enter TECNICUS [*with a scroll*].
ARMOSTES. Welcome; thou com'st in season, reverend
    man,
  To pour the balsam of a [suppling]* patience
  Into the festering wound of ill-spent fury.
ORGILUS [*aside*]. What makes he here?
TECNICUS.   The hurts are   120
  yet but mortal,
  Which shortly will prove deadly. To the king,
  Armostes, see in safety thou deliver
  This sealed-up counsel; bid him with a constancy
  Peruse the secrets of the gods.— ꓳ Sparta,
  O Lacedemon! Double-named, but one
  In fate! When kingdoms reel (mark well my saw),*
  Their heads must needs be giddy. Tell the king
  That henceforth he no more must inquire after
  My aged head; Apollo wills it so.
  I am for Delphos.
ARMOSTES.   Not without some conference   130
  With our great master?
TECNICUS.   Never more to see him;
  A greater prince commands me.—Ithocles,
    When youth is ripe, and age from time doth part,
    The lifeless trunk shall wed the broken heart.
ITHOCLES. What's this, if understood?
TECNICUS.   List, Orgilus;
  Remember what I told thee long before;
  These tears shall be my witness.
ARMOSTES.   'Las, good man!
TECNICUS.   *Let craft with courtesy a while confer;*
    Revenge proves its own executioner.
ORGILUS. Dark sentences are for Apollo's priests;   140
  I am not Oedipus.*
TECNICUS.   My hour is come.

---

  suppling: healing.   saw: maxim.
  Oedipus: who guessed the riddle of the Sphinx, the monster
threatening Thebes.

Cheer up the king; farewell to all.—O Sparta,
O Lacedemon!

Exit TECNICUS.

ARMOSTES.   If prophetic fire
Have warmed this old man's bosom, we might construe
His words to fatal sense.

ITHOCLES.   Leave to the powers
Above us the effects of their decrees;
My burden lies within me. Servile fears
Prevent no great effects.—Divine Calantha!

ARMOSTES. The gods be still propitious!

Exeunt. Manet ORGILUS.

ORGILUS.   Something
    oddly
The bookman prated, yet 'a talked it weeping: 150
    "Let craft with courtesy a while confer;
    Revenge proves its own executioner."
Con it again. For what? It shall not puzzle me;
'Tis dotage of a withered brain.—Penthea
Forbade me not her presence; I may see her
And gaze my fill. Why, see her, then, I may
When, if I faint to speak, I must be silent.

Exit ORGILUS.

[IV.ii]

Enter BASSANES, GRAUSIS, *and* PHULAS.

BASSANES. Pray, use your recreations; all the service
I will expect is quietness amongst 'ee.
Take liberty at home, abroad, at all times,
And in your charities appease the gods
Whom I, with my distractions, have offended.

GRAUSIS. Fair blessings on thy heart!

PHULAS [*aside*].   Here's a rare
    change!
My lord, to cure the itch, is surely gelded;
The cuckold in conceit* hath cast his horns.

BASSANES. Betake 'ee to your several occasions;
And, wherein I have heretofore been faulty,   10
Let your constructions mildly pass it over.
Henceforth I'll study reformation; more

_____

in conceit: in imagination.

I have not for employment.
GRAUSIS.   O sweet man!
   Thou art the very "Honeycomb of Honesty."
PHULAS. The "Garland of Goodwill." °—Old lady, hold
   up
   Thy reverend snout and trot behind me softly
   As it becomes a moil ° of ancient carriage.
                                   Exeunt. Manet BASSANES.
BASSANES. Beasts, only capable of sense,° enjoy
   The benefit of food and ease with thankfulness;
   Such silly creatures, with a grudging, kick not   20
   Against the portion nature hath bestowed;
   But men, endowed with reason and the use
   Of reason, to distinguish from the chaff
   Of abject scarcity the quintessence,
   Soul, and elixir of the earth's abundance,
   The treasures of the sea, the air, nay, heaven,
   Repining at these glories of creation,
   Are verier beasts than beasts; and of those beasts
   The worst am I—I, who was made a monarch
   Of what a heart could wish for, a chaste wife,   30
   Endeavored what in me lay to pull down
   That temple built for adoration only
   And level't in the dust of causeless scandal.
   But, to redeem a sacrilege so impious,
   Humility shall pour, before the deities
   I have incensed, a largeness of more patience
   Than their displeasèd altars can require.
   No tempests of commotion shall disquiet
   The calms of my composure.
                        Enter ORGILUS.
ORGILUS.   I have found thee,
   Thou patron of more horrors than the bulk   40
   Of manhood, hooped about with ribs of iron,
   Can cram within thy breasts. Penthea, Bassanes,
   Cursed by thy jealousies—more, by thy dotage—
   Is left a prey to words.
BASSANES.   Exercise
   Your trials for addition to my penance;
   I am resolved.

_____

   Honeycomb . . . Goodwill: popular miscellanies.
   moil: mule.   sense: sensuality.

ORGILUS.   Play not with misery
  Past cure; some angry minister of fate hath
  Deposed the empress of her soul, her reason,
  From its most proper throne; but, what's the miracle
  More new, I, I have seen it and yet live!   50
BASSANES. You may delude my senses, not my judgment;
  'Tis anchored into a firm resolution;
  Dalliance of mirth or wit can ne'er unfix it.
  Practice yet further.
ORGILUS.   May thy death of love to her
  Damn all thy comforts to a lasting fast
  From every joy of life! Thou barren rock,
  By thee we have bee[n] split in ken of harbor.
    Enter ITHOCLES, PENTHEA, *her hair about her ears,*
      [ARMOSTES], PHILEMA, CHRISTALLA.
ITHOCLES. Sister, look up; your Ithocles, your brother,
  Speaks t'ee; why do you weep? Dear, turn not from
  me.—
  Here is a killing sight; lo, Bassanes,   60
  A lamentable object.
ORGILUS.   Man, dost see't?
  Sports are more gamesome; am I yet in merriment?
  Why dost not laugh?
BASSANES.   Divine and best of ladies,
  Please to forget my outrage; mercy ever
  Cannot but lodge under a roo[f] so excellent.
  I have cast off that cruelty of frenzy
  Which once appeared impostors and then juggled
  To cheat my sleeps of rest.
ORGILUS.   Was I in earnest?
PENTHEA. Sure, if we were all Sirens, we should sing
    pitifully;
  And 'twere a comely music when in parts   70
  One sung another's knell. The turtle* sighs
  When he hath lost his mate, and yet some say
  'A must be dead first. 'Tis a fine deceit
  To pass away in a dream; indeed, I've slept
  With mine eyes open a great while. No falsehood
  Equals a broken faith; there's not a hair
  Sticks on my head but, like a leaden plummet,
  It sinks me to the grave. I must creep thither;

---

turtle: turtledove.

The journey is not long.

ITHOCLES.   But thou, Penthea,
Hast many years, I hope, to number yet   80
Ere thou canst travel that way.

BASSANES.   Let the [sun] first
Be wrapped up in an everlasting darkness
Before the light of nature, chiefly formed
For the whole world's delight, feel an eclipse
So universal!

ORGILUS.   Wisdom, look 'ee, begins
To rave.—Art thou mad, too, antiquity?

PENTHEA. Since I was first a wife, I might have been
Mother to many pretty, prattling babes;
They would have smiled when I smiled, and for certain
I should have cried when they cried.—Truly, brother,   90
My father would have picked me out a husband,
And then my little ones had been no bastards;
But 'tis too late for me to marry now—
I am past child-bearing; 'tis not my fault.

BASSANES. Fall on me if there be a burning Etna
And bury me in flames! Sweats hot as sulphur
Boil through my pores! Affliction hath in store
No torture like to this.

ORGILUS.   Behold a patience!
Lay by thy whining, gray dissimulation;
Do something worth a chronicle. Show justice   100
Upon the author of this mischief; dig out
The jealousies that hatched this thralldom first
With thine own poniard. Every antic* rapture
Can roar as thine does.

ITHOCLES.   Orgilus, forbear.

BASSANES. Disturb him not; it is a talking motion*
Provided for my torment. What a fool am I
To [bandy] passion. Ere I'll speak a word,
I will look on and burst.

PENTHEA [to ORGILUS].   I loved you once.

ORGILUS. Thou didst, wronged creature, in despite of
      malice;
For it I love thee ever.

PENTHEA.   Spare your hand;   110
Believe me, I'll not hurt it.

---

antic: referring to a stage clown.   motion: puppet.

ORGILUS.   Pain my heart, too!
[PENTHEA.] Complain not though I wring it hard. I'll
    kiss it;
    O, 'tis a fine soft palm! Hark, in thine ear:
    Like whom do I look, prithee?—Nay, no whispering.
    Goodness! We had been happy; too much happiness
    Will make folk proud, they say—but that is he—
    (*Points at* ITHOCLES.)
    And yet he paid for't home. Alas, his heart
    Is crept into the cabinet of the princess;
    We shall have points* and bride-laces. Remember,   120
    When we last gathered roses in the garden,
    I found my wits; but truly you lost yours.
    That's he, and still 'tis he.
ITHOCLES.   Poor soul, how idly
    Her fancies guide her tongue.
BASSANES.   Keep in, vexation,
    And break not into clamor.
ORGILUS.   She has tutored me;
    Some powerful inspiration checks my laziness.—
    Now let me kiss your hand, grieved beauty.
PENTHEA.   Kiss it.—
    Alack, alack, his lips be wondrous cold.
    Dear soul, h'as lost his color; have 'e seen
    A straying heart? All crannies! Every drop
    Of blood is turn[è]d to an amethyst,   130
    Which married bachelors hang in their ears.
ORGILUS. Peace usher her into Elysium!—
    If this be madness, madness is an oracle.

                                        Exit ORGILUS.
ITHOCLES. Christalla, Philema, when slept my sister?
    Her ravings are so wild.
CHRISTALLA.   Sir, not these ten days.
PHILEMA. We watch by her continually; besides,
    We cannot any way pray her to eat.
BASSANES. O, misery of miseries!
PENTHEA.   Take comfort;
    You may live well and die a good old man.
    By yea and nay, an oath not to be broken,   140
    If you had joined our hands once in the temple—
    'Twas since my father died, for had he lived

---

points: tagged laces that attach to hose to fasten clothes.

He would have done't—I must have called you father.
O, my wracked honor, ruined by those tyrants,
A cruel brother and a desperate dotage!
There is no peace left for a ravished wife
Widowed by lawless marriage; to all memory
Penthea's, poor Penthea's, name is strumpeted.
But, since her blood was seasoned by the forfeit
Of noble shame with mixtures of pollution,   150
Her blood ('tis just) be henceforth never heightened
With taste of sustenance! Starve; let that fullness
Whose plurisy* hath fevered faith and modesty—
Forgive me; O, I faint!

ARMOSTES.   Be not so willful,
Sweet niece, to work thine own destruction.

ITHOCLES.   Nature
Will call her daughter monster!—What? Not eat?
Refuse the only ordinary means
Which are ordained for life? Be not, my sister,
A murd'ress to thyself.—Hear'st thou this, Bassanes?

BASSANES. Foh! I am busy, for I have not thoughts   160
Enow to think; all shall be well anon.
'Tis tumbling in my head; there is a mastery
In art to fatten and keep smooth the outside,
Yes, and to comfort up the vital spirits
Without the help of food; fumes or perfumes,
Perfumes or fumes. Let her alone; I'll search out
The trick on't.

PENTHEA.   Lead me gently; heavens reward ye.
Griefs are sure friends; they leave, without control,
Nor cure nor comforts for a leprous soul.

                    Exeunt the Maids supporting PENTHEA.

BASSANES. I grant t'ee and will put in practice instantly   170
What you shall still admire.* 'Tis wonderful,
'Tis super-singular, not to be matched;
Yet, when I've done't, I've done't. Ye shall thank me.

                                        Exit BASSANES.

ARMOSTES. The sight is full of terror.

ITHOCLES.   On my soul
Lies such an infinite clog of massy dullness
As that I have not sense enough to feel it.—

---

plurisy: excess, overabundance.   admire: wonder at.

See, uncle, th'augury* thing returns again;
Shall's welcome him with thunder? We are haunted
And must use exorcism to conjure down
This spirit of malevolence.

ARMOSTES.   Mildly, nephew.   180
    Enter NEARCHUS *and* AMELUS.

NEARCHUS. I come not, sir, to chide your late disorder,
Admitting that th'inurement to a roughness
In soldiers of your years and fortunes, chiefly
So lately prosperous, hath not yet shook off
The custom of the war in hours of leisure;
Nor shall you need excuse since y'are to render
Account to that fair excellence, the princess,
Who in her private gallery expects it
From your own mouth alone. I am a messenger
But to her pleasure.

ITHOCLES.   Excellent Nearchus,   190
Be prince still of my services and conquer
Without the combat of dispute; I honor 'ee.

NEARCHUS. The king is on a sudden indisposed;
Physicians are called for. 'Twere fit, Armostes,
You should be near him.

ARMOSTES.   Sir, I kiss your hands.
    Exeunt. Manent NEARCHUS *et* AMELUS.

NEARCHUS. Amelus, I perceive Calantha's bosom
Is warmed with other fires than such as can
Take strength from any fuel of the love
I might address to her. Young Ithocles,
Or ever I mistake, is lord ascendant*   200
Of her devotions—one, to speak him truly,
In every disposition nobly fashioned.

AMELUS. But can your highness brook to be so rivaled,
Considering th'inequality of the persons?

NEARCHUS. I can, Amelus; for affections injured
By tyranny or rigor of compulsion,
Like tempest-threatened trees unfirmly rooted,
Ne'er spring to timely growth. Observe, for instance,
Life-spent Penthea and unhappy Orgilus.

AMELUS. How does your grace determine?

---

augury: foreboding; angry (?).
lord ascendant: in the favored position (astronomically).

NEARCHUS.   To be jealous   210
In public of what privately I'll further;
And, though they shall not know, yet they shall find
    it.

                                                        Exeunt omnes.

[IV.iii]
        Enter LEMOPHIL *and* GRONEAS *leading* AMYCLAS,
        and placing him in a chair; followed by
        ARMOSTES [*with a box*], CROTOLON, *and*
                        PROPHILUS.
AMYCLAS. Our daughter is not near?
ARMOSTES.   She is retired, sir,
Into her gallery.
AMYCLAS.   Where's the prince our cousin?
PROPHILUS. New walked into the grove, my lord.
AMYCLAS.   All
    leave us
Except Armostes and you, Crotolon;
We would be private.
PROPHILUS.   Health unto your majesty!
                Exeunt PROPHILUS, LEMOPHIL, *et* GRONEAS.
AMYCLAS. What! Tecnicus is gone?
ARMOSTES.   He is to Delphos,
And to your royal hands presents this box.
AMYCLAS. Unseal it, good Armostes; therein lies
The secrets of the oracle. Out with it.
[ARMOSTES *takes out the scroll.*]
Apollo live our patron! Read, Armostes.   10
ARMOSTES.   *The plot in which the vine takes root*
                Begins to dry from head to foot;
                The stock soon withering, want of sap
                Doth cause to quail° the budding grape;
                But from the neighboring elm a dew
                Shall drop and feed the plot anew.
AMYCLAS. That is the oracle. What exposition
Makes the philosopher?
ARMOSTES.   This brief one only:
                The plot is Sparta, the dried vine the king,
                The quailing grape his daughter; but the
                        thing   20

_____
quail: dry up (and, therefore, die).

> *Of most importance, not to be revealed,*
> *Is a near prince, the elm; the rest concealed.*
> > *Tecnicus.*

AMYCLAS. Enough; although the opening* of this riddle
Be but itself a riddle, yet we construe
How near our lab'ring age draws to a rest.
But must Calantha quail too? That young grape
Untimely budded! I could mourn for her;
Her tenderness hath yet deserved no rigor
So to be crossed by fate.

ARMOSTES. You misapply, sir— 30
With favor let me speak it—what Apollo
Hath clouded in hid sense: I here conjecture
Her marriage with some neighb'ring prince, the dew
Of which befriending elm shall ever strengthen
Your subjects with a sovereignty of power.

CROTOLON. Besides, most gracious lord, the pith of oracles
Is to be then digested when th'events
Expound their truth, not brought as soon to light
As uttered. Truth is child of Time; and herein
I find no scruple, rather cause of comfort, 40
With unity of kingdoms.

AMYCLAS. May it prove so
For weal of this dear nation!—Where is Ithocles?—
Armostes, Crotolon, when this withered vine
Of my frail carcass on the funeral pile
Is fired into its ashes, let that young man
Be hedged about still with your cares and loves.
Much owe I to his worth, much to his service.—
Let such as wait come in now.

ARMOSTES. All attend here!

> *Enter* ITHOCLES, CALANTHA, PROPHILUS, ORGILUS,
> > EUPHRANEA, LEMOPHIL, *and* GRONEAS.

CALANTHA. Dear sir! King! Father!

ITHOCLES. O my royal master!

AMYCLAS. Cleave not my heart, sweet twins of my life's
solace, 50
With your forejudging fears, there is no physic
So cunningly restorative to cherish
The fall of age, or call back youth and vigor,

---

opening: interpretation.

As your consents in duty. I will shake off
This languishing disease of time to quicken
Fresh pleasures in these drooping hours of sadness.
Is fair Euphranea married yet to Prophilus?

CROTOLON. This morning, gracious lord.

ORGILUS.   This very
        morning,
Which, with your highness' leave, you may observe too.
Our sister looks, methinks, mirthful and sprightly,   60
As if her chaster fancy could already
Expound the riddle of her gain in losing
A trifle maids know only that they know not.
Pish! Prithee, blush not; 'tis but honest change
Of fashion in the garment, loose for strait,°
And so the modest maid is made a wife.
Shrewd business—is't not, sister?

EUPHRANEA.   You are pleasant.

AMYCLAS. We thank thee, Orgilus; this mirth becomes
        thee.
But wherefore sits the court in such a silence?
A wedding without revels is not seemly.   70

CALANTHA. Your late indisposition, sir, forbade it.

AMYCLAS. Be it thy charge, Calantha, to set forward
The bridal sports, to which I will be present;
If not, at least consenting.—Mine own Ithocles,
I have done little for thee yet.

ITHOCLES.   Y'have built me
To the full height I stand in.

CALANTHA [aside].   Now or never.—
May I propose a suit?

AMYCLAS.   Demand and have it.

CALANTHA. Pray, sir, give me this young man, and no
        further
Account him yours than he deserves in all things
To be thought worthy mine; I will esteem him   80
According to his merit.

AMYCLAS.   Still th'art my daughter,
Still grow'st upon my heart.—[To ITHOCLES.] Give me
        thine hand.—
Calantha, take thine own. In noble actions

---

strait: tight.

Thou'lt find him firm and absolute.—I would not
Have parted with thee, Ithocles, to any
But to a mistress who is all what I am.

ITHOCLES. A change, great king, most wished for 'cause
the same.

CALANTHA [*aside to* ITHOCLES]. Th'art mine. Have I
now kept my word?

ITHOCLES [*aside to* CALANTHA]. Divinely.

ORGILUS. Rich fortunes, guard to favor of a princess,
Rock thee, brave man, in ever-crownèd plenty.
Y'are minion of the time; be thankful for it.—   90
[*Aside.*] Ho! Here's a swinge in destiny. Apparent,*
The youth is up on tiptoe, yet may stumble.

AMYCLAS. On to your recreations!—Now convey me
Unto my bedchamber. None on his forehead
[Wear] a distempered look.

OMNES.   The gods preserve 'ee!

CALANTHA [*aside to* ITHOCLES]. Sweet, be not from my
sight.

ITHOCLES [*aside to* CALANTHA]. My whole felicity!
Exeunt, carrying out the King; ORGILUS *stays* ITHOCLES.

ORGILUS. Shall I be bold, my lord?

ITHOCLES.   Thou canst not,
Orgilus.
Call me thine own, for Prophilus must henceforth
Be all thy sister's. Friendship, though it cease not   100
In marriage, yet is oft at less command
Than when a single freedom can dispose it.

ORGILUS. Most right, my most good lord, my most great
lord,
My gracious, princely lord—I might add, royal.

ITHOCLES. Royal! A subject royal?

ORGILUS.   Why not, pray, sir?
The sovereignty of kingdoms in their nonage
Stooped to desert, not birth; there's as much merit
In clearness of affection* as in puddle
Of generation.* You have conquered love

---

apparent: obviously, clearly.
clearness of affection: nobility of feelings.
generation: birth (puddle of generation: the mysteries of here-
dity).

Even in the loveliest; if I greatly err not,   110
The son of Venus hath bequeathed his quiver
To Ithocles his manage,* by whose arrows
Calantha's breast is opened.

ITHOCLES.   Can't be possible?

ORGILUS. I was myself a piece of suitor once,
And forward in preferment, too—so forward
That, speaking truth, I may without offense, sir,
Presume to whisper that my hopes and (hark 'e)
My certainty of marriage stood assured
With as firm footing (by your leave) as any's
Now at this very instant—but—

ITHOCLES.   'Tis granted;   120
And, for a league of privacy between us,
Read o'er my bosom and partake a secret:
The princess is contracted mine.

ORGILUS.   Still,* why not?
I now applaud her wisdom; when your kingdom
Stands seated in your will, secure and settled,
I dare pronounce you will be a just monarch:
Greece must admire and tremble.

ITHOCLES.   Then the sweet-
    ness
Of so imparadised a comfort, Orgilus!
It is to banquet with the gods.

ORGILUS.   The glory
Of numerous children, potency of nobles,   130
Bent knees, hearts paved to tread on!

ITHOCLES.   With a friend-
    ship
So dear, so fast as thine.

ORGILUS.   I am unfitting
For office, but for service—

ITHOCLES.   We'll distinguish
Our fortunes merely in the title—partners
In all respects else but the bed.

ORGILUS.   The bed?
Forfend it, Jove's own jealousy!—till lastly
We slip down in the common earth together;

---

manage: management.   still: even so.

And there our beds are equal, save some monument
To show this was the king and this the subject.
(*Soft, sad music.*)
List! What sad sounds are these? Extremely sad ones! 140
ITHOCLES. Sure, from Penthea's lodging.
ORGILUS.   Hark! A voice,
     too.

A Song [*within*].

> *O, no more, no more, too late*
>   *Sighs are spent; the burning tapers*
> *Of a life as chaste as fate,*
>   *Pure as are unwritten papers,*
>   *Are burnt out: no heat, no light*
>   *Now remains; 'tis ever night.*
> *Love is dead; let lovers' eyes,*
>   *Locked in endless dreams,*
>   *Th'extremes of all extremes,*   150
> *Ope no more; for now Love dies,*
>   *Now Love dies, implying*
>   *Love's martyrs must be ever, ever dying.*

ITHOCLES. O, my misgiving heart!
ORGILUS.   A horrid stillness
Succeeds this deathful air; let's know the reason.
Tread softly; there is a mystery in mourning.

                                        Exeunt.

[IV.iv]

Enter CHRISTALLA *and* PHILEMA, *bringing in*
     PENTHEA *in a chair, veiled: two other*
     Servants placing two chairs, one on the
     *one side, and the other with an engine**
     on the other. The Maids sit down at her
     feet, mourning. The Servants go out;
     meet them ITHOCLES *and* ORGILUS.

SERVANT [*aside to* ORGILUS]. 'Tis done; that on her
     right hand.
ORGILUS.   Good; begone!

                                     [*Exeunt Servants.*]

ITHOCLES. Soft peace enrich this room!

---

engine: mechanical contrivance.

ORGILUS.   How fares the
    lady?
PHILEMA. Dead.
CHRISTALLA.   Dead!
PHILEMA.   Starved.
CHRISTALLA.   Starved!
ITHOCLES.   Me
    miserable!
ORGILUS.   Tell us
    How parted she from life?
PHILEMA.   She called for music
    And begged some gentle voice to tune a farewell
    To life and griefs. Christalla touched the lute;
    I wept the funeral song.
CHRISTALLA.   Which scarce was ended
    But her last breath sealed up these hollow sounds,
    "O, cruel Ithocles and injured Orgilus!"
    So down she drew her veil, so died.
ITHOCLES.   So died!   10
ORGILUS. Up! You are messengers of death; go from us.
    Here's woe enough to court without a prompter.
    Away; and—hark ye—till you see us next,
    No syllable that she is dead.—Away;
    Keep a smooth brow.—

                  Exeunt PHILEMA *et* CHRISTALLA.
                  My lord—
ITHOCLES.   Mine only
    sister!
    Another is not left me.
ORGILUS.   Take that chair;
    I'll seat me here in this. Between us sits
    The object of our sorrows. Some few tears
    We'll part among us; I perhaps can mix
    One lamentable story to prepare 'em.   20
    There, there; sit there, my lord.
ITHOCLES.   Yes, as you please.
    (ITHOCLES *sits down, and is catched in the engine.*)
    What means this treachery?
ORGILUS.   Caught! You are caught,
    Young master; 'tis thy throne of coronation,
    Thou fool of greatness! See, I take this veil off:
    Survey a beauty withered by the flames

Of an insulting° Phaëton,° her brother.

ITHOCLES. Thou mean'st to kill me basely?

ORGILUS.   I foreknew
The last act of her life and trained° thee hither
To sacrifice a tyrant to a turtle.
You dreamt of kingdoms, did 'e? How to bosom   30
The delicacies of a youngling princess,
How with this nod to grace that subtle courtier,
How with that frown to make this noble tremble,
And so forth whiles Penthea's groans and tortures,
Her agonies, her miseries, afflictions
Ne'er touched upon your thought? As for my injuries,
Alas! they were beneath your royal pity;
But yet they lived, thou proud man, to confound thee.
Behold thy fate, this steel!

[*He draws a dagger.*]

ITHOCLES.   Strike home! A courage
As keen as thy revenge shall give it welcome.   40
But, prithee, faint not; if the wound close up,
Tent° it with double force and search it deeply.
Thou look'st that I should whine and beg compassion,
As loath to leave the vainness of my glories;
A statelier resolution arms my confidence,
To cozen° thee of honor. Neither could I,
With equal trial of unequal fortune,
By hazard of a duel; 'twere a bravery
Too mighty for a slave intending murder.
On to the execution, and inherit   50
A conflict with thy horrors!

ORGILUS.   By Apollo,
Thou talk'st a goodly language! For requital
I will report thee to thy mistress richly.
And take this peace along: some few minutes
Determined, my resolves shall quickly follow
Thy wrathful ghost; then, if we tug for mastery,
Penthea's sacred eyes shall lend new courage.

---

insulting: arrogant.
Phaëton: son of Helios (the sun); for his arrogance in taking
over his father's chariot, which he was unable to control, and for
nearly burning the earth, Zeus struck him down with a thunderbolt.
trained: lured.   tent: probe.   cozen: cheat.

Give me thy hand; be healthful in thy parting
From lost mortality! Thus, thus I free it.
([*He stabs*] *him.*)

ITHOCLES. Yet, yet, I scorn to shrink.

ORGILUS.   Keep up thy   60
  spirit:
I will be gentle even in blood; to linger
Pain, which I strive to cure, were to be cruel.
[*He stabs him again.*]

ITHOCLES. Nimble in vengeance, I forgive thee. Follow
Safety, with best success. O, may it prosper!—
Penthea, by thy side thy brother bleeds—
The earnest° of his wrongs to thy forced faith.
Thoughts of ambition or delicious banquet,
With beauty, youth, and love, together perish
In my last breath, which on the sacred altar
Of a long-looked-for peace—now—moves—to heaven.   70
(*Moritur.*) °

ORGILUS. Farewell, fair spring of manhood. Henceforth
  welcome
Best expectation of a noble suff'rance.
I'll lock the bodies safe till what must follow
Shall be approved.°—Sweet twins, shine stars for-
  ever!—
In vain they build their hopes whose life is shame;
No monument lasts but a happy name.

                                                           Exit ORGILUS.

ACTUS QUINTUS

[V.i]

                         Enter BASSANES *alone.*

BASSANES. Athens, to Athens I have sent, the nursery
Of Greece for learning and the fount of knowledge;
For here in Sparta there's not left amongst us
One wise man to direct; we're all turned madcaps.
'Tis said Apollo is the god of herbs;
Then certainly he knows the virtue of 'em.

---

earnest: payment.   *moritur:* he dies.
be approved: be tested by experience.

To Delphos I have sent to. If there can be
A help for nature, we are sure yet.

Enter ORGILUS.

ORGILUS. Honor
Attend thy counsels ever!

BASSANES. I beseech thee
With all my heart, let me go from thee quietly; 10
I will not aught to do with thee of all men.
The [doubles] of a hare° or, in a morning,
Salutes from a splay-footed witch, to drop
Three drops of blood at th' nose just, and no more,
Croaking of ravens or the screech of owls
Are not so boding mischief as thy crossing
My private meditations. Shun me, prithee;
And, if I cannot love thee heartily,
I'll love thee as well as I can.

ORGILUS. Noble Bassanes,
Mistake me not.

BASSANES. Phew! Then we shall be troubled. 20
Thou wert ordained my plague—heaven make me
thankful;
And give me patience, too, heaven, I beseech thee.

ORGILUS. Accept a league of amity, for henceforth
I vow by my best genius,° in a syllable,
Never to speak vexation. I will study
Service and friendship with a zealous sorrow
For my past incivility towards 'ee.

BASSANES. Heyday! Good words, good words! I must believe 'em
And be a coxcomb for my labor.

ORGILUS. Use not
So hard a language; your misdoubt is causeless. 30
For instance, if you promise to put on
A constancy of patience, such a patience
As chronicle or history ne'er mentioned,
As follows not example but shall stand
A wonder and a theme for imitation,
The first, the index pointing to a second,

---

doubles of a hare: referring to the superstition that ill luck
attends one whose path a hare has crossed.
genius: guiding angel.

I will acquaint 'ee with an unmatched secret,
Whose knowledge to your griefs shall set a period.
BASSANES. Thou canst not, Orgilus; 'tis in the power
Of the gods only; yet, for satisfaction,   40
Because I note an earnest in thine utterance,
Unforced and naturally free, be resolute
The virgin bays shall not withstand the lightning
With a more careless danger than my constancy
The full of thy relation. Could it move
Distraction in a senseless marble statue,
It should find me a rock. I do expect now
Some truth of unheard moment.
ORGILUS.   To your patience
You must add privacy, as strong in silence
As mysteries locked up in Jove's own bosom.   50
BASSANES. A skull hid in the earth a treble age
Shall sooner prate.
ORGILUS.   Lastly, to such direction
As the severity of a glorious action
Deserves to lead your wisdom and your judgment,
You ought to yield obedience.
BASSANES.   With assurance
Of will and thankfulness.
ORGILUS.   With manly courage
Please then to follow me.
BASSANES.   Where'er, I fear not.
                                        Exeunt omnes.

[V.ii]
        Loud music. Enter GRONEAS *and* LEMOPHIL,
    leading EUPHRANEA; CHRISTALLA *and* PHILEMA,
        leading PROPHILUS; NEARCHUS *supporting*
        CALANTHA; CROTOLON *and* AMELUS. *Cease
            loud music; All make a stand.*

CALANTHA. We miss our servant Ithocles and Orgilus;
On whom attend they?
CROTOLON.   My son, gracious princess,
Whispered some new device, to which these revels
Should be but usher, wherein I conceive
Lord Ithocles and he himself are actors.
CALANTHA. A fair excuse for absence. As for Bassanes,
Delights to him are troublesome. Armostes
Is with the king?

CROTOLON.   He is.

CALANTHA.   On to the dance!—
Dear cousin, hand you the bride; the bridegroom must be
Intrusted to my courtship. Be not jealous,   10
Euphranea; I shall scarcely prove a temptress.—
Fall to our dance.
   (*Music.*)

   NEARCHUS *dance with* EUPHRANEA, PROPHILUS *with*
      CALANTHA, CHRISTALLA *with* LEMOPHIL,
      PHILEMA *with* GRONEAS. *Dance the first
      change,** during which enter* ARMOSTES.

ARMOSTES (*in* CALANTHA'*s ear*). The king your father's
   dead.

CALANTHA. To the other change.

ARMOSTES.   Is't possible?
   (*Dance again.*)

           Enter BASSANES.

BASSANES [*in* CALANTHA'*s ear*].   O,
   madam!
Penthea, poor Penthea's starved.

CALANTHA.   Beshrew thee!—
Lead to the next.

BASSANES.   Amazement dulls my senses.
   (*Dance again.*)

           Enter ORGILUS.

ORGILUS [*in* CALANTHA'*s ear*]. Brave Ithocles is murdered, murdered cruelly.

CALANTHA. How dull this music sounds! Strike up more
   sprightly;
Our footings are not active like our heart,
Which treads the nimbler measure.

ORGILUS.   I am thunder-
   struck!
   (*Last change. Cease music.*)

CALANTHA. So! Let us breathe awhile.— Hath not this
   motion   20
Raised fresher color on your cheeks?

NEARCHUS.   Sweet princess,
A perfect purity of blood enamels
The beauty of your white.

---

change: figure.

CALANTHA.   We all look cheerfully;
  And, cousin, 'tis, methinks, a rare presumption
  In any who prefers our lawful pleasures
  Before their own sour censure to interrupt
  The custom of this ceremony bluntly.
NEARCHUS. None dares, lady.
CALANTHA. Yes, yes; some hollow voice delivered to me
  How that the king was dead.
ARMOSTES.   The king is dead.   30
  This fatal news was mine; for in mine arms
  He breathed his last and with his crown bequeathed 'ee
  Your mother's wedding ring, which here I tender.
CROTOLON. Most strange!
CALANTHA.   Peace crown his ashes! We
  are queen, then.
NEARCHUS. Long live Calantha, Sparta's sovereign queen!
OMNES. Long live the queen!
CALANTHA.   What whispered Bas-
  sanes?
BASSANES. That my Penthea, miserable soul,
  Was starved to death.
CALANTHA.   She's happy; she hath finished
  A long and painful progress.—A third murmur
  Pierced mine unwilling ears.
ORGILUS.   That Ithocles   40
  Was murdered—rather butchered—had not bravery
  Of an undaunted spirit, conquering terror,
  Proclaimed his last act triumph over ruin.
ARMOSTES. How? Murdered!
CALANTHA.   By whose hand?
ORGILUS.   By
  mine; this weapon
  Was instrument to my revenge. The reasons
  Are just and known; quit° him of these, and then
  Never lived gentleman of greater merit,
  Hope, or abiliment° to steer a kingdom.
CROTOLON. Fie, Orgilus!
EUPHRANEA.   Fie, brother!
CALANTHA.   You have done
  it?

---

  quit: acquit.   abiliment: ability.

BASSANES.   How it was done let him report, the forfeit   50
  Of whose allegiance to our laws doth covet
  Rigor of justice; but that done it is,
  Mine eyes have been an evidence of credit
  Too sure to be convinced.*—Armostes, rent* not
  Thine arteries with hearing the bare circumstances
  Of these calamities. Thou'st lost a nephew,
  A niece, and I a wife. Continue man still;
  Make me the pattern of digesting evils,
  Who can outlive my mighty ones, not shrinking
  At such a pressure as would sink a soul   60
  Into what's most of death, the worst of horrors.
  But I have sealed a covenant with sadness
  And entered into bonds without condition
  To stand these tempests calmly.—Mark me, nobles,
  I do not shed a tear, not for Penthea!
  Excellent misery!

CALANTHA.   We begin our reign
  With a first act of justice.—Thy confession,
  Unhappy Orgilus, dooms thee a sentence;
  But yet thy father's or thy sister's presence
  Shall be excused.—Give, Crotolon, a blessing   70
  To thy lost son; Euphranea, take a farewell,
  And both be gone.

CROTOLON.   Confirm thee, noble sorrow,
  In worthy resolution.

EUPHRANEA.   Could my tears speak,
  My griefs were slight.

ORGILUS.   All good[n]ess dwell amongst
      ye!
  Enjoy my sister, Prophilus; my vengeance
  Aimed never at thy prejudice.*

CALANTHA.   Now withdraw.—
          Exeunt CROTOLON, PROPHILUS, *and* EUPHRANEA.
  Bloody relater of thy stains in blood,
  For that thou hast reported him, whose fortunes
  And life by thee are both at once snatched from him,
  With honorable mention, make thy choice   80
  Of what death likes thee best; there's all our bounty.—

---

convinced: confuted, overcome.   rent: rend.
prejudice: injury.

But, to excuse delays, let me, dear cousin,
Entreat you and these lords see execution
Instant before 'e part.

NEARCHUS.   Your will commands us.

ORGILUS. One suit, just queen, my last: vouchsafe your
    clemency
That by no common hand I be divided
From this my humble frailty.

CALANTHA.   To their wisdoms
Who are to be spectators of thine end
I make the reference. Those that are dead
Are dead; had they not now died, of necessity   90
They must have paid the debt they owed to nature
One time or other.—Use dispatch, my lords;
We'll suddenly* prepare our coronation.

                    Exeunt CALANTHA, PHILEMA, CHRISTALLA.

ARMOSTES. 'Tis strange these tragedies should never
    touch on
Her female pity.

BASSANES.   She has a masculine spirit;
And wherefore should I pule and, like a girl,
Put finger in the eye? Let's be all toughness,
Without distinction betwixt sex and sex.

NEARCHUS. Now, Orgilus, thy choice?

ORGILUS.   To bleed to
    death.

ARMOSTES. The executioner?

ORGILUS.   Myself, no surgeon;   100
I am well skilled in letting blood. Bind fast
This arm, that so the pipes may from their conduits
Convey a full stream; here's a skillful instrument.
[*He takes out his dagger.*]
Only I am a beggar to some charity
To speed me in this execution
By lending th'other prick to th'tother arm
When this is bubbling life out.

BASSANES.   I am for 'ee.
It most concerns my art, my care, my credit.—
Quick, fillet* both [his] arms.

ORGILUS.   Gramercy, friendship!
Such courtesies are real which flow cheerfully   110

---

suddenly: immediately.   fillet: bind.

Without an expect[at]ion of requital.
Reach me a staff in this hand.
[*They give him a staff.*]
                                                    If a proneness
Or custom in my nature from my cradle
Had been inclined to fierce and eager bloodshed,
A coward guilt, hid in a coward quaking,
Would have betrayed fame to ignoble flight
And vagabond pursuit of dreadful safety;
But look upon my steadiness and scorn not
The sickness of my fortune, which, since Bassanes
Was husband to Penthea, had lain bedrid.   120
We trifle time in words: thus I show cunning
In opening of a vein too full, too lively.
[*He pierces a vein.*]

ARMOSTES. Desperate courage!
ORGILUS.   Honorable infamy!
LEMOPHIL. I tremble at the sight.
GRONEAS.   Would I were loose!
BASSANES. It sparkles like a lusty wine new broached;
The vessel must be sound from which it issues.
Grasp hard this other stick; I'll be as nimble—
But, prithee, look not pale. Have at 'ee!—Stretch out
Thine arm with vigor and unshook virtue.
[*He pierces the other vein.*]
Good! O, I envy not a rival, fitted   130
To conquer in extremities. This pastime
Appears majestical; some high-tuned poem
Hereafter shall deliver to posterity
The writer's glory and his subject's triumph.
How is't, man? Droop not yet?

ORGILUS.   I feel no palsies.
On a pair-royal° do I wait in death:
My sovereign, as his liegeman; on my mistress,
As a devoted servant; and on Ithocles,
As, if no brave, yet no unworthy enemy.
Nor did I use an engine to entrap   140
His life out of a slavish fear to combat
Youth, strength, or cunning,° but for that I durst not
Engage the goodness of a cause on fortune,
By which his name might have outfaced my vengeance.

---

pair-royal: three of a kind (in cards).   cunning: skill.

O, Tecnicus, inspired with Phœbus' fire!
I call to mind thy augury; 'twas perfect:
"Revenge proves its own executioner."
·When feeble man is bending to his mother,
The dust 'a was first framed on, thus he totters.
BASSANES. Life's fountain is dried up.
ORGILUS.   So falls the
          standards   150
Of my prerogative in being a creature:
A mist hangs o'er mine eyes; the sun's bright splendor
Is clouded in an everlasting shadow.
Welcome, thou ice, that sitt'st about my heart;
No heat can ever **th**aw thee.
          (*Dies.*)
NEARCHUS.   Speech hath left him.
BASSANES. 'A has shook hands with time; his funeral urn
Shall be my charge. Remove the bloodless body.
The coronation must require attendance;
That past, my few days can be but one mourning.

                                                          Exeunt.

[V.iii]

> *An altar covered with white; two lights of*
> *virgin wax, during which music of recorders.*
> *Enter Four bearing* ITHOCLES *on a hea[r]se,*
> *or in a chair, in a rich robe and a crown on*
> *his head; place him on one side of the altar.*
>
> > *After him enter* CALANTHA
> > *in a white robe and*
> > *crowned;* EUPHRANEA,
> > PHILEMA, CHRISTALLA, *in*
> > *white;* NEARCHUS, ARMOS-
> > TES, CROTOLON, PROPHILUS,
> > AMELUS, BASSANES, LEMO-
> > PHIL, *and* GRONEAS. CA-
> > LANTHA *goes and kneels*
> > *before the altar; the Rest*
> > *stand off, the Women*
> > *kneeling behind. Cease re-*
> > *corders during her devo-*
> > *tions. Soft music.* CALAN-
> > THA *and the Rest rise, do-*
> > *ing obeisance to the altar.*

CALANTHA. Our orisons are heard; the gods are merci-
　　ful.—
　　Now tell me, you whose loyalties pays tribute
　　To us your lawful sovereign, how unskillful*
　　Your duties or obedience is to render
　　Subjection to the scepter of a virgin,
　　Who have been ever fortunate in princes
　　Of masculine and stirring composition!
　　A woman has enough to govern wisely
　　Her own demeanors, passions, and divisions.
　　A nation warlike and inured to practice　　　　　　　10
　　Of policy and labor cannot brook
　　A feminate authority; we, therefore,
　　Command your counsel how you may advise us
　　In choosing of a husband whose abilities
　　Can better guide this kingdom.
NEARCHUS.　　　　　　　　　　　Royal lady,
　　Your law is in your will.
ARMOSTES.　　　　　　　　We have seen tokens
　　Of constancy too lately to mistrust it.
CROTOLON. Yet, if your highness settle on a choice
　　By your own judgment both allowed and liked of,
　　Sparta may grow in power and proceed　　　　　　　20
　　To an increasing height.
CALANTHA.　　　　　　　　Hold you the same mind?
BASSANES. Alas, great mistress, reason is so clouded
　　With the thick darkness of my infinite woes
　　That I forecast nor dangers, hopes, or safety.
　　Give me some corner of the world to wear out
　　The remnant of the minutes I must number,
　　Where I may hear no sounds but sad complaints
　　Of virgins who have lost contracted partners;
　　Of husbands howling that their wives were ravished
　　By some untimely fate; of friends divided　　　　　30
　　By churlish opposition; or of fathers
　　Weeping upon their children's slaughtered carcasses;
　　Or daughters groaning o'er their fathers' hearses;
　　And I can dwell there, and with these keep consort
　　As musical as theirs. What can you look for
　　From an old, foolish, peevish, doting man
　　But craziness of age?

---

unskillful: unwise.

CALANTHA. Cousin of Argos—

NEARCHUS.   Madam?

CALANTHA.   Were I pre-
     sently
     To choose you for my lord, I'll open freely
     What articles I would propose to treat on   40
     Before our marriage.

NEARCHUS.   Name them, virtuous lady.

CALANTHA. I would presume you would retain the
     royalty
     Of Sparta in her own bounds; then in Argos
     Armostes might be viceroy; in Messene
     Might Crotolon bear sway; and Bassanes—

BASSANES. I, queen? Alas, what I?

CALANTHA.   Be Sparta's marshal.
     The multitudes of high employments could not
     But set a peace to private griefs. These gentlemen,
     Groneas and Lemophil, with worthy pensions,
     Should wait upon your person in your chamber.   50
     I would bestow Christalla on Amelus;
     She'll prove a constant wife. And Philema
     Should into Vesta's temple.

BASSANES.   This is a testament!
     It sounds not like conditions on a marriage.

NEARCHUS. All this should be performed.

CALANTHA.   Lastly, for
     Prophilus,
     He should be, cousin, solemnly invested
     In all those honors, titles, and preferments
     Which his dear friend, and my neglected husband,
     Too short a time enjoyed.

PROPHILUS.   I am unworthy
     To live in your remembrance.

EUPHRANEA.   Excellent lady!   60

NEARCHUS. Madam, what means that word "neglected
     husband"?

CALANTHA. Forgive me.—[*To* ITHOCLES's *body on the
     hearse.*] Now I turn to thee, thou shadow
     Of my contracted lord! Bear witness all,
     I put my mother['s] wedding ring upon
     His finger; 'twas my father's last bequest.
     Thus I new-marry him whose wife I am;

Death shall not separate us. O, my lords,
I but deceived your eyes with antic gesture
When one news straight came huddling on another
Of death and death and death. Still I danced forward;   70
But it struck home, and here, and in an instant.
Be° such mere women, who with shrieks and outcries
Can vow a present end to all their sorrows,
Yet live to vow new pleasures and outlive them.
They are the silent griefs which cut the heartstrings;
Let me die smiling.

NEARCHUS.   'Tis a truth too ominous.

CALANTHA. One kiss on these cold lips, my last! Crack,
    crack!—
Argos now's Sparta's king.—Command the voices
Which wait at th'altar now to sing the song
I fitted for my end.

NEARCHUS.   Sirs, the song!   80
               A Song.

ALL.   *Glories, pleasures, pomps, delights, and ease*
               Can but please
        [Th'] outward senses when the mind
        Is [or°] untroubled or by peace refined.

1 [VOICE].   *Crowns may flourish and decay;*
        Beauties shine, but fade away.

2 [VOICE].   *Youth may revel, yet it must*
        Lie down in a bed of dust.

3 [VOICE].   *Earthly honors flow and waste;*
        Time alone doth change and last.   90

ALL.   *Sorrows mingled with contents prepare*
             Rest for care;
        Love only reigns in death though art
        Can find no comfort for a broken heart.

[CALANTHA *dies.*]

ARMOSTES. Look to the queen!

BASSANES.   Her heart is broke, in-
    deed.
O, royal maid, would thou hadst missed this part!
Yet 'twas a brave one. I must weep to see
Her smile in death.

AMOSTES.   Wise Tecnicus, thus said he:

---

be: there are.   or: either.

"When youth is ripe, and age from time doth part,
The lifeless trunk shall wed the broken heart."   100
'Tis here fulfilled.

NEARCHUS.   I am your king.

OMNES.   Love live
Nearchus, King of Sparta!

NEARCHUS.   Her last will
Shall never be digressed from; wait in order
Upon these faithful lovers as become us.—
   The counsels of the gods are never known
    Till men can call th'effects of them their own.

                                [*Exeunt.*]

FINIS.

The Epilogue.
Where noble judgments and clear eyes are fixed
To grace endeavor, there sits truth, not mixed
With ignorance: those censures° may command
Belief which talk not till they understand.
Let some say, "This was flat"; some, "Here the scene
Fell from its height"; another, that the mean
Was "ill observed" in such a growing passion
As it transcended either state or fashion.
Some few may cry, " 'Twas pretty well," or so,
"But—" and there shrug in silence; yet we know   10
Our writer's aim was in the whole addressed
Well to deserve of *all* but please the *best*,
Which granted, by th'allowance of this strain,
The *Broken Heart* may be pieced up again.

FINIS.

-----

censures: opinions.

Afterword

Of all the later Jacobean and Caroline playwrights, Ford probably gives us the truest picture of the Cavalier attitude. Middleton's is the negative picture—of the undirected good, of the inner corruption stemming from failure to assume responsibility. Ford's, however, is the positive—of the beautiful, even heroic, gesture of embracing death as the only satisfying gesture in a world of conflicting loyalties and shifting values. However artificial and unreal it may seem to us today, in less than a decade after its publication in 1633 *The Broken Heart* was to be re-enacted in the lives of many Cavaliers. As the civil wars tested their code, life frequently imitated art.

In 1640, his treasury exhausted from his recent religious wars with the Scottish Presbyterians and from the lavish expenditures to maintain an elegant court, Charles twice was forced to summon Parliament to vote taxes. So numerous, however, were the stored-up grievances of the Commoners, particularly of the second or "Long" Parliament, that, before voting the desired funds, they issued an ultimatum to the king to surrender his prerogative powers concerning the church, the creation of peers, and the appointment of ministers, councilors, military commanders, and royal guardians. Instead of agreeing with these terms, Charles, so long used to his "divine right," raised his standard at Nottingham on August 22, 1642. So began the first of the civil wars that were to lead to his capture, his trial, and, finally, his execution by Parliament on January 30, 1649. No longer was the "middle mood" possible, at least in life: the wars forced a decision of loyalty upon men in a quarrel that they did not wholly em-

brace. Clarendon has Edmund Varney, the king's standard-
bearer at Nottingham, express the Cavalier dilemma:

> . . . for my part I do not like the quarrel, and do heartily
> wish that the king would yield and consent to what they
> desire; so that my conscience is only concerned in honor
> and in gratitude to follow my master. I have eaten his
> bread, and served him near thirty years, and will not do so
> base a thing as to forsake him; and choose rather to lose my
> life (which I am sure I shall do) to preserve and defend
> those things which are against my conscience to preserve
> and defend . . .

So, too, Lord Falkland, who revered the institution of Parliament and was equally devoted to the person of the king,
chose "not [to] do so base a thing as to forsake" his royal
master. But this decision, as Clarendon describes its effects,
had its toll: "From the entrance into this unnatural war, his
natural cheerfulness and vivacity grew clouded, and a kind
of sadness and dejection of spirit stole upon him, which he
had never been used to." Lord Falkland's desire for peace was
so passionate that people shamefully whispered that he would
have bought it at any cost. To discharge this affront to his
honor, on the morning of the battle of Newbury in September,
1643, looking "very cheerful" and putting himself "into the
first rank of the lord Byron's regiment," he rode to his death.

Like Calantha, Lord Falkland died smiling, worthily anti-
cipating his monarch, who also met his death as resolutely as
a martyr. From the scaffold Charles was to say that he was
going "from a corruptible to an incorruptible crown; where no
disturbance can be, no disturbance in the world."

"*They are the silent griefs which cut the heartstrings.*" "*No
monument lasts but a happy name.*" "*He cannot fear/ Who
builds on noble grounds.*" "*They die too basely who outlive
their glories.*" "*Our home is in the grave.*" "*O, that I would
take/ So sound a sleep that I might never wake.*" "*. . . by the
gods it is a joy to die;/ I find a recreation in't.*" "*Man and his
sorrow at the grave must part.*" "*Integrity of life is fame's best
friend,/ Which nobly, beyond death, shall crown the end.*"

With a nation up in arms, the theater could not be expected
to flourish. Moreover, on September 2, 1642, the Puritan Long
Parliament, whose members had been alienated from the thea-

ter for over three decades, issued an order "concerning stage-plays":

> It is therefore thought fit, and ordained by the Lords and Commons in this Parliament assembled, that, while these sad causes and set times of humiliation do continue, public stage-plays ["spectacles of pleasure"] shall cease and be forborne. Instead of which are recommended to the people of this land the profitable and seasonable considerations of repentance, reconciliation, and peace with God . . .

In time Parliamentary soldiers tore down the Blackfriars to make room for "tenements," and other London theaters were wrecked or dismantled. The actors, most of whom had eaten the king's bread and had worn his livery, rallied to their royal master's side during the wars; but afterward they fell on hard times, their few attempts at public performances harassed by soldiers. One fortunate result was that many actors, to sustain themselves, took to publishing plays that had been lying around in manuscript before that time; we owe, for instance, *The Changeling* to such a circumstance.

Although much of it went underground, theatrical activity did not come to a complete halt. Strolling players, as before the great surge of Elizabethan theater building, managed to perform, at country fairs and elsewhere, *drolls* or farcical play-lets often composed of the comic elements of the more serious earlier plays—as *The Gravediggers* (Act V, scene i, of *Hamlet*), *Bottom the Weaver*, *The Bouncing Knight* (Falstaff). The advantage of drolls to the actors was that they could easily be moved on when Commonwealth soldiers threatened. The homes of noblemen and even, in Cromwell's time, of the more cultured Puritans welcomed players and took up contributions for them. One of the most intriguing figures in theatrical history in the last years of the Interregnum is Sir William Davenant, a playwright-courtier and theatrical entrepreneur who did not follow Charles II into exile although he remained a Royalist. Possibly owing to Cromwell's own love of music and moderate pageantry, Davenant managed to obtain Puritan permission to stage semi-private performances of semi-operatic, semi-oratorical "moral representations" in London. The most famous and influential of these was his own *Siege of Rhodes*—sometimes considered the first English opera—which he elaborately staged at Rutland House in September, 1656.

Designed by Inigo Jones' nephew, John Webb, and greatly influenced by the scenic splendor of the late Caroline masques and by the court taste for the tragicomic heroic, the play, as well as its playwright, was destined to be a major link with the drama of the Restoration.

Amid general rejoicing Charles II was restored to his throne on May 29, 1660. Within a few months the "Merry Monarch" issued to two favorite courtiers, Sir Thomas Killigrew, who shared his exile with him, and Sir William Davenant, a "patent" to form companies and build theaters for the "innocent and harmless divertisement for many of our subjects." And thus, directly under royal patronage, the Silver Age of English drama was born. The narrowing of range and vitality that had accompanied the movement of drama indoors in the early Jacobean era became further pronounced in the new type of theater that developed in the Restoration. The actors still performed on a shortened version of the Elizabethan stage, a half-oval apron or forestage that projected far into the pit; but an elaborately decorated proscenium arch, flanked by curtains that remained parted from the beginning to the end of a play, separated them from a backstage that contained grooves for painted scenery or "flats" to slide apart to "open" or together to "close the scene" (as the numerous stage directions in the texts of the period phrase it). The grooves were an innovation elaborated from court masques and from Davenant's "operas." The scenery functioned merely as background; but the actor, even in front of it, was no longer universal man on a bare stage that universalized the scene. The world had become more circumscribed, and the scene—though far from the verisimilitude of modern picture-frame staging—placed man in a particular society and emphasized by its two-dimensional effect the artificiality of his situation. Against this background the major Restoration playwrights, not possessing the strong faith that sustained the greatest playwrights at the beginning of the century in their struggle to reaffirm a moral universe, sought, much as Ford did, to make life meaningful by defining an elaborate code of manners through the action of their plays. The beheading of Charles I had executed also the idea so potently suggestive for drama that "divinity doth hedge a king" and, consequently, man himself; the figure of Charles II contained less kingly divinity than his father's to restore the idea.

Selected General
Bibliography

COLLECTED EDITIONS

Baskervill, C. R., V. B. Heltzel, and A. H. Nethercot, eds. *Elizabethan and Stuart Plays*. New York: Holt, 1934.

Brooke, C. F. T., and N. B. Paradise, eds. *English Drama: 1580–1642*. Boston: Heath, 1933.

Harrier, R. C., ed. *The Anchor Anthology of Jacobean Drama*. 2 vols. Garden City, N. Y.: Doubleday, 1963.

Knowland, A. S., ed. *Six Caroline Plays*. London: Oxford University Press, 1962. (The World's Classics.)

Spencer, H., ed. *Elizabethan Plays*. Boston: Little, Brown, 1933.

Spencer, T. J. B., and S. W. Wells, gen. eds. *A Book of Masques, In Honor of Allardyce Nicoll*. Cambridge: Cambridge University Press, 1967.

BIBLIOGRAPHIES AND GUIDES

Bentley, G. E. *The Jacobean and Caroline Stage*. 7 vols. Oxford: The Clarendon Press, 1941–1968.

Chambers, E. K. *The Elizabethan Stage*. 4 vols. Oxford: The Clarendon Press, 1923. *Index*, compiled by B. White, 1934.

Greg, W. W. *A Bibliography of the English Printed Drama to the Restoration*. 4 vols. London: Oxford University Press, for the Bibliographical Society, 1939–1959.

Harbage, A. *Annals of English Drama (975–1700): An Analytical Record of All Plays, Extant or Lost, Chronologically Arranged and Indexed by Authors, Titles, Dramatic Companies, etc.*, rev. by S. S. Schoenbaum. London: Methuen, 1964.

Henslowe, P. *Diary*, ed. R. A. Foakes and R. T. Rickert. Cambridge: Cambridge University Press, 1961.

STUDIES OF THE THEATER

Beckerman, B. *Shakespeare at the Globe: 1599–1609.* New York: Macmillan, 1962.

Bentley, G. E. *Shakespeare and His Theatre.* Lincoln: University of Nebraska Press, 1964.

Hillebrand, H. N. *The Child Actors.* University of Illinois Studies in Language and Literature XI. Urbana: University of Illinois Press, 1926.

Hodges, C. W. *The Globe Restored: A Study of the Elizabethan Theatre.* London: Benn, 1953.

Hosley, R. "The Origins of the Shakespearian Playhouse," *Shakespeare Quarterly,* XV (1964), 29–39.

Hotson, L. *The Commonwealth and Restoration Stage.* Cambridge, Mass.: Harvard University Press, 1928.

Joseph, B. L. *Elizabethan Acting,* 2nd ed. London: Oxford University Press, 1964.

Nagler, A. M. *Shakespeare's Stage.* New Haven, Conn.: Yale University Press, 1958.

Reynolds, G. F. *The Staging of Elizabethan Plays at the Red Bull Theater, 1605–1626.* New York: Modern Language Association of America, 1940.

Simpson, P., and C. F. Bell. *Designs by Inigo Jones for Masques and Plays at Court.* London: Oxford University Press, for the Walpole and Malone Societies, 1924.

Smith, I. *Shakespeare's Blackfriars Playhouse: Its History and Design.* New York: New York University Press, 1964.

———. *Shakespeare's Globe Playhouse: A Modern Reconstruction in Text and Scale Drawings. Based upon the Reconstruction of the Globe by John Cranford Adams.* New York: Scribner, 1956.

Wickham, G. *Early English Stages: 1300 to 1660.* Vol. II: *1576 to 1660, Part I.* New York: Columbia University Press, 1963. (Part II forthcoming.)

HISTORICAL AND CRITICAL STUDIES

Bluestone, M., and N. Rabkin, eds. *Shakespeare's Contemporaries: Modern Studies in English Renaissance Drama.* Englewood Cliffs, N.J.: Prentice-Hall, 1961.

Boas, F. S. *An Introduction to Stuart Drama.* London: Oxford University Press, 1948.

———. *An Introduction to Tudor Drama.* Oxford: The Clarendon Press, 1933.

Bowers, F. T. *Elizabethan Revenge Tragedy, 1587–1642.* Princeton, N. J.: Princeton University Press, 1940.

Bradbrook, M. C. *The Growth and Structure of Elizabethan Comedy.* London: Chatto and Windus, 1955.

———. *Themes and Conventions of Elizabethan Tragedy.* Cambridge: Cambridge University Press, 1935.

Brown, J. R., and B. Harris, eds. *Elizabethan Theatre*. Stratford-upon-Avon Studies 9. London: Edward Arnold, 1966.

———. *Jacobean Theatre*. Stratford-upon-Avon Studies 1. London: Edward Arnold, 1960.

Campbell, O. J. *"Comicall Satyre" and Shakespeare's "Troilus and Cressida."* San Marino, Calif.: Huntington Library, 1938.

Clarendon, Edward Hyde, the First Earl of. *Selections from "The History of the Rebellion" and "The Life by Himself,"* ed. G. Huehns. London: Oxford University Press, 1955. (The World's Classics.)

Cruttwell, P. *The Shakespearean Moment and Its Place in the Poetry of the Seventeenth Century*. London: Chatto and Windus, 1954.

Davis, G. *The Early Stuarts: 1603–1660*. Oxford: The Clarendon Press, 1945. (With corrections.)

Doran, M. *Endeavors of Arts: A Study of Form in Elizabethan Drama*. Madison: University of Wisconsin Press, 1954.

Dunlap, R. "King James's Own Masque," *Philological Quarterly*, XLI (1962), 249–256.

Eliot, T. S. *Elizabethan Essays*. London: Faber and Faber, 1934.

Ellis-Fermor, U. *The Jacobean Drama: An Interpretation*, 4th ed., rev. London: Methuen, 1961.

Farnham, W. *The Medieval Heritage of Elizabethan Tragedy*. Berkeley: University of California Press, 1936.

Ford, B., ed. *The Age of Shakespeare*, rev. Pelican Guide to English Literature 2. Baltimore, Md.: Penguin Books, 1964.

Haller, W. *The Rise of Puritanism*. New York: Columbia University Press, 1938.

Harbage, A. *Cavalier Drama: An Historical and Critical Supplement to the Study of the Elizabethan and Restoration Stages*. New York: Modern Language Association of America, 1936.

———. *Shakespeare and the Rival Traditions*. New York: Macmillan, 1952.

Harrison, G. B. *Elizabethan Plays and Players*. Ann Arbor: University of Michigan Press, 1956.

Herrick, M. T. *Tragicomedy: Its Origin and Development in Italy, France, and England*. Illinois Studies in Language and Literature 39. Urbana: University of Illinois Press, 1955.

Hill, C. *Society and Puritanism in Pre-Revolutionary England*. London: Secker and Warburg, 1964.

Kaufmann, R. J., ed. *Elizabethan Drama: Modern Essays in Criticism*. New York: Oxford University Press, 1961.

Kernan, A. *The Cankered Muse: Satire of the English Renaissance*. Yale Studies in English 142. New Haven, Conn.: Yale University Press, 1959.

Leech, C. *Shakespeare's Tragedies, and Other Studies in Seventeenth Century Drama*. London: Chatto and Windus, 1950.

Ornstein, R. *The Moral Vision of Jacobean Tragedy*. Madison: University of Wisconsin Press, 1960.

Parrott, T. M., and R. H. Ball. *A Short View of Elizabethan Drama*. New York: Scribner, 1943.

Prior, M. *The Language of Tragedy*. New York: Columbia University Press, 1947.

Reed, R. *Bedlam on the Jacobean Stage*. Cambridge, Mass.: Harvard University Press, 1952.

Ribner, I. *Jacobean Tragedy: The Quest for Moral Order*. New York: Barnes and Noble, 1962.

Tomlinson, T. B. *A Study of Elizabethan and Jacobean Tragedy*. Cambridge: Cambridge University Press, 1964.

Wilson, F. P. *Elizabethan and Jacobean*. Oxford: The Clarendon Press, 1945.

Wright, L. B. *Middle-class Culture in Elizabethan England*. Chapel Hill: University of North Carolina Press, 1935.

NOTE: *Many works listed above devote chapters to specific playwrights and plays included in this volume.*

MODERN LIBRARY COLLEGE EDITIONS